The Craft of
System Security

The Craft of
System Security

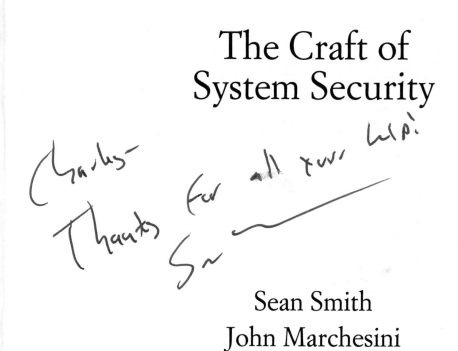

Charles—
Thanks for all your help!
Sn

Sean Smith
John Marchesini

Addison-Wesley

Upper Saddle River, NJ • Boston • Indianapolis • San Francisco
New York • Toronto • Montreal • London • Munich • Paris • Madrid
Capetown • Sydney • Tokyo • Singapore • Mexico City

Many of the designations used by manufacturers and sellers to distinguish their products are claimed as trademarks. Where those designations appear in this book, and the publisher was aware of a trademark claim, the designations have been printed with initial capital letters or in all capitals.

The authors and publisher have taken care in the preparation of this book, but make no expressed or implied warranty of any kind and assume no responsibility for errors or omissions. No liability is assumed for incidental or consequential damages in connection with or arising out of the use of the information or programs contained herein.

The publisher offers excellent discounts on this book when ordered in quantity for bulk purchases or special sales, which may include electronic versions and/or custom covers and content particular to your business, training goals, marketing focus, and branding interests. For more information, please contact:

U.S. Corporate and Government Sales
(800) 382-3419
corpsales@pearsontechgroup.com

For sales outside the United States please contact:
International Sales
international@pearsoned.com

This Book Is Safari Enabled
The Safari® Enabled icon on the cover of your favorite technology book means the book is available through Safari Bookshelf. When you buy this book, you get free access to the online edition for 45 days.

Safari Bookshelf is an electronic reference library that lets you easily search thousands of technical books, find code samples, download chapters, and access technical information whenever and wherever you need it.

To gain 45-day Safari Enabled access to this book:

• Go to http://www.awprofessional.com/safarienabled
• Complete the brief registration form
• Enter the coupon code SRGV-LMXF-TLQH-TKFB-NPRD

If you have difficulty registering on Safari Bookshelf or accessing the online edition, please e-mail customer-service@safaribooksonline.com.

Visit us on the Web: www.awprofessional.com

Library of Congress Cataloging-in-Publication Data
Smith, Sean W., 1964-
    The craft of system security / Sean Smith, John Marchesini.
        p. cm.
    Includes bibliographical references and index.
    ISBN 0-321-43483-8 (pbk. : alk. paper)

ISBN 13: 978-0-321-43483-8

ISBN 10:   0-321-43483-8

Text printed in the United States on recycled paper Courier in Stoughton, Massachusetts.
First printing, November 2007

To Nancy, Hannah, Natalie, and the community
at St. Francis of Assisi in Norwich, Vermont
—Sean Smith

For Wendy
—John Marchesini

Contents

List of Figures

Preface

Computer security, once the arcane concern of specialists, is becoming everyone's problem in society. Because so many aspects of society now depend on computing, coaxing or tricking a computer into misbehaving can have serious consequences. Attempts to grasp the nuances of this problem are bedeviled by its sheer complexity—in the individual components and computer hardware, in the operating systems that make this hardware useful, in the application programs, in the network protocols—and in the human processes that use and maintain these systems.

Since security is everyone's problem, a natural question is how to give each cybercitizen the knowledge and perspective needed to reason about these issues. In navigating their careers as software engineers, managers, lawyers, or anything else, students and practitioners need to be exposed to not only the breadth of the space of this security challenge but also what trends and principles to look out for.

Too many existing texts seem to focus on hacks-du-jour or system administration or cryptographic specialists or the Orange Book/NSA criteria. The computer science student or computer security practitioner can easily find books detailing particular tools that can be used to assess the security of a system but not books that take the reader into the deeper world of why these tools exist or explain how and when to apply the appropriate tool to a particular problem. Furthermore, many of the popular texts fail to aid one who is trying to build a system; many of the tool catalogs out there are geared toward the auditor, not the artisan.

We wrote this book to be that missing doorway. This book presents the modern security practitioner's toolkit; more important, this book also explains why these tools exist and how to use them in order to solve real problems. We want to give students enough practical knowledge to be useful and to give practitioners enough of the fundamentals to foster a deep understanding of the issues. Such mastery of the toolkit is necessary to understand the craft of system security.

How does one get such a security education? One could read through a bookshelf of material or access a large set of CD-ROMs to get the necessary depth, but most people do not have that time. Furthermore, much of that material may pertain to fine details of current systems and is thus doomed to a short shelf life. The material will likely be stale by the time the reader finishes reading it all.

This book itself grew out of a college course the first author developed (and then the second author helped with) to solve just this problem: to provide the right security education to students who may only ever take one security course and then move on toward a wide range of professional careers. We wanted to arm these students with a deep understanding of what they need to know in order to meet today's and tomorrow's security challenges. In the course, and throughout this book, we draw on our experience as security practitioners and try to relay some of the lessons we have learned.

One of us had the good fortune to be working in a government security laboratory at the dawn of the Web—when the very first forward-thinking government agencies started considering using this new medium for service delivery to wide populations.[1] This experience provided some important lessons to frame what has followed. Computing technology will keep changing explosively, in ways that affect everyone, not only computer scientists—compare the state of home or office computing and of the Web in 1994 to today. However, security must be viewed in the context of the social impact of the systems. If one is going to build, deploy, work with, manage, or perhaps simply use the systems that keep flooding society, one needs to understand these issues.

The other author has spent time working in the security software industry, shipping security products to such institutions as banks, airlines, and government agencies. This experience has made it clear why vendors deal with security by shipping patches on a regular schedule. Software vendors are under continual pressure to release products that are loaded with new features and must get these releases out as quickly as possible. At every stage of the development cycle, security is at odds with this goal. The requirement phase tends to favor features—and thus complexity—over robustness; the design phase typically favors elegance and reuse over durability; the implementation phase usually favors speed over safety; the quality assurance phase traditionally focuses on feature testing rather than crash testing. The result is that many companies ship software that is neither robust, durable, nor safe and that has not been tested to see how well it holds up against *malicious* users. An essentially infinite list of BugTraq [Sec06] identifiers is just waiting to get assigned to such products. If one hopes to build systems that break this mold, one needs to understand these types of issues as well.

---

1. In 2006, this same author renewed his amateur radio license and carried out the entire process via the FCC Web site. It's amazing to think how far e-government has come in these 12 years.

The dynamic nature of the security game makes it different from other types of engineering, such as building a bridge or building a safe. When building a bridge, one calculates the strength required, buys the appropriate materials, and constructs the bridge according to the specification. In security, the building blocks age quickly—sometimes faster than predicted and sometimes dramatically faster. Staying on top of this situation requires continued vigilance, as well as a solid grasp of the fundamentals. That's why we wrote this book.

Structure of the Book

We begin by presenting the historical background of computer security (Part I). We then describe the modern computing landscape (Part II), present the basic building blocks for securing systems (Part III), apply these blocks to modern computing applications (Part IV), and consider emerging tools and trends that will change the future landscape of system security (Part V).

History

Part I looks at history. Today, computers permeate nearly every aspect of life. Decades ago, however, the migration of computation from laboratory toys to real-world applications was just beginning. Military and defense provided many of these early applications, as well as significant funding. These domains traditionally featured real adversaries interested in such matters as espionage, sabotage, and war fighting. The move into computerized settings brought along these concerns. These early days of computing gave rise to much thinking about new problems of computer security. Some in our field regard this thinking as gospel, never to be challenged or extended; others dismiss it out of hand. We believe that the truth lies somewhere in between.

Introduction.   We use these roots as the foundation for our journey. Our discussion of computer system security starts out in Chapter 1 with discussions of the terms *security* and *system*. We consider the standard notion of "system" as a computer providing simple information applications and "security" as the standard *confidentiality, integrity*, and *availability* (CIA) rubric. We also introduce the basics of access control/protection—subjects, domains, and objects—and the matrix that describes who can do what to whom when. We finish by talking about the theoretical implications and practical instantiations of this matrix.

The Old Testament.   A subset of the security community believes that all computer security problems were solved a few decades ago, in the body of *Department of*

Defense (DoD)-sponsored work popularly identified with the *Orange Book* [DoD85].
When Roger Schell espoused this view at a December 2001 talk [Sch01], a curmudgeon in the audience characterized him as the Old Testament prophet Jeremiah,
castigating the community for turning away from the true path. It is important to
understand Schell's point of view, whether or not one accepts it. In Chapter 2, we
present this point of view.

Old Principles, New World.   In Chapter 3, we discuss how the "ancient history"
from Chapters 1 and 2 applies—and fails to apply—to modern computing scenarios.
We look at how the confidentiality-integrity-availability rubric can, when applied
carelessly, miss important aspects of system security, and we present an alternative
characterization in terms of *correctness* against adversaries. We also look at the
difficulty of establishing the system boundary. We critique the Orange Book—what
works now and what doesn't. We close by reviewing some other system design
principles and discuss how they still apply to this new world.

Landscape

After studying the history, we examine where that history has taken us. In Part II,
we look at the security of the elements used to build applications.

OS Security.   In the cyber infrastructure, the *operating system (OS)* lies between a
user's computing experience and the rest of the world. The OS provides the first
line of defense between the user and external adversaries and, since it shapes and
confines the user's computing experience, also provides the first line of defense
against internal adversaries. Chapter 4 presents the basic structures and tools the
OS brings to the security battle. We present the basic principles and discuss how
they are manifested in common Windows systems and the UNIX family (e.g., OS X,
Linux, BSD, Solaris).

Network Security.   Funny things happen when one lets computers talk to each
other. In Chapter 5, we present some of the basic pieces of networking and highlight some of the principal areas of concern for security practitioners. We also focus
on the emerging networking technology of wireless. Rare four years ago, wireless
technology is now standard on new laptops. For hotels, industrial campuses, and universities, not offering wireless almost seems as backward as not offering electricity.
However, the new technology also comes with risks. As we have personally seen,
information practices that were safe with a tethered network become rather dangerous when migrated to wireless; one can enliven boring conferences by discovering

and browsing the Bluetooth-equipped devices in range that have accidentally been left open to the world.

Implementation Security.   Abstractions are all well and good, but computing eventually consists of real code executing on real machines. A longtime source of computer security problems consists of basic flaws in these implementations. In Chapter 6, we survey these flaws—both common blunders, such as buffer overflow, lack of argument validation, escape sequences, and time-of-check/time-of-use, and more subtle problems, such as development process, tool-chain issues, and hardware issues. For each, we present real examples and general principles and discuss defensive coding practices and other countermeasures. We also discuss how programming language techniques and software development processes can impact security—and what we can do about it.

Building Blocks for Secure Systems

In Part III, we survey the basic building blocks critical to designing, building, and deploying secure systems today.

Using Cryptography.   Cryptographic primitives are a fundamental building block for secure systems today. Computer professionals need to have a good working understanding of what these primitives are and how to use them in larger applications. Chapter 7 introduces the standard primitives (public key, symmetric block ciphers, and so on) and the standard ways of using them (hashing functions, padding algorithms, hybrid cryptography, and MACs, and so on). In our teaching experience, we have encountered too many students who have "learned RSA" but have not known about all the steps involved in constructing digital signatures.

Subverting Cryptography.   Humans like to deal with simple abstractions. However, dangers have often lurked in the messy details of realizing cryptographic primitives in real systems. These dangers can break a system that seemed safe when examined as clean abstractions. As with cryptographic primitives, computer professionals need to have a good working understanding of the types of issues that can arise in practice. Chapter 8 considers problem areas and real-world case studies in order to help cultivate a healthy wariness.

Authentication.   Talking about "secure systems" makes sense only when there's a possibility of more than one player being involved. Chapter 9 covers the basics of authentication, as well as techniques when authenticating humans and systems in various settings: direct machine access, over an untrusted network, or over an untrusted network through an untrusted client. We also discuss the difference between authentication and authorization.

Public Key Infrastructure.   By removing the need for sharing secrets a priori, public key cryptography enables trusted communication across boundaries of space, time, and organizations. However, the *infrastructure* necessary to realize the public key vision is still emerging; some dissidents even feel that the whole approach is fundamentally flawed. In Chapter 10, we look at the problem space, the main approaches, the issues that complicate deployment and progress in this space, and the dissenting points of view.

Validation, Standards, and Testing.   Why should one believe that a given system is secure? Whether one is a vendor, an implementer, an administrator, or a customer, this question is fundamental. In Chapter 11, we talk about penetration testing, validation, and standards: how they can work to help achieve security and privacy and what their limitations are. We draw on our own experience in validation and testing and provide some suggestions to guide the reader through the cloud of emerging standards.

Applications

We have examined the history and the building blocks. In Part IV, we now apply these principles and tools to principal ways in which our society uses computing.

The Web and Security.   Created by physicists too lazy to go to the library, the Web is now the central medium for electronic services in our society. We review how the Web works and then present the various security and privacy threats it faces—and the principal solutions. In Chapter 12, we cover both the standard material (e.g., SSL and cookies) and more subtle material.

We also discuss recent case studies of how institutions that should have known better ended up inadvertently disclosing information via Web-based services. For example, had editorial writers read this chapter, they would not have condemned the business school applicants for "hacking" the ApplyYourself site to learn application decisions prematurely; had the schools in question read this chapter, they might have disciplined the IT staff who approved that site, rather than summarily reject the applicants.

Office Tools and Security.   Productivity tools, such as the Microsoft Office suite, Lotus 1-2-3, and rich graphical HTML email, etc., have become standard in nearly all settings. However, the richness and the complexity of these tools have continually led to interesting security and privacy issues. Since these tools work with electronic objects that look like familiar paper objects and provide manipulation functions that feel like familiar paper manipulation, users tend to assume that electronic objects behave like their paper counterparts and proceed to make trust decisions based on this assumption. However, this assumption is incorrect, and often, so are the resulting trust decisions. Chapter 13 explores these issues.

Money, Time, Property.   Bits are not paper. Our social systems rest on the properties of paper, which we've had millennia to understand. In Chapter 14, we discuss some problems—and some tools—in making bits act like paper money and notarized documents. Another important distinction between bits and paper is that we have evolved techniques for traditional media—books, magazines, and even recordings—that make it easy to enforce notions of intellectual property. Bits provide no such natural physical reinforcement; the area of *digital rights management (DRM)* and associated areas, such as watermarking, information hiding, and policy expression, are attempts to design and build secure systems that enforce certain types of "good" states despite certain types of malicious behavior.

Tools

In this book, we aim to equip the reader with the knowledge necessary to navigate the security field not only now but also in the future. In Part V, we look at computer security techniques and tools that promise to play an increasingly important role in this future. Consequently, some of these chapters are "lighter" than the previous material. The topics of Chapters 15 and 17 are full-fledged fields in their own right but often fall outside the view of the security artisan. Chapter 18 surveys a field that didn't even exist until recently.

Formal Methods and Security.   One of the main challenges in ensuring secure behavior of contemporary computing systems and applications is managing their ever-increasing complexity. If the system is too complex to understand, how can any stakeholder—let alone the designers and implementers—have any confidence that it works securely?

Industrial-strength formal methods are emerging as potent weapons in the security and privacy arsenal (e.g., [CW96, Win98]). Holzmann's SPIN even won the ACM Systems Award in 2002. The computer professional should be aware that, if one formally specifies what one's system does and what it means for a state to preserve "security" and "privacy," semiautomatic methods exist to verify whether the system, as modeled, has these properties. Chapter 15 surveys these tools.

Hardware-Based Security. Research on computer security and privacy typically focuses on computation. However, since computation ultimately requires computer hardware at its base, the structure and behavior of this hardware can fundamentally shape properties of the computation it hosts. A subset of the computer security community, including at least one of the authors, has long advocated and explored using hardware-based techniques to improve security. In recent times, with e-commerce creating a market for cryptographic accelerators, with enterprise authentication creating a market for user hardware tokens, and with the computing industry advancing TCPA/TCG hardware, we see the feasibility of such techniques increasing. Chapter 16 presents the state of the art in research into the design, use, and evaluation of hardware techniques to achieve security and privacy properties in higher-level computation.

In Search of the Evil Bit. The field of artificial intelligence provides a grab bag of learning and recognition techniques that can be valuable tools in the security arsenal. (For example, it led to a Los Alamos research project that made a profit.) In Chapter 17, we survey these tools and how they can be applied in security to look for known bad patterns as well as unusual patterns and to look at not only system and network intrusion but also higher-level application data.

Human Issues. For the most part, security and privacy are issues in computing systems only because these systems are used by humans for things that are important to humans. The area of *human/computer interaction (HCI)* has studied how humans interact with devices: the principles that guide this interaction and how bad design can lead to amusing annoyance or major disaster. In Chapter 18, we look at the field of *HCI–security (HCISEC)* and at some fundamental design principles—nicely expressed in Norman's book *The Design of Everyday Things* [Nor02]—and their implications in computing security. We also look at the increasing attention that security researchers are paying to this human angle (e.g, [AS99, BDSG04, Gar05, Smi03c, Yee04]).

End Materials

We conclude the book with a final wrap-up chapter, and an appendix containing some background from theoretical computer science to shed more light on some of the topics covered in the main text. The bibliography takes the reader further into the primary sources and cutting-edge research—which should be in a reference book but, for the most part, wasn't until this one was published.

Acknowledgments

Although only two authors are listed on the cover of this book, many people helped us make this project a reality. We'd like to thank Jessica Goldstein, Catherine Nolan, Elizabeth Ryan, and Mark Taub at Addison-Wesley for giving us the opportunity to write the book and keeping us on task when we needed prodding. We would also like to thank the anonymous reviewers for their feedback. We would also like to thank those who offered their technical input and support: the Product Security Group at Symantec, the crowd at the Dartmouth PKI/Trust lab—home of the nicest coffee machine on the Dartmouth campus—the folks at Dartmouth Computing Services, the students whose participation in the Security and Privacy course over the years made it so much fun, and all our other colleagues in the computer science and computer security communities.

About the Authors

Professor Sean Smith has been working in information security—attacks and defenses, for industry and government—since before there was a Web. As a post-doc and staff member at Los Alamos National Laboratory, he performed security reviews, designs, analyses, and briefings for a wide variety of public-sector clients; at IBM T.J. Watson Research Center, he designed the security architecture for (and helped code and test) the IBM 4758 secure coprocessor, and then led the formal modeling and verification work that earned it the world's first FIPS 140-1 Level 4 security validation. In July 2000, Sean left IBM for Dartmouth, since he was convinced that the academic education and research environment is a better venue for changing the world. His current work, as PI of the Dartmouth PKI/Trust Lab, investigates how to build trustworthy systems in the real world. Sean was educated at Princeton (A.B., Math) and CMU (M.S., Ph.D., Computer Science), and is a member of Phi Beta Kappa and Sigma Xi.

Dr. John Marchesini received a B.S. in Computer Science from the University of Houston in 1999 and, after spending some time developing security software for BindView, headed to Dartmouth to pursue a Ph.D. There, he worked under Professor Sean Smith in the PKI/Trust lab designing, building, and breaking systems. John received his Ph.D. in Computer Science from Dartmouth in 2005 and returned to BindView, this time working in BindView's RAZOR security research group. He conducted numerous application penetration tests and worked closely with architects and developers to design and build secure systems. In 2006, BindView was acquired by Symantec and he became a member of Symantec's Product Security Group, where his role remained largely unchanged. John recently left Symantec and is now the Principal Security Architect at EminentWare LLC.

Part I

History

Introduction
1

So just what is security, anyway? When asked to define the word *security*, many people give a definition that deals with being protected from danger or malice. A common belief is that *secure* is a state of being: Something is secure, or it is not. Marketing departments, managers, and executives seem to like this definition. They make such press release statements as, "Our product is secure." We have seen requirements for a software release that included a checkbox for "product is secure," as if security is some magic configuration setting. If only security were that simple!

In this chapter, we consider some basic definitions of security.

- Section 1.1 introduces the rubric traditionally used for defining security.
- Section 1.2 discusses the concept of the access control matrix, for framing security.
- Section 1.3 presents some alternative frameworks.
- Section 1.4 considers the general problem of determining whether a system can remain secure.
- Section 1.5 considers some other hard questions about security.

1.1 The Standard Rubric

Security texts usually start by defining security with the acronym *C-I-A*. In deference to tradition, we start by presenting that definition, even though we don't quite believe it. In this traditional view, a system is secure when it possesses the following three properties:

1. *Confidentiality.* The system does not reveal data to the wrong parties.
2. *Integrity.* Data the system stores does not get changed in inappropriate or illicit ways.
3. *Availability.* The right parties can always use the system when they need it.

These definitions have their genesis in the early days of computer security and computing, when machines were multiuser and centralized, not personal or distributed over the Internet. If one thinks about the security problem for military and defense applications of these early computers, the C-I-A taxonomy makes perfect sense. We don't want spies seeing or sabotaging sensitive data, but we do want the right people to see it. (In fact, one can trace the trail of this rubric back through Carl Landwehr's seminal computer security taxonomy [LBM + 93], to his early formal models work developed explicitly for this setting [Lan81].)

As we hinted earlier, we object to this definition of security. The C-I-A properties are all good things to have, and much good thinking arose from the early efforts to figure out how to achieve them. (We go into this thinking in more detail in Chapter 2.) However, we do not agree that these properties are always *sufficient* for security. Too often, we see them defined too narrowly; even when defined broadly, they can still lead one away from the important points. We attribute this mismatch to the complexity of the modern computing and computing applications landscape.

- Modern computing applications are tightly embedded with real-world social and economic processes. In these settings, a Bad Thing at the process level corresponds to a computer security problem at the technology level. However, it's not always clear how these security problems fit the C-I-A rubric. For example, from the point of view of the *Recording Industry Association of America (RIAA)*, if college student Alice can subvert the DRM protections in her online music service and create an unprotected MP3 of her favorite Pogues song, she is a Bad Hacker doing a Bad Thing. (See rant on page 6.) However, which C-I-A principle is she violating? We might stretch the idea of confidentiality violation to include producing a copy of this music data without the accompanying usage restrictions; we might stretch the idea of integrity violation to include fooling the music application into providing a service that it wasn't supposed to. We might also conclude that we're trying to stretch a rubric to fit a problem it wasn't designed to handle.

- Modern computing environments feature a diversity of parties and points of view. Clear, universal definitions of "right party" and "wrong party" no longer exist. To continue with our example, from the point of view of the RIAA, end users, such as Alice, are the potential adversaries because they want to distribute music without paying; from the point of view of many end users, the RIAA is the adversary[1], because its technology prevents users from exercising their legitimate "fair use" rights. The vast distribution of the Internet complicates things further: In addition to conflicting views of the adversary, all parties are faced with the additional challenge of never quite being sure who is on the other end of the wire and who else is listening.

- Modern computing environments consist of highly complex—perhaps even overly complex—software. This complexity leads to malleability and uncertainty, almost straight out of *Alice in Wonderland*: One needs to run and run and run, just to stay in the same place. One can never be sure whether one's own software—or the software on remote machines, allegedly acting on behalf of a remote party—has not been coopted into acting on behalf of unknown adversaries. Most users aren't even sure what services their machines are happily offering to anyone who queries on the Internet. These features don't easily factor into traditional ways of reasoning about C-I-A. For an enterprise—or even an individual—dependent on Internet-connected Windows machines, current best security practices dictate that one make sure to install all the latest security patches and updates for the OS and the applications and to disable all unnecessary network services. The vexing thing is that these actions do not guarantee a system free of vulnerabilities. Indeed, almost the opposite is true: We can guarantee, with extraordinarily high confidence, that serious vulnerabilities exist but that neither the defenders nor, we hope, the attackers have discovered them yet. (To support this guarantee, we only need to look backward at the continual history of announcements of vulnerabilities in deployed code. In Chapter 6, we discuss some strategies to reduce the number of vulnerabilities; in Chapter 11, we discuss some strategies to help discover them.)

---

1. Not long ago, Windows guru Mark Russinovich discovered that certain Sony music CDs silently install a rootkit on users' machines to allow Sony to enforce copy protection [Rus05]. Such tactics, along with threatening lawsuits, make the anti-RIAA standpoint easy to understand.

- Somewhat in contrast to early systems, modern computing environments tend to focus on applications pertaining to the everyday life of end users in the general population. These users have notions of *privacy* and would regard computer-enabled violation of this privacy as a security problem. However, how does privacy fit into the C-I-A rubric?

- Similarly, security technology is effective only if the human users use it to solve real problems. This requires users to generate an accurate model of the system and can determine the right way to interact with the system in order to get the results they are expecting. How does usability fit into this rubric?

Where the C-I-A rubric applies in modern settings, the relative importance does not always follow the order C-I-A. We cite some examples from domains in which we have worked.

- In the power grid, availability is so important that the domain uses "security" as synonym for "availability."

- A government benefits provider was considering providing citizens with a Web-based way to check their private information. From the outside, common sense dictated that the Bad Thing—to be prevented—was violation of confidentiality: Carlo should not be able to trick the system into divulging Alice's data. However, the client had an even more urgent requirement: This service would provide a data path between the Internet and the critical internal databases; continued integrity of those databases against attackers who might exploit this connection was a much more significant worry.

- We once helped advise a government medical benefits system. From the outside, common sense dictated that the Bad Thing, which our security measures needed to prevent, was the paying of fraudulent claims. (Since money is flowing to the wrong parties, is this a confidentiality violation?) However, the client had an even more urgent requirement: Correct claims needed to be paid within a tight time limit. Timely availability of the service dominated fraud suppression.

Rant.   Perhaps as a relic of its early applications in national defense, discussions of security often implicitly incorporate some notion of a conflict and *right* and *wrong* sides. *We* are good; *they* are bad; they want to cause this *Bad Thing* to happen; we want to stop them. However, in reality, which is the right side and even what the conflict itself is may not always be clear. KGB versus CIA? RIAA versus college students? Whistle-blower (or inside attacker) versus large corporation? Loss of confidentiality versus loss of integrity? It all depends on one's point of view and the context of the situation.

1.2 The Matrix

This early work on computer security focused on individual systems and framed the security question in terms of preventing the wrong people from doing the wrong things. This line of inquiry, nicely stated by Lampson [Lam74], raised questions about what can go on in a computer system, anyway. Who can do what to whom?

Developing this line of inquiry leads to a useful framework for thinking about security. In this framework, *subjects* are the actors, the entities performing the actions. Typically, these subjects are users, but sometimes subjects may be programs acting on their behalf. *Objects* are the entities that are acted on. Typically, these objects are files or other passive data items, but they can also be more general. The informal security statement of this view translates to "Subjects shouldn't have inappropriate access to objects." However, this translation still implicitly assumes that some types of access are appropriate and some aren't.

We need to specify what exactly is appropriate. Here in the safety of a book, we can do that by drawing an *access control matrix* (Figure 1.1):

- A row for each subject S
- A column for each object O
- In each S-O entry, a list of the *access rights* that subject S has for object O

	(Objects)			
	/home/alice	/home/bob	/home/carlo	/etc/passwd
Alice	read, write, cd			read
Bob		read, write, cd		read
Carlo	read, write, cd	read, write, cd	read, write, cd	read, write

Figure 1.1 An *access control matrix* expresses who can do what to whom in the system. This example shows how some subjects are allowed to read, write, and change directory (cd) to various directories in a file system.

Sometimes, we list the rows as *domains* and then worry about the mapping of subjects to domains. Think about how you might install software updates on your laptop: Usually, you're simply a user, but sometimes, you need to enter the admin password and thus change your domain. However, be careful. In the literature, one will see the terms *principal* and *domain* used in many ways. Good luck!

This access control matrix is sometimes referred to as a *security policy* for the system, although this term also can be used for many other things. The matrix is useful for many aspects of secure system development. One can tack the matrix on the wall for use in guiding a design and implementation, as we have. One can use the matrix to do the implementation. One can use the matrix to manage, change, display, and administer permissions. One can use the matrix to reason about what it is one means when talking about security—and perhaps even to prove properties about the security of a design.

However, a general matrix is hard to reason about, understand, code, and modify in a way that preserves global security properties. So, throughout this process, we start taking shortcuts—ways to reduce the complexity of the matrix—so that reasoning, proving, implementing, and so on, all start becoming tractable. Two common approaches follow from the structure of the matrix.

- We might break the matrix into columns and associate with each object a list of who is allowed to act on it and how. This list is called an *access control list (ACL)*.
- We might break the matrix into rows and associate with each subject a list of what each is allowed to do. The elements of this list are called *capabilities*.

(We revisit both approaches in Chapter 4.)

In general, the issue of how to enable expression, display, and management of policy is a vexing issue. Many of the same principles—such as modularity, least surprise, and encapsulation—that govern programming and system design also apply to policies. (We discuss some of these principles in Chapter 3.) Common software engineering flaws map to common "policy engineering" flaws. For example, good software engineering practice warns against cut-and-paste programming that repeats the same code in multiple places. If a bug fix or functionality change is necessary, will we remember to fix all the instances? In an access control matrix, if multiple boxes are supposed to be doing the same thing, will they always do that? We offer two real-world examples.

1. In older versions of some of Microsoft's Web servers, users could bypass certain configuration settings, such as whether to use SSL encryption, by

requesting a URL in different ways [Mic04]. To this day, Microsoft filesystems understand two names for each file in the system: the short (8 characters, a dot, then 3 characters) filename, such as for legacy applications, and the standard long filename. The OS correctly maintains the ACL for each file regardless of name, but older versions of the Microsoft Web servers related configuration information only to the long filenames. If Alice asked the server for a URL and used the short filename instead of the long filename, the server would fail to understand that its configuration should apply to the version with the short name. Thus, by using the short filename in the URL, Alice could bypass SSL or IP restrictions on the file being requested.

2. At the Department of Computer Science at Dartmouth, students and faculty share a common NFS-based filesystem. By default, the NFS permissions allow users to read one anothers' files. We also make heavy use of Web pages to house course material. When preparing a new offering of a standard course, instructors often want to keep the previous homework and exams, which had been on the class Web site, accessible to themselves and their staffs, but private from the students. Thinking in terms of Web access control (Chapter 12), instructors are tempted to use .htaccess techniques to implement this restriction: Only certain users can see these directories via the Web.

   However, the Web directories live *both* as Web-accessible sites, governed by Web access control, and NFS directories, governed by standard NFS access control. Instructors who protect their private pages with .htaccess leave them world-readable to students who know how to traverse the filesystem.

1.3   Other Views

In our experience, security is not necessarily the C-I-A properties, and the real security question is not: Is our system secure? A more appropriate outlook is: Given a model of the threats to our system, how much of our resources should we expend to mitigate the risk and impact of an attack? We develop these two aspects—model and risk—separately.

1.3.1   Correctness

Rather than thinking about C-I-A, we like to think about security in terms of *correctness*. We can think of the system as being in some state, an element of some larger space of possible states. Some subset of these states are "good," based on the semantics of the system. The system can change states, depending on various

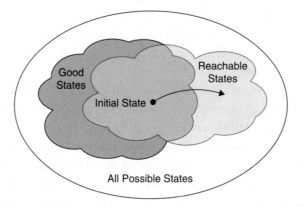

Figure 1.2 We like to think of security in terms of state spaces. User actions and environmental events and perhaps other things, can change the state of the system. The semantics of the system give us a notion of good, correct behavior. The goal of security to keep the adversary from coaxing the system into a state that is not good.

events: the actions of users, the actions of adversaries, computation, environmental or component failure, or even the passage of time. One hopes that the system begins in a state within this good set. The design of the system then leads to a larger set of states that are reachable, given adversarial behavior. We can reframe the security question as: Is this set of reachable states contained within the good set or can the adversary lead the system into an incorrect state? (See Figure 1.2.)

(Strictly speaking, we'd like to keep the state good despite *any* possible environmental or user behavior. The disciplines of *reliability* and *fault tolerance* deal with that more general battle. For our discussion of *security*, we're going to focus mainly on behavior by malicious actors, perhaps opportunistically exploiting other failures. Nonetheless, we do admit that some researchers assert that there is no difference between security and fault tolerance.)

When we get down to building real software systems, measuring the risk and impact of an attack has to do with the states that the system is in, and the security question boils down to keeping the system out of bad states. A single program can transition through billions or more states during a single run, and this number increases if one considers nuances, such as network or hardware behavior. An attacker wins by getting the system into a bad state or taking advantage of a system already in a bad state.

Let's consider some real-world examples.

- Users can often get systems into states that were not anticipated by the designers. The world of ATMs provides an amusing example. One deployed design had a door that covered the slot where the machine dispensed cash. If a user performed a withdrawal transaction, the machine opened that door and spat out the cash; when the user took the cash, the machine shut the door.

This all seems sensible. However, what should happen when the user carries out a withdrawal transaction but neglects to take the cash? As one user discovered, the machine shuts the door. Since cash is there that shouldn't be given to anyone else, the machine keeps the door shut through subsequent transactions—even if those transactions are withdrawals [Fis88]. The result is a denial of service: These subsequent withdrawal users have money removed from their bank accounts and placed behind a door that no one can open.

- The Tenex operating system contained a bug that allowed attackers to gain unauthorized access to the system. In the system's intended operation, a party needed to enter the correct password to log in to an account. If an attacker did not know the password, it might seem that the attacker could do no better than guess. If passwords consisted of a string of 8 characters each chosen from an alphabet of size 50, that's 50^8 possible passwords. On average, the attacker would have to try $\frac{50^8}{2}$ guesses before succeeding. (That's $19,531,250,000,000$ tries.)

  However, the Tenex system had two critical properties that, together, made the attacker's life significantly easier. First, the system checked password guesses character by character and rejected an incorrect guess at the first wrong character. Second, it was possible for the user to arrange the password to span a critical boundary in memory and to observe whether the system needed to cross that boundary when checking the password.[2] (This unintended output avenue— through which the attacker can observe useful data—is sometimes called a *covert channel*, or a *side channel*.) Consequently, the attacker could arrange to place only the first character before the boundary—and with 25 guesses on average, determine what the first character was. The attacker could then repeat this for each subsequent character and log in successfully after only 200 tries on average.

  This attack was possible because the state space of the system was a bit more complex and messy than the designers imagined, and the attacker was able to take actions to cause the system to enter a state the designer would consider bad: permitting the attacker to log in.

---

2. In case you're curious, this memory boundary is the boundary between two *pages* in the virtual memory system. Yes, Tenex allowed the user to lay out the guessed password so that the tail end was in a memory page that was not currently resident.

As a system's complexity grows—typically, via the addition of new features—the state space grows as well, and thus the risk of an undetected bad state increases. When an attacker finds unexpected states, security trouble often follows.

- Many common security exploits are a form of a category of attacks known as *buffer overflow attacks* (discussed in Chapter 6). In such a scenario, an attacker injects into the system's memory data that expands the functionality of the system. In some sense, the attacker modifies the space of reachable states of the system while it is running. This injected data typically gives the attacker unauthorized superuser access to the machine in the form of a root shell, thus the data is typically referred to as *shellcode*.

    Once the code is in place, the attacker forces the program to transition into bad states by tricking it into executing the shellcode. Typically, the result is that the attacker gains unauthorized access to the victim machine. When an attacker can control a system's state space, security trouble often follows.

- Another common attack vector involves tricking users so that their perception of the system—and the consequences of their actions—differs from reality. In Chapter 13, we discuss ways that the electronic versions of standard office documents can contain content that substantially differs from the virtual "piece of paper" that a user sees when opening it through the standard application program. As one consequence, when sending a document on to an external colleague, the user may end up transmitting far more information than intended. When an attacker can exploit differences between users' mental model of the system's state space and the actual state space, security trouble often follows.

In addition to the state space being more complex than designers can imagine, nailing down the notion of correctness can also have some surprising subtleties.

- In the U.S. federal income tax system, the government estimates what a citizen's tax payment will be and requires the citizen's employer to withhold that amount from the citizen's wages and send it to the government instead. Generally, the government overestimates—to be on the safe side, from its point of view. The annual income tax return process that so many of us dread involves filling out forms and filing them with the government in order to retrieve the extra that was overpaid.

    What criteria specify correctness for the tax form evaluation process? The natural rules one thinks of are something like this:

1. Verify that the form was really filled out by the alleged citizen.

2. Verify that the income numbers and other parameters that determine the tax payment are correct.

3. If the preceding checks are OK and the amount withheld is greater than the tax payment owed, send the citizen a check for the difference.

   In fact, the Internal Revenue Service implemented a process that targeted exactly this definition of correctness. However, this definition of correctness, although obvious and straightforward, neglects to consider whether a tax return for this citizen has already been processed. Consequently, until the IRS caught on, a popular[3] method of tax fraud was for a citizen whose employer withheld more than necessary to simply file a correctly filled-out form multiple times. The IRS would dutifully send multiple checks.

- Even the more basic process of having a client fill out a form and return it can have subtle problems. Straightforward correctness leads us to evaluate whether the answers in fact came from that citizen. However, this straightforward correctness condition neglects to consider whether the answers matched the questions the form asked. In one IRS case, a citizen didn't like the fine-print waiver on a form, altered the waiver with whiteout, and then signed it. The IRS initially didn't notice; when it did, courts held that it was bound to the altered waiver, since the IRS had accepted it.

   Mismatch can bite the citizen as well. In the U.S. security clearance process as practiced at Los Alamos National Lab, which is part of the Department of Energy, applicants were given an official clearance form with questions and spaces for answers but then were also given a sheaf of mimeographed papers with additional instructions that modified the questions and, if memory serves, each other as well. Some of these questions were of the form "Have you smoked marijuana in the last N years?" Some of the modifications adjusted the value of N. The modification sequence changed over time, but the original form remained the same. According to rumor, one honest and law-abiding citizen got in trouble at clearance renewal time because the changing value of N caused his answer to change, despite the continued passage of time. But the investigators merely looked at the original forms and asked, "Were you lying then, or are you lying now?"

---

3. According to an insider.

The saga continues. In their analysis of Diebold electronic voting systems, Kohno et al. observe that the system records that a user voted for Candidate #3 but does not record the order in which the candidate names were shown to that user on the screen [KSRW04].

- Most readers are probably familiar with the way that ATMs authenticate users: via a card and a PIN. Should a user who requests a withdrawal be given money? The natural rules one thinks of are something like this:

1. Verify that the entered PIN matches the one stored on the card.

2. Verify that the one on the card was properly encrypted by the bank.

3. Verify that the bank account on the card is a real account and has sufficient funds.

4. If the preceding checks are OK, debit the account and spit out the money.
   In the early days of ATMs, machines were deployed that targeted exactly this definition of correctness. However, this definition of correctness, although obvious and straightforward, neglects to consider whether the bank account matches the PIN. If adversarial Alice has an account at the bank but also knows Bob's bank account number, she could build her own magnetic stripe card that features Bob's account number but her own encrypted PIN. She could then withdraw money from Bob's account. Until the banks caught on, this *jackpotting* technique was allegedly rather lucrative.

1.3.2 Risk Management

Another common view of security is that it is about managing risk. (For example, see CERT's OCTAVE approach for dealing with information security needs [CER].) Systems grow too large and budgets too small for one to defend against *every* possible attack. One instead needs to start figuring out how to balance one's resources to achieve the best effect; however, evaluating what is this best effect is tricky and includes estimating such things as how likely a particular adversarial action is and how costly it is if the system enters a particular bad state. The field of *risk management* has produced tools to enable rational decisions in such areas as fire safety or financial investment; the fact that, for the most part, insurance companies and banks remain solvent testifies to the success of these tools.

Many researchers believe that the same approach needs to be applied to security. Blakley et al. go even further and assert that information security *is* risk management [BMG01]. Geer has subsequently evangelized for development of sound security metrics so that information security can be as well founded as financial risk management. Colleagues of ours at Dartmouth's Tuck School of Business also work in this area. Can a corporate chief information officer say whether too much or too little is being spent on security? Right now, the CIO has no way of knowing.

System designers not only have to deal with an enormous amount of complexity but also are forced to deal with rapid change. In our version of the security question, we start with a model of the threats to our system. In practice, this model changes regularly and rapidly, forcing designers to revisit their decisions about managing risk.

For example, consider the long sequence of dangerous security holes announced and patched in Microsoft Windows in the past few years. Some notable exploits include the DCOM exploit that enabled the Blaster worm, the SQLServer exploit that gave birth to the Sasser worm, and the Windows metafile vulnerability. All these exploits give unauthorized users the ability to run commands on the victim machine. One can always hire a security expert or buy software to configure one's system to be safe, and many enterprises do just that. If one did this in 2003, the expert or software would have left the enterprise with a system that contained all these holes. In the security game, things become stale very quickly.

This substantial qualitative difference from other forms of engineering and design bears repeating. That things decay is not surprising. For an example from another domain, if one installs pressure-treated lumber on an outside porch, one might expect the lumber to gradually decay over time; eventually, the lumber is too weak and must be replaced. However, with enterprise-quality computing systems, the weaknesses are *already there* when one first installs them. The *discovery* of these weaknesses is what happens gradually over time. (Well, at least one hopes that it's gradual.)

Another factor working against security is the ever-increasing computing power available to the attacker. At the turn of the millenium, fast desktops had a processor speed of around 500MHz. Just 6 years later, that speed had increased by almost an order of magnitude.

To illustrate the security consequences of such power increases, consider an attacker performing a *dictionary attack* on a user's password: that is, guessing every password from a large set of common choices. In 2000, an eight-character password that was not in the dictionary was sufficient to discourage attackers looking for an easy kill. Today, password policies force users into passwords that are longer, not found in the dictionary of any language, contain numbers and special characters as well as letters, and comply with restrictions about what type of characters can go into the first and last positions.

1.4 Safe States and the Access Control Matrix

In Section 1.1, we discussed the traditional way of thinking about security in terms of information access and C-I-A. In Section 1.2, we modeled security via the access control matrix: who can do what to whom when. In Section 1.3, we discussed how we disbelieve the C-I-A approach and suggested that a better way might be to think about whether reachable states satisfy some system-specific notion of goodness.

A natural question is whether we can put this all together. The access control matrix describes the state of the system. However, the state may change via operations themselves expressed in the matrix. Thus, we can end up with our space of reachable states, each described by an access control matrix and with each transition permitted by the matrix for its originating state.

Suppose that we had a predicate to describe whether any particular state was good. Is there a way we can look at an initial state and determine whether all reachable states are good?

1.4.1 Computability Theory

If we're going to talk about whether there's a way we can decide something, we need to first talk about what it means to be able to decide something. Computer science studies computation. (That should come as no surprise!) However, for some readers, it might come as a surprise that the "computation" studied goes beyond the structure of real-world computers and programs. Computer science also studies the essence of what it means to *compute*.

Mathematics frames the notion of a *function* as a map taking each item in its *domain D* to an item in its *range R*. Drawing on the work of early-twentieth-century logicians, computer science extends these notions to consider *computability*. A function f is *computable* when there exists an algorithm to compute it: a formal and finite specification of how to obtain $f(d)$, given d. Theoretical computer science gives many ways to precisely flesh out what such specifications must be like; for now, we might think of it simply as a program.

A maddening and fascinating result of theoretical computer science is that there exist functions that cannot be computed. These functions are reasonable and well defined; however, no program can compute them: There will always be inputs for which the program either gives the wrong answer or gives no answer at all. The appendix contains more information on these topics.

Punch Line.   Be careful about assuming that it's always possible to write a program to solve a problem. Logicians have proved a negative: Interesting functions exist that *no* algorithm can compute.

1.4.2 The Safety Problem

In Section 1.2, we introduced the traditional matrix model for access control. This approach lets us model who can do what to whom in the system. At first glance, we might regard this model as expressing what is permitted *now* and wonder about what will be permitted later. However, we can embed this potential future behavior in the matrix as well, by two simple tricks.

1. We regard the matrix itself as an object that can be manipulated.
2. We can express the rights to manipulate the matrix themselves as rights within the matrix.

If Q_1 is the current configuration of the matrix and a subject can change it to Q_2 by taking an action permitted in Q_1, we can write

$$Q_1 \vdash Q_2.$$

Suppose that we have a sequence of configurations $Q_1, Q_2, \ldots, Q_n$ such that

$$Q_1 \vdash Q_2 \vdash Q_3 \vdash \ldots \vdash Q_{n-1} \vdash Q_n.$$

We can write $Q_1 \vdash^* Q_n$: Some sequence of transitions takes us from Q_1 to Q_n.

One of the motivations for boiling security policy into a simple matrix model is to make it easy to reason about the behavior of the system. For example, we might define a predicate *BAD* on configurations, such that $BAD(Q)$ is true if and only if something really bad is permitted in configuration Q. In the historical treatment of this problem, "something bad" translates to "a given right r suddenly appears in the (s, o) cell in the matrix." However, what we really want to know is whether the current configuration is safe or whether it can lead to such a bad state. We can formalize this concern with the predicate *UNSAFE*. $UNSAFE(Q)$ is true if and only if there exists a Q' such that $Q \vdash^* Q'$ and $BAD(Q')$.

When considering system behavior, safety is a natural thing to reason about. If we let the system run from the current configuration, can we guarantee that nothing bad will happen? Since, as good computer scientists, we take it as an article of faith[4]

---

4. More formally, this is called the *Church-Turing Thesis*.

that computer programs or algorithms embody what we mean by "reasoning," we might then try to write a program that takes a Q as input and outputs whether $UNSAFE(Q)$ holds.

However, in 1976, Harrison, Ruzzo, and Ullman used the tools of computability theory to prove a surprising result: This problem is not computable! If a program existed that correctly decided the safety problem in all instances, we could modify it and produce a program that correctly solved the Halting Problem (a classic function shown to be not computable; see the appendix) in all instances. According to their seminal paper [HRU76, p.466]:

> it is in general undecidable whether, given an initial access matrix, there is some sequence of commands in which a particular generic right is entered at some place in the matrix where it did not exist before. Furthermore, in some restricted cases where safety is decidable, the decision procedures are probably too slow to be of practical utility.

In reality, then, we need to use other methods to ensure safety. Usually, this is done by restricting the problem so much that only safe states are possible.

1.5 Other Hard Questions

1.5.1 Who Is the Adversary?

Computer security people are a paranoid lot and continue to discuss "the adversary" as if it were a specific entity. This abstraction embodies several useful concepts. The failure scenarios we need to consider are not random but intelligent and adaptive; we need to tolerate the worst case, not the expected case, and, ideally, consider this tolerance from the very beginning of the design process. Furthermore, we also need to consider who has access to what parts of the system, what motivation those with access might have, and how well funded they might be. From the popular media, one might conclude that the adversaries are mysterious outside hackers; however, insiders and ordinary users also might be adversaries. Who might profit financially or politically? Who has the motivation or opportunity? Furthermore, not all adversaries are necessarily intentionally attacking the system; they might simply not know what they're doing or not know what the designer thought they should be doing.

When examining system security in the real world, one may also encounter some common fallacies.

- Sometimes, attacks will be left undefended simply because "no one would ever do that." History shows that the adversary can be more creative and motivated than we allow.

- Sometimes, attacks will be left undefended simply because "that attack is far too difficult." History shows that attacks only get easier, as Bruce Schneier likes to observe.

- Sometimes, attacks will be left undefended because "no one would know to do that." History show that such "security through obscurity" doesn't work.

- Sometimes, attacks will be left undefended because "we've never been hacked." One colleague likes to retort: "How do you know?"

- Sometimes, attacks will be left undefended because the attacker will be stopped at an outer perimeter; however, history shows that perimeter barriers break, leading to a doctrine of *defense in depth*.

1.5.2   Where Is the Boundary of the System?

It's easy for those of us who work in computer technology to forget that it is useful only when it is embedded in larger social and business processes. Consequently, when we think about securing systems, it can sometimes be hard to define exactly where the perimeter of the system is and how the adversary may act on it. We offer a few examples.

- Colleagues hired to do a penetration test on a computer installation intended to protect classified information completed their work in a few seconds: by grabbing some floppy disks and tossing them (Frisbee-like) over the fence.

- In the early 1990s, one of us advised an enterprise that takes great pains to protect the data on its computer systems but then shipped it, unencrypted, on back-up tapes in a truck driven by a low-paid contractor. Given $10K to spend on breaking the security, where do you think an adversary would spend it?

- A colleague of ours who was a senior scientist at the NSA once observed that although it's easy to assume that advanced mathematical cryptanalysis was necessary to break enemy ciphers, this was seldom needed in practice. Usually, the three Bs—burglary, bribery, and blackmail—were sufficient.

- A client for which we consulted scoffed at our concerns that adversaries might try to subvert computation by physically modifying the computers. However, the client later admitted that it had a problem with RAM modules being stolen from systems overnight.

- When considering software-based computer systems, it's easy to focus attention on the source code. In our industrial work, another branch of the company once reported a bug in a security-related product. We reproduced the same source tree, built the system, and tested it under the same input and environmental conditions, but the buggy behavior did not happen. After much work, we finally determined that the version of the compiler we were using differed from the one our colleagues were using by one subsubrevision level, and that was the source of the bug.

1.5.3 How Do We Quantify the Possible?

Technical people often scoff at the process of crafting regulation and law, perhaps because those who craft such things often appear not to have strong technical expertise. This perception may follow because the regulations often do not appear to assume much technical acumen on the part of the reader. However, this is exactly what regulations need to do: to specify rules precisely and unambiguously. If we as a society decide that personal medical information should be held carefully in order to preserve personal privacy, then someone has to write down clear, enforceable rules.

Unfortunately, the nature of computer science and the relative speed of technological versus policy development both work against this goal. As we discuss later, computer scientists tend to say "impossible" when they mean "intractable": If limited to foreseeable computing power and only a few centuries, the adversary cannot solve that problem. However, the power of what is foreseeable and our understanding of the underlying algorithms continue to evolve—not to mention the continuing revolutions in cost and ubiquity of computing devices. Twenty years ago, 56-bit keys were considered strong; Windows 95 did not exist; iPods did not exist; the Web did not exist; USB thumbdrives were unthinkable. Good advice for reasonable computing practices then would sound silly and dated now. Why will the rules we write now sound any better 20 years from now?

1.5.4 Detect or Prevent?

Considering system security can also lead to two potentially conflicting approaches. We can try to *prevent* the adversary from carrying out a bad action; alternatively, we can focus energy on simply trying to *detect* it and, we hope, recover from it. Banks use strong and visible vaults rather than cardboard boxes to store money for a reason: Even though it's against the law to steal the money, thick iron walls help prevent the problem in the first place. On the other hand, many bad scenarios are very hard to formally characterize *a priori*.[5] In modern desktop computing, it seems that society has decided that it's more effective to detect known malware than to build operating systems that resist penetration in the first place. On the other hand, as we saw earlier, automated detection of bad states may not even be computable without restrictions.

1.5.5 What's the Cost?

It's easy to assert that no price is too high to pay for saving a human life. However, most of us still drive automobiles. Such an act has a significant chance of causing death; furthermore, it's likely that automobile manufacturers could make much safer cars if the median retail price were a factor of 100 higher, but we, as a society, wouldn't stand for that. As ugly as it sounds, society has decided that preventable death is an acceptable outcome, and an acceptable cost benefit tradeoff exists for life-saving technology, at least in such domains as transportation.

We need to keep this lesson in mind when we consider computer security. We will not reduce the risk to zero, and a tradeoff exists between cost and effectiveness of security technology. By cost, we must consider not only the dollar price but also other negative impacts, such as the computational resources and the user inconvenience.

1.6 The Take-Home Message

We hope that in this chapter, we have given you the impression that security is hard to define and without a solid definition, and it's almost impossible to achieve. When someone asks you to build a secure system or tells you that he or she has built one, your first response should be to ask yourself what that means. Does the system have C-I-A? Does it use ACLs or capabilities? How is the security of the system measured? Does the system prevent malicious use or simply detect it?

In the course of our experience, we've found that considering the state space of our systems is the most useful approach. We like to think of the security of a system as its ability to stay in good states. This is the definition of security that we'll use throughout the book.

We also believe that measuring security in absolute terms is meaningless. We are leary of those who brag that they have built a secure system. How do they know? Just because the penetration testing lab didn't find any vulnerabilities doesn't mean that they don't exist—the testers simply didn't find them. A more useful approach

---

5. If you don't believe this, try to write down the precise rules that can enable a bank's computer to distinguish between a genuine credit card transaction and a fraudulent one.

is defining the adversary and seeing whether the system can remain in a good state despite that adversary. This makes the security of the system something we can reason about: "Our system is secure against an adversary that can do X."

Finally, it's important to understand that there are no magic silver security bullets. The most useful approach we've found is risk management: "How much of our resources should we expend to mitigate the risk and impact of our adversary?" Although this type of approach might make you unpopular with your marketing department, it will likely lead to systems that hold up on the battlefield.

1.7 Project Ideas

1. Find in your computing environment some things that claim to be secure. Look at Web sites, programming libraries, software products you use, and so on. Think about what the designers' definition of security was: C-I-A? Something else? Can you think of some bad states for the system? What type of attacker did they design against? What type of attacker did they leave out? What are the risks and impacts of a compromise? How would you improve the security situation?

The Old Testament 2

Although the topic of computer security seems to have emerged in relevance in lockstep with the Internet—or perhaps the Web—certain sectors of the population have been thinking about the topic for a long time. In this chapter, we discuss some of the early, foundational thinking about secure systems.

- Section 2.1 outlines the basic framework of this thinking.
- Section 2.2 introduces the notion of formal security models.
- Section 2.3 explains how this old thinking transformed into an explicit standard: the Orange Book.
- Section 2.4 considers some more recent activity that has evolved as a result of this early work.

2.1 The Basic Framework

As we already noted, much of the early thinking about computer security coincided with the early days of computing, when the U.S. military and associated agencies found themselves in a quandary.

- They had lots of information they needed to store and process.
- This information was very sensitive.

- There were real adversaries (e.g., other countries) that wanted to learn this information.

- However, the United States wanted to use these new computers to help store and process this information.

This quandary led to a challenge: How can one build computing systems that preserve this correctness property against these adversaries? This challenge then led to a lot of foundational thinking in security—definitions, concepts, models, standards, all very much theoretical in flavor—as well as to a set of rigid standards regarding the features and assurance process governing computing systems that met this notion of security.

Informally, this set of thinking is often summed up as the *Orange Book*, which itself is slang for one of the main standards for what the U.S. government termed a secure computing system [DoD85]. Much of this thinking persists even today in certain places. In his talk at the 2001 Annual Computer Security Applications Conference (ACSAC), Roger Schell said, basically, that most current security work was garbage and that the Orange Book thinking told us how to solve all problems, if only we'd pay attention. (We discuss his paper later [Sch01].) Marshall "Curmudgeon" Faulk,[1] likened Schell to the Old Testament prophet Jeremiah, castigating the people for turning away from the true path. We chose this metaphor for the chapter title because it resonates on several levels. Much of Western thought has roots in biblical concepts; however, the typical educated westerner will disregard the Bible as irrelevant—without ever having read it.

This situation is similar to the Orange Book thinking and current security work. The majority of sophisticated, educated security people tend to dismiss the Orange Book thinking with a knee-jerk reaction[2]—without even knowing what's in there. Whether or not one agrees with the Orange Book, it holds significant history—and maybe even a useful concept or two. It's irresponsible to reject it without reading it. There are no branches without roots.

In this chapter, we take a look at the Orange Book concepts and the standard itself. In Chapter 3, we examine why it perhaps didn't work as well as hoped and consider what lessons and tools we can take with us.

---

1. His name tag actually said "Curmudgeon."
2. Be very suspicious of knee-jerk reactions.

2.2 Security Models

The real world is complex. Real systems are complex. Trying to reason about what happens in a real system using the real system itself is fraught with peril. The system itself may be too critical to experiment on. The system may also be too large for us to effectively understand what parameters can be tuned and what the effect of this tuning is. A logician friend of ours liked to use the analogy of how to determine whether it's safe for Professor Smith to run across a rickety abandoned bridge. Evaluating this question by having Professor Smith try to run across the bridge has disadvantages, if the bridge in fact is not strong enough. Some of our other work in performance analysis of Internet-scale security protocols faces a different problem: People keep complaining when we ask them to shut the Internet down for a week so we can run our experiments on it.

In order to deal with the complexity of reasoning about security, early thinkers adopted the same principle: Abstract the real system to a simpler *model*. In this early world of defense and intelligence computing, designers were worried about various bad things happening in their systems, usually with regard to information flow, and therefore built mathematical specifications of what a system might do, usually with regard to information flow. These models provided an escape hatch from the undecidability of the general safety problem, since they provided well-structured restrictions of the general problem. This approach allowed the designers to prove security properties about the reachable states within this model and then to assert that if a real system conformed to this model, these properties would hold in the real system.

2.2.1 Information Flow and Partial Orders

Let's start with the basic access control matrix model for system security. We want to make sure that information doesn't flow to the wrong parties: the *information confinement* problem. However, in order to talk about this, it would help to have a clean formulation of what we mean by *wrong* and by *flow*.

Clearances. We can look to the national defense roots of computer security for inspiration here. For example, we might consider the set

$$\textsc{ClearanceLevels} \;=\; \{\textit{"Top Secret", "Secret", "Confidential", "Unclassified"}\}.$$

We can label each subject with the member of ClearanceLevels that indicates how trustworthy they are (e.g., according to a background investigation).

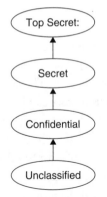

Figure 2.1 This directed graph shows how our example set of clearance levels would be ordered according to sensitivity: $n_1 \leq n_2$ if and only if a directed path exists from n_1 to n_2.

We can label each object with the member that indicates how sensitive it is. As Figure 2.1 shows, we can also put an order on these labels: Top Secret is stricter than Secret, which is stricter than Confidential, and so on. We can now talk clearly about information flow; if we then ensure that, no matter what, information flows only upward in the order, we can be sure that unprivileged subjects can't read sensitive information.

Categories.   For a slightly more complex example, we might think instead of *categories* (also known as *compartments*). For example, consider

$$\text{Categories} = \{\text{``Vermont''}, \text{``New Hampshire''}, \text{``Maine''}, \text{``New York''}\}.$$

In this case, we might label each subject with the *subset* of Categories describing what topics that subject is allowed to know about. We can label each object with the Categories *subset* that indicates what topics it pertains to. As before, we can put an order on these labels, but things are slightly more tricky. Since we're dealing with sets of topics, the more topics we add to a set, the stricter it becomes. Consequently, we use the subset relation for our order: set S_2 is "above" set S_1 when $S_1 \subseteq S_2$. Figure 2.2 shows the resulting order on Categories.

Again, we can now talk clearly about information flow: If we then ensure that information only flows upward in the order, then we can be sure that subjects can't read information that pertains to topics they don't need to know about.

Partial Orders and Lattices.   However, we can now be left with pairs of labels that have no order relative to each other. For example, both of these relations are true:

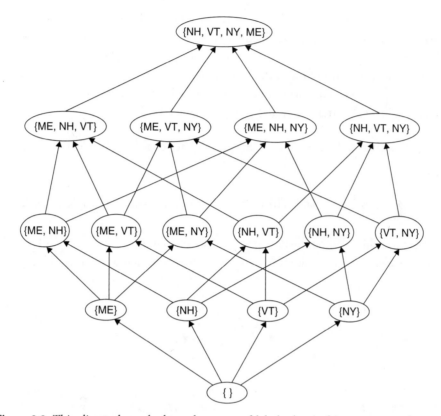

Figure 2.2 This directed graph shows how sets of labels drawn from our example set of categories would be ordered according to need-to-know $n_1 \leq n_2$ if and only if a directed path exists from n_1 to n_2 (or n_1 and n_2 are the same).

- {*"Vermont", "New York"*} ⊆ {*"Vermont", "New York", "Maine"*}
- {*"Vermont", "Maine"*} ⊆ {*"Vermont", "New York", "Maine"*}

However, *neither* of these is true:

- {*"Vermont", "New York"*} ⊆ {*"Vermont", "Maine"*}
- {*"Vermont", "Maine"*} ⊆ {*"Vermont", "New York"*}

A *partial order* is the mathematical construct for orders, such as this one, that can leave some pairs unordered. A *lattice* is a partial order with a few additional properties. (See the appendix for more discussion.)

The General Story.   In the traditional military and defense setting, we want to order information according to both sensitivity level and need to know. To do this, we consider the classes formed by putting together both the clearance levels and categories we discussed earlier: Each label is of the form form $\langle c, d \rangle$, where $c \in$ CLEARANCELEVELS and $d \in 2^{\text{CATEGORIES}}$ (that is, $d \subseteq$ CATEGORIES).

For our information flow formalism to work out, we need to define a partial order on these labels. However, we can do that easily by gluing together the orders on each element. We define $\langle c_1, d_1 \rangle \leq \langle c_2, d_2 \rangle$ when both

- $c_1 \leq c_2$: that is, the clearance level c_2 dominates or equals the clearance level c_1
- $d_1 \subseteq d_2$

Figure 2.3 shows a set of labels from this example and how they would be ordered.

The MLS World.   When the flow partial order has a unique maximum and unique minimum element, the maximal element is usually called *system high*, and the

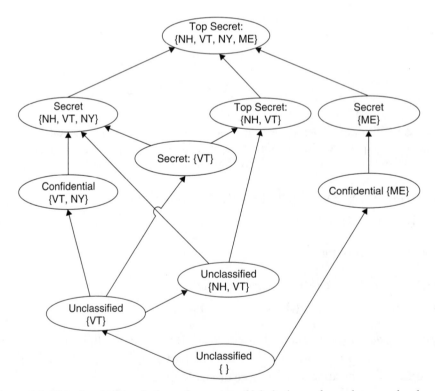

Figure 2.3 This directed graph shows how a set of labels drawn from clearance levels and compartment sets would be organized according to the information flow partial order. $n_1 \leq n_2$ if and only if a directed path exists from n_1 to n_2 (or n_1 and n_2 are the same).

minimum element is called *system low*. The term *multilevel security (MLS)* refers to this general approach of partial orders and information flow. Systems that prohibit actions unless they abide by certain flow rules within this framework are said to practice *mandatory access control (MAC)*. In contrast, systems that permit owners of objects to specify access control rules are said to practice *discretionary access control (DAC)*. (These approaches are not necessarily mutually exclusive; a system could enforce MAC rules and permit users to specify additional discretionary restrictions, as long as they do not contradict the MAC policy.)

2.2.2 The Bell-LaPadula Model

Bell and LaPadula built a formal model that tried to describe a variant of the *Multics*[3] operating system that would be secure, in this traditional sense of preserving confidentiality of information.

Building a formal model describing a real-world OS, even one a few decades ago, is not a simple task. Consequently, we give only a high-level sketch of the model here; the original report contains more details [BL76].

The Bell-LaPadula model puts subjects and objects in clearance/category classes. It then defines three security properties:

1. *The Simple Security Property.* A subject can read an object only if the class of the subject dominates or equals the class of the object. This is also known as the *no-read-up rule:* a subject can't read data from an object "above" it in the lattice.

2. *The *-Property.* If a subject has simultaneous read access to object O_1 and write access to O_2, then the class of O_2 must dominate or equal the class of O_1. (See Figure 2.4.) This property is also known as the *no-write-down rule.* Intuitively, the idea is that a subject shouldn't be able to write data to an object below it in the lattice, in which case information would be flowing in the illegal direction. However, the rule is a bit more subtle than that; in our model, subjects themselves don't possess information and don't remember it unless they store it somewhere. This is why we have O_1 and O_2 in the rule: A subject that can read data in some class can't write to lower class; such a write could violate the information flow rules. (This concept is also known as the

---

3. Multics was a historically important OS that no longer sees use. The UNIX OS, which still persists in many forms, was more or less a skunkworks project intended to be a simplification of Multics; UNIX was so named to highlight this intention.

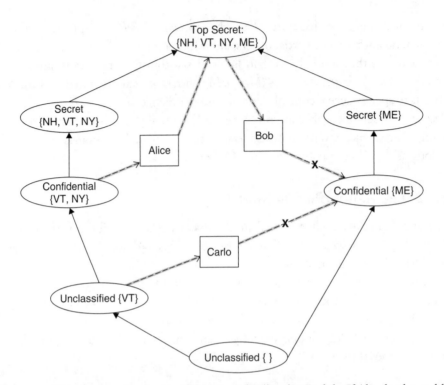

Figure 2.4 This diagram sketches the *-Property of Bell and LaPadula. If Alice has been able to read confidential data about Vermont and New York, then she can write Top Secret data about all the states. However, if Bob has read Top Secret data about all the states, he cannot write to an object that is only Confidential and only needs to know about Maine. Similarly, if Carlo has read unclassified data about Vermont, then he cannot write to an object that has no need to know about Vermont, even though "Confidential" dominates "Unclassified."

> *high-water mark:* The subject is marked by the highest level of data to which it has had access and thus by which it may have been contaminated.)

3. *The Discretionary Security Property.* A subject S can perform an access on an object O only if that access is permitted in the S-O entry of the current access control matrix.

Bell and LaPadula then prove a *Basic Security Theorem:* If we start in a secure state and if each transition abides by some rules derived from the preceding properties, then the system remains in a secure state. (This theorem doesn't violate the undecidability result from Section 1.4.2, because the Simple Security and * Properties keep us away from the general case.) Bell and LaPadula then attempt to work out the details of how a Multics variant can follow all these rules.

However, one starts to wonder how a program can meaningfully embody the *-property. What about the initialized data within text of the program? Should the program itself have a security level or implicit read access to itself? What if a program opens, reads, and then closes a sensitive file: How do we express that data may remain in the program state?

2.2.3   Other Security Models

Lattices.   Dorothy Denning extended the partial-order model even further by organizing the security structure into a *lattice*[4] and using it to model the information flow at each step in execution [Den76]. The extra features a lattice offers over a partial order come in handy. For example, the existence of least upper bounds lets us always describe the level of information that arises from an operation on two arguments, each of which may be a different security level.

The standard MLS structure of

$$\text{ClearanceLevels} \times 2^{\text{Categories}}$$

is already a lattice. We'll leave that as a proverbial exercise for the reader.

Integrity.   The Bell-LaPadula model provides for confidentiality but not for *integrity*. The *Biba* model tries to address this problem by essentially turning Bell-LaPadula upside down. We organize subjects and objects according to integrity levels and prevent subjects from reading objects with lesser integrity or writing objects with greater integrity. Rather than trying to prevent information from flowing to weaker parties, we try to prevent contamination from flowing to stronger parties. (Biba's 1977 technical report is considered the seminal reference, but obtaining a copy is not easy [Bib77].) Clark and Wilson subsequently developed a formal model that took a different approach to ensuring integrity: ensuring that users can act on data items only via *well-formed transactions* [CW87].

Chinese Wall.   Consider an enterprise, such as investment banking or legal counsel, that may have clients who compete with each other. For example, suppose that Alice and Bob are getting divorced but are using the same law firm. Carlo, a lawyer in that firm, can look at Alice's file or Bob's file. However, once he looks at one of them, looking at the other becomes a conflict of interest.

The *Chinese Wall* security model formalizes this notion. We put objects into conflict classes. Before accessing anything in a class C, a subject S is allowed to

---

4. See the appendix.

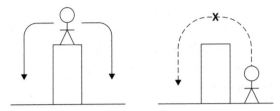

Figure 2.5 When Carlo is standing on top of the Chinese Wall, he is able to jump to either side, as we see on the left. However, once he jumps to one of the sides, he is no longer able to jump to the other one, as we see on the right.

access anything in C. However, once it accesses an $O \in C$, S can no longer access any $O' \in C$ where $O' \neq O$. When standing on top of the Great Wall of China, it's possible for Carlo to jump to either side; however, once he jumps off to one side, it's no longer possible for him to jump to the other side (see Figure 2.5).

The Chinese Wall model received attention in the research literature because it handled useful scenarios that the traditional MLS approach could not handle. The Chinese Wall model receives attention in practice, too, because real enterprises, such as investment banking, require such access control rules. Colleagues in that industry tell us that potential clients now use security as a differentiator when choosing a firm—however, they define security by asking how many *insiders* will have access to their data. (Everyone assumes that firms already have good perimeter control.) The industry also implements *timed* Chinese Walls: If S accesses $O \in C$ at time t, then S is prohibited from accessing $O' \in C$ during the interval $[t, t + \Delta]$.

RBAC. What exactly are the actors in the access control matrix? In Chapter 1, we called them *subjects* but also noted that some treatments call them *domains*. The idea there is that although the subjects, such as human users or an operating system process, may do the acting, their permissions may change according to what hat they are wearing. Hence, it can be easier to set up the matrix in terms of these hats, or domains, and then worry about which domain a subject currently maps to.

The concept of *role-based access control (RBAC)* generalizes this idea [NIS07b]. Developed in the 1990s, RBAC associates permissions with *roles* [FK92, SCFY96]. However, it goes beyond simple domains by allowing fairly rich and expressive structure on the roles and on the mapping of subjects to roles. For example, RBAC allows roles to be organized into hierarchies. This structure can simplify security management; for example, an enterprise may set up permissions for the generic role of *employee* and then set up a *manager* role that inherits the permissions of *employee* but has additional permissions. This structure can also allow enforcement of organizational policy, such as *separation of duties*; for example, a subject may be allowed to take on the role of *trader* or *auditor* but not both. As a consequence, RBAC can be more expressive than simple user-group approaches of the UNIX family.

2.3 The Orange Book

The U.S. Defense Department, concerned that using computers—Automatic Data Processing systems, as they were called—would lead to secrecy violations, sponsored much of this early research and then tried to codify the resulting conclusions as a set of standards. The standards documents themselves lay out their purpose:

- To give users a "yardstick" to measure security
- To guide manufacturers
- To guide all those poor souls needing to decide what computers to buy for Defense Department applications

A series of documents were published. Each document had a different color cover and became known by that color. The full set was known informally as the *Rainbow Series*.

The *Orange Book* presented the main criteria for trusted computer systems [DoD85]. The idea was to have two types of requirements:

1. *Functionality:* What must it do?
2. *Assurance:* Why should anyone believe it does that?

Figure 2.6 sketches this space.

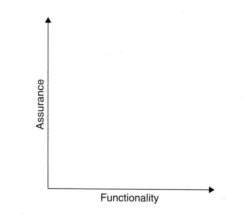

Figure 2.6 To evaluate the security of systems, we often use two independent axes: what *functionality* the system must have and what degree of *assurance* we require it to have.

A system was then put in place whereby vendors could submit systems to receive ratings according to the resulting yardstick. (It's tempting to use *certification* and *validation* as synonyms for this type of process, but certain programs get picky about which term is used. For example, the *Federal Information Processing Standards (FIPS)* process insisted on *validation*.)

The Orange Book is upfront about its goals, declaring on p. 9 that one had better define *security* first before talking about how to achieve it; the Orange Book defines it as being sure that classified data doesn't fall into the wrong hands.

2.3.1 Within the Matrix

This goal drives much of the requirements and features. Some of them follow right from the abstract model. For example, if we don't want to leak data, we might want to consider certain techniques:

- *Discretionary access control (DAC).* We'd better make it possible for subjects to specify access restrictions for objects they care about.
- *Mandatory access control (MAC).* If we really care about it, we'd better make sure that subjects and objects actually follow the lattice model.
- *Identification and authentication (I&A).* We need to know who subjects are.
- *Labels.* We'd better have labels on objects to indicate their security level. We also probably want to worry about input/output (I/O) devices, so that output is properly labeled.
- *Reference monitor.* If we care about the access rules and have labeled subjects and objects in order to know what rules should apply, we'd better have a module within this system that actually checks the rules. (Some texts use the term *security kernel* as an approximate synonym for the reference monitor.)
- *Complete mediation.* If the reference monitor is to do its job, we'd better make sure that the rules are checked for each and every access.
- *Audit.* We may also want to be able to go back later to see what was going on, so it would be good to have audit capabilities.

2.3.2 Beyond the Matrix

Some of the requirements come from more subtle issues about information flow in real systems. At a high level of analysis, the access control matrix, which must always comply with no-write-down and no-read-up rules, governs information access and all other security-relevant actions in the system. A subject or an object that does not appear in the matrix does not exist. A method of access that is not even in the set of possible methods does not exist, let alone if it is possible but simply not listed in a particular cell. However, the matrix is only a model: a simpler abstraction of what the system actually does. Unfortunately, this abstraction simplifies away details that can be relevant to information flow. The Orange Book identifies some of these details.

Object Reuse.   As part of its ordinary operation, an operating system may reuse an element for a different purpose. For one example, consider memory. Processes and programmers operate under the convenient illusion that they have a full 2^n bytes of addressable memory, where n is the number of bits in the address bus. However, the area of *memory management* (within OS design) focuses on how to allow processes to operate under this illusion—or *virtual memory*—while in fact giving them only much smaller pieces of physical RAM. Furthermore, which pieces they have can change dynamically over time, as which and how much memory they really need right now changes.

   This give and take of physical memory frames can provide an avenue for information flow. Right now, frame 23 in physical memory may contain page 42 of the address space of process A. However, various events may cause the OS to revoke this mapping: Perhaps process A is going to be blocked for a while, or perhaps it hasn't been using page 42 very much. The OS may then save the contents of page 42 out on disk, in order to get it back the next time process A needs it, and reuse frame 23 for another process, B.

   If frame 23 shows up as a newly allocated page within process B's address space rather than simply a place to store a page restored from disk, the old data from process A may still be there. Rather than zeroing out frame 23 as soon as it's evicted from process A's space, many modern operating systems preserve it as long as possible, which can greatly lower the cost of handling the page fault should process A turn out to need page 42 again quickly. (Chapter 4 discusses more security implications of operating system structure.) Memory reuse can thus provide a way for data to flow from A to B, completely outside the purview of the matrix model.

   Memory reuse can also provide an avenue for information flow between elements of an individual program. For example, a program might execute a cryptographic subroutine that stores highly sensitive keys as local variables. By convention, these variables live on the stack. Unless the programmer takes countermeasures, that data is still there in the part of the stack abandoned when that subroutine exits, and may show up as the initial value of local variables in a later subroutine. Even if the programmer does take countermeasures, such as zeroing out the sensitive variables before the subroutine exits, the compiler may still cause problems, since an overly clever one might realize that there's no point in writing these zeros that are never read. (See Figure 2.7.)

The heap can provide another avenue for leakage: Without additional countermeasures, memory that is `malloc`'d and `free`'d and then `malloc`'d again by the same process may contain relics of its first usage. (Recently, researchers from Stanford used some advanced hardware simulation techniques to examine these issues in modern systems, with interesting results [CPG⁺04].) We might be tempted to conclude that, within this Orange Book thinking, we're exempt from worrying about all this if we treat each process as a single entity. However, the *operating system* itself is a long-lived program with stacks and heaps and subroutines and static buffers. Careless reuse of these objects can cause trouble.

Yet another family of trouble areas lies in nonvolatile storage, such as disk. From the high-level view, the disk provides a place to store an item, such as a file. When we delete the file, it disappears; when we rewrite or truncate the file, the old parts disappear. The reality is more complicated. In traditional filesystem design, the abandoned parts may persist as now-unallocated blocks. Modern log-structured filesystems save files as a series of updates, so *all* the previous data may persist. Computer systems that use FLASH memory for nonvolatile storage have similar issues, since each erase/rewrite of a FLASH sector consumes a nontrivial part of its working life. Even if the programmer is careful about object reuse via filesystem calls, the fact that the OS will typically use nonvolatile storage as a backing store for virtual memory creates yet another avenue.

Covert Channels. Typical operating systems provide methods of *interprocess communication (IPC)*. These communication channels should show up in the access control matrix; the reference monitor should check this matrix to determine whether a particular instance of channel use should be allowed.

This is all well and good. However, since the matrix is a simplifying abstraction of the real system, *covert* communication channels may exist that do not show up in the matrix, and thus never get checked. Malicious subjects can use these channels to communicate information in ways that violate policy.

Historically, the Orange Book community worried about covert channels and identified two flavors. In *storage channels*, one can send a message by manipulating statically observable structure, such as filenames or disk usage. Some simple examples would be creating or deleting a file with a certain name or growing or shrinking a file. If Alice is not allowed to tell Bob about the result of a computation but Bob is still allowed to `ls  -l` on a common directory, then Alice can still tell him.

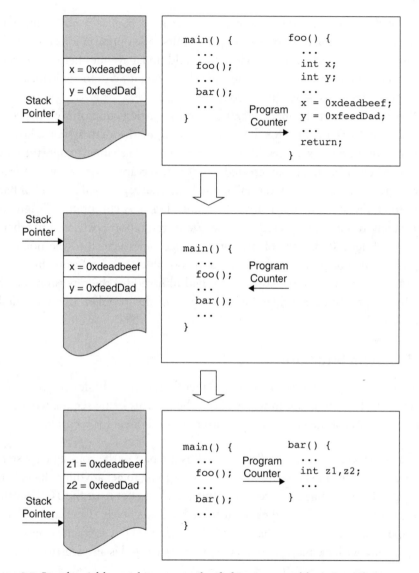

Figure 2.7 Local variables can be an example of *object reuse* problems in modern computing environments. On the top, function foo() leaves important secrets in local variables x and y. In the middle, foo() has exited, but these secrets persist in now free space on the stack. On the bottom, these secrets show up again as the unitialized values of local variables z1 and z2 in function bar().

In *timing channels*, one can send a message through dynamically observable structure such as the timing or frequency of page faults. The optimizations that modern systems use for memory usage provide many additional avenues here. If process B invokes a dynamic library routine and times how long it takes to get loaded, it can learn whether process A had just used it.

Whether a covert channel *requires* the active participation of both the sender and the receiver is a matter for the pedantic to argue. Modern systems, however, offer many interesting examples of covert communication channels where the sender did not quite realize that it had created a useful observable. For example, advance knowledge of whether a corporation's annual financial report will be good or bad is useful to an investor but legally forbidden knowledge. A corporate colleague told us of having recently discovered that the *size* of the report correlated to whether it was good news (long, lots of bragging) or bad news (short, to the point) and that, in advance of publication, it had been possible for a malicious investor to observe how much space the corporation had reserved for the report on the Web site. (In Chapter 8, we consider some instances of this problem in cryptographic implementations.)

2.3.3 System Structure

Additional Orange Book security requirements flow from basic structure of the system itself. If we're going to worry about the systems being secure, we'd better identify the parts of the system where correctness is critical for security:

- *Trusted computing base (TCB)*. The TCB is the part of the computing system that absolutely must be trustworthy if we're going to get anything done. This usage of *trusted* may seem counterintuitive: We do not trust the TCB because it's worthy of trust but rather because we have no choice.[5] Consequently, it's important both to know what the TCB is and to keep it as small as possible. That way, we have more assurance that what's trusted is also trustworthy.

- *Security perimeter.* The TCB is sometimes defined indirectly, by defining the *security perimeter* that separates it from the rest of the system.

- *Security kernel.* The reference monitor is sometimes called a security kernel.

- *Trusted path*. The user had better be sure whether he or she is communicating with the TCB. The term *trusted path* usually denotes a mechanism through

---

5. A friend who served on a Navy submarine gave a similar definition: "Trust" is what you do to the crewmates who can kill you if they make a mistake.

which the user can do this. Sometimes, *trusted path* refers only to a channel from the TCB to the user; a *secure attention key* is the mechanism used in the other direction, so that the TCB can be sure input came from the user.

In modern times, the trusted-path concept has generalized somewhat to refer to channels between the user and a particular trusted application, as well as to channels between a nonuser entity and a particular trusted application. Some in the field use the term *trusted channel* to distinguish this latter item.

2.3.4 Software Engineering Practices

The Orange Book also requires that system design and development follow what its authors considered to be good software engineering practices:

- *Layering.* The software should be broken into well-defined layers; each layer *n* should make use of services provided by the layer below it.
- *Abstraction and data hiding.* A layer should hide the details of how it performs its services. Rather than exposing these internals, a layer should simply provide an interface for the layers above to call.
- *Configuration control.* When building systems composed of many source files and developers, it can be easy to lose track of updates. Procedures to avoid this sloppiness are needed to ensure security.

Subsequent research in operating system design and system software engineering raises questions about whether strict layering and strict data hiding are always good, but that's an argument for a different book. However, in our experience, the importance of good configuration control continues to be overlooked.

2.3.5 System Assurance

In addition to specifying features the system should have, the Orange Book enumerates techniques to help answer the question of why one should believe that the system does in fact work:

- *Trusted facility management.* It's important that the system not become corrupted while it's being built. Consequently, we might want to consider the procedures for protecting the production tools, such as source code repositories, editors, compilers, and so on.

- *Trusted distribution.* It's important that the system arrive at the user site in one piece. Consequently, we might want to consider what the distribution channel is and what protections might be appropriate there.

- *Testing.* It's important that we can verify that the system works. Consequently, we might want to consider procedures for testing, at start-up as well as on the fly, at runtime. We might want to test each interface and, potentially, consider how to test that the interfaces do not do what they are not supposed to do. We might also want to figure out how to test that the system does not have flaws and holes that can enable the adversary to move the system into an incorrect state. Proving the absence of such holes is, of course, not necessarily possible; however, we should at least try.

- *Documentation.* It's important to tell the users (and analyzers, and maintainers, and developers) what the system actually does.

- *Formal top-level specification.* In some sense, we require documentation in order to know what the system actually does and to force the designers themselves to think about that issue. We might even go further and require that the documentation include a formal specification of system behavior. In order to show that this behavior is what was wanted, we might want to verify that the specification matches the security policy; in order to show that the behavior is what the system does, we might want to verify that the specification matches the code. (The Orange Book requires formal methods for the former but allows informal methods for the latter.)

The resulting yardstick consists of four *divisions* (D–A) and then various *classes* within each division. (Divisions get more secure as the letters go down toward A; classes get more secure as the numbers go up away from 1.) Each successively more secure category raises the bar in feature and assurance requirements:

- D: "minimal protection"
- C: "discretionary protection"
- B: "mandatory protection"
- A: "verified protection"

(No, we've never been happy with these verbal names for the divisions, but there they are.) Systems in class C1 must have some mechanisms to let users restrict access to data. C2 adds login and auditing. B1 adds labeling, MAC, and an informal security policy. B2 makes it formal and requires more thought about the TCB. B3 requires a stronger reference monitor. A1 adds more formal methods. (Systems that

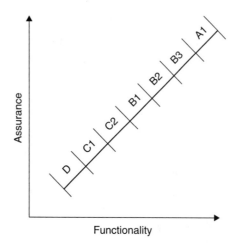

Figure 2.8 The Orange Book strikes one path through the two-axes space: As we move along the classes and divisions, we require more functionality and more assurance.

fail to meet any of these standards earn the D rating.) Figure 2.8 sketches how these standards land in the functionality-assurance space.

2.3.6 Case Studies

VAX Security Kernel.   As a case study of a real-world commercial product pursuing Orange Book validation, we'll consider the VAX Security Kernel designed and built by Paul Karger and his colleagues [KZB+91]. They were on track for an A1 rating.

The VAX Security Kernel was not a general-purpose OS. Rather, it was a high-assurance way of *virtualizing* the machine so that different classes of operation could safely take place on different virtual machines. (This notion of virtualization—secure or otherwise—has become fashionable again of late; we consider the modern approaches in more detail in chapters 4 and 16.) Karger and his colleagues chose to make multiple virtual instances of the hardware rather than, say, virtual instances of an OS API. This work required changing the hardware in order to virtualize the instruction set.

The project demonstrated real-world wrangling with various Orange Book concepts. The authors identified subjects and objects, secrecy levels and access classes, and the rules of both mandatory and discretionary controls. The authors identified the TCB and designed it around a hierarchy of many layers; worried about trusted path and the secure attention key; used multiple physical environments, including a "cage" and an airgap to ensure trusted facility management; and developed an extensive set of tests, including a suite that tested "illegal and malformed requests."

This last action demonstrates a principle deserving special emphasis: *Everyone tests that systems do what they should do. But it's easy to overlook testing that they do not do what they shouldn't.*

The authors set up invalid *guard* pages to protect against wild addressing; shipped elements of the software along separate paths to protect against compromise along the shipping channel; exhaustively surveyed for storage channels and timing channels; and used an automated theorem prover to show that their *top-level specification (TLS)* matched their security policy. The authors noted that the TLS turned out to be one-sixth the size of the kernel itself.

They also bragged about how the discipline of "verified protection" led to robustness [KZB+91, p. 1161]:

> The kernel regularly remained up for nearly three weeks while under a heavy production load of real users! Most new OSes (and VMMs) consider themselves lucky to stay up a few hours when in initial field test.

Some would assert, not without foundation, that an inevitable consequence of security is robustness.

Unfortunately, the A1-verified VAX Security Kernel never shipped as a product. The U.S. government deemed that such a high-assurance product would be treated as a munition and be subject to strict export controls, and Digital Equipment Corporation (DEC) decided that it would not be profitable to market it under those conditions.

GEMSOS. GEMSOS is another example of a real-world kernel that underwent a series of high-level validations over its long development lifetime [NCS95, STH85, STT88]. The GEMSOS architecture was inspired by the layered separation of Multics. For secrecy, GEMSOS used the Bell-LaPadula approach; for integrity, a combination of a software-based Biba approach as well as hardware enforcement. The design and development process consciously tried to not sacrifice too much performance to achieve security. The process also paid attention to commercial realities, by framing the kernel as a "sealed unit" that could be adapted and used in other platforms and by tracking advances in commercial hardware; the OS evolved from the Intel 286 through to the 486 with multiprocessor support.

The GEMSOS security kernel was used in the core of such systems as BLACKER, rated A1 against the Orange Book; a later commercial embodiment of GEMSOS earned an A1 rating against the "Trusted Network Interpretation" of the Orange Book [NCS87]. Even today, GEMSOS is touted as "the only general-purpose kernel in the world rated Class A1" according to sales material found at [AES06].

2.4 INFOSEC, OPSEC, JOBSEC

Although the Orange Book may have passed into the recycle bin of history, much military-driven thinking about security persists. One still hears discussions of the distinctions among *information systems security (INFOSEC)*, *communication security (COMSEC)*, and *operations security (OPSEC)*. (Of course, some wags assert that this is all part of *JOBSEC*.)

The NSA promulgates a set of security-training standards that academics may encounter when applying to be an NSA Center of Excellence in security education. As part of these standards, the *Comprehensive Model of Information Systems Security* considers the $3 \times 3 \times 3$ matrix of confidentiality-integrity-availability versus information states (transmission, storage, processing) versus approaches (technology, policy and practices, and education/training/awareness) [Nat94]. With all seriousness, the documentation elaborates on the comparison between states of information and states of water, which serves to weaken its intellectual credibility.

2.5 The Take-Home Message

Folks have been thinking hard about security for a number of decades. It's almost easy to take the position that since we still don't have secure systems, the old thinking must have been wrong. We believe that's a narrow point of view. Although it's certainly true that it didn't solve world hunger, the Orange Book did introduce and cleanly define a number of security concepts that are still relevant today.

If nothing else, the Orange Book gave the community a giant stake in the ground, to use as a reference point. It's had quite an impact on the field, and we believe that it's still a worthwhile resource to consult when faced with system-level security problems.

2.6 Project Ideas

1. Read the Orange Book. What parts are relevant? What parts aren't? Why aren't they relevant anymore? (Were they ever?)

2. What's the difference between a storage channel and a timing channel? Implement one of each.

3. Bell and LaPadula's no-write-down rule is a bit more complex than the simple rule that you can't write to a class lower than your own. Why?

4. Show that the standard MLS structure of CLEARANCELEVELS $\times$ $2^{\text{CATEGORIES}}$ is a lattice. (You may need to consult the appendix.)

5. Take your favorite OS or system and try to find any Orange Book concepts that might be present. Does the OS use DAC or MAC? How does the OS do I&A? Does the OS use labels? Does it implement complete mediation and keep audit logs? If you have source code, can you find the TCB and the security perimeter?

Old Principles,
New World

In Chapter 1, we offered our working definition of *security*: when the system state remains correct, despite potential actions of some class of adversaries. It's clear from looking at history, headlines, or even the latest posts to the BugTraq mailing list that we, as a community, are not managing to develop and deploy secure systems. The causes for this problem are grist for lively debate and good classroom exercises. Is it because we don't know how to build secure systems? Is it because we can build them but somehow cannot deploy them in the real world? Is it because we don't quite know what the correct state is? In Chapter 2, we looked at some of the early thinking that tried to address these problems. In this chapter, we look at trying to build on these historical foundations to solve the problems of today.

In 1975, Jerome Saltzer and Michael Schroeder wrote down a set of eight design principles intended to help designers of time-sharing systems protect information. The two men were involved with the Multics system, and their work has been widely cited throughout the years, as it represents some of the earliest thinking on building secure systems.

For the military and defense world in the early days of computer security, correctness roughly meant that information didn't flow to the wrong people. These pioneers then developed a rigid set of rules—exemplified by the Orange Book—to try to ensure that systems were secure. However, even its True Believers regard the Orange Book as a failure: It did not lead to a wealth of commericial or even noncommercial systems that met that definition of security. What went wrong?

Why do computer security problems persist, even though the Orange Book was published more than 20 years ago?

- Section 3.1 looks at whether the Orange Book was solving the wrong problem.
- Section 3.2 shows how the U.S. government failed to follow through.
- Section 3.3 considers whether the Orange Book's rigid mindset made it too inflexible and unwieldy.
- Section 3.4 examines the Saltzer and Schroeder principles in detail.
- Section 3.5 explores whether any of these old approaches to building secure systems are relevant today or whether they all missed the mark in some way. Some of this thinking has been around for three decades, and we're still not building secure systems.

3.1 Solving the Wrong Problem?

The main focus of the Orange Book is on confidentiality of data within an MLS environment. With labels on data and I/O channels and worries about write-down and write-up rules, the standard expends much energy on the topic of confidentiality. Consequently, artisans following its advice must also expend much energy thinking about their systems in that way.

Is this the right problem? Is this the right way to think about the security of our system? One might ask who really cares about multiple levels of secrecy. With the Biba and Chinese Wall models, we already saw divergences from the MLS approach within the space of standard models. Most important, what are the right notions of correctness and security in today's enterprise systems?

One could argue that modern notions of correctness and security are rooted in *interface security*. A vast majority of the known and exploited vulnerabilities in systems stems from advertised interfaces that provide unintentionally dangerous functionality. For example, the `fingerd` network daemon was intended simply to let remote parties query a machine for some basic state information. In terms of our state reachability definition, the authors of this daemon did not intend to provide a "run your code at my privilege" service; that would not have shown up in their model of the system's state space. Nonetheless, that's what it really did, in a well-known and well-exploited vulnerability!

Modern worms propagate not because modern systems fail to implement labeled protection but because core boundary functions fail to properly check their input. It's possible that systems that followed the Orange Book in letter and spirit could still be vulnerable to these types of issues. In Chapter 6, we discuss interface security and input validation in more depth.

One could argue that modern correctness and security are about *isolation*. As we discuss further in Chapter 6, software consumers demand increasingly fancy features, which lead modern software to be increasingly complex. Making matters worse is the fact that business drivers force software development to be quick. This combination of factors makes it unreasonable to engineer, label, and add high-assurance protections within any one application installation. As a consequence, we might assert that it makes more sense to ensure that separate installations cannot contaminate each other. In some sense, this is a security motivation behind the renewed interest in virtualization, both at an OS level (Chapter 4) and a hardware level (Chapter 16). Rather than making Windows secure, we'll simply make sure that the damage that an exploit can cause is confined. Orange Book–style information flow techniques should apply between, rather than within, virtual machines.

Then there's the question of who really uses multiuser general-purpose machines anymore. Arguably, the primary desktop model is single-user box with interfaces and specialized services—arguing the case for intermachine isolation and controls, not intramachine controls. Alternatively, if we look at back-end machines, such as mail servers or e-commerce Web servers, we still have data for many individuals—but these individuals are not users of the machine, in the traditional sense of having general accounts and logging in.

One could argue that correctness and security are about *performance*. Rather than putting data confidentiality or data integrity first, we should put availability first. However, we stretch the definition and apply *availability* to include the development of the software, rather than only its execution. As we stated before, customers want the latest fancy features to be available. Vendors wanting to stay in business will eye functionality and time to market and usually skip spending an extra n months improving the assurance of the system. In a different embodiment of this idea, enterprises can so desire the availability of their mission-critical applications that they decline to update outdated and vulnerable operating systems, for fear that the updates will be incompatible with the applications. We have seen numerous cases in which an organization's cost of updating its systems is greater than its cost of being attacked. (In one case we know of, the fear belonged not to the organization but rather to the regulators: If the end enterprise applied the update, the application lost its validation.)

Of course, some old-guard graybeards[1] dissent from this view that Orange Book thinking solved the wrong problem. They argue that it's still relevant. Buying commercial software that is ridden with vulnerabilities in contemporary times is like buying from the KGB back in the cold war: We need *verified protection.* The importance of an e-merchant's cryptographic keys requires MLS, covert channel analysis, and the whole package. (Schell's "Flying Pigs" essay [Sch01] is an excellent exposition of this point of view. His new company, AESec, has in fact purchased the rights to his A1-rated GEMSOS system and is marketing it as an e-commerce solution.)

Rant.   The "Flying Pigs" essay raises many good points but also raises many we object to. For example, the essay derides cryptography as not a real science, because of its basis in unsolved intractability issues. At the same time, the essay asserts a blind faith in "verified protection." It is true that crytpography is based on assumptions about intractability that might be false. However, "verifiable protection" is meaningful only if one's model is complete, one's theorem prover works, one's model actually expresses the properties that one really cares about, and the system actually matches the model. For another example, requiring programmers to have security clearances might make them less susceptible to blackmail and treason. But does it make them smarter? Are cleared programmers less likely to have buffer overflow errors? The essay scoffs at building trustworthy systems from untrustworthy components. Why not? We build reliable systems that way. We build secure social systems (e.g., voting) that way (e.g., by ensuring that the observers' tendencies to cheat cancel each other out). Any system that has real users has at least one untrustworthy component: a human.

We believe that the truth likely lies somewhere in between.

3.2 Lack of Follow-Through?

Another potential reason for the failure of the Orange Book to save the world was the bad interaction of economics with government policy. Building a high-assurance system is a lot of work—and, as noted earlier, can delay a product's time to market. Businesses exist to make a profit or at least make enough revenue to stay in business.

---

1. We use the term *graybeard* as one of honor. In one of our early workplaces, people who had worked in information security from the early days and had personally seen its evolution and history were reverently called "graybeards," no matter their gender or facial hair. By no means do we mean to imply anything pejorative.

Rational businesses will thus build high-assurance systems only if this action aligns with these goals: if a sufficient market exists and will pay a sufficient price for the systems.

By promulgating the Orange Book, the U.S. government purported to establish metrics for vendors to target when building, and for federal customers to require, when procuring systems. However, somehow this didn't happen: Sufficient demand never arose, and systems that were built were never purchased. Many old-timers bemoan this as a failure of the U.S. government to create a marketplace for the systems built to the standards it requested. Government budgets determined the demand for these types of systems, and they failed to generate enough demand to keep the suppliers in business.

This problem persists with newer security standards, such as FIPS 140-n (see Chapters 11 and 16). Federal law requires that federal customers buy a FIPS-validated product when they have a choice—unless they get a waiver. It is rumored that everyone receives waivers.

One can also make a strong argument that the lack of success of the Orange Book, as well as the broader lack of security in modern systems, stems from another aspect of poorly crafted public policy: the U.S. government's long-running stranglehold on cryptographic research and subsequent draconian export restrictions. In this case, government regulation restricted demand and increased costs. As was discussed in Chapter 2, the $A1$-rated VAX Security Kernel was canceled because the government deemed it a munition and restricted its export. This action led DEC to decide that it could not market it successfully. (We discuss the "crypto wars" further in Chapter 7.)

3.3 Too Unwieldy?

One can also develop another line of thought: The Orange Book might have solved the right problem, but the features it required were too unwieldy and inflexible for real systems and real situations. For example, the principle of keeping flow in the right direction can become excruciatingly hard to follow in practice. We offer two quick examples.

1. How can a cleared subject jump to an uncleared one? On a machine level, jumping to another section of code requires writing to the *program counter*. Normally, an executing program can read its own program counter. However, if a subject with a high security label writes a value here, a subject with a low security label is not supposed to be able to read it.

2. What about the manageability of security? Who's going to add all those labels? (Recently, Cheng et al. have been doing some promising research here [CRK⁺07].)

When philosophical consistency forces undue contortions, perhaps the philosophy is wrong. Some Orange Book graybeards tell stories that MLS systems in practice end up running at "system high" all the time, so that people can get work done. Just as Web users now simply keep clicking to make warning windows go away, users of MLS systems were reputed to keep clicking "I don't care" when warned about upgrading the high-water mark.

Another source of trouble was the way that these principles of secure operating system design and construction became embedded in formal standards in a military setting. This process led to rules that were too rigid and admitted no reevaluation for new scenarios. We can readily think of numerous scenarios for which the Orange Book advice is too unwieldy for a particular problem or system.

- Auditing sounds like a good idea in practice, and audit logs would appear to be necessary for an audit to occur. However, does audit make sense in an embedded device with limited memory? As we recall, this requirement nearly killed the e-check project, in which many players, including the U.S. banking industry, cooperated to introduce electronic checks into the U.S. banking system. The checks were generated electronically from a small embedded device that would serve as a user's e-checkbook.

- Some tout GEMSOS as a solution to modern computing problems, but GEMSOS's security model insists that subjects are "active" and objects "passive" [STH85]. However, ever since the dawn of the Web, one of the problems most vexing to ordinary computer users has been that objects are no longer passive. If objects can act independently on their own, what assumptions are broken?

- The traditional view touts the Bell-LaPadula model as gospel. However, researchers have questioned the notion that the Bell-LaPadula Basic Security Theorem actually means something. McLean offers such a dissenting view, asserting that it is about induction rather than system security [McL85].

- It's clearly important that a system believe commands only if they are issued by the appropriate entities. In the early days of computing, these entities were humans, sitting in front of the machine, and their authority was derived from their identity. The computer security principles that resulted conflated the basic truth—that command should be authorized—with this initial usage scenario, that no longer exclusively describes the world. As a result, we see, as gospel, assertions that security should start with identification and authentication, even though a strong case can be made that, in many scenarios, *authorization*, which is what's really important, requires neither (see Chapter 9).

In our own experience with FIPS 140-1 validation, we had difficulty getting security validators to accept the notion that the "user" authorizing the command may be a remote entity who indicated authorization via a digital signature at some point in the past. Modern trusted computing hardware work (see Chapter 16) stretches this thinking even further: Authorized commands may come not from human subjects but from programmatic entities—a form of troublesome active object—living in a suitably trustworthy environment.

- The nature of computing systems has also changed in other ways since the Orange Book principles were developed. What if we want higher assurance for different functionality? (The *Common Criteria* splits functionality from assurance, but Schell does not have kind words about that strategy [Sch01].) As we build the systems of the future, all signs point to the nature of systems changing even more. For example, why must we have an administrator? Can we build systems for which no one is in charge, or one for which everyone's in charge of a small portion of the system?

- Orange Book–style thinking leads to strict layering in operating systems. (GEMSOS documentation boasts about its 11 layers.) However, newer thinking suggests that strict layering may not be good. As Lampson observes, "if there are six levels of abstraction, and each costs 50% more than is 'reasonable,' the service delivered at the top will miss by more than a factor of 10" [Lam83]. Other developments, such as upcalls, microkernels, and extensible kernels, don't easily fit into this layered thinking, either. Even though the Orange Book has stopped, system engineering has kept developing.

- Even the level of abstraction represented by modern high-level language can be problematic. The old-style thinking stressed the importance of coding the TCB in a high-level language in order to facilitate formal modeling and reasoning about its behavior. However, developments in computing have outstripped this thinking in two directions. On the one hand, the need for performance drives most modern operating systems to have many pieces written in assembly, making this requirement overly burdensome; on the other hand, advances in programming languages and compilers, as well as CPU support for out-of-order and speculative execution, make the notion of inferring well-defined behavior from high-level source code rather questionable.

- The reference monitor sounds like a good idea in the abstract. Security-critical actions ought somehow to get vetted against a policy. However, why is the subsequent requirement of a *centralized* reference monitor absolutely necessary? With public-key cryptography, it's probably possible to build a lattice system that automatically enforces its rules in a distributed, decentralized way. In many application scenarios, this might be a better way of doing things.

- Finally, many of these traditional discussions of security use the word *trustworthy* as if it were a single, well-defined concept and as if it were possible to measure. In the modern computing environment, that may not always be true: We often see a diversity of viewpoints. For example, the RIAA may regard a DRM-enforcing OS component as trustworthy, whereas the end user may regard it as dangerous spyware. For another angle, consider the code-quality aspects of the debates we have seen in recent times between open source and closed source.

In addition to inflexible rules for engineering systems, the Orange Book also put forth a somewhat inflexible mindset. It's true that the hacker mentality often features a subtle cruelty. Announcements and discussions of newly discovered software vulnerabilities often ring with undisguised chortling. This attitude overlooks the fact that software engineering is in fact a difficult field, not populated by stupid people, and that cackling is not perhaps the best way to build a better future. The hacker mentality also echoes gnosticism: Value lies in secret knowledge, hinted and smirked at, rather than in open, rational discussion.

The Orange Book mentality has its own unproductive side effects. The trusted/cleared notion has a tendency to create "us versus them" cliques. Furthermore, this traditional view has a tendency to use such terms as *trusted* and *secure* often enough that these uses become the definitions.[2] Perhaps most dangerous is the traditional view's tendency to accept pronouncements and conclusions as true, never to be questioned again. As scientists and scholars in pursuit of truth, we should be ready to question anything.

---

2. One of us recalls a critique of AI that notes that using the name *thought* for a data structure can lead to the fallacious belief that the program manipulating these structures is "thinking." One worries that an analogous conclusion applies here.

3.4 Saltzer and Schroeder

Ten years before the Orange Book was published, Saltzer and Schroeder wrote their seminal paper: "The Protection of Information in Computer Systems" [SS75]. In the early 1970s, much of the buzz in the computer world centered on the development of multiuser time-sharing OSes, such as Multics and UNIX. Saltzer and Schroeder had been working on the Multics OS and had spent a bit of time considering how to protect information from different users on a multiuser system.

They were solving a different problem than the Orange Book system designers would solve years later: They were building a commercial system, not a military one. As such, their approach to protecting information was quite different in spirit from the Orange Book methodology.

Saltzer and Schroeder began with the admission that no one at the time knew how to build completely secure systems. Although much research was going on at that time—some of which would later form the underpinnings of the Orange Book—no "methodical techniques" existed. So, instead of giving system designers a rigid prescription for how to build a secure system, Saltzer and Schroeder offered eight useful principles based on their experience with building systems to protect information. (Actually, their paper surveys a wide range of systems topics; interested readers should have a look at the original paper.) Here, we focus solely on their eight design principles:

1. *Economy of mechanism*, or keep the design simple. As we discuss in Chapter 6, complexity is one of the largest enemies of security. Keeping security-critical components simple reduces the probability that an error exists in the component and facilitates careful review, perhaps by reading each line of code.

2. *Fail-safe defaults*. The default action of the system should be to deny access to someone or something until it has been explicity granted the necessary privileges. If the system has an error in judgment, perhaps caused by a programming error in the access control mechanism, the system is more likely to refuse access to an authorized party than to grant access to an unauthorized party. Clearly, this is the better of the two outcomes.[3]

3. *Complete mediation*, or every object access needs to be authorized. Saltzer and Schroeder call this the "primary underpinning of the protection system."

---

3. This principle can admit dissent, however. For example, in crisis situations, in some "boomable" industries (in which things may literally blow up) the cost of denying access far outweighs the cost of granting access to someone who cannot formally authenticate. Similarly, IT systems in financial investment services can permit users to break some rules, as long as those users have a good reason.

If any object access goes unchecked, some information in the system cannot be protected.

4. *Open design.* The idea behind this principle is that the security of a particular component should not rely on the secrecy of its design. As we discuss in Chapter 7, this principle is widely held in the cryptographic community. In modern parlance, we say that systems built on secret designs try to achieve "security by obscurity." With some of the reverse-engineering techniques we discuss in Chapter 6, such systems can often be broken. (On the other hand, as we discuss in Chapter 4, whether this principle applies to publishing source code of critical software is a question on which not all vendors agree.)

5. *Separation of privilege.* Systems that require multiple keys or pieces of information to get a job done are more secure than systems that require only one. Requiring multiple parties to each wield a secret—or one party to wield multiple secrets—in order to participate in a transaction means that a potential attacker must compromise more pieces of the system in order to be successful.

6. *Least privilege.* The idea here is that users and machine processes should operate with the smallest set of privileges necessary to complete the given task. For example, many modern best practices encourage users to run as nonsuperusers on their machines. However, some OSes encourage users to run with superuser privileges. Should their account get compromised, the attacker now has superuser access to the target system. If the account had fewer privileges, the attacker would have less power on the victim system.

7. *Least-common mechanism.* Designers should minimize the sharing of tools, resources, and systems mechanisms between processes and users. This principle has motivations both in security and in fault tolerance. From a security perspective, the more state shared between different users, the more likely it is that this shared state may become a conduit for inadvertent (or maybe even "vertent") information flow. Furthermore, system surfaces touched by many users can become an attractive attack target for the adversarial user. From a fault tolerance perspective, the more users that depend on a single mechanism, the more critical it is that the mechanism work flawlessly. (In some sense, then, this principle relates to the dictum of minimizing the TCB.)

8. *Pyschological acceptability.* As we dicsuss in Chapter 18, designers must create user interfaces that allow users to generate appropriate mental models of the system. Saltzer and Schroeder state that "to the extent that the user's mental image of his protection goals matches the mechanisms he must use, mistakes will be minimized" [SS75].

Table 3.1 Security Implications of Saltzer and Schroeder's Design Principles

Principle	Description
Economy of mechanism	Keep the design simple. Complexity breeds vulnerabilities.
Fail-safe defaults	Fail the right way. Denial of service is often preferable to more substantial system compromise.
Complete mediation	Check each access. If you don't check, how can you be sure?
Open design	No security via obscurity. Kerckhoff's Principle applies to system design too.
Separation of privilege	Require the adversary to break multiple components.
Least privilege	The more privileges you have, the more damage you can do.
Least-common mechanism	You wouldn't share a toothbrush, so why share your data files?
Psychological acceptability	If users can't understand the system, they won't use it correctly.

Table 3.1 summarizes these principles.

The Saltzer and Schroeder paper presents some interesting precognition for a paper that's more than 30 years old. Furthermore, in contrast to the Orange Book, the Saltzer and Schroeder principles "do not represent absolute rules—they best serve as warnings" [SS75]. Much as we will try to do throughout this book, Saltzer and Schroeder offered what they believed to be best practices that arose from their experience with designing and building secure systems. Many of their principles are still applicable today.

One important observation was that it's impossible to build a secure computer without support from the underlying hardware. They noted that an attacker who simply waits for a hardware failure may be able to defeat the system. Many modern systems implement some sort of hardware protections; in Chapter 16, we explore the role of specialized security hardware in modern OSes. (Also, the emergence of effective side-channel attacks (see Chapter 8) validates Saltzer and Schroeder's concerns about waiting for hardware failure.)

Another important observation is the realization that it's not enough to have an access control policy that keeps the adversary from reading the system's objects; the adversary must also not be able to modify the policy. Furthermore, they note that attempts to cache access control decisions for the sake of performance can often lead to security trouble. We discuss these issues in detail in Chapter 9.

Finally, their principle of psychological acceptability is making a comeback in the field of *HCISEC*, which looks at *human–computer interaction* and *security* together, as we discuss in Chapter 18.

3.5 Modern Relevance

Admittedly, it's easy to adopt the viewpoint that the Orange Book and Saltzer and Schroeder's principles must have been wrong. After all, we still ship insecure systems, and the technologies and paradigms of the 1970s and 1980s are radically different from those of today. If we believe this, then it's easy to dismiss these bodies of work and start from scratch.

We grant that the community still ships insecure software. We understand that the Orange Book didn't solve all the community's problems. However, we also believe that this pile of work contains some gems. If we remove ourselves from the Orange Book mindset and look at it from an outside perspective, we can find numerous tools and techniques that are useful to those trying to build secure systems.

- Formally defining a system's correctness is a healthy exercise. In the worst case, it gives designers a clearer picture of the problem that their system is trying to solve, as well as establishes some concrete goals for the system to achieve. We discuss this topic further and present tools for doing this type of work in Chapter 15.

- Checking that the design matches the correctness goals and that the code then matches the design are also good habits to develop when building secure systems. We explore some tools and techniques to accomplish this in Chapters 6 and 15.

- Flagging the code that is necessary for the system to operate securely is also an important exercise. This idea has found a rebirth in an approach known as *threat modeling*, which we explore in detail in Chapter 6. This approach also underlies the notions of trusted computing base (Chapter 4) and plays a role in newer trusted-computing initiatives (Chapter 16).

- There is nothing wrong with adhering to good software engineering principles, such as the ones offered by Saltzer and Schroeder. Although these principles— or any other principles, for that matter—are not guaranteed to yield a secure system, they reduce the likelihood that a serious security error exists, and they tend to have a side effect of producing more robust systems in general.

- Spending resources to test the security of a system can also be highly productive. In Chapter 11, we discuss the importance of testing and some of the modern approaches. Furthermore, we discuss the process of having a third party test a system against an established standard.

- Finally, recognizing that cryptography is not a magic silver bullet is also important. As discussed in Chapter 8, there is a never-ending battle between folks who make crypto and folks who break crypto. Furthermore, correctly implementing cryptography is no simple task. Even if the math in your cryptosystem is provably secure, that doesn't stop a developer from storing keys in plaintext.

3.6 The Take-Home Message

Building secure systems is hard. People have been at it for quite some time, and yet we still seem to be no further along as a community than when we started. We still ship systems that get patched on a regular basis—in fact, the second Tuesday of every month is affectionately known as Patch Tuesday in IT circles because that's when Microsoft releases its updates.

For the past three decades, we've been trying to solve this problem. We've adopted best practices, written formal criteria, and developed thousands of tools and techniques to help us build more secure software. What happened?

As we've explored in this chapter, the earliest comprehensive set of guidelines for building such systems—the Orange Book—failed to produce generations of secure software. Maybe it solved the wrong problem, maybe it wasn't executed properly, or maybe it was simply too much.

Nevertheless, we believe that the Orange Book was a beginning, not an end. To dismiss it entirely is like dismissing Newtonian physics because it does not explain electromagnetic forces. The Orange Book represents an important first step in trying to explain how to build secure systems. Even though it is old, by modern technological timelines, it is full of useful and relevant techinques for building secure systems today.

As we progress through this text, we challenge readers to continuously look for a relation between the topic at hand and the principles put forth by the Orange Book and Salzer and Schroeder. It is surprising to see how much of our modern thinking about security stems from these decades-old texts.

3.7 Project Ideas

1. Would the VAX Security Kernel have helped for an e-commerce Web server? What about GEMSOS? It's easy for those not in the old guard to assert that these "old" operating systems will simply not be appropriate for modern computing applications and environments. However, argument by assertion should never suffice. What kind of data would support or refute this assertion? How would you go about obtaining it?

2. Mitre's list of *common vulnerabilities and exposures (CVEs)* describes and categorizes known vulnerabilities in software [MIT06]. Pick a set of the vulnerabilites (e.g., all the vulnerabilities for 2005), and determine which problems are the direct result of violating a principle in the Orange Book or from Saltzer and Schroeder. Which problems are entirely independent of these ancient bodies of work?

3. Pick a piece of software for which you have access to the source code and understand its design. Which of Saltzer and Schroeder's principles are followed? Which ones are disregarded?

4. Using that system, assume that you are submitting it to get an Orange Book rating. What rating is it closest to? What would you have to do to get it there? Is the rating worth the effort? Why or why not?

Part II

Security and the Modern Computing Landscape

OS Security 4

As interesting as the image might be, most users don't execute computation themselves. They use computers for that.

Earlier, we defined security as keeping the adversary from subverting the important properties of your system. "System" consists primarily of "computation." In order to subvert computation, an adversary must somehow have a way to get into it, such as via some type of input or some other computation. Computers use an *operating system* to bring some order and control to the computation they host. Consequently, operating systems become a natural arena for security attacks and defenses.

In this chapter, we explore the arena of OS security.

- Section 4.1 looks at the general background of OS construction.
- Section 4.2 considers OS security primitives.
- Section 4.3 focuses on the complexity of modern OS behavior.
- Section 4.4 examines how this complexity has led to security issues.
- Section 4.5 considers where to go next.

4.1 OS Background

We begin this chapter with a quick review of what operating systems are.

4.1.1 Computer Architecture

Believe it or not, using a computer once required using a soldering iron and wire-wrapping tools and knowing what a hex inverter was. The past several decades, however, have brought technology advances that have also raised the level of abstraction that shapes how users think of computers. The operating system plays a key role in all that abstraction. However, to appreciate it, we need to see through the layers. So, we start with a simplified view of what's at the bottom: the hardware.

Computers operate in binary. This is the literal truth: At the bottom level, things are binary numbers, each bit is some wire, and the value of that bit is the voltage level on that wire. The CPU and memory use buses to send bits back and forth (see Figure 4.1). Physical memory is an array of bytes. Each physical address names the location of 1 byte. You can think of each byte of physical memory as a register: either eight flip-flops (for static RAM) or eight capacitors (for dynamic RAM). With simple Boolean gates, we can build a decoder that recognizes an N-bit address from an AND gate and up to N inverters. Thus, we can think of memory as an array of 1-byte registers, each with a decoder circuit that enables that byte for reading or writing. If it wants to read a byte from memory, the CPU spits out the address on the address bus and issues a read signal on the control bus. The memory sends that byte back out. If it wants to write a byte to memory, the CPU spits out the address on the address bus and the value on the data bus, and issues a write signal on the control bus. The memory loads that byte in.

In modern systems, the program, at its basic level, consists of a sequence of machine instructions. These instructions are literally simply binary values—*opcodes* and data—living in memory. The CPU has an internal *program counter (PC)* register that contains the address of the next instruction it should execute. The CPU issues that address on the address bus and fetches the instruction. The CPU then uses its internal logic circuits to decode this instruction and figure out what it's supposed to be doing (e.g., "move the contents of CPU register B to the memory location whose address is the next 4 bytes that follow the opcode") and does it. As part of

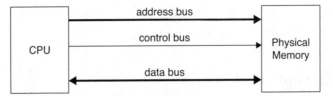

Figure 4.1 In a basic model of physical computer architecture, the CPU reads and writes memory locations via its buses.

executing the instruction, the CPU's circuits will update the PC to be the address of the next instruction to be executed.

That's it—that's computation. The user might be pointing and clicking or typing into a word processor or running a large payroll application, but it all reduces to this basic process.

Again, recall our caveat: The model we presented here is simplified. The reality on modern computers is more complicated, owing to the use of various tricks to improve performance. For example, CPUs now are typically *pipelined*, using tricks to start executing the next instruction before the first one is finished, and much *caching* of instructions and data occurs. But those are just optimizations; what we have presented is the basic idea.

4.1.2 The Need for an OS

Dealing with computation on this very low level can be exasperating, especially if we think of all the kinds of complex tasks we expect a modern computer to perform, usually all at the same time. Operating systems arose in order to make it more convenient and efficient to set up and coordinate all these tasks. We might even stand on a professorial soapbox and declaim that an OS makes our lives easier in three main ways:

1. *Freedom from low-level annoyances.* An OS can prevent each new program from having to deal with the picayune details of the same low-level tasks; an OS can prevent a program from having to redo its handling of these low-level details when it moves to another machine. For example, the need to read and write files is a common task for programs. However, think of all the work involved in enabling a program to read in some part of a file: We need to figure out where that file is on disk, where that part is within that file, and then how to bring it in. It would be much easier to provide a common service that handles this for everyone.

2. *Multiprogramming.* Andrew Birrell once quipped that "humans are actually quite good at doing two or three things at a time, and seem to get offended if their computer cannot do as much" [Bir89, p.2]. An OS can make it easier for a computer to do many things at once. Being able to switch back and forth between programs enables increased convenience and efficiency. If a program is waiting for a disk transfer to complete, the CPU can run another program; if the CPU can rapidly switch back and forth between two programs, then the user can do such things as run a lengthy calculation in one window while simultaneously typing in another one.

3. *Process isolation.* When the computer has more than one thing going on at the same time, the OS can protect these things from each other. Since this is a security book, the first thing we might think of here is protecting a target process from a malicious one. However, isolation is useful in less paranoid scenarios as well: A programmer doesn't have to worry about another process's clumsiness trashing her memory or causing her program to crash.

4.1.3 Basic Elements

Operating systems use several basic elements, in conspiracy with the computer hardware, to try to achieve these goals.

Userland and Kernel Mode. Modern CPUs typically run in two modes:

1. *Kernel*, also known as *privileged* and, in Intel x86 parlance, *Ring 0*
2. *User*, also known as *unprivileged*, or *Ring 3*

The hardware will allow only certain types of privileged instructions and operations if the current CPU mode is, as the name implies, privileged. According to conventional wisdom, the OS should run in privileged, or kernel, mode; everything else should run in unprivileged mode, or *userland*. However, current reality often departs from this model, as we'll discuss shortly.

Obviously, if the protection provided by the privileged mode is to be meaningful, unprivileged code cannot freely change modes. In the standard model, the only way to go from userland to kernel mode is by triggering a special hardware *trap*, such as

- An *interrupt* from some external hardware, such as I/O or a clock
- An *exception*, such as trying to divide by zero or trying to access illegal memory or memory that does not belong to the process
- Executing an explicit *trap instruction*

The consequences of these actions are similar: The CPU suspends execution of the userland program, changes modes to kernel model, looks in a table—for example, the *interrupt vector*—to see where to go, and starts running the OS code specified by that table.

Memory Management. If we're to protect userland processes from each other, then we had better be able to keep them from reading and writing each other's memory and from reading and writing the operating system's memory, which includes its code. The standard way systems achieve this is by having a *memory-management*

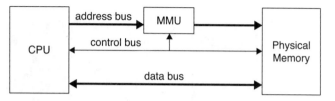

Figure 4.2 In modern systems, a *memory-management unit* translates the virtual addresses the CPU issues into actual physical addresses. The ability to control and change this translation enables an OS to give each process its own address space and to keep userland code from stepping on data it shouldn't.

unit (MMU) sit on the address bus, between the CPU and the rest of the system (see Figure 4.2). The CPU issues addresses as it sees fit, but the MMU *translates* each such logical address to a physical address. The OS sets up and controls this translation, via privileged instructions.

This concept of memory management enables further abstraction. From the perspective of the program running on the CPU, memory may appear as one large, contiguous region of physical locations. However, the MMU will typically break memory up into chunks called *pages*, or *frames*. The pages that comprise a logical address space do not need to appear in order in physical memory; indeed, some may not even appear at all.

MMU translation also lets us mark certain regions of memory as read-only (for userland code); if the CPU, in userland, tries to issue a write to that address, the MMU will refuse to translate it and will trap back to the kernel.

Similarly, MMU translation can keep userland code from even reading memory it shouldn't. Typically, the kernel sets up memory that only it can see and uses this memory to store userland process bookkeeping data, buffers for I/O, and so on. However, *how* this is done depends on both the hardware architecture and OS design choices. Figure 4.3 shows a typical textbook presentation. Each userland process has its own address space; however, the MMU tables are set up so that the kernel's private memory appears in the same place in *each* address space. This way, when a userland process traps to kernel mode, we don't need to change the MMU tables; furthermore, kernel-level code can easily see and change userland data. Again, *where* in the userland address space the mapping goes varies from OS to OS. Also, this arrangement is only typical, not *necessary*. In some systems, such as Solaris on SPARC, the kernel has its own address space, which necessitates additional tricks for the kernel to reach out and touch userland memory. The ability to completely switch both what userland code is running and the address space it sees gives rise to the notion of *process* as a fundamental element controlled and managed by operating systems.

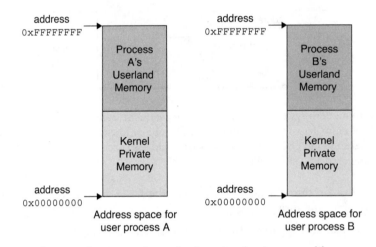

Figure 4.3 In the typical setup, each userland process has its own address space, but the kernel's private memory is mapped to the same part of each space. (Pedant's note: Yes, we've simplified away the kernel stacks.)

Most modern systems also permit the OS to evict selected pages from memory to a backing store—typically, a hard disk, although newer technologies are emerging. Since most processes do not use all their memory all the time, this technique can greatly improve performance—that is, depending on how we measure performance.

System Calls. Userland code needs to request services of the operating system. Typically, the way this is done is via a *system call*, or *syscall*: The userland code leaves in some agreed-on place, such as one of the CPU registers, a value representing which OS service it wants. If the service requires parameters, the userland code leaves them in some agreed-on place as well. The userland code then issues a trap instruction. As with other types of interrupts, the system reacts, saving the state of the userland process by recording the value of the program counter and the other hardware registers, the process stack, and other process data. The hardware switches into kernel mode and starts running the system call trap handler function. This function typically looks up the requested service in a table, in order to figure out what subroutine to call to carry it out. This entire process is often called a *context switch*. Once the requested service is complete, the state of the userland process is restored, and control is passed back to that process.

However, programmers may make frequent use of these services—for example, fork() or exec()—without ever being aware that this trap instruction stuff is going on. The reason is that when programmers want such a service, they typically call a *library function* (userland code that is usually precompiled and linked into the program at build time or later); the library function then does all this trap stuff

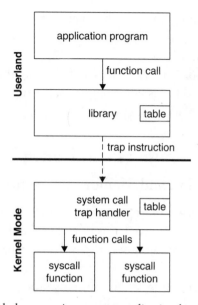

Figure 4.4 To interact with the operating system, application-level code in userland typically makes function calls into prebuilt library code, also in userland. These library functions in turn make system calls by issuing trap instructions, which causes the CPU to change to kernel mode, suspend userland execution, and begin in the system call trap handler, which in turn calls the appropriate kernel function. Often, both the library and the system call handler use tables of function pointers to figure out where to go.

(see Figure 4.4). This subtlety can make it hard for many programmers to answer quickly whether that subroutine they just looked up in the manual and invoked is a library function, a system call, both, or perhaps even neither.

Bookkeeping. In order to manage all these processes, the OS must perform a lot of bookkeeping: tracking which processes are running, which are blocked waiting for something, and so on. Some system calls permit userland code to inspect some of this bookkeeping. Some operating systems provide other ways to inspect this bookkeeping. For example, Linux makes a set of pseudofiles appear under /proc in the filesystem; each process has its own subdirectory, each containing bookkeeping and resource usage information about that process.

User Interaction. Users typically have two main ways of interacting with a computer system: via a command line *shell* and via a *graphical user interface (GUI)*. Neither way is necessarily part of the OS itself. For example, a shell is typically itself a userland process that catches typed commands and then decides what to do. Sometimes, the shell executes the command itself; sometimes, it looks in some predefined places for a program with that name. If it can find this program, the shell uses OS syscalls to set that program up running inside a new process. GUIs are similar but more complicated.

Often, users talk about an OS in terms of the way they interact with it, not realizing that this look and feel is not necessarily an artifact of the kernel itself but rather an artifact of the shell or GUI packages.

4.2 OS Security Primitives and Principles

4.2.1 Process Isolation and Memory Protection

As we have seen in Section 4.1, one of the main tasks of the OS is to isolate processes from each other. Also as we observed, this task has other benefits besides security. However, when it comes to ensuring security, this is a primary contribution the OS can make.

Some aspects of ensuring isolation are fairly straightforward, such as using memory management to ensure that one process can neither read nor write memory that belongs to another process. However, even making this simple idea work in practice can lead to some subtleties. For example, if a userland process A can figure out how to rewrite parts of the kernel's memory, then A might be able to rewrite the parts of the OS that keep it from touching B's data. We have also heard of more subtle tricks, such as convincing the system that it has twice as much physical memory as it really does, with the result that the same physical byte will appear at two places in the physical address space.

More complications arise when we consider that, in practice, we often don't want processes to be completely isolated; rather, we want them to interact, a little bit. We want them to able to communicate via some standard mechanisms, such as pipes or message passing or other forms of *interprocess communication (IPC)*; we want them to be able to share memory; we want them to be able to read and write some of the same files. Each such hole we poke through the wall of complete isolation makes it harder to reason about what isolation really means. Under what conditions should process A be able to map part of process B's address space into its own address space? What if process A asked for less than a page but the OS rounds the shared amount up to a page, which might happen in systems where a page is the natural granularity of memory management? For another example, what happens if a A sends a message to B, but B exits before the message can arrive? We know of one system where, if a process C managed to come into being with the same identifier number that B had, then the message would be delivered to C, much the same as a new occupant of an apartment may receive mail addressed to the previous occupant.

In the course of building a system, one might not even think to ask this question until late in the game, at which point, going back to rework things to find and delete not-yet-delivered messages is easier said than done. It's hard to get all this right.

As Section 2.3 discussed, isolation can break down in other ways too. Reuse of such objects as memory frames or kernel heap regions can leak information. Observable temporal variations, such as being able to figure out what shared code might be in memory or even in cache, may allow one process to infer things about the operations of another.

Finally, we would be remiss in not pointing out that contemporary operating systems are big pieces of code, with many potential internal configurations and external input scenarios, that, in theory, never terminate. It's much harder to test an OS than it is to test, say, a routine that sorts its inputs and then terminates. (It's hard to even specify what it means for an OS to be correct!) A Boeing 747 jet has 6 million parts, but Windows XP has 40 million lines of code; one could argue that your laptop's OS is more complicated than six jumbo jets. Even if the design principles are sound, the opportunity for bugs is enormous.

Again: It's hard to get all this right.

4.2.2 Users

In Section 1.2, we talked about modeling and managing system security in terms of the access control matrix: who can do what to whom. In order to manage this access, an OS needs to have some notion of "who."

Traditionally, these actors have been *users*. The system maintains some notion of account or identity for a set of users. Naively, each account belonged to a real, human user, who needs to authenticate via a password or other human authentication technique. (We discuss this topic further in Section 9.2.) This notion of "user = human" quickly generalized to special accounts for groups of humans, such as the staff of a college class, and for no human in particular, such as "guest" or "games."[1]

It also quickly became apparent that, to paraphrase George Orwell, some users needed to be more equal than others. Some systems take the approach of creating a special account (often called *root*, *superuser*, or *admin*) that contains maximal privileges over the rest of the accounts and systems. Others take a different approach and mark specific users as also having admin privileges.

Staying at maximum privilege level can be dangerous, because blunder or attack may then lead to considerable damage. For example, when one of us had to walk

---

1. One of us got some of his first programming experience via compromising the "games" account on the big time-sharing system at the local community college.

through a bad neighborhood in Pittsburgh to do a cash transaction at the AAA, we carried just enough cash to carry out the transaction; computer security scholars call this the principle of *least privilege*. (It was even one of Saltzer and Schroeder's principles.) Consequently, systems may instead force even privileged users to operate with ordinary privileges and only wield their full power when necessary, by entering a special admin password to a pop-up window or by invoking the command sudo ("do as superuser").

The context of how computer systems are used sometimes leads to a mismatch with this user structure. Single-user laptops can be configured to boot into that user's account, without logging in. Ordinary end user actions on PCs often require admin privileges, resulting in all users being admin by default. Web server software is often configured to run with maximal privileges, giving maximal privileges to any adversary who might subvert it. Yet again: It's hard to get all this right.

4.2.3 Filesystem Access Control

Talking about who can do what to whom also requires thinking about the objects on which the users act. In typical modern systems, we usually think about these in terms of the *filesystem*. In modern systems, both data and programs appear as files. Some of these program files are key parts of the system functionality, such as the programs that carry out the key commands of the shell; some of these data files define key parts of the system configuration, such as /etc/passwd. *Pseudofiles*— such entities as the /proc filesystem and /dev/kmem, with which a process can interact via the standard file system interface—can also show up here.

The permissions on files are typically read, write, and execute; for directories, *execute* means *descend into*. Note that we said that this list is typical, not exhaustive. Systems can end up with more elaborate permissions as well. A good example of this is the setuid permission in the UNIX family (a concept known as *impersonation* in Windows), which can enable the user running a program to take on the privileges of the owner of the program, but only while running that program. This permission can be useful when a file needs to be updated by anyone but only in a carefully guarded way. For example, consider a file that records the high scores earned by the players of a game: If *everyone* can write this file anytime, then no one can trust the scores that it reports. Often, administrators of enterprise systems might use techniques like setuid privileges to allow specific users to do specific tasks that require root privileges; the admins write up a program or shell script to carry out this task, have it owned by root, but give it setuid privileges so the user can be root when needed. However, this technique can backfire: An adversary who can trick such a program into carrying out action of his or her own choosing can have this action carried out as `root`.

In Section 1.2, we presented the access control matrix and talked about two approaches. The column-based approach stores an *access control list* (ACL) with each object; the row-based approach stores *capabilities* with each subject. Modern Windows systems use the ACL approach. Every object in the system—directories, files, network shares, and so on—has an ACL attached to it. This ACL is a list of *access control entries (ACEs)* that contain a user or group; an operation, such as read or write; and a permission, either allow or deny. When Alice attempts to operate on an object, such as opening a file, the kernel checks the ACL on the object to determine whether the operation should be permitted. If Alice or a group of which she is a member is explicitly denied access to the file, then the check immediately fails, and Alice's access is denied. Otherwise, the system goes through all the ACEs in the ACL to determine the set of privileges that Alice has. If the operation she is attempting is within the set of her privileges, the operation is allowed; if not, it fails.

In contrast, systems in the UNIX family, including Linux and OSX (which is based on FreeBSD), use a hybrid system. Each file has an owner and a group. The owner of a file can change its group. Groups consist of sets of users; a user can belong to many groups. Each file then carries three permission sets: one for the owner, one for the group, and one for everyone else; each set is a subset of

$$\{\text{``read,''} \text{ ``write,''} \text{ ``execute''}\}.$$

If a user A asks to operate on a file, the OS checks these sets in order.

- If A is the file owner, then the owner permission set decides whether A can carry out the operation.
- Otherwise, if A is the member of the file's group, then the group permission set decides the issue.
- Otherwise, the "everyone else" permission decides the issue.

The UNIX approach is sort of like an ACL, in that objects carry their permission list; however, in that things like group membership can give a subject blanket access to certain rights, the approach is also like capabilities. We note that in both schemes, the administrator, or root account, overrides all the permission checking—meaning that the superuser has full control over all the objects in the system.

These approaches are merely typical—not necessarily the way all systems do it and not necessarily the right way to do it for all scenarios. For one example, recalling the terminology of Section 2.3, we might not be satisfied with a *discretionary access control* policy that gives users free reign over the objects they own; we might instead want the system to enforce *mandatory access control* in support of some greater goal, such as *MLS*. For another example, we might be frustrated by the inarticulateness of traditional UNIX filesystem permissions[2] and instead try build in support for other models, such as RBAC or Chinese Walls (see Section 2.2.3).

4.2.4 Reference Monitors

Many in computer science preach the principle of *separating policy from mechanism*. Here, we take the weaker position of simply noting that the two are not always the same thing. Our OS design might include nice structure for subjects and objects and access controls; however, if the system as built takes actions without checking permissions, then we've somewhat failed in our goal. As discussed in Sections 2.3 and 3.4, it's good if a system can practice *complete mediation*: checking permissions on each action. An OS can package all its checking into a central module called a *reference monitor*; one of the contributions of the NSA's *Security Enhanced Linux (SELinux)* effort was the introduction of a formal "pluggable" framework for reference monitors in Linux [LS01, NSAa, WCS+02].

4.2.5 The Trusted Computing Base

In some sense, all these protection structures within an OS are about shifting and reducing trust. For example, it might be a bad bet to trust that everything on a typical PC will act correctly and nonmaliciously. That's a large set of code and users; who knows if any one element might go bad? However, we might be able to structure the system to reduce this set. Maybe if we trust the OS and the CPU/MMU protections to work, then we don't have to trust every userland process to act correctly and nonmaliciously. That's a better position to be in: The collection of things we have to take on faith is smaller and more controlled.

   Again, as we discussed in Section 2.3, this is the concept of the *trusted computing base (TCB)*: the set of things that we're forced to trust—but if we do, then we don't have to trust anything else. As our example suggested, a computer's OS seems to be a natural candidate for its TCB—at least at first glance. In practice, we often discover that the TCB might be much larger—for example, in the case of OSes that permit arbitrary device drivers to run in kernel mode; we also might discover that the TCB is too poorly engineered to merit our trust.

   At the risk of seeming like a broken record: It's hard to get all this right.

---

2. We note that we know one UNIX zealot who will insist that all useful scenarios can be handled by the standard permissions plus `setuid`.

4.3 Real OSes: Everything but the Kitchen Sink

Real operating systems go far beyond the simple abstractions we have presented. At one time, operating systems consisted of a kernel, drivers, a command interpreter, and a filesystem. Modern operating systems are crammed with programs, services, and utilities aimed at making users' lives easier. Many operating systems come with libraries that go beyond giving programmers access to system calls and convenient string-copying routines; we see remote procedure calls, cryptography, and more. Some vendors have even gotten in trouble with the U.S. government for trying to bundle applications, such as a Web browser, with the OS. Because operating systems have such a broad audience—standard users, application developers, and hardware manufacturers—they have become the Swiss Army knives of software. Trustworthiness can lose out.

4.3.1 Access to the OS

Operating systems provide services to application developers to accomplish tasks that user-level applications are not authorized to do, or simply can't perform. Some examples include providing IPC mechanisms and access to kernel-level data structures, such as semaphores, kernel-level threads, and shared memory. Since applications sometimes have a valid reason to violate the boundaries put forth by the OS, such as memory protection, the OS must provide mechanisms to facilitate this behavior.

As discussed in Section 4.1, the system call is the usual method through which userland code communicates to the OS. The set of system calls available to applications makes up the operating system interface. This interface differs from OS to OS, despite efforts to standardize an interface to work across operating systems.

POSIX.   In the mid-1980s, the IEEE specified a set of interfaces for UNIX operating systems and called the family of standards the *Portable Operating System Interface (POSIX)* [IEE04]. At that time, and even today, there were many flavors of the UNIX OS, and programs written for one flavor did not necessarily run on another flavor, because of the difference in system APIs. The idea behind POSIX was to fix an interface so that code written for one flavor could run on another.

The standard has a number of parts, and different operating systems are free to implement different parts of the standard, often defeating the goal of true portability. Even the Windows NT kernel implements a portion of the POSIX standard. Linux, which in this context is defined as the Linux kernel and GNU utilities, has its own set of standards so that applications can run across the various distributions. Although

Linux isn't strictly POSIX-compliant, many parts of the Linux standards are in line with POSIX.

The Win32 API.   The Windows OS places a layer of abstraction between application and system calls: the Win32 API. The "Win32" derives from the fact that it's the Windows OS for Intel's IA32 architecture. (To relate this to the background concepts of Section 4.1, the Win32 API would be the library.)

This abstraction layer allows Microsoft to change system calls at will, and frees application developers from having to change also. Of course, when the Win32 API itself changes, application developers will have to change, but Microsoft typically tries to keep some interface around so that legacy applications do not have to update.

Although the concepts are similar to the POSIX API, the semantics are different. Although they both have C-style function semantics, the Win32 API requires the use of numerous specialized data structures and techniques. One example is the heavy use of making the same API call numerous times with different arguments so that the application can get information on how much memory to allocate for a target buffer. Documentation is freely available online at Microsoft's Web site [Mic06].

4.3.2 Remote Procedure Call Infrastructure

Another common component that is usually bundled with an OS is *Remote Procedure Call (RPC)* support. Developed in the late 1970s and early 1980s, RPC allows code on one machine to invoke code on another machine by making what appears to be a standard procedure call [Nel81]. Underneath the hood, the RPC library intercepts the procedure call, packages the call and *marshals* its arguments,[3] and sends the request to the destination machine. On the destination machine, the RPC library unpacks the call and arguments and sends it to its intended destination. When the procedure completes, the RPC library at the destination machine packs up the return value and sends it back to the calling machine.

In theory, a programmer could code all this up each time he or she wanted to have a program on machine call procedures on another machine. In practice, that would quickly grow tiring and create too many opportunities for bugs—in code that wasn't part of the programmer's main purpose, anyway. It would be much easier to have the programmer call the procedure, write the procedure, and have the build environment take care of the rest. That's why RPC libraries came into existence.

---

3. When you call a procedure locally, the procedure expects its parameters to be arranged in memory in a certain way. To send the parameters across the network, we need to walk through this local arrangement and turn it into a linear sequence of bytes. This process is called *marshaling*. On the other end, we rebuild things.

RPC functionality isn't necessarily part of the OS, but RPC libraries are often bundled with the OS. Since access to the network stack is usually governed by the OS, placing RPC services there makes sense. It also gives remote attackers a way onto your OS, as we discuss later.

DCOM.   Two popular RPC technologies are in use today: *SunRPC* for UNIX-based systems and *MSRPC* for the Windows family. (The latter is based on DCE RPC) [Ope97, Sun88]. Beyond MSRPC, Microsoft systems also support a technology called the *Component Object Model (COM)*. The idea behind COM is to allow developers to write software components in the language of their choice and then publish them so that other developers can use them—possibly from a program written in a different language.

COM allows developers from different organizations to share their components, as long as the component is installed on the machine where it is used. Microsoft then developed *distributed COM (DCOM)* with the intent of allowing developers to use COM components on a remote machine. DCOM, which is built on top of MSRPC and allows remote access to system services, has provided a steady stream of fun for security researchers for years.

4.3.3 Integrating Cryptography

In more recent years, operating systems have started to offer access to cryptographic services via system calls and system-level APIs. *Cryptographic API (CAPI)*, a subset of Microsoft Win32 API, gives developers access to cryptographic routines, as well as to certificate management functions. Windows operating systems even have certificate and private-key stores built in; they use a specialized storage system called the *Windows registry*[4] to store their data. (Chapter 10 discusses certificates and private keys in more detail.) Including all this functionality in the OS makes life nice for application developers, but makes life fun for security researchers. (As we discuss in Chapter 8, we've even poked around at CAPI [MSZ03, MSZ05].)

Part of the reasoning behind this seems to have to do with the ability to support the cryptographic needs of Microsoft's browser, Internet Explorer (IE). Browsers had an early need for cryptography, as they had (and still have) to support the *Secure Sockets Layer (SSL)*. (We discuss SSL further in Chapter 7.) Without OS support,

---

4. The registry is a storage system that many Windows applications, and the OS itself, use to store configuration information. The registry roughly serves the same role as the /etc directory on *nix systems.

browsers have to implement their own cryptographic subsystems. For example, the Mozilla browser has quite an elaborate cryptographic subsystem used for SSL and S/MIME (the latter is for encrypting MIME-encoded messages, such as email attachments).

In the Linux world, systemwide cryptographic support has been slower to be adopted. At the time of this writing, the most recent kernel is the first version to contain a cryptographic API. Designed to be easy to use, the *Linux kernel cryptographic API* provides services to code running inside the kernel, such as the network stack, and to other modules, as well as to application code running outside the kernel. Although it doesn't provide certificate storage, this API does provide the necessary tools to implement filesystem security and integrity.

4.3.4 Extending the Kernel

So far, we've described some of the common services one is likely to find bundled as part of a modern OS. Typically, these services are packaged by the OS vendor or are included by the group of developers maintaining the OS. In addition to these services, operating systems typically provide an API that allows *anyone* to extend the OS. The most common use of this technique is to allow third-party developers to write programs that allow the OS to speak to peripheral hardware, such as printers, network cards, and video cards; such programs are called *device drivers*. Since drivers have access to kernel-level data structures and execute with kernel privileges, another (much more fun) use of these APIs is to attack the OS. (We discuss such attacks in Section 4.4.3.)

Windows operating systems have a well-defined API that device drivers must implement. When a user installs a device driver, it registers with the *Hardware Abstraction Layer (HAL)*, which allows the OS to use the hardware without having to know the details of the particular devices; that's the driver's job, after all.

In Linux, device drivers are either compiled directly into the kernel or are implemented as dynamically loadable kernel modules. Like Windows device drivers, Linux kernel modules implement a well-defined interface. Unlike Windows, the kernel modules can be loaded and unloaded from the kernel dynamically, without requiring a reboot. For both systems, in general, suitably privileged users can write and load a kernel module and thus effectively get access to the kernel's execution thread and its data structures.[5]

---

5. It is possible to configure Windows so that it (in theory, anyway) will not load any drivers that haven't been signed by Microsoft, but the default action is to simply issue a warning to the user.

4.4 When the Foundation Cracks

As the central program in a computer system, the OS fulfills many roles. It is responsible for executing user programs and keeping them protected from one another. Additionally, it offers a host of services to the other programs in the system. Finally, it stores and protects the information stored in the filesystem.

From an attacker's perspective, the OS is a lucrative target for a number of reasons. First, the OS may be an end in itself if that computer holds information that an attacker wants, perhaps corporate or military data. Second, it may be a means for an attacker to carry out an attack on someone else. For example, an attacker may use the victim OS to run a program that floods the victim's network with malformed or malicious network traffic. Third, an OS can provide a means for hiding a remote attacker's tracks. Carlo may break into Bob's machine first and from there launch an attack on Alice's machine. If Carlo has done a good job, the investigators will believe that Bob was the attacker. In this section, we examine some of the common OS attack patterns.

4.4.1 Common Attack Strategies

Regardless of the attacker's motivation, the goal is typically to *own*, or *root*, the victim's machine, meaning that the attacker has complete control to install and run programs, has access to all the files in the filesystem, and can modify user accounts. (In hacker lingo, these terms are often spelled *0wn* and *r00t*.) Sometimes, the attacker is lucky enough to gain this level of access with only one exploit (suppose the vulnerability is directly in part of the OS, such as a DCOM vulnerability). Other times, an attacker may have to work a little harder. An attacker who can gain access to only a low-privilege user account may be forced to *escalate* privileges in order to own the machine.

(We offer a caveat to the reader. There's a natural ordering to privilege level: We think of "low privilege" as not having very many privileges and "high privilege" as having lots of them. In computing systems, it may also be natural to encode things privilege level or priority as a number. Numbers also have a natural order: $\geq$ and $\leq$. Unfortunately, there are *two* natural ways for these orders to correspond! Should low privilege be a low number or a high number? Be warned: In real systems, you'll see *both* approaches used.)

As we have discussed, many modern operating systems ship with numerous services, some of which even run at the OS's privilege level. Many of these services, such as DCOM, face the network, thus giving remote attackers a way to access the OS of the victim machine. One class of attacks is for the remote attacker to exploit such a service and then transfer a program to the victim OS, which performs some tasks on the attacker's behalf. This pattern is called a *remote code execution* vulnerability.

One common example is for the attacker to install a *keystroke logger* program, which allows the attacker to capture the keystrokes of all the legitimate users of the system. (Think about this the next time you visit an Internet cafe.) This is a good way for the attacker to find other passwords and, possibly, elevate his or her privilege level. Sometimes, the keylogger is part of a larger set of attack tools called a *rootkit*. We discuss these attack tools in more detail in Section 4.4.3.

Another thing that an attacker may do once finding a remote code execution vulnerability is install a program that is used to launch *denial-of-service (DoS)*[6] attacks against another site, perhaps simply by bombarding the site with requests that are apparently legitimate but whose only real purpose is to consume all the site's resources. Such programs are often called *bots*—robots—because they are remotely controlled by the attacker, sometimes via an *Internet Relay Chat* (IRC) server. Sometimes, an attacker may have compromised a number of machines, and placed a bot on all of them; this is often referred to as a *botnet*. An attacker can acquire a botnet via hard work—getting code on each of the victim operating systems—or by purchasing one on the black market. Botnets can be used for massive *distributed DoS (DDoS)* attacks, which can shut down Web sites indefinitely.

Why would the attacker bother? One of the things we've encountered examining vulnerabilities in the real world is a gap between the discovery of a way to break system security and the discovery of real-world motivation to do it. Often, this gap translates to managers insisting that an enterprise need not defend against some attack, because "no one would ever try that." Usually, this short-sighted view is simply a failure of imagination. In the case of botnets, for example, attackers can use the threat of DDoS to blackmail companies that depend on an Internet presence. (This case also raises some interesting social questions: The parties with the vulnerable systems who can thus do something to prevent the attacks are not the ones being hurt by them.)

Another class of attacks allows attackers running with low-level privileges to gain higher-level privileges (as we mentioned). In this scenario, an attacker may start by obtaining access to a low-level account and then using an exploit to elevate his or her privilege level. In the bad old days, many systems shipped with guest accounts enabled by default.[7] These accounts often have weak or no passwords and provided a launch pad for privilege-escalation attacks.

---

6. It's tempting to make some connection between a DoS attack and the ancient operating system of the same name—but we'll refrain.
7. As noted elsewhere, this practice helped the first author learn to program.

The final use of remote code execution vulnerabilities we discuss is propagating worms or viruses. An attacker who can find a remote code execution vulnerability that doesn't require any user interaction to trigger—for example, doesn't require that the victim navigate to a URL—may be able to write a self-propagating program to scan and exploit the vulnerability. For this reason, such vulnerabilities are sometimes called *wormable*. (Section 6.4 discusses worms, viruses, and other malware further.)

4.4.2 Common Attack Techniques

Throughout this book, we discuss various techniques to make systems, in general, break. At this point, we introduce some of these topics and give some detail to attacks that are unique to the OS.

One of the oldest tricks in the book is tricking someone into giving away his or her credentials. This strategy is typically referred to as *social engineering*. Some of the stereotypical social engineering attacks involve the attacker's calling a help desk, posing as a legitimate system user. The attacker then goes into a sob story about having lost his or her password, hoping that the help desk will simply provide a new one. To increase the effectiveness of social engineering, attackers will often try to structure the attack so that natural human psychology reinforces the deception. Attractive young females can be good at coercing male technical workers; an attacker who dons the persona of an angry, impatient senior-level manager can be good at cowing a lowly IT person.

More resourceful attackers will have already gone on a *dumpster dive* to gather useful information from the target's trash. Although many institutions have become much better about training personnel to resist this type of attack, many still view humans as the weakest link in an OS; we discuss this further in Chapter 18. Admittedly, this example has become so common that it is unexciting, but the sad part is that it is still effective. Readers interested in learning more about social engineering should read Kevin Mitnick's *The Art of Deception* [MS02].

Another technique that attackers often use involves *reverse engineering* a piece of software—perhaps an OS or a service that is a part of the OS, such as DCOM—in search of a vulnerability. (Indeed, the fear that attackers might easily find bugs if they can see the source often drives vendors to keep their source proprietary, which at least forces the would-be attacker to overcome the barrier of reverse engineering first. We discuss more on this debate later.) Once a vulnerability has been discovered, attackers write a program, called an *exploit*, that exploits the vulnerability. The exploit typically gives the attacker a remote, privileged shell on the victim machine, in order to run arbitrary commands on the victim machine, or directly allows the attacker to run code on the victim's machine. (We discuss how this is done in Chapter 6.)

A final technique that attackers often use in order to gain access to the OS is to take advantage of an application that is tightly coupled with the OS. Internet Explorer is a prime vector for this style of attack. Since the browser does a lot of work using kernel-level privileges and is accessible from Web servers, via Web pages, attackers can cleverly craft Web pages that trick users into installing the attacker's code on their machines. We discuss these kinds of attacks and similar attacks, such as *phishing*, in Chapter 18.

4.4.3 Keyloggers and Rootkits

As briefly discussed earlier, a common modern attack scenario involves installing software on the victim's machine. Keylogger programs fall into a category of malware known as *spyware*; they allow the attacker to remotely spy on the victim.

A system's user or administrator who can discover the existence of the attack software can begin to take corrective action, such as removing the software or at least taking the infected machine out of use. As a consequence, attackers can put considerable engineering effort into keeping their software from being detected and removed. A *rootkit* is attack software that attempts to hides its presence even from root. In Section 4.1.3, we discussed how one of the tasks of an OS is to keep track of processes and report this to the user via syscalls and shell commands; consequently, rootkits go to great lengths to make themselves disappear from the standard reporting tools and the filesystem. Some rootkits contain different versions of system binaries used to report on the system. For example, on UNIX systems, the ps command reports the running processes; hence, a process that wishes to hide its presence might rewrite that code, so that ps will not report its existence. Other rootkits modify kernel data structures directly to achieve the same effect; for example, many kernel-level Windows rootkits pull their own entry out of the process table.

Rootkits started as a set of tools that an attacker installed after successfully "rooting" a machine to hide his or her tracks. Rootkits are the topic of entire books and Web sites, so in this section, we simply cover some of the basics. Readers interested in more detailed information should check the literature [HB05, Hog06].

Windows Rootkits.   Windows has two classes of rootkits: ones that run in user space and ones that run in kernel space. Ones that run in user space are much easier to detect but menacing nonetheless. Typically, these rootkits get started by injecting themselves into a number of programs that report system status (such as

Windows Explorer, used to browse the filesystem). Using a technique known as *dynamic link library (DLL) injection*, the rootkit coerces the Windows loader into loading the rootkit code into the victim process—in this case, Windows Explorer. Another approach is to use a Win32 API call, `CreateRemoteThread`, to create a thread of execution (with code chosen by the attacker) in the victim's process; thus, the attacker's code can see and modify the victim's address space. Such tricks have legitimate uses as well and thus are covered in detail in the Windows system programming literature [Pie00, Ric99].

Once installed in the victim process, one of the first orders of business is for the rootkit code to redirect any Win32 API calls it is interested in by redirecting the victim process's *import address table (IAT)*. The IAT is a table of pointers that the loader uses to look up where an API call should be directed. Redirecting the victim's IAT to point to the rootkit allows it to intercept any API calls that it chooses; it is by this means that userland rootkits achieve stealth. For example, when it needs to display the contents of a directory, Windows Explorer makes an API call. If a rootkit such as Vanquish [xsh06] is installed, it hijacks this call and removes the return value that reports the rootkit binary itself. The net effect is that the Vanquish rootkit is hidden from anyone who uses Windows Explorer to browse the filesystem. This technique is known as *API hooking*, and rootkits that use this technique are sometimes called *hookers*.

More difficult to detect are Windows rootkits that are installed as drivers and have access to a number of the kernel data structures. Instead of redirecting the IAT of one victim process, kernel rootkits can hook the *system service descriptor table (SSDT)*, also known as the *system call table*. This technique allows the rootkit to intercept the system calls it is interested in from *every process on the machine*. Additionally, kernel-level rootkits may use such techniques as *direct kernel object manipulation (DKOM)* to modify the kernel's internal state. Using this method, a rootkit can modify data structures such as the process table, which effectively makes it disappear.

Detecting rootkits is more difficult and more painful than it might seem. Most antivirus software will detect some of the more common rootkits, but more modern rootkits have figured out a way to hide from such software. There are a few specialty tools for detecting rootkits. In 2004, Microsoft Research released a tool, *Ghostbuster*, that can be used to detect some rootkits [WBV+05]. This tool works by taking a scan of the infected system from an API level and comparing it with a scan of the system from the raw disk level. If the API fails to report bytes that are on disk, then a rootkit is probably installed on the system. In 2005, Bryce Cogswell and Mark Russinovich released a tool, the *Rootkit Revealer*, that uses similar techniques to detect rootkits.

Linux Rootkits.   Linux is not without its own rootkit woes, although there are some differences in approach. Older Linux (and UNIX) rootkits work by simply replacing system binaries that are responsible for reporting system status to the administrator, or root. It is not uncommon for these older rootkits to begin execution by shutting down the system logging daemon—the component responsible for logging system changes—and then replacing some of the critical binaries on the system with versions of its own. These typically include such programs as `netstat`, `ps`, and `top`, to name a few.[8] By replacing these programs, the rootkit can hide any network connections or processes that it is using. However, an administrator who used or wrote a program not replaced by the rootkit could easily detect the rootkit.

The more sophisticated Linux rootkits work much as the Windows ones do: by hooking system calls and directly modifying kernel data structures. Since the Linux kernel allows users and attackers to extend the kernel via modules, many kernel-level rootkits are implemented as a module. Once installed, the rootkit typically redirects portions of the system call table to point to itself, so that it gets a chance to intercept system calls made from any process on the machine.

As in the Windows world, there are a number of detection methods—none of them perfect. One method is to monitor the disk for changes by using a filesystem integrity tool, such as Tripwire, which checks whether file contents have changed illegitimately. (We ourselves have used this technique to recover rootkits in the wild on both Windows and Linux systems.) Although rootkits are great at hiding themselves from other programs within the system, hiding its image on disk is much harder, though not impossible. Other approaches attempt to detect when kernel modules hijack the system call table [KRV04]. The theory here is that a kernel module that hijacks the system call table can be only one thing: a rootkit.

4.5 Where Are We?

During the course of our careers, we are all faced with the decision of what OS to use. Maybe the decision will be what OS to install on a new computer or what to recommend for deployment at a customer site or what platform to target in building a new application. For many, the decision of which OS to use is a religious or philosphical issue or is decided by someone else. In this section, we discuss the security-relevant portions of this decision.

---

8. Curious readers should refer to the man pages for a detailed description of what the genuine versions of these programs do.

4.5.1 Windows Versus Linux

One of the oldest arguments in the ongoing debate over Windows versus Linux is which one is more secure. Every year or so, one side enlists some "disinterested" third party to conduct a study and determine which OS is more secure. These third parties usually compare the number of vulnerabilities published on the BugTraq mailing list [Sec06], the number of worms and viruses, the number of security patches, and so on. Interestingly, the side that sponsors the study is almost always[9] the superior OS. The loser always questions who did the study, usually followed by a claim that the entity is never really "disinterested," and typically finds flaws in their methodology.

The real story is that both operating systems have security problems—and, probably, always will, if anyone is going to use them. As we discuss in Chapter 18, there is a direct tradeoff between security and usability. If these operating systems are to be adopted or purchased by the general population, then they have to be usable. But if they're easy to use, they're harder to secure. For environments in which security is a top priority, certain configurations of these operating systems— and even other operating systems—may make more sense. (We discuss some of these alternative operating systems momentarily.)

Given that both operating systems have had their share of security trouble, an obvious question is: Well, why not just use a Mac? Some think that because the Mac has not received the same negative security publicity as Windows and Linux, then it must not have the same security issues. Others argue that the Mac doesn't have the market share to warrant attackers' attention. Finding a vulnerability on Windows has a much higher payout than finding one on the Mac, as the attacker can infect more systems. Who is right? We don't know.

What we do know is that there have been some recent efforts to investigate Mac security. A number of new worms have recently appeared, perhaps because of the rise in Mac's popularity with OSX [Win06]. Some feel that the Mac provides numerous easy targets because security researchers haven't been prodding at it as long as they have been prodding at Windows [Kot06]. In any case, as the OS gets more popular, it will certainly receive more attention from the security community.

Mac OSX does have the advantage over Windows of being more principled about what goes in kernel mode and of being based on the longer heritage of BSD and the Mach microkernel. The core of the Mac OSX kernel is available as

---

9. If not always, but we don't have good statistics.

open source. Amit Singh's book is a good starting point for more information on the engineering inside of OSX [Sin06b].

4.5.2 Alternatives

OpenBSD. The OpenBSD OS is a BSD-style UNIX system built with security in mind. The Web site proudly proclaims: "Only two remote holes in the default install, in more than 10 years!" [Ope06]. OpenBSD was one of the first UNIX distributions to contain integrated cryptography. This can be seen in the cryptographic services available to developers and in internal systems, such as the password storage mechanism; OpenBSD uses the Blowfish algorithm to encrypt passwords.

The distribution strives to be secure in the default configuration, so that administrators don't have to perform a lengthy checklist of tasks before plugging the machine into the network. The project undergoes continual security review and produces a number of freely available security utilities.

SELinux. A few years ago, the NSA released a version of Linux that addressed numerous security concerns. *Security Enhanced Linux (SELinux)* [NSAa] uses mandatory role-based access control, which protects users from one another—as well as from root. At the center of SELinux is a large and complex policy statement that assigns roles to subjects and types to objects and then explains how subjects in a particular role can interact with the types.

We can use this policy document to create *software compartments:* places where applications run that disallow them to access other processes' memory or data. Using the policy document, one can restrict how the compartments interact. SELinux is available for download from the NSA's project site and has become part of some RedHat Linux distributions.

OpenSolaris. *Solaris*, the line of UNIX operating systems from Sun Microsystems, developed a reputation for reliability (particularly for higher-end servers) and observability via some pretty fun inspection tools. Recent releases have also developed stronger notions of *process rights management* and *containers* [PT04, TC04]. Sun sales literature, not an unbiased source, touts that "the Solaris 10 Operating System ... —the result of a $500-million plus investment in development by Sun—is the most advanced operating system on the planet"; see [Suna].

What's particularly exciting here is that, recently, Sun released a version of Solaris as open source [Sunb]: Users can read code, modify and rebuild it, and offer contributions back, although Sun engineers retain the final say. This opportunity provides the community with the opportunity to observe the internals of a highly engineered system with a long evolution.

The Open Source Debate.   We often need to field questions about open source software and security, particularly with respect to operating systems. Our answers usually disappoint zealots on both sides of the issue.

First, it's important to clarify what is meant by "open source." We see a progression of classes:

1. Software whose source is published, so it can be examined
2. As in the preceding, but the user/customer also has the ability to modify and rebuild it—and the legal right to then deploy this modified version within their enterprise
3. As in the preceding, but the source itself was written in a large, volunteer community

Some will argue that publishing source weakens security because it makes it easier for adversaries to find vulnerabilities. Our gut instinct goes against this dictum: Historically, "security through obscurity" does not fare well, and recent events with the alleged source for Diebold voting machines suggest that the "secret source" mantra serves only to cloak and excuse bad engineering. The ability for end users to rebuild and redeploy can enable them to patch vulnerabilities when needed rather than being beholden to the proprietary vendor's schedule—but may require more software engineering and testing skill than an enterprise may be ready to bring to the table.

Software from a large community (#3) is a trickier matter [Ray99]. One of us once had a manager who objected to using freeware in products, because she was concerned about who would take responsibility for fixing its bugs down the road. National security colleagues worry about the ability of one malicious coder, in a large, anonymous community, to insert something malicious. As one example, a few years ago, a contribution to an open source OS was discovered to have a line of the form:

```
if ((options == (__WCLONE|__WALL))&&(current->uid = 0))
        retval = -EINVAL;
```

A one-character omission turned an innocuous error check

```
current->uid == 0
```

into privilege escalation that sets the caller to root (0) privileges.

Personally, we have always found that a small, passionate team produces better results than a large, ambivalent one.

4.6 The Take-Home Message

Operating systems serve a vital role in modern computing systems: protecting computation and information. For this reason, they are also continually under attack.

Many desktop operating systems are not prepared to handle the barrage of attacks aimed at them. The more an OS strives to be usable—by developers or users—the harder it is to secure. As they pile on the features, operating systems pile on complexity. We hope to have impressed on you that getting all the details right when building a system isn't easy. Numerous moving parts interact with one another; the complexity of a modern OS is maddening. Too often, complexity is the enemy of security.

4.7 Project Ideas

1. Read the source code for a real OS. The source for the Linux OS is freely available from www.kernel.org, or you can look at Linux's simpler parent: Minix, available from www.minix3.org. To gain an appreciation for the complexity, attempt some simple task that requires you to modify the code, such as implementing a system call.

2. Compare and contrast the security benefits of having an application, such as Windows Explorer, in userland. Is it part of the TCB? Should it be? Does part of it need to be in the TCB? Should any applications or services run in kernel space? Can you come up with a list of requirements that would suggest putting an application in kernel space?

3. Survey your friends and colleagues. What operating systems do they use? If Windows, do they operate on a day-to-day basis as admin or as an ordinary user?

Network Security

Funny things happen when you let computers talk to one another. Although we can hardly imagine a world in which they don't, worrying about what happens when they do was, until the mid-1990s, the concern only of government agencies, academics, and system administrators. Although they allow us to share massive amounts of information very quickly, computer networks also open our machines up to remote attackers.

The topic of *network security* covers a range of topics from how to construct an enterprise network to the underlying protocols that allow various components to communicate with one another. Traditionally, the job of securing an organization's network belonged to the system administrator. However, as modern software increasingly relies on the presence of a network, having an understanding of networks and network security is becoming more important to system architects and developers as well.

Most modern enterprise applications use and/or deploy Windows services and UNIX daemons. These applications may open up sockets or register Remote Procedure Call (RPC) servers; they may be accessible via a Web Service interface. In all these scenarios, anyone with access to the network can send or request potentially malicious information to and from the application.

In this chapter, we explore some of the fundamental concepts of networks and network security that system builders should be aware of. We hope that these concepts will be useful in design and implementation discussions, as well as give testers ways to crash test the network-facing parts of their applications before the bad guys get to.

- Section 5.1 reviews some of the basic networking concepts. We review the concept of a network stack and how it works in the OS. We also explore how networks are arranged from a high level.
- Section 5.2 looks at some of the network protocols that are particularly important when thinking about building secure systems.
- Section 5.3 considers some of the classes of attacks that system builders should be aware of. We also discuss some of the common defenses against some of these attacks.
- Section 5.4 explores some recent developments in networking technology that open up new avenues for attack.

5.1 Basic Framework

As you can imagine, the subject of computer networks has been covered extensively in numerous other books. In this section, we present just enough background to illustrate the relevance to system security. For more detail on the general topic of networks, look at Andrew Tanenbaum's *Computer Networks* [Tan02] or Kurose and Ross' *Computer Networking* [KR07].

We start by looking at the big picture of how computers talk to one another over the Internet. We then shift to the core concept behind networking software: the *network stack*. We then zoom out and discuss how and where the stack fits into modern computers. Finally, we explore some of the basic concepts in building a network for an organization.

5.1.1 The Big Picture

Perhaps the first thing to consider here is the question of the networks themselves: the electrical interconnections among the computers. We generally see two flavors: the *local area network (LAN)* and the *wide area network (WAN)*. *Gateway* machines connect LANs to other networks (see Figure 5.1).

LANs are, by definition, local, such as within an enterprise. They tend to be more expensive per foot but also provide much higher performance. *Ethernet* is a common medium for LANs. Traditionally, Ethernet-based LANs operate as broadcast protocols, meaning that every machine on the LAN can see every packet for every machine on that LAN. Consequently, many enterprises have moved to *switched LANs*, which put each host on its own LAN (see Figure 5.2).

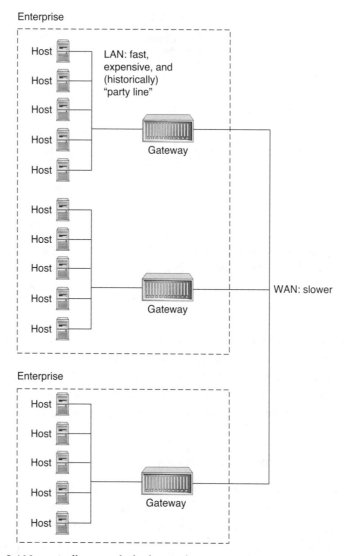

Enterprise

Host — LAN: fast, expensive, and (historically) "party line"

Host
Host
Host
Host

Gateway

Host
Host
Host
Host
Host

Gateway

WAN: slower

Enterprise

Host
Host
Host
Host
Host

Gateway

Figure 5.1 LANs typically provide high-speed connections within an enterprise; WANs provide lower-speed connections across larger distances.

WANs are, by definition, wide-area. They tend to be slower but much cheaper per foot. WANs in the real world use pretty much any media one can imagine: telephone lines, satellite, and so on. Wide-area nets give rise to wide-area concerns, such as *topology* and the risk of *partitioning*.

Network topology in the real world can be fun. For one example, the somewhat recent deregulation of telecommunication in the United States can lead to a mismatch between the designer's mental models of network topology and its

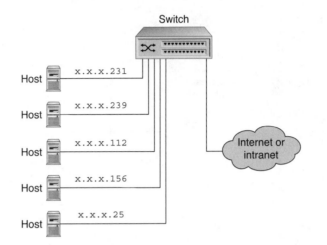

Figure 5.2 Traditionally, an Ethernet LAN was a "party line," enabling any host to easily listen in on all traffic. Many enterprises have migrated to *switched* Ethernet, which prevents that.

physical reality; on more than one occasion, a single backhoe has managed to disrupt both a critical network line *and* its redundant backup, which, through complex business relationships, ended up on the same cable. For another example, exercises in mapping wide-area network topology have revealed links between corporations that were merging but whose merger had not yet been announced.

5.1.2 Finding Networked Machines

Once we have a network connecting a large set of machines, the next step is trying to find those machines. First, we need to figure out how to name them. We start with a *hostname*: a human-understandable name, such as "www.cs.dartmouth.edu." These names follow a standard hierarchy: the ".edu" domain, the ".dartmouth" enterprise within that domain, the ".cs" subgroup. Naively, one might think that hostnames form a unique naming: Each machine has one hostname and vice-versa. In reality, we see exceptions to these expectations on both sides. For example, a server name may map to many real machines, for load balancing; an individual machine may appear with two different names.

We then move to the *IP address*, a machine-understandable name for each host. In the current Internet, using IP version 4, these names are 32-bit values expressed in *slot-dot* notation: The 32 bits are broken into 4 bytes, and each byte is then expressed as a decimal value. (IP version 6 addresses are 128 bits in length

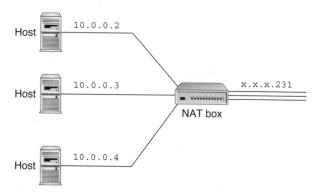

Figure 5.3 A *NAT* box enables multiple machines on a LAN to share the same IP address, from the perspective of the outside world.

and offer a much larger range of addresses.) As with hostnames, one might expect IP addresses to uniquely name machines, but exceptions occur. *Multihomed* machines may have multiple IP addresses at the same time. Enterprises may configure a LAN with the *Dynamic Host Configuration Protocol (DHCP)*, which gives an individual host an IP address when it comes online but may give it a different one the next time it comes online and give the old one to someone else. Enterprises with insufficient IP address space might use *network address translation (NAT)* to enable multiple machines on a LAN to share the same IP address, from the perspective of the outside world (see Figure 5.3). This is also common in home networks.

Suppose that Alice wants to send a message to a particular machine: "www.cs. dartmouth.edu." Her computer needs to find out the IP address to which this name maps. The *Domain Name System (DNS)* is the Internet-wide infrastructure to support this mapping. A hierarchy of *nameservers* exists, following the hierarchy of hostnames. In theory, if Alice's machine is completely lost, it could ask the top-level nameserver, which would tell it where the "edu" nameserver is; that nameserver could tell Alice's machine where the "dartmouth.edu" nameserver is; that nameserver could tell Alice's machine where the "cs.dartmouth.edu" nameserver is. In practice, DNS allows for all sorts of other optimizations, such as asking peers, and caching.

Once it knows the IP address of the host she wants, Alice's machine needs to find a route to get to that host. The term *routing* refers to the hierarchical process that Alice's machine will use to accomplish this task, and there are numerous *routing protocols* to aid Alice's machine in its quest. Some of these protocols will help Alice's machine find Bob's machine if it's in her LAN, some will help it find Bob's machine if it's in her enterprise, and some will help it find Bob's machine across the Internet.

Within an enterprise, such protocols as *Open Shortest Path First (OSPF)* are used to help construct routes. Across the Internet, the *Border Gateway Protocol (BGP)* supports the establishment and maintenance of cross-enterprise routing information. With BGP, each *autonomous system*, such as an enterprise, maintains tables of its preferred routes to each range of IP addresses. If it has information announcing or withdrawing routes, an autonomous system sends updates to its peers; depending on policy, each peer might update its own tables and send out further announcements. For example, system S_1 might announce: "I can now reach addresses starting with prefix P via this sequence R of enterprises." If its peer S_2 likes that, it might update *its* tables and announce that *it* can now reach P via the new sequence consisting of S_2, then R.

Once Alice's machine manages to get a message to the LAN close to the destination machine, we need to figure out which physical hardware should get that message. Each network device itself has a *media access control (MAC)* address, typically 48 to 64 bits. Vendors conspire to try to ensure a unique MAC address to each device, although for many types of devices, it's quite easy to reprogram them with a MAC address of one's choosing. The *Address Resolution Protocol (ARP)* is the Internet-wide infrastructure to support this mapping: A machine can query to see who has what IP address. (Figure 5.4 sketches these relationships.)

5.1.3 Using Networked Machines

The namespace and protocol infrastructure can, in theory, enable Alice's machine to get some packets to the machine she had in mind. However, usually that's not her end goal; Alice is probably thinking about getting a service, such as accessing a Web page or getting a login shell. In the infrastructure that's evolved for this, hosts offer *ports*, numbered endpoints for network connections. Alice's machine can send data to a particular port at the destination machine; different programs on the destination machine may listen for traffic arriving on different ports there. For each standard[1] network protocol (such as http, ftp, ssh, and email) designers have worked out how the two machines should dance together, by sending certain data to certain ports, listening on other ports, and so on (see Figure 5.5).

Through tradition and historical process such as *Request for Comments (RFC)* documents, *Internet Engineering Task Force (IETF)* drafts, and so on, different

---

1. As well as the nonstandard ones, we suppose.

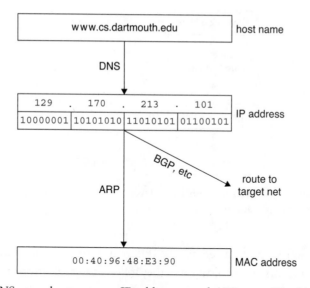

Figure 5.4 DNS maps hostnames to IP addresses, and ARP maps IP addresses to MAC addresses. Routing protocols, such as BGP, build and maintain routes.

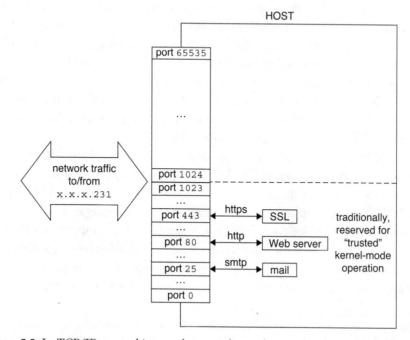

Figure 5.5 In TCP/IP networking, packets are directed toward *ports* on a host machine, which may have various services wired to various ports.

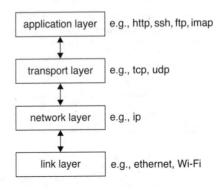

Figure 5.6 A typical network stack consists of layers of protocols. Each layer works directly only with the layers above and below it.

services come to be standardized against different ports. Internet know-it-alls will pull these assignments out of thin air, as if they followed logically from first principles.

5.1.4 Yet Another Stack

How does Alice's machine work with the network? One of the fundamental concepts in computer networks is the *network stack*, sometimes called a *protocol stack*. (Yes, we'll encounter "stacks" elsewhere in this book; this is a different one. Sorry.) The stack is essentially a set of services that deal with a particular set of network protocols and is arranged so that each layer in the stack can use only the services of the layer below it—but essentially ends up communicating its counterpart layer in another machine. Textbooks like to teach the *ISO OSI* seven-layer stack, even though one never sees that in the real world. The protocol stack you are most likely familiar with is the *TCP/IP stack* (see Figures 5.6 and 5.7).

The TCP/IP stack has four layers: the *link layer*, the *network layer*, the *transport layer*, and the *application layer*.[2] The link layer is primarily responsible for getting data—encapsulated in data structures called *frames*—between two hosts on the same LAN. Some examples of link-layer protocols are Ethernet and Wi-Fi (which we discuss more in Section 5.4). The network layer—typically, the *Internet Protocol (IP)*—is concerned with getting packets from the source to destination; it deals with such issues as addressing, routing, and network congestion. The transport layer gives applications a way to send traffic between two hosts in a seamless fashion.

---

2. The original TCP/IP reference model contained four layers, but some folks now claim that the model contains a fifth layer: the *physical layer*, which consists of the raw medium that is used to transmit link-layer frames. Most of the common physical-layer protocols are covered in the IEEE 802.x family of standards.

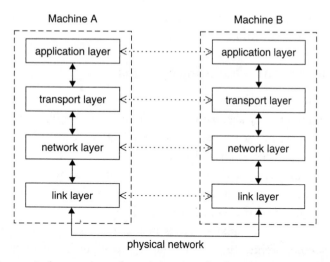

Figure 5.7 In a typical network stack, each layer works directly only with the layers above and below it but works virtually with its peer layer on a peer machine, by going all the way down the stack, across the net, then up the stack on the other side.

In contrast to the link layer, the transport layer provides an end-to-end connection between two hosts, even if they are separated by a WAN. Some protocols at this layer, such as the *Transmission Control Protocol (TCP)*, deal with such issues as in-order delivery of messages and error recovery; others, such as the *User Datagram Protocol (UDP)*, provide fewer frills but cost less. Finally, the application layer covers the set of protocols that applications use directly to talk to one another. For example, applications called Web browsers often use http to talk with Web server applications.

Data flows down the sender's stack, across to the receiver, and then up the receiver's stack. To illustrate this, let's continue with our example of the Web browser and server. Let's assume that in this case, the browser is sending a request to the server. The browser makes an http request message and uses the transport layer to connect to the server. In many cases, the application will use a transport-layer construct known as a *socket* to connect to the server. The browser will use the socket's `send()` function to send the http request on its way. The transport layer will append a header and send the message down to the network layer, where the message will be fragmented into packets, each prepended with a network-layer header. The network layer will in turn place the packets in some sort of link-layer construct, such as an Ethernet or Wi-Fi frame, which will travel over the physical medium to the destination (or nearest switch or router). Once all the IP packets have reached their destination, they are reassembled and are then delivered to the Web server via the socket that the browser established with this server. When it reads from the socket, the server receives the http request that the browser sent and then performs the appropriate operation.

5.1.5 Networks and Operating Systems

In modern computing systems, users typically do not interact with the network stack directly; rather, they access the network via services offered by the OS. For example, developers can write networking applications with the help of TCP/IP sockets or other services, such as DCOM (discussed in Chapter 4). Putting the stack in the OS abstracts the details of the network stack away from the user and the userland programmer, allowing them to focus instead on the services offered. It also allows the OS to process network packets in kernel mode, which greatly reduces the number of context switches necessary to send and receive packets. (Many *microkernel* architectures leave the network stack out of the OS kernel proper, but that's a research topic.)

If we go back and think of the OS as a collection of states, we see some interesting properties emerge when the network becomes part of the OS. Without the network, the typical OS state space and the avenues for interacting with it are quite large. Adding users and applications to the systems increases the state and interaction space, as both interact with the OS (e.g., via syscalls). Accordingly, most OSes put much effort into authentication and authorization so that users and applications can only affect the OS's state space in a well-defined manner; of course, this is not always successful.

However, adding the network to the OS explodes things. Any packet coming from any other entity must be processed by the receiving OS: Anyone on the network becomes a potential requester of OS services; any service the OS offers over the net is offered potentially to the whole world; any flaw in any API or implementation is exposed to the whole world. The network gives attackers the ability to remotely affect the target OS's state, either by causing unexpected transitions or by injecting new states. This "feature" of computer networks is what has traditionally made them the medium that attackers rely on to get into a victim machine (we discuss this in Section 5.3).

To give a concrete illustration of this point, we'll pick on the Windows NT OS. An administrator so inclined could configure the OS in such a way that it met the Orange Book requirements for a level-C2 system. (Rumor has it that this was necessary in order to sell the OS to military clients.) However, one crucial part of the configuration was that the machine was not plugged into a computer network; the second the administrator configured the system to send and receive network traffic, it was no longer considered that secure [Sch00].

5.1.6 Enterprise Network Architecture

Once having acquired multiple computers, a person or organization needs to arrange them on the network to accomplish the desired task. Such an arrangement is typically called a *network architecture*, and there are literally hundreds of books on this topic (e.g., [McC03, Opp04]). Many of these texts cover such topics as routing, topologies, and best practices for building a network. The question we are interested in is: How do we arrange the machines to minimize the risk and impact of a remote attack?

As we discussed in Section 5.1.3, most modern operating systems receive network traffic through one of the OS's numbered *ports*. From the outside, ports are entryways into the target computer's network stack. Programs or services that are expecting network input often *bind* to a port, so that any traffic sent to that port is delivered to the program. As an example, Web servers typically bind to port 80; this port is reserved by the *Internet Assigned Numbers Authority (IANA)* for http traffic.[3] When it sends a page request to the server, a browser sends that request to port 80 on the Web server machine, and the server's network stack delivers the request to the Web server program proper, such as Apache.

If we simply plug a machine into the network, anyone can send network packets to any of the open ports on that machine. If we think about the system's state space, it becomes clear that simply plugging the machine into the network allows anyone to potentially affect the machine's state. Minimally, an attacker can cause unexpected transitions between system states; maximally, an attacker can introduce new states into the system and force a transition to those new states. Obviously, this is a very risky network architecture; it has been the cause of numerous security incidents over the years.

One way to decrease the risk of a remote attack is to shut down as many port-bound services as possible. In the extreme case—all such services are disabled—potential attackers can still send packets to all the target's ports; however, the stack drops the packets, since it has no services set up for those ports. (However, an attacker might still mount a denial-of-service attack simply by flooding the machine with more useless packets than it can handle.) In practice, this extreme but effective solution may be impossible to do on some OSes, since the OS itself registers services on particular ports. As an example, many flavors of the Windows OS open port 139 so that they can participate in file and printer sharing.

---

3. IANA has reserved a set of low-numbered ports for use with common, well-known services, such as mail, ftp, and ssh traffic. In theory, these ports are reserved for use only by the OS kernel, so some have called them "trusted." In practice, it's not clear they should be.

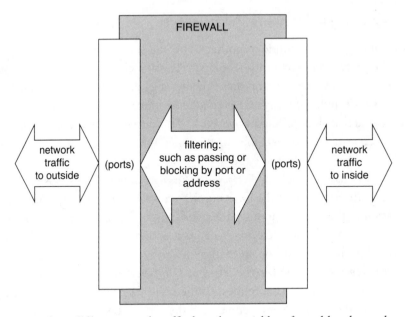

Figure 5.8 A *firewall* filters network traffic, based on quickly enforceable rules, such as ports and addresses.

Another way to decrease the risk of a remote attack is to install a *firewall:* a program that blocks access to particular ports (see Figure 5.8). Firewalls can be installed on the machine itself or at the network's border, so that the ports are blocked on all machines inside the firewall. In practice, many organizations install firewalls at the network border, as well as on the individual machines, as part of a *defense-in-depth* strategy.

Putting a firewall at the border to block all port traffic to the network decreases the risk of a remote attack but may also kill productivity. For example, if we were running a Web business and had one Web server, we would like port 80 to be accessible. If we block port 80 traffic, no http requests can hit our server; if we allow port 80, *all* the machines in our enterprise accept http requests—or any other traffic sent over that port. To remedy this situation, many enterprises have a *demilitarized zone (DMZ)* (see Figure 5.11), which is a part of the network that is outside the firewall. In our example, we would probably lock the Web server down as much as possible, most likely by disabling all the services except for the Web server and installing a host-based firewall that blocks everything except port 80. We would then place the server in the DMZ, allowing the server to be accessed by any remote machine but, we hope, only in ways we expect. Meanwhile, all the other machines in our enterprise would be behind the firewall and thus inaccessible from the outside world. (Section 5.3.2 provides more discussion on firewalls and DMZs.)

5.2 Protocols

Many modern software systems are designed to interact with the network at some point during their operation. For example, consumer software may receive updates from the network and get or reference information on the Internet. Enterprise software may use the network to allow subsystems, potentially running on different machines, to communicate with one another. Such network applications allow data to flow over the network, using some sort of network protocol. As we discuss in Section 5.3, this flow of data can give potential attackers a wealth of information that can be used to attack the software, gain access to the underlying OS, or compromise data, such as a credit card number.

As security artisans, our primary duty is building systems that protect such data from attackers. When building network applications, some of the most valuable tools in our box are network security protocols.[4] These protocols can give us a way to authenticate parties communicating over a network, create a private channel for data to pass through, provide integrity to ensure that data is not tampered with in transit, and so on.

5.2.1 SSL/TLS

Perhaps the most useful security protocol widely used in practice is the *Secure Sockets Layer (SSL)*. More recent versions of SSL have been renamed as the *Transport Layer Security (TLS)* protocol.[5] As we mentioned in Section 5.1, most network applications access the kernel's network stack via the sockets interface. In the mid-1990s, the Netscape team developed, standardized, and released a secure protocol that could be used by applications to add security measures to traditional TCP sockets.

The Netscape protocol (SSL) was designed to run on top of TCP, which allowed it to be run from user space. This meant that applications could start using SSL without having to wait around for operating systems to start building it into their network stack. Furthermore, much of SSL's interface is similar to TCP's, allowing programmers to transition from building TCP-based applications to SSL-based applications rather seamlessly.

Systems that would normally implement application-layer protocols using sockets should look to SSL to provide a secure alternative. SSL was designed to

---

4. Well, to be properly pedantic, we should call these "secure" protocols—they're not necessarily impenetrable, but they're darn useful.
5. Much has been written about SSL/TLS over the years, and we encourage readers to consult the literature for a detailed description of the protocol [KPS02, Res00]. We provide more description in Chapter 12, after we've gone through the necessary cryptography.

provide an authenticated, private, and tamper-evident channel between two machines on a public network. Some of the early applications that drove much of SSL's requirements were e-commerce applications conducted over the Internet.

In such applications, a user at an SSL-enabled Web browser would attempt to make an SSL connection to an SSL-enabled Web server. In a standard *server-side SSL* session, the server responds to the client by presenting its certificate. (We discuss certificates further in Chapter 10.) Once it receives the server's certificate, the client's browser checks that the certificate was issued by an entity that the browser trusts. Concretely, these trusted entities are represented by a set of root certificates that come preinstalled in the browser. If the server's certificate checks out (that is, it was issued by a trusted entity, it hasn't expired, and the server proves possession of the corresponding private key), then the client has authenticated the server.[6] (Again, if you're confused about all this, wait for Chapter 10.) Once the authentication step has occurred, the parties derive a set of symmetric cryptographic keys they use to encrypt/decrypt data and integrity checks over that data.

To date, numerous implementations of the SSL protocol exist. The decision of which one to use is typically dictated by the programming environment. Those developing in a C/C++ environment on virtually any modern OS should look at the *OpenSSL* library [VMC02, YH06]. Java developers have access to Sun's SSL implementation via the Java Foundation Classes [Sun04]. Sun's Java Developer Kit includes all the necessary tools to build SSL-enabled applications. Finally, .NET developers have access to SSL via third-party commercial libraries, such as *Secure-Blackbox* [Eld06].

5.2.2 IPsec

Another common suite of security protocols used in practice today is *IP security (IPsec)*. As the name suggests, the IPsec protocols are aimed at securing traffic at the IP layer of the TCP/IP stack. Unlike SSL, IPsec implementations cannot run from user space, since the IP layer is below TCP and is typically buried pretty deep in the kernel. In order to use IPsec, support must be built into the OS. Additionally, since application developers don't use IP directly but instead use transport-layer sockets, which in turn, use IP, they don't deal with IPsec directly, either.

IPsec is typically used by developers who write OSes, network hardware (e.g., routers), that must implement the TCP/IP stack, or security vendors that

---

6. The SSL specification also describes a similar process whereby the client presents a certificate as well, resulting in a *mutually authenticated* SSL channel. This variant is called *client-side SSL* and is discussed further in Chapter 12.

make specialized appliances that must process each network packet as it crosses
the security boundary. One of the most common applications of the IPsec family of
protocols are *virtual private networks (VPNs)*. VPNs allow parties to communicate
privately, even if they are connected over a public network, such as the Internet.
Many corporations use VPNs to give employees outside the firewall access to the
internal network.

IPsec supports two modes of protecting IP packets. In *transport mode*, the
payload of the IP message is encrypted while the header remains in plaintext. In this
mode, the packet can be routed like any other IP packet, as routers need the header
information only to make routing decisions. (An optional *authentication header* can
provide an integrity check on both payload and header.) Typical uses of transport
mode include scenarios in which two hosts are communicating directly. Since the
header is unencrypted, the packet can be routed from endpoint to endpoint without
any intermediate entity having to unencrypt the packet, which makes it ideal for end-
to-end security. However, the use of *network address translation (NAT)* can make
transport mode with authentication headers unusable, as it changes the destination
address in the header, thus breaking the cryptographic hash over the packet.

In *tunnel mode*, the entire IP packet is encrypted and is placed in the payload
section of a new IP packet. Tunnel mode is most often used when networks must
communicate, such as during router-to-router or host-to-network communication.
In tunnel mode, the destination network must unencrypt the original IP packet and
read its header so that it knows how to route the packet to the correct destination.
Tunnel mode is ideal when only some part of the packet's journey is dangerous, such
as when a remote employee makes a VPN connection to his or her organization's
network. Once it reaches the firewall, the packet can be unencrypted, parsed, and
sent to its final destination behind the firewall.

Readers interested in learning more about IPsec should start with the two
chapters that deal with the topic in [KPS02]. Those wanting to understand it from
a source-code level should refer to the FreeSwan project, which has added IPsec
support to the Linux kernel [Fre06].

5.2.3 DNSSEC

A critical part of making the Internet work is the ability to map hostnames to IP
addresses. However, as a paranoid reader might have inferred from our discussion,
the DNS was designed for a previous world, when the parties operating machines
on the network could trust on another to act in good faith. This assumption does
not hold in the current world. As a result, adversaries have had considerable success disrupting this mapping; see [AA04, DNS, ISC] for overviews. Attacks have

occurred on the protocol level: In *domain cache poisoning*, for example, the attacker fools a nameserver into accepting and then serving incorrect mapping information. Attacks have occurred in the human level: In *domain cache hijacking*, for example, the attacker fools the network registrar into thinking that the attacker owns a hostname. Attacks have also occurred on the software level: The *BIND* software, for example, that runs on many nameservers has had a long history of vulnerabilities. Attacks have even occurred on the basic network level: The nameserver may happily serve correct information, but the attacker impersonates it or alters the information in transit.

We leave as an exercise for the reader the various fun networking scenarios an attacker can arrange to subvert a nameserver.

The *DNSSEC* protocol [AAL$^+$05a, AAL$^+$05b, AAL$^+$05c, WI06] has been developed to address some of these risks. With DNSSEC, nameservers use digital signatures (see Chapters 7 and 10) to authenticate the senders of mapping information—and thus presumably authenticate the mapping information itself. (Unfortunately, DNSSEC still seems to be future tense.)

5.2.4 (S)BGP

Section 5.1.2 explained how the enterprises that make up the Internet use the Border Gateway Protocol to distribute routing information and maintain their own routing tables. As with DNS, this critical infrastructure implicitly assumes a more trustworthy world than we currently have.

The first kind of attack that comes to mind is simply forging or lying about routing information. By doing so, an attacker can claim an IP address that belongs to someone else. (We understand that this is a popular trick with spammers [Hou06].) An attacker can also create other distortions in the infrastructure, such as *blackholing* a host (cutting off all the host's traffic) overloading part of the network, or even partitioning it. However, the complexity of BGP permits another level of attack: Deviously timed route-update announcements can introduce considerable instability into the routing infrastructure and hence into the Internet itself. Murphy wrote the classic document on this topic [Mur06].

How to address BGP insecurity is an ongoing research topic. We might start by splitting it into two problems:

1. *Path authentication.* Suppose that autonomous system A announces to its peer B that it can now reach addresses starting with prefix P via this sequence R of autonomous systems. How can B know that this path exists? Even if A was honest, someone earlier along R might have lied.

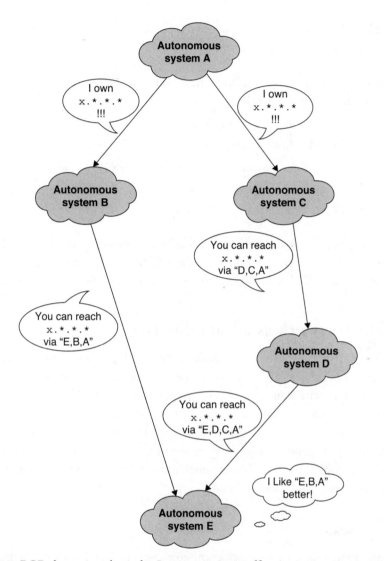

Figure 5.9 BGP determines how the Internet routes traffic: An autonomous system announces that it owns part of the IP address space, and then other systems propagate potential routes. However, nothing stops these parties from lying.

2. *Origin authentication.* Suppose that the sequence R ended with S_P. How can B or A or anyone else verify that autonomous system S_P in fact owns the IP addresses that start with a particular prefix P? (See Figure 5.9.)

The classic solution to this problem is *S-BGP* (see [Ken03, KLS00]): having each party along a route R digitally sign a statement about how it extends the route.

Although S-BGP may be classic, many researchers have found many drawbacks. Some principal ones are the following.

- The cryptography lengthens the time it takes for the network to stabilize after significant routing disruptions.
- The cryptography makes messages longer.
- The cryptography taxes router caches.
- The system does not allow for incremental deployment.
- The system pays a high price to secure the claim of a route but still cannot ensure that those parties will do that routing.

As a consequence, securing BGP remains an active area of research (e.g., [HPS04, SRS+04, WKvO05]) even in our own lab (e.g., [ZSN05a, ZSN05b]). Kent has also recently proposed a PKI-based solution to the origin authentication problem [Ken06].

5.3 The Network as a Battlefield

Numerous movies portray a stereotypical hacker gaining access to remote machines from the comfort of home. Indeed, computer networks are the battlefield on which many computer security incidents occur, as they open the world of remote exploitation. As more institutions take advantage of networking technology and adopt electronic processes, more critical information flows through the network. As a result, many institutions spend the bulk of their security budget on efforts to secure their networks. We look at some of the common tactics involved in network warfare from both perspectives: attack and defense.

5.3.1 Attacks

There are numerous ways to attack computer systems. In Chapter 4, we discussed attacking the OS itself. In Chapters 6 and 8, we discuss how to attack programs and some of the fundamental building blocks of secure systems. Here, we focus on attacking machines that are connected to a network.

A number of good texts cover various attack tools and techniques. *Hacking Exposed* [MSK05] covers the attacker's toolkit in great detail and has broadened into different editions for different OSes. *Gray Hat Hacking* [HHE+04] covers some of the latest attack tools, as well as penetration-testing process. *Counter Hack* [SL05] gives a good treatment of attacks and defenses. Readers seeking more detail on the network aspects of security should consult one or more of these texts.

A network attack can be used to accomplish a number of objectives. Perhaps the attacker is after critical information, such as new product designs or financial information. Perhaps the attacker is attempting to compromise machines to participate in a larger attack, such as a DDoS, or to cover his or her tracks. Perhaps the attacker is simply out for a thrill or to vandalize the target. Regardless of the particular objective, tool, or technique that an attacker uses, most network attacks comprise one or more of the following steps: *scanning* the network for potentially vulnerable machines, *sniffing* network traffic, *spoofing* network addresses to cover tracks, and executing an *exploit* of some sort.

Scanning.   Regardless of whether an attacker is targeting an enemy on the battlefield, a physical bank, or a computer system, the first step usually involves reconnaissance. In terms of network combat, this is done by scanning the target environment.

Scanning a network is not a crime in itself but is typically categorized as suspect behavior, since it is usually one of the first stages of an attack.[7] Scanning can produce all sorts of useful information to a potential attacker, such as basic network topology, the types of OSes in the environment, and which ports and services are running on the individual machines. At the core, scanners gather such information by sending packets to the target machine and evaluating responses. Often, the scanner tries to connect to the target by using TCP or UDP. Although attempting to make a connection to a machine seems rather uninteresting, all sorts of useful information can be gathered by how the machine responds.

First, since the TCP/UDP connections target a particular port on the target machine, the scanner can immediately determine whether the port is open or closed. Since IANA reserves some ports for particular well-known protocols, such as ftp, ssh, and so on, successful connections to these ports mean that there is a good chance that a particular service is running; however, the IANA port reservations are only a convention—technically, one can bind another service to a reserved port. Unreserved ports may also accept connections; these ports are typically used by third-party software vendors or hand-rolled services deployed by the machine's owner. In this case, a technique known as *banner grabbing* can be used to attempt to guess at what service is attached to the port. Since many protocols begin with

---

7. During a transition in our research lab's networking environment, an oversight left an unprotected lab machine on the network for a weekend. Needless to say, the machine was compromised. Apparently, the attacker used the machine to scan a national laboratory belonging to the U.S. Department of Energy. The national lab swiftly contacted us and requested that "we" stop scanning its environment. Of course, we disconnected the machine and traced the attack back to its source. All in all, it was a great experience, but it serves to show that scanning the wrong people can get you in hot water.

the servers sending some sort of message and/or challenge to the client, matching what is sent by a service on a particular point against a database of known messages can allow the scanner to identify the service. From just a simple set of connection attempts, an attacker can get a useful list of services running on the machine.

A second piece of useful information that can be ascertained by attempting to make TCP connections to a machine is the type of OS. Recall from Section 5.1.5 that the network stack is a part of the OS itself. By examining some subtleties of the return packets, such as the distribution of sequence numbers and the state of such variables as the TCP initial window size and many others, it is possible to learn what OS is running on the target. Fyodor—creator of the popular network scanner *nmap* [Fyo06a]—has a great article that covers various techniques for OS fingerprinting and how they are implemented in nmap [Fyo06b].

Scanning can also be used to discover the network topology of the target environment. By sending *ping* packets to a range of IP addresses, a potential attacker can learn which machines are up in a given network; this technique is called *ping sweeping*. Other tools, such as `traceroute`, use the packet's *time-to-live (TTL)* field[8] to determine the path that packets take through a network. With enough paths, it's possible to reconstruct a pretty good picture of the network topology.

At the end of the scanning phase, a potential attacker should have a decent idea of what the target environment looks like as a whole and should have a clear path to the target, know what OS the target uses, and have an idea of what services the target is running. This is usually enough information for an attacker to start thinking about what type of exploits will work against the target.

Sniffing. Another useful network information-gathering technique is *sniffing*, which involves putting a piece of software, called a network sniffer, on the target's network to capture, or sniff, all the network traffic. Such efforts can usually turn up a gold mine: usernames and passwords; open network shares; the location of important machines, such as Windows domain controllers and databases; and the location of vulnerable services.

On many older, nonswitched, Ethernet-based networks, this approach easily turned up volumes of useful information. An attacker simply had to obtain access to one machine on the network; put its network card in *promiscuous mode*, allowing it to capture *all* the Ethernet frames on the network; and run a sniffer, such as WireShark, (previously known as Ethereal [Com06]) to store and analyze the data.

---

8. This TTL is not to be confused with the *transistor-transistor logic* TTL, once a dominant technology in digital electronics.

Although Ethernet is a broadcast protocol, many enterprises have begun to use switches to help Ethernet traffic get to its destination and thus improve network performance. As noted earlier, a side effect of using a switched network is that sniffing is more difficult. The scenario in which an attacker has compromised one machine and uses it as a sniffer is no longer effective. Even though the machine's network card will accept all Ethernet traffic, the switch lets the machine see only traffic that was destined for it in the first place.

To overcome this limitation, modern sniffers, such as Ettercap [OV06], use a technique known as *ARP cache poisoning*. As we discussed in Section 5.1.2, ARP is a simple network protocol that allows networked devices to associate MAC addresses with IP addresses. Under normal circumstances, machine A would formulate an ARP request and send it out to the local network or subnet. The effect of this request is A asking the other machines on the network who has IP address x.x.x.x. Assuming that machine B has that IP address, it would formulate an ARP reply that lets A know that B has that IP address and that the MAC address for machine B is y:y:y:y:y:y. Machine A places this association in its ARP cache table so that it does not have to send an ARP reply every time it wants to communicate with B. Now, if it wishes to communicate with B, A can do so by using B's MAC address.

The weakness of this protocol is that there is no authentication: A will believe any machine that sends an ARP reply claiming to be B. In fact, many machines will accept unsolicited ARP replies—those for which there is no corresponding ARP request. By taking advantage of this fact, a malicious machine C may send an ARP reply to the network, claiming that it has IP address x.x.x.x and that its MAC address is z:z:z:z:z:z. C has effectively tricked all the machines that accept the reply into thinking that it is in fact machine B and thus intercepts B's traffic. C has implemented a *man-in-the-middle* attack.

If B is a network switch instead of an ordinary computer on the network, C may try to send so many ARP replies that the switch goes back into hub mode and broadcasts packets to every switch segment. This attack is known as *MAC flooding* and allows an attacker to resume normal sniffing operations, if successful.

Spoofing.   One of the fundamental tactics in network warfare is stealth. Typically, this is accomplished by an attacker covering his or her tracks in the victim's logs and attacking from a machine that does not physically belong to the attacker. The idea is that an attacker A wanting to hit some target in C's network should perform the attack from a machine in B. The more hops between the attacker and the final target, the harder the attack is to reconstruct, and the harder the attacker is to find.[9] Of course, one way to do this is for A to directly attack B first, using the standard arsenal of techniques. Another way to accomplish this is for the attacker to use *IP spoofing* techniques [Bel89]. IP spoofing allows an attacker to change the network packets so that they appear to have originated somewhere else. This is useful only in attacks where the target does not need to reply to the attacker. If A sends packets to C and makes the packets look like they are from B, when C replies, the reply goes to B. Although this would not work for some types of remote attacks, it is particularly useful for asymmetric attacks,[10] such as DoS attacks, in which the attacker sends as many packets as possible to the host so that it becomes overwhelmed with network traffic. Since the attacker doesn't care what the target has to say as a reply, simply changing the source address of the packets can be useful in hiding the attacker's tracks.

MAC spoofing is another useful technique but not necessarily for covering one's tracks. Many wireless networks (which we discuss more in Section 5.4.1) use MAC addresses for authentication. For example, Alice may set up a wireless network in her house such that only her laptop and XBox 360 are allowed to use the network. Since Alice is unlikely to change the network hardware on either device, she decides to use the devices' MAC addresses as authenticators to the wireless network. If Carlo is outside her house with a wireless sniffer, he can easily learn the MAC addresses of Alice's laptop and XBox 360. If Carlo wants to use Alice's network, he can change the MAC address of his laptop—for example, using the `ifconfig` command on Linux—to be the MAC address of Alice's XBox 360. When Alice turns her XBox off, Carlo can easily board her wireless network, since the network believes that his computer is the XBox.

If the reader feels that this example is too innocuous, think instead of a corporation that wants to restrict wireless LAN access to insiders, since it goes straight to the corporate intranet, but does so simply by checking the MAC address of the wireless card in the client's laptop. (Sadly, such an approach to network admission is common.)

Vulnerabilities, Exploits, and Automation. Once an attacker has mapped out the target, gotten enough information to plan the attack, and taken the appropriate steps to cover his or her tracks, there's only one thing left to do: attack the target. Typically, this involves trying to get a remote shell—ideally, with root or administrator

---

9. We've even encountered victim enterprises—the C in this scenario—whose legal counsel advised *not* pursuing the attacker back through enterprise B's machines, because that itself might constitute an attack on B.
10. That is, attacks in which the resource posture of the attacker and victim substantially differ.

privileges—so that the attacker can install software, access the desired information, destroy the hard drives, and so on. Often, the attacker accomplishes this step by using an *exploit* that exercises a *vulnerability* in one of the network-facing services that the attacker discovered. (We discuss exploits in detail in Chapter 6.) If successful, the attacker is on the target machine and can carry out the rest of his or her battle plan.

In the discussion thus far, we have assumed that the attacker has nefarious intentions. However, people attack systems for other reasons as well. For example, a system administrator or security consultant may attack the target environment to locate and repair weaknesses in the environment's defenses. In this type of exercise— often referred to as a *penetration test*, or *pen test* for short—the "attacker's" objective is to find as many exploitable vulnerabilities as possible.

In recent years, a number of automation tools have been developed in order to reduce the time, cost, and complexity of performing a pen test. Such tools as Metasploit [Met06], Core Impact [Cor], and Nessus [Ten06] perform many, if not all, the preceding steps and allow administrators and pen testers to quickly assess the security of the target environment. Of course, these tools are often used for "unauthorized" pen tests as well. (We consider penetration testing further in Chapter 11.)

5.3.2 Defenses

Defending a computer network is hard work. Attackers have to be good at only one thing in order to get into a network; often, it takes only one well-executed exploit. Defenders, on the other hand, have to be prepared for anything. Defending an organization against numerous types of attacks coming from various places, even within the organization itself, requires careful planning, flawless execution, and continual maintenance.

Just as there is a set of common attack tools and techniques, there are a number of common defense tools and tactics that find their way into many organizations. Ideally, these tools and tactics should serve to reduce the complexity of running a secure environment—one with a low risk of compromise. We start by discussing some of the design philosophies involved in architecting a secure network environment. We then discuss some of the common tools used to accomplish this task.

Security Domains and Defense in Depth.   Before network architects were overly concerned about security, computers were typically placed directly on the network, with no protection other than what the computer itself had to offer. Potential attackers could directly communicate with services running on such computers, with no restrictions other than what the computer or service imposed, such as password-based authentication. This open arrangement gave attackers direct access to the machine's state space and effectively put each machine in its own *security domain*, meaning that an effective attack on one machine might be ineffective on another. However, in order to reduce the administration overhead, many machines run the same services in the same configurations, thus placing them in the same security domain.

As network attacks became more of a threat, network architects began to build perimeters around their network. Typically, this was done using a piece of software—and sometimes specialized hardware—called a *firewall* (disussed earlier). The basic idea is to keep particular types of network traffic away from the computers inside the firewall. For example, a user workstation inside the firewall probably has no business accepting file transfer protocol (ftp) traffic from anyone on the Internet.

Conceptually, firewalls place an entire network in a security domain different from the outside world. Firewalls also keep potential attackers away from the individual machines' state spaces. For some time, many enterprises relied only on their firewalls for security. This strategy allowed organizations to concentrate all the security effort on one spot and reduce the cost of having to manage the security of individual machines inside the firewall. The downside is that if the firewall is breached, the entire enterprise is vulnerable to attack.

Modern thinking is to architect networks along security boundaries, thus creating multiple security domains inside the firewall. For example, an enterprise may partition its intranet into *subnets* (see Figure 5.10). Mission-critical servers may get placed on one subnet and have very strong access controls, such as PKI; noncritical

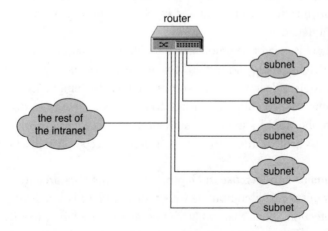

Figure 5.10 An enterprise may use *subnets* to partition its intranet into separate security domains.

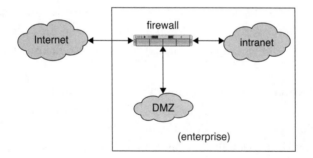

Figure 5.11 An enterprise having machines that need more external access than is appropriate for its intranet but less than the open Internet often places them in a *DMZ*.

servers may get placed on another subnet with more lax access controls; workstations may get placed on yet another subnet; and publicly accessible servers, such as Web servers, may get placed in a DMZ (again, discussed earlier) so that they can be reached by the outside world (see Figure 5.11).

The motivation behind this strategy is to contain firewall breaches to particular security domains of the enterprise. This way, an attacker who was able to get through the firewall and compromise a workstation might not be able to gain access to mission-critical servers. Ideally, the machines themselves may also have defenses on them, such as machine-level firewalls, antivirus software, and integrity checkers, as mentioned earlier. This strategy of having multiple lines of defenses is often referred to as *defense in depth* and has become a best practice when designing modern networks.

Firewall Details.   As we've previously discussed, the first line of network defense is often the firewall. At the core, firewalls are used to block network connections from the outside world to machines behind or inside the firewall. Firewalls are typically governed by a set of rules that specify what IP addresses, ports, and, potentially, even types of traffic are allowed to connect to machines inside the firewall.

Firewalls can also be used to protect the host machines themselves. In fact, modern versions of Windows come with such a "personal" firewall, and the Linux OS has had support for the `ipchains` and `iptables` firewalls for years. Such personal firewalls are similar in concept and operation: They block connections to particular ports on the host machine. Typically, there is a set of firewall rules that specify how the firewall should behave. The rules are similar (at least in concept) to regular expressions in that, as it passes over the network interface, each packet is matched to a particular rule. The actions for the matching rule will determine whether the packet is allowed to cross the interface. (Surprisingly, some enterprise IT departments request that users do *not* enable personal firewalls, because they complicate the life of the remote sysadmin trying to install security patches.)

Intrusion Detection.   Another common type of defense tool is the *intrusion detection system (IDS)*. IDS tools, such as Snort [Sou06], work by examining network traffic in real time and matching the traffic against known attack patterns, sometimes called signatures. If it sees that some incoming traffic matches an attack signature in its database, the IDS alerts the appropriate authorities.

As with many security systems, attackers and IDS designers have an ongoing arms race. IDS designers are continually trying to keep attack databases up-to-date with the latest signatures, whereas attackers are continually finding new ways to obfuscate their attacks so that they can slip by the IDS. In fact, clever attackers can use IDS systems as a diversion. Knowing that an attack will trigger the IDS and attract attention, an attacker can first send a "false" attack. Then, while the victim's security personnel are watching the "false" attack, the attacker can perform the real attack, which either gets lost in the noise or, ideally, doesn't trip the IDS at all.

(We examine the technology behind intrusion detection in Chapter 17.)

Host-Based Defenses.   The last line of defense in a defense-in-depth strategy occurs at the host machine itself. In addition to personal firewall support, which blocks traffic to specific ports on the machine, there are also *host-based intrusion prevention systems (HIPS)*, which are essentially IDS solutions running on the end host itself and can inspect and block traffic in real time. Additionally, many organizations rely on antivirus and antispyware tools to scan the host machine's hard drive in an attempt to locate viruses, rootkits, and other malware.

Finally, some enterprises deploy filesystem integrity checkers, such as the Tripwire system [Tri06], to ensure that critical files on the host system are not modified. (We discussed these briefly in Chapter 4.) Essentially, these tools work by taking a snapshot of the file, calculating a hash value for the file (see Chapter 7) and periodically comparing the file on disk against the snapshot. If the versions do not match, then the user is alerted.

5.4 The Brave New World

In this section, we discuss how using radio waves to carry packets makes the security game different. Techniques such as air gaps that worked back in the bad old days can break down when cutting the cord no longer cuts the connection.

5.4.1 WLANs

The last few years have seen a major paradigm shift to *wireless* networking from the older, traditional form, which is now derided as "tethered." It's become ubiquitous: A technical conference or a high-end hotel that does not offer its guests wireless networking is as unthinkable as one that does not offer its guests electricity. (Many hotels will still attempt to charge extra, however.) Corporations and universities are still thinking it through, owing to the difficulties of access control: sorting out who's an insider deserving inside access and who's an outsider.

Standards and technology for wireless are undergoing considerable churn; it would be inappropriate to try to make a definitive statement here. Nevertheless, we offer a rough guide to the alphabet soup. The IEEE *802.11* set of standards describes wireless. These standards have different letters after their names. One might think that the set of names of the form "802.11 plus a letter" all talk about the same thing; however, that's not the case. For example, *802.11a* refers to particular ways of stuffing the bits through at high speeds, and *802.11i* refers to security, with *802.1x* a more general networking security standard included in 802.11i. (No, "802.1x" does not refer to "things of the form 802.1 + one more digit.") The term *Wi-Fi* is used as both a generic term for wireless stuff and a specific term for a certification process established by the *Wi-Fi Alliance*, a vendor consortium.

In *ad hoc* wireless networking, computers talk directly to each other. (In airports and meetings, you can usually find lots of laptops happily offering to make an ad hoc wireless connection with anyone who asks.) The more common use is *infrastructure* networking, whereby computers talk to a tethered *access point*. The term wireless LAN (*WLAN*) refers to the cloud of service around an access point. A *supplicant* is a computer that is requesting to join a WLAN (see Figure 5.12).

Paradigm Change.   Users like wireless; the ability to do networked computing anywhere one opens up one's laptop is surprisingly enchanting. Here at our own university, we've seen users complain about the slow wireless—while they sit in front of unused Ethernet jacks that offered ample capacity. We also planned not to put

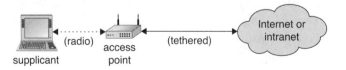

Figure 5.12 In basic WLAN architecture, a *supplicant* connects to the *infrastructure network* via an *access point.*

```
0000  00 00 18 00 0f 18 00 00   c8 b0 20 02 00 00 00 00    ........ .. .....
0010  32 0b 9e 09 80 04 00 17   08 02 3a 01 00 16 cb b5    2....... ..:.....
0020  e1 0e 00 19 07 96 72 a0   00 50 e8 01 7a 36 a0 48    ......r. .P..z6.H
0030  aa aa 03 00 00 00 08 00   45 00 05 8c 67 d4 40 00    ........ E...g.@.
0040  34 06 2f 01 42 a5 ba 81   ac 1e 01 52 00 50 c0 ae    4./.B... ...R.P..
0050  b0 eb 40 1a c6 d0 ae 61   80 10 06 b4 67 5d 00 00    ..@....a ....g]..
0060  01 01 08 0a 7b 58 e8 1c   1f da 15 28 64 65 78 2e    ....{X.. ...(dex.
0070  68 74 6d 6c 27 20 74 61   72 67 65 74 3d 27 5f 62    html' ta rget='_b
0080  6c 61 6e 6b 27 3e 32 30   30 37 2d 30 33 2d 31 39    lank'>20 07-03-19
0090  3c 2f 61 3e 20 2d 20 31   37 20 70 69 63 74 75 72    </a> - 1 7 pictur
00a0  65 73 20 63 75 74 69 65   20 64 65 74 61 69 6e 65    es cutie  detaine
00b0  65 20 67 65 74 74 73 20   65 72 20 61 6b 73 20 6e    e getts  er aks n
00c0  6e 73 70 65 63 74 65 64   20 62 79 20 61 20 6a 61    nspected  by a ja
00d0  69 6c 20 6f 66 66 69 63   65 72 3c 62 72 3e 0d 0a    il offic er<br>..
00e0  3c 61 20 68 72 65 66 3d   27 2f 63 6c 69 63 6b 2e    <a href= '/click.
00f0  70 68 70 3f 75 72 6c 3d   68 74 74 70 3a 2f 2f 77    php?url= http://w
0100  77 77 2e 62 6f 6f 74 79   6a 75 6e 6b 69 65 2e 63    ww.bootyjunkie.c
0110  6f 6d 2f 72 61 67 65 63   61 73 68 32 2f 73 6c 65    om/ragec ash2/sle
0120  65 70 61 73 73 61 75 6c   74 2f 70 69 63 73 2f 31    epassaul t/pics/1
0130  37 2f 69 6e 64 65 78 2e   68 74 6d 6c 27 20 74 61    7/index. html' ta
0140  72 67 65 74 3d 27 5f 62   6c 61 6e 6b 27 3e 32 30    rget='_b lank'>20
0150  30 37 2d 30 33 2d 31 39   3c 2f 61 3e 20 2d 20 31    07-03-19 </a> - 1
0160  38 20 70 69 63 74 75 72   65 73 20 62 72 75 6e 65    8 pictur es brune
0170  74 74 65 20 68 6f 74 74   69 65 20 67 65 74 74 69    tte hott ie getti
```

Figure 5.13 Wireless sniffing in a hotel room at a conference revealed much interesting traffic, including this packet. The user whose session we sniffed was also doing employment-related browsing; it would not have been difficult to determine the user's identity.

wireless in the dormitories, since we already have one jack per bed. Nevertheless, we deployed it there anyway—and subsequent usage measurement showed that the dorms were the most popular places for wireless.

However, computing activities that were somewhat safe on switched LAN and only moderately risky on broadcast LAN become downright dangerous when anyone within radio range can join your LAN, listen to your packets, and add his or her own. This is the case for naively deployed access points and naively migrated applications. A small programming exercise can put an off-the-shelf wireless card into promiscuous *passive* mode; standard tools then enable the attacker to reassemble packet streams. We can watch users access the Web (see Figure 5.13). We can watch users read their email and watch the mail too (see Figure 5.14). As part of a classroom exercise, one student even managed to impersonate critical back-end servers—not by hacking into machines or wires but simply by listening for a request to those servers and transmitting a forged response; since he was within short radio range of the victim, his forgery often got to the victim first. (See Chapter 9 and Figure 9.9 for more discussion.)

Wardriving. The ability for anyone within radio range to join an enterprise's LAN creates the potential for *wardriving*: physically traveling through a new area to see

```
0300   7e 7e 7e 7e 7e 7e 7e 7e   7e 0d 54 68 65 20 6d 61    ~~~~~~~~ ~.The ma
0310   74 65 72 69 61 6c 73 20   69 6e 20 74 68 69 73 20    terials  in this
0320   6d 65 73 73 61 67 65 20   61 72 65 20 70 72 69 76    message  are priv
0330   61 74 65 20 61 6e 64 20   6d 61 79 20 63 6f 6e 74    ate and  may cont
0340   61 69 6e 20 50 72 6f 74   65 63 74 65 64 20 48 65    ain Prot ected He
0350   61 6c 74 68 63 61 72 65   20 49 6e 66 6f 72 6d 61    althcare  Informa
0360   74 69 6f 6e 2e 20 49 66   20 79 6f 75 20 61 72 65    tion. If  you are
0370   20 6e 6f 74 20 74 68 65   20 69 6e 74 65 6e 64 65     not the  intende
0380   64 20 72 65 63 69 70 69   65 6e 74 2c 20 62 65 20    d recipi ent, be
0390   61 64 76 69 73 65 64 20   74 68 61 74 20 61 6e 79    advised  that any
03a0   20 75 6e 61 75 74 68 6f   72 69 7a 65 64 20 75 73     unautho rized us
03b0   65 2c 20 64 69 73 63 6c   6f 73 75 72 65 2c 20 63    e, discl osure, c
03c0   6f 70 79 69 6e 67 20 6f   72 20 74 68 65 20 74 61    opying o r the ta
03d0   6b 69 6e 67 20 6f 66 20   61 6e 79 20 61 63 74 69    king of  any acti
03e0   6f 6e 20 69 6e 20 72 65   6c 69 61 6e 63 65 20 6f    on in re liance o
03f0   6e 20 74 68 65 20 63 6f   6e 74 65 6e 74 73 20 6f    n the co ntents o
0400   66 20 74 68 69 73 20 69   6e 66 6f 72 6d 61 74 69    f this i nformati
0410   6f 6e 20 69 73 20 73 74   72 69 63 74 6c 79 20 70    on is st rictly p
0420   72 6f 68 69 62 69 74 65   64 2e 20 49 66 20 79 6f    rohibite d. If yo
0430   75 20 68 61 76 65 20 72   65 63 65 69 76 65 64 20    u have r eceived
0440   74 68 69 73 20 65 6d 61   69 6c 20 69 6e 20 65 72    this ema il in er
0450   72 6f 72 2c 20 70 6c 65   61 73 65 20 69 6d 6d 65    ror, ple ase imme
0460   64 69 61 74 65 6c 79 20   6e 6f 74 69 66 79 20 74    diately  notify t
0470   68 65 20 73 65 6e 64 65   72 20 76 69 61 20 74 65    he sende r via te
0480   6c 65 70 68 6f 6e 65 20   6f 72 20 72 65 74 75 72    lephone  or retur
0490   6e 20 6d 61 69 6c 2e 30   31 30 20 4f 6b 2e 0d 0a    n mail.0 10 Ok...
```

Figure 5.14 Wireless sniffing at a college dorm revealed much interesting traffic, including this packet. It is interesting to note that the campus medical service includes dire privacy warnings on email but then proceeds to send it in plaintext over publicly accessible radio.

what networks can be found. (For some researchers, wardriving also implies preparing and publishing maps of what open networks can be found where.) This is risky for an enterprise that regards its WLAN as part of its internal network; an outsider who connects might land inside the firewall and have access to internal services, such as databases, intended to be confined to internal users only. Wardriving can also be risky for the wardriver; in the United States, we're starting to see cases of people prosecuted for borrowing an open connection.

Personally, we feel that limited borrowing of an open connection is as ethical as limited use of a trash can or electrical outlet—particularly since putting up the electronic equivalent of a "no trespassing, please" sign is trivial. One colleague even went further and reconfigured his neighbors' access points so they wouldn't interfere with each other; he thus improved everyone's lot. (Those who would use a burglar metaphor to vilify wardrivers must now grapple with the case of someone who breaks and enters—and then washes the dishes.) On the other hand, another colleague reports an ISP customer service call in which the customer complained of slow service. After nothing worked, the call handler suggested that the customer unplug his access point. The customer replied, "The service is still slow." For all these months, the customer had been using someone else's connection.

Access Control.   Fun with open networks and open network traffic is possible because the traffic is not protected and because the networks let anyone join. As a consequence, the field has had a long history of trying to address these problems.

The first major approach promulgated was *wired equivalent privacy (WEP)*. (The name alone made us worry: privacy? and equivalent to what?) Cam-Winget et al. give a nice rundown of what happened [CWHWW03]. WEP used a single shared key, used a cyclic redundancy checksum (CRC) rather than a cryptographic hash for integrity, and used a complicated way to derive keys. As a result, attacks progressed from a theoretical attack in August 2001 [FMS01] to practical, working code a few weeks later [BGW01].

More recently, the Wi-Fi Alliance promulgated *Wi-Fi Protected Access (WPA)*, which lays a much stronger foundation for both session protection and network admission. We see a range of current approaches to controlling network admission.

- Some enterprises restrict entry to anyone who knows the "secret" *SSID* of the network—except that this information can usually be obtained simply by listening to the broadcasts.

- Some enterprises restrict entry to supplicants whose MAC addresses lie on a special access control list—except that an eavesdropper who can learn a blessed MAC address can reprogram his or her own wireless card to have that one.

- Some enterprises tunnel other protocols through the access point. Names of the form *EAP-Foo* refer to network admission based on Foo pulled into this new setting. (EAP stands for *extended authentication protocol*.) These range from *EAP-TLS*—which uses PKI-based mutual SSL—down to ones that simply use passwords.

- Some enterprises leave the access point open but shunt all traffic outside the firewall (see Figure 5.15).

Adding network admission to a WLAN often requires that access points be able to handle two modes of supplicant traffic; even before a supplicant is allowed "on the net," it may need to send traffic through the access point to an authorization server—which is on the net (see Figure 5.16).

The security artisan trying to build a WLAN security solution must work though many issues. Should all supplicant traffic first be routed to a *captive portal* that lets them authenticate? How do we cause an authenticated supplicant to re-associate with an internal WLAN? What about special-purpose devices that do not speak WPA? Will an enterprise's legacy RADIUS authorization server—a relic from

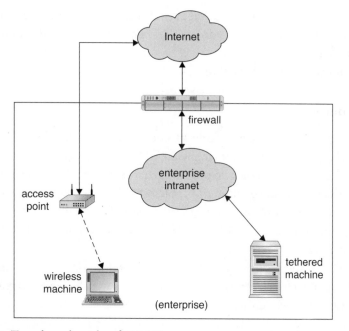

Figure 5.15 To reduce the risks of WLAN access, some enterprises choose to connect the wireless infrastructure *outside* the firewall.

dial-up days that often becomes the backbone of authorization decisions in enterprise IT (discussed further in Section 9.8)—speak to the access points in the right way? (We found that they didn't [GKS⁺04].)

So far, we've been worried about how an enterprise might protect network access and network traffic from rogue outsiders. However, WLANs offer other risks as well. An adversary might set up a *rogue access point* that bridges to an enterprise's real services but also sniffs userids and passwords that the users are

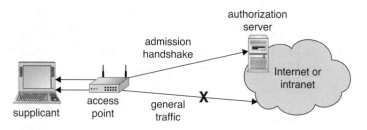

Figure 5.16 Before it can get on the internal network, a supplicant may need to authenticate, which itself may require access to the internal network.

trained to enter into the captive portal page. Furthermore, many access points fail to authenticate their control and administration messages, creating another avenue for malfeasance.

As we noted, there is lot of churn here.

5.4.2 Bluetooth

Another popular wireless networking protocol is *Bluetooth*. Like 802.11x, Bluetooth uses short-range radio waves in the 2.4GHz frequency band to send messages between devices. Although the two protocols share some of the same characteristics, they were designed to solve different problems: 802.11x, to create wireless LANs, or a wireless equivalent to common Ethernet-based LANs; Bluetooth, to facilitate the creation of *personal area networks (PANs)*, a shorter-range network of one's personal devices.

The 802.11x standard is typically used to connect two or more fairly large network devices, such as laptop computers, or to allow such devices to connect to a preexisting wired network, such as a corporate LAN. Since such devices usually have a fair amount of power, 802.11x uses more power and results in throughput (around 11Mb/s originally and now up to about 50 Mb/s) on par with wired Ethernet. The power consumption of 802.11x also allows devices to connect at fairly long ranges— around 300 feet originally, and longer ranges are possible by using newer protocols and signal-extending hardware, such as an antenna.

Bluetooth, on the other hand, was designed to allow smaller devices, such as cell phones and *personal digital assistants (PDAs)*, to communicate wirelessly. Since these types of devices do not typically have the same level of power as such devices as laptops, Bluetooth was designed to use much less power than 802.11x. The reduction of power also limits the bandwidth—Bluetooth can do about 1Mb/s—and limits the range to about 30 feet[11].

Bluetooth Applications.   Much like 802.11x, Bluetooth becomes more widespread on a daily basis. Bluetooth hardware is finding its way into a number of modern digital devices. Most major cell carriers offer a number of Bluetooth-enabled cell phones, and most laptops are now equipped with a Bluetooth transceiver as well. Various other types of hardware, such as computer peripherals, are also shipping with Bluetooth capabilities.

---

11. Bluetooth devices are placed in different classes, based on their radio range. Technically, class 1 Bluetooth devices have ranges up to 300 feet. Most Bluetooth radios that are found in cell phones and the like are class 3 devices, which have a range of around 30 feet.

One of the original usage scenarios for Bluetooth involves replacing cables. In such a scenario, users could link together devices, such as computer peripherals, using Bluetooth and spare the hassle of run cable. In the past few years, such applications have started to arrive on the market. A number of commercially available printers, keyboards, and mice rely on Bluetooth for communication, thus alleviating the need for cords to connect the devices.

In the world of cell phones, a large number of Bluetooth headsets have been sold in recent years. These headsets have a microphone and a receiver that communicate with the owner's cell phone over Bluetooth. When the user speaks, the voice signal is carried over Bluetooth to the cell phone, where it is then forwarded to the user's cellular network.

Another Bluetooth use scenario involves personalizing a particular space to fit the user's preferences. The idea behind this scheme is that a user, Alice, is carrying a Bluetooth-enabled device with all her preferences. As she approaches the space, a Bluetooth device in the space and the user's device discover each other, and Alice's preferences are sent to the space. The space then configures itself according to Alice's preferences—for example, the seats are adjusted to the proper position, Alice's favorite radio station is selected, and the temperature controls are set according to Alice's taste.

Bluetooth is ideal for sharing small amounts of data between devices. For example, Alice may want to synchronize the contacts in her laptop, PDA, and cell phone without having to plug everything in to each other. The range and data rate of Bluetooth make it ideal for this type of application.

Bluetooth also does a decent job of sharing connections across devices. Before the advent of cellular broadband, especially in areas where a WLAN is unavailable, it was often difficult to get a dial-up Internet connection with a laptop. Many laptop users solved this problem by using the Internet connection on their cell phones over a Bluetooth connection between their laptop and phone.

Bluetooth and Security.   Before we examine some of the security issues with Bluetooth, we need to understand the basics of how Bluetooth connections are made. Bluetooth devices within range of each other learn of each other's capabilities via a process known as *discovery*. The discovery process has two phases: *device discovery*, whereby a device learns what Bluetooth-enabled devices are within range, and *service discovery*, whereby the device learns what services are available on each of those devices. Once it sees a service that it is interested in connecting to, a device makes a connection by using one of the communication-layer protocols available in the Bluetooth stack.

The discovery process by itself can have some security ramifications. By allowing a Bluetooth device to be *discoverable*—this is usually a setting in the device's user interface and is often on by default—anyone within range of your device can "see" it by performing a device discovery. Furthermore, if your device has any applications running that register services, then anyone in range can see what applications are running by doing a service discovery. On a traditional wired network, this is roughly analogous to portscanning.

After obtaining a list of services within range, an attacker would likely begin attempting to connect to those services in order to gain information, execute code on the remote device, and so on. Fortunately, Bluetooth does contain mechanisms for authentication, authorization, and encryption.

Bluetooth's optional authentication scheme relies on a shared key derived from a *personal identification number* (PIN) that all devices wanting to mutually authenticate must share. The PIN is used to derive a shared key that is used for authentication and is never directly transmitted over the air. This type of scheme offers some authentication but doesn't scale well and can't offer such features as *nonrepudiation*. (We discuss these topics in more detail in Chapter 9.)

Bluetooth also supports a basic authorization scheme, by letting Alice maintain a list of *trusted devices*. If an application running on Alice's phone requires authorization, it will allow Bob to connect only if Bob authenticates and Bob's device is trusted.

Finally, Bluetooth has mechanisms to support symmetric encryption of data in transit (discussed in detail in Chapter 7). In order for a Bluetooth connection between Alice and Bob to be encrypted, the client (let's say Bob) must have authenticated to Alice's device using a shared PIN. Once the authentication challenge/response protocol is complete, a shared encryption key is generated using the PIN and some other information that both parties know. From then on, any data sent over the connection is first encrypted using the shared key.

Although Bluetooth supports some security measures, we have found that it can lead to security trouble fairly quickly if one isn't careful. First, most devices have Bluetooth enabled and discoverable by default, and some even run server applications that accept anonymous connections—those with no authentication, authorization, or encryption. Devices in this configuration are susceptible to *bluejacking*, whereby an attacker within Bluetooth range connects to your device and pushes data to it or reads data from it.

Some companies, such as Filter, take advantage of such devices and offer them unsolicited advertisements [Fil06]. Although some devices (such as most Nokia phones we've played with) now ask whether the user wishes to accept the connection by default, some do not.

As an example, one of us was at a conference and noticed a discoverable Bluetooth device, presumably a PDA, in range. He was then able to connect to the PDA and gather all sorts of information, including a username and password to an email account; the other of us verified that these authenticators worked. Of course, the first author alerted the PDA's owner, but a malicious person could have done quite a bit of damage in such a scenario.

Second, the security measures supported by Bluetooth are not that strong in comparison to other wireless technologies, such as 802.11x. All the security features rely on the use of a shared PIN. Depending on the length of the PIN, it may be possible for an attacker with a little time to try all the possible PINs until coming across the right one. Once knowing the PIN, an attacker can authenticate and read all traffic between parties who rely on the PIN. In fact, the only thing the attacker can't do is authorize himself or herself to a particular server.

5.5 The Take-Home Message

Networks are scary places filled with risks. Plugging your machine into a network is roughly analogous to driving your car through a bad part of town. For one reason or another, people are out to get you.

If you're designing and building software that uses the network to communicate, then you should be aware of the way that people are going to use and abuse your software on the network. You should expect that potential attackers will be watching every piece of data your code places on the wire. You should assume that potential attackers will modify the data your application is sending and receiving, causing your application to receive input that you may not have ever imagined. As a result, when designing network applications, your motto should be: Trust No One.

5.6 Project Ideas

1. Pick your favorite piece of software that uses a network, install a sniffer, and watch it communicate with the outside world. Does anything look suspicious? Is sensitive information being sent over the network?

2. Write a small program to send unexpected data to one of the network-facing services on your machine, and see what happens. Can you make it crash?

3. Download and use a wireless sniffer. How many wireless networks can you find in you neighborhood? Can you tell what kind of security they use?

Implementation Security

6

Eventually, system designs give way to actual implementations: real code running on real hardware that, in theory, realizes the design and turns it from collection of ideas into a real piece of software. This transformation has long been a source of security problems. Some blame these blunders on programmers, as they are the ones who carry out the transformation. Others blame their tools: the long and rapidly changing list of languages, environments, and technologies that programmers use to carry out their craft. Others blame the broader economic and engineering processes by which modern software is made.

So, which perspective is right? We believe the answer is yes; all these perspectives are valid to an extent, (and we might throw in some others, too, such as not including security throughout the entire lifecycle). In some cases, security issues are caused by smart programmers trying to do the right thing. Why is it so hard to get it right? In other cases, the system design makes security difficult, as well. Recall our definition of security from Chapter 1: Does the system remain in a correct state, despite foreseeable adversarial actions? Implementation blunders often embody the problem of the system's not anticipating reasonable adversarial stimuli or not quite getting "correctness" correct.

The underlying issue is that implementing modern software is a complex process, and as we've discussed, complexity is the enemy of security. Many modern software designs do not fit in one's head, and the software development process may only make that worse; for example, a programmer may be given only one subsystem to implement and have very little knowledge of what the rest of the application does. Furthermore, if we go back to our notion that a system is a set of states and a set of transition rules between states, then one can imagine how much larger the state space becomes—and how much more complex the system becomes—once we shift from a program's high-level source code to the programming running on a real machine with a real OS.

In this chapter, we look at some of the common classes of security mistakes that programmers make and that systems allow.

- Section 6.1 reviews one of the oldest tricks in the book: *buffer overflow*.
- Section 6.2 examines what happens when systems make assumptions about the type of input they receive. We also look at some other common blunders, such as format string bugs, integer overflows, and escape sequences.
- Section 6.3 talks about race conditions.
- Section 6.4 reviews some of the common forms of malware that often exploit these blunders.
- Section 6.5 looks at the core properties of programming languages that make these errors possible.
- Section 6.6 discusses how the typical software development lifecycle opens the doors for security trouble and what some development shops are doing to correct this.

Within the scope of one chapter, we can only begin to cover the topics we'll be discussing. Implementation security, or software security, is a large and growing field within the security space, and entire volumes are dedicated to the topic. We encourage readers wanting more depth on this topic to go to the relevant literature. The Hoglund, McGraw, and Viega "boxed set" is one of the most comprehensive sources of material on this topic [HM04, McG06, VM01]. Howard and LeBlanc's *Writing Secure Code* is also a great source of detailed information on the topic [HL03]. *The Shellcoder's Handbook* provides a wealth of information on regarding various attacks [KLA+04].

6.1 Buffer Overflow

Probably one of the oldest and most common vulnerabilities is the infamous buffer overflow, which gives attackers remote access to machines. Far too many worms and viruses have propagated themselves using a buffer overflow exploit of some kind—including the first Internet-scale worm: the *Morris worm* (discussed later).

In concept, buffer overflows are quite simple. Let's say that you're writing a piece of code that is taking input from somewhere: a human, a remote program, a user interface (UI) control, whatever. In order for your program to use the data, you need to store it in a variable somewhere in your program—in a *buffer* of some sort. So, what happens when the input is longer than the buffer? Well, that depends on what language you're using and where the buffer is.

Modern, controlled languages, such as C# and Java, will throw a runtime error under these conditions. However, lower-level languages, such as C and C++, will gladly copy the long input into the short buffer, overwriting memory beyond the buffer. The C programming language and its standard libraries made these types of mistakes easy. The C library assumes that strings are a sequence of bytes terminated by a byte with 0x00; so, library functions, such as the now-infamous strcpy or gets, will gladly keep copying bytes until they see an 0x00. This can corrupt memory, perhaps in interesting ways.[1]

6.1.1 Detour: Program Memory Environment

In Section 4.1, we reviewed how computer and operating system architecture conspire to give a running program its own address space. In order to clarify the fun and games one can have with buffer overflow, we now look at what goes in there.

Typically, a process's address space is a chunk of virtual memory, organized as a linear array of slots, each of which can hold a byte. On typical modern 32-bit systems, these slots are indexed from 0x00000000 to 0xFFFFFFFF. Figure 6.1 shows the typical contents. We start from the bottom and go upward:

- *Text segment.* Recall from Section 4.1 that on a fundamental level, program execution consists of the CPUs fetching and executing machine-level instructions. The main sequence of instructions for a program live in the *text segment.*

- *Data segment.* Global variables and other data whose existence and size can be deduced when the program is created go in the *data segment.*

- *Heap.* Data whose sizes need to grow dynamically as the program runs go in the *heap.* (In C, this is where malloc'd regions live.)

- *Libraries.* As discussed in Section 4.1, programmers typically expect to use *library* code that the build process automatically links in. Such libraries

---

1. The Morris worm propagated by overflowing a buffer in the finger service, which relied on the gets function.

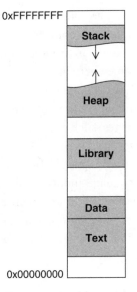

0xFFFFFFFF

Stack

Heap

Library

Data

Text

0x00000000

Figure 6.1 The typical contents of a process's address space. Not to scale.

typically get linked into a vacant part of the address space, usually in well-defined locations.

- *Stack.* As shown in Figure 2.7, an executing process stores context specific to the currently executing routine on the *stack*. The stack grows downward; that is, calling a subroutine creates a new stack frame, for this new subroutine context, physically below the caller's stack frame. Yes, as things get pushed *onto* the stack, they cause the stack to grow *downward* in memory. Thus, in terms of the data structure abstraction, the top of the stack is really the bottom, in terms of the memory layout, and vice-versa.

Figure 6.2 shows the typical contents of a stack frame, relative to a subroutine invocation. Going downward in memory, we typically see

- *Return address.* The stack frame stores the address to which control should return when the subroutine exits. (For example, this will contain the address of the instruction after the `call` instruction that took us to this subroutine.)
- *Arguments.* The stack frame stores the arguments that were passed to this subroutine.
- *Local variables.* The stack frame then stores the local variables for this subroutine.

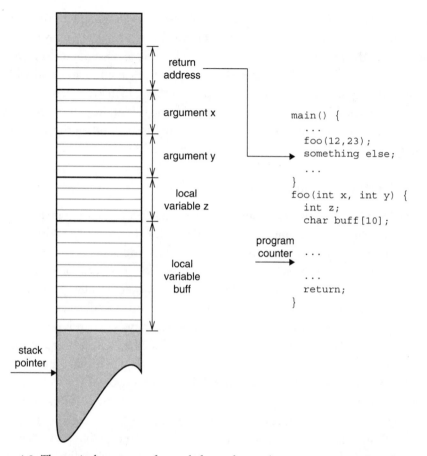

Figure 6.2 The typical contents of a stack frame for a subroutine `foo()`. We assume that an integer is 4 bytes and that a char is 1 byte, as is common—for now, anyway. Not to scale.

6.1.2 Stack Smashing

The "classic" buffer overflow attack does *code injection* directly onto the victim process's stack. Aleph One's seminal paper "Smashing the Stack for Fun and Profit" goes into great detail on this style of attack [Ale96].

Suppose that your program has a function, called `foo`, that takes two integer arguments and locally declares a character array of size ten (see Figure 6.2). When `foo` is called, perhaps from `main`, a new stack frame is created, and the argument values and the return address are pushed onto the new frame. Additionally, space is allocated for `buff` on the new frame. Now, the pattern of a buffer overflow attack consists of an attacker's supplying input that gets written into `buff`. The attacker's input is longer than ten characters and is carefully crafted so that it puts a valid value into the stack location storing the return address to which we should return when foo exits. If successful, the attacker can overwrite the stack in such a way that, when foo returns, the return address on the stack will take the program to code that the attacker chooses. This code will then execute—in the victim's name and with the victim's privileges. The end result is that the attacker can get the victim's machine to execute code of the attacker's choosing—with the victim program's privileges. If you're running as the superuser, as most Windows users do, then the attacker has administrative privileges on the target machine.

6.1.3 Anatomy of an Exploit

An attacker who can manage to control the execution flow of a program running on a remote machine—for example, by controlling a function's return address—has a foothold on the victim. In order to complete the task and gain complete control of the victim machine, the attacker needs to execute code that does something on his or her behalf. Back in the old days, that something would usually spawn a remote shell (recall Section 4.1.3) on the victim's machine—and with the victim's privilege level—that would allow the attacker to execute arbitrary commands on the remote machine. To this day, the term *shellcode* is used to describe the code that the attacker places and executes on the remote machine. Modern shellcode may actually spawn a shell or may instead perform a host of other nefarious tasks.

Regardless of the goal, most exploits typically have three sections: a series of repeating return addresses that will overwrite the function's return address stored on the stack frame (there are a number of them so that the attacker has a few chances to get position and alignment right); a *payload* that is executed when the function with the vulnerable buffer returns; and a NOP *sled*. (NOP is an assembly instruction for "no operation.") In general, the shellcode is delivered as the payload part of the attacker's exploit. In a successful attack, the entire exploit is copied to—and beyond—the vulnerable buffer, placing one of the repeating return addresses into the return address on the stack frame. Ideally, the overwritten return address points into the NOP sled, so that when the function returns, it returns somewhere in the NOP sled.[2] The machine keeps executing NOPs until they expire, leaving the first line of the attacker's shellcode as the next instruction. At that point, the attacker "owns" the machine.

---

2. The NOP sled allows the return address to be a little off, giving the exploit some room for error. Without the sled, the exploit would have to return *exactly* to the first line of the attacker's code. With the sled, the exploit has to return somewhere close to the attacker's code, as the machine will "slide down the NOPs" until it hits the attacker's code.

Writing shellcode is a bit of an art. The attacker needs a good understanding of the victim program's memory layout. Also, for attacks that use unchecked C string copies, the injected shellcode cannot include any `0x00` bytes—because otherwise, the string copy would stop at that point. This constraint necessitates much cleverness, such as writing encoded shellcode that decodes itself as a first order of business.

As we discussed, some shellcode actually gives the attacker a remote shell on the machine. The shellcode could also be one of the rootkits we discussed in Chapter 4 or any other program that an attacker may find useful. Interested readers should have a look at the Metasploit project, which has a number of high-quality payloads that can be used for various things [Met06].

6.1.4 Other Smashing Ideas

Buffer overflow can achieve other goals besides tricking the victim into executing code that one has just injected onto the stack. One technique is known as *heap smashing*. In such an attack, the attacker overflows heap-allocated buffers and gets similar results to a stack-smashing attack, except that the code goes on the heap instead of on the stack. Because of the many subtle variations in the way the heap is laid out, exploiting the heap is a bit trickier than exploiting the stack. Thus, many heap-smashing exploits are targeted to a particular platform and software configuration, often including particular versions of the libraries that the target depends on.

In a nutshell, heap smashing works by taking advantage of the way in which the memory block allocator uses bookkeeping information. In most systems, heap blocks have a header that keeps track of bookkeeping information; these headers are kept in some sort of data structure, such as a doubly linked list. By overwriting a heap block, it may be possible to overwrite some of the header information and/or one of the data structure's pointers. This may give the attacker a way to get shellcode into the system or a way to control the execution flow of the target process.

Attackers can also enlist the help of system libraries or exception handlers. One such method is known as a *return-to-libc* attack. In this type of attack, the return address of the function is overwritten with the address of a standard library function. (The library functions usually reside in a well-known memory location.) Before overwriting the return address of the function, the attacker ensures that his or her arguments are properly placed on the stack, just as the library function expects to find them once its stack frame gets created. When the vulnerable function returns, control is passed to the library function, using the attacker's arguments.

For example, if the library function is the C library's `system` function, then the victim's computer will execute whatever code the attacker chooses.

Buffer overflow attacks don't have to directly alter control flow to be useful. For example, instead of overwriting return addresses, the attacker can overwrite critical data that the program may rely on. Peter Neumann discusses an example from the early days of UNIX (Section 3.7 in [Neu95]). To authenticate a user, the system would copy stored information about the user's real password into one buffer and copy the password the user entered into a second buffer below the first; the system would then check whether the user's entered password matched the stored information. An attacker could log in as any user chosen: When prompted for a password, the attacker could provide overly long input that filled both buffers—and structured so that the part that filled the second buffer matched the part that filled the first.

When designing and reasoning about a system, the programmers might have had a mental model of the states of the system, which states were "correct," and which states were reachable. By not anticipating that an attacker might provide much longer input than expected, buffer overflow vulnerabilities let the attacker inject new states into the model—for example, by adding shellcode—and then force a transition to that state—in this case, by overwriting a function's return address. In Chapters 15 and 17, we discuss some techniques for, and the difficulty of, determining which states are bad and which transitions we should allow. However, the existence of buffer overflow should caution us: The model we reason about may not necessarily match the system as implemented.

6.1.5 Defenses

Buffer overflow vulnerabilities have been hunted, found, and exploited for decades. It's hard to find a discussion of software security that does not mention this attack—which, unfortunately is still effective. Over the years, numerous techniques have attempted to protect software against the dreaded buffer overflow attack.

Nonexecutable Stacks. In response to stack-smashing attacks, some operating systems use a *nonexecutable stack*, which ensures that code on the stack can't be run. Since many stack-smashing exploits lay their shellcode on the stack and then attempt to execute it directly from there, a nonexecutable stack stops the shellcode from running; even though an attacker may get shellcode into the system, he or she cannot execute it.

Making a stack nonexecutable is not as trivial as it might sound, because many legacy compilers and other tools depend on putting executable code on the stack.

One successful attempt is Solar Designer's Linux kernel patch, which implements a nonexecutable stack on the Linux OS [Sol06]. Well, as you might have guessed, attackers have found ways to wreak havoc in spite of the nonexecutable stack [Woj98]. Attackers can use the heap-smashing techniques discussed earlier to inject code on the heap or the return-to-libc techniques discussed previously to maliciously exploit code that's already present in the victim's library. Furthermore, as we noted, one can have fun with overflows that merely change variables.

In an attempt to protect against heap-smashing, projects such as *PAX* use a technique that includes making writable memory pages nonexecutable [PaX06]. Imagine that a program has a heap-allocated buffer that is capable of being over-flowed. Once the attacker overflows the buffer, his or her shellcode likely resides in the same memory page as the buffer. Clearly, this page must be writable, or the buffer could never have anything written to it. However, it doesn't need to be executable; in fact, making the page nonexecutable stops the shellcode from ever being executed.

Canaries.   Another common defense against stack-smashing attacks is to put a known value on the stack just before the return address. This known value is often called a *canary*, or a *canary word*, because of its similar role to canaries in coal mines. When the canary died, perhaps because the level of toxic gas was too high, the miners knew that something was wrong and that it was time to get out of the mine.

In the context of stack smashing, the idea is that if a buffer overrun takes place and successfully overwrites the return address, then the canary will be overwritten with a new value as well. When the function is ready to return, the canary is checked to see whether it is still intact. If the canary is destroyed, the stack has been smashed, and the system has a chance to react before returning from the function and likely jumping into shellcode.

Crispin Cowan's *StackGuard* pioneered this approach [CPW+98]. StackGuard is an extension to the Gnu `gcc` compiler that supported various types of canaries. StackGuard is not a magic bullet, however; there are methods to circumvent its protection [Ric02]. In 2001, Microsoft added to its C++ compiler a feature based on Cowan's StackGuard approach. Unfortunately, as McGraw and Hoglund point out, the Microsoft version is not only defeated easily but also makes programs compiled with that version of the compiler susceptible to a new type of attack [HM04].

Address Randomization.   Another defense against buffer overflow vulnerabilities involves randomizing the address space of the program [BSD05, PaX06]. This tech-nique, called *address space randomization (ASR)*, essentially shuffles the locations of variables and other static data stored on the stack. This way, when a buffer is overflowed, there is no telling what stack information got overwritten. Since the stack is typically randomized at the beginning of each program execution, an exploit that works during one run of the target program will likely not work on the next. (Nonetheless, researchers have shown that attackers can work around some types of address randomization [SPP+04].)

Code Analyzers. Since the types of errors we've been discussing so far in this chapter are visible in the program's source code itself, one might wonder: Why not simply scan the source code for security errors? In fact, many software development processes recommend some sort of *code review*: a process whereby one human manually reviews another human's code (we revisit this topic in Section 6.6). However, for any sufficiently large system, reviewing each line of code—or even only the security-relevant features—can be an enormous undertaking.

To assist reviewers in their hunt for security bugs, a number of *code scanners* have been developed. ITS4 [Cig], Rats [Seca], and BOON [Wag] scan through C/C++ code and can identify program statements that are likely to yield security trouble. Such scanners can locate unsafe functions that can lead to buffer overflow attacks. In addition, some of these scanners, as well as Coverity's Prevent [Cov] and FXCop [Mic06], can detect format string errors, integer errors, and even *time-of-check/time-of-use (TOCTOU)* errors.

The biggest drawback of these types of tools is the large number of false positives they generate. Additionally, such static analysis tools don't always find every instance of an overflow, either. This is troublesome for many who rely on the tool as the final word in the security of their software. Although some would like to replace code reviews with code analysis tools, we've found that the two are complementary: The tool generates a good set of starting points for code analysis.

6.2 Argument Validation and Other Mishaps

Q: Why did the chicken cross the road?
A: 42

During design and implementation, it's easy to start thinking of a system's interactions with outside parties or even with internal modules as a conversation. At each point the program may collect input, only some subset of possible values make sense in the context of the conversation so far. As a consequence, the programmer implicitly expects that the input value falls in this subset. However, the adversary doesn't have to follow these rules.

Such scenarios give rise to another common class of vulnerabilities: when programs fail to validate their input. Concretely, this could be input from the user, the network, or some other process or program. While in the midst of writing software, it's often easy to think of what the program *should* do—and thus what the inputs *should* be. To some extent, it breaks the natural flow of writing software to sit and think about all the possible inputs and their ramifications on the system. Yet, considering a range of possible inputs to each subsystem and function is the cornerstone of coding defensively.

6.2.1 Fuzz Testing

One of the first tricks many reverse engineers use to find such "soft spots" in software is *fuzz testing*, or *fuzzing* [MFS90]. During this exercise, an attacker will throw potentially large amounts of random data to different spots in the application. This may start with network-facing or user-facing inputs, such as listening sockets, GUI text box controls, and command line arguments. Potential attackers may probe deeper into the code by using API hijacking to insert random data into the function calls in your module (see Section 8.4.4).

Most times, such fuzz testing will simply cause an application to crash, perhaps even dumping core. However, such behavior is often indicative of an underlying problem, typically having to do with argument validation and/or memory management. A potential attacker who can find a spot in your code to supply input that isn't validated and that causes memory corruption has probably found a spot to start trying a buffer overflow attack.

The moral of this story is that the practice of validating function arguments and other inputs is necessary if one wishes to build a secure system. However, it's not sufficient, as we'll explore momentarily. We return to fuzz testing in Chapter 11.

6.2.2 Format Strings

Another source of vulnerabilities stems from programmers' failing to validate input to the C `printf` function family. These API functions rely on *format strings* to get arguments from the stack and display them. Consider the following C statement: `printf("%s", buf)`. This statement fetches the value of `buf` from the stack, substitutes it for the format string `%s`, and displays the result to the screen.

Now, consider a function that takes the format string from a potential adversary. (See Listing 6.1.) This function, unlike the statement `printf("%s", buf)`, allows the format string to be supplied by the caller. If the program contains an

```
 void bar (char *str)
{
    printf(str);
}
```

Listing 6.1 A C function that is susceptible to a format string attack

execution path that allows user input to be supplied to this function, we've found a vulnerability that we can exploit to read the contents of the stack.

In short, imagine that we supply the string %08x as an argument to the function in Listing 6.1. The string tells the printf statement to print the first word on the stack as eight hexadecimal characters. To see more of the stack, we could simply add to our string %08x%08x%08x%08x. We could also supply the format string %s, which will print the stack contents until the first null character is reached. In any case, format string errors let us read stack contents, which can be very useful if we are trying to read stack-stored information, craft exploits, and the like.

Hoglund and McGraw have a good explanation and example of this issue, and we encourage interested readers to consult pages 317–324 of *Exploiting Software: How to Break Code* [HM04].

6.2.3 Integer Overflow

Yet another tricky error that arises from a lack of input validation is called *integer overflow*. Down in the bowels of the machine, computers encode numbers as a fixed sequence of bits, in binary. How to interpret this sequence of bits is usually guided by two questions:

1. How many bits do we look at?
2. Is the value *unsigned* or *signed?*

Integer overflow errors occur when two operations on the same binary value use different answers to these questions.

The basic overflow scenario occurs when we add two numbers but store the result in a space that's too small. For example, an unsigned 16-bit integer can represent only the numbers n in the range

$$0 \leq n \leq 2^{16} - 1 = 65,535.$$

It's quite possible to pick two numbers in this range whose *sum* lies beyond it:

$$
\begin{aligned}
65535 + 1 &= 65,536 \\
&= 2^{16}.
\end{aligned}
$$

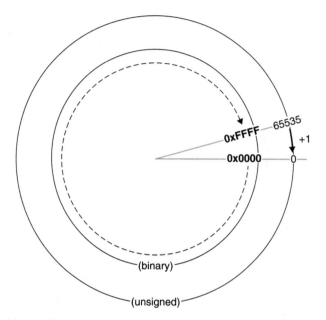

Figure 6.3 Addition of unsigned integers can yield incorrect values, if the result is forced to be an unsigned integer of the same bit length.

When written as a binary integer, 2^{16} takes 17 bits: 1 followed by 16 zeros. Unfortunately, if the code simply assumes that the result is also 16-bit integer, it typically will throw out that seventeenth bit—the most significant one. We then end up operating on the incorrect result:

$$65,535 + 1 \longrightarrow 0.$$

(See Figure 6.3.) We could also wrap around the other way:

$$1 - 3 \longrightarrow 65,534.$$

Typically, signed binary numbers are encoded by subtracting from zero but wrapping around. For example, signed 16-bit integers represent n in the range

$$-32,768 = 2^{16} \leq n \leq 2^{16} - 1 = 32,767.$$

As Figure 6.4 shows, if we're using signed integers, addition may cause us to wrap around to large negative numbers; subtraction could give us large positive numbers.

Inadvertently converting one type of integer to another can also cause problems. For example, an unsigned 32-bit integer can represent the numbers n in the range

$$0 \leq n \leq 2^{32} - 1 = 4,294,967,295.$$

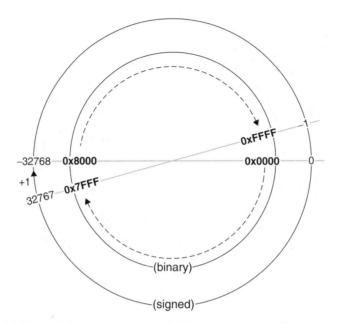

Figure 6.4 Addition of signed integers can yield incorrect values, if the result is forced to be a signed integer of the same bit length.

If one part of the program treats variable x as a 32-bit integer but then a later part treats it as a 16-bit integer, then the later part may likely end up with an incorrect value that is far lower than it's supposed to be. For another example, if we build up an integer as unsigned but then use it as signed—or vice-versa—we can have surprising value shifts; see Figure 6.5.

Although the direct security ramifications are not as bad as a buffer overflow, integer overflow errors can be problematic nonetheless. One common pattern occurs when an overflowed integer is used directly in pointer arithmetic or as an index to an array; integer overflow errors can let the adversary access a memory location that is out of bounds of the array. Errors can also arise when the overflowed integer is used as a parameter for memory allocation; the adversary can trick the program into allocating a far smaller buffer than it thinks it has, enabling various memory-management attacks. Another common pattern for overflow vulnerabilities is when the program does a sanity check on the result of an operation but overlooks the implicit truncation or sign conversion that happened when that result was generated.

Making matters worse is that this type of error is difficult to find. Some compilers will generate warnings about possible signed/unsigned mismatch, but many programs will happily continue after an overflow or sign error has occurred. The real solution to this class of problems is for programmers to sanity check integer

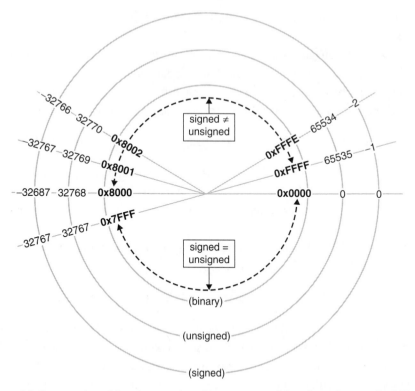

Figure 6.5 Interpreting a bit string as a signed integer can yield a value substantially different from interpreting it as an unsigned integer.

values before they are used in memory-sensitive operations, such as array indexing. (See [ble02] for more discussion.)

6.2.4 Escape Sequences

Another common type of validation blunder involves the use of *escape sequences*. An escape sequence is basically a sequence of characters used to send a command to a program or a peripheral device. For example, in C, the sequence \n tells the program to print a newline character to the output device (e.g., the screen). Security problems can arise when programs do not carefully validate user input, allowing malicious users to embed escape sequences in their input. In such a scenario, the user is able to send control messages to the program or its underlying environment—probably not a good thing.

One large category of attacks that uses escape sequences is known as *SQL injection*. SQL *(Standard Query Language)* is a common language used for reading and writing to databases. SQL uses the single-quote character as an escape character to delimit input; if the user input contains this character, interesting things can result.

For example, imagine that we have an application that performs access control based on the presence of the user's name in our database. We take the user input—possibly from a Web page or rich client—assign it to the `username` variable, and check whether it's in the Users table in our database with the following SQL query:

```
SELECT * FROM Users WHERE Name = 'username'
```

In theory, if the user is in the database, this statement returns the row or rows containing the user; if the user is not in the database, this statement returns the empty set. Thus, we can test whether the user is authorized by testing whether the statement returns any rows.

When the legitimate user Alice uses the system by entering **alice** into the `username` field, the SQL statement becomes

```
SELECT * FROM Users WHERE Name = 'alice'
```

Since the `SELECT` statement returns a row, we allow Alice to use the application—not a great access control mechanism, we know, but it illustrates the point. Now, assume that a malicious user Carlo enters **'carlo' or '1' = '1** instead of **alice**. This peculiar input turns the SQL statement into the following:

```
SELECT * FROM Users WHERE Name = 'carlo' or '1' = '1'
```

Since `'1' = '1'` is always true, the statement always returns rows; thus, the system will grant Carlo access, because it will incorrectly conclude that Carlo's name is in the database.

In some sense, escape sequences are carefully constructed puns. When systems have two different components each acting on the same user input, one can find the potential for escape sequence fun. A Web server might want to ensure that only file requests satisfying certain rules (such as "ends in 'html'") get returned, but the adversary might work around this restriction by embedding, in the requested pathname, an escape sequence that causes the server software and the underlying filesystem to have different opinions about which was the last character in the request.

6.2.5 Internal Validation

The preceding cases focused on vulnerabilities that can arise when a system makes assumptions about the input an external attacker can provide. However, security trouble can also arise when a system makes assumptions about communication between its own internal components.

For one example, in standard programming practice, a subroutine will return a special error code should it run into trouble when carrying out its requested work. A standard programming bug is to forget to check the subroutine's return code but instead to simply assume that the call succeeded. (As we discuss later in the book, this almost caused a fatal flaw in a high-end security product one of us helped work with.) Another standard bug is to check the return code but to get confused about whether a particular value means "success" or "failure." (In one well-regarded operating system, successive nested subroutine calls alternated between "0" for success and "0" for failure.)

6.3 TOCTOU

Another source of errors—both general errors and security errors—involves a program's checking the property of a resource and then assuming that the property still exists when the resource is used. These types of errors are called *time-of-check/time-of-use (TOCTOU)* errors, or *race conditions*. The former term derives from the nonzero duration between the time the system makes an observation and the time the system acts on the result of that observation; if the universe has changed in the meantime, the system may have problems. The latter term comes from the framework of concurrent programming, when the correctness of what happens depends on a "race" between different entities (e.g., for the same resource).

Identifying and preventing race conditions is a significant challenge in lower-level systems programming, with multiple processes and multiple threads within a process potentially sharing resources or other dependencies. Systems typically provide *synchronization* frameworks to help here. Processes or threads must acquire a *lock*, or *mutex*, before they can begin executing a particular block of code, often called a *critical section*.[3] In a naive implementation, the lock might be a data value stored somewhere. Once it checks the state of the lock and determines that it is available, the process or thread acquires the lock by changing its state and continues executing. Race conditions can occur when two processes A and B both attempt to acquire a free lock. Unless the act of checking the state and acquiring it is a single machine instruction, there is a chance that process A may believe that the lock is

---

3. In Windows, there is actually a synchronization mechanism called a Critical Section that is a type of lock.

available and decide to take it; however, before it can change the lock's state, process B checks the state and also decides to take it. However, even providing a correct implementation of these basic synchronization primitives doesn't solve the problem if programmers don't correctly identify and coordinate critical sections. Many programmers who deal with multithreaded programs have seen these types of scenarios; programs often act in a seemingly nondeterministic fashion when this occurs.

In a security context, TOCTOU problems can lead to all sorts of trouble. For one example, consider shell commands implemented as setuid programs that an ordinary user can invoke but that execute with root privileges. In a typical scenario, a user might invoke such a command to provide the name of a file the command should operate on; the command program would check and consequently believe that a user has permission to access that particular file. However, before the program performs the file operation, the devious user replaces the file with another one to which the user does *not* have access. If the shell program is operating at higher privilege levels, then the operation will succeed anyway. Malicious users have used such TOCTOU flaws in shell command programs to trick privileged code into reading and writing files the users themselves were not allowed to see.

Another example of TOCTOU occurred in an OS in which modules communicated by passing messages to each other. A caller process would request a service, such as "give me my private data", by sending a message to the service provider; when the service was complete, the provider would respond with a message. However, senders and receivers were identified with process identifiers, and a devious user might construct a scenario whereby the caller would die or be killed and an imposter would inherit its identifier. The imposter would then receive the response message, much the same way that college students often receive postal mail addressed to the previous occupants of their dorm room.

6.4 Malware

No security book would be complete without at least some mention of *malware*. Colloquially, malware is that evil software from bad people that exploits all these blunders in your information infrastructure.

More seriously, yes, the root of the word, *mal*, comes from *evil*. But we wouldn't go so far as to say that malware is, by definition, evil. Some of it is intended as a harmless prank. Some of it is intended as customer service. Some of it is petty vandalism. And, of course, some of it is intended as activism or protest or espionage or warfare or theft. The "moral correctness" of malware serving these latter purposes is, like any other action in these camps, not, shall we say, a matter of universal consensus. So, we think a safer definition is: Malware is software that intentionally causes its system to depart from the advertised notion of "correctness."

6.4.1 Types

The community tends to use several standard terms to denote specific types of malware.

- A *Trojan horse* is code that does what it's supposed to do and also secretly does something else.
- A *virus* is a piece of code that inserts itself or somehow transforms innocent programs to do something nasty, usually including propagation of the virus.
- A *worm* is a free-standing nasty self-propagating program. (But the distinction between "virus" and "worm" is a bit pedantic, when you get down to it.)
- A *rabbit* is a virus or worm that multiples without bound.
- A *trapdoor*, also called a *backdoor*, is a feature/bug by which a party can access services other than through the standard, authenticated channels. (Note that the term *trapdoor* also shows up in some treatments of public-key cryptography, where it more or less refers to the private-key operation.)
- A *logic bomb* is dormant malicious code, triggered by something specific, such as a date. (Typically, one sees these left by disgruntled employees.)
- An *Easter egg* is "cute" but harmless behavior triggered by special input: for example, if the user types in a specific parameter and the program displays a picture of the developers. Some people tend to get quite irate about this. Others don't. (We recall a rumor about a security colleague getting very upset about some unidentifiable bytes showing up in ROM, only to discover that they were an ASCII encoding of the lyrics to "Sweeney Todd.")

Sometimes, one will hear the assertion that viruses cannot get into hardware. This is perhaps misleading and perhaps should be consigned to the dustbin of history, along with the assertion that "you can't get infected from reading email." Old-timers will tell you about PostScript files you could print only once (on any one printer). A colleague of ours here at Dartmouth showed us a trick that corrupts a printer until you reboot it. The Kriz and Magistr viruses re-FLASH a computer's BIOS. One of the themes in an OS course is "Gee, we're moving more computation into previously dumb peripherals, such as disks."—There's a cynical prediction one might make. Furthermore, even old-style malware would go for your hard disk, in order to make itself permanent.

6.4.2 Notable Examples

Ken Thompson's Turing Award speech [Tho84] provides a seminal discussion of Trojan horses. In a style that sheds some light on the "code-jock chic" popular in that generation, Ken describes the "cutest program" he'd ever written: a C compiler with two extra features.

- When it recognizes that it's compiling the login program, it inserts a trapdoor for Ken.
- When it recognizes that it's compiling a C compiler, it inserts code that inserts both the above feature and this one.

So, once you get a compiler *executable* with these features, all further compiler executables it builds will have these features, even if they're not in the source code!

The Morris worm mentioned earlier is another seminal malware example. In the late 1980s, Robert T. Morris, a grad student at Cornell, released a worm that spread itself to numerous computers hooked up to the Internet, which was at that time made up largely of government, military, and academic machines. The Morris worm used a number of techniques to spread itself: It tried commonly used passwords and the dictionary file against the encrypted password file; it used buffer overflow in fingerd; and it used a DEBUG trapdoor in sendmail. The worm propagated itself around the Cornell network and eventually spread to other machines connected to the Internet. Either by blunder or by intention, the worm became a rabbit and spread too rapidly to control. Even though there was no destructive payload—all the worm did was spread; it did not destroy infected machines—everyone got furious. Estimates of damage range to up about $100 million. Eugene "Spaf" Spafford gives a detailed view and some anti-Morris rants [Spa89]; Eichin and Rocheis give a more technical analysis [ER89].

There's still no consensus about what should have been done to Morris. Spaf represents the one extremum: *String him up!* Neumann has a typically pithy summary of the other endpoint: "The Internet Worm's exploitation of sendmail, fingerd, and rhosts required NO authorization! Debate over whether Morris exceeded authority is somewhat moot" [Neu95, p. 133].

As much as we respect Spaf, we are inclined to disagree with him here. His arguments may be more telling than he intended: "The claim that the victims of the worm were somehow responsible for the invasion of their machines is also curious. . . . The attempt to blame these individuals for the success of the worm is equivalent to blaming an arson victim for the fire because she didn't build her house of fireproof metal" [Spa89, p. 685].

Perhaps. But try getting fire insurance if you ignore basic practices and current building codes! (And vilifying Morris only deflects attention from the main problem.)

6.5 Programming Language Security

Programming languages are the fundamental tool for building software. They give programmers a way to turn the concepts in their heads into a set of instructions that a machine can execute. Languages often succeed or fail on the basis of their power, expressiveness, and efficiency. But what about security? Could the safety and security of a system be determined by the language it's implemented in? What properties make a language secure? In this section, we look at these questions in some detail and examine some of the initial efforts to get answers.

A large number of security problems are the result of a programming error that, when exploited, puts the system in an unsafe state. So far in this chapter, we've been discussing specific types of errors that can lead to such security trouble as buffer and integer overflow, format strings, and so on. In this section, we look at the issue from a different perspective; we look beyond specific programming errors at the properties of the programming language itself.

6.5.1 Memory (Mis)management

Many of the scenarios we've been discussing in this chapter involve an attackers being able to get some sort of evil data into the target program's memory space. Protecting that memory space is vital to ensure the program's security. If we think of a program or a system as a collection of states and rules to transition through those states, then we see that the program's memory space holds the state of the program—the value of all the program variables, as well as the rules that govern how the program can transition through states.

A programming language that allows programs to access only intended memory locations is said to have *memory safety*. Without this feature, it is impossible or, perhaps, rather imaginative for a programming language to make any claims about being secure. A language without this feature can allow programs to arbitrarily read and write memory and thus gives attackers a means to alter the program state. A program written in a memory-safe language would never be able to overflow a buffer or write data to a memory location that it should not be able to.

Consider the C programming language for a moment; it is clearly not memory safe. As we discussed in Sections 6.1 and 6.2, programs written in C will gladly copy input into portions of memory where they don't belong. This lack of memory safety is responsible for buffer overflow attacks, as well as the format string errors we discussed in Section 6.2 and the consequences of many integer overflow attacks.

Memory safety is a key language feature when it comes to considering the security of a particular programming language. Many newer languages, such as Java and C#, are memory safe. Trying to read or write to an inaccessible memory location in these languages causes the underlying runtime to throw an exception, possibly halting the program.

Although memory safety is necessary for security, it is not sufficient. Memory-safe languages can still have security problems, many of which are the result of bad system design, such as passing sensitive information in cleartext.

6.5.2 Type Safety

Another important consideration when evaluating the security of a programming language is *type safety*. Loosely speaking, a type-safe language will enforce that variables of a certain type can be assigned values only of that type. For instance, assume that we have a program variable y that is a pointer (that is, y has the type "pointer"). A type-safe language would allow us to assign only valid pointers to y, whereas a type-unsafe language would allow us to assign different types of values to y, possibly using a *type cast*, such as is often done in C programs.

So, what does type safety have to do with security? The answer is that type-safe languages are memory safe as well, and memory safety is a necessary property for security. To see why this relation is true, let's expand the previous example a little and assume that we are working in the C language, which is both type and memory unsafe. Since x is an integer, we could assign the value 123456 to x. Now, let's assume that we have some *pointer* variable y. Since C is type unsafe, we could assign x to y, essentially telling the system that y points to the address 123456. Listing 6.2 illustrates the scenario.

```
void foo ()
{
    int x;
    char *y;

    x = 123456;
    y = x;
}
```

Listing 6.2 A type-unsafe and memory-unsafe C function that generates a compiler warning

```
void foo ()
{
    int x;
    char *y;

    x = 123456;
    y = (char*) x;
}
```

Listing 6.3 A type-unsafe and memory-unsafe C function that doesn't generate a compiler warning

When compiling the last line of code, the compiler will generate a warning that the assignment makes a pointer from an integer. The compiler's suggestion is to force the types to match via a *type cast*. Indeed, changing the program to Listing 6.3 makes the compiler happy.

Even in this case, the program is still memory unsafe. The moment that it tries to read or write data from *y*, the program will be reading or writing from the memory location 123456, which is just an arbitrary number, possibly input from the adversary. Without the ability to enforce type safety, such memory-safety violations are possible. (Furthermore, integer overflow vulnerabilities can essentially be blamed on a lack of type safety.)

It is also true that memory-unsafe languages cannot be type safe. To see why this is true, imagine that we have declared our variable *x* to be an integer again. Now, assume that we copy the appropriate number of bytes from memory into the value of *x*. How do we know that the bytes we've copied represent an integer? We don't, and since we can assign *x*'s value from anywhere in memory, there's no way to enforce that *x* takes on only integer values. (Figure 6.6 shows the relationships between memory safety and type safety.)

If security is a driving force behind your choice of programming language, choose a type-safe language, if possible. Of course, using a type-safe language is no magic bullet; improper handling of sensitive data will make any system vulnerable, no matter what language it's written in. Using a type-safe language does free you from the buffer overflow issues of Section 6.1.

6.5.3 Information Flow

Another property that should be considered when evaluating a language's ability to construct secure systems is *information flow*. The idea here is that a language

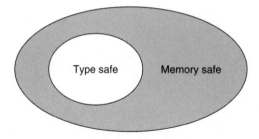

Figure 6.6 Type-safe languages are memory safe. Type-unsafe languages may or may not be memory safe. A memory-safe language could be type safe, although there is no guarantee, but a memory-unsafe language cannot.

should allow information and execution to flow only to appropriate portions of the system. This covers numerous aspects of the system: how information flows to external libraries and the underlying OS and its resources and how information flows between the objects and subsystems. (Recall from Chapter 2 the Old Testament focus on information flow.)

Thinking about information flow in the context of programming can raise some tricky issues. Suppose that we're concerned about standard multilevel security. Let L be a low-security variable and H a high-security variable. Clearly, information leaks if we assign H to L:

```
L  ⟵  H
```

However, Listing 6.4 shows how information can leak in more subtle ways as well. Sabelfeld and Myers provide a thorough survey of such issues [SM03].

One of the fundamental flows of information that deserves consideration occurs at the boundary between the application and the underlying OS and/or core APIs. In some cases, applications need a certain privilege level in order to perform specific operations. At the extreme, programs can be *sandboxed:* run in a virtual

```
H  ⟵  {0,1}
if (H == 0)
    L  ⟵  0
else
    L  ⟵  1
```

Listing 6.4 This code permits bad information flow even though the high-security information in H is never written directly to L

compartment such that it has the least amount of privileges necessary to accomplish its task. At the extreme, such support can be built into the OS itself, as in SELinux—see Section 4.5.2. A step down from using such an OS is to use a tool such as *systrace* to generate and enforce access policies for the OS's system call interface [Pro06]. Additionally, the Java and .NET runtimes have a policy mechanism that governs how various code packages can interact. Although none of these approaches are features of the programming language proper, they all serve to govern how the application interacts with other portions of the system.

Inside the application itself, the flow of information can be governed by access protections on portions of code. This is standard practice in *object-oriented (OO)* languages. Such languages often rely on special keywords—typically, `public`, `private`, and `protected`—to specify the access policy on a particular object. `Public` data and methods are accessible by any program entity, such as another object in the system; `protected` data and methods can be modified and invoked by subclasses of a particular class; and `private` data and methods can be modified and invoked only by a particular object itself.

Some languages use other keywords or properties to specify a particular policy on data members. For example, in C#, the `readonly` keyword applied to a data member disallows any program entity other than the object's constructor to assign a value to a variable. C/C++ programs can use the `const` keyword to achieve similar effects and more, since `const` can be applied to methods as well.

6.5.4 The Once and Future Silver Bullet

With all these advanced programming language tools, one might wonder why we still have insecure implementations, especially when it seemed that all the common implementation security blunders arose from the C programming language.

The answer is complex. A widely held belief in the systems programming community is that a low-level language like C is necessary for the required efficiency. Management of hardware—with bits, bytes, addresses, and such—requires data manipulation that does not easily lend itself to type safety. Just because a programming language will constrain behavior according to some type of policy (or type policy) doesn't imply that the policy itself is correct or is in fact easy or quick to write and maintain. Finally, many of these tools have yet to reach the level of reliability necessary for production-grade code.

Programming language researchers offer counterarguments against all these issues. Nonetheless, the Internet runs on C and C++ and will continue to do so for the foreseeable future.

6.5.5 Tools

What should the security artisan do? One approach is to continue to use C but augment it with additional protection tools. One can run *static analysis* tools, such as *Splint* or *ITS4* on the source code. (Trent Jaeger and his colleagues even used type-based static analysis to verify that SE/Linux made calls to the Linux Security Module at the right times [ZEJ02]). One can run *dynamic analysis* tools, such as *Purify* or *Valgrind*, at runtime. One can build with safer libraries and compilers to help defend against stack smashing via such techniques as canaries and address space randomization, discussed earlier.

Another approach is to move to a type-safe variant of C, such as *CCured*, *Cyclone*, or *Clay*. (Unfortunately, when we surveyed the field, it appeared that these tools were not yet ready for production use.) Or, one could listen to the evangelists and move to a more advanced language, such as Java or OCaml. (See [DPS07] for a longer survey of these techniques.)

6.6 Security in the Development Lifecycle

It's easy to wonder why the software industry as a whole allows products with the types of flaws we've been discussing to make their way into customers' hands. It's much more difficult to find a good answer. If we compare the software industry to the automobile industry, for instance, it would be a fair conclusion that the software industry gets away with murder in comparison. For example, automobiles don't get sold with known defects. The price to "patch" units in the field is much higher for cars; it's called a recall. So, why is that we have come to terms with the fact that software will have security problems but are unwilling to accept the fact that our car may shut down at any moment? More important, why has the software industry come to terms with that? Put simply, the software industry hasn't had to make secure products and hasn't really wanted to—it's hard.

6.6.1 The Development Lifecycle

We won't discuss the issue of legal liability in this section but do discuss the difficulty of making a secure product from a process point of view. To review, the traditional software development lifecycle comprises five phases.

1. In the *requirements* phase, someone sits and talks to the customer in an effort to try and understand the customer's problem and what the requirements for a good solution are.

2. In the *design* phase, architects and developers come up with the basic product design. Depending on the organization's methodology, this phase may be very rigorous and thorough and produce a rigid design when done; or, it may be more flexible and just provide a starting point for development.

3. In the *implementation* phase, the code actually gets written. Again, depending on the organization's philosophy, this phase may revisit the design phase periodically and even incorporate parts of the testing phase—via nightly unit testing, for example.

4. In the *testing* phase, the bulk of the product testing happens. Bugs are often submitted back to the developers for consideration.

5. Finally, in the *support* phase, the product is shipping to customers.

The goal of most commercial software companies is to build a product that has more features than the competition and get it to the market faster. With these overall goals in mind, many organizations have architected the development lifecycle to get as close to the goals as possible.

Under this type of regime, the requirements phase becomes a feature-maximization problem, limited only by the amount of time that is "acceptable" between releases. The design phase focuses on making reusable components and reusing components from the last release, so that the system can be built more quickly. The implementation phase is almost always highly clock driven. Midlevel managers keep a close eye over developers' time estimates and continually check progress against the product's schedule. The testing phase is focused primarily on testing the features; they have to work if anyone's going to use them. Finally, the support phase is about keeping the customers happy enough with what they bought so that will buy the next version. This is where the software is "patched," when necessary.

6.6.2 Never the Twain Shall Meet

Viewed this way, it becomes clear why software with security problems gets out the door: Security is opposed to the intent of nearly every phase of the development lifecycle. Unfortunately, building a secure product goes against the very essence of the "build a feature-rich product and get it to market fast" mentality. At each phase of the development lifecycle, security detracts organizations from their goals.

If our primary concern were to build a secure product, then our process would be different. The requirements phase would focus on finding the fewest number of features that make the customer happy. Features add complexity, and complexity makes security difficult. The design phase would focus more on robustness rather than reuse. Demolition experts and architects would have to work together to consider how the system will hold up under attack. Implementation would focus on argument validation and careful memory management rather than time to market. The testing phase would focus on crash-testing the software—using such techniques as fuzz testing to make things break—in addition to feature testing. The support phase would remain largely unchanged; no matter how hard you try, there will likely always be something that needs fixing once the product is out in the field. As is the case in many software shops today, security-related issues would get a higher priority than functionality bugs.

You may be thinking that this is unrealistic in many places, and you're probably right. However, we are trying to illustrate the point that building a secure product is in almost complete opposition to what most organizations practice. Until organizations are aware of and want or have to fix this—and probably even after that, to some extent—we'll continue to see software that requires patching on the second Tuesday of every month.

6.6.3 Baking Security In

Some of the common thinking in the software engineering literature is that the cost of fixing problems increases by a factor of 10 during each phase that the problem persists. So, for example, a design problem that isn't fixed until the support phase costs 1,000 times more to fix than fixing it in the design phase itself. Catching security problems early has a financial advantage.

Some organizations are beginning to realize this. Microsoft and other companies are beginning to pay much more attention to security and are starting to modify their development processes to incorporate security [Lip04]. The basic idea behind these efforts is to incorporate security folks into the development lifecycle so that they can raise the security awareness of the product. As we discussed in Chapter 1, security is really a form of risk management. By letting security professionals get involved in the development lifecycle, they can help decision makers quantify the security risk involved at each step in the process.

In the requirements phase, a member of the security team may join the dialog and point out which features are likely to be a high risk and should thus require more careful design, implementation, and testing. During the design phase, security professionals may conduct design reviews and start the *threat-modeling* process to see how the design can stand up against potential adversaries [SS04b].

The first phase in threat modeling is to look at the application under consideration from the adversary's point of view. Concretely, this process begins by looking at the entry points to the application: any network-facing remoting services, RPC channels, special files and registry entries, and the like. In this process, we strive to enumerate all the ways that an adversary can supply input into the application.

Once the entry points have been identified, the modeling team then identifies the assets of the application: things that an attacker may want to get. Assets might include credentials, cryptographic material, the ability to execute certain code, and so on.

Finally, the modeling team identifies the trust level necessary to access the entry points and assets outlined in the previous steps. The result of the first phase is a mapping of entry points to assets and trust levels. The idea is that from this map, it should be clear what level of trust is necessary to supply input to specific parts of the application and particular assets.

In the second phase of the threat-modeling process, the modeling team looks at the application as a system in motion. This begins by considering security-relevant use case scenarios for the application. The modeling team looks at the scenarios that have been given consideration at design time and tries to brainstorm ones that have not been given any consideration. The modeling team also enumerates any security-relevant design assumptions and external dependencies, such as the use of third-party components. Finally, the team constructs data-flow diagrams for the security-relevant use scenarios.

In the final phase of threat modeling, the team constructs the threat profile of the application. This process starts by identifying all the possible threats to the application: for each entry point, considering what security-related processing occurs and what might a malicious external entity do to attack that processing or otherwise use an asset for another purpose.

Once the threats have been identified, the team considers particular attack scenarios. This can be done by starting with known vulnerabilities as well as the application's assets and then assigning a threat classification, such as *STRIDE*, to each scenario. (In STRIDE, such a classification will indicate whether the scenario results in spoofing, tampering, repudiation, information disclosure, denial of service, or elevation of privilege.)

Once the list of threats has been constructed and attack hypotheses have been formed and classified, the team can then identify vulnerabilities: unmitigated threats. Once the system's vulnerabilities have been identified, they can be ranked according to severity and prioritized.

During the implementation phase, the security team typically conducts code reviews, looking for the types of implementation problems that we have been discussing in this chapter. During the testing phase, security professionals can be conducting application security audits in an effort to break the product. Finally, during the support phase, members of the security team work with engineering and marketing to develop and test patches, as well as supply details for press releases regarding the incident.

6.7 The Take-Home Message

Good design is critical, but implementation is where the rubber meets the road. Even with the best of intentions, common programming errors, programming languages, and the development process itself can make it hard to do the right thing.

In our experience, most security trouble will get introduced into a system when the programmers are actually building the system. Sure, many systems often have design problems, most likely some form of incompleteness, but implementation is where design flaws and programming mistakes get turned into real, potentially exploitable vulnerabilities.

However, implementation is also the right time to pick the best tools for the job. The choice of development process, programming language, and security tools (e.g., code scanners, fuzz testers, etc.) can have an enormous impact on the security of the finished product. It's unrealistic to assume that you'll get it right every time, but picking the best tools for the job certainly reduces the risk of a major disaster.

6.8 Project Ideas

1. Read some BugTraq mailing list archives, which are available online from the site www.securityfocus.com. Can you find some examples of escape-sequence vulnerabilities or input-validation vulnerabilities? What about TOCTOU issues?

2. Code up a buffer overflow from the Aleph One paper [Ale96]. Why do such vulnerabilities still exist if we know so much about this attack?

3. Code up a return-to-libc attack.

4. Play with some fuzz testers, or write one yourself. Be sure you have control of the target system—be ethical—and then see what you can do by supplying random or malicious input to it. This may end up being an important testing tool for your system.

5. Even though it makes it easy to write code with all sorts of security problems, C remains the ubiquitous language for much security-relevant system code. Why?

6. Tools exist to help mitigate the security problems of C. (For example, consider CCured, Cyclone, Vault*, OCaml, .NET Framework, Splint, ITS4, RATS, Purify, or Valgrind.) Pick one of these and try it out. What installation and usage issues did you find? What performance and security impacts did the tool have?

Part III

Building Blocks for Secure Systems

Using Cryptography

To a large extent, computers and computation consist of information: bits and bytes, some stored locally and some sent over a network wire or carried on a CD-ROM. Ensuring that the adversary cannot coax such systems into bad behaviors can thus depend on ensuring that the adversary cannot do bad things with this information, such as spy on or alter or forge it. Focusing on how to prevent the adversary from doing such bad things to information, the field of *cryptography* provides many useful items for the computer security toolkit. In this chapter, we survey these tools.

- Section 7.1 sets the stage and introduces some basic terminology.
- Section 7.2 discusses the importance of randomness to cryptography.
- Section 7.3 explores the topic of symmetric cryptography.
- Section 7.4 discusses some of its applications.
- Section 7.5 covers the topic of public-key cryptography.
- Section 7.6 explores hash functions.
- Section 7.7 illustrates some of the practical issues to be aware of when using public-key cryptography in the real world.
- Section 7.8 outlines some of the issues to be aware of when using cryptography.

For a more detailed treatment of cryptography, we refer the reader to dedicated books, such as Schneier's *Applied Cryptography*, which provides a great introduction to the field [Sch96]. The depth of its bibliography compensates for the occasional shallowness (and bugs) in its text. Menezes, van Oarschots, and Vanstone's *Handbook of Applied Cryptography* is a better source for hard-core detail but is not the sort of thing that many would read cover to cover [MvOV96]. Kaufman, Perlman, and Speciner's *Network Security* does a good job of explaining theoretical background, as well as covering many practical implementation details that designers and developers should be aware of [KPS02]. Levy's *Crypto* provides interesting, and more lightweight, tales of the recent history of this topic, focusing in particular on the interplay between the technological and the political [Lev03]. (Kahn's history goes much farther back but gives short shrift to the recent politics [Kah96].)

7.1 Framework and Terminology

The term *cryptography* derives etymologically from *secret writing*. One also encounters the terms *cryptanalysis* and *cryptology*. The former term refers to how to break cryptography; the latter term refers to the field consisting of cryptography and cryptanalysis together.

7.1.1 Transformations

A way to start thinking about cryptography is to think about *transformations*. We start with a set of possible *plaintexts:* messages that might arise naturally within the context of our application or system. We have another set of possible *ciphertexts:* messages that appear to make no sense whatsoever. We can then imagine a function that maps each plaintext onto a unique ciphertext and an inverse of this function that does the reverse mapping. (Figure 7.1 sketches this mapping.) Intuitively, we might think of the forward mapping as *encryption:* We're taking a plaintext message and transforming it in such a way that hides its information from prying eyes. Similarly, we might think of the reverse mapping as *decryption.*

We admit right away that this approach is overly simplistic. For example, exactly what does it mean for ciphertexts to "make no sense"? (A government client once

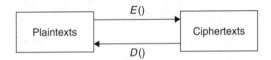

Figure 7.1 As an organizing framework, we can think about cryptography as a pair of transformations between a set of possible plaintexts and a set of possible ciphertexts. The transformations should invert each other: that is, for any x, we have $D(E(x)) = x$.

objected to this definition by observing that the citizenry regarded all that agency's naturally arising messages as making no sense, even without encryption.) In fact, modern cryptosystems typically treat both plaintext and ciphertexts as sets of arbitrary bit strings, frequently with a direct length correspondence. Furthermore, we caution the reader to be careful about using the terms *encryption* and *decryption* for these maps; although these are intuitive, better choices might be *encipherment* and *decipherment*. (We'll explain shortly.)

With this framework of two sets and two transformations, we might start thinking about privilege. Who should be able to perform which transformation? If everyone can do both, then there's not much point to anyone's doing either. Consequently, we end up wanting to restrict at least one direction to specially privileged parties. We do this by breaking the transformation into two pieces: a *key* (e.g., a long number) that embodies the privilege to carry out the transformation and an *algorithm* that tells how to do the transformation, once given a key as input. The key is used as a parameter to the algorithm; each choice of key gives a different instantiation. (Figure 7.2 sketches this revised mapping.)

Designers aspire to the idea that this core algorithm can be published—even to the adversary—without weakening the system; this aspiration is known as *Kerckhoff's Principle* and echoes the old adage of "no security through obscurity." The cryptographic research community relishes this principle; the give and take of new cryptosystems followed by new cryptanalysis is part and parcel of that community's literature.

However, not everyone subscribes to this "publish the algorithm" philosophy. One may encounter several classes of counterexamples. One class consists of proprietary vendor encryption; sales literature often touts a brand-new "perfectly secure" algorithm. It's a safe bet that such systems are extremely weak. (Some experts assert that if it's proprietary, it must be considered broken, by definition.) Another class consists of "high-grade" cryptosystems used for sensitive and classified government applications. The working assumption here is that these cryptosystems

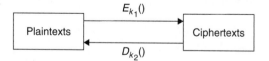

Figure 7.2 We need to expand our framework to embody the *privileges* necessary to perform these transformations. We express these as keys (long numbers). Each general algorithm $E()$ and $D()$ can be made public; each choice of key gives a different transformation within its family.

are strong but kept secret only in order to make it easier for the government in question to break the cryptosystems of other governments. (How does this mesh with the dictum of mistrusting proprietary cryptography, on principle? On the one hand, one assumes that these government agencies have large pools of smart cryptographers, so "proprietary" does not necessarily equal "not peer reviewed" here. On the other hand, this working assumption has not always been borne out; witness Matt Blaze's discovery of weaknesses in Skipjack. See [Lev03, pp. 256–260] for a discussion of that incident.) Sometimes, industrial players withhold details of otherwise strong cryptosystems in order to protect their trade secrets. RSA did this with its *RC4* cipher—licensing only the executable—only to have someone post source, which came to be known as *Arcfour*. Interestingly, RSA asserted that although this source worked, it did not appear to be an obfuscated version of the original source.

7.1.2 Complexity

The preceding discussion made several assertions about impossibilities. One *cannot* perform the required transformation without knowing the right key; one *cannot* derive information about a plaintext simply by examining the corresponding ciphertext. Building on early work by logicians, computer science has developed elaborate and elegant theory about what can and cannot be computed. (Recall Section 1.4.1, or see the appendix.) *Computability* examines what can be computed at all; *complexity* examines the amount of resources (e.g., time and memory) required to compute something. Complexity theory is full of fascinating and annoying open questions. Classes of problems exist that all appear to be equivalently "hard": If we could solve one efficiently, we could solve all of them efficiently, but no one knows whether we can solve one efficiently. (Usually, the working assumption is no, the problems cannot be solved efficiently.)

In light of complexity theory, when computer scientists say "cannot be done," they usually mean "cannot be done with tractable resources"—and sometimes they forget to add "as we all believe, but no one has conclusively shown." Rest assured, more formal treatments of cryptography are well founded in this framework.

7.1.3 Some Attack Strategies

We can also use the preceding framework to build a taxonomy of some attack strategies. In a *ciphertext-only attack*, the adversary has access only to ciphertext. In a *known-plaintext attack*, the adversary knows plaintext/ciphertext pairs. In a *chosen-plaintext attack*, the adversary can choose plaintexts and then see the ciphertexts to which they encrypt. In a *chosen-ciphertext attack*, the adversary can choose cipher-texts and then see the plaintexts to which they decrypt. In the *adaptive* variants of the chosen-text attacks, the adversary can delay picking another choice until he or she sees the result of the previous choice.

7.2 Randomness

Since the possession of a key embodies privilege in many cryptosystems, it is worth asking: Where do we get these keys from? Cryptographic applications frequently require random bit strings for generating cryptographic keys. (Other applications, such as large-scale simulations in computational science, also require randomness.) One could imagine having a universally trusted person flipping a perfectly fair coin; however, it would not be practical to scale that process to the number, rate, and locations where these bits are required. This situation thus brings up two challenges. Where can computers get these random bits? And what do we mean by "random," anyway?

Let's start with the second challenge. The image of a trusted person flipping a fair coin raises two ideals worth aspiring to. First is the ideal of *distribution*: We expect a random bit sequence to have the same statistical distributions as a sequence of flips of a fair coin. We want these properties to hold not only when we look at individual bits but also as we look at wider windows of consecutive bits. The FIPS 140-2 validation process even offers some explicit procedures for testing for this distribution property [NIS01]. Second is the ideal of *unpredictability*: Even having seen the result of every coin flip so far, the adversary cannot predict the result of the next one with better than 50 percent accuracy. Formal treatments of this property use the complexity tools discussed earlier. Figure 7.3 sketches these ideals.

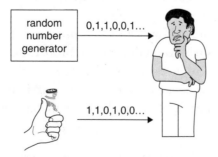

Figure 7.3 An ideal random-number generator produces a sequence of bits that is as distributed and unpredictable as a sequence of flips of a fair coin.

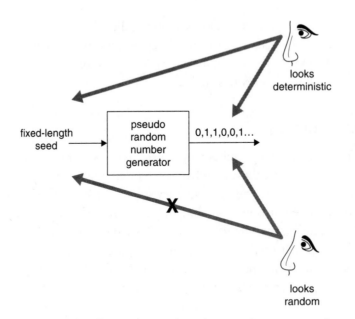

Figure 7.4 A cryptographically strong *pseudorandom number generator* deterministically amplifies a fixed-length seed into an arbitrarily long sequence that, ideally, would be indistinguishable from a random sequence—as long as one does not know the seed.

Where can a computer get sequences of bits that satisfy these properties? One approach is to use physics: Find a physical process that behaves randomly and somehow harness the bits inside a computing device. Techniques that have been used here include noisy diodes and radioactive decay. However, a more common approach is to use computational means[1] to take a *seed* input and amplify it to an (ideally) arbitrarily long sequence that appears random. Since this sequence is in fact completely deterministic, we usually use the phrase *pseudorandom* for such sequences and call such a program module a *pseudorandom number generator (PRNG)*. (See Figure 7.4.)

Typically, simulation applications require pseudorandom-number generators that produce sequences with good distribution properties. Unpredictability is not as important. In fact, in some cases, complete predictability can be useful; it can sometimes be useful to generate the same test data again by using the same seed. However, since simulation applications have a long history in computing, many

---

1. Kaufman et al. provide a wonderful quote from Von Neumann: "Anyone who considers arithmetical methods for producing random digits is, of course, in a state of sin" [KPS02].

of the random number generators that show up by default in computing environments and computing textbooks fare poorly when it comes to unpredictability; for example, consider `rand ()` and `srand ()` in the standard C library. In practice, one should take care to use a *cryptographically strong* PRNG.

For cryptographic applications, another important item to consider is where to get the seeds from; an adversary who can predict the seeds can predict the random numbers. To alleviate this problem, many current systems consciously try to accumulate difficult-to-predict values, such as keystroke and disk timings, and make them available to application code (e.g., see `/dev/random/`). Many PRNG constructions also permit on-the-fly reseeding.

7.3 Symmetric Cryptography

Recall again the view of cryptography as a pair of keyed transformations between plaintexts and ciphertexts. From the dawn of time to the age of disco, mankind thought of doing cryptography only one way: using the same key for each transformation. To decrypt a message, one needed to know the key that was used to encrypt it. Figure 7.5 sketches this approach.

Because both transformations used the *same* key, this approach is now known as *symmetric-key cryptography*. Sometimes, one will also encounter the terms *private-key cryptography* or *secret-key cryptography* for this approach, because the key in question needs to be kept at least somewhat secret in order for its use to mean anything.

The classic example of a symmetric cryptosystem is the *one-time pad*. Let the plaintext space be some subset of the bit strings, perhaps those consisting of sequences of ASCII bytes or perhaps the full set itself. The key is a string of random bits as long as the message. We encrypt the message by bitwise-XORing the plaintext against the key; we decrypt the message by bitwise-XORing the ciphertext against the same key. This works because XOR—that is, exclusive OR—is associative; because XORing the same value against itself yields zero; and because XORing against zero is the identity. For example, for a message bit b_i and the corresponding

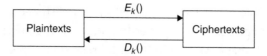

Figure 7.5 In *symmetric* cryptography, the same key is required for both transformations. Whoever can do one can also do the other.

key bit k_i, the ciphertext will be $b_i \oplus k_i$, and its decryption will be

$$
\begin{aligned}
(b_i \oplus k_i) \oplus k_i &= b_i \oplus (k_i \oplus k_i) \\
&= b_i \oplus 0 \\
&= b_i
\end{aligned}
$$

We might ask ourselves some questions about the one-time pad. Can the adversary break this algorithm via brute force—that is, by trying decryption with each possible key until he or she got the right answer? What information does the ciphertext betray? How would we go about doing this in the real world? What would happen if we reused a key?

For now, let's consider the first question. If brute force is used, how can the adversary tell whether he or she got the right answer? Naively, we might think something like: "Gosh, since the plaintext is an ASCII string in English, if a test decryption yields some ASCII in English, then the adversary must have the right one." The reality is more annoying. Suppose that the real plaintext is p_r and the real key is k_r. Pick another arbitrary plaintext p_f the same length as p_r. The bit string $k_f = k_r \oplus p_r \oplus p_f$ is one of the keys the adversary will try. Consider what happens when the adversary tries that on the ciphertext:

$$
\begin{aligned}
(p_r \oplus k_r) \oplus k_f &= (p_r \oplus k_r) \oplus (k_r \oplus p_r \oplus p_f) \\
&= p_r \oplus (k_r \oplus k_r) \oplus p_r \oplus p_f \\
&= p_r \oplus p_r \oplus p_f \\
&= p_f
\end{aligned}
$$

For *any* possible plaintext p_f of the same length as the original p_r, a key exists that decrypts the ciphertext back to p_f. The adversary's situation is reminiscent of "The Library of Babel," J. L. Borges's short story that considers a library that contains a copy of every possible book-length sequence of characters [Bor64].

A similar calculation shows why it is dangerous to use a one-time pad to encrypt two different plaintexts p_1 and p_2 with the same key: By XORing the two ciphertexts together, the adversary learns $p_1 \oplus p_2$, which can be rather interesting if these plaintexts have nontrivial structure. (Indeed, reuse of one-time pads has been blamed for enabling the decryption of the Soviet *Venona* ciphers [NSAb].) The facts that keys should never be reused and that each key must as long as the plaintext are fundamental obstacles to using one-time pads in practice. How do we generate all these keys and then distribute them to the right parties?

7.3.1 Information Theory

You might be wondering how many different keys will decipher a ciphertext to something that makes sense.

Claude Shannon developed *information theory* to describe, in robust mathematical terms, what *information* and *noise* mean in communication.[2] Central to information theory is the concept of *entropy:* The entropy $H(M)$ is how many bits are necessary to specify the information in a message M. (Some wags characterize entropy as measuring how *surprising* the message is.[3])

Information theory can help us answer our second question about the one-time pad: How much information is present in the ciphertext? Viewed through the lens of information theory, keys and plaintext messages both have entropy. So, given a key and a plaintext, one could add up the "entropy in key" (denoted $H(K)$) and the "entropy in plaintext" (denoted $H(P)$).

A ciphertext also has entropy, $H(C)$. One can imagine seeing a progressive sequence of prefixes of the ciphertext and asking about the entropy in each prefix. When we see one bit of ciphertext, we have at most one bit of entropy. Each additional bit might give us some more entropy. But there might exist a U where, once we've seen U bits of ciphertext, the entropy in what we've seen—denoted $H(C_U)$—equals the sum of the entropy in the key and the entropy in the plaintext: i.e., $H(C_U) = H(K) + H(P)$. This U, when it exists, is called the *unicity distance* for that cryptosystem in that scenario.

We care about the unicity distance of a given cryptosystem with a given plaintext space because this tells us how many keys can decrypt a ciphertext back to a possible plaintext. Suppose that the adversary is sneakily trying to learn the plaintext by observing the ciphertext. If the adversary gets more than U bits of ciphertext, the plaintext has probably been uniquely identified; that is, the uncertainty approaches 0. For the TDES cipher (discussed in Section 7.3.4) with ASCII plaintext, the unicity is less than 19 bytes. This means that an adversary who has more than 19 bytes of ciphertext, guesses a key, and gets ASCII characters almost certainly has the right key! However, for one-time pads, the unicity distance is infinite: One can never have enough ciphertext bits to determine whether one guessed the key correctly. In that sense, the one-time pad hides *all* information about the plaintext—except, of course, its length.

(The appendix gives some more discussion and rants.)

---

2. Cover and Thomas's *Elements of Information Theory* covers this field in depth [CT91].
3. "'Information,' as technically defined, is proportionate to surprise; the more surprising a message is, the more information it contains. If someone listening over the telephone heard 'Hello' at the beginning of a conversation, he would not be very surprised; but his gain of information would be quite large if he were suddenly electrocuted" [Coh63, p.85].

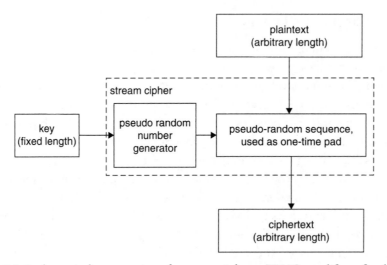

Figure 7.6 In the typical construction of a stream cipher, a PRNG amplifies a fixed-length key into a longer pseudorandom sequence that is then used as a one-time pad.

7.3.2 Stream Ciphers versus Block Ciphers

Building symmetric cryptosystems has seen the emergence of two main approaches: *stream ciphers* and *block ciphers*. In the general *stream cipher* approach, we encrypt each bit one at a time. That is, we process each bit in the context of the state determined by the key and previous history. In the typical construction, the key seeds a PRNG and uses the resulting pseudorandom number as a one-time pad (see Figure 7.6). RC4 appears to be a good example, although strictly speaking, one can't quite officially say what RC4 does, because the details were protected by trade secret.

In the general *block cipher* approach, we fix a block size (typically much larger than 1 bit, of course). The key determines a permutation on block-size sequences of bits (see Figure 7.7). To encrypt a message, we partition the message into a sequence of blocks and apply the permutation to each block individually. Common examples of block ciphers include DES, TDES, and AES.[4] Until recently, DES was probably the most commonly used block cipher. It used 8-byte blocks and 8-byte keys; however, one bit in each byte was parity, yielding a real key length of only 56 bits.

In general, one finds that the computer security field emphasizes block ciphers over stream ciphers. The reason appears to be mixed. Block ciphers are more suited

---

4. These stand for *Data Encryption Standard*, *Triple DES*, and the *Advanced Encryption Standard*, respectively, but everyone simply thinks of DES and AES as words.

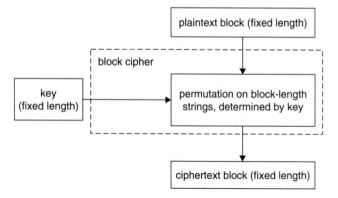

Figure 7.7 In a block cipher, the key determines a particular permutation on block-length strings.

to software implementations and are also more general. Thus, block ciphers are more useful as basic building blocks in computer and network security. Good block ciphers exist in the open literature.

Stream ciphers are good for lossy transmission channels in hardware; as one consequence, they tend to be popular in telecom and military applications. But as another consequence, they tend to be kept proprietary or secret. (Schneier gives some discussion [Sch96]; so does Chapter 6 in the *Handbook of Applied Cryptography* [MvOV96].)

7.3.3 Chaining

In the preceding presentation on block ciphers, we encrypted a message by applying the block permutation to each successive block of the message. Without additional techniques, this approach has many problems. For example, if the same block appears twice in the plaintext, then the same block will appear twice on the ciphertext. The same message getting encrypted twice with the same key will produce the same ciphertext. If two different messages with a common prefix (longer than one block) get encrypted with the same key, then the ciphertexts will have a common prefix.

To avoid the problem of same-plaintext-block encrypting the same way in the message, we use *chaining*. The literature describes many *modes* of chaining, sometimes called *modes of encryption*. The most common we see in practice is *cipher-block chaining (CBC)*. Let $P_1, P_2, \ldots, P_n$ be the blocks of plaintext. We obtain C_1, the first block of ciphertext, by performing the block permutation on P_1. However, for $i > 1$, we obtain C_i by first XORing P_i with C_{i-1} and then running the block permutation.

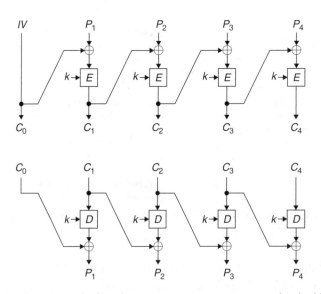

Figure 7.8 In block ciphers, the key determines a permutation on individual blocks. Using block ciphers in the real world requires chaining these block operations together. Here, we sketch the commonly used *CBC* approach to encrypt a plaintext consisting of blocks P_1, P_2, P_3, P_4 (above) and to decrypt the resulting ciphertext (below).

To avoid the problem of the same message encrypting the same way, we use *initialization vectors (IVs)*. Basically, we pick a random block-length IV, declare that to be C_0, and XOR the IV against P_1 before we do the block operation on P_1. Decryption with CBC works the other way around: We do the inverse block operation on a C_i and then XOR the result against C_{i-1} to obtain P_i. Figure 7.8 sketches these operations.

7.3.4 Multiple Rounds

A block cipher's weak point can be its key length. With a fixed key length acting on arbitrarily long plaintexts, real-world application scenarios regularly exceed the unicity distance. An adversary can always try breaking the cipher by trying every possible key, even if the block operation is otherwise strong. If the key length is too short, this brute-force approach may be feasible. Even if the key length is sufficient at the time of deployment, increases in computing power may make the brute-force approach become feasible.

If the key length of a block cipher is insufficient, we can try using the cipher multiple times with different keys. This natural idea has some subtle hazards, however. One hazard: Does the cipher constitute an algebraic *group*? That is, suppose that E_k is the block permutation function for key k. We can denote the set of possible permutations under this cipher as $\{E_k \mid \forall k\}$. If we apply E_{k_1} and then E_{k_2}, this yields a new block permutation, $E_{k_2} \circ E_{k_1}$. Is this new permutation also in the set $\{E_k \mid \forall k\}$? That is, does there exist a k_3 such that $E_{k_3} = E_{k_2} \circ E_{k_1}$? If so, then performing multiple rounds of permutation hasn't really helped us!

For a long time, DES was the standard block cipher in use. However, its 56-bit key length grew worrisome. After verifying that DES is not a group, the field started deploying new block ciphers consisting of multiple rounds of DES. The design parameters here include how many rounds, how many keys, and how to do chaining.

Typically, these new ciphers used three rounds of DES, and so they all tend to be known by the ambiguous name *TDES*, or *3DES*. In practice, the most common way to structure the rounds is (1) encrypt with a key k_1, (2) decrypt with a key k_2, and (3) encrypt again with k_1. This is often known as *EDE with two keys*. One may immediately wonder: Why only two keys, and why this decryption step in the middle?

Let's consider the first question. One reason that TDES often uses only two keys is that developers deemed an effective key length of 112 bits to be sufficient. Of course, one may then wonder why, if two keys are sufficient, we don't simply use 2DES by DES-encrypting with k_1 and then DES-encrypting the result with k_2? To answer this, suppose that the adversary has a plaintext/ciphertext pair. To break 2DES with brute force, one might think that the adversary has to try every possible choice of two DES keys, or 2^{112} possibilities. However, with a lot of storage, the adversary can try every possible DES encryption of the plaintext and save the results (2^{56} ciphertext results) and can then try every possible DES decryption of the ciphertext and see whether one of these matches. That takes another 2^{56} operations—and 2^{57} is much less than 2^{112}. (Figure 7.9 sketches this *meet-in-the-middle* attack.) Thus, to use two keys but *not* be subject to this somewhat theoretical attack, we need to use at least three rounds. Furthermore, if we used three keys on three rounds, a similar style of attack might reduce the work factor to not much more than 2^{112} anyway.

That leaves us with the question: Why use EDE instead of the more obvious EEE? The answer here is that using the middle decryption step does not weaken things and does permit an EDE TDES black box to perform single DES, if one sets $k_1 = k_2$.

The next question is how to chain. More than 200 ways exist to do chaining with three steps. (Biham even has a paper that analyzes all of them [Bih99].) The popular ones are *inner CBC* and *outer CBC*. With inner-CBC EDE, we use CBC

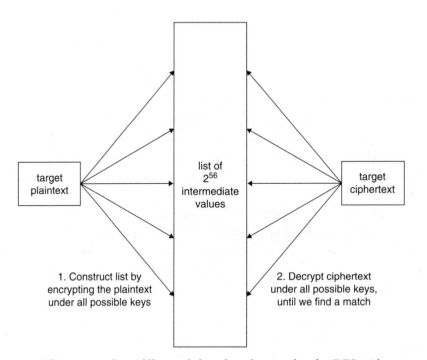

target plaintext

list of 2^{56} intermediate values

target ciphertext

1. Construct list by encrypting the plaintext under all possible keys

2. Decrypt ciphertext under all possible keys, until we find a match

Figure 7.9 The *meet-in-the-middle* attack lets the adversary break 2DES with not much more work than breaking single DES—provided the adversary is willing to store 2^{56} intermediate values.

DES to encrypt the entire message with k_1; we then CBC-DES-decrypt the entire result with k_2; we then CBC-DES-encrypt again with k_1. With outer-CBC EDE, we build a new block permutation by applying the DES permutation for k_1, applying the inverse permutation for k_2, and applying the forward permutation for k_1 again:

$$New_{k_1,k_2} = E_{k_1} \circ D_{k_2} \circ E_{k_1}.$$

We then encrypt the message using New_{k_1,k_2} as the block permutation and CBC chaining. One can remember the terminology by looking at the structure in Figures 7.10 and 7.11, which sketch these two modes. Three steps times N blocks gives us a $3 \times N$ matrix of boxes. With inner CBC, the arrows for chaining fly around inside this matrix; with outer CBC, the arrows connect points outside the matrix. (Note that, because of the D step, the arrows in inner CBC may appear somewhat counterintuitive; many respected published sources get this wrong.)

Real-world DES implementations—particularly in hardware—often have an expensive per-operation cost—to set up the internal key schedule that drives the block permutation—but a very cheap per-block cost once that setup is done.

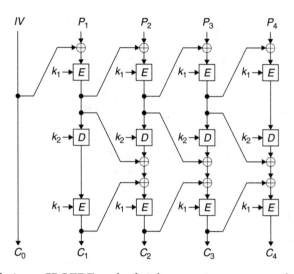

Figure 7.10 In the inner-CBC EDE mode of triple encryption, we encrypt the entire plaintext with single-mode CBC, then decrypt the entire result, and then encrypt it all again. (Different implementations handle the IV differently; this is a typical usage.)

Consequently, inner-CBC TDES can be desirable in practice because, if we're building on a DES subroutine, we pay that per operation cost only three times for the whole message. With outer CBC, we have to pay that cost three times for each block in the message. Unfortunately, because of some theoretical weaknesses, ANSI did not include inner CBC when it issued its TDES standard, discouraging its use in new applications.

Newer symmetric ciphers, such as AES, permit much longer key lengths, obviating these worries about multiple rounds. However, many existing systems

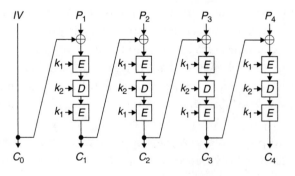

Figure 7.11 In the outer-CBC EDE mode of triple encryption, we treat the composition of three-block permutations as a new block permutation and then do CBC on that.

use TDES. We caution the reader to watch out for the ambiguity in what DES or 3DES can stand for and also to consider the potential for pessimal outer-CBC implementations when evaluating TDES benchmarks.

7.4 Applications of Symmetric Cryptography

Suppose that we become stranded on a desert island with nothing but a symmetric cipher. What can we do? (If desert islands seem fanciful, consider instead that we might be working on a software project or embedded system that has only a DES or AES core.)

7.4.1 Encryption

Probably the most natural use of symmetric cryptography is to *encrypt*. If Alice wants to send a message to Bob and would rather the eavesdropper not learn the content of the message, she can encrypt it with a symmetric cipher.

Of course, this encryption requires a key. To generate a key, Alice needs access to random numbers—or a cryptographically strong PRNG seeded with a value that the adversary cannot predict. (If Alice is using CBC, she'll need a random IV as well.) If Bob is to be able read the message, then Alice and Bob need to share knowledge of the key beforehand. For stream ciphers, this requirement can be cumbersome, since, owing to the way stream ciphers are typically modeled on a one-time pad, it is dangerous to reuse the key. For block ciphers, such as TDES and AES, the shared key can be reused, although too much reuse can give the adversary data that can assist cryptanalysis.

7.4.2 MACs

For encryption to be effective, cryptosystems aspire to the property that the encryption transformation can be carried out only by a party that knows the key. With block ciphers, Alice can use this property to preserve *integrity* and *authenticity* of a message she sends to Bob. Rather than encrypting M with her secret key k, Alice can use k to derive a *message authentication code* (*MAC*), sometimes also called a *message integrity code* (*MIC*), from M. An adversary might try to modify M and perhaps also modify the MAC. However, not knowing Alice's key, the adversary will not be able to produce a new matched pair. When Bob receives a message, he can also calculate its MAC, since he shares the key with Alice. If his calculated MAC does not match the one that was sent, he knows that the transmission has been altered since Alice sent it.

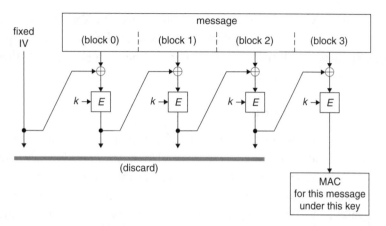

Figure 7.12 We can use a block cipher to construct a *message authentication code* by CBC encrypting the message with a secret key but then throwing away all the blocks of output except the last one. (Since this basic approach permits forgery if varying-length messages are permitted—see project idea 2—the current "best practice" is to append an encoding of the length to the message, before the residue is calculated.)

For example, Alice could use her key to calculate the CBC encryption of M from a known IV, except that she throws away all the output except the last block of ciphertext. This *CBC residue* of M has the property that only a party who knows k can calculate it, so Alice can use that as a MAC and send it along with her message across an open channel (see Figure 7.12). However, if varying message lengths are permitted, this basic CBC-residue approach has a flaw: An adversary who knows the residue of a message M under an unknown key can calculate the residue of extensions of M. (See project idea 2.) Cryptographers address this flaw by appending an encoding of the length of the message before calculating the residue [Dwo05].

Section 7.6 discusses how to use *hash functions* to build MACs.

In practice, Alice would usually like to both have integrity and secrecy on her transmission. This goal requires encrypting and using a MAC. In general, using the same or related keys for these operations leads to trouble; the best practice is to use independent keys. Some cryptographers also worry about whether the cryptosystems in question possess *nonmalleability*, or whether an adversary might be able to alter ciphertext and MACs so things still check. Another question that has received recent research attention is whether to MAC first and then encrypt or the other way around. We also advise the reader that using CBC residue for integrity in situations when things may be more exposed or when more than two parties are involved can lead to trouble.[5]

---

5. More on this topic can be found in Section 21.16 in Kaufman et al. [KPS02].

In the past few years, clever chaining schemes have emerged that give integrity and secrecy in one pass over the data, at the cost of slightly more complicated chaining complications. Jutla seemed to open this field up [Jut01], but there has been much follow-on work (e.g., [Dwo07]).

7.4.3 One-Way Functions

With encryption, Alice performs an operation that only she or Bob can undo, assuming that only she and Bob have the key. With MACs, Alice performs an operation that only she or Bob can perform. However, we can also use a symmetric cipher to build an operation that *anyone* can do but *no one* can undo. For example, we might build a function $F(M)$ by deriving a sequence of keys from the message M and then repeatedly encrypt some known quantity with those keys. Anyone can take M to $F(M)$, but, if we've done our job properly with the underlying cryptosystem, going from $F(M)$ back to M should be rather difficult, if not impossible. Such *one-way functions* frequently find use in the design of secure systems and protocols. As an example, a variant of the DES algorithm was used to store password hashes in many UNIX systems. Given only a password hash $F(M)$, it is infeasible to find out that the original password was M.

7.4.4 PRNGs

Intuitively, if it is to not reveal any information about its plaintext, a ciphertext should appear essentially random to an adversary who does not possess the proper key. Cryptographers have formalized and verified this intuition. As a consequence, we can use a symmetric cipher to build a reasonably strong PRNG. For example, we might divide the seed into two pieces, use one as key and the other as a plaintext—after extending it to an indefinite sequence—and then CBC encrypt. The resulting ciphertext is our pseudorandom bit string.

7.5 Public-Key Cryptography

7.5.1 Basics

As noted earlier, from the dawn of time to the age of disco, only symmetric cryptography was used. As Figure 7.5 shows, the same key must be used for both transformations. Then, the world changed. Many parties (Whitfield Diffie, Martin Hellmann, and Ralph Merkle in the public world; researchers at the GCHQ—the British "NSA"—in the secret world) independently began asking: What if the keys for each transformation could be different?

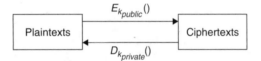

Figure 7.13 With public-key cryptography, each transformation requires a different key; one can be published without compromising the secrecy of the other. Doing the public-key operation on a plaintext produces a ciphertext that only the holder of the private key can decrypt.

We want the two transformation keys k_1 and k_2 to be more than just *different*; we want them to be sufficiently independent so that one of them (say, k_1) could be published without compromising the secrecy of the other. Recall our earlier discussion of complexity theory: A formal treatment would describe the (hopeful) intractability of computing k_2 from k_1. We describe this k_1, k_2 as a *key pair*. In this example, k_1 would be the *public key*, and k_2 would be the *private key*. Because the keys are different, this approach is called *asymmetric cryptography*. Because one of the keys can be published, this approach is also called *public-key cryptography.*

7.5.2 Encryption

As with symmetric cryptography, one of the first applications that comes to mind is encryption. If Bob wants to send a secret message M to Alice, he simply transforms M with the public key of Alice; only Alice can retrieve the plaintext, since she's the only one who knows the corresponding private key. Figures 7.13 and 7.14 sketch this situation.

As with symmetric cryptography, Alice requires a key pair, which must be generated with sufficiently strong randomness so that an adversary cannot predict Alice's private key. However, unlike with symmetric cryptography, Alice and Bob do not need to share a secret beforehand—*or ever*. In fact, until she receives the message, Alice does not even have to be aware of Bob's existence.

We can start to appreciate the power of the public key if we compare the work required to enable pairs of individuals to communicate securely. If 30 students at

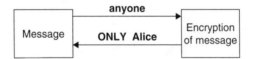

Figure 7.14 Anyone can encrypt a message for Alice by using his public key, but only Alice can decrypt it.

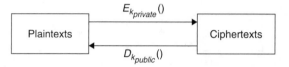

Figure 7.15 In public-key cryptography, doing the private-key operation on a plaintext produces a ciphertext that anyone can verify was produced from that plaintext by the holder of that private key.

Dartmouth wanted to be able to communicate securely, they would need to negotiate $\frac{30 \cdot 29}{2} = 435$ shared keys. If these 30 students each want to be able to communicate with 30 students at the University of Houston, that's another $30 \cdot 30 = 900$ shared secret keys, to be negotiated between parties half a country apart. However, with public-key cryptography, all we need is a key pair for each student. If the respective universities publish directories of public keys for their students, that eliminates the need for cross-country establishment of pairwise shared secrets.

7.5.3 Signatures

With public-key cryptography, we don't need to use the public key for the transformation from plaintext to ciphertext. We could use it for the other transformation. Figures 7.15 and 7.16 sketch this scenario: Anyone in the world has the ability to transform Alice's ciphertext back to the original plaintext, but only Alice can produce this ciphertext.

This arrangement enables *digital signatures.* For a message M, its transformation under Alice's private key constitutes a *signature* on M that only she can produce but that anyone can verify. The fact that Bob and Alice need never have met opens up worlds of applications.

It is interesting to contrast digital signatures with MACs (see Section 7.4.2). In both scenarios, receiver Bob can verify that sender Alice produced the message. However, MACs require that Bob share Alice's secret, which prevents Bob from ever turning around and proving to anyone else that Alice sent M. (It does no good

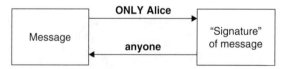

Figure 7.16 Only Alice can generate the signature from her message, but anyone can check that the signature matches it.

to exhibit the MAC, because he could have generated it himself; furthermore, in order for anyone else to verify it, he would have to expose the secret key.) In this sense, digital signatures provide *nonrepudiation* to third parties; MACs do not.[6] (Sometimes, however, this drawback of MACs can be useful. For example, it enables integrity on communications that Alice is sending to Bob but would otherwise like to not be tied to her.)

7.5.4 Terminology Warning

When we introduced the transformation model (see Section 7.1), we included a warning: Although it might be natural to think of the transformation from plaintext to ciphertext as "encryption," one should be careful using that term. Public-key cryptography is the reason. Some members of the community define "encryption" and "decryption" not in terms of the message spaces but rather in terms of the amount of privilege required. For this audience, "decryption" is, by definition, the *private-key* operation. We find this interpretation awkward, since it requires the first step in generating a signature to be to "decrypt the plaintext," but there it is. Be warned.

7.5.5 RSA

In the open literature, credit for discovery of public-key cryptography is given to Diffie, Hellman, and Merkle. Diffie and Hellman published their seminal 1976 paper, "New Directions in Cryptography," which marked the beginning of a new era [DH76]. Just two years later, Rivest, Shamir, and Adlemen developed the first known implementation of the full public-key concept [RSA78]. Their work literally changed the world and enabled modern e-commerce, among other things.

Like many historic events, this one is awash in rumors. Stories are told that the NSA pressured them to suppress the work, so they published before filing the patent. This move lost them patent rights outside the United States, since Europe requires filing a patent before public disclosure, thus adding a few more ironic wrinkles to the U.S. government's unfortunate former policy of protecting U.S. interests by suppressing the export of strong cryptography.

RSA uses *modular math*, which means working with the integers $0, \ldots, N-1$. If we need to add 1 to $N-1$, that takes us back to zero. Algebra and number theory give all sorts of useful results here.

---

6. *Nonrepudiation*, a word borrowed from the legal world, means that, if Alice signs a contract at some point in time, she cannot deny signing the contract at some later point in time.

The field uses "mod N" to refer to operations in modular arithmetic, although the notation is a bit sloppy. To be strict, it should really modify the equality symbol. "A is congruent to B mod N" when A and B have the same remainder, when divided by N; or more formally, there exists an integer K such that $A = B + KN$.

If Alice wants to generate an RSA key pair, she picks two large primes, p and q. These are secret. She then sets her *modulus* $N = pq$. She picks her *public exponent* e to be some integer that is relatively prime to the product $(p-1)(q-1)$; pretty much any such integer will do. Alice then calculates her *private exponent d* to be the multiplicative inverse of e, or nothing at all mod $(p-1)(q-1)$. That is,

$$de = 1 \bmod (p-1)(q-1).$$

Calculating multiplicative inverses is a cookbook application of some *greatest common divisor (GCD)* algorithms; however, knowing $(p-1)(q-1)$ would certainly appear to require Alice's secret knowledge.

For this key pair, the plaintext and ciphertext space are both integers mod N. The public key is (e, N). The private key is (d, N), or simply d, although Alice can do some calculations more efficiently if she remembers p and q as well. The public-key transformation consists of raising the input to e modulo N; the private-key transformation consists of raising the input to d modulo N.

RSA works because the magic of number theory gives us, for any X, that

$$X^{de} = X \bmod N.$$

RSA is considered strong because it appears to require $(p-1)(q-1)$ to calculate d—and it seems that calculating $(p-1)(q-1)$ from the public N requires factoring N. Breaking RSA thus is no harder than factoring a larger number, which most people consider to be intractable; many people believe that it cannot be much easier.

(In this aspect, public-key cryptography tends to be more intellectually satisfying, because its algorithms typically have some basis in complexity theory. Symmetric ciphers, in contrast, tend to be more of a "black art.")

7.5.6 Other Algorithms

We focus on RSA because it was the first (public) full implementation of the public-key concept, it remains the de facto standard, and it serves as a good illustration of the concepts. However, it is far from the only public-key system out there. Another principal one is the *Digital Signature Algorithm (DSA)*, a cryptosystem promulgated by the U.S. government to enable digital signatures only (not encryption) and designed to avoid patent encumbrances. The *Diffie-Hellman* system predates RSA

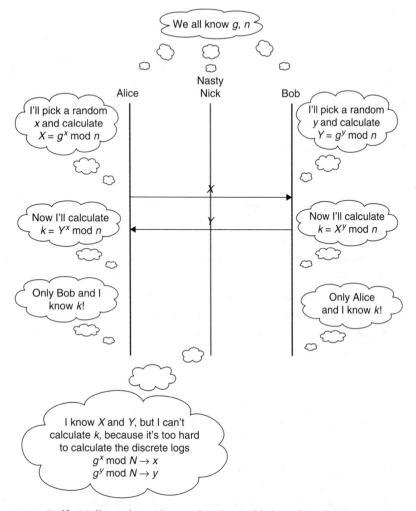

Figure 7.17 Diffie-Hellman lets Alice and Bob establish a shared secret over an open channel. (However, Diffie-Hellman alone does not enable them to *authenticate*: Each has no idea who the other is, only that they share a secret.) The parameters g and n can be published; n is a prime, and g has a special number theoretic relation to n. Diffie-Hellman works because that *discrete log* problem (calculating z, given g^z mod n) is considered intractable.

but only allows establishing a shared symmetric key between parties who haven't met; in particular, it does not allow for *authentication* (see Figure 7.17). Since symmetric cryptography is typically faster than public-key cryptography, many communication protocols rely on Diffie-Hellman to establish short-lived symmetric keys, sometimes called *session keys*, so that the cryptography does not bottleneck the communication channel.

Elliptic curve cryptography (ECC) provides an alternative mathematical setting for public key; because it gets more security "bang" for computation and memory expenditure, ECC is receiving much attention in embedded systems applications and resource-constrained devices, such as PDAs and cell phones. We urge curious readers to refer to Schneier [Sch96] and Menezes et al. [MvOV96] for details on these and other public-key cryptosystems.

7.6 Hash Functions

7.6.1 Overview

Earlier, we mentioned one-way functions: functions that everyone can calculate but no one can invert. Cryptography makes frequent use of a special set of one-way functions called *hash functions*.

In practical settings, a hash function H maps an arbitrarily long input to a bit string of some fixed length. The term *hash function* also shows up in other computer science concepts, such as *bucket hashing* and the hash table data structures, but the term used there has fewer implications. In practical cryptographic settings, a hash function H needs to be one-way. This goal tends to get formalized as two main properties:

1. *Preimage resistance.* Given some hash output value z, it is not feasible to calculate a message x such that $H(x) = z$.

2. *Collision resistance.* It is not feasible to calculate two messages x and y such that $H(x) = H(y)$.

Sometimes, we also see a third property:

3. *Second preimage resistance.* Given a message x, it is not feasible to calculate a second message y such that $H(x) = H(y)$.

7.6.2 Construction

Typically, hash functions are built by starting with a *compression* function on two inputs. We break the input message into blocks and then iterate the compression function on each block and the output of the previous iteration. Typically, these hash functions finish with a concluding block that encodes the length of the message. Figure 7.18 illustrates this approach, known as the *Merkle-Damgard* framework.

In the past 15 years, the primary hash functions in use are *MD5*, which maps messages onto 128-bit strings, and *SHA-1*, which maps messages onto 160-bit strings. (We revisit the topic of hash function security in Chapter 8.)

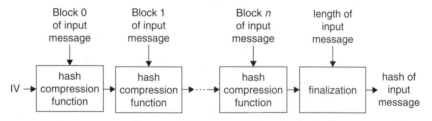

Figure 7.18 In the basic Merkle-Damgard approach to hash function construction, we break the input message into blocks, append a block dependent on the length of the message, and then iterate a compression function on each new block and the output of the previous iteration.

7.6.3 Basic Application Techniques

As a colleague once quipped, "hash functions are the duct tape of cryptography." In order to prepare the reader for the myriad places in system and protocol design where hash functions can be useful, we'll quickly cover a few representative application techniques.

In perhaps the most straightforward scenario, one can use a hash function to calculate a "secure checksum" of a larger value. For example, suppose that we're building a "thin device" that has very little space for internal nonvolatile storage but instead must fetch most of its system image from a remote file server. How can we be sure that the adversary hasn't modified the image that we're going to load and run? Naively, we might try calculating the checksum of the genuine image, using a standard parity-based approach, and storing that internally; when we get the alleged image, we'll calculate that checksum and compare. However, we'd have a problem: Although they may perform well at detecting some types of random errors, these standard checksum functions won't work against an adversary, since they don't have second-preimage resistance. Given the correct image x and the evil y the adversary wants to run, it's generally pretty easy to find a functionally equivalent y' that will give the same checksum as x. However, if we use a cryptographic hash instead, we'll be safe.

In this straightforward approach, we need to see all of M if we want to verify whether $H(M)$ equals some h. For settings where this might not be appropriate, we can build a set of messages into a *Merkle tree* (see Figure 7.19). Message hashes go at the leaves; each parent then gets the hash of the concatenation of the hashes on its children. A Merkle tree lets us prove that a leaf message contributed to the root, by exhibiting the leaf hash and the path from that leaf to the root. For example, in this diagram, we could show that M_3 contributed to h_6 by exhibiting M_3, h_2,

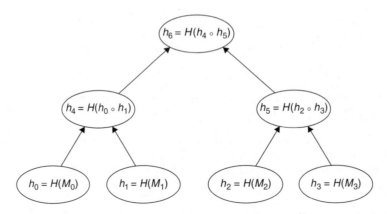

Figure 7.19 In a Merkle tree, we build a hash value representing 2^N messages by building a depth-N binary tree.

and h_4. The verifier can produce h_3 by hashing M_3 and combine it with h_2, which we presented, to generate h_5. Then, by combining h_5 and h_4, which we presented as well, the verifier can generate h_6. Note that we didn't have to disclose any other messages; verification relied only on our message and some other hashes in the tree.

In Section 7.4.2, we showed how one might build a keyed MAC from a block cipher. We can also use hash functions to build keyed MACs. Naively, one could simply prepend the key to the message before hashing. However, the slightly more complex *HMAC* construction has better security properties [NIS02].

In the preceding approaches, we were using hash functions to achieve integrity. We can also use hash functions for authentication. Suppose that Alice has published $H(x)$. If someone is claiming to be Alice and Bob wants to verify that claim, then he can ask her to exhibit x. Bob can then quickly check whether the offered x hashes to the published $H(x)$. Of course, this approach has some problems: Once Alice reveals x, it's no longer secret. She can extend the lifetime of her x by *iterating* H on it (see Figure 7.20). If she publishes $H^k(x)$ and keeps records carefully, she might be able to authenticate k times before using up the power of her secret knowledge.

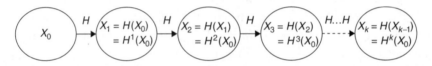

Figure 7.20 Another useful construction is iterating a hash function repeatedly on the same initial value. If Alice keeps X_0 secret but publishes X_k, then only she can calculate the sequence $X_1 \ldots X_{k-1}$.

7.7 Practical Issues: Public Key

Theoretical treatment is nice. However, these cryptographic concepts are useful in real systems only if we can build them into real systems. Consequently, it is important to look at some of the practical aspects involved in using public-key cryptography.

(This material is important in the real world but is commonly neglected in security and cryptography curricula. So, we advise you to read it two or three times.)

7.7.1 Coding

RSA all comes down to *modular exponentiation*: taking x to x^y mod N for some exponent y and large integer N. Perhaps the most straightforward way to perform this operation is to loop on y: to keep multiplying x by itself y times but reducing modulo N at each step. However, this takes y large-integer operations and can thus be slow.

A faster way is to use the *square-and-multiply* approach. We start by setting our running total to be 1. We then loop for each bit in the exponent, from most significant to least significant. First, we square the running total and reduce modulo N. Then, if the exponent bit under consideration is 1, we multiply the running total by x and reduce modulo N.

To understand this approach, let's think about the loop invariant. Let $\circ$ denote concatenation of bit strings. Then we can write $y = y_L \circ y_R$, where y_L is the sequence of bits we've handled so far, and y_R is what's left to go. Suppose that, at this point, the running total is x^{y_L} mod N.

- If the bit under consideration is 0, we square the running total and reduce modulo N. This gives us x^{2y_L} mod N. However, $2y_L = y_L \circ 0$.

- If the bit under consideration is 1, we square and then multiply. This gives us x^{2y_L+1} mod N. However, $2y_L + 1 = y_L \circ 1$.

In either case, we preserve the loop invariant: After looking at y_L, the running total is x^{y_L} mod N. (If you are worried about the base case, pretend that we prepended y with 0 and used that 0 as the initial y_L.) See Figure 7.21.

With this optimization, the execution time grows with the number of 1s in the exponent. Since Alice can choose her public exponent e fairly arbitrarily, she generally chooses an e with a small number of 1s. Common choices include

$$
\begin{aligned}
17 &= 2^4 + 1 &&= 10001_2 \\
65537 &= 2^{16} + 1 &&= 10000000000000001_2.
\end{aligned}
$$

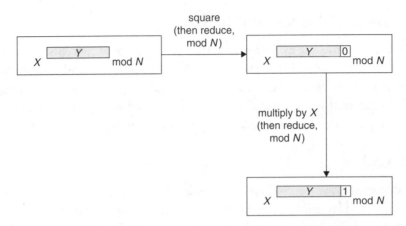

Figure 7.21 In the *square-and-multiply* implementation of modular exponentiation, we iterate through the exponent bits from left to right. If the bit is 0, we square our intermediate value; if the bit is 1, we square it and then multiply in X.

In performance-critical applications, such as SSL servers, one can find even more optimizations, such as *Montgomery multiplication*, in this vein.

7.7.2 Performance

Using cryptography in the real world brings us up against some facts of life: Public key is slow; symmetric key is fast. As a consequence of this differential, we do many things to minimize how many bits we have to run through the slow public-key algorithm.

For encryption, we almost always pick a random *session key k*, run all our bits through a symmetric-key algorithm with this k, and then encrypt the k with the public key. In this setting, sometimes called *hybrid encryption*, we treat both items—the symmetric-encrypted message and the public-encrypted symmetric key—as the public-key ciphertext. Figure 7.22 sketches this approach.

For signatures, we usually run all the bits through a *cryptographic hash* function H that transforms arbitrary-length messages to some fixed-length digest. We then transform this (short) hash with the expensive private-key operation and send this transformed hash along as the "signature." Figure 7.23 sketches this approach.

7.7.3 Padding

The preceding performance issues lead us into the some of the less-well-publicized functional elements of public-key cryptography. Cryptosystems such as RSA operate on modulus-length integers. In practical public-key encryption, we operate on a

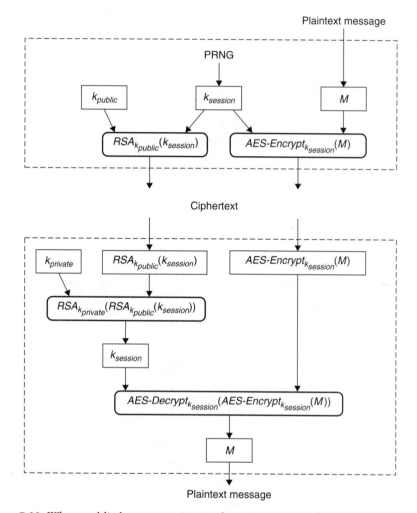

Figure 7.22 When public-key encryption is done in practice, the message is typically encrypted with a much faster symmetric cipher; the slower public-key operation encrypts this cipher's key, usually much shorter than the message. This diagram sketches example encryption (above) and decryption (below), using RSA for the asymmetric cryptosystem and AES for the symmetric one.

symmetric key; in practical signatures, we operate on a hash value. However, both of these values are typically much smaller than the public-key modulus. How do we pad out these values to a full modulus length?

Doing the obvious thing, such as padding out the short value with zeros, can lead to subtle problems. For encryption, conventional cryptographic wisdom suggests *optimal asymmetric encryption padding (OAEP)* [BR94]. For signatures,

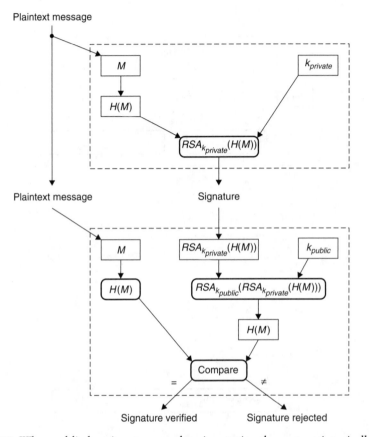

Figure 7.23 When public-key signatures are done in practice, the message is typically hashed first; the slower private-key operation encrypts the hash value, usually much shorter than the message. This diagram sketches signature generation (above) and verification (below), using RSA for the asymmetric cryptosystem.

conventional wisdom had suggested ISO 9796 [ISO97] but has recently reconsidered. RFC 3447 covers many of these practical issues involved in building systems that use public-key cryptography [JK03]. In general, it's good to use a standard padding function, but there are many to choose from, and they keep changing. Good luck!

7.8 Past and Future

The recent history of cryptography has been rather interesting. For many decades, the United States has dominated both the computer industry and computer research. However, for decades, the U.S. government also greatly restricted the strength of cryptography that could be exported and, some have alleged, attempted to restrict research as well. As a side effect of these restrictions, many U.S. vendors would simply default to the weaker exportable cryptography on all products. As we observed in Section 3.2 and discuss in Section 8.1.1, there's a rich vein of public policy issues here. (See Levy for a starting point [Lev03].) Fortunately, as of this writing, things have become much saner, as some of these restrictions have been relaxed.

As for the future, NIST[7] has been reworking its recommendations for cryptography, to take into account both recent developments and long-term trends. In recent strawman taxonomies, NIST separates *discrete logarithm cryptography* (DLC), which includes ECC, from *integer factorization cryptography* (IFC) and is reworking long-term key forecasts. This situation is too fluid for us to commit to in writing; however, one thing to note is that many parameters that have been regarded as strong for the foreseeable future, such as 1024-bit RSA moduli and 160-bit hashes, are now recommended to be phased out by the year 2010.

7.9 The Take-Home Message

We hope that in this chapter and the next, you gain familiarity with what these basic cryptographic elements—symmetric-key cryptography, public-key cryptography, hash functions, and so on—*are*, if you haven't run into them already. In this chapter, we hope that you gain an intuition about how you'd go about coding and using them in a system; in the next chapter, we hope that you gain an intuition about where the *cracks* might be in a system that uses them.

7.10 Project Ideas

1. Code some functions to generate and verify MACs, using CBC-DES on arbitrary strings.

2. Demonstrate how an adversary who knows the CBC-residue R of a message M under a key k can calculate the residue of a longer message M' under that key—even without knowing the key.

3. Implement TDES, using both inner CBC and outer CBC.

4. Use a crypto library, such as OpenSSL or the CryptoAPI, to write a program that generates self-signed certificates, digitally signs arbitrary messages with the private key, and verifies the signatures with the public key found in the certificate.

---

7. The National Institute for Standards and Technology. Chapter 11 discusses more about NIST and other standards bodies.

Subverting Cryptography 8

One of the most useful tools in the security toolkit is cryptography. Cryptography often plays a key role in the design and implementation of secure systems. However, often when we use cryptography in a practical setting, what we really think about is an abstract model of how cryptography ought to work. Unfortunately, reality is often messier than abstract models.

In this chapter, we present cautionary tales, discussing many areas where this gap has caused security problems.

- Section 8.1 examines attacks made against symmetric-key cryptosystems that do not require brute force.

- Section 8.2 looks at some of the popular brute-force attacks on DES.

- Section 8.3 discusses a variety of attacks on public-key cryptosystems.

- Section 8.4 considers attacks made possible because cryptography doesn't exist simply as ideas on paper; to be useful, it must be embodied in electronic devices in the real world.

- Section 8.5 discusses some of the background involved in quantum computing and how such machines could potentially change the game of public-key cryptography.

8.1 Breaking Symmetric Key without Brute Force

It's tempting to think of a symmetric cryptosystem as a nicely behaved black box. We plug in a key and a plaintext, and out comes a ciphertext that hides all the information about the plaintext (that is, at least all the information that is computationally available). If we use a standard, off-the-shelf (and thus, one hopes, well-vetted) cryptosystem, the only way the adversary can break things is via *brute force*: trying every possible key until finding the one that works. Consequently, as long as we pick a system with a key length long enough to make brute-force attacks impractical, then we have nothing to worry about.

This mental model is attractive and convenient. Unfortunately, history provides numerous examples of its failure to match reality.

8.1.1 Random-Number Generation in Closed-Source Code

Symmetric cryptography requires keys. Where do these keys come from?

In 1996, the Web was just beginning to take off. Most users browsed the Web with Mosaic or the newer Netscape clients. Various approaches for securing Web connections were proposed; the *Secure Sockets Layer (SSL)* from Netscape came to dominate. (Chapter 12 discusses this topic in more detail.)

SSL protects transmissions with symmetric cryptography, using a random session key. In those bad old days, U.S. firms were not allowed to export products that used symmetric keys longer than 40 bits. As a consequence, two versions of Netscape were released: a *domestic* version that allowed the full 128-bit keys and an *international* version that restricted the key length to 40 bits. One was supposed to be able to obtain the domestic version only if one established—to some lawyer's satisfaction, presumably—that it was not leaving the United States.

The release of the international version with its somewhat crippled cryptography generated a bit of a fuss. (One of the authors remembers not being able to determine whether his government-provided machine was running the domestic or international version—and the system administrators didn't know, either.)

Ian Goldberg and Dave Wagner, then graduate students at Berkeley, were curious about these random keys. Their discussion gives a good overview of pseudo-random-number generation and of attacks on software that uses a PRNG for random keys [GW96]. We do not need to determine the random key itself but rather only the seed for the PRNG. (Remember Figure 7.4.) If we have a way to verify a guessed key, we don't need to determine the seed exactly; rather, we only need to collect enough data about it to trim the size of the search space down to something reasonable.

Goldberg and Wagner couldn't easily examine Netscape, because the code wasn't published. So, they reverse-engineered it and discovered some interesting things. The PRNG seed depended on the time of day, the process ID (i.e., the `pid`), and the parent process ID (`ppid`). As a consequence, even the 128-bit U.S. version had only 47 bits of randomness for a remote attacker. With an account on the browser machine, the attacker could get enough data to obtain the key with about 10^6 guesses. Without an account, the attacker could also exploit rules of thumb about the `ppid`, or the fact that such services as `sendmail` leak the `pid`.

Punch Line.   The attacker could mount an effective brute-force attack on strong cryptography with long keys—because the attacker could learn enough about the seeds used to generate those keys to reduce his or her uncertainty sufficiently to make brute force feasible.

8.1.2 Random-Number Generation in Open-Source Code

One of the conclusions Goldberg and Wagner drew in their analysis of the Netscape PRNG was that "open source"—meaning, at least, published source—and "peer review" were good for security. If the Netscape browser source had been exposed to more eyes, they reasoned, then the weaknesses in PRNG seeding might have been found.

Purdue graduate students Bryn Dole and Stephen Lodin read Goldberg and Wagner's paper in a cryptography course and wondered whether they could find something similar, However, rather than reverse engineering code, they looked at publicly available source code for highly scrutinized software in widespread use: *Kerberos version 4 (Kv4)* [DLS97]. (We talk more about Kerberos in Chapter 9.)

In Kerberos, it all came down to single-DES session keys. In Kv4, the PRNG was seeded by taking the exclusive-OR of some 32-bit quantities: some time values, the process ID, the count of keys generated, and the host ID. The resulting seed is 32 bits long. Right away, we can see a problem here. The 56 bits of the DES key—or perhaps even the 112 bits of the TDES key, if we tried to strengthen the cipher—reduce, in reality, to the 32 bits of entropy of the PRNG seed.

In 1997, a brute-force search on 32 bits took 28 hours. However, Dole and Lodin noticed that the adversary could do much better. Each of the 32-bit quantities contributing to the exclusive-OR includes some bits the adversary can predict. For each of these quantities, these predictable bits are on the left—that is, they're the most significant bits in each of these 32-bit words. Since the exclusive-OR of predictable values is predictable, the most significant 12 bits of the seed are predictable!

This reduces the search space down to 20 bits, which could be done in a few seconds, with some cleverness.

Dole and Lodin's further exploration revealed more history. In 1988, Ted Anderson statistically discovered the 20 bits of entropy in the Kv4 PRNG. A stronger PRNG was written and checked into the source but was never used! Among other things, function names were changed with `#define` preprocessor statements, making it very hard to inspect the code and determine which set of functions was really being called. The authors lamented that code review can lead to a "false sense of security" and that "everything that is a potential source of randomness is insulated by abstraction and high level interfaces" [DLS97]. (This latter point would be good grist for software engineering and operating system classes!)

Punch Line.   In security code that was widely used in real enterprises, and whose source had been published and inspected, the use of strong (at the time) cryptography was subverted by poor seeding of the PRNG. The cryptography and key length were irrelevant. An adversary could easily do all sorts of mischief, such as eavesdrop on communications, impersonate someone else, or get unauthorized services.

8.2 Breaking Symmetric Key with Brute Force

In a brute-force attack, we assume that the adversary knows what cryptosystem is being used and has some text, usually a ciphertext. But missing the key, the adversary tries each one until finding one that works. On average, the adversary will need to search half the keyspace before this happens. Furthermore, for brute force to work, the adversary must have some way of testing whether the key is the right one. The *unicity distance* results from information theory (discussed in Section 7.3) help here: For commonly used cryptosystems, plaintext sets, and messages longer than a trivial length, a guessed key that decrypts the ciphertext to a valid plaintext is the right key.

During the years in which DES was the dominant symmetric cryptosystem, there was much speculation on the feasibility of brute-force attacks on DES. In 1993, *Wiener boxes* were proposed: specialized hardware that would cost $1 million but search through the keyspace in 3.5 hours [Wie96]. Jean-Jacques Quisquater and Yvo Desmedt speculated about a "Chinese Lottery": the potential for a country to leverage its large population by building key-checking hardware into radio and TVs and farming out key searches via media [QD91]. In the days when exportable Netscape browsers were restricted to 40 bits, many groups organized distributed key-cracking efforts to demonstrate the folly of this policy. (Unfortunately, these demonstrations somewhat backfired. Keys were cracked but with considerable computational efforts.)

Much of this speculation had strong political overtones. The U.S. standard—DES—was derived from IBM's *Lucifer* algorithm. However, the U.S. government had shortened the key length to 56 bits, a move that made many believe that the government deliberately weakened it in order to enable the NSA to break domestic cryptography, which would be against the law, most believed. Similar concerns were raised about the cryptographic export restrictions. Many worried that the difficulty of determining which end customers were domestic and which were not would result in the default of all commercial products, even those used domestically, using the weaker exportable key lengths. In response, the U.S. government kept claiming that such attacks on DES were infeasible. Many believed this claim. A well-regarded computer security textbook published in February 2000 even asserted, "nor do people really believe that hardware power has reached the point of feasibility."

This assertion is interesting, because in preceding years, it had shown to be wrong. In 1997, John Gilmore, Paul Kocher, and others in the *Electronic Frontier Foundation (EFF)*[1] started looking at how to build clever DES search hardware, basically as an "up yours" to the U.S. government position on cryptographic regulation.

First, they considered a simple hardware module. They assumed that "interesting plaintext" is specifiable as strings over some set of interesting bytes. So, their module takes as input a 256-bit vector specifying these interesting bytes. Their module also takes two blocks of ciphertext and has control register bits to specify chaining, IV, and so on. The module then takes a guessed key and tries it on the first block. If each byte of the plaintext is interesting—that is, is in the set specified by the vector—the module tries the second block. If the bytes are still interesting, the module reports the key as interesting. The module then increments the guessed key, tries that one, and so on.

The EFF researchers then built *Deep Crack*, a massively parallel machine with 1,500 chips that each contained 24 of these search modules. Software set these chips up and checked the interesting results. The resulting machine cost $250,000 (in 1997 dollars) and could consistently search the full keyspace in 9 days. If you want to build one, go ahead: The EFF published the designs and specifications in machine-scannable form and placed it all in the public domain [EFF98].

---

1. Put simply, the EFF is the Internet equivalent of the ACLU. Their aims probably sound good to most of the population. Many support the group whole-heartedly, but others can be put off by the group's choice of battles.

Punch Line. DES was the dominant symmetric cryptosystem in the open world. The prevailing wisdom among most players was that brute-force attacks on 56 bits were not worth worrying about, because building hardware to carry them out efficiently would be far too expensive to be feasible. This prevailing wisdom was wrong.

8.3 Breaking Public Key without Factoring

Just as with symmetric cryptography, it's tempting to think of public-key cryptography as a black box with one warning label. Yes, if the adversary can factor the modulus (or otherwise efficiently solve the "hard problem" on which the cryptosystem is based), then the game is over. But otherwise, the adversary has no hope of learning details of encrypted data or forging signatures without knowing the private key.

Again, as with symmetric cryptography, we use this convenient mental model of public key when building secure systems. However, the mental model does not quite match reality. We now survey a few interesting departures.

The first of these are of historical interest:

- Problems that emerge because RSA encryption does not actually hide all information about its plaintext (Section 8.3.1).

- Problems that emerge if we simply give everyone a key pair and start encrypting and signing (Section 8.3.2).

The remainder are ongoing causes for concern:

- Some relatively recent breaks in the *padding* functions used in public key encryption and signatures (Section 8.3.3).

- Some relatively recent breaks in the *hash* functions used in signatures and in many other places (Section 8.3.4).

8.3.1 Cheating at Mental Poker

As we just noted, system designers like to think that public-key encryption computationally hides all information about the plaintext. (The information is still present, but the adversary cannot feasibly extract it without knowledge of the private key.)

As discussed in Section 7.5, RSA works because of number theory. Another piece of number theory magic is the *Jacobi symbol*, written $J()$. For an integer A and modulus N, the Jacobi symbol $J(A, N)$ will be $-1, 0$, or 1.

We can build a number of fun protocols with public key; one is for *mental poker*. This protocol includes a way for two players to shuffle and deal a deck of cards over the telephone [GM82]. In a note with the marvelous title *How to Cheat at Mental Poker*, Dick Lipton points out that some public key encryption schemes preserve the Jacobi symbol: that is, the ciphertext has the same Jacobi symbol as the plaintext [Lip81]. This is somewhat like shuffling a deck of cards but still having the color of the suit show through the back of each card.

Punch Line.   A short-term solution to this sort of problem is to structure the plaintext space so they all have the same Jacobi symbol. However, the reader might justly worry that such a solution is just a Band-Aid. Encryption should hide everything, but suddenly, here's a property it doesn't hide. What *other* properties are there that it doesn't hide?

8.3.2 Naive RSA

After learning the RSA cryptosystem, we might be tempted to go off and start using it for signing and encryption in larger secure systems. However, naive application of RSA can get us into trouble. (Remember what *naive* means in computer science: the obvious, straightforward way, until we figured out better ways.)

Suppose that our system uses RSA to sign messages by ensuring that the message is always smaller than the modulus and then doing the private-key operation directly on the message. We can trick Alice into signing a message M she didn't intend to. Let e be Alice's public exponent and N be her modulus. We pick a random X and calculate $X^{-1} \bmod N$. We calculate $Y = X^e \bmod N$. We then calculate a decoy message $M_D = YM \bmod N$. Because of the random-looking nature of Y, the decoy message M_D looks nothing like M. We innocently ask Alice to sign M_D, and, since it looks OK, she returns $U = M_D^d \bmod N$. Using substitution and the fact that (modulo N) $X^{ed} = X$, we calculate

$$
\begin{aligned}
U X^{-1} \bmod N &= M_D^d X^{-1} \bmod N \\
&= Y^d M^d X^{-1} \bmod N \\
&= X^{ed} M^d X^{-1} \bmod N \\
&= X M^d X^{-1} \bmod N \\
&= M^d \bmod N.
\end{aligned}
$$

The final result is Alice's signature on M. (Cue maniacal laughter.)

Suppose that our system uses RSA to sign and encrypt by operating on raw data and also has players use the same key pair for both signing and encryption. Here's how we can trick Alice into decrypting something she didn't want to and didn't realize she was doing. Suppose that C is the ciphertext of M, encrypted for Alice under her public key. (That is, $C = M^e \bmod N$.) We pick a random R less than the modulus N and then calculate the following:

$$
\begin{aligned}
X &= R^e \bmod N \\
Y &= (XC) \bmod N \\
T &= R^{-1} \bmod N.
\end{aligned}
$$

We ask Alice to sign Y, which gives us $U = Y^D \bmod N$. We then calculate

$$
\begin{aligned}
TU \bmod N &= TY^d \bmod N \\
&= TX^d C^d \bmod N \\
&= TR^{ed} C^d \bmod N \\
&= TRC^d \bmod N \\
&= R^{-1} RC^d \bmod N \\
&= C^d \bmod N \\
&= M^{ed} \bmod N \\
&= M \bmod N.
\end{aligned}
$$

We have tricked Alice into decrypting C for us! (For a nice discussion of these "gotchas," see Schneier [Sch96, p. 471].)

Suppose that our system uses RSA to encrypt by operating on raw data. Alice can get into trouble all by herself, without any help. Suppose that she sends message M to all her friends and encrypts it for them. However, suppose also that these friends are all following the standard practice of having a low public exponent, and they've all chosen the same one (say, $e = 3$). Obviously, they have different moduli (say, N_1, N_2, N_3).

Thinking that she's secure, since she's using strong public-key cryptography, Alice sends her three messages out on the public net:

$$
\begin{aligned}
Y_1 &= M^3 \bmod N_1 \\
Y_2 &= M^3 \bmod N_2 \\
Y_3 &= M^3 \bmod N_3
\end{aligned}
$$

We eavesdrop on these values. Using the *Chinese Remainder Theorem*, a standard number-theory technique, we can easily calculate

$$
\begin{aligned}
Y &= Y_1 Y_2 Y_3 \bmod (N_1 N_2 N_3) \\
&= M^3 \bmod (N_1 N_2 N_3).
\end{aligned}
$$

Since $M < N_i$ for each i, we have $Y = M^3$. We know how to calculate cube roots in $\mathbb{Z}$, so we can get M. Thanks, Alice!

Hastad's *Broadcast Attack* showed a more general result [Has88]. If Alice ends up doing operations in K different public keys where the operations in question turn out to be polynomials of degree d on one unknown and satisfy a few other restrictions, then we as the eavesdropper can efficiently solve for the unknown, if $K > d^2$.

Punch Line. It's easy to abstract RSA and other cryptosystems as these magic black boxes. Although this abstraction makes it easier to use these tools in large systems, the abstraction can also make us overlook the fact that these black boxes actually have a rich internal structure. Now and then, smart people reach into this structure and pull out scary weaknesses.

8.3.3 Padding Functions

The troubles in the previous section stemmed from the *multiplicative homomorphism* of RSA. For data X, Y, and exponent z, this property gives us that

$$(X^z \bmod N)(Y^z \bmod N) \quad = \quad (XY)^z \bmod N.$$

In the previous section, we were encrypting and signing by using RSA to operate on raw data. However, since these operations were simply modular exponentiations, we ended up with multiplicative homomorphism on our various cryptographic primitives. That is, for a primitive F, we had

$$F(X)F(Y) \bmod N \quad = \quad F(XY \bmod N).$$

Section 7.7.3 introduced the use of *padding functions* for public-key operations. One of the main purposes of these functions is to defeat attacks in the spirit of Section 8.3.2. Requiring data to go through a padding function before going through modular exponentiation breaks the multiplicative homomorphism—as well as other weaknesses in that vein, we hope. Requiring randomization in the padding function helps further—for example, by ensuring that the same plaintext does not keep encrypting to the same ciphertext.

In the late 1990s, *ISO 9796* [ISO97] was considered the right way to pad for signatures. Then, something interesting happened. In 1999, Coron et al. [CNS99] showed that, for padding schemes very close to real-world ones, such as ISO 9796, theory suggests that complicated but tractable computations can calculate new signatures from old signatures. This was not a fatal problem, yet.

However, 2000–2001 subsequently brought a flood of follow-on work. Coppersmith, Halevi, and Jutla pushed the technique through to a complete break, but carrying it out required the adversary to trick the victim into signing thousands of messages chosen by the adversary [CHJ99]. Grieu then had a chosen message attack that breaks ISO 9796 for a given message, given signatures on only three selected others [Gri00]. (Furthermore, if the exponent is even, the attacker can factor the modulus!) Girault et al. then discussed some proposed fixes and why none of them work [GM00].

Consider the progression here. We had an international standard that was widely regarded as the best way to pad for signatures. A few theoretical weaknesses show up. Researchers find more holes and suggest fixes. More researchers then find more holes, even in the fixes.

In general, the problem is that these padding schemes lack complexity-based arguments for security. The conventional wisdom for now appears that OAEP [BR94] is good and that for the near future, hashing the message first will protect us. In the medium term, we advise the reader to always use a recognized standard—ANSI X9.31 exists, finally—and to test that the code in question does in fact comply with the standard.

Punch Line.   When designing secure systems using cryptographic tools, it is important to keep asking oneself: What happens if step Y breaks? Over and over, such things happen. In the case of ISO 9796, this happened in only a few years.

8.3.4 Hash Functions

A comforting fact about public-key cryptosystems, such as RSA, is that they are founded in complexity and computability theory. RSA is built on factoring, which everyone believes to be hard. (Sections 8.4.5 and 8.5 discuss these issues further.)

However, *hash functions* are another key component of public-key-based digital signatures. Unfortunately, hash functions generally seem to be based on black magic (e.g., ad hoc techniques) instead of well-founded theory. This lack of a strong foundation might cause the paranoid to worry; history has shown they might have due cause to do so.

Recall from Section 7.6.2 and Figure 7.18 that, in general, hash functions work by initializing a *chaining variable*, then repeatedly updating it by applying a *compression function* as they iterate through the message. In 1996, Hans Dobbertin, of the German equivalent of the NSA, announced that with ten hours on a slow Pentium, he'd calculated a collision on the MD5 compression function [Dob96b].[2] With this announcement, we all expected to see more data and to see all of MD5 fall apart. For almost a decade, nothing happened—except for the more cautious designers shying away from using MD5 in new systems.

Given a 20-byte hash value h, how big does a set S of messages need to be before something in S hashes to h? The simple pigeonhole principle gives us that once we have at least 160 bits of variation in our messages, collisions will exist. Furthermore, many standard message formats, such as text documents, Word files, or an electronic rendering of a driver's license, may easily permit 160 bits of variation *without* changing the semantics of this message. Colleagues of ours have discussed including photographs as part of personal digital certificates, but think of how much noise a photograph contains! Indeed, this all suggests a backward way of looking at steganography: Rather than adding structure to low-level noise, in order to hide messages, we're adding noise to low-level structure, in order to cause malicious hash collisions. (Chapter 14 will look at steganography and the more traditional way.)

More formally, suppose that our hash function generates values of length L bits. Intuitively, the brute-force way of finding a *preimage*—an x that hashes to a given h—would thus take 2^L guesses—that is, the number of possible hash values. The odds that a randomly chosen x hashes to h are $\frac{1}{2^L}$, so if we have a set $S = \{x_1, ..., x_k\}$ of guesses, we would need to get $k = 2^L$ before we would expect one of them to work. (If a coin lands heads with probability $\frac{1}{2^L}$, we need to flip it 2^L times before we can expect heads.)

However, the brute-force way to find a *collision*—an x and y such that $H(x) = H(y)$—takes only $2^{\frac{L}{2}}$ guesses (that is, the *square root* of the number of possible hash values). Although this may seem unintuitive, it follows from the same intuition that it takes 2^L flips if the coin lands heads with probability $\frac{1}{2^L}$; the key distinction is that we now need to think about *pairs* of messages rather than individual messages. The odds that any randomly chosen pair of messages hash to the same value are $\frac{1}{2^L}$; since the first element of the pair hashes to some h, getting the second element to collide is the same as randomly choosing a preimage of h. So if we have a set $P = \{p_1, ..., p_n\}$ of random pairs of messages, we would need to get $n = 2^L$ before we would expect one of them to work. However, a set of $S = \{x_1, ..., x_k\}$ messages gives us just about k^2 pairs. So, if we take $k = 2^{\frac{L}{2}}$ messages, that's 2^L pairs, so one of them should work. This phenomenon is known as the *Birthday Paradox*, owing to

---

2. The original Dobbertin paper is a maddening exercise in brevity! Dobbertin offered some more explanation in a subsequent RSA Laboratories technical newsletter [Dob96a].

	x_1	x_2	x_3	$\cdots$	x_{k-1}	x_k
x_1		$H(x_1) \overset{?}{=} H(x_2)$	$H(x_1) \overset{?}{=} H(x_3)$	$\cdots$	$H(x_1) \overset{?}{=} H(x_{k-1})$	$H(x_1) \overset{?}{=} H(x_k)$
x_2			$H(x_2) \overset{?}{=} H(x_3)$	$\cdots$	$H(x_2) \overset{?}{=} H(x_{k-1})$	$H(x_2) \overset{?}{=} H(x_k)$
x_3				$\cdots$	$H(x_3) \overset{?}{=} H(x_{k-1})$	$H(x_3) \overset{?}{=} H(x_k)$
$\vdots$	$\vdots$	$\vdots$	$\vdots$	$\ddots$	$\vdots$	$\vdots$
x_{k-1}				$\cdots$		$H(x_{k-1}) \overset{?}{=} H(x_k)$
x_k				$\cdots$		

Figure 8.1 A population of k elements gives us $\frac{k^2 - k}{2}$ pairs. If our hash function H yields L-bit values, then a pair of randomly chosen values has a $\frac{1}{2^L}$ chance of colliding. So, when our population is about $k = \sqrt{2^L}$, we'll have 2^L pairs and so can expect a collision. This phenomenon is known as the *Birthday Paradox*.

the classroom demonstration of considering how big a crowd has to be before two people have the same birthday. See Figure 8.1.

The brute-force method to find a collision for MD5, where $L = 128$, is 2^{64}. That's a lot of work. However, 2004 and 2005 were exciting years for hash functions. In 2004, Wang et al. announced that MD5 and other hash functions contained collisions [WFLY04]. Vlastimil Klima then described a method for finding collisions in about 8 hours with a standard Pentium laptop [Kli05]. In the spring of 2006, Klima reduced that to 17 seconds, and it's probably still going down [Kli06]. It's fair to say that this improves on the brute-force approach.

Let C be the MD5 compression function, and let I be a chaining value that we choose. These methods let us derive two pairs of message blocks: B_0, B_1 and B_0', B_1'. B_0 and B_0' differ only slightly; B_1 and B_1' differ only slightly. However, these pairs have an interesting property:

$$C(C(I, B_0), B_1) = C(C(I, B_0'), B_1').$$

See Figure 8.2.

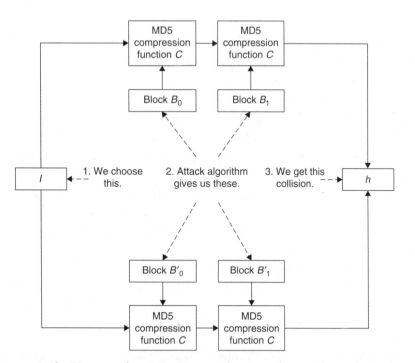

Figure 8.2 In the Wang attack on MD5, we can choose a value I. (This might be the IV for MD5 or the intermediate value of calculating MD5 on the first part of a message.) The attack lets us efficiently compute two pairs of blocks—B_0, B_0' and B_1, B_1'. B_0 differs only slightly from B_0', and B_1 differs only slightly from B_1'. However, when we iterate the compression function from I through these blocks, we get a collision.

Let's consider what these results mean. We can choose a base message M. We can then choose two consecutive blocks—let's say k and $k + 1$—in M. Starting with the initial chaining value IV, we iterate the MD5 compression function on the blocks of M until we're ready to do block k. Using the current chaining value as I, we do the magic and come up with two pairs B_0, B_1 and B_0', B_1'. We then substitute these blocks into M to obtain M_1 and M_2, respectively. We can then show

$$MD5(M_1) = MD5(M_2).$$

In March 2005, Lenstra et al. used this technique to construct two digital certificates with different public keys—*and the same hash* [LWW05]. Researchers have demonstrated other semantically interesting collisions.

These are interesting times.

In the summer of 2005, Wang et al. demonstrated weaknesses in the SHA-0 and SHA-1 hash functions [WYY05a, WYY05b]. The attack on SHA-1 involves finding a pair of messages that have a higher than normal probability of hashing to the same value. Wang et al. took advantage of mathematical weaknesses in the early rounds of the algorithm and were able to show that they can find a collision in 2^{63} operations; to find a collision with brute force takes 2^{80} operations. Their results show that one can find a collision using 2^{17} fewer operations than using brute force—that's six orders of magnitude!

To be fair, 2^{63} is still a lot of work to do, but recall from Section 8.2 that the EFF's DES-cracking machine worked on a problem of the size 2^{56}: the search space for 56-bit DES keys. A problem of this size is just on the edge of modern computing capability.

Furthermore, it's worth noting that these researchers showed that they could find a collision in 2^{63}; this is different from finding a message that has the same hash value as a given message. Such *preimage attacks* still appear to be infeasible, for both MD5 and SHA-1.

In light of these attacks, NIST held a Halloween Hash Bash on October 31, 2005, to try to decide what to do next. How deep are the current breaks going to go, and how big a family of hash techniques will they affect? One senior colleague at NIST laments his Catch-22 position:

- If the entire field is to securely migrate to a new hash function, it would take ten years.

- Currently, standard hash functions might not last ten years, so we need to start the migration now.

- We do not know what *new* function is secure enough to migrate to.

Punch Line. As Schneier pointed out on his blog in the days following the announcement, there's an old saying in the NSA that "attacks only get better, not worse" [Sch05]. We saw the MD5 attacks progress from Dobbertin to Wang to Klima over the course of nine years. At this point, we've seen the first shots fired at SHA-1. The conventional wisdom for practitioners is to start using SHA-256 or SHA-512; the conventional wisdom for researchers is to start looking for the next generation of hash functions.

8.4 Breaking Cryptography via the Real World

As we have discussed, it's easy to think of cryptographic tools as black boxes. However, even when lifting the veil of that abstraction, it's easy to still think of cryptographic tools as algorithms and mathematics. We forget that, to be used in the real world, these algorithms and mathematics need to be turned into real code running on real circuits. Even if the cryptosystem, abstracted as an algorithm, is strong, the physical nature of its real-world physical embodiment may introduce weaknesses.

8.4.1 Timing Attacks on RSA

For example, let's revisit the standard square-and-multiply approach to RSA (Section 7.7 and Figure 7.21). To calculate X^d mod N, we set our running total R to be 1 and then traverse each bit in the exponent, from most significant to least significant. For each bit, we replace R with R^2 mod N; if the bit is 1, we then replace R with $R \cdot X$ mod N.

In 1995, Paul Kocher announced some observations about this style of implementation [Koc96]. Suppose that someone has a machine that does square-and-multiply RSA with a private key we don't know but would like to know. Suppose that this machine performs its private-key operation on some data X. If we know what X is, we can try *guessing* what the exponent is. If we guess the first bit correctly, then we know exactly how long the first round should take; this means that we also then know what the R will be for the second round. This pattern repeats; if we also guess the second bit correctly, then we know what R is for the third round, and so on. However, if our initial guess was wrong, then the value of R for the second round is essentially unrelated to our prediction, so the time will be unrelated to our prediction. Furthermore, a wrong guess will give a wrong R for the next round, so the time that round takes will also be essentially unrelated to what we might predict from X and our guessed exponent.

To generalize, suppose that the private exponent has w bits. The time that the private-key operation takes on X is the sum of the individual times for each of the w rounds. We can use our guessed exponent to predict how long the overall operation should take. If the first k bits of our guess are correct but bit $k+1$ is wrong, then the first k terms of this sum will be correct, and the remaining $w - k$ will be essentially random. Thus, the difference between our guess and the real time will have these $w - k$ random values in there. Consequently, over a large enough sample of X, the difference between how long we predict X^d mod N to take, based on our guess of d, and what it actually takes will be a distribution whose *variance* will be linearly proportional to k. (See Figure 8.3.)

These observations enable us to learn the private exponent if we have a good model of how the target implementation works and if we can get the keyholder to perform the private-key operation on a large number of samples while we time how long each operation takes. We guess the first k bits of the w bits in the exponent.

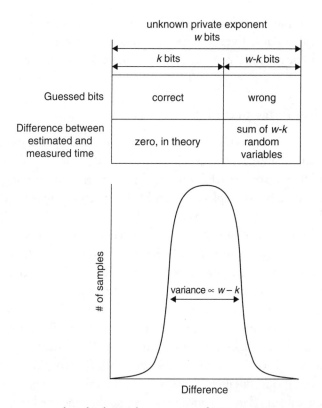

Figure 8.3 The square-and-multiply implementation of RSA permits a timing attack. Suppose that we guess the private exponent but that only the first k bits of our guess are correct. Then we can accurately estimate the time it will take to do that part of the operation, but our estimate for the rest of the operation will be off. If we look at this difference over a large enough set of samples, its variance will be proportional to how many bits we got wrong. We can thus determine the exponent with an $O(w)$ search, instead of $O(2^w)$. (For a review of this notation, see the Appendix.)

For each sample, we use our implementation model to calculate the time that the first k rounds should take, if our guesses were correct. We then measure how long the target takes and find the difference between the actual time and our estimate. By looking at the variance on the distribution of the differences of the measured times from our predicted times, we can learn whether our guess for the first k bits was correct. So, we repeat this for $k = 1, 2, \ldots, w$ to progressively learn each bit of the private exponent.

The attack extends to other public-key systems. More advanced optimizations of RSA make things trickier, and additional sources of statistical noise make the attacker's job more difficult but not impractical. In 2003, Boneh et al. even demonstrated how to carry out a timing attack against OpenSSL-based Apache servers across the Internet [BB03].

   To address these attacks, one needs to make the time of the operation be unrelated to the data and the key. Simply adding noise doesn't work; the statistics will make the noise fall right out. One approach is to use *blinding* to transform the data before the operation and to do the inverse operation afterward. Another approach is simply to force all modular exponentiations to take the same constant time.

Punch Line.   Cryptographic computation takes places in the real world. Artifacts of the physical instantiation of this computation, such as how long the computation takes, can betray information that an adversary, armed with a stopwatch and statistics, can exploit.

8.4.2 Cache Timing Attacks

As we've discussed, cryptographic software can sometimes cause the mental model and the real world to diverge. Theoretically, we can code our way out of software issues, but what happens when the hardware gives us away? In the spring of 2005, Daniel Bernstein found such a problem with the AES algorithm on a variety of processors: the Pentium III, Pentium M, IBM PowerPC RS64IV, and the Sun UltraSPARC III [Ber05]. The attack is also a form of timing attack.

   AES is a block cipher that takes a 16-byte message m and operates on it using a key that is 16 bytes or longer. Internally, AES relies on a number of arrays to hold results for particular rounds of computation. These arrays are indexed by a number that is the output of a function that takes part of the key as an argument. For example, if we let one of the internal arrays be called A, the ith element of array A is $A[m[i] \oplus k[i]]$. It turns out that measuring the time it takes to do an array lookup leaks some information about the key. Intuitively, the reason is that these private bits can influence whether the data the lookup seeks is entirely in cache or out in memory. Bernstein showed that by sending enough messages to the server, recording the time it takes for the AES software to compute the result, and doing sufficient statistical magic, an attacker can obtain the key.

   So who is at fault here: the AES algorithm or the software that implements it (in this case, OpenSSL)? As it turns out, neither the AES algorithm nor the OpenSSL library is at fault: The CPU is; more precisely, the memory access time is. At the time AES was standardized, NIST made the assumption that array lookups take constant time. This assumption turns out to be wrong and is the reason that this attack exists. The time it takes to do an array lookup depends on whether the array element is in a CPU cache and even further, whether it is in the $L1$ cache or the $L2$ cache or out in memory and is thus nonconstant. The variance in timing allows an attacker to compute $k[i]$ from the distribution of AES timings over $m[i]$ and eventually gives away the key.

Punch Line. In this case, the separation between the abstract model and the underlying reality was subtle. Even NIST can overlook such things. In response to reading the Bernstein paper, one of the AES algorithm designers replied that such attacks are irrelevant to designing cryptosystems. Although this might be true in theory, it certainly isn't in practice.

8.4.3 Hardware Side-Channel Attacks

Timing attacks are an example of *side-channel analysis:* examining ways a device can inadvertently transmit information, in addition to its official I/O channels.

Kocher's timing attacks were touted as brilliant and revolutionary. Lurking in the shadows were rumors that the attacks had already been known by certain government agencies, perhaps; someone recalled a European smartcard that took constant time. At the time Kocher's attacks were in the news, one of our own colleagues harrumphed: "That's nothing: if not time, you can use power, heat, or EMF."[3] In hindsight, we wish we had listened! The next wave of side-channel research results focused on *power analysis* [KJJ]; EMF has received attention more recently [GHT05].

Semiconductors require power. When CMOS[4] semiconductors switch, they consume power. If we can measure this power consumption, we can learn things about what gates are switching and when—which statistically can betray things about the computation the circuit is performing. Kocher et al. [KJJ] presented two approaches. With *simple power analysis (SPA)*, we simply look at the power trace and figure out what was going on. (We have seen this done to a commercially released smartcard that performed DES; the power trace showed 56 spikes, each one of two heights, which corresponded to the device checking parity on its key. We could read the key, by eye, from one power trace.) *Differential power analysis (DPA)* looks at much more subtle data correlations. We capture a large number of traces and ciphertexts. We pick a function that depends on these observables, a secret,

---

3. EMF stands for *electromagnetic field*; we are not discussing the one-hit wonder band that is responsible for the early 1990s song "Unbelievable." We doubt that the group is interested in cryptanalysis.
4. CMOS is one of the standard ways to build the components in digital electronics. If you're curious, it stands for *complementary metal-oxide semiconductor*.

and some aspect of the crypto processing, such that if we guess the secret wrong, the function is randomly 0 or 1. We look at the difference between the average traces where the function (with our guess) is 1 and where it's 0. If our guess was wrong, we have two uncorrelated sets; the differential trace becomes flat. If our guess was right, the differential approaches the correlation of the target function and power: the trace becomes spiky.

Defending against DPA is rather difficult. One approach is to try to build circuits that self-compensate; another way is to try to decorrelate the power from the secret through k-way secret splitting. Chapter 3 in [Smi04c] provides greater discussion of side-channel attacks.

Punch Line.   Again, cryptographic computation takes place in the real world, and real devices can generate signals that our clean abstractions do not allow for.

8.4.4 Keyjacking

During the past several years, we have seen a number of PKI companies, such as Thawte, Verisign, Aladdin, and Spyrus, try to get end users to begin using public-key cryptography. The core pitch in all the marketing literature is that using cryptography is much more secure than passwords—and in theory, it is. In practice, inspired in part by the work of Peter Gutmann, we wondered just how well an OS that requires patching on a regularly scheduled basis (i.e., Windows) can protect end users' private keys [Gut97]. Forget the elegant math and the subtleties of memory access time! What happens when we take a crowbar to the system-level cryptographic APIs? The result is something we call *keyjacking* [MSZ03, MSZ05].

The basic idea behind the keyjacking attack is to inject some code into the victim's application, such as Internet Explorer, which hijacks calls to the cryptographic APIs (i.e., the CryptoAPI). (Standard "dark arts" techniques let us do this if we can run a single user-level executable on the target machine.) Since many of the API calls take plaintext and private key *handles* as arguments, the attack code can get access to sensitive information: It can see the plaintext and use the handles to invoke its own operations on with these keys. This is essentially a software man-in-the-middle attack between a cryptography-using application and the CryptoAPI. Depending on the configuration of the victim's machine, we were able to capture plaintext, export private keys, or use the victim's private key to sign data, such as email or client-side SSL challenges.

As it turns out, moving the key off the desktop and into a token (e.g., a USB dongle) does not thwart this attack. Since applications still interact with the device through the CryptoAPI, we were still able to misuse the victim's key.

Unfortunately, no OS or browser configuration that we've seen can stop this attack. The attack is possible because the system designers operated under the assumption that the entire system is trustworthy. The implication is that if we as an attacker can convince the victim to run one user-level executable on their machine, then minimally, we can use the victim's private key at will.

Punch Line.   Even if the cryptosystem is strong, the keys are well chosen, and the implementation is not at risk of side-channel attacks, we still need to worry about whether the cryptography is being invoked by the code we thought, with the data we thought.

8.4.5 Theoretical Evidence

Everyone assumes that *factoring* equals *breaking RSA*. Is this true?

Reductions.   First, we should consider what such a statement must mean. (The tools of theoretical computer science—see the Appendix—come in handy here.) "Problem X is easy" means that an algorithm exists to solve this problem for a standard computational model with resources considered reasonable. For example, "X is in P" means that a polynomial-time Turing machine can solve X. "Problem X is no harder than problem Y" means that there exists a *reduction R* that maps X to Y.

Complexity theory gives us a range of specialized definitions of *reduction*. For an example view, we might think of R as simply an algorithm. We run on it an instance of X, and it generates zero or more instances of Y. If A is an algorithm for Y, A composed with R (written $A \circ R$) gives us an algorithm for X. That is, we simply run R on our X instance and then run A on every Y instance that this run of R produces.

In more formal treatments, we need to qualify all these statements by saying such things as "relative to the complexity class $\mathcal{C}$." We also need to cook up the math carefully so that things stay true relative to the complexity classes of interest. That is, if $A \in \mathcal{C}$ and $R \in \mathcal{C}$ or an easier class, $A \circ R \in \mathcal{C}$. The upshot of all this is that if Y is "easy," and such a reduction exists, X too is "easy."

Breaking RSA.   In order to use the tools of complexity and reduction to discuss the weakness of RSA, we need to formulate "breaking RSA" as a computational problem. Boneh and Venkatesen give a formulation that gets right to the point: They define "breaking RSA" as, given the public key, being able to do the private-key operation on arbitrary data [BV98].

Let's return to our original question: Is breaking RSA equal to factoring? To start, breaking RSA is clearly no harder than factoring. If we can factor easily, we can obtain p and q from N; as Section 7.5 discussed, knowing p and q and the public exponent e quickly lets us calculate the private exponent d.

However, what about the other direction? Is factoring no harder than breaking RSA? Initially, we might think that this is a vacuous question, because knowledge of both the private exponent d and the public exponent e will let us factor N efficiently.[5] However, recall Boneh and Venkatesen's characterization: breaking RSA requires only being able to do the private-key operation, which does not *necessarily* require knowing the private exponent.

One way to prove that factoring was no harder would be to exhibit an "easy" reduction R from factoring to breaking RSA. With such an R, we could argue that if we had an efficient algorithm for breaking RSA, we could use it with R to build an algorithm that solved the factoring problem with essentially the same work.

Boneh and Venkatesen showed that the situation was more interesting. First, they restricted their consideration to *low-exponent* RSA: the common case, when the public exponent is chosen to be small for efficiency. They also restricted their consideration to reductions that are *algebraic* and satisfy a few other esoteric properties. However, with these assumptions, they show that if such a polynomial time reduction R exists, then we can convert it to an algorithm of similar complexity that also factors—but doesn't bother using the RSA oracle.

Punch Line.   This result implies that, under these restrictions, breaking RSA does not help us factor! If a polynomial time reduction exists (that satisfies some additional properties), then factoring is as easy as the reduction. This means that if breaking low-exponent RSA is as hard as factoring via a reduction they analyzed, then *both* are easy. However, the common belief is that factoring is hard. If this belief is true, then Boneh's theorem is strong evidence that breaking low-exponent RSA is *easier* than factoring.

8.5 The Potential of Efficiently Factoring Moduli

As discussed in Chapter 7 and the Appendix, computer science looks at problems in terms of the resources necessary to solve them. If solving the problem requires too much computation, then we regard the problem as essentially unsolvable.

---

5. For the algorithm, see [MvOV96, p. 287].

As we have discussed in this chapter, RSA and related cryptosystems depend on the factoring problem, which computer science regards as being one of these essentially unsolvable problems. In theory, one could factor a number N by trying every possible divisor from $2, \ldots, \sqrt{N}$; in practice, this takes $\Omega(2^k)$ time for a k-bit integer.[6] Yes, there are optimizations, but nothing is known that does better, asymptotically. However, these apparent lower bounds hold only for traditional computers.

8.5.1 Quantum Mechanics and Quantum Computing

In the past century, we have seen an evolution in how physics models the universe. In particular, the field of *quantum mechanics* has emerged as a way to model how the universe appears to behave when we look at things on a very fine scale. This model has some unintuitive features.

- Objects can be in a *superposition of states*, or more than one state at the same time.

- We never "see" an object in more than one state, because the act of observing an object causes its superposition to *collapse* into one of its member states.

- When two objects interact, each part of each object's superposition gets involved, in a fairly complex way.

The Appendix gives more discussion and mathematical detail.

Calculating iterations of quantum processes becomes fairly complex fairly quickly. In the example in the Appendix, if we have a pure state coming in, we need two terms in our equation. If the input is a superposition of two states, then we need four terms. If the example hadn't been cooked up so nicely, we would have kept doubling the number of terms with each step.

This doubling turned out to be a problem for quantum physicists: Computerized simulations of their systems quickly grew intractable. In the 1980s, physicist and legendary character Richard Feynmann observed that, since simulating quantum systems with traditional computers was so hard, maybe we should consider building computers using quantum mechanics. As a consequence, research started developing theoretical models of quantum computing: hooking up *circuits* out of *quantum gates*. Traditional Boolean circuits operate on signals that are either 1 or 0; a quantum gate can operate on *qubits* signals that are superpositions of 1 and 0. (Again, the Appendix gives more detail.)

---

6. For a review of this notation, see the Appendix.

The question then arises: For reasonably-sized circuits (e.g., polynomial in the size of the input), what functions can be computed this way, and can we compute functions that aren't possible with reasonably sized traditional computers?

The class of functions computable by quantum circuits is formally characterized as *BQP*: languages "recognizable" by a uniform family of polynomial-size quantum circuits. Since obtaining an output from a quantum circuit requires making an observation that collapses the wave function, and wave functions collapse probabilistically according to the superposition, we have some randomness involved. The definition of "recognizable" must take the randomness into account: for example, a string s is in the language recognized by a circuit C exactly when, for some δ with $0 < \delta < \frac{1}{2}$, the circuit C will accept string s with probability at least $\frac{1}{2} + \delta$.

(Readers familiar with complexity theory will recognize that this is the type of construction typically used for randomized complexity classes. The term *BQP* derives from the elements involved in defining this class: *bounded* error, owing to the randomization; *quantum* gates; and *polynomial* size.)

8.5.2 Nagging BQP Questions

Trying to characterize the computational power of BQP is maddening. On the one hand, it would seem that BQP should be very powerful indeed, compared to traditional computers. We might conclude that, for an n-qubit input, we can cook up a superposition of all 2^n possible states of an n-bit vector in a polynomial number of states. If F is some polynomial-size classical circuit on n bits, then we could evaluate F on all possible n-bit sequences by cooking up this superposition of all of them and then running F on the superposition. Readers familiar with complexity theory might immediately recognize this approach as practically a way to calculate anything in the complexity class NP: functions whose solution can be verified in polynomial time.[7] Tractable *NP* is a long-sought-after Holy Grail and has generally been regarded to be impossible, so this would be big news indeed.

Indeed, the preceding construction will give us a polynomial-size circuit that calculates F on every possible n-bit input. So why doesn't BQP obviously contain NP? The answer lies in the fact that we have to somehow obtain a useful output from this circuit. To have an NP engine, we need to be able to reliably observe a 1 when there exists at least one n-bit vector x such that $F(x) = 1$. However, when we observe the result of circuit, the wave function collapses and the output is probabilistic, based on the squared modulus of the amplitude. Quantum mechanics

---

7. The term *NP* derives from *nondeterministic polynomial*: polynomial time on a nondeterministic Turing machine.

will give us that F acts on all the states in the superposition at once. However, we need to cook things up so that, somehow, the amplitudes of the right answers to reinforce each other and the amplitudes of the wrong answers cancel each other out, in order for us to have a better than random shot at having the wave function collapse to the right answer.

Punch Line.   What has been shown is that factoring, the basis for RSA, and discrete logs, the basis for DSA and Diffie-Hellman, are both in BQP. If the physicists and engineers can build quantum computers for large bitsizes, that's the end of most public-key cryptography in use. Furthermore, the authors have colleagues, albeit starry-eyed ones, who insist that we will see practical quantum computation in our lifetime.

This perhaps small but certainly nonzero risk underscores the tricky nature of building secure systems based on cryptographic tools: Advances in science and engineering may lead to the rapid decay of our building blocks!

8.6 The Take-Home Message

We chose these cautionary tales deliberately. It can be easy to abstract cryptography into convenient mental models and then use them to design, build, and reason about systems. These models can lead one into the traps of commonly held but untrue beliefs. We targeted these cautionary tales to illustrate the falsehood of these beliefs.

For example, it can be easy to think of a cryptosystem as a perfect black box; the only practical way to get a particular key is via a brute-force search. We saw that one way around this is to instead attack the method by which the key is chosen. To avoid this pitfall, one could be sure to use strong PRNGs with sufficient entropy. It can also be good to use validation tests that evaluate whether the implementation matches the strong algorithms (see Chapter 11).

It can be easy to believe that brute-force attacks are never feasible. The EFF showed otherwise, with DES. To avoid this pitfall, one should be sure that cryptosystems have sufficiently large keyspaces.

It can be easy to believe that the only way to break public-key cryptography is to factor the modulus: So as long as the modulus is secure, the key pair will be secure. We saw that many ways exist to break the public key without going after the modulus. To avoid these pitfalls, one might use distinct key pairs for signing and encrypting and to stay abreast of the latest wisdom on such components as hashing and padding.

It can be easy to think of cryptosystems as abstract, clean mathematical objects. However, to be useful, they must end up as real implementations in the real world.

As we have seen, real-world objects possess observables beyond the official output of the function.

It can be easy to believe that problems, such as factoring or "inverting" a hash function, are intractable. As we have seen, developments in science have led to enhanced understanding of these problems, which is leading to potential weaknesses. To avoid these pitfalls, one might try to design a system to allow for any particular cryptographic component to break.

These tales also illustrate the point that the field of cryptography is far from static. What works today may not work tomorrow. When designing and implementing systems that use cryptography, it would be wise to plan for change. One of the principles of *object-oriented design* is to find what changes and encapsulate it, so that changes can be localized to one or a few spots in the code. This strategy can be particularly useful when dealing with cryptography. If all your system's SHA-1 routines are in one place (the same interface, object, subsystem, and so on) the changes are minimal when SHA-1 gets broken.

Finally, these tales illustrate that attacks typically travel in one direction: better. Once the seal on a cryptosystem is broken, it is time to start thinking of alternatives. Even if the initial attacks are not quite feasible on today's machinery, the safe bet is that feasible attacks will follow. As a designer and/or implementer of a secure system, it's probably time to start thinking about moving on.

8.7 Project Ideas

1. Write a tool that can carry out Kocher timing attacks on RSA key pairs with a modulus length of at least 512 bits.

2. See whether you can recreate Bernstein's timing attacks on AES.

3. Calculate the time it would take a computer of your choice to brute force a 2,048-bit RSA key.

4. Produce two program binaries that do different things but still have the same MD5 hash value.

Authentication

9

So far, we've been talking about what it takes to build and break secure systems. We started with our own personal view of what *secure* means: *Does the system remain correct?* We then went on with common *implementation blunders* that cause insecurity, the building block of *symmetric-key cryptography* and how it can be attacked, and the building block of *public-key cryptography* and how it can be attacked.

But talking about secure systems makes sense only when there's a possibility of more than one player involved. We now consider the issue of *authentication*. The systems we're interested in building typically consist of many kinds of entities—people, machines, programs on machines, data—distributed across space and time. This structure leads to a fundamental question: How do we figure out who the entity on the other end is?

Probably the first manifestation of this problem is how a machine authenticates a human user, although there are many other issues as well. This chapter covers the basics of authentication, as well as techniques for authenticating humans and systems in various settings: direct machine access, over an untrusted network, or over an untrusted network through an untrusted client.

- Section 9.1 lays out some basic definitions we use when talking about authentication.

- Section 9.2 explores some of the issues one should consider when attempting to authenticate human users.

- Section 9.3 considers the effect that human perception has on the security of an authentication system.
- Section 9.4 looks at authentication from the machine's perspective and discusses some of the common solutions to the authentication problem.
- Section 9.5 explores some advanced techniques for authenticating users.
- Section 9.6 explores two common authentication systems: Kerberos and SSH.
- Section 9.7 wraps up by covering some of the broad issues that are related to authentication, such as naming, authorization, and trust.

9.1 Basic Framework

The literature of computer security and, in fact, of computer science in general is full of discussions of *protocols.* In fact, we've probably already used the term several times without your even noticing!

However, it's good to define terms. What is a protocol, really? To start with, we might think of a protocol as a dance between two parties. (Let's call them *Alice* and *Bob*, to keep with cryptographic tradition.) However, their dance is very organized and rigid; all the rules are spelled out in advance, so that we have no ambiguity. When we design protocols for authentication (or for other things), we often think of them in terms of an interaction between Alice and Bob: a serial exchange of messages across time. We draw *ladder diagrams* to illustrate this exchange; see Figure 9.1 for an example.

In Chapter 1, we framed computing as a series of state transitions determined by such things as user actions; we then framed security as ensuring that these reachable states remain correct despite adversarial action. In this setting, what is *correctness* for an authentication protocol? Eventually, the dance ends with Alice making a

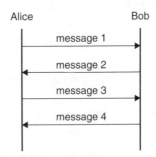

Figure 9.1 Authentication protocols are often illustrated with a *ladder diagram* showing how each party sends a particular message after receiving a particular message.

decision about Bob and perhaps with Bob making a decision about Alice as well. To be correct, these decisions should match the reality of the situation.

In particular, we as humans might think of each interaction in the context of this sequence of dance steps. However, the machines, particularly servers, that carry out these protocols don't think of it that way. Instead, the machines might think of it as "if X happens, I do Y." The protocol steps are simply services that the machines offer.

If we as adversaries start thinking about protocols that way, we can often find *other* ways to put the pieces together so that although everything still works, the decision doesn't match reality anymore. To break the protocol, we might think of each step as a service and find a way to make it useful to us. (The first two sections of Bird et al. give a good overview of this material [BIH+93].)

9.2 Authenticating Humans

Perhaps the most tangible and immediate incarnation of authentication is the login process. How can a machine figure out what human is standing at the keyboard?

The standard story, seemingly told by every proper security professor and text-book, is that authentication is achieved via *authenticators*. Authenticators come in three flavors. *Knowledge-based authentication* focuses on what the user *knows*. *Token-based authentication* is based on what the user *has*. *Biometric authentication* focuses on what the user *is*. Typically, such proper pedagogy stresses the need for *two-factor* authentication: using more than one factor. The thinking here is that, even if an attacker bypasses one authentication mechanism, that is insufficient to gain access to the system. Two-factor authentication creates more work for an attacker.

9.2.1 Passwords

Passwords are probably the most common authentication scheme. Typically, the user tells the machine his or her identity, either explicitly or implicitly, and then types in a password for that identity. This is a knowledge-based scheme, founded on the assumption that if an entity knows the password matching some userid or role (such as the administrator) then that entity is indeed that human.

Common attacks on password schemes center on the adversary simply trying to guess the correct password for the targeted victim. In an *online* attack, the adversary enters guesses directly into the authentication interface. Countermeasures for online attacks include *exponential backoff*—after each incorrect password entry, the system waits an increasing amount of time before accepting another guess—and *blacklisting*, or locking an account after some number of consecutive incorrect guesses. Traditionally, this number has been 3, although some researchers have tried to use

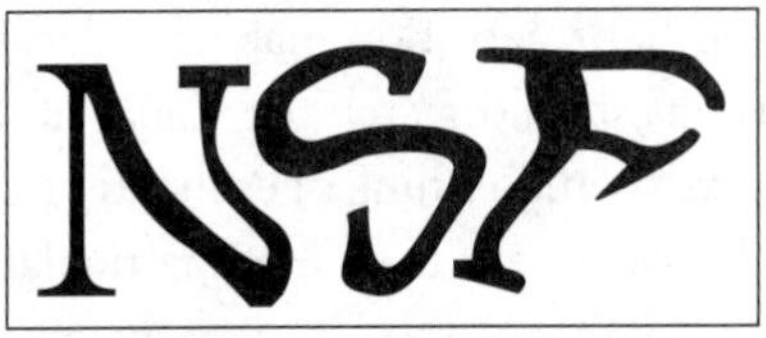

Figure 9.2 This image shows a sample CAPTCHA (from www.captcha.net). It's easy for humans to read "NSF" in this image but hard for a computer to do this efficiently.

real data to decide a better threshold [BS03]. The blacklisting countermeasure, of course, enables a denial-of-service attack. Alice can block out Bob, so perhaps he can't issue a competing bid in the auction, by entering "foobar" three times as his alleged password.

In an *offline* attack, the adversary is able to capture some information, such as the hash of a user's password, that enables him or her to go somewhere else, away from the system, and check guesses. In *dictionary* attack, the adversary can precompute such information (e.g., from a "dictionary" of likely passwords) once, thus facilitating offline attacks against a number of users.

A reverse Turing test, or *completely automated public Turing test to tell computers and humans apart (CAPTCHA)*, is another class of countermeasures against automated password guessing. In addition to a password, the server challenges the user to do a task that a human can do easily but that a computer might find challenging. Figure 9.2 shows an example. (In his early theorizing about computing and AI, Alan Turing proposed to determine that computers had achieved artificial intelligence when a human communicating with a computer and with a human could not distinguish between them; this came to be known as the *Turing test*. CAPTCHAs turn this around.)

9.2.2 Biometrics

With biometric approaches, a device typically measures a physical aspect of the user and compares it to a *template* stored for that user. Some common methods include *hand geometry* and *fingerprints*; newer methods include *iris patterns.*

Biometrics raise some challenges not found in the simpler password model. For one thing, the biometric reader may make a somewhat different measurement each time it examines the same user—so the system can't get away with doing an exact comparison to the stored template. For another thing, the human feature being measured, such as my right hand, may change from day to day, so the system may also need a way to let a user's template evolve over time. As a consequence

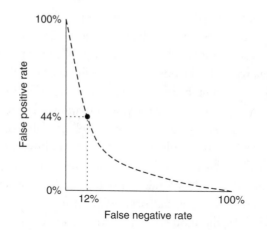

Figure 9.3 An example ROC curve. The device in question can be tuned to anywhere along the curve; for example, at the example point, we have a 12 percent false negative rate, at the expense of a 44 percent false positive rate.

of such challenges, biometric authentication systems are usually *tunable:* We can adjust them to be forgiving, leading to fewer *false negatives* at the price of more *false positives*, or exacting (vice-versa). (In this context, a false positive is when the system mistakenly authenticates an impostor; a false negative is when the system mistakenly rejects a legitimate user.)

This tradeoff between false positives and false negatives is often illustrated by a *receiver operations characteristics (ROC) curve* such as that shown in Figure 9.3. The device's behavior determines the curve, but we can tune it to select what point on the curve we desire. Picking the correct point raises additional challenges: A false positive means that we have let an adversary in, but a false negative means that we might have irritated a legitimate customer. (It seems that one can't win.)

Biometric authentication also comes with other tricky issues. Some wags characterize it as having a large password that one can never change[1] but must use everywhere. Indeed, we recall security technology trade shows where biometric vendors encouraged passersby to hand over a business card and then stick their hands and thumbs and such into their devices—and users happily complied. We doubt that asking passersby to type their userids and passwords into a terminal would have had the same success, even though the net effect was the same.[2]

The binding of authentication to body parts has other ramifications as well. A friend of ours doing a penetration test of a biometric-protected installation managed

---

1. Recent research attempts to address this limitation [RCBC06].
2. However, see Chapter 18.

to defeat the system by wrapping a bandage around his hand and claiming that it was injured, so he couldn't put it in the hand geometry reader; a fake driver's license then sufficed. One also might imagine an adversary collecting the thumbs of victims, although the media seems to document only one instance of this.

Another challenge is that, historically, vendors have often been close-mouthed about the internals of the details of their implementations. Furthermore, in practice, the technology does not always quite work as well as claimed. We know of one financial services provider that deployed a certain type of fingerprint reader because of its low cost and alleged accuracy. Much to the provider's chagrin, the deployers soon discovered that the readers achieve this accuracy only when their glass faces were kept clean, and no budget had been allowed for someone to go around to all the kiosks and clean the biometrics regularly. To make matters worse, it was rumored that simply breathing warm air onto a dirty reader would cause the reader to "measure" the fingerprint of the previous user. As another case in point, a friend of ours has managed to fool iris-recognition devices simply by holding up a photograph of someone else's iris.

9.2.3 Tokens

We talk about *tokens* in Section 9.5 and in Chapter 10.

9.3 Human Factors

By definition, authenticating humans requires working with humans. Consequently, the success or failure of an authentication technique can often depend on human factors. Do users find the system too intrusive? Do they find the system easy to use? Does the system capture the trust relationships important to users?

9.3.1 Passwords

Although password-based authentication is popular and relatively simple, it suffers from some fundamental usability problems. In a talk once, Bob Blakely put it well when he presented the following "Rules for Passwords":

1. "A good password should be too complex to remember."
2. "You should never write a password down."

Passwords are hard to remember. How many passwords do you have? Can you remember them all? Can you remember that one that you use only every 2 months?

People who study HCI[3] point out that this spontaneous, context-free recall is exactly what humans aren't good at. Do you use the same password at multiple sites?

What makes things worse is that a password that can be easy to remember can also be easy to guess, particularly if the adversary can mount a large-scale offline attack. This risk leads to the standard guidelines for picking strong passwords—e.g., passwords that can't be found in a dictionary, that use a "mixture of capitalization," that "include punctuation," and so on. Some systems enforce such rules, forcing a user to make several guesses. Some systems go ahead and pick strong passwords for users, which can be even more annoying (although sometimes systems use heuristics to pick pronounceable ones, which may help).

Other difficulties come from the lifetime of passwords. If a system or account came with a default password, did you change it? How often should you change passwords? In theory, it is a good idea to change them on a regular basis. In practice, having the system automatically enforce password change can generate considerable user ill will and forgotten passwords, if the forced change takes the users by surprise, occurring while they were in a rush to do something else and did not have time to select strong but memorable new passwords.

These struggles can often lead to the dreaded problem of users writing passwords down on Post-It notes stuck to the computer. (At trade shows, some vendors even hand out Post-Its emblazoned with "Don't Write Your Password on This!" When we need to write down a password, we usually try to pick such a Post-It. We have also heard that a well-known infotech retailer used to sell notebooks with two columns: one for "systems" and the other for "passwords.") One friend who managed security for a Wall Street firm has observed that, whenever he walks through a trading room, he can always find passwords taped to the bottoms of keyboards. The conventional wisdom is that this practice is Very Bad. On the other hand, it's not clear that this conventional wisdom is true; a colleague observed that he's never yet seen a remote attacker, coming in over the network, reach through the computer and grab a Post-It attached to the monitor.

9.3.2 Credential Recovery

Sooner or later, some users will forget their passwords. This scenario leads to the *credential-recovery* problem. Before registering a new password for that user, we need to authenticate that it's really them. But how can we authenticate the user when we can no longer authenticate the user?

---

3. "HCI" stands for *human-computer interaction*. We'll discuss HCI further in Chapter 18.

This problem can be particularly vexing in scenarios such as remote Web applications, where nonelectronic human-to-human channels don't exist. Typically, such enterprises resort to a knowledge-based scheme, such as the infamous[4] "place of birth" and "mother's maiden name."

Risks here include the *spouse effect*—a user's spouse or other close companion can often do a very good job of answering these questions—as well as the problem of revoking and reissuing such credentials. Some enterprises leverage the (relative) difficulty of an adversary's reading a user's email account and instead send a new password there.

9.3.3 Other Knowledge-Based Approaches

Of course, passwords aren't the only way to do knowledge-based authentication of humans. Many authentication systems exist based on a user's knowledge of graphics or images. For example, when registering in one system, a user chooses a subset of *faces* from a larger set [Pas06]. When the user logs in, the system presents various groups of faces randomly chosen from this larger set; the user must select those from this group that belong to his or her subset. Interestingly, follow-on research has shown that users, both male and female, tended to choose attractive women from their own race; thus, an apparently natural human tendency can greatly weaken the "keyspace" of this system.

Other image-based systems have users select more abstract images, such as *visual hashes* of random strings. Naturally, many graphical schemes rely on the user's ability to recognize a set of images. However, newer methods ask the user to input the secret over a graphical channel. *Draw a Secret (DAS)* schemes ask the user to input the secret—some sort of drawing—using a stylus. If the drawing is "close enough" to the user's original, the user succeeds. Thorpe and van Oorschot examined a number of attack possibilities on such schemes and proposed a method whereby the user first picks a particular part of the screen to draw on [TvO04a, TvO04b]. DAS schemes are still an active area of research.

9.3.4 Biometrics

Biometric approaches can engender conflicting human reactions. On the one hand, users often find such systems invasive and threatening. ("Want to use my ATM? Just press your face against this glass and let me bounce a laser off of your retina!") On the

---

4. Interestingly, human factors researchers regard these authenticators as infamous because U.S. e-government efforts believed that they were sufficient to authenticate humans in the first place.

other hand, such systems can also have an exotic, high-tech appeal, like something out of a science fiction film. Sometimes, users show both tendencies simultaneously. Colleagues doing user tests on a biometic device they were considering deploying found that users felt threatened—and were also eager to "queue up around the block" to try the device.

9.3.5 Sharing

A property of many authenticators, such as passwords, is that they are de facto transferable. Alice can tell Bob her password. Whether this is a bug or a feature depends on one's point of view. The conventional wisdom is that this is a Bad Thing. After all, if the foundation of access control, resource management, and such things is that knowledge of password implies identity, then sharing passwords subverts everything.

On the other hand, this point of view is rather technocentric and neglects to ask *why* the users are sharing authenticators. When we look into this, we can find some interesting scenarios. Locally, Dartmouth students still away for break share passwords in order to successfully complete check-in services that must be done on campus. Sharing her password is also the only way Alice can have Bob pick up her output from the campus printer service. A colleague team-teaching a security course at another university needed to share a password with her coteacher, since the system did not allow any other way of letting the two coteachers share access. A colleague at an investment bank worries about what he calls the *access control hygiene* problem: the exigencies of quickly getting the right data to the right analysts, coupled with the inarticulateness of off-the-shelf access control [DNSW01]. Such a scenario can lead to an unmanageable mess.

To summarize, we often see users transfer credentials, against policy, because their real human processes require some type of transfer or delegation, but the authentication system was not designed for this. We revisit these issues in Section 9.8.

9.4 From the Machine's Point of View

So far, we've been discussing authentication of humans from the point of view of humans, and we've been using passwords as a central example. Let's now look at this process from the machine's point of view. What does the machine do that makes it conclude that Alice is there? What can the adversary do to disrupt this conclusion?

Let's start by trying to solve the problem. Alice types in her userid and her password. The machine wants to check whether this is valid. The most straightforward approach would be to store a table somewhere of userids and passwords and then look up Alice's real password in that table and compare it to the one Alice typed in. Although perhaps natural, this approach has a problem: This table of userids and passwords would become a highly attractive target for attackers—because once having read it, the attacker can log in as anyone.

To fix this weakness, we need a way to make these table entries less useful to adversaries but still be able to compare Alice's typed password to one. The tools of cryptography (Chapter 7) come to the rescue here. Building from first principles, we might be tempted to use a symmetric or public-key cipher somehow and keep the table entries encrypted when not in use. This, however, would raise the problem of where to keep the key, which the system needs to know, in order to decrypt the table. Alternatively, if we can always encrypt the same plaintext to the same ciphertext, then we can encrypt Alice's typed password and compare the result to the ciphertext stored in her table entry. This would still require storing a key. However, further speculation might show that we never actually need to *decrypt* the table, so we could instead use a keyless one-way function, such as a good cryptographic hash.

This final approach is now the standard practice in operating systems. On UNIX systems, the table is traditionally stored in a file called /etc/passwd. On Windows systems, the table is maintained by a subsytem known as the *Security Accounts Manager (SAM)*. However, reality is never quite as simple as a nice first-principles discussion. For one thing, the idea of first transforming the passwords under a one-way function was devised before the formal theory of cryptographic hashes was created, so rather than using MD5 or SHA-1, traditional UNIX systems use a one-way function derived from DES. For another thing—and just to keep us on our toes—this transformation is traditionally called "encryption" instead of "hashing."

The approach, as we've sketched so far, still has some risks. An adversary who obtains a copy of /etc/passwd or the password hashes from the SAM can perform *offline attacks* by guessing passwords, hashing them, and comparing the hashes. An adversary can precompute hashes of dictionaries and look for matches in each new /etc/passwd obtained. Even by looking at one /etc/passwd, the adversary can learn which users share the same password.

One countermeasure includes the use of *salt*. Suppose that user U has registered password p and that H is our password hash function. In the plain approach, without salt, we store $H(p)$ in the user's entry. With salt, we generate a random r (the "salt"), and store $H(p, r)$ and r instead of $H(p)$ in the entry. We can still quickly verify whether alleged Alice typed in Alice's password—we simply read her salt and use that when generating the hash. An adversary who obtains /etc/passwd or dumps the password hashes from the SAM can still mount a brute-force attack against one targeted account. However, the precomputation necessary for dictionary attacks has now gone up by a factor of $2^{|r|}$: The adversary needs to hash each guess for *each* possible salt value. (Our colleague Mike Atallah suggested[5] a further twist: not recording the salt in the password entries. Verifying each guess now takes $2^{|r|}$ checks, since we need to try each salt, but on a modern CPU, that may be only a few seconds. Furthermore, he suggests that users are happier when the machine seems to need to "think" a bit before completing a task as important as authentication—that fits with the principle of perceived proportionality.)

Another countermeasure to offline attacks is simply not to let the adversary read /etc/passwd. However, this is easier said than done; during the long period when /etc/passwd was world readable, various useful user-specific data found its way into the file, and various programs and applications grew accustomed to looking at /etc/passwd to get that data. This scenario led to the compromise countermeasure of a *shadow* password file: typically, /etc/shadow. The standard /etc/passwd still exists for the things that need it, except that its password entries are garbage. The real hashed passwords live in /etc/shadow, whose read access is restricted to root.

On Windows systems, the game is slightly different. There is no text file containing password hashes. Instead, the hashes are stored in an encrypted format in the Windows registry and are thus not world readable. However, a number of techniques exist to get at the raw hashes, although many of them require administrator-level privileges. The standard technique for recovering the unencrypted MD5 hashes (i.e., something similar to /etc/passwd) is to inject a DLL into the Local System Authority, which then recovers the hashes from the SAM at runtime. Tools such as Todd Sabin's pwdump2 are based on this technique [Sab00].

Of course, the adversary can try other things. If the user is logging in over an unencrypted connection, such as via telnet, the adversary can observe the password in transit. An adversary who can obtain sufficient control over the user's screen can put up a fake login window and collect passwords that way. An adversary who feels like being considerate or hiding his or her presence can even collect a password from the user but then turn around and actually log in for the user, who thus does not perceive that anything is wrong. (This approach is variously known as a *man-in-the-middle* attack, *bucket brigade* attack, or a *chess grandmaster* attack. The latter name comes from how an unskilled chess player can play two grandmasters simultaneously and be guaranteed not to lose to more than one of them if the games

---

5. At least, we remember Mike suggesting that. He might deny it, however.

are in different rooms and if the unskilled player can be black in one and white in the other.)

Both in our own classroom exercises—as well as in the wide world of successful *phishing* attacks (see Chapter 18)—users are quite happy to type their authentication credentials into a window controlled by the adversary. This behavior underscores the often-overlooked need for *mutual authentication*: Just who is the party to whom one is giving one's credentials? For example, college students might be trained to show their college ID and drivers' licenses for various services but wouldn't show them to simply anyone who asked. (Well, maybe they would.)

Other attack avenues include *TOCTOU*: in this case, taking over the communication channel after the user has authenticated. This embodiment of a TOCTOU attack is often called *session hijacking* (see Section 9.5.4). Passwords can also fall to *social engineering* attacks—basically, mimicking the ordinary communications of social networks in order to trick users into divulging secrets. Chapter 18 discusses these further.

9.5 Advanced Approaches

Passwords are a basic form of knowledge-based authentication: Alice proves herself via her knowledge of her password. However, she's been doing this in a rather basic way: by divulging the password. This approach has the unfortunate consequence that an adversary who is listening in or has successfully impersonated the login screen gains sufficient knowledge to impersonate Alice. This approach also implicitly assumes that Alice trusts the machine to which she's authenticating; this implicit assumption prevents us from even considering scenarios whereby Alice might authenticate herself to a peer user Bob. However, other approaches exist that don't force Alice to divulge her secret each time she authenticates. In this section, we survey some of those approaches.

9.5.1 One-Time Passwords

Rather than disclosing her password each time she authenticates, Alice can disclose a temporary value somehow derived from her permanent secret. Such temporary values are called *one-time passwords*. In some schemes, a temporary value can be used only once; in others, it can be used for a short period of time.

In one family of one-time password schemes, Alice carries around a *token*, a small computational device that looks like a tiny calculator, with a keypad and an LCD. This token contains a real-time clock. When Alice needs to authenticate, her token generates a temporary password from the clock time, via some function $P(t)$.

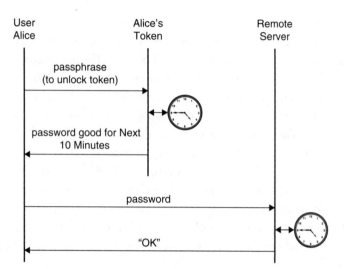

Figure 9.4 We can build a one-time password scheme by giving user Alice a hardware token that has a real-time clock.

We can turn this into a two-factor scheme by requiring Alice to type in some type of secret to the token, which then uses this secret as a parameter in calculating the one-time password. To complete the picture, the machine to which Alice wants to authenticate must be able to verify that $P(t)$ is indeed the current password for Alice. (RSA Security's *SecurID* tokens are a common commercial instantiation of this technique.) Developing schemes to generate one-time passwords from Alice's secret, the token's secret, and time is a straightforward exercise in cryptography. (See Figure 9.4, and the projects at the end of this chapter.)

Taking this idea into the real world requires worrying about some additional details, however. For one thing, we need to take into account the fact that users, devices, and networks don't follow as clean a model of time as we might like. The user may have non-negligible delay between when the token displays the password and when she types it; the network may have some delay in routing. Our protocol needs to take this time window into account. Furthermore, inexpensive electronic devices may suffer clock drift. Our protocol needs to take into account that the token's clock may not be accurate; perhaps the remote host should maintain some correction delta, updated after successful logins. (Of course, both of these features may themselves introduce new opportunities for the creative adversary.) What secrets must the token know? What if the user loses the token, or maliciously opens it up and reverse engineers it? (We consider hardware attacks and countermeasures in Chapter 16.) In order to verify the user's temporary password, what secrets about the user and token must the remote host know?

Rather than a time-based temporary password, we can also use iterated hash functions to build a sequence-based approach. (Recall Section 7.6.3 and Figure 7.20.) Suppose that Alice has a secret seed value s. For Alice, the host records a logins-left count n and also $H^n(s)$, the n-times iterated hash of her seed. When Alice goes to log in, the host tells her n. To log in, Alice or her computational proxy iterates H on the seed $n - 1$ times: that is, she calculates $H^{n-1}(s)$ and uses that as her one-time password P. The host can easily verify that $H(P) = H(H^{n-1}(s)) = H^n(s)$; if the authentication is successful, the host replaces its stored n with $n - 1$ and its stored $H^n(s)$ with $P = H^{n-1}(s)$. (See Figure 9.5.) The S/KEY system follows this approach [HM96]. The iterated hash approach works because the host can verify an alleged preimage, but (presumably) only Alice can generate such a preimage. On the other hand, the approach, as we've sketched it, can suffer from a man-in-the-middle attack: An adversary claiming to be the host and offering an n' that's much

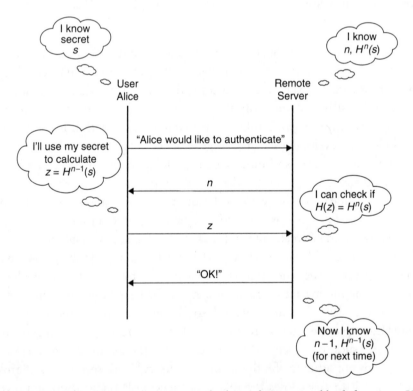

Figure 9.5 We can build a one-time password scheme from iterated hash functions. Here, Alice's secret knowledge of the beginning of the hash chain enables her to calculate all values along it—including H^{n-1}, as the server asks. The server's knowledge of the end of chain lets it verify Alice's response.

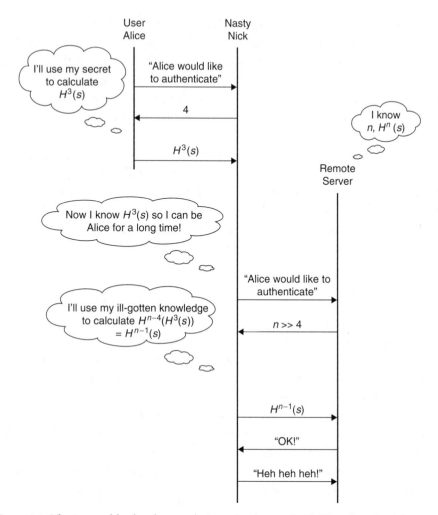

Figure 9.6 The iterated hash scheme admits a simple attack: If Alice doesn't authenticate the server, the adversary can impersonate the server once, obtain an early value in the hash chain, and then authenticate as Alice for a long time.

less than the real n can claim to be Alice for a quite a few logins, since knowledge of $H^{n'-1}(s)$ will let the adversary calculate all the $H^k(s)$ for $k \geq n' - 1$. (See Figure 9.6.)

9.5.2 Cryptographic Approaches

We've been focusing on variations of knowledge-based authentication: that Alice proves it's really her because of a secret she knows. Cryptography gives us a lot of things we can do with secrets other than simply give them away or hash them. Let's consider some various approaches.

Remembering Keys. To begin with, if Alice is going to do something crypto-graphic, she needs to remember her key somehow, and she also needs to perform cryptography with it. Since humans aren't very good[6] at the latter, these schemes generally require that Alice have access to a computer to help her log in. Sometimes, this can be her own portable token; sometimes, it can be the workstation or laptop in front of her. (Sometimes, she has both, particularly if the token does not have direct user I/O.)

If Alice carries a token, it can remember her key. However, humans can some-times remember passwords. Schemes can leverage this ability by deriving keys from this remembered data. For symmetric systems, we might hash the password. (As we shall discuss shortly, one scheme in use at Dartmouth uses the password itself, in ASCII.) For public-key systems, some researchers have suggested using the hash of the password as a seed for a PRNG and then using this PRNG to drive randomized generation of a keypair.

Public Key. Suppose that Alice has a key pair and the machine Bob knows her public key. Alice might authenticate by using her private key to sign a random value Bob provides. Alternatively, Alice might authenticate by decrypting a random value that Bob has encrypted with her public key. Of course, an implementation this sim-plistic is susceptible to various attacks. Chapter 8 showed various problems Alice can get herself into if she simply wields her private key on unknown data provided by a potential adversary. In addition to these esoteric attacks, this simplistic imple-mentation is vulnerable to something much more direct: Alice has no idea whether the challenge really came from Bob; it could have come from Carlo, carrying out a man-in-the-middle attack. In cryptographic protocols such as this, such random challenge values are known as *nonces*.

Symmetric. Perhaps Alice and Bob instead share a symmetric key K_{AB} just for Alice to authenticate. Alice might authenticate by encrypting a nonce supplied by Bob and then returning this encrypted value to Bob. Since Bob shares the key with Alice, he can check whether Alice encrypted the nonce he gave her. This is essentially how the legacy *Dartmouth Name Domain (DND)* authentication protocol works at our university (see Figure 9.7). Coupled with the way DND derives keys from passwords and with Dartmouth's move to an open wireless network, the prevalence of this authentication approach provides no end of fun in our security class.

---

6. Actually, researchers have explored *visual cryptography*, essentially doing one-time pads with trans-parent overlays, as well as some more esoteric ways of enabling humans to do cryptography. However, we don't see these in widespread use yet.

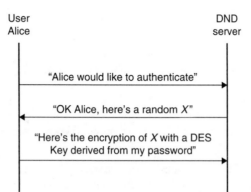

Figure 9.7 In our college's legacy DND protocol, Alice authenticates by encrypting a challenge with a DES key trivially derived from her password.

- Because of the open WLAN, it is very easy for the adversary—or the inquisitive security student doing a class project—to monitor challenges and responses.

- The single-DES symmetric cipher in use makes it almost feasible to determine a user's key via sheer bruteforce on machines lying idle around campus.

- However, the key itself is derived from concatenating the 8 ASCII bytes representing the (typable) password. Such ASCII bytes always have their most significant bit zero, but the DES standard requires that, when representing a 56-bit DES key as 64 bits, the *least* significant bit in each byte be considered as parity. (Implementations always seem to simply ignore the parity bit.) As a consequence, the effective key length is down to 48 bits (see Figure 9.8). Using assumptions about which characters a user might choose makes it even smaller.

- This weak key derivation makes brute force even more feasible. However, we would still need to do this work anew for each new user. One thing in our favor is that the open wireless network lets us observe when a user requests a challenge. Along with the lack of authentication of the DND server, the WLAN lets us send a forged response to this request. If we are in physical proximity to the user (e.g., in the same large common room at the library), we can typically get our response to the user before the genuine one comes from the DND server (see Figure 9.9). As a consequence, we can *choose* the random challenge the user encrypts and observe the ciphertext. This lets us do the brute force once on a random challenge we make up, to create a dictionary, and then use this dictionary against every user.

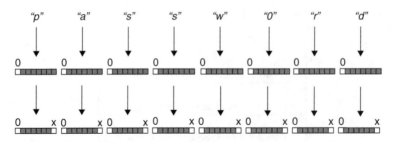

Figure 9.8 Our college's legacy DND protocol derives a DES key from a user password by concatenating the ASCII encodings of each character. However, the least significant bit of each byte is thrown out, and the most significant bit is always zero—giving an effective keyspace size of at most 2^{48}.

- Access to the WLAN lets us also observe the time it seems to take a user's machine to encrypt a challenge and respond. Some students have observed that this duration appears to be proportional to the length of the password. If the password is shorter than eight characters, the DND scheme pads it with zeroes, which would enable us to identify keys that have even fewer than 48 bits of entropy and thus are more easily searchable. We haven't yet followed up on these ideas, however.

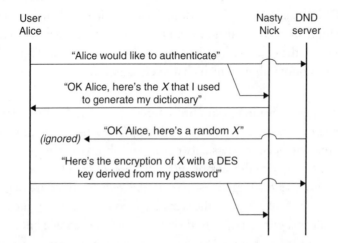

Figure 9.9 When users attempt the legacy DND authentication protocol over our open wireless network, the adversary—here, Nasty Nick—can exploit the ability to eavesdrop and the lack of authentication of the DND server in order to impersonate the DND response. This enables the adversary to look up the user's encrypted nonce in a precomputed dictionary.

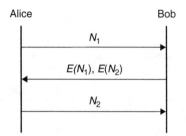

Figure 9.10 In the ISO SC27 authentication protocol, Alice and Bob use nonces to establish knowledge of a shared symmetric key.

9.5.3 Mutual Authentication

As we've seen from the weaknesses in simplistic versions of cryptographic authentication, one of the properties that's nice to have is *mutual authentication:* a dance between Alice and Bob whereby each can end up concluding that it's really the other—but neither discloses anything important if it turns out that the other one is an impostor.

All sorts of subtle issues can show up here. Bird et al. provide a rather enlightening exposition of some of them [BIH+93]. (This is recommended reading!) They consider the ISO SC27 protocol, sketched in Figure 9.10. Alice challenges Bob with a nonce. Bob encrypts the nonce but then also challenges Alice with the encryption of a second nonce. If Alice verifies it's Bob because he correctly encrypted the first nonce, then she sends back the decryption of the second.

Although an ISO standard, this protocol suffers from a number of interesting flaws. One basic flaw is that the adversary Carlo could use the chess grandmaster approach: pretend to be Bob to Alice, pretend to be Alice to Bob, and wait until Alice tries to authenticate (see Figure 9.11). In a more subtle game, Carlo could simply claim to be Bob; when Alice tries to authenticate with him, Carlo turns around and initiates a parallel authentication instance with her and uses those results to successfully complete the first session (see Figure 9.12).

In general, authentication protocols can suffer from many similar risks, sometimes rather subtle. As we discussed at the chapter's opening, it's easy to think of these protocols only as one dance between two parties; we can forget that in practice, we might have additional parties and multiple dance sessions going on.

9.5.4 Session Hijacking

As we mentioned earlier, authentication protocols can also suffer from a TOCTOU problem: Alice and Bob might mutually authenticate now, but if Alice sends a

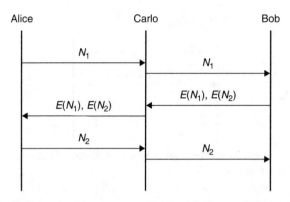

Figure 9.11 The adversary Carlo can wait until Alice initiates authentication and then perform a chess grandmaster attack.

message a little while later, is it still Bob? Was it still Alice? Or has the adversary hijacked the session?

A good countermeasure here is to set up strong *session keys* and tie them to the authentication process. Typically, deployers want both secrecy and integrity on these channels but often forget the latter. Consequently, as we saw in Chapter 7, a common approach is to establish two keys: one for a MAC and one for encryption. Typically, these keys are derived from short-lived data, such as the nonces, that only the two parties would know.

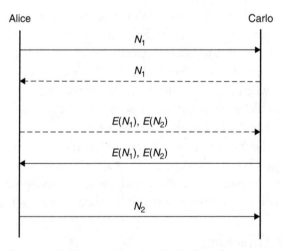

Figure 9.12 The adversary Carlo can pretend to be Bob and start a parallel session back with Alice (dashed lines) in order to learn the data necessary to complete the original session (solid lines).

9.5.5 Elements to Look For

Designing authentication protocols is an art in itself deserving its own handbook. Generally, when designing protocols or evaluating someone else's design, it's good to try to break symmetries but to enforce links. The use of nonces can complicate replay attacks. The use of direction and sequence numbers on the messages (e.g., "Alice to Bob") can make it harder for the adversary to reuse the messages for another purpose or context.

However, the hazards are many. As noted earlier, the designer must worry about *replay* attacks, when the adversary saves old messages and reuses them later: *reflection* attacks (as we saw in Figure 9.12); *oracle* attacks, when the adversary tricks a party into unwittingly answering authentication queries (e.g., by starting and abandoning authentication sessions); and extra players. On a cryptographic level, authentication protocols can do many things to make cryptanalysis easier, such as revealing plaintext/ciphertext pairs and perhaps even letting the adversary choose his or her own plaintext or ciphertext.

In general, we recommend that you *not* design an authentication protocol but instead adopt a standard, well-vetted one from one of the many cookbooks.

9.5.6 Zero Knowledge

As we discussed in Chapter 8, it can be easy to think of cryptosystems as magic black boxes that work cleanly and perfectly. In practice, these mathematical and computational functions don't cleanly hide information so much as transform it. As a consequence, each time we do something with a private or secret key, it's as if we give a little bit of it away.

Given this framework, one might wonder whether Alice can prove knowledge of her secret to Bob without giving *anything* away—not even a plaintext/ciphertext pair. The field of cryptography is a wonderland, full of suprising nonintuitive results. One of these is the existence of *zero knowledge authentication*: ways to do just that.

As an example, we start with a problem that's considered hard (in the computational sense), such as *graph isomorphism*. In this context, we use the term *graph* to represent the standard data structure made up of a set V of vertices and a set E of edges. A graph G is defined in terms of these sets: $G = (V, E)$. Given graphs G_1 and G_2, is there some permutation π of nodes such that $\pi G_1 = G_2$? Such a π would then be an isomorphism between the two graphs.

Alice's secret is that she knows such an isomorphism between G_1 and G_2:

$$\pi \;\; : \;\; G_1 \longrightarrow G_2.$$

She publishes G_1 and G_2 and announces that she knows an isomorphism. Bob might respond "Oh, yeah? Show me!" Should Alice simply say OK and reveal π?

Of course not. That would ruin everything—because Bob would then know Alice's secret. Instead, Alice generates another graph, G_3, that is also isomorphic to G_1 and G_2. She can do this simply by relabeling the nodes. Because she just did this herself and because she also knows how to get G_1 and G_2 to match up, she can also calculate two more isomorphisms:

$$\pi_1 \;:\; G_1 \longrightarrow G_3,$$
$$\pi_2 \;:\; G_2 \longrightarrow G_3.$$

(See Figure 9.13.)

So, instead of revealing her secret π, Alice reveals this new graph, G_3, and asks Bob to pick π_1 or π_2. She then shows him the permutation he asked for; Bob can verify that it's a valid permutation.

If Alice really knows π, then she can provide either π_1 or π_2. However, if "Alice" is really the adversary Carlo, he certainly could calculate either a $\langle G_3, \pi_1 \rangle$ or $\langle G_3, \pi_2 \rangle$ pair correctly. For example, Carlo could pick direction 1 and obtain a G_3 by relabeling the nodes in G_1; π_1 then follows from this relabeling. However, Carlo cannot calculate both π_1 and π_2 correctly, because that would imply that he can calculate $\pi_2 \circ \pi_1$, which, as an isomorphism between G_1 and G_2, is supposed to be Alice's secret knowledge. So as long as Alice's secret remains secret and Bob chooses

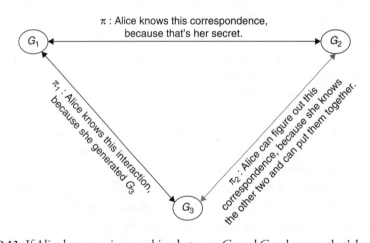

Figure 9.13 If Alice knows an isomorphism between G_1 and G_2—because that's her secret— and also knows an isomorphism between G_1 and G_3—because she generated G_3 from G_1— then she can calculate an isomorphism between G_2 and G_3.

his challenge randomly, the adversary will fail Bob's challenge with probability $\frac{1}{2}$. Each additional round of the protocol lowers the chance of the adversary's escaping undetected by another $\frac{1}{2}$, so k rounds take us down to $\frac{1}{2^k}$.

We thus see how this protocol can work to authenticate Alice. To see how Alice leaks no other information, consider what Bob or an eavesdropper observes: In each round, the adversary sees an $i \in \{1, 2\}$, a graph G_3, and an isomorphism between G_i and G_3. However, given an $i \in \{1, 2\}$, the adversary knowing G_i, which was published, can easily calculate a G_3 isomorphic to G_i, and so has learned nothing.

Punch Line.   Implementing zero knowledge protocols in practice requires dealing with many additional subtleties, such as how to generate hard instances of hard problems (and probably how to avoid patent infringement). However, we mention this protocol here to illustrate a couple of points. First, the technique Alice and Bob use of *cut-and-choose*, whereby Alice offers π_1 or π_2, but Bob chooses which one, can be a useful way of bringing fairness into protocols. (The term derives from how to share the last remaining piece of birthday cake fairly: Alice cuts the cake into two allegedly equal pieces, but Bob chooses which piece he gets. Bob's ability to choose keeps Alice honest.) Second, this technique of taking something with a rather high failure rate—with probability 50 percent that Carlo can impersonate Alice successfully for one round—and repeating until the error drops to an acceptably low rate is useful. Finally, the very idea that zero knowledge protocols can exist— and their relative ease of explanation—serves to emphasize the counterintuitive wonderland the cryptography can be.

9.6 Case Studies

9.6.1 Kerberos

Kerberos is a widely used protocol for authentication in distributed enterprise systems. The protocol came from MIT; the principal architects were Jeff Schiller and Cliff Neumann. The name *Kerberos* is derived from the three-headed guard dog of Hades in Greco-Roman mythology—*Cerberus* is the Latin spelling sometimes found in mythology.

Kerberos was developed for human users on somewhat untrusted machines, who need to access services on other somewhat untrusted machines. Developed before the emergence of public-key cryptography, Kerberos depends on symmetric-key instead.

Like most well-used, long-lived systems, Kerberos has gone through several evolutions and versions. We leave explicit details of various principal versions to other textbooks[7], and simply give a quick presentation.

In Kerberos, all parties have secret keys: usually, single-DES. For users, these are derived from passwords. The central authorities know everyone's secrets. When two parties need to communicate, they and central authorities work together to establish a symmetric key shared between—and sharable only by—the two parties who need to work together.

As we have seen, the main way a party can prove that he or she knows a secret key is to somehow use it. In Kerberos, a client does this in two steps: It uses its secret key to decrypt a message that includes a session key; it then uses that session key to encrypt a message that includes the current time. The idea is that to produce this second message, a party must have known the session key. But to get the session key from the first message, the party must have known the client's secret key.

Now, let's put this in context. Suppose that client C wishes to use a service S. If C wants to authenticate using a shared secret, then C needs to share a secret with S. It doesn't make sense for S to know C's main secret—let alone for each service S to know, a priori, secrets for all possible clients. So, Kerberos adds another party, the *ticket-granting server (TGS)* and another level of indirection in the secrets. Here's what happens.

- Assume that C shares a secret $K_{C,TGS}$ with the TGS.
- When it wants to use a service from S, C asks for a *ticket* for S from the TGS.
- C proves who he or she is by constructing an *authenticator* for this request, using $K_{C,TGS}$.
- The TGS then constructs and sends the ticket to C. This ticket is encrypted with S's secret key and includes a session key $K_{C,S}$ for C and S.
- The TGS also sends this $K_{C,S}$ session key to C, encrypted with $K_{C,TGS}$.

(See Figure 9.14.) Now, presumably only C can figure out the $K_{C,S}$ from the encrypted transmission to C, and only S can figure out $K_{C,S}$ from the encrypted ticket. So, C asks S for the service and sends the C-S ticket and an authenticator for this request, constructed using $K_{C,S}$.

To request a service ticket, the client needs to know the $K_{C,TGS}$ shared secret. Naively, this could be the user's master secret. However, it's risky for the client to

---

7. Schneier has a nice overview [Sch96, pp. 566–571]; Kauffmann et al. go into considerable detail [KPS02].

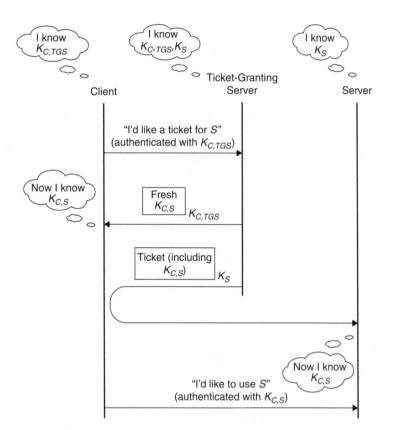

Figure 9.14 In Kerberos, two parties can authenticate by using a shared secret. In order for the client and the server to obtain a shared secret, the client requests a ticket from the TGS, which generates the fresh secret and sends it to the client in two ways: encrypted under the client's key and in a ticket encrypted under the server's key.

keep this in memory, since it's the user's master secret; it's annoying as well as risky if the client keeps asking the user to enter a password. Consequently, Kerberos introduces a second level of indirection: the $K_{C,TGS}$ shared secret is not the client's permanent secret but is rather simply a short-lived secret shared between C and the TGS. How do C and the TGS establish this secret? The same way that C and S do! C asks the master Kerberos server—which knows everyone's secrets—for a *ticket-granting ticket (TGT)*. The server responds with this TGT, which is encrypted with the TGS's secret key and includes a session key for C and TGS. The server also sends this C-TGS session key to C, encrypted with the C key (see Figure 9.15). After getting this encrypted C-TGS key, the client decrypts it, then *deletes the client key*—so that the client key is exposed on the machine only for that short period.

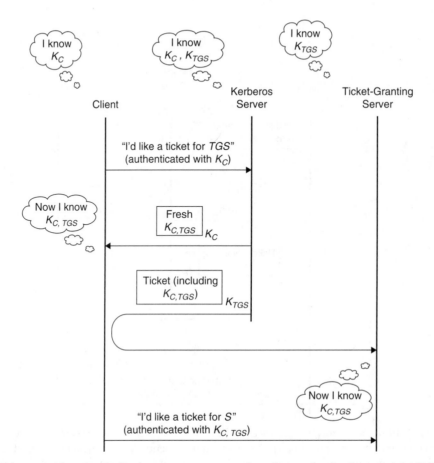

Figure 9.15 The main Kerberos server generates a shared secret for the client and the TGS. The Kerberos server sends it to the client in two ways: encrypted under the client's key and in a ticket encrypted under the TGS's key.

When it needs a ticket for S from the TGS, the client uses the C-TGS secret that the server sent to build an authenticator and then sends the authenticator and the encrypted C-TGS ticket to the TGS. With one extra step, the S server can authenticate to the client; C and S can use a shared secret for subsequent communication.

Kerberos has risks. In Chapter 8, we saw how use of a bad PRNG can undermine the system. With single-DES, session keys may be vulnerable to brute-force attacks. With human users and designers, we might see bad choices of passwords and bad mappings of passwords to keys. The master Kerberos server itself may be attacked.

When mobile users share public platforms, revoking the TGT when a user leaves a machine can be a problem.

Because vanilla Kerberos is based on symmetric cryptography, it can be difficult to use this infrastructure to get nonrepudiation of user actions. It also can be difficult for Alice to work with a party she's never met, in a different organization.

9.6.2 SSH

Not all that long ago, it was standard practice for Alice to use `telnet` when she needed to connect to a remote machine and to use `ftp` to move files to or from remote machines. However, as we discussed in Chapter 5, both of these protocols expose Alice's userid and password on the network, enabling an eavesdropper to subsequently impersonate Alice.

Even when the big, bad Internet started to be regarded as a dangerous place, these tools were still commonly used within local environments. However, the growing presence of malware in the environment made even this dangerous. In many cases, any machine on the LAN could monitor traffic; an attacker who compromised one machine could thus install a *password sniffer* that looked for the beginnings of `telnet` and `ftp` sessions and recorded the userids, destination machines, and passwords. Indeed, a common scenario we encountered was a two-sniffer attack: The adversary would leave a sniffer in a very obvious place and another in a more subtle place. The adversary's intention was that our sysadmin would discover the first sniffer, remove it, and alert everyone to change their passwords—thus enabling the second sniffer to achieve a larger catch.

Many people tried various complex solutions. The de facto standard solution that emerged was *Secure Shell (SSH)* (see Figure 9.16). SSH has the implicit goals of enabling use of comfortable legacy software while also trying to avoid the a priori shared-secret dance of Kerberos. To do this, SSH uses public-key cryptography. In its standard configuration, SSH uses public key in two ways.

1. SSH uses Diffie-Hellman key agreement (see Figure 7.17) to establish shared secrets that neither the client nor the server could have chosen on its own. This permits the client and the server to estabilish a cryptographic tunnel for encrypted, integrity-protected information.

2. During key agreement, the remote server also presents a public key and digitally signs some elements of the exchange. This permits the client to authenticate that it really is the intended host at the other end of the tunnel.

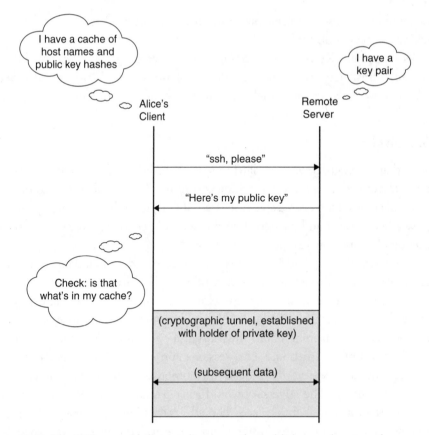

Figure 9.16 The SSH protocol allows a client to easily establish an authenticated, encrypted, and integrity-protected channel with a remote server. However, an ongoing challenge is how the client knows that the host matches that public key.

SSH thus essentially provides "drop-in" secure[8] replacements: ssh for tel-net, scp for ftp. SSH also lets the client authenticate the server, based on verifying a signature against the public key of the server. SSH has options to let users set up a key pair and leave the public-key and some other parameters on the server side and thus not have to enter a password again.

However, current deployments of SSH still possesses a risk: How does the client know what the public key of the remote machine really is? Ideally, some wonderful PKI would exist (see Chapter 10): All client machines know the public key of some

---

8. Some implementations of SSH sent each password character encrypted but separately. Some researchers have shown that, for restricted alphabets, the timing of these characters—which would be visible to an eavesdropper—can help the adversary figure out what the password is [SWT01].

trusted root and would be able to obtain and verify a certificate chain from this root to the desired host. Sadly, we don't live in an ideal world. The IETF standard advises users not to simply accept a host key blindly, but that's often what the client does. Most users simply press the Return key to keep it going. If Alice's client doesn't a priori know the server public key, she's susceptible to DNS spoofing. If the adversary can get Alice's packets to go to his or her machine, Alice loses. However, one could argue that this weakness results from a deliberate tradeoff: trading speed of deployment against security.

Punch Line. Don't ever use `telnet`; use `ssh` instead. Don't ever use `ftp` (other than anonymously); use `scp` instead. Don't blindly accept a public key unless it's on the same LAN and you have good reason to think that things are as they seem. If you go on travel, get the public keys of the servers you want to connect to first. Realize that, with the rapid evolution of the protocols and implementatations, things may change overnight.

9.7 Broader Issues

So far, we've identified the problem of authentication as determining the identity of a human user. In the real world, however, the problem is often trickier than this. For example, what we want to know about the entity is not necessarily "identity," and the entity might be a computational service of some kind. We close this chapter by considering some of these broader issues.

9.7.1 Names

We start by taking a closer look at the initial problem setting: humans and identity. It's easy to implicitly identify "identity" with "name." (In fact, we did that already in this chapter, and you didn't even notice.) Within the mental model of any one individual, these terms might be almost synonymous: each name denotes exactly one individual. However, once we expand to multiple individuals and perhaps even throw organizations into the mix, the situation becomes murky. The same name may denote different humans for different individuals; the same human may be known by multiple names. In computerized authentication systems—which typically involve many individuals and typically take things rather literally—the resulting ambiguity can be a source of trouble.

Our friend Carl Ellison calls this the *John Wilson problem*. Carl's former employer had two employees named John Wilson, an arrangement that led to no end of confusion with regard to things like travel arrangements and email. Carl observes that whenever he mentions this, listeners always say "that's nothing" and proceed to top it with an even better John Wilson story from their own experience. We are no exception. In graduate school, the first author had been only "Smith" at cs.cmu.edu, and his userid was also smith. At one point, a new email disambiguating system was put in place that led to email for other Smiths being delivered to smith@cs.cmu.edu instead,[9] unless the sender used the right Smith's exact userid. For another example, a fellow student whose first name was Dean found that using his full name in phone calls could make the wheels of academic bureaucracy turn rather quickly. Here at Dartmouth, a senior professor and occasional dean shared a first name and last name with his nephew, an undergraduate; apparently, this arrangement led to the Dean's being inadvertently invited to quite a few parties.

Some researchers might argue that globally unique names for humans do not exist. A more acceptable assertion might be that (as Carl Ellison puts it) "globally unique names are not humanly usable," and vice-versa. Some colleagues disagree and point to names based on street addresses and hometowns; we would counter with the large number of home addresses we each have had over the past 15 years.

Punch Line.   These anecdotes serve to underscore a deeper point: In large settings, the names that humans use for each other may no longer be unambiguous, which may spell trouble for computerized authentication systems based on names. As Carl Ellison would observe, email that is securely encrypted for and transmitted to the wrong John Wilson isn't really secure.

9.7.2 Authorization

Names aside, the prevailing emphasis on authentication as confirmation of identity can lead us to miss the point that often what matters is not the precise identity of the party but rather some other property he or she possesses. For example, in action movies, the police officer pounding out the door doesn't shout out his or her name and Social Security number but rather "police!" At the physician's office, a patient wouldn't care whether the doctor's name was J. Douglas Tiger rather than Douglas Tiger; what matters is that he is qualified to give medical advice.

Researchers who worry about this thus preach that *authorization* is not the same as authentication. Considering authorization as a question independent from

---

9. I would forward it on to the correct Smith; sometimes, that Smith would reply to me instead of the original sender, forcing me to forward again. I thus was a "Smith-in-the-middle."

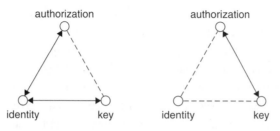

Figure 9.17 Carl Ellison uses a triangle of authorization, identity, and key to illustrate the problem of authorization. Identity-based PKI (shown on the left) requires verifying two bindings; thinking about authorization directly (shown on the right) requires verifying only one.

identity leads to several alternative models and approaches. In Chapter 10, we consider some cryptographic approaches to expressing nonidentity authorization. The classic OS access control techniques from Chapter 4 also apply: We might consider expressing authorization via access control lists or capabilities. Researchers have expanded the notion of basing authorization not on an identity but also on a special hat (e.g., "instructor") that a user could choose to wear into *role-based access control (RBAC)*. Note, however, that RBAC has come to denote that specific family of work rather than the generic idea of authorization based on roles. Other researchers have formalized the nonidentity approach as *attribute-based access control.*

Our friend Carl Ellison likes to describe the authorization problem in terms of a triangle (see Figure 9.17). We want to determine whether a user has rights to a service. The user has a secret or key or other tool for an authentication protocol. Building on identity-based authentication requires traversing two edges of this triangle; thinking about authorization directly requires traversing only one edge [Ell02].

Promoting authorization to a first-class issue worthy of deeper consideration complicates the task of *deciding* whether a party issuing a request is appropriately authorized to be granted that request. It's no longer sufficient simply to check a userid or ask for a password. As a consequence, the task of making an authorization decision about a service has begun to be abstracted away from the service itself; standards are emerging for both this decision maker and the process of asking for a decision. *Remote authentication dial-in user service (RADIUS)* is a protocol for accessing for authorization decisions that emerged in the old days of dial-up modems—so the modem could ask whether to let the caller into the network—that has found new use in enterprise WLANs and other services. Authorization servers that handle these queries have come to be known as *RADIUS servers. XACML* is a newer emerging standard for allowing a *policy enforcement point* to ask a *policy distribution point* to make an authorization decision.

Using identities can also inconveniently eliminate *delegation*. If the system is designed so that only Alice sees this data, then only Alice can see it. But if Alice needs to let Bob see it too, then she may very well end up having to disclose her password to him. The world is full of scenarios in which such *delegation* is reasonable. But if the system doesn't provide it, then users figure out a workaround. For example, here at Dartmouth, we have seen the administrative assistant to the dean of first-year students log in as the dean herself, in order to proceed with a demo.

As a final note, some researchers and practitioners will sometimes assert the existence of an inevitable tradeoff between anonymity and accountability. According to this view, if one doesn't want a service to be abused, one must require its users to authenticate—and thus reveal their identities. However, more careful thinking suggests that what matters here is that users prove they are authorized—and that proving authorization does not have to require revealing identity. Indeed, the wonderland of cryptography gives us ways to prove authorization while otherwise retaining anonymity; Chapter 14 will present some cryptographic tricks whereby identity is revealed only when a user is *illegitimate*.

9.7.3 Trust Negotiation

Authentication in the real world can thus require generalizing away from the simple notion of global identity. However, when user Alice ends up with a "wallet" full of authenticators, credentials, and attributes, she then is faced with the problem of which of these she needs to disclose to Bob in order to receive a service from him. This problem can lead to further wrinkles. What if Bob would rather keep his authorization policy secret? What if Alice herself has access control policies on her credentials: How does Bob figure out what credentials *he* should disclose in order for Alice to disclose hers? Researchers call this general problem *trust negotiation* and have pursued theoretical and applied work in this area.

9.7.4 Trust Management

As we've discussed, access to a particular resource is granted based on authorization rather than authentication. *Trust-management* systems are designed around the concept of checking whether the entity that presents a set of attributes should have access to a requested resource. The KeyNote and PolicyMaker systems embody this approach [BFIK99a, BFIK99b, BFL96, BFS98].

The trust-management approach simplifies the management of ACLs at the resource. For example, if Bob wants to access Alice's file, he presents his set of attributes to Alice. Alice first decides whether the attributes are authentic—that is, whether she believes that Bob really matches the attributes: if so, she examines Bob's attributes to check whether he should have access. For example, if the file is accessible to the group developers, Bob's attributes must state that he is a member of the group.

A number of trust-management (TM) languages handle this scenario, such as Delegation Logic [LGF03] and others [LWM03]. These languages can not only tell Alice that Bob has a certain set of credentials but also evaluate Bob's credentials and Alice's policy to determine whether she should allow the file access. Although TM languages are typically framework-specific—KeyNote, PolicyMaker, and SDSI/SPKI have their own policy languages—there have been efforts to generalize across languages [Wee01].

9.7.5 Attestation

So far, we have considered authenticating primarily humans.[10] However, in many scenarios, we want to authenticate some type of computing entity, such as a Web server or trustworthy e-wallet application. Formally defining the thing-to-be-authenticated here raises numerous sticky questions. What *is* the foo.com Web server? Is that hardware? If so, what if the operator upgrades the hardware, or even simply replaces a memory card? Is it the software stack? If so, what if the operator upgrades the software, or another vendor loads the same software stack? For any of these answers, how does remote Alice verify what she wants to know?

The rise of *trusted computing* technology has led to considerable attention on this problem of *attestation*: how a computational entity "authenticates" who it is. The same identity/authorization issues arise here as well: Does Alice really care what the hashes of the software stack are, or does she want to know whether this stack possesses certain properties? We discuss some of these issues further in Chapter 16.

9.8 The Take-Home Message

If you design and build real systems for real users, sooner or later, you'll be faced with the issue of authentication. You may want to restrict access to areas of your system or site, you may want to ensure that you use the right credit card for the right electronic shopping cart, or you may want to be sure that users have the right game stats and items when they visit your game server.

---

10. However, many of the cryptographic approaches could easily extend to the computer that wields the secrets.

In this chapter, we've outlined the basic tools for doing authentication: from passwords to biometrics to cryptographic approaches and beyond. No matter what you end up implementing, we strongly urge that the day after it's done, turn your hat around and try to break it. Authentication subsystems—the proverbial "front door" that attackers will likely knock on at least once—make some of the juiciest targets for attackers.

As with cryptography, we recommend using what's out there as opposed to "rolling your own." Use battle-tested protocols, such as SSH and Kerberos, and integrated authentication services, when available. For example, Windows has a rich set of APIs that allow developers to write authentication code that does not expose credentials.

Finally, as with just about everything in the security game, authentication technologies change. The best practices of today can hold the vulnerabilities of tomorrow.

9.9 Project Ideas

1. See how many passwords you can get! Try the variations from [Smi04b].

2. Explore the Windows authentication APIs, such as `LogonUser()`. If you hijack `advapi32.dll` and hook this call, you should be able to obtain any password on a Windows box (from a local login). This exercise requires that you get a thread running in the LSA context—not for the feint of heart but a real kick when you figure it out. *Hint:* Check out `CreateRemote Thread()`.

3. How can we use cryptography to implement the time-based one-time password scheme of Figure 9.4—while requiring no secret data to live at the server and also no secret data to live at the token, except when Alice is using it?

Public Key Infrastructure

Public key cryptography can be a wonderfully useful tool. Without sharing any secrets, Alice can sign statements that Bob can verify, Bob can encrypt things for Alice, and Alice and Bob can authenticate each other. Alice and Bob can belong to different enterprises and need never have met. Chapter 7 presented the steps involved in sending a signed message, receiving and verifying one, sending an encrypted message, and decrypting it. Chapter 9 presented the steps involved in using a public-key handshake to conclude something about the entity on the other end.

Suppose that Bob gets a message, a signature on the message, and a public key, and that he then verifies the signature on that message against that public key. If the cryptosystem hasn't fallen victim to any of the fun padding attacks described in Chapter 8, Bob can conclude that the signer of that message knew the private key matching this public key. However, in our application, we want him to be able to conclude that it was Alice. Reaching this conclusion requires a few additional premises. Usually, the main one is that Bob believes that a binding exists between this public key and "Alice"; if we get picky, we might also worry about whether Alice ever knew the private key and whether anyone else might have known it as well.

Public-key cryptography enables effective trust judgments about information services across boundaries, because parties don't need to share secrets a priori. For this to work, it is critical that Bob be able to conclude that, because an entity used a private key, that said entity must have some property (e.g., the identity "Alice"). *Public key infrastructure (PKI)*, broadly defined, is all the stuff that needs to be in place if public-key cryptography is actually going to do this in the real world.

- Section 10.1 defines some of the basic terms we use when discussing PKI systems.

- Section 10.2 develops the basic PKI model into something that represents the way PKI is deployed in the real world.

- Section 10.3 discusses the impact that complexity has on PKI systems.

- Section 10.4 illustrates some of the models for arranging particular elements in a PKI.

- Section 10.5 discusses one of the nastier parts of PKI: revocation.

- Section 10.6 describes the sometimes bizarre world of X.509, including some of its variations and alternatives.

- Section 10.7 echoes the voices of dissent in the PKI world.

- Section 10.8 discusses some of the new directions on the PKI horizon.

10.1 Basic Definitions

How do we use public-key cryptography to achieve effective trust judgments in the real world? We need a lot more than some algorithms and intractability assumptions. We sometimes like to stand on a soapbox and insist that the correct definition of *public key infrastructure* is as we stated earlier: "all the stuff" necessary. In the field, however, the more common definition focuses on the key pairs and the bindings, so that Bob can draw the correct conclusion.

In the standard, clean "textbook" presentation, we assume the existence of a trusted (and, we hope, trustworthy) Carlo who knows Alice's public key. Carlo signs a statement saying "Alice has public key E_A, N_A." Bob verifies this statement—since he trusts Carlo, by assumption, and he knows Carlo's public key, by magic—and thus can conclude that Alice has that alleged public key.

We can use this basic model to introduce some standard PKI terms. In the preceding scenario, Alice is a *principal*,[1] since she has a public key. Bob is a *relying party*. Bob is using the public key of Carlo as a *trust anchor*, also called *trust root*. The signed statement that Carlo issues is a *certificate*.[2] If he makes a habit of doing this, we say that he is a *certification authority (CA)*. (Some also call this role a *certificate authority*, although when they do, they often hear a few grumbles.) Figure 10.1 sketches this basic arrangement.

---

1. In case you're wondering what a "principal" really is, Kaufman et al. define it as "thingy" [KPS02]. We salute them.
2. A concept introduced in an undergraduate thesis! [Kor78]

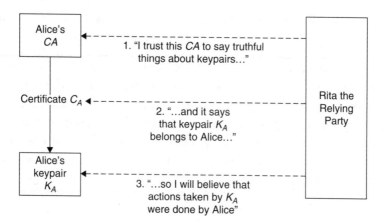

Figure 10.1 In a basic PKI architecture, the relying party believes the certificate issued by a CA that the relying party has chosen as a trust root.

However, be wary of terminology confusion more serious than simply what CA stands for. In particular, we just used the term *certificate*. In its most general sense, a certificate is a signed statement, by someone who presumably is in a position to say, binding some property to some type of entity. Typically, a certificate binds an *entity name* to a *public key*, although other variations are possible. However, some people automatically assume that a "certificate" means an "X.509v3 identity certificate." (Probably, if one counts them, these are the most common certificates in existence; however, X.509 allows more than identity certificates, and there are other formats besides X.509.)

One can also be tempted to think of a certificate as a credential like a driver's license or a passport. However, this thinking can lead one to the fallacy that a certificate is valuable in and of itself, like a big password. It can be so common to hear discussion of how a certain service requires "presenting your certificate" that it can be easy to forget that a certificate typically can be public knowledge and that "presenting a certificate" is useful only if the private key matching a public key has been used in some fashion. There needs to be an *action* as well as a credential.

In discussion, many in the field also confuse certificates with key pairs and talk about certificates that "contain a private key." This confusion is understandable. Often, when one wants to build code to deal with these things, one ends up with a certificate for each key pair; it's convenient to keep these as one data object and even to export them as one bundle (with the private key suitably protected, one hopes). As a result, one can end up calling this data structure a "certificate." Furthermore, in many PKI scenarios, a key pair has one and only one certificate, and the first thing a user does when generating a key pair is get it certified. Thus, one ends up saying things like "If you want to use these services, just install a certificate in your browser, and you're all set."

Rant.   In our opinion, conflating "certificate" with "key pair" is a serious and dangerous misuse of terminology. Certificates and private keys have different security and usage properties. Lumping them together (e.g., in a browser's security UI) is asking for trouble. A key pair may have many certificates or none at all and still be useful. It can be useful for a certificate to be issued that the keyholder never knows about. Finally, as we noted, this use of terminology can lead to thinking about a certificate as "one big password."

10.2 Basic Structure

Let's develop this basic PKI model into something more suitable for the real world.

- *Strawman 0.* The CA signs a statement about Alice's public key. Bob knows the CA's public key.

  This basic strawman has some problems, not the least of which is that neither Bob nor the CA has any reason to know that Alice really belongs to this key pair. So, let's revise it.

- *Strawman 1.* As in the preceding, but the CA generated Alice's key pair for her and then issued it to her somehow.

  Now the CA knows that the key pair belongs to Alice (and anyone she shares it with or accidentally discloses it to). However, Alice and Bob might both worry that the CA may store or accidentally disclose a copy of the private key.

- *Strawman 2.* As in the preceding, but Alice generates her key pair herself and then brings the public key to the CA.

  Now Alice can be sure that the CA hasn't snuck off with her private key. However, the CA might worry that Alice hasn't done a good enough job generating a random key pair. More important, both the CA and Bob, as well as the genuine keyholder (if it's not Alice) might worry that Alice doesn't really know the private key.

- *Strawman 3.* Alice generates her key pair herself. However, when she brings the public key to the CA, she also brings along some type of signed request showing that she knows the private key.

  This is a simple, generic PKI model that folks imagine. One can see this "certificate request" if one does something like generate a key pair for an

SSL-protected Web server with OpenSSL and follow the directions to get it certified. The CA[3] verifies that Alice is who she says is, more or less, and then verifies that Alice knows the private key matching the public key she claims. If satisfied, the CA signs off on the certificate.

Even this relatively simple scheme leaves several design choices: Should Alice carry around her certificate and offer it to those who need it? Should the CA leave it in a *repository*[4] where Bob can know to look for it? (If so, should Bob somehow have to authenticate himself first?) The security of this whole scheme also rests on the fact that the CA's private key remains private and is used only when it is supposed to be used, on the appropriate data. This raises questions of how to protect not only the CA's key but also the machines and software that invoke its use.

10.3 Complexity Arrives

Can it really be that simple? Of course not!

10.3.1 Registration

For one thing, we haven't really considered the details of the *registration* process, through which Alice convinces Carlo that she really possesses whatever properties Carlo intends on putting in Alice's certificate. We start with some basics. How *can* Alice convince Carlo that she possesses those properties? In some settings, Alice and Carlo may already have a close enough relationship—say, as coworkers or neighbors—to make that work. Here at Dartmouth, we've taken to issuing certificates to each fall's incoming students at the same time they receive their Dartmouth photo ID, in order to bootstrap off an existing process. However, such direct face-to-face contact—not to mention the numerous mouse clicks that standard tools require—imposes a minimum cost that doesn't scale well to larger user populations. In our first year trying to enroll freshmen, we achieved less than 10 percent success; human bottlenecks, such as help desk lines, choked off progress. It took much more careful logistical planning to get penetration up into the 80 percent range.

In broader settings, however, things become trickier. We recall one proposed nationwide-scale PKI that intended to register users based on driver's licenses.

---

3. If you are indignantly wondering about the *registration authority (RA)*, be patient; we'll get to that shortly.
4. The first author once had a patent filed that, owing to a clerical error, discussed *public-key suppositories.* To our lasting disappointment, the error was corrected before the patent was granted.

Those familiar with the ways of college students younger than the U.S. drinking age can testify that forging such credentials is far easier than factoring RSA moduli.

The issue of how to register also raises structural questions that tend to be "religious" in nature; that is, sizable camps emphatically hold opposing positions that are not quite supported by or amenable to reason. One issue is the relationship of the CA to the user. One might think that the closer the relationship beforehand, the greater the accuracy of the CA's assertions. However, an opposing school argues that the greater the separation, the less likely it will be that the user will unduly influence the CA. Another issue is the relationship of the CA to the party doing the registering. Naively, it would seem that they are one and the same: The CA's signature on a certificate means something only if the certificate's assertions are true. However, some formally assert a model whereby the CA is separated from the *registration authority (RA)*. Essentially, the CA outsources its judgment to one or more third parties.

Where should a CA keep its private key? Because an adversary who learns this key can probably cause considerable damage, a market niche has arisen for *hardware security modules (HSMs)*. HSMs are specialized devices that store and wield cryptographic keys and protect them from various types of physical and logical attack. Their design reflects mixed motivations: Offloading cryptographic key storage and operation from the main host may improve both performance and security. (However, if the adversary still controls the host that tells the HSM to sign certificates, it's not clear what good the physical security of the HSM has achieved.) Chapter 16 discusses principles of physical attack and defense in more detail.

A final contentious issue is whether the CA should be "online." We put this in quotes because objections seem to be raised to the idea both of the CA machine being on a network and of automated processing of certificate requests (e.g., over the Web), although the latter does not *require* the former, necessarily. The objection to network connectivity should be understandable after our discussions in Chapters 4, 5, and 6 about how, historically, operating systems and other large pieces of code have been attacked over the services they expose on the network. Secrecy of the CA's private key is paramount; the system breaks down if the adversary learns it. The objection to automated online processing otherwise is less clear, but probably stems from the absence of human operator judgment.

Although both strictures sound reasonable, both can lead to problems in practice. Keeping a CA separated from the network for a deployment not funded sufficiently for 24×7 staffing but nonetheless required to issue CRLs regularly (see Section 10.5) can drive one to consider Rube Goldberg–style devices involving things like hamster wheels. At Dartmouth, we even considered this technology

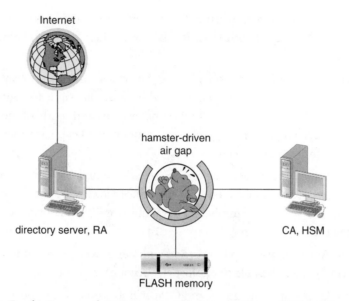

Internet

hamster-driven
air gap

directory server, RA

CA, HSM

FLASH memory

Figure 10.2 For the Dartmouth PKI, we wanted to keep the CA and HSM offline, to protect the private key and its interfaces from remote adversaries. At the same time, we needed to provide timely response to external requests and be able to issue CRLs without manned operation. To achieve these goals, we initially planned a hamster-driven air gap. (In deployment, however, we replaced the hamster with an electronic switch.)

(see Figure 10.2) but opted for something involving electronically controlled switches instead. Furthermore, designing CA tools to never operate online can make them hard to use where online access is reasonable. At Dartmouth, our initial low-assurance certificates, targeted for the security-relevant goal of getting population and services used to this new idea, were issued over a Web site, but adapting OpenCA for this purpose was hard enough that we have since considered rewriting OpenCA.

10.3.2 Key Escrow and Key Recovery

In our enumeration of strawmen, we raised and handled the concern that the CA might know Alice's private key. From the admittedly paranoid perspective of a security technologist, private keys should be private, and that should be the end of the story. In the more practical light of the real world, the case isn't so simple, particularly when it comes to private keys used for encryption. (Recall from Chapter 7 that typically, the user's private key decrypts an encoding of a symmetric key; this latter key then decrypts the encrypted file.) We enumerate some example scenarios.

- User Alice has encrypted her files but forgotten the passphrase to unlock her private key. She might appreciate it if Bob at the help desk can help her recover it.

- Citizen Alice might keep her health records on a smartcard for easy availability but also keep them encrypted because she wants to control their disclosure. However, if Alice is found unconscious at the side of the road after a cycling accident, she might prefer that random medical personnel be able to decrypt it for emergency care.

- Engineer Alice might keep her source code encrypted, to protect company secrets; however, her manager, Bob, might need access to that data should Alice be hit by a bus or simply be unavailable for 40 hours because she's off running the Barkley Fun Run.

- Student Alice might be up to no good with her university account, and Dean Bob would like to be able to explore her account for evidence.

- Citizen Alice is up to no good, and Officer Bob would like to be able to explore her account.

- Citizen Alice in another country is up to no good, and Spy Bob would like to explore her account.

- User Alice has not practiced safe computing hygiene, and her computer has become infected with malware that has encrypted her critical data files and demands a ransom before it will disclose the keys used. She might appreciate it if her OS's cryptographic library, which the malware used, had automatically escrowed the keys with which it was called so she could recover the data without paying the ransom. (Adam Young and Moti Yung [YY04] call this *kleptography* and have written a proof-of-concept virus that does just this; the malware's use of the Windows CAPI keeps it from having to carry around cryptographic implementations itself.)

Key escrow is a technology that enables a party other than the nominal keyholder to access a key, presumably only in special, emergency scenarios. In the context of PKI, the escrow question typically arises when considering an enterprise CA certifying key pairs used for encryption; such scenarios usually suggest the sane approach of having users wield *two* key pairs—one for signing and one for encryption—and having the CA escrow only the latter private key, perhaps even after generating it itself. However, we can also look at key escrow and *key recovery* techniques in the context of the symmetric ciphers used on the actual data; some proposals suggest limiting the key lengths Alice can use, to make brute force feasible for Bob or allowing him to recover only some of the bits, so he still has to use some brute-force searching, thus limiting his ability to abuse his privilege.

In theory, the technology behind escrow and recovery sounds rather straight-forward. In practice, more subtle problems arise. For example, unless we take additional steps, if Bob recovers Alice's escrowed private key, he has access to all the symmetric keys encrypted under her key pair, so he has access to all her traffic. This is problematic if the accepted policy permitted him to decrypt only some of this traffic. (These—along with rumored backdoors in the code—were some of the objections raised to the U.S. government's ill-fated Clipper/Skipjack proposal for escrowed encryption, in the previous century.) Another issue to consider is time: As we saw in Chapter 8, brute force continually gets easier. A technique that uses the difficulty of brute-force searches to limit abuse of Bob's powers may find that these barriers erode quickly.

A more serious problem with escrow and recovery is that, essentially, we are deliberately building a hole into the cryptosystem. In theory, this hole permits ap-propriate access only by appropriate parties, but it is a hole nonetheless; history (e.g., Chapter 6) shows that, in software systems, we often up with broader functionality and broader access than intended. One of us recalls a U.S. government workshop on escrow in the mid-1990s—the heady days of the cryptography export wars. The attendees were split between public sector and private sector and between pro-escrow and anti-escrow camps. However, these divisions did not correlate; gener-ally, the younger attendees (no matter their employer) opposed escrow, worrying about the future it might create for our children. One older industrial representative insisted that we needed escrow, so the U.S. government would approve strong cryp-tography, so that "we can protect General Motors from the French secret service"; this is a paraphrase, from memory. We in the opposing camp insisted that unless we move carefully, the French secret service and other adversaries could attack GM precisely *because* of the escrow hole that we deliberately installed.

A government gentleman who (through memory) looked and acted just like the title character from *Dr. Strangelove* rationalized along these lines:

> Young man, you work for Los Alamos National Lab. When I worked for Oak Ridge National Lab, we had safes in our office. Our secrets went in the safes. The combination to my safe was in my manager's safe; the combination to his safe was in his manager's safe, and so on. Get used to it.

At that time, young men working for Los Alamos were familiar with the recently published memoirs of Richard Feynman [Fey84], who worked at Los Alamos in the Manhattan Project days. He also worked at Oak Ridge. His hobbies included lock picking. In his memoirs, he observes that, at Oak Ridge, the higher in the management chain, the bigger the safe—and the more likely the officer was to have never changed the well-known default combination it shipped with. Escrow is a hole that, when implemented in the real world, can lead to subtleties that can bring the whole system down.

However, we chose this litany of example scenarios deliberately to underscore another set of issues: the wide range of types of applications of escrow and the fairly deep social and ethical implications that underlie many of these applications. The standard schoolbook vision in the United States is that government monitoring of domestic private citizen communication is permitted and moral only when an impartial court has issued a warrant; however, foreign communication might be subject to monitoring by the National Security Agency. As a consequence, this vision often provides an implicit framework for discussion of the use and ethics of escrow. However, this implicit assumption has at least two problems. For one thing, no matter how tempting it can be, especially for those of us born and raised in the United States, to believe otherwise, this vision is a cultural artifact, not necessarily following from the first principles of universal natural law. Other cultures may have different underlying firm beliefs.[5] A colleague who grew up in the "bad old days" of the Soviet Union distrusts all government and other sources of power. There are probably citizens of France who can argue why it is correct that the French secret service spy on GM.

A second reason to be wary of this assumption is that a significant gap may exist between this vision as preached and this vision as practiced. The off-the-record story from United States law enforcement is that illegal wiretaps happen all the time; once one uses these illegal methods to find out who's guilty, one uses legal methods to gather evidence for court. As of this writing, the Bush administration is practicing a wider program of domestic spying that many feel violates the fundamental rules.

Punch Line.   Be careful. Technology doesn't care who uses it.

10.4 Multiple CAs

In the initial vision for PKI and the preliminary strawmen proposals, one central trusted party would certify everyone. However, the simplicity of this model does not fit the real world. Many reasons exist for this mismatch. Some reasons pertain

---

5. To underscore this point, a colleague teaching in Switzerland set up a Web site that linked to three interesting sites: a U.S.-based hate group, pornography, and something about whiskey; the United States, Switzerland, and Saudi Arabia might each strongly object to the legality of at least one of these sites, but their views would not be consistent. Chapter 13 tells what happened.

to performance: It can be difficult for a single global CA to keep up with demanded operations. Some reasons pertain to other forms of scalability. For example, when a community grows beyond a certain size, it's not clear how effective registration verification can be or how the namespace issues will hold up (recall Section 9.7).

Another angle to consider is start-up: One should be cautious if the first step in a proposed plan is "first, assume that this global system is in place." Some reasons pertain to organizational structure. When N organizations each get impatient and start their own PKIs, how should these merge? How do we map the different organization's policies and practices to each other?

Multiple CAs are now a fact of life. Many schemes have been proposed to try to bring order to the resulting infrastructure. A clean, universally accepted taxonomy does not exist, so we offer an unclean one instead. Initially, we might start with small generalizations of the single-CA approach. In what Kaufmann et al. call the *oligarchy* approach [KPS02] but others call *extended trust lists*, a set of CAs exist, each certifying its own population; each relying party accepts some local subset of them as trust anchors. (This is what browsers do.) Generalizing in the other direction, we might form a *hierarchy* by organizing the CAs into a tree. One CA is king.

Alternatively, we might keep with independent CAs forming peer agreements. With *cross-certification*, one CA decides to trust another one and signs a statment saying "Hey, people in my domain can trust the public key of this other CA." Generally, this cross-certification is symmetric; the two CAs do it for each other. It's important to see that cross-certification is different from the parent/child relationship in a hierarchy. With cross-certification, each CA's user population still has that CA as its trust root. For example, from the perspective of the users of CA_1, CA_2 appears to be a subordinate CA attesting to another subset of the populace, but for the users of CA_2, it's CA_1 that appears to be subordinate (see Figure 10.3).

One way to use cross-certification is to randomly link together PKIs. This approach is often optimistically called a *mesh* topology; however, alternative approaches exist. In cross-certification, work needs to be done for each pair of CAs; for N CAs to interconnect, they need to set up $\Omega(N^2)$ cross-certificates: essentially, a clique on these N nodes. The *bridging* model simplifies this by introducing a *bridge CA* whose sole purpose in life is to cross-certify with other CAs in a way that enables these cross-certifications to compose (see Figure 10.4). A bridge CA is a hub in a hub-and-spoke model: Each interested CA cross-certifies with the bridge, which brings the work down to $O(N)$. Principal existing bridges include the U.S. Federal Bridge, linking together federal agency PKIs; SAFE, linking together PKIs in the pharmaceutical industry; and CertiPath, linking together aerospace corporations. Here at Dartmouth, we've been building the *Higher Education Bridge CA*

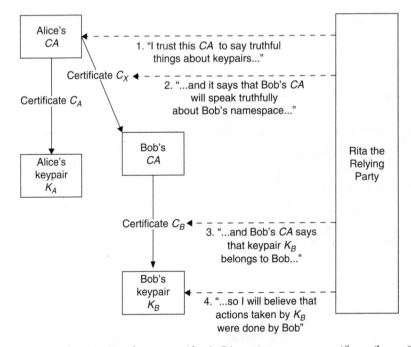

Figure 10.3 In a basic PKI architecture, Alice's CA can issue a cross-certificate (here, C_X) to another CA. This cross-certificate tells the relying parties who hold Alice's CA as a trust root to believe the assertions this second CA makes. Typically, the cross-certificate C_X includes some constraints limiting which of these assertions the relying party should believe. Note that, if Alice's CA revokes C_X, then Rita can still draw conclusions about Alice's key pair, and a relying party who trusts only Bob's CA can still draw conclusions about Bob. Typically, cross-certification is symmetric; in such a case, Bob's CA would also have issued a certificate to Alice's CA.

(HEBCA) for Educause and Internet2. Besides simplifying topology and reducing set-up work, bridging also solves a political problem: "Everyone gets to be King," as one of the U.S Federal Bridge scientists puts it.

As the organization of CAs becomes more interesting, using the PKI becomes more interesting. In general now, a relying party, Bob, no longer needs a single certificate to verify Alice's signature but rather a *certificate chain* rooted at one of Bob's trust anchors. The question of how the players find such a chain raises challenges of *path discovery;* Alice's certificate is the *target*. Formal tools for evaluating strategies for path discovery is an area of ongoing research (e.g., [EAH+01, ZSN05b]).

The introduction of more than one CA introduces issues of *key usage*. Naively, a certificate tells one that the signer asserted that a specific entity belongs to a specific public key. It does *not* tell one whether that entity is in a position to make

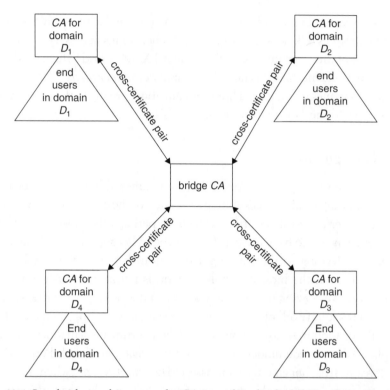

Figure 10.4 In a bridge architecture, the CA in each individual PKI still certifies its own users, and the end users in each individual PKI can still retain only their own CA as a trust root. However, users can still form trust paths to users in other domains.

key-entity assertions of its own, and, if so, for which entities. (Should harvard.edu be in a position to make meaningful statements about students at yale.edu?) Linking two certificates together as part of a chain also raises questions of *policy*, which, in the PKI world, means something a bit more specialized than the policies we saw in Chapters 4 and 5. For example, trust is not always transitive. The existence of a correctly signed path from one of Rita's trust roots to the target Bob does not necessarily imply that Rita should trust things done with Bob's private key. Rita or her enterprise may require that the intermediate CAs all follow certain practices or that the certificates have certain properties; Bob's requirements may even change depending on the context. Consider Figure 10.3 again: If Rita doesn't believe the intermediate assertions 2 or 3, the existence of the certificate path doesn't justify her final conclusion, 4. (As one practitioner put it, even if a U.S. federal CA cross-certifies with Canada's, and Canada cross-certifies with Cuba, the U.S. State Department still doesn't trust Cuba.)

As a consequence of these issues, mechanisms emerged to uniquely and precisely express these issues of key usage, policies, and other things necessary to understand the semantics of these certificates. In the standard X.509 world, which we discuss in Section 10.6, these mechanisms take the form of *object identifiers (OIDs)* and fairly complex policy rules (which, in all honesty, contribute greatly to the perception that X.509 is unwieldy and overly complex).

10.5 Revocation

A certificate binds a property to a public key. Sometimes, things can happen that can render this binding invalid, necessitating *revocation* of the certificate: Relying parties should no longer accept its assertion as true. In perhaps the most straightforward scenario, Alice needs to have her certificate revoked because her machine has been compromised, leading to the working assumption that the adversary knows the private key. In fact, the most common scenario is perhaps that Alice herself has lost her private key, owing to something as innocuous as forgetting the passphrase needed to unlock it. (Both of these scenarios have direct analogs in the credit card system.) Revocation may also be necessary when certificate semantics, other than the implicit "Alice is the unique wielder of this private key," fail. Perhaps Alice's certificate came from her employer and asserted her employment; when Alice resigns in order to form a start-up, the employer may wish to revoke her certificate. Alice still is the unique key wielder, but she's no longer an employee.

A colleague who used to work in the U.S. government tells an even more subtle revocation story. In the first Gulf War, a key part of keeping the U.S-led coalition together was keeping Israel out of the coalition. Allegedly, cryptography helped achieve this goal; overnight, the U.S. revoked the ability of the jets from Israel, a former ally, to authenticate themselves as friends, not foes.

10.5.1 Mainstream Approaches

The field takes two natural approaches to revocation. (Again, we can draw on credit cards for analogs.) In one approach, someone—typically the CA—maintains a *certificate revocation list (CRL)*: a signed statement identifying the currently revoked certificates. Although natural, CRLs raise concerns. One is network performance: Downloading the CRL can lead to performance issues for an individual user on a slow connection, as well as to broader network congestion if all users must download the latest CRL. Colleagues both in the Department of Defense and in industry tell of problems owing to congestion, following from unexpectedly large CRLs. The CRLs were unexpectedly large because, owing to various logistical and UI snags, many users unexpectedly forgot their passphrases; many of these users ended up "blacklisted" from the tokens holding the private keys. Another issue with the CRL approach is the nonzero and usually regular interval between issuance of CRLs. What if a certificate is revoked *during* this interval? More subtle issues can arise because of time; for example, an attacker who wants to trick a relying party into accepting a revoked certificate might try to substitute an older CRL, issued before the certificate was revoked.

Various optimizations and alternatives have been proposed to try to mitigate these problems. An extreme alternative approach is to dispense with CRLs altogether; with the *Online Certificate Status Protocol (OCSP)*, the relying party checks the status of the certificate online, similar to what is commonly done with credit cards today. In the OCSP scheme, servers called *OCSP responders* are connected to the CA's certificate database. Clients wishing to check the revocation status of a particular certificate connect to the responder and simply ask for the certificate's status.

10.5.2 Alternative Approaches

CRLs and OCSP are the mainstream approaches to revocation. However, they are not the only ones.

Revocation can be an annoying problem. How do we check? What about the lag between revocation and notification or between compromise and revocation? As a consequence, some researchers preach the virtues of *monotonic* systems, whereby certificates can never be revoked, although they can expire.[6] Monotonicity has theoretical appeal: Those who formally model and prove theorems about PKI often prefer monotonic systems, because it makes things much cleaner. Monotonicity also has practical appeal: Those who worry about building PKI for mobile, disconnected devices also often prefer monotonic systems—because it's hard for mobile, disconnected devices to check an OCSP or download fresh, large CRLs.

In his *NOVOMODO* system [Mic03], Silvio Micali uses iterated hashes (recall Section 7.6.3) to simplify certificate management. Let H be a strong cryptographic hash function, and let K be the number of time units (say, days) in the lifetime of a certificate. When it issues a certificate, the CA picks random values X_0 and Y_0, each

---

6. The reader may be puzzled about why the term *monotonic* is used in this context, especially because in real analysis, a *monotonic* function is one that never decreases. Logic and formal methods (branches of mathematics not typically encountered in general education or, unfortunately, computer science) extend the term to talk about assertions that never "decrease" from true to false.

the length of a hash image, and calculates the two sequences:

$$X_0 \quad X_1 = H(X_0) \quad X_2 = H(H(X_0)) \quad \dots \quad X_K = H^K(X_0)$$
$$Y_0 \quad Y_1 = H(Y_0).$$

The CA includes Y_1 and X_K in the certificate itself.

NOVOMODO supports both revocation and proof of validity. At any day, to revoke a certificate, the CA can publish Y_0. This announcement takes only 20 bytes, and the relying party can verify it with a simple hash operation. On the other hand, to prove that a certificate is still valid on day i, the CA publishes X_{K-i}. Again, both the announcement and the verification work compare favorably to more traditional signature-based schemes.

Pretty Good Privacy (PGP) takes a more egalitarian approach to PKI. The PGP *web of trust* model does not distinguish any nodes as CAs. Everyone is an end user; end users issue "certificates" about keys of other end users and use some essentially ad hoc heuristics to decide whether a certificate is trustworthy. Perhaps as a consequence of this democracy, it's up to Alice herself to issue a revocation certificate for her public key. (This may be problematic if Alice needs to revoke her key because she no longer has access to her private key.) Section 10.6.3 discusses PGP further.

The premise underlying revocation is that, unless the certificate has been explicitly revoked, the relying party should believe its assertions: that is, if the signature is valid, and if the relying party believes that the signer is in a position to make such assertions. Some organizations take the opposite approach and maintain their own *directory* of currently valid certificates; in this scenario, the organization "revokes" a certificate by deleting it from this directory.

10.5.3 Complexity and Semantics

The existence of all these wrinkles makes the problem of how to validate certificate chains nontrivial. Certificate semantics and policies lead to varying opinions about whether a relying party should accept a particular certificate as appropriate in a particular place in a trust chain. Revocation approaches lead to varying opinions about whether the signature on a given certificate is even valid. (We haven't even mentioned the potentially thorny issues of why a relying party should believe the signature on a CRL or an OCSP response!) Complex PKI topologies create the potential for multiple chains from a trust anchor to the same certificate; what should the relying party do if these chains give different answers?

It's important to remember that we're pushing certificates around and defining validation rules because we want the relying party to be able to draw the "right" conclusions about trust. Ueli Maurer has done some great formal-logic work trying to get a handle on all of this (e.g., [KM00b, Mau96]). Essentially, he asks "yes, but is it well-founded?" Do the conclusions our fancy system draws actually match any realistic notion of trust and truth? (We ourselves have made some contributions here [MS05a].) It's always good to ask these questions.

10.6 The X.509 World

What do we need to put in certificates? For the "natural" identity certificate, one clearly needs the public key and the identity of the entity. However, if we start thinking about all the other functionality discussed earlier, the need emerges for other detail as well. When does the certificate expire? When does the certificate become effective? Where does one look to find the CRL? Who signed this certificate? What cryptosystems were used for this signature? Where is the signature of this certificate? To what cryptosystem does the certificate's public key belong? What about key usage and policy?

10.6.1 The Basic View

As we can see, certificates, in general, may need to contain a lot of information. Many parties need to be able to unambiguously find and parse these fields within a certificate. Many parties need to do standard sorts of things with certificates (e.g., directory lookup, CRL check, etc.). Often, it can help if everyone speaks the same language. As a consequence, standards have emerged for formats, services, and players in PKI.

The *X.509* family dominates here—so much so that, for all intents and purposes, discussion of PKI in the real world can quickly *become* a discussion of X.509.

X.509 has a reputation for being cumbersome. If one checks the IETF material on X.509, one finds much complexity: in the certificate format, in the X.500 directory services, in the *CMP* (*Certificate Management Protocol*, which our irreverent friend Peter Gutmann describes as the *certificate mismanagement protocol*). If one talks to implementers trying to deploy X.509 PKI in the real world, one will hear further stories of how various tools from major vendors neglect to follow the standard in critical ways, thus adding to the complexity.

10.6.2 X.509 Variations

Is identity of the keyholder always enough to enable your trust decision? Most people would probably agree "no". But then they immediately disagree on what to do about it. Here, we consider some example scenarios and how X.509 has been extended to handle them.

Extensions. In many cases, the *identity* of the keyholder is not what the relying party needs to know. Rather, the relying party wants to know some other property. The dominant X.509 certificate format (X.509v3) permits *extension* fields, in which the certificate issuer can store other items meaningful to the issuer and relying-party population.

This approach has downsides, however. By definition, extensions contain assertions made by the issuer of the identity certificate; by construction, these assertions have the same lifetime as the containing certificate; by construction, these assertions go anywhere the certificate goes.

Attribute Certificates. Suppose that Dartmouth arranged with the University of Illinois to allow students in a particular class at Illinois to view the class Web site for CS38 at Dartmouth. We could keep an ACL of those Illinois students who are allowed to see it, and we could use SSL client-side authentication to let them in. However, this would require us, at Dartmouth, to maintain a list of those students at Illinois taking this class. How do we know? Wouldn't it be much easier if we let someone at Illinois say who's in the class? In theory, we could put this information in an extension in each student's identity certificate. However, this would require the Illinois CA to know about our security course arrangement before we could do this. Furthermore, how often do students change their class enrollments? Must Illinois reissue identity certificates every term and revoke certificates when students drop a class? What if the Illinois professor would also like to grant access to students and staffers who are informally auditing the course but not "taking it" in the eyes of the registrar?

In the X.509 world, one scheme to support this approach involves the use of *attribute certificates.* An *attribute authority (AA)* issues a signed statement binding an *attribute* to an entity, which is usually specified as a name but apparently sometimes can be specified as a public key. When she approaches the Web site, Alice at Illinois might present her identity certificate signed by the Illinois CA, to prove that Illinois says that the party who knows the private key matching a particular public key really is Alice at Illinois, and an attribute certificate signed by the Illinois CS38 AA, saying that whoever proves she's Alice is OK to see the material. Placing the AA at Illinois (perhaps in the hands of Prof. Nicol, teaching the course) makes sense, since it mirrors the way trust flows in the real world: Prof. Smith at Dartmouth to Prof. Nicol at Illinois to Prof. Nicol's students.

David Chadwick and others have even formalized a whole *privilege management infrastructure (PMI)* framework as an analog to PKI, with a *source of authority*

(*SOA*) replacing a trust anchor. Chadwick's *PERMIS* system might be the principal deployment of attribute certificates to date [COB03].

Research questions persist here, as we discuss in Section 10.7.

Proxy Certificates.   In some cases, the relying party cares about neither the identity nor other personal attributes of the keyholder. Rather, the relying party wants to know who the keyholder is representing.

For example, suppose that Alice wants to run a program on Bob's computer. This program needs to run a long time, while Alice is off doing something else. This program also needs Alice's privileges, in order to access restricted services and data. However, Alice doesn't want to download her private key to Bob's computer!

Scenarios like this occurred with regularity in the *Grid*, a distributed computing environment developed to support cooperative scientific computing. As a consequence, Grid security researchers introduced *proxy certificates* into X.509. Alice generates a special key pair and signs a short-lived proxy certificate saying that the keyholder can act as Alice. (We've even explored using X.509 extensions to let Alice restrict the certificate's rights as well as its lifetime [MS05b].) Alice then leaves the certificate and private key with the program, which acts as Alice.

The real world gives many human-to-human scenarios as well. Suppose that it's the beginning of the Dartmouth spring term but that student Alice is still away skiing in the White Mountains. Alice would like her fellow student, Bob, to complete the required term-start sign-in for her. Unfortunately, the proxy certificate specification seems to deliberately discourage delegating rights to a public key that exists in any other certificate, which seems, on the face of it, to unreasonably exclude many useful scenarios. (Anecdotes claim that the X.509 leadership insisted that X.509 "is not going to become PGP!")

Of course, things always become interesting when one tries to actually carry out ideas in the real world. In particular, we've been finding that X.509 attribute certificates can be a nice solution to some real-world authentication problems. Nonetheless, we've also ended up using X.509 proxy certificates and pretending that they're attribute certificates, thus probably annoying zealots on all sides, primarily because standard cryptographic software handles proxy certificates but not attribute certificates.

10.6.3 Alternatives to X.509

Various alternative schemes have been proposed over the years.

PGP. The principal alternative is *Pretty Good Privacy (PGP)*, developed by Phil Zimmerman more as a political act—to enable the right to "whisper in someone's ear, even if their ear is 1,000 miles away"—rather than a mere technological one. In contrast to the hierarchical bent of X.509, with CAs and end users, PGP takes an egalitarian approach. Users are equal; users sign statements asserting a belief that a friend's public key matches his or her identity and exchange these assertions. Each user can then use draw trust conclusions about the keys accumulated in his or her *key chain*, based on confidence in the parties involved in the assertion's provenance. As we noted, the PGP community uses the term *web of trust* for this distributed, ad hoc system. (See [Zim95] and [CDFT98] for a good introduction to PGP; [KM00] gives a sharp criticism of its trust methodology.)

SDSI/SPKI. The *Simple Distributed Security Infrastructure (SDSI)* and *Simple PKI (SPKI)* merged into *SDSI/SPKI*, occasionally pronounced "sudsy spooky." (One sometimes hears *SPKI/SDSI* instead.) As the name stresses, a key design factor here is *simplicity*: principals *are* public keys; global names do not exist; certificates merely assert local properties, such as the signer's delegation of authorization. (See [CEE+01, EFL+99, Ell99, RL96] for more discussion.)

Even so, it remains an X.509 world. One wonders whether a better way exists or whether the complexity of X.509 PKI itself somehow follows inevitably from the complexity of the human and organizational trust fabric it is trying to express.

To those dissuaded by the messiness of X.509, we can only offer the following balm: There may be lots of reasons to dislike X.509, but one must pay attention to it if one wants to be relevant to real-world infrastructure.

10.7 Dissent

Many researchers and deployers continually raise some significant objections to the X.509 approach to PKI. Some of these objections are obvious. X.509 is incredibly, incredibly complex. (Imagine you were a student, and the professor assigned "prove that this X.509-based scheme is correct" as a homework problem.) X.509 was built on the *ASN.1* notation, which might be described as a way to optimize the information encoding in the days when data storage space was expensive. ASN.1 is horribly complex; that alone was why the first author decided not to use X.509 in the IBM 4758, in 1996. The ASN.1 notation is so horrible that, in the beginning of 2004, it was revealed that all the Microsoft ASN.1 parsers suffered from numerous dangerous buffer overflow problems. Kaufman, Perlmann, and Speciner raise some additional objections: The name field matches nothing useful; the directory concept ignores the most useful Internet directory out there; and the policy rules make reasonable path-discovery schemes needlessly inefficient [KPS02].

In order to illuminate some of the dissent to the X.509 gospel, we summarize the thinking of some of the principal reseachers here: Carl Ellison, Alma Whitten, Simson Garfinkel, and Peter Gutmann.

10.7.1 Ellison

Carl Ellison—formerly at Intel, now at Microsoft—criticizes the conventional approach to PKI: "Cryptographers and lawyers have dominated much of the PKI discussion." In his 1996 paper, he stresses that authorization is not the same as authentication and that conventional PKI has given undue attention to the latter [Ell96]. He discusses the namespace problem again: PKIs are built on global namespaces, but, as discussed in Section 9.7, globally unique names are not humanly usable. Carl also notes that X.509 emerged from an attempt at telephone books. Is this really the right foundation for Internet security? In conversation, Carl adds comments about X.509's close binding of certificate validity with certificate chains. Within enterprises, certificate chains betray information about organizational structures, but corporations frequently regard this data as private.[7] The "existence of valid path" is important and should be public information, but the path itself may be considered confidential.

Two alternatives to the X.509 approach emerged from Ellison and others: SDSI and SPKI (discussed earlier). SDSI/SPKI stresses local namespaces and is tuned specifically to authorization. It was supported by attractively simple code libraries from MIT. This simplicity enticed student interest, although one wag characterized it as "the Libertarian Party of PKI": intellectually seductive, but one can't help feel that it will never work in the real world.

Carl revisits and extends these issues in his 2002 paper [Ell02]. He notes with surprise that people took the idea of a centralized directory literally and observes that this traditional approach to PKI simply replaces a key-management problem with a name-management problem. (How many different identities do *you* have?)

For an example, consider the natural way to integrate PKI with SSH, so that we don't have to rely on the server's word for its public key.[8] We use a *name-constraint*

---

7. The first author notes: At IBM, I never managed to convince the IBM Web Police to approve my Web page for external visibility; one of their objections was that it listed my office number, considered private, allegedly because the adversary might mine this information and infer group structure.
8. Essentially, we did this: see [AS04]. This solution was also an example of a scenario in which key pairs may have many certificates, many of which are never known by the keyholder.

model, whereby we tie the hostname to a domain where that host lives. In that domain, a well-defined officer takes charge of certifying the hosts's public keys. We build a PKI for those officers, and in theory, this approach should work. We assume that names humans use for the hosts they wish to connect to trivially map to their global hostnames (e.g., add the domain suffix). We assume that this "local namespace" is small enough to avoid the John Wilson problem; we also assume that all organizations have a reasonable person who can do the certifying. When we proposed this to Carl, he pointed out that at Intel (his previous employer), the second two assumptions don't hold!

10.7.2 Whitten

Most PKI work ignores the gap between the program and the user. Even if the cryptography and certificates all work, have we enabled effective trust judgments for the user? In the late 1990s, Alma Whitten and Doug Tygar chose the PKI tool that allegedly had the best user interface and did a study of how a dozen educated but not security-knowledgeable subjects could use it [WT99]. In a 90-minute test session, only 3 of 12 users managed to "successfully send encrypted email and decrypt a reply." The same number also managed to send the secret message in plaintext by accident. No one managed to successfully create a backup revocation certificate.

In Chapter 1, we framed system security as things that can be done in reachable space. Alma's work showed that, from the starting state of users familiar with email but not security, transitions (consisting of what users do) take the system to many unexpected places. In general, the system did not reach the desired states.

10.7.3 Garfinkel

In 2005, Simson Garfinkel revisited Whitten and Tygar's examination of the usability of PKI software [GM05]. His approach was based on a technique called *key-continuity management* (*KCM*) [Gut04]. KCM uses X.509 certificates, but instead of forcing Alice and Bob to validate a chain of certificates back to a common trust anchor, they can simply decide to trust each other explicitly; for example, the entity is still Bob, because the entity is still using Bob's key. In fact, this is similar to the way modern SSH implementations operate.

For his experiment, Garfinkel tried to replicate the Whitten and Tygar work with a mail client that implemented the KCM technique. The mailer alerts Alice the first time she sees Bob's public key but doesn't alert her again unless Bob's public key suddenly changes. In general, they found that KCM improves email security.

10.7.4 Gutmann

Peter Gutmann is another vocal critic of the conventional PKI wisdom. In his 2002 paper, Gutmann highlights a number of problems with the X.509 approach to PKI and explains how such things came to be [Gut02]. Essentially, the X.509 PKI scheme was developed to solve a specific problem: guarding access to X.500 name directories. Since that problem was well defined and tightly controlled by a few telephone companies, X.509 provided a somewhat reasonable solution. Much of the X.509 wackiness complained about now resulted from trying to solve that particular problem.

Today, we try to use X.509 to solve a wide variety of problems that are unrelated to its original intent; it should be no surprise that X.509 does not meet all our requirements. Instead of building a PKI that fits the real world, we try to bend the real world to fit in the PKI. Gutmann points out that X.509 has become a "one-size-misfits-all" solution.

10.8 Ongoing Trouble

A standard lament about PKI is how it's remained "the field of the future" even after all these decades. Although the underlying cryptography is relatively simple, the mechanics of effectively deploying and using PKI in the real world continue to be messy and challenging. Pinning down the exact reasons for this continuing challenge is grounds for lively debate (and perhaps a good homework exercise). However, the observation that effective deployment continues to raise new obstacles is not controversial. In this section, we review some of the obstacles that, as of this writing, seem to present some of the more vexing issues.

10.8.1 Key Storage

How should end users store their private keys? One factor that complicates this problem is that users want to use their private keys for applications that run on their desktop or laptop. Unfortunately, standard commodity operating systems are not particularly good at protecting themselves from external adversaries or (as we discussed in Section 8.4.4) protecting key storage, even hardware tokens, from use by code those adversaries plant. Another problem is that in many enterprise settings, such as our university, end users want to carry out their business from multiple machines, including borrowed ones and shared-access ones. Private keys somehow need to be mobile or portable. Among the challenges we have faced here is that USB hardware security modules don't always seem to have drivers available for all our target operating systems.

10.8.2 Expression of Trust Flow

Current PKI deployment focuses primarily on central authorities binding keys to identity. However, if we look at the type of authorization problems that arise in the real world, the near-exclusive focus on these two factors is too limiting.

1. The central authority is not always in the position to make the assertion. In the legacy world of passwords, users often end up sharing passwords because there is no other way for an end user to delegate some limited aspect of his or her privileges to another user. The X.509 PKI world offers proxy certificates and attribute certificates, but both of these require some stretching before end users can issue certificates to other end users.

2. As Carl Ellison preaches, the "identity" of the keyholder is not necessarily what the relying party wants to know. For example, noted PKI evangelist Ken Klingenstein stresses that academia needs PKI because someone at Yale canceled classes by forging email from the dean. The week he said that, one of us received email from the dean here at Dartmouth, except that it wasn't from the dean but from Effie Cummings, his new assistant, whom we hadn't yet met. X.509 PKI that would have assured us that yes, indeed, the email came from Effie Cummings but would not have told us that she was speaking for the dean. (We elaborate more on these shortfalls in our Allerton paper [SMS04].)

10.8.3 End User Trust Judgments

The fact that *phishing* remains an ongoing problem demonstrates that, at least within the context of email and Web browsing, the current infrastructure for enabling end users to make effective trust judgments about communication does not work. Adding the extra features of trust paths, bridges, revocation, and complications such as attribute certificates, will not make things better. We need a revolution in user interface design if the PKI revolution is ever to take place.

10.8.4 Historical Perspective

Existing PKI standards and practices are geared toward the here and now: Is this signature valid at this moment? However, as business and government practices start to move from paper-based to electronic processes, the notion of *historical* validation is becoming an issue. Was this signature valid when it was generated 5 years ago? Did these bits even exist 5 years ago? Has a revolution in the understanding of hash functions made this all meaningless?

10.9 The Take-Home Message

In Chapter 7, we introduced the wonderful world of public key cryptography, an attractive solution to numerous problems we may face when trying to design a secure system. Part of its appeal is the clean abstraction of elegant mathematics. When clean abstractions meet the messiness of the real world, interesting things often result, such as PKI.

In Diffie and Hellman's original paper on public key cryptography, they envisioned using a "Public File" to locate other parties' public keys [DH76]. We hope that in this chapter, we have given you some appreciation for the challenges involved in implementing such a "Public File." What Diffie and Hellman probably considered an implementation detail has spawned numerous standards, companies, and research topics in itself.

As with many of the topics we've discussed so far, getting PKI right is harder than it seems. Although on paper PKI may appear to be clean and simple, building a real PKI for real users means dealing with such issues as names, policies, certificates, revocation, software usability, and desktop security. On top of that, recall from Chapter 8 that the underlying cryptography is in a state of flux as well. What works today may not work tomorrow.

10.10 Project Ideas

1. Enroll in an X.509 PKI and figure out how to send and receive S/MIME encrypted and signed email. (CAs exist that let you enroll for free; inspect the list of baked-in trust roots in your machine.)

2. Investigate your S/MIME email client's user interface. Can you tell whether and how it checks revocation? When it accepts a signature as valid, can you tell what trust root and certificate path it used? When it rejects a signature as invalid, can you tell why?

3. Try translating different certificate formats into one another.

4. Revisit the experiments of "Why Johnny Can't Encrypt" [WT99] and see whether the state of usability has changed.

5. Use a library, such as OpenSSL or the CryptoAPI, to build a basic certificate authority.

6. In NOVOMODO, why doesn't the CA's release of the proof of validity enable a relying party to forge false proofs of validity?

Standards, Compliance, and Testing

Let's assume that you've used the tools and techniques mentioned throughout this book so far to try to build a secure system or that someone has handed you an allegedly secure system. How do you know that the system is safe? How safe is it really? What we'd really like to know is: How likely is it that the system will get into an unsafe state either by accident or by malice? Whether one is a vendor, an implementer, an administrator, or a customer, these questions are critically important.

It would be ideal if we could map the entire state space of our system and then look for system paths that lead to unsafe states; we could then simply avoid such paths. The complexity of modern software makes such a task more difficult than it may appear. For starters, even mapping the entire state space of a system is a daunting task likely to bring many modern computers to their knees. Nevertheless, such approaches at using formal methods to verify software are a lively topic in the research community and are explored in detail in Chapter 15.

Meanwhile, modern practitioners are left with three main tools to assist with this task: standards, compliance, and testing. It is important to note that such tools cannot provide a conclusive answer about the security of a system: They cannot *prove* that a system will not get into a harmful state. However, such tools can show that a system meets some security criteria or follows some guidelines for best practice. Furthermore, these tools can more directly prove that a system is *not* secure. A fundamental point that we explore throughout the chapter is that proving insecurity is *much* easier than proving security; finding one hole in the system completes the proof, whereas proving security means showing that no holes exist.

In this chapter, we explore the basics of standards, compliance, and testing.

- Section 11.1 covers some of the basic standards that have been put in place, mostly by the U.S. government, to rate the security of various systems. We also explore some of the limitations of these standards.
- Section 11.2 looks at what is currently driving much of the security spending: *policy compliance*. Although this area is geared more toward IT practices, anyone building software for enterprise IT or even simply managing infrastructure should be aware of some of the issues and limitations.
- Section 11.3 examines techniques that are often used to test the security of the system. Sometimes called *penetration testing*, testers may use these techniques to validate a system against a particular standard; a software company may use them to test the security of its own product; or a reverse engineer/attacker may use them to break into a deployed system.

Figure 11.1 sketches a timeline of some of the relevant standards and laws.

11.1 Standards

During the 1970s, the U.S. government underwent a paradigm shift: No longer would it exclusively create its own secure systems; rather, it would also allow itself to use commercial systems. However, how could the government ensure that these commercial systems were secure enough? The government went with a multi-pronged approach:

- It created *standards* specifying what a suitable secure system should do. (It had hoped that this would stimulate the development of these products in the commercial sector.)
- It created a *validation* process to determine whether products met these standards.
- In theory, it created laws and regulations to ensure that appropriate federal players needed to purchase an appropriately validated product, if one was available among the choices.

As discussed in Chapter 2, one of the first widespread embodiments of this approach was the Orange Book, formally titled the *Trusted Computer System*

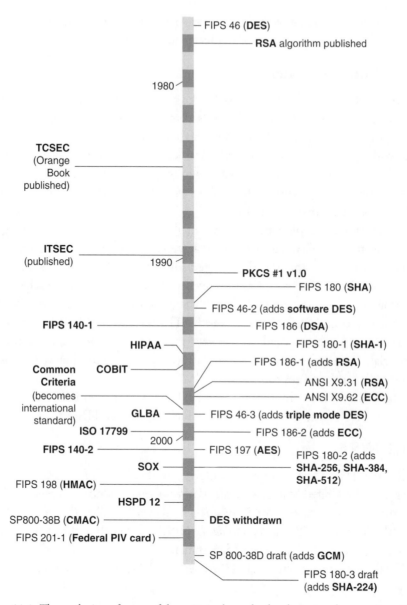

Figure 11.1 The evolution of some of the principal standards relevant to the security artisan.

Evaluation Criteria (TCSEC), and the rest of the Rainbow series. Although most of the Orange Book validation levels did not include a formal model and a proof of the system's correctness, they did allow the government to reason about various security aspects of the system under consideration. For example, the government could tell what types of adversaries the system was designed to protect against and what technologies the system used to protect its critical assets.

11.1.1 Common Criteria

In recent decades, the Orange Book has given way to new standards and rating systems. Although the TCSEC and friends were national efforts, computer security, particularly in this networked age, knows no boundaries. Several European nations were working on their own standards (and we have heard some of these parties insist that they invented material that was in the U.S. FIPS standards). From this work emerged the *Information Technology Security Evaluation Criteria (ITSEC)*, a multinational standard based in Europe.

In Chapter 2, we discussed how we might characterize standards along two axes: what functionality a device should have versus what level of assurance we should use to validate that. TCSEC charted a linear path through this space (recall Figure 2.8), allowing for an increasing sequence of security levels, with each new step requiring more (and specific) functionality and increased assurance scrutiny. One of its main innovations over TCSEC was that ITSEC replaced TCSEC's linear path with a matrix. A vendor could craft a *security target* that specified the functionality appropriate for some type of box and then have it evaluated to whatever *evaluation assurance level* seemed appropriate.

The United States started updating its TCSEC, but then both the U.S. and Europe united[1] on the *Common Criteria*, which supplanted ITSEC.

11.1.2 NIST

Besides the TCSEC and Common Criteria, another suite of security standards emerged in the United States: the *Federal Information Processing Standards (FIPS)* from the *National Institute for Standards and Technology (NIST)* (see [NIS07a]). Formerly the *National Bureau of Standards,* NIST is a branch of the Department of Commerce, part of the U.S. federal government.

For the security artisan, most of the relevant FIPS standards focus on cryptography.

- *FIPS 180-2* specifies SHA. (In FIPS parlance, the *-n* suffix usually denotes the revision number.)

---

1. Perhaps "united" might be an overly ambitious word choice here. In general, the countries recognize each other's evaluations only up to EAL4, although subsets of the countries may have special arrangements to go further.

- *FIPS 186-2* specifies digital signature algorithms: initially only DSA but now extended to include RSA and ECC.
- *FIPS 197* specifies AES, the new standard symmetric cipher.
- *FIPS 198* specifies HMAC, the standard keyed MAC algorithm.

Validation of a product or module against one of these crypto standards can give you strong assurance that the product implements the algorithm in question (e.g., it doesn't skip a few rounds or use the wrong S-box tables). Validation also ensures that, when there are options (e.g., chaining modes for block ciphers), the product chooses options that are considered secure.

NIST is also probably the world leader in charting out a long-term road map for cryptography. NIST is the first place we would go to gauge what key lengths for RSA, DSA, elliptic curve, and AES would be considered secure in 15 years or what to do about hash functions. On the other hand, the drive to maintain an accurate long-term vision sometimes makes the standards a bit dynamic. With the standards themselves, new revisions get issued; with the validation process, new "derived test requirements," clarifications, and precedents emerge. This dynamism can complicate the life of an artisan trying build a secure system, since it makes the goal a bit of a moving target.

Besides cryptography, NIST also provides some other standards relevant to secure systems.

- *FIPS 140-2* specifies standards for "secure cryptographic modules." Security for such modules typically requires that they still house and run the correct software and that they keep cryptographic secrets secret. Such modules often exist as specialized hardware: chips soldered onto a motherboard, PCI peripherals installed in a PC, USB dongles and smart cards carried by users. It is important that such systems have these security properties. However, it may be also important that other devices, such as secure coprocessors, electronic postal meters, or even voting machines, have these security properties. As a consequence, FIPS 140 becomes a catch-all for validation of computational devices that need to remain secure despite physical attack. FIPS 140 offers four levels of validation; Level 4 is the most stringent. FIPS 140 also offers different sets of rules depending on the device type (e.g., "single-chip," "multichip," "stand-alone," "embedded"). (Chapter 8 in [Smi04c] provides gory details on the first author's experience taking a product through the world's first FIPS 140-1 Level 4 validation.)

- *FIPS 201-1* is an emerging NIST standard that may have consequences for some security artisans. Pertaining to *personal identity verification (PIV)*, this standard responds to *Homeland Security Presidential Directive (HSPD) 12*, a recent directive aimed at "promulgation of a Federal standard for secure and reliable forms of identification" [Bus04]. Right now, this seems to have something to do with PKI-enabled RFID cards[2] for federal employees and contractors. Your guess is as good as ours—and from what we hear, as good as federal PKI scientists—as to where this ends up.

Be careful. When it comes to FIPS standards and probably others, a world of difference exists between a vendor's declaration that a product is "FIPS *NNN compliant*" and a certification that it is "FIPS *NNN validated*" (or "*certified*"). *Compliance* simply means that someone squinted and said "Hmm, that looks like it fits;" in other words, it means nothing. *Validation* implies that a NIST-sanctioned laboratory has tested the product against the rules and that it passed.

11.1.3 ANSI

Another set of relevant standards comes from the the *X9* group of the *American National Standards Institute (ANSI)*. Despite a name that sounds synonymous with NIST, ANSI is a voluntary industrial consortium and is not a part of the U.S. government. X9 is a nonprofit organization accredited by ANSI to "develop, establish, maintain, and promote standards for the Financial Services Industry."

Two relevant ANSI standards are *X9.31*, which specifies a standard way of doing RSA-based signatures, and *X9.62*, which specifies elliptic curve DSA. Some standards also cite X9.31 not for RSA but rather for its specification of suitably strong PRNGs.

NIST standards often cite ANSI X9 standards. However, for the artisan, a crucial difference exists: The NIST standards are available for free download, but one must pay for the interesting ANSI standards.

11.1.4 PKCS

We have NIST standards for public-key cryptography. We also have ANSI standards for public-key cryptography So, why stop there?

RSA Laboratories—an applied research arm of *RSA Data Security, Inc.*, initially formed to market RSA, acquired in 1996 by *Security Dynamics*, acquired in 2006

---

2. RFID stands for *radio frequency identification*. We talk more about RFID in Chapter 16.

by *EMC Corporation*—maintains *Public Key Cryptography Standards (PKCS)* [RSA], another set of voluntary standards for things related to public key, such as message formats for handling and transporting data in PKI protocols. For example, *PKCS #7* deals with signature formats, and *PKCS #12* deals with transporting credentials.

Historically, PKCS standards seem to move more quickly and go farther than NIST standards.

11.1.5 RFCs

Another set of standards relevant to the security artisan are the Internet standards promulgated by the *Internet Engineering Task Force*. The IETF runs a more ad hoc, cooperative, and voluntary process by which ideas are proposed first as *Internet drafts* and then codified as *Requests for Comments*, which despite their name are usually considered finished documents. RFCs are where one should go to find a formal definition of such things as communication and network-security protocols. One should remain shrewd, however; rules can be ambiguous, and gaps can exist between rules and practice, particularly when no formal process exists to validate that practice conforms to the rules.

11.1.6 Flaws in Standards

Some wags quip that the nice thing about standards is that there are so many to choose from. Security is no exception. Like so many other things in the security artisan's toolbox, standards are useful but have limits.

Some standards, particularly NISTs, tend to be overly conservative. This can be a good thing, since slow movement tends to codify only things that are trustworthy. On the other hand, conservatism can also lead to frustrating and tortuous situations. For example, in the 1990s, RSA was the de facto universal way to do digital signatures. For reasons of patents and politics, the U.S. government promulgated DSA instead, although NIST kept hinting that an RSA standard was coming. So (brace yourself now):

- In the first author's group at IBM, we initially supported only RSA for signatures in our security product.
- We had customers who needed *U.S. Postal Service (USPS)* certification of our device.
- USPS rules required FIPS validation but permitted RSA instead of DSA.
- FIPS rules required NIST-approved algorithms.
- NIST allowed only DSA.

- So, we had to add code for DSA options for all signatures, in order to make FIPS happy, in order to make the USPS happy, in order to make customers happy—except that said customers immediately proceeded never to use the DSA options.

Other strangeness derived from the fact that cryptographic weaknesses can move faster than standards. In the 1990s, it was known that the single-DES key was not able to withstand brute-force attacks running on modern hardware. One government rule that required DES for all secure communications recognized that fact and said, in essence, "Fine, TDES counts as DES for the rule but actually provides the required security." Another government rule, for a different scenario, decided that "if it says DES, then DES it shall be—not TDES." (We also ran into trouble because the FIPS notion of "NIST-approved secure PRNG" lagged behind the common beliefs of the cryptographic community, even if they used NIST-approved algorithms to build secure PRNGs.)

Another set of limitations comes from drawing a boundary around exactly what is being validated. To be meaningful, standards need to be applied to a well-defined module. (Otherwise, what should the validator look at?) This need can cause confusion, however, as the validation may assume options or configurations that do not necessarily apply when the artisan goes to use the module in the real world. As we mentioned earlier, Windows NT received a C2 rating under TCSEC but only as long as one didn't connect the computer to a network.

One encounters fundamental contradictions: Too few variations make it impossible for labels to adequately describe products; too many variations make it impossible for designers to make good decisions. Almost by definition, standards cannot address the whole system. Another source of related trouble is how much of a module's development and maintenance process is considered during the validation: Does the validation examine only the module, or does it also examine such things as the source code repository and the product-testing process?

11.2 Policy Compliance

In recent years, there has been a lot of buzz around the topic of *policy compliance*. Many IT organizations, particularly in the medical field and in publicly traded U.S. companies, are now being forced to comply with numerous regulations. Such regulations often span the entire organization and have a real impact on the way that IT organizations run their environments. In order to comply with a particular regulation, an IT organization may be forced to implement certain *controls* that govern how data is accessed and transmitted, what happens to critical data during a disaster recovery scenario, and so on.

Since regulations are fairly vague, they are sometimes mapped to *best practice frameworks*, which give IT organizations more prescriptive guidance on how to administer their environments in order to comply with a particular regulation. Frameworks give IT organizations a set of industry-accepted processes and tools for setting and measuring the effectiveness and security of their environments.

Regulations and best practice frameworks govern IT organizations but are of importance to software vendors as well. Vendors wishing to have their products deployed in regulated environments must be aware of the types of controls and policies their customers rely on and are likely get audited against. For example, if a medical facility mandates that all patient information that goes over the network must be encrypted, and vendor X attempts to sells the facility a workflow application that sends information in plaintext, that vendor is going to have a hard time selling its product.

One positive outcome of recent regulatory pressure is that numerous organizations are becoming more security aware. In the past few years, we have seen an increase in the number of software consumers who include things such as particular cryptographic algorithms and key lengths in their product requirements. Since they are under regulatory pressure to protect their critical data, such consumers have become a forcing function for software vendors to make more secure products.

Numerous regulations affect enterprise IT security today. In this section, we narrow the focus to the three regulations that have had the largest impact in recent years. We certainly don't have the space to give a detailed description of each one here; entire books are devoted to that.

11.2.1 HIPAA

As the name suggests, the *Health Insurance Portability and Accountability Act of 1996 (HIPAA)* is a regulation that governs the health care industry [U.S.96]. HIPAA has two goals, each covered by one of its *titles*: (1) providing health care coverage to people as they move between jobs, and (2) preventing health care fraud and abuse. HIPAA's second title includes a *Privacy Rule* for keeping patient data private and a *Security Rule*, or *Security Standard*, that prescribes administrative, physical, and technical safeguards for *protected health information*.

The physical-access safeguards specify that computer hardware and software must be properly guarded using physical-access control mechanisms. Such hardware and software must also be disposed of properly, so that critical information cannot be recovered from things such as discarded disks. The safeguards also specify that computers with critical data should be monitored, such as by camera, that they should not be in public places, and that their screens should not face the public.

Although the physical safeguards have broad implications, the technical safeguards are directly targeted toward IT organizations. The safeguards specify that critical data that travels over an open network must be encrypted, that machines housing such data must be locked down and use authentication, and that digital signatures and MACs be used for data integrity. Furthermore, IT organizations must have documented policies, procedures, access records, and configuration settings for all components on the network.

By April 21, 2006, all institutions that handle protected health information needed to comply with HIPAA. In Section 11.2.5, we discuss how to determine whether an organization complies with a given regulation. Failure to comply with HIPAA can result in some weighty fines for the organization.

11.2.2 SOX

The *Sarbanes-Oxley Act (SOX)* was signed into effect in 2002 as a result of several high-profile corporate accounting scandals, such as those of Enron and World-Com [U.S.02]. SOX applies to all publicly traded U.S. companies and governs the manner in which companies handle financial data. Like HIPAA, SOX affects numerous departments and procedures throughout the organization. Also like HIPAA, since much of the critical data that the regulation protects flows through and is stored on computer systems, IT organizations play a significant role in a company's ability to comply with SOX.

Section 404 of the SOX regulation specifies that certain IT controls be in place in order to secure and audit critical financial data. These controls specify such things as access control to systems that store or perform processing on financial data, application logic that deals with financial data, and the integrity of financial data. SOX also specifies that financial records be managed properly, retained for a certain amount of time, and that electronic communications about such records be retained as well.

SOX differs from HIPAA in its stance on particular conditions that must be met in order to comply. Although HIPAA's Security Rule specifies particular measures that must be in place, SOX mandates use of a Best Practice Framework to define the set of particular controls. In fact, the *Securities and Exchange Commission (SEC)* states that the *Committee of Sponsoring Organizations of the Treadway Commission (COSO)* framework for financial processes be used to demonstrate compliance [COS04]. Most IT organizations rely on the *Control Objectives for Information and Related Technology (COBIT)* framework to help them achieve SOX compliance [Inf07]. (See Section 11.2.4 for more on COBIT.)

SOX brought about numerous changes to the way companies do business. As one might imagine, the cost—measured in both dollars and time—of complying with SOX or HIPAA is significant. Some even argue that SOX has created such a barrier for small companies wanting to go public that it has disrupted innovation. Failure to comply with SOX results in a public disclosure of the failure—the real impact being that shareholders will likely lose confidence in the organization.

11.2.3 GLBA

The *Gramm-Leach-Bliley Act (GLBA) of 1999*, also referred to as the *Financial Services Reform Act of 1999*, is a regulation that applies to the financial services industry [U.S.99]. Much like the other regulations we've discussed in this section, the Safeguards Rule of GLBA requires that financial institutions follow administrative, physical, and technical safeguards in order to protect customer information.

In order to comply with GLBA, financial institutions must have controls and policies in place that serve to protect their customers' personal information. Institutions must also demonstrate that they have identified threats to information security and have controls in place that address those threats. Finally, institutions must show that they have formal, documented access control policies in place that govern who has access to customer data.

As with HIPAA, failure to comply with GLBA results in some heavy fines—both to the institution and to the executives and board members.

11.2.4 Best Practice Frameworks

Regulations have an inherent tension between being specific and being applicable. A very specific regulation would give an organization clear guidance on how to administer its environment; for instance, a regulation may give an organization a specific set of IT controls to use and measure compliance against that set of controls. However, organizations that are not close to the regulation's prescription—because they use different technologies or have different processes—may have to spend large sums of time and money to retool parts of their organization in order to comply. On the other hand, a vague regulation leaves room for interpretation and does not give clear guidance to organizations. Instead, a vague regulation describes processes and procedures that can apply in any type of environment, regardless of particular technologies.

In practice, many regulations have been designed to be vague, since they are intended to be applied to a diverse set of organizations. Typically, they give an organization a list of *what* should be done; they are rather silent about *how* to do it. Therefore, most organizations rely on some sort of best practice framework for guidance on how to implement what a regulation calls for. Although organizations are technically audited against a regulation (see Section 11.2.5), implementing a framework can increase the chances that an organization will pass the audit. In fact, in many cases, organizations that align with a framework surpass the requirements of a regulation.

Numerous frameworks and best practice guides exist. We narrow our focus to discuss today's most popular IT frameworks: COBIT and ISO 17799.

COBIT. In the early to mid-1990s, the *Information Systems Audit and Control Association (ISACA)* developed a system of best practices that IT organizations can use to build stable and secure environments. The result, COBIT, has become very popular since the passing of SOX. Many organizations follow COBIT guidelines in an effort to comply with the IT-specific portions of SOX. According to version 4 of the framework, COBIT links IT to business requirements, organizes IT activities into an accepted process model, identifies major IT resources, and defines control objectives. As we'll see, COBIT helps IT organizations develop human-level processes but is light on specific technical details.

COBIT is divided into four high-level areas, or domains: *Planning and Organization*, *Acquisition and Implementation*, *Delivery and Support*, and *Monitoring*. Each of these domains contains a number of *high-level control objectives* that outline an IT process and a number of the 215 specific *control objectives* that serve as guidance to the organization.

The *Planning and Organization* domain deals with the overall picture of how the IT organization fits into the larger business. The objectives in this domain are geared at finding out how well the organization at large understands and manages IT and its inherent risks. Some of the high-level objectives include such processes as defining a strategic IT plan, defining an information architecture, and determining technological direction. The detailed control objectives break the tasks down even further and include such items as defining and implementing procedures to ensure the integrity of stored data, establishing a data-classification scheme, and establishing a process to monitor relevant standards.

Although these detailed control objectives give some specific guidance, it is still up to the organization—and the auditor (see Section 11.2.5)—to come up with a set of concrete things to do to meet the objective. For example, one of the detailed control objectives indicates that we should ensure the integrity of stored data in our enterprise. It is still up to us to determine the exact mechanisms we need to use. Maybe we should hash and verify all the data in our databases, or maybe we should hash and sign all our backups.

The *Acquiring and Implementation* domain governs how organizations build, buy, integrate, and maintain IT systems. One of the high-level control objectives in this domain states that organizations should have a process to acquire and maintain application software; clearly, this process is particularly relevant to software vendors. Detailed objectives here specify that an organization should evaluate the application's security: how well it deals with access control, data protection, authentication, and so on. In practice, as a result of these controls, many IT organizations formulate security-specific requirements for software vendors and expect them to explain the security-relevant details about the applications they use.

The *Deliver and Support* domain covers how IT organizations deliver their services, as well as how they secure and manage their facilites. The high-level objectives in this domain cover the range of IT operation, from training users to running a help desk to securing systems. The security objectives specify that organizations should have an identity-management solution, have policies for managing user accounts, regularly test the security of their environment, and have a policy put together to deal with security incidents. Furthermore, the detailed control objectives state that organizations should construct policies and procedures for managing network security, malicious software, and cryptographic keys.

Finally, the *Monitor and Evaluate* domain governs how an IT organization monitors its environment over time. This domain states that organizations should continually evaluate their performance. Part of this process involves undergoing an audit, which we discuss in Section 11.2.5.

ISO/IEC 17799.   ISO 17799 is another best practice framework that IT organizations rely on to secure their environment [ISO05]. ISO 17799 grew from British Standard 7799-1 and is now technically an ISO standard, but its role in the organization is somewhat similar to COBIT's. Unlike COBIT, ISO 17799 has IT security as its focus and defines security as the preservation of confidentiality, integrity, and availability. Many organizations that must comply with the HIPAA regulation adopt ISO 17799, as it covers much of what HIPAA calls for.

ISO 17799 is made up of 12 *clauses*, each containing control objectives and specific controls that are used to achieve the objectives. The 12 control objectives are roughly analagous to COBIT's 34 high-level control objectives, and the specific controls are somewhat similar to COBIT's detailed control objectives. The clauses include such topics as:

- Risk Assessment and Treatment
- Security Policy
- Organizing Information Security
- Asset Management

Unlike COBIT, ISO 17799 does not stop at the construction of human-level policies. A number of controls in ISO 17799 give specific technical guidance to organizations. For example, the "Access Control" clause contains a control for configuring operating system access control. The implementation guidance for this control specifies that a password-management system should be in place and that it should enforce quality passwords, enforce regular password changes, force users to change temporary passwords at first login, and store passwords in encrypted or hashed form.

Software vendors should be aware of the "information systems acquisition, development and maintenance" clause. The controls in this clause specify that security requirements for an application be discussed upfront. Another control involves ensuring that applications correctly process data; the control gives a list of things to check for, such as out-of-range values and invalid characters. Additionally, this clause contains controls that require applications to validate input and output data, ensure message integrity, properly manage cryptographic material and system files, and use development processes, such as version control.

11.2.5 Audit

As we've seen, frameworks give organizations varying levels of guidance on how to run their environments. Ultimately, the responsibility to comply with a particular regulation rests with an organizational leader, such as the *chief information officer (CIO)*. One of the first tasks at hand for such an individual is to map the control objectives of whatever framework is in place into concrete corporate *policies*. As Jay Grieves observes in a personal communication: "Policies are an organization's pre-made decisions. Your policies are your plan for implementing the requirement that the regulation is mandating" [Gri06]. Policies are environmentally specific and, since they are constructed to satisfy somewhat generic control statements in a framework, subjective.

At some point in an organization's lifespan—assuming that the organization has to comply with a particular regulation—it will get *audited* by a third-party auditing firm. An audit scores to what degree an organization meets the regulation in question. By their nature, regulations are not designed to make organizations perfect. Instead, regulations are designed to install accountability and visibility into critical information processes.

Regulations, frameworks, and the audit process do not aim to make all organizations alike. Rather, they force organizations to control their own environments; they are concerned mostly with the organization's demonstrating *due care*, or *due diligence*, to protect critical assets. Part of demonstrating due care is policy coverage: An organization should have a plan for everything. Another part deals with how well an organization is able to realize and deal with violations; detection and remediation of such violations is evidence of due care.

As we noted earlier, it is important to realize that compliance is different from validation. Since regulations and frameworks are somewhat generic and allow for imperfections, organizations can be only *compliant* with a regulation. In contrast, systems that are trying to achieve a particular rating against a standard, such as the Common Criteria (Section 11.1.1), must meet a very specific set of requirements in order to be *validated* against the standard.

11.3 Testing

Testing plays a critical role in building and deploying software systems. Many software companies employ testers to perform such testing on their products before they are shipped to customers. Thorough software testing can translate into great improvements in stability, reliability, performance, and security. In this section, we are concerned primarily with testing software security, although much of the discussion could be applied when testing for other properties, such as reliability.

Testing cannot ensure that a system is secure. In the best case, testing can show that the system doesn't have any major flaws that the test plan could find. One might hope that sufficient test coverage might provide a statistical basis to extrapolate to wider claims of safety—but one never knows. Testing is only as good as the test plan (Section 11.3.2). If the test plan itself is flawed or incomplete, then testing is of little value.

It is also important to realize that testing in "the lab" can produce different results from testing in "the field." Lab environments are typically near-ideal situations for the software, and testers have detailed product knowledge as well as access to developers. Field environments are usually much messier than labs. For instance, real customers likely run the software alongside numerous applications on different platforms. Usually, security researchers test deployed products as part of their effort to reverse engineer the product and find security vulnerabilities. Sometimes, the very fact of testing can change the code or its environment enough to remove or induce the error. We have personally seen conditional compilation affect memory layout in a critical way and running a program in a debugger appear to eliminate race conditions. (Some wags use the term *heisenbug* for bugs whose appearance is affected by whether they are being observed.)

Finally, as we discuss in Section 11.3.4, explicit testing for security is different from typical software testing. First and foremost, testing for security requires a different mindset: one that gets testers thinking like attackers.

11.3.1 Testing in the Lab

In general, testing strategies can be broken down into at least two categories: *black-box* testing and *white-box* testing. Black-box testing treats the software as a black box: Testers are given no visibility into how the code actually works but instead simply test the interface that the software presents to users. In white-box testing, the software is tested at the subsystem, or API, level. Testers typically write programs that exercise parts of a code module by calling its functions and checking their return values for correct results.

To illustrate the point on something more concrete, imagine that we are testing a car. A black-box test would involve our driving the car. We would likely be testing the car's handling, testing that the radio and windows work properly, and so on. A white-box test would involve pulling components out of the motor and testing them individually. We might pull the alternator out and test that it functions properly.

Unfortunately, many organizations perform only black-box lab testing as the final step before a product is shipped. Testers employed or contracted by the company devise and execute a test plan and inform developers when they find a problem with the software. The developers then fix the problem and the testers validate the fix. This process continues until the test plan is complete and all the known issues have been *resolved*. It's important to note that "resolved" does not mean "fixed"; resolution may involve postponing a fix until the next release.

In our experience, the most successful testing strategies are more *gray box* in nature. They do white-box testing of individual components throughout the entire development cycle and perform black-box testing on well-defined, though not necessarily complete, milestones. Such strategies are likely to catch problems early—when they are less expensive to fix. Discovering a design flaw after the system has been entirely written is quite expensive to fix.

However, it's worth mentioning that even good gray-box approaches can miss significant items when it comes to testing composite systems. Breaking a composite system into components and then testing them is a natural way to decompose the enormous task of testing a piece of modern software. This deconstructionist view can often overlook subtle or not-so-subtle vulnerabilities that may arise as the result of interaction between various subsystems. It's important to consider the system as a whole, perhaps performing black-box testing on the finished product in addition to the other testing efforts.

11.3.2 The Test Plan

A good testing effort starts with a good test plan. One of the core properties of a test plan is *coverage*: how much of the system the plan tests. In a perfect world, a test plan would incorporate black-box and white-box testing and would maximize the coverage of both types of testing. Attaining black-box coverage is probably the easiest; testers should execute test cases for nearly all possible valid inputs into the system. White-box coverage is harder to come by, as there is much more testing surface. White-box coverage can be measured by how many classes and functions are exercised by the test suite. Since this surface is typically too large and complex to test by hand, developers often rely on automated testing for help. (We discuss this topic shortly.)

Security-conscious software shops may also incorporate security testing into their normal testing process. We discuss some security-testing techniques in a bit, but from a test plan perspective, it is important to focus on particular issues. Many times, the security-relevant portions of a test plan come from security-specific requirements and early architectural analysis. In fact, one outcome of the threat-modeling process, discussed in Chapter 6, can be a solid security-based test plan.

The desire or requirement for the system to adhere to a particular standard may also drive the creation of the test plan. Most standards publish their requirements so that vendors can build their systems with those requirements in mind from the beginning. A test plan that encompasses the standard's requirements and is executed in-house before going up for validation can greatly reduce the time and money needed to get validation.

There is no right or wrong way to build a test plan for software. Even though different types of software have different testing requirements, all test plans try to achieve maximum coverage in the time allotted. One strategy that we use is to do an initial risk assessment of the system, build a broad test plan, and then spend extra time achieving depth in the riskiest parts of the system: in security-specific and mission-critical features.

11.3.3 The Role of Developers

Back in the bad old days, most testing was done by professional testers; developers were often exempted from testing duties. One argument for this approach was that the testing efforts remain objective, as testers often act as a disinterested third party. However, the argument against this approach is that testing is done too late and without the developer's intimate knowledge about the software.

In our experience, the most successful software projects are ones in which developers are involved in the testing efforts from the beginning. Involvement of developers places them in a mindset whereby they pay more attention to correctness and security from the very beginning. Using such tools as threat modeling (see Chapter 6), developers can begin testing their designs before code is ever written. As we've pointed out, the earlier you find a problem, the better.

Once code starts getting written, the use of code scanners (see Section 6.1.5) and other such tools can decrease the likelihood of introducing bugs into the code base. Additionally, performing code reviews—especially in security-critical or mission-critical areas—can be priceless. Although code reviews for general-feature testing are valuable, they are essential for security testing, owing to the size and complexity of modern software. As usual, developers have to balance these activities against time, but the overall benefit to the product's correctness and security justifies this type of testing.

Another useful technique is for the developers themselves to perform the white-box testing every day as the product is being developed. Although this sounds like an enormous amount of overhead, it doesn't have to be.[3] Automated testing frameworks allow developers to write small programs called *unit tests* that exercise small portions of the system. For example, a developer may write a set of unit tests that thoroughly exercise the objects and functions that make up a subsystem.

A number of unit-testing frameworks exist that will run the tests and calculate passes and fails. *Junit* is such a framework for Java developers, *Nunit* for .Net developers, and *Cppunit* for C++ developers [cpp, jun, TPCF]. Another useful item is a *code-coverage* tool, such as *Ncover*, which calculates a percentage of the system covered by unit tests [nco].

---

3. However, since it's the *managers* rather than the developers who decide how the developers spend their time, it's the managers who would need convincing here.

One strategy that we often use is to execute the unit tests as part of the build process. If the tests fail, the build fails. Using unit testing, code coverage, and some simple processes, the white-box portion of a test plan can be done entirely by developers as they are developing the software.

11.3.4 Negative Testing

Most test plans focus on testing the advertised behavior of the system. The test cases cover common and uncommon usage scenarios in an effort to verify that the system's features function as advertised. Since the number of features is finite, test plans of this sort are measurable and therefore manageable.

Although this type of testing is necessary to evaluate the overall quality of the product, it is not sufficient. Many bugs, design problems, and security problems surface because users do the unexpected. Users rarely interact with the software in the exact way that developers designed them to. Unfortunately, most test plans don't focus on this type of unexpected behavior. *Negative testing* focuses not on what the product *should* do but on what it *can* do. This type of testing involves testers using the software "the wrong way" in an effort to see how the system handles the unexpected. It is useful for testing the reliability of a system; it is essential for testing a system's security.

To revisit our car analogy, negative testing is roughly equivalent to crash testing cars. Much in the same way that automakers are concerned about how well their cars hold up in an accident, software makers are concerned with how well their systems can handle faults and malicious users.

Negative testing requires testers to get creative—even downright evil—with the system they are testing. Testers should be asking themselves questions like:

- What happens if I put garbage into this input?
- What happens if I don't put in anything at all?
- What happens to my data if I pull the network or power cord?

One useful technique to get started is called *fuzz testing*, which involves sending random and malformed input to various parts of the application (see Sections 6.2.1 and 11.3.7). If we take this mindset to its extreme, we find a place to start security testing. To be an effective security tester, one has to go beyond testing features and even beyond testing for the unexpected. Being a good security tester means being malicious. A security test plan has as its goals such things as compromising the integrity of the application or gaining unauthorized access to critical information, such as passwords or cryptographic keys. Good security testers can also make good attackers (and vice-versa); both share the same adversarial mindset.

11.3.5 Testing in the Field

Although testing in a lab environment is a necessary step in assuring the quality of a software system, seeing how the system operates in a real production environment can be illuminating as well. Many larger software companies can afford to build large testing environments and hire administrators to configure the lab so that it looks something like a customer's environment. However, there is almost always a gap between the environment in which testers test and the environments in which users use the system. It would be extremely difficult to reproduce the exact applications, configurations, and processes that constitute a customer's environment.

Software manufacturers can sometimes get a feel for how their software will perform in the field by enlisting the help of the customers. In a *beta* release, a vendor gives a (sometimes) limited set of customers a version of the system that is not quite complete. Commercial vendors may offer a discount or provide some other incentive to get beta customers to try the software and give the vendor feedback.

Software manufacturers can also employ third-party testing companies to test their systems. Many companies use such services in order to get their systems validated against a particular standard. In order to get a Common Criteria certification, for instance, a system must be evaluated by an approved third-party testing organization. The rationale is that third-party firms are more objective than the manufacturer, and they typically possess specialized testing skills, such as security testing.

Some third-party security testing firms "test" the security of a vendor's product free of charge. Security software companies that sell vulnerability scanners and vulnerability-management products, such as *eEye* and *ISS* (recently acquired by IBM), employ security researchers to look for vulnerabilities in shipping products [eey, ISS]. Although there is no direct compensation from the vendor for finding a vulnerability, there are some indirect forms of payment: The testing company gets credit for the find, and its tool becomes the first to locate the problem.

The type of testing that security researchers perform is quite different from what testers do back in the lab. Security researchers typically have no access to the target application's developers; in fact, the relationship between the testing company and the vendor may be adversarial. Additionally, many vendors do not release the source code of their products, so security researchers are typically limited to do some form of black-box testing.

Because the constraints of the job are different, security researchers and traditional testers use different sets of tools and techniques. A number of excellent texts on this topic exist, so we limit this discussion to an overview of some of the most common techniques. Interested readers should consult Hoglund and McGraw's *Exploiting Software* [HM04], Kaspersky's *Hacker Dissassembling Uncovered* [Kas07], Harris et al.'s *Gray Hat Hacking* [HHE+04], Kozoil et al.'s *Shellcoder's Handbook* [KLA+04], and Dowd et al.'s excellent book *The Art of Software Security Assessment* [DMS06].

11.3.6 Observation

A good place to start testing a piece of deployed software is to simply watch it. Specifically, watching what ports it opens up on the network is useful in defining the application's *attack surface*—the portion of the application that can be accessed by an attacker. Once the network entry points have been established, watching the network data that flows in and out of the application is useful. Simply passively sniffing the network data can give testers insight into application-layer protocols. If the target application has multiple components, as most enterprise applications do, then watching the data exchanged between different components, possibly over the network, can also be a great way to get some information about the application.

Another useful observation technique is to watch how an application interacts with its local environment. Applications typically store configuration information in the Windows registry or in `/etc`. Such configuration information can tell a tester where other components (e.g., log files) are, which objects are available over particular network services, and so on. Applications can also leak all sorts of information in files that it uses—particularly log files. Many developers use the log file to print debugging information, which can be extraordinarily useful to a security tester.

In the Windows environment, a systemwide debugging mechanism is accessible to developers via the `OutputDebugString()` API call. A developer can pass a debugging string as an argument and then capture all the debugging information by using a tool such as `dbgview` [Rus07]. In fact, *anyone* running `dbgview` (not only the developer) can capture the debugging output. Some software companies do not disable the debugging information before shipping, allowing any customer/tester with a copy of `dbgview` to watch the debug stream. In practice, we have seen all sorts of sensitive information, such as usernames and passwords, leaked via this mechanism.

Finally, testers can dig into system-level resources to get more information about a deployed application. Watching kernel objects, such as semaphores and shared memory segments, can sometimes turn up interesting information. Using techniques similar to keyjacking (see Chapter 8), testers can inject code into the running application and watch API calls, their arguments, and their return values.

11.3.7 Fuzzing

Another useful tool for testing deployed software is *fuzz testing*, or *fuzzing*: sending unexpected and/or malformed data to the application. (Recall Section 6.2.1.) Fuzz testing typically produces interesting results on network-facing services. According to anecdote, fuzz testing stems from a dark and stormy night when Bart Miller [MFS90] dialed into a time-shared UNIX system and noticed that the storm-induced electrical noise was introducing random changes to what he was typing—but these randomly changed commands still caused the computer to *do* something. Fuzz testing has evolved considerably since then and is sometimes called *dumb fuzzing* or *smart fuzzing* depending on how much the test harness exploits the structure of the data it is fuzzing.

Connecting to the network-facing portions of an application and then sending all sorts of data can show testers how robust the application-layer protocols are. Although the initial impact of these types of tests is limited to denial of service, the tests are useful in finding weak spots in the protocol, as well as potential memory-management problems.

In addition to the network, putting random data into the application's local environment can be useful as well. Putting unexpected data in configuration files, temporary working files, and log files can produce some interesting results. These tests will likely simply cause the application to crash, but they show where data-handling problems exist in the application.

By injecting test code into the application and hijacking the application's API calls, testers can perform fuzz testing at the API level. The idea is for the test code to capture API calls; modify their arguments and/or return values, exchanging valid data with garbage; and then pass control back to the application to see how it deals with the garbage. Such techniques are sometimes called *software fault injection*, and there are even commercial testing products based on these ideas [Secb, VM97].

11.3.8 Crafting an Exploit

Armed with information gathered during observation and a list of places where data may be mismanaged, a tester may attempt to dig deeper and find a vulnerability. This process usually requires some level of visibility into the application. Since testers may not have access to the application's source code, they may have to *disassemble* the program in order to get assembly from the shipped binaries.

Once the application has been disassembled, testers can then look for suspect programming structures, such as the now-infamous `strcpy()` C library function.[4] Once a target has been identified, the tester has the tedious job of trying to locate a code path that begins from user or network input and finishes at the suspect call. If such a path is found, then the tester has found a vulnerability, and the final step is to construct some interesting input that will exercise the vulnerabilty. This interesting input is called an *exploit*. An internal tester could use the exploit to help convince management of the severity of the problem. An external tester, armed with an exploit, may call the vendor in order to resolve the issue, may publish it in black-hat circles, or may use it as a propagation vector for a worm or other attack.

11.4 The Take-Home Message

In this chapter, we've covered a number of criteria and approaches that can aid in determining how likely it is that a given system can end up in an unsafe state. If we drill into this concept a bit, we can imagine that the system is in a particular state at a given moment in time. We can also think of the *behavior* over time as consisting of various sequences of states that the system has transitioned through. Some behaviors are good; others aren't.

It's worth mentioning that examining a behavior (i.e., a sequence of states) is better than simply examining some static state. Often time, you can see a system's security problems only if you look at the broader context of the system and how it is has progressed through the state space over a period of time.

Theoretically, there exists some function F that can determine whether a particular behavior is bad. In Chapters 15 and 17, we discuss some emerging research that attempts to build such tools. Until such quantitative methods of validation and testing are commonplace—if they ever are—we are left with such things as compliance, accountability, and negative testing. Although such methods aren't absolute, using them early and using them often can certainly reduce the risk that your system is compromised in the field. That's the best that the current state of the art will allow.

---

4. We say that `strcpy()` is infamous because, as we discussed earlier, it is responsible for numerous buffer overflows throughout the years. The function is used to copy string but does so without consideration for the source and destination string length. If the destination is not large enough to hold the string being copied, buffer overflow occurs. Interestingly, this is not an implementation "flaw"—This is what the API for this library function says it's supposed to do!

11.5 Project Ideas

1. Download and read some of the standards and best practice frameworks. Do they apply to your school or workplace? If so, how are they implemented there? How much does that environment spend keeping up-to-date?

2. If you work with software, try to instrument your environment with unit tests and possibly a coverage tool. How much of your code can you test during the daily build this way?

3. Download a software product, perhaps one for which the source code is available as well, or take one that you work on and perform a security audit on it. Can you craft an exploit against it?

4. Take a small piece of code and try to craft an F that determines whether the system is well behaved. If you can come up with F, try to code it up and run it over the system. If you can't come up with F, why can't you? Are there any heuristics that may give a good approximation?

5. See whether you can find anything interesting with dbgview.

6. As we noted, attackers and security testers share considerable mindset. Discuss the challenges this overlap creates. Should an enterprise hire former attackers as testers? Should experience in crafting malicious attacks disqualify a job candidate (as unethical), or should the lack of such experience disqualify a job candidate (as incompetent)? How does a skilled hacker obtain these skills? Should schools teach hacking?

Part IV

Applications

The Web and Security 12

With any luck, we two coauthors are still in the first halves of our lives. As relative youngsters, it's strange to be able to start talking like an old-timer. But old-timers we are, for we can remember the Dark Ages before there was a Web.

Yes, Virginia, there was such a time. Public networked interaction took place on such things as USENET newsgroups (all ASCII text). Indeed, there once wasn't even an "Internet"; and email via BITNET and UUNET required knowing not only your colleague's email address but also the route by which a message could get from your site to your colleague's site.

However, thanks to lazy physicists in Switzerland, we now have the World Wide Web. We could spend quite a bit of time on this topic; it seems that every time we try to nail down some specific behavior or issue, we discover a few more wrinkles. Indeed, the Web offers a microcosm of security's overarching issues. We see a continual churn of evolving standards, code, and practices—one of the reasons it's hard to nail down details. We see code that doesn't always work, including different versions of the same browser that do not work the same way. We see a notion of "correctness" that is very hard to pin down. We see a history of implementation blunders. And we also see a technology that nonetheless has become central to the way modern society operates.

Discussing the Web uses many of the elements we've talked about so far. We need to talk about "correctness" (Chapter 1), networks (Chapter 5), implementation blunders (Chapter 6), cryptography (Chapter 7), authentication (Chapter 9), and PKI (Chapter 10). This material also relates to topics we deal with later: policy and models (Chapter 15), secure hardware (Chapter 16), and human behavior (Chapter 18).

- Section 12.1 goes through the big picture to refresh the pieces of the basic structure.
- Section 12.2 discusses standard security techniques for Web interaction.
- Section 12.3 focuses on some of the privacy implications.
- Section 12.4 quickly reviews the emerging area of *Web services.*

However, the Web is a rapidly evolving field where standards seem to be regarded as even more optional and flexible than is normal. Consequently, we need to raise a big, visible caveat here: Although the issues we discuss are current at the time of this writing, one never knows what the future will bring.

12.1 Basic Structure

12.1.1 Basic Action

Reasoning about the security and privacy issues involved in a process, such as Web interactions, requires starting with a mental model of the process. Since humans seem to like building mental models from what they experience, and since every reader has probably experienced using the Web, we start with the model that experience suggests.

Let's suppose that user Alice is visiting a Web page at Bob's site. At first glance, we have these elements:

- Alice and Bob
- Alice's machine, running a Web browser
- Bob's machine, running some type of Web server
- Bob's web page P.

We then have this action:

- Alice pointing her browser to Bob's site
- Bob's server sending back the page P
- Alice's browser displaying P

However, reality is more complex than this simple model, and this is where the fun comes in. The Web has become the primary portal for all sorts of information and service delivery. As a consequence, stakeholders of all types need to make rational decisions about security and privacy implications of their actions in this medium. These stakeholders range from ordinary (or even savvy) users, to individuals setting up Web pages, to enterprises contemplating Web servers—to legislators, lawyers, and insurers making policy decisions about responsible and negligent behavior in this realm. When a user's mental model omits crucial complexity, that user may make important decisions (with important real-world ramifications) based on a pretend view of the situation. Such mistakes may be significant. We thus use this mismatch as a stepping stone to exploring Web security issues.

12.1.2 The Page Request

The Browser's Request.   We might start by thinking about Alice's request: the *uniform resource locator (URL)* that she might have typed in to the location bar. Consider:

> http://www.cs.dartmouth.edu/~sws/

- The http indicates that it is the network protocol to be used. We think of the Web as synonymous with the *Hypertext Transport Protocol (http)*. In fact, this identification is often implicit: Web sites sometimes omit the protocol part when advertising URLs; Web browsers often fill in the http protocol by default, if a protocol part isn't specified.

  However, browsers often also happily speak other network protocols, such as ftp and telnet, as well as https, which we discuss later. The protocol issue is further complicated by the fact that many browsers will also act as a portal into Alice's own filesystem; so a protocol name, such as "file", might send the browser not into outer cyberspace but rather into Alice's own machine.

- The hostname "www.cs.dartmouth.edu" indicates the external Web site at which the page lives. Bob will have configured the server software at this machine to look within some special directory there for Web material.

- The path "~sws" indicates where the material Alice wants lives within this directory at Bob's machine. In this case, in standard filesystem semantics, Bob's machine will look in the home directory of user sws, within a directory called public_html. (We should point out that the directory may not always be on Bob's physical machine; things like failure and load balancing may move the material to different machines, even though the address doesn't change.) If the URL specifies a directory rather than a filename, the server will default to looking for a well-defined index file, such as index.html; if no index file can be found, the server may, depending on its configuration, provide instead a listing of the directory.

- Of course, this behavior does not follow from the laws of nature but rather from tradition mixed up with various standards. The server software can in fact do whatever it wants to, and Bob may have several standard configuration options, such as *redirecting* requests for certain URLs to other places.

Of course, this complexity may have security ramifications. What server is Alice's machine working with, really? What file at Bob's machine is being shown?

Alice's Request.   In the preceding discussion of URLs, we casually observed that Alice may have typed the URL into her browser. At one point, perhaps, that might have been the dominant way users began their Web exploration. However, the dominant way today has gone through several levels of changes.

- Alice cuts-and-pastes rather than types the URL into her browser. (Is she paying as much attention to the details for the URL?)
- Alice simply clicks on a link from another page. Sometimes, if she mouses over the link without clicking, the URL may appear on the *status bar* at the bottom of the browser. Is she paying attention?
- Alice simply clicks on a link inside an email, PDF file, or some other content that does not even explicitly appear to be Web content.

These subtleties are significant because the first level of access control and authentication occur inside Alice's head, based on her perception of what site she's visiting. Even if she sees the URL, it's not clear that Alice will make the correct decision. (Indeed, *phishing* attacks exist precisely because enough users do not make good decisions about the URLs their clicks invoke.)

- In the hierarchical way that hostnames are decided, an organization that controls a name may set up hosts with essentially arbitrary prefixes added to that name. For example, in theory, nothing stops dartmouth.edu from setting up a hostname

    www.trustworthy.bank.com.dartmouth.edu.

    Would customers of

    www.trustworthy.bank

    notice the difference? For another interesting example, an enterprise recently registered the hostname and set up an automated system so that requests to URLs with the suffix

    name.edu.com

came back with Web content that appeared to represent the university "name." (Universities were not happy.)

- The tendency of some browsers to helpfully expand incomplete URLs into what they think the user intended can also cause the user to end up somewhere other than where she intended. We recall a classroom demonstration in which typing in the partial URL "whitehouse" caused the browser to go not to "www.whitehouse.gov," the site of the U.S. president's residence, but to "www.whitehouse.com," which was at that time a pornographic site.

- *Typejacking* is another old approach to subverting the user's perception of where he or she is going. Here, the adversary uses creative typography to pick a domain name that appears deceptively similar to the intended one. One of the first well-known cases was "paypai.com," which, when rendered lowercase in standard fonts, looks an awful lot like "paypal.com." One suspects that "paypal.com"—substituting a numeral for the lowercase l—might also work.

    In recent years, *Unicode* encoding of characters has begun supplanting ASCII, in order to accommodate the much larger sets of fonts required for internationalization. Researchers have speculated on the potential for typejacking using similar-looking characters from fonts other than the standard Roman ones that Western users expect.

- Web standards also permit users to specify a user name and password as well as the hostname: "username:password@hostname." This feature can also be used to deceive users: for example, the adversary can provide a link with a URL where the "username" component itself looks like the intended URL and the remaining components are obscured. Some versions of IE even had an escape sequence bug (recall Section 6.2.4) that, if the URL had the correct escape characters before the "@," the browser would not even display the "@" and what came after, thus leaving the user to make a trust judgment based only on the fake part of the URL [Int04].

- Even if the user is perceptive enough not to be fooled by deceptive URL tricks, the adversary can do an end run around this wisdom. Web pages can consist of more than simply passive content, as we discuss in Section 12.1.3. Some spoofing sites have packaged links with event handlers for mouse events, in order to tell the browser to render a fake URL on the status bar when the user moves the mouse over the link.

Chapter 18 considers further these issues of how humans make trust judgments based on user interfaces.

Interaction.   In her mind, Alice may be doing more than simply requesting pages from Bob's server; she may be trying to fill out a form or otherwise interact with the Web content. HTML provides a standard set of tools for this. The Web page code can include `form` elements. A `form` element includes a URL to which the form information should be sent when submitted, a `method` by which to submit it, as well as `input` elements. These `input` elements create such things as radio buttons to click, boxes to type text into, and even ways for a user to name a file to upload. Each `input` element can specify a `name` of the parameter it collects. Filling out the input attaches a value to this parameter. Sometimes, the `input` code can even include a default value to use, if the user provides none; the specifications also allow for `hidden` input fields that provide a default value without letting the user know about it.

When the form is submitted, Alice's browser sends a request to the URL that the `form` element specified in its `action` field. Her browser also sends back all the parameter information associated with the input elements for that form. However, *how* her browser sends these parameters depends on the `method` of the `form`:

- If the page does it via GET, the answers to the questions are appended to the URL sent back.
- If the page does it via POST, the answers to the questions are sent back separately.

(*How* a Web form works might be considered a bit arcane for the average user. However, the question of whether a URL will contain the user's private responses certainly is not!)

Typically, the server on the other end of this URL will be configured to grab these parameters and respond somehow. Usually this is done by the URL's specifying a CGI script (although it could be any other kind of executable), which turns around and spits out HTML code to send back, perhaps after interacting first with some back-end service code.

Web Form Processing.   Alice's interaction with the Web form may involve providing sensitive information, such as her income or prescription information. Consequently, it is important to understand what happens to the information she's provided to the Web page in front of her.

- This information is going off to the server at the other end of the `action` URL.

- Unless countermeasures are taken to encrypt the channel, the entire set of questions and answers will be sent in plaintext over the network. This data will thus be visible to—and changeable by—any network-level adversary.
- If the parameters are sent back via GET, they formally become part of the URL the browser requests. This means that they will perhaps be visible in Web logs and history lists, as well as in the location bar of the browser. As part of the URL of the owning page, the information may even be passed on to third parties; see Sections 12.1.4 and 12.3.3.

Unfortunately, even if Alice is trained to examine the target URL that appears on the status bar when she mouses over a link, there is generally no easy way for her to determine the action URL of a form or whether the parameters will be sent via GET or POST.

Cross-Site Scripting   Server-side CGI scripts have been a common medium for *escape sequence* attacks over the years. Another family of evil-input attack is *cross-site scripting (XSS)*, by which a server injects code that appears to be from a different server. This approach is a bit tricky, so we'll walk through some examples.

- Alice is a Web user.
- Bob is a server operator.
- Alice trusts Bob. Unfortunately, Bob is not trustworthy; although he is not malicious, he's not as vigilant as he should be about how his interactive pages handle unexpected client input.
- Carlo has some malicious Web material M. He would like to have Alice render this material in her browser. However, Alice, wisely, does not trust Carlo.

In cross-site scripting, Carlo exploits Bob's carelessness by embedding the malicious content M within a page offered by Bob, or at least to make it appear that way. This enables Carlo to achieve his goal: Alice will accept this content because it comes from Bob, and she trusts him. How does Carlo do this? We offer two common scenarios:

- Bob's site might offer a blogging capability that lets third-party users upload content but does not sufficiently screen this content for escape sequences and other issues. Carlo enters M as part of an entry.
- Bob may have set up a site that lets Alice ask for complicated things via a URL; maybe Alice generates a complicated request based on a form response and GET. However, Bob's code fails to allow for bizarrely crafted input.

Carlo creates such an input and offers to Alice—for example, embedded in phishing email. She clicks on it, because it goes to Bob—but causes Bob's site to get Alice's browser to run the malicious M.

As a real-life example of the latter, we received some eBay phishing email that intended to harvest the recipient's eBay userid and password by offering this long link:

```
http://signin.ebay.com/ws/eBayISAPI.dll?
SignInMCAlert&
ru=http://client-66-116-24-226.consolidated.net:82
/signin.ebay.com/reg.php
```

It looks safe, since it goes to eBay. However, what's this `ru=` stuff all about? (It appears to redirect the user to this second URL, on successful login at eBay. We speculated that this second site may claim that login failed and offer a spoof of the eBay login page.)

12.1.3 Page Content

In the basic model, the user Alice points her browser (via typing or clicking) to Bob's site, the page P comes back, and Alice's browser renders it. Reality differs in many aspects.

Alice's Browser. To start with, this basic model might lead one to conclude that "rendering a page" is a well-defined action that all browsers do the same way. As many conscientious Web site designers have discovered, this is not the case. Different browsers act differently on content; we have even noticed that the *same* browser, on different OS platforms, acts differently.

Another fallacy with this model is that the rendering is done entirely by Alice's browser. Although standard html content probably is, many other types of content may get sent to other applications on Alice's machine; for example, PDF documents may get sent to Adobe Acrobat. Sometimes, this rerouting of content to a particular handler is very explicit and "transparent" to the user.

- Alice may see the separate application get invoked and thus know that this separate application is involved.
- Some browsers may even make it very easy for Alice to configure what application programs should be invoked for what type of content.

Unfortunately, this rerouting more often simply happens without the user's awareness (another version of "transparent").

- The rendering via a separate application may occur *within* Alice's browser's window, leading to an impression that this is part of the browser itself.

- On some platforms, how to configure or even investigate how the browser maps content types to separate applications may be rather elusive for the ordinary or even savvy user.

From a software engineering perspective, invoking a separate application can make sense. Why absorb the full source for a complicated task *within* the browser when we can plug in the appropriate module instead? Why maintain *two* different programs that process the same content type? From a security perspective, this approach can sometimes be useful: It reduces the size and complexity of all the applications involved. However, this approach can also be dangerous. In the current de facto Internet security model, the external network is full of adversaries, and OS and application software are full of design and implementation blunders. As a consequence, it's critical to know where one's front line is: The applications whose APIs are exposed to the outside world are the ones the user has to be scrupulous about patching and mindful about using. When browsing the Web, the user may naturally think that the browser is the front line; however, transparent invocation of separate programs to handle untrusted content undermines the truth of that perception.

Active Content.   Another potentially deceiving aspect of Web browsing is the potential illusion that the page P is just that: a passive page consisting of text and graphics. In fact, Web pages can include various types of active, executable content. Trying to put an exhaustive list in a book like this is daunting; it seems that people are continually coming up with new ways to add flashy functionality to the medium. In the early days of the Web, active content came via three primary vehicles:

1. *Java applets*, small programs that could be embedded in a page, as if they were images

2. *JavaScript*,[1] code that was embedded in the HTML itself and could be called from places within the page

3. *ActiveX controls*, software components that could expose functionality to other programs or Web pages

---

1. Note, however, that JavaScript is used for more than simply active code within a Web page. The language has other uses: For example, in the Web context, it might be used for parts of the browser itself, as well as to write the server-side programs that catch and respond to forms submissions. When you hear "It's JavaScript," be sure to distinguish where in this space the JavaScript is running.

However, many more vehicles have emerged: flashy animations, Flash movies, Shockwave, sound.

As we noted earlier, the user's mental model of the systems state and the implications of the user's actions guide the implementation of the user's implicit security policy. Is this safe? Should I do this? A reasonable-sounding rule of thumb is that passive content is harmless; indeed, this led to the early guideline that "one cannot get infected from reading email," which may have been true when email was only ASCII text. Because of the potential for active content, this rule of thumb does not apply in the context of the Web. What programs are you downloading? What can they do? What parts of your system configuration are responsible for seeing that they don't do anything bad? Are they updated with the latest patches, and do you believe that no problems remain? (On some systems, we've seen that the browser depends on the Java environment it finds in the OS, so making sure that the browser is updated is not enough.)

During the early days of the Web, randomly and unwittingly downloading executable content was considered sufficiently dangerous that, at the first author's Los Alamos job, browsing the Web with Java or JavaScript enabled was considered a security violation, even though the computer itself was open and unclassified. As time progressed, however, more and more Web content required such features to work; disabling them left one's browser too crippled to function. (We also recall a Netscape version on which the browser quietly ignored the configuration request to disable JavaScript, but that's a different story.)

Trying to investigate what a Web page really does can be tricky. Suppose that the server operator Bob puts up a Web page P whose HTML contains some JavaScript code so that when Alice's browser renders it, it spits out HTML code P' instead. We've noticed at least one occasion when Alice tries to investigate the page content via the "view page source" feature on her browser, she sees the source HTML for P', even though the browser saw P.

One Page. The natural mental model of fetching a Web page suggests that a Web page is one atomic unit, fetched in one action. Reality differs from this model in many respects.

To start with, pages commonly include images. For example, the HTML source code for the page may have a line

```
<img align="right" src="wakely.jpg"></img>.
```

As part of rendering this page, Alice's browser needs to obtain this image. Fulfilling this need may break the "one page" model in several ways:

- To save time, Alice's browser might first look in a local cache for the image. If Alice has visited a page with this image recently, which is likely if the image is something like a logo common to many pages at Bob's site, then it's quite possible that it's already in her browser's cache.

  Alice thinks that she's fetching an atomic page from Bob, but in fact, parts of it were already on her machine and may persist as state there after she's stopped browsing. (Web site authors can recommend whether an item should be cached and can suggest how quickly it might go stale. On the other end, some browsers provide tools to allow users to set cache properties and perhaps even flush it.)

- If the image is not in the cache, Alice's browser may issue a separate URL request to Bob's site to get the image. Alice may think that that she's engaged in one request/response interaction with Bob's site, but her browser may do several.

- The image may in fact live on a site different from Bob's, so Alice's browser may send a request there instead. Alice may think that she's engaged in an interaction with Bob's site, but her browser may silently be carrying on interactions with other sites as well.

- Bob may even have made the image so small that Alice will not even see it when her browser renders it.

As we shall see in later discussion, each of these departures from the standard mental model can lead to security issues.

Bob's page could also include an image tag whose source is a CGI script instead of an image. Web development guides tout this technique as a feature, since it enables the page author to provide a script that is executed whenever the user visits the page; however, we can imagine more devious uses.

Framesets (sketched in Figure 12.1) are another Web element that breaks this "one page" model. With a frameset, Web page author Bob can partition a page into frames and specify a separate URL for each frame. When rendering a frameset, Alice's browser will, for each frame, fetch the URL and render that page within that frame. Alice may think that she has just fetched a page from Bob's site, but her browser may have silently fetched full-blown pages, not just images, from other sites as well. (See our keyjacking work for details [MSZ03, MSZ05].)

Framesets can also have amusing consequences for isolation. Web page author Cathy may write her page thinking that the user will interact directly with it. If Cathy's page gets rendered within a frame in Alice's browser, user Alice may also implicitly assume that her interactions with Cathy's site will be confined to clicks she makes within Cathy's page. However, framesets permit tricks whereby clicks within a

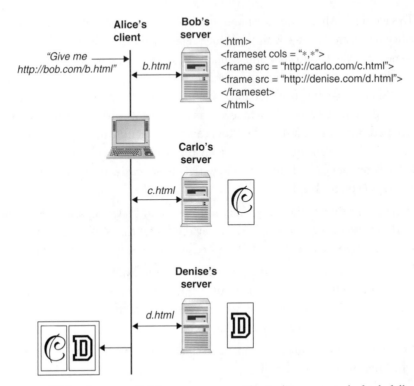

Figure 12.1 With a frameset, Bob's server can get Alice's client to quietly fetch full pages from other servers and render them.

slightly deviously crafted frame (e.g., from Bob) can cause Alice's browser to interact with the pages loaded into other frames, unbeknownst to Alice. Reality does not quite match the mental model—and user security judgments made according to the model may not match reality. Indeed, as this book is going to the printer, this general approach of Bob's using his page to trick Alice's browser into unwittingly launching requests is starting to get broader attention as *cross-site request forgery (CSRF)* (e.g., see [Hig07]).

12.1.4 State

In the early days of the Web, a standard mantra was that "http is stateless." To each request from Alice's browser, Bob's server responds as if it's never heard from Alice's browser before.

From the perspective of a modern Web user, this statelessness sounds rather annoying. Alice doesn't simply click to get information; more typically, she engages in a longer-term interaction with a site. She might be browsing a vendor's online store, adding items to her shopping cart, and then checking out; she might be engaged in a long sequence of answering questions as part of obtaining an e-government service, such as renewing her ham radio license with the FCC.

Because http is stateless but many types of interesting Web applications required state, folks figured out workarounds to give the user the illusion of a long-lived session. The main workaround is the use of *cookies*, specially formatted data items exchanged between servers and browsers according to certain rules.

When Alice's browser visits Bob's page, Bob's server can leave a cookie at Alice's browser. With this cookie, Bob's server can set an *expiration date* as well as *domain* and *path* policy specifications. When it visits a page whose domain and path satisfy the specifications for a cookie that hasn't expired, Alice's browser will send the cookie to that server. Over the years, browser developers have offered user-side tools for managing cookies, beginning with an option to reject all of them, and growing to permit more increasingly sophisticated policy. (Cynically, we note that such tools haven't always worked, as is often the case of complex software—recall Chapter 6.)

Servers can track browser state and thus provide the illusion of a continuous Web session in other ways as well. One way is by maintaining a hidden `form` field in each page, in order to enable the server to correlate a request with a previous request. Another way is via the (misspelled[2]) `REFERER` field, by which a browser informs a server of the "current" page when the browser generates a request for a new one. For example, a newspaper Web site might use the `REFERER` field to make sure that users can access individual articles only by coming through the "front page" page first.

As with other Web elements, the devious reader might immediately think of interesting "corner" cases regarding `REFERER` behavior. In order for the browser to report the "current" URL as in the `REFERER`, must the user explicitly click within that page? If the user clicks within a frame, which URL gets reported? What if the user types in a new URL? What if the user selects a URL from a bookmark instead? As with other Web elements, one might check the current standards to see what is *supposed* to happen, although a safer bet might be to check the intended browsers instead. Reality can differ from standards—and from itself, for that matter.

In theory, other methods of tracking state exist as well—for example, a server might examine network-level information, such as the TCP/IP session. In practice, one doesn't see this happening.

---

2. Phil Hallam-Baker has taken credit for this misspelling, but we are not sure whether to believe him.

Web pages also rely on *asynchronous JavaScript and XML (AJAX)* to provide the illusion that a Web page is stateful. Many of the emerging "Web 2.0" applications rely on AJAX to deliver a desktop-style user experience, even though the application is running on a server across the Web somewhere.

Of course, all this work of using state-preserving techniques in order to accommodate the user's and the service provider's mental models of what a Web session should be raises a natural question. Can we in fact define what a Web session is? We can start with a few natural observations.

- It should be between a human user and a service.
- The duration should be longer than a single click/return, if the user is staying with that server longer.

However, even these natural observations raise challenging corner cases:

- Should a Web session accommodate families of individual server machines within the same site?
- Should a Web session accommodate alliances between separate domains cooperating in some service? (For example, shopping at bikeman.com can take the user to paypal.com and back; the front page of cnn.com may take a reader to time.com.)
- Should a Web session allow interruptions, that is, the user goes off to another site and comes back? (For example, when shopping at bikeman.com, the user might go check a price at a competitor site or a specification at a manufacturer site.)
- What if the user goes away and then comes back via a different window?
- What if the user comes back in from a different browser?
- What if the user doesn't want to come back as him- or herself? (For example, perhaps a roommate wants to check something, and it's a shared computer.)
- What if the user has two windows (or two browsers or two frames) going simultaneously?
- What about disconnected operation?

Generally speaking, the Web has undergone continual evolution, without much thought to what it "meant." Features get added when they appear fun. So, generally speaking, if one pokes around and tries to formalize, one will find that the details keep getting fuzzy.

Because these state-preserving techniques are intended to provide context about the user's interaction, their existence raises security concerns for the user. What state *is* preserved? Which servers get to see it? What might adversaries with access to Alice's computer learn about her past browsing patterns? These issues are important, and we discuss them later. However, concern over these user security issues can obscure the security issues that *servers* face, because they may be making security-relevant decisions based on information the user—a potential adversary—is providing. In theory—and also in practice, with not that much work—nothing stops a user from modifying a browser to report an arbitrary REFERER field or hidden form field or a hand-edited cookie. History offers examples of this happening already.

- Amazon was (reported to be) using cookie state to determine what price to offer users; by sharing cookies, users could pass their discount on to friends. More recently, *Money Magazine* alleges the opposite behavior: online travel agents using cookies to give a user the same price they quoted earlier, rather than a better one [Ros06].

- An *ISS E-Security Alert* from 2000 warned of Web shopping cart software that used hidden fields in HTML forms to hold parameters, such as item price; item price is not supposed to be a user-modified field, but nothing stopped the user from modifying it—to a lower price, presumably.

- Graduate students at MIT set up a fun "cookie cutter" project whereby they systematically reverse engineered and broke cookie-based user authentication for real Web sites [FSSF01].

These are all classic examples of the permitted functionality exceeding the intended functionality. If Bob is using a cookie to store state information about the client at the client, how does he know it's still the same state information?

12.1.5 Network Issues

Because Web interaction works over the Internet, the network issues discussed in Chapter 5 have relevance to Web interaction. To start with, plaintext traffic can be eavesdropped. On WLANs and many LANs, it's a very easy exercise; at conferences, producing a mosaic of images from Web pages visited on the conference's wireless net is a fun party trick. Attacks at other levels of the network infrastructure also have Web implications. DNS and BGP attacks can let the adversary send a browser to the wrong site, even if the user was following all the rules. Cached DNS translations can let an adversary (such as one's employer) with access to the nameserver examine access patterns. As discussed in Section 5.4.1, the potential in a WLAN for an adversary to simply forge packets allegedly from someone else creates some interesting opportunities for attacking Web surfing: by spoofing DNS responses, Web server responses, or even Web browser responses.

12.2 Security Techniques

12.2.1 Basic Access Control

Computer security is traditionally framed in terms of access to information. One of the first questions when thinking about security of Web interactions might be how to control what users can access a site's information.

At a basic level, a Web site administrator can specify some basic access control policy via a `.htaccess` file established in the directory in question. This technique permits Bob to restrict access based on such things as IP address and domain name of the user or to require that a user log in with a username and password: *basic authentication*, in Web parlance. These techniques are in fact rather basic and do not provide a significant barrier to the adversary wishing to overcome them. The alleged IP address or domain name of the accessing computer can be forged via standard network attacks (Chapter 5). The username and password are typically sent in plaintext over the open Internet; the username–password pair also seldom changes and may be shared among many users. Even after authentication, the Web content itself will be sent over the open Internet; the information is subject to eavesdropping and modification; the connection, to hijacking.

Shortly before the turn of the century, the *digest authentication* method was standardized. This is an improvement over basic authentication in that, rather than sending the password in plaintext, the browser sends a hash of the username, password, site-specific information, and a nonce provided by the server [F+99].

Nonetheless, such basic access control still has some uses. For example, most course Web pages at Dartmouth are restricted to Dartmouth IP space, in order to keep nonaffiliated personnel from casually wandering in. Online information archives that make data available only to subscribing enterprises may also authenticate a requester via IP address.

In practice, a Web site administrator using `.htaccess` for access control may run into stumbling blocks. Here are some we have seen:

- The domain name rules have somewhat counterintuitive semantics. For example, the policy

  ```
  deny from all
  allow from dartmouth.edu
  ```

may look as though it permits access only from hosts within the Dartmouth domain. In fact, it permits access from hosts whose names literally end with the suffix "dartmouth.edu". A user at "hackers.notdartmouth.edu" will be allowed in.

- Things grow. Enterprises may find that they have more hosts than easily fit into their IP space and instead resort to *network address translation*—so that internal hosts may have either a standard address within the enterprise's range or a local address (e.g., `10.0.0.1`). When Dartmouth started silently doing this, Web pages restricted to

```
deny from all
allow from 129.170.0.0/16
```

stopped being reachable for students who were getting `10.` addresses in their dorm rooms.

- In some enterprises, each user `foo` may have a Web site accessible at
      http://domainname.org/~foo/.
  When asked for that path, the enterprise's Web server will look for a directory called `public_html` within the home directory of `foo`, within the enterprise filesystem. In order for the server to find this information, the directory `~foo/public_html` typically must be world-readable within the filesystem.

      As discussed in Chapter 1, we have often seen users, such as course instructors, attempt to make parts of a Web site, such as the part with last year's solutions, private by dropping an `.htaccess` in there—and forgetting that the material is still readable to students who access it via the filesystem instead of via the Web.

12.2.2 Server-Side SSL

The Protocol. Although basic authentication has its uses, it still isn't very secure. Early on, it became apparent that something stronger was needed. The first author remembers those ancient days, when there was no Internet Explorer. The breakthrough browser that everyone used was *Mosaic*, from *NCSA*. As we recall the story, a portion of the Mosaic team left NCSA to form *Netscape*; however, a portion of the Mosaic team remained at NCSA. Both teams claimed to be the "real" Mosaic team. Both teams also developed security solutions for the Web.

- The Netscape team designed *Secure Sockets Layer (SSL)* and shipped it with their free browser.

- The Mosaic team very slowly designed *Secure HTTP* with the CommerceNet consortium and shipped it, eventually, with a browser one needed to buy.

There's an interesting systems tradeoff between the two: SSL is more general, since it's not specific to HTTP, but S-HTTP (potentially) was more efficient, since it was tuned to HTTP. Microsoft also tried to enter the game later with its *PCT (private communication technology)* protocol but, oddly, backed down and backed SSL instead.

Of course, we wrote the preceding descriptions with the benefit of hindsight, which makes it clear that SSL was logically positioned to dominate. However, at the time, the outcome wasn't as clear. We recall allusions to the "Betamax versus VHS" technology debate and to e-government pioneers worrying which horse to back.

Like most things that make it into the real world, SSL allows for many options and variations. We start by considering what is probably the most common instantiation: what happens when Alice initiates a "secure" Web interaction.

- She starts this by clicking on a link that specifies an https: protocol rather than the typical http.

- Alice's browser and Bob's server then negotiate a mutually acceptable *ciphersuite:* the set of cryptographic algorithms they will use in this connection. For the latest versions of the protocol, this will include a symmetric cipher, for encryption, as well as a method of checking integrity of messages (e.g., a hash function). (Recall Chapter 7.)

- Bob's server has a public/private key pair and an X.509 identity certificate binding the identity of the server to the public key (see Chapter 10). Bob's server sends this certificate to Alice's browser, which goes through some magic, discussed shortly, to decide whether to trust this certificate.

- Alice's browser picks some random bits (the pre_master_secret), and sends them back to Bob's server—but first encrypting them with Bob's public key.

- At this point, both Alice and Bob know this random seed value—but no eavesdropper should be able to know both, because pre_master_secret was encrypted with Bob's public key. Both Alice and Bob then use this secret seed value, along with some other public values, to derive a set of keys that also should be secret. (In the true spirit of Kerckhoff's Principle, this derivation is done via a published function that uses these values as parameters.) This set includes an encryption key for browser-to-server communications, as well as one for server-to-browser communications; if the

ciphersuite's integrity-checking function also is keyed, this set will include a
pair of keys, one for each direction, for that as well.

- Subsequent communications between Alice's browser and Bob's server—
within this SSL session, anyway—will then be encrypted and integrity-checked
using the algorithms in the negotiated ciphersuite and the derived keys. This
communication will include the URL, form responses, cookies, and so on.

(See Figure 12.2.)

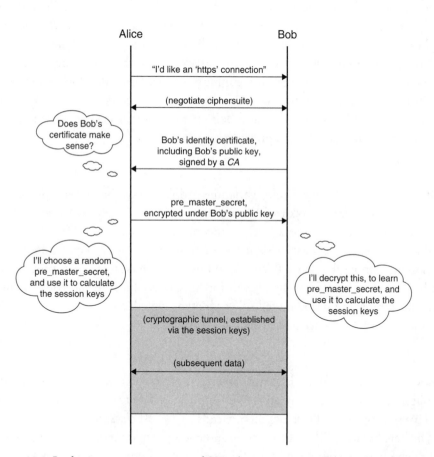

Figure 12.2 In the most common usage of SSL, the server presents a certificate that binds
its identity to a public key. In theory, Alice's browser checks that this identity makes sense
for the session in question. Alice's browser then picks a random seed, encrypts it with the
server's public key, and sends it back. Alice uses this seed to establish a cryptographic tunnel
and can conclude that the party on the other end is the holder of the private key matching
the server's certificate.

This standard flavor is also called *server-side SSL*, since the server is the one presenting a PKI certificate. After going through several evolutions, SSL was standardized as the *Transport Layer Security (TLS)* protocol [DR06], which is why one will see it referred to as SSL/TLS or perhaps even simply TLS sometimes.

In theory, server-side SSL provides several protections for Alice and Bob. First, since Bob must present a certificate and (in order to complete the handshake) know the private key matching the public key to which the certificate testifies, we have authentication: Alice can be sure that it's Bob on the other end. Since the communications are encrypted, Alice and Bob are protected against an adversary who eavesdrops. Since the communications are checked for integrity, Alice and Bob are protected against an adversary who tries to alter the plaintext by altering the ciphertext. Since the keys differ for each direction, Alice and Bob are protected against an adversary who tries *reflection* attacks. Since the communications have sequence numbers within the cryptographic boundary, Alice and Bob are protected against an adversary who tries to reorder messages. Since the keys are generated fresh for each SSL session, Alice and Bob are protected against an adversary who tries to replay messages from a previous session.

SSL Variations.   Of course, other variations of SSL are possible as well. SSL permits the client and the server to skip certificates altogether and simply use Diffie-Hellman to establish shared session keys. This is sometimes called *anonymous SSL*. The second author has come across this variation numerous times during security audits. It's important to note that since this variation doesn't use certificates, it provides no authentication. It provides a handy way for Alice to establish an encrypted channel with something, but it doesn't tell Alice who that something is.

Section 12.2.3 discusses the client-side variation.

Uses.   Server-side SSL finds nearly universal use in e-commerce and e-government applications, as well as many other Web applications that require users to send or receive sensitive data. (This popularity leads to a good classroom or lecture trick: "Who here has used PKI?" In a general audience, not many hands will go up. Then: "But who here has purchased something online?") If one's enterprise provides an SSL server, SSL combined with basic Web authentication can be an easy way to set up a private Web site.

Furthermore, many standard network protocols have been adapted to layer over SSL.

Problems.   Note that we used the caveat "in theory" in our earlier discussion of the security properties of SSL. In practice, many issues can undermine these properties: such as UI trouble, PKI trouble, bugs, and post-SSL privacy spills.

Probably the first issue that comes to mind is *user interface* issues. Can Alice easily tell that she's entered an SSL-protected site—and the site she intended? (We discuss these issues in great detail in Chapter 18.) Even beyond those UI issues, there are some design issues regarding correlation of SSL and sensitive data. Bob might offer a form page via SSL, but how does Alice know that the answers will be sent via SSL? The fact that cryptography can hurt performance leads Web sites to often move back and forth between HTTP and HTTPS—so Alice may be trained to ignore any SSL signals her browser gives her anyway.

Another set of issues come from *PKI* (recall Chapter 10). Authentication of Bob's server comes from Bob's certificate. However, what does this certificate mean? The teaching of PKI lays out several criteria by which Alice should decide to accept this certificate. Was it signed by a root CA she trusts? If not, can she construct a trust chain from a root she trusts to Bob's certificate? Have any of the certificates in this chain expired? Have any been revoked?

Unfortunately, the supporting infrastructure for servers and standard Web browsers does not do a particularly good job at these tasks.

- Standard browsers come with dozens of built-in trust root CAs. These are in the form of preinstalled-root CA certificates. Whether Alice even knows what these are—let alone whether she should trust them—is uncertain. Each browser has a different way of showing them—and if Alice finds hers, she will see that many of the roots may be enterprises that she's never heard of, and many may be out of business. For some of these defunct CAs, the key pair and certificate have literally been purchased by other parties; for others, who knows? Furthermore, according to at least some involved in the process, becoming included as a built-in trust root did not involve a thorough scrutiny for trustworthiness as much as it did paying a large fee [Smi03b].

    Alice may add a new trust root to her browser, but this process is rather cumbersome and, for the average user, a bit mysterious. This can lead to an ironic situation. If Alice belongs to a large enterprise that operates its own CA and mints certificates for its own SSL-protected Web servers, *those* servers—the ones that Alice *should* trust—will be flagged as untrustworthy; ones certified by the unknown built-in roots will be OK.

- From current investigation, it appears that standard browsers will not explicitly do certificate-chain discovery. However, if a server sends a chain, the browser will attempt to verify it, as long as it has a trust root at the one end.

- Browsers have begun to check revocation of server certificates, by default. However, their behavior when this check times out might be less than desirable—sometimes, they give the questionable certificate the benefit of the doubt.

- Users will typically click "OK" no matter what warning a browser raises, including warning about certificate expiration.[3]

- This situation is becoming only murkier. As they become more aware of PKI and perhaps other credentials, operating systems and user application suites start to offer their own credential and certificate-management stores and services—and these start to merge with the browser's store and processing of Web site certificates.

Suppose that Alice's browser succeeds in discovering and verifying a trust chain to Bob's certificate. This means that, according to the trust rules it uses, Alice's browser is going to carry out SSL with the party identified in that certificate. However, is this party the one with whom Alice believes she is communicating? Real life gives several examples where the certificate identity information does not seem to match what Alice intended.

- It used to be the case that www.palmstore.com had an SSL-protected page through which the user could purchase Palm computing equipment. If Alice clicked there and interrogated the site certificate, she would find that she has a secure connection to Modus Media International. Who on earth is Modus Media International? (It turns out it was the third party that Palm hired to run the Web store—but Alice has no way of knowing that.)

- In 2006, Alice could go to http://www.ual.com to see the Web site for United Airlines. If she clicked on the option to buy a flight, she got another page that still has the United Airlines logo on it. However, the location bar now read "https://www.itn.net". Furthermore, its certificate belonged to travelocity.com. (Thanks to Jothy Rosenberg for pointing this one out.)

---

3. Besides expiration dates, certificates also have "not valid before" dates. We ran into an issue once when, owing to failure of a backup battery, a laptop needed to do an SSL handshake with a server whose certificate appeared not to be valid until several decades in the future. This scenario did not leave laptop and browser in a clean failure mode—it was quite a while before we figured why the connection was failing.

• In the United States, an important component of applying to graduate school is having faculty members file letters of recommendation on behalf of the candidate. Soliciting and receiving these letters online may be convenient, but setting up the infrastructure for this is awkward. As a consequence, many universities, including Dartmouth, have begun outsourcing letter collection to third parties, which provide this service online.

The content of recommendation letters is sensitive and is usually considered confidential. Thus, these third parties usually have "secure" Web sites to collect this sensitive information. Unfortunately, neither the host domain name nor the information in the SSL certificate (e.g., ssl.linklings.net) betrays any clear relationship to the university in question. (Indeed, setting up a fictional third-party college application site could be great way for a dishonest student to learn what faculty recommenders are really saying.)

Experimentally, it seems that Web browsers will check the hostname of the URL in the browser's original request against the hostname in the certificate—but only if the original request was HTTPS. For example, as of this writing, a request to

https://www.gmail.com

will be redirected to a URL beginning with

https://www.google.com/accounts/

The server www.google.com can successfully carry out the SSL handshake with a certificate issued to www.google.com, but the browser will complain because

www.google.com ≠ www.gmail.com

However, if the browser request initially goes to

http://www.gmail.com

then the redirection to

https://www.google.com/accounts

still happens, but the browser doesn't complain—presumably since the SSL negotiation didn't start until after the redirection occurs. This delay creates the opportunity for attack: An adversary can use standard network attacks to "become" www.gmail.com to the user. Then, the adversary redirects the user's original request for www.gmail.com to an HTTPS request for another site—one with a valid SSL certificate and that the attacker controls. The user's browser will happily complete the SSL connection with no complaints.[4]

Historically, another source of trouble with SSL security has been bugs. As we discussed earlier, the session keys in SSL are derived from various nonces. However, only one, the `pre_master_secret`, will be secret from an eavesdropper. As we discussed in Section 8.1.1, when they were grad students at Berkeley, Ian Goldberg and David Wagner discovered significant trouble in how this seed was generated— and showed how an adversary could discover it and thus derive the session keys. This situation itself suggests an interesting research angle. All the entropy here comes from the client, but it's the server that can afford expensive hardware random number generators. How much work has there been into crypto protocols between parties with asymmetric resources?

There have also been occasional cryptographic bugs (e.g., [Hay03]) and subtle flaws in the ciphersuite negotiation protocols.

Another problem with server-side SSL is that, even if everything works, it protects the data only in transit. To use the words of Gene Spafford, it's the "equivalent of arranging an armored car to deliver credit card information from someone living in a cardboard box to someone living on a park bench" [Tri]. In theory, an adversary could monitor the network for things like credit card numbers sent in plaintext; a Web user should worry about sending such information to an SSL Web site that would accept only ciphersuites with 56-bit keys. In practice, the real risk appears to be the continual privacy spills suffered by e-commerce servers that collect information from their online customers—and then get hacked into, disclosing large amounts at once. SSL (alone) says nothing about that.

12.2.3 Client-Side SSL

The Protocol. As we discussed earlier, SSL typically involves one certificate—as part of the handshake, the server presents its certificate to the browser. Successful completion of the handshake proves that the server knows the private key matching the public one to which the server certificate attests. However, the protocol also permits the browser to present a certificate as part of the handshake (see Figure 12.3). In this option, successful completion would also prove to the server that the browser knows the private key matching the one to which the browser certificate attests.

---

4. Thanks to Gun Sirer for suggesting this attack.

Alice   Bob

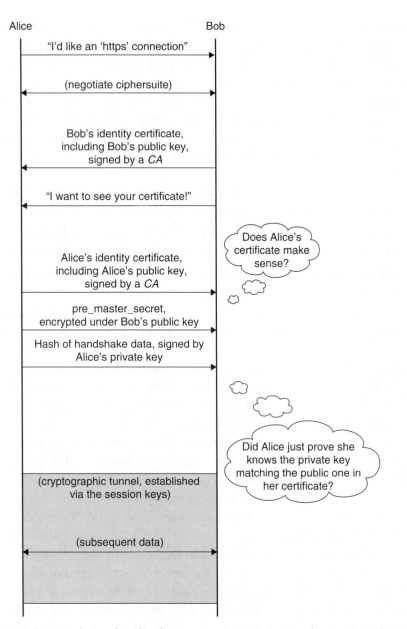

Figure 12.3 Server-side SSL lets the client use PKI to authenticate the server. In the *client-side* variation, the server requires that the client present a certificate and also prove knowledge of the private key matching the public one in that certificate.

Standard server tools will also make the information in the browser certificate available to the Web material. As a consequence, the server can then use this data—both successful authentication and details of the certificate—to make decisions about subsequent content and interaction.

For Web-based services whose users have certified key pairs, client-side SSL can be a vehicle for easy authentication and authorization of users. For example, Dartmouth offers a wide range of online information services to its population. These services range considerably in nature. For example:

- "Computing Sales and Services" wants to distribute its pricelist only to personnel associated with Dartmouth.
- The only party who should be able to access the college's "Blitzmail" (Dartmouth's hand-rolled email solution) account for a given user is that user.
- The only party who should be able to register a student for classes is that student.
- However, many parties might be able to see a student's grades and placement test scores: that student, that student's academic adviser, and various deans.

As the information age dawned, services such as these moved from paper to electronic; as the information age matured, these services moved onto the Web. As the Web matured, however, the college moved the authentication from various legacy password-based systems into client-side SSL. The college set up a CA and is issuing certificates to the user population. (By the time this book goes to print, the entire user population should have a key pair and certificate). The college also modified the back-end information service engines to accept client-side SSL.

As a consequence, users need only log in by unlocking their key pair. They no longer need to remember N different ways to log in for N services or worry whether their particular machine or network configuration supports a particular service's legacy authentication scheme. On the back end, the information service systems can use the information that the browser's certificate provides to make authorization decisions. For example, a faculty member serving as academic adviser for a half-dozen freshmen does not need to remember who they are or how to navigate deep into a system to find their records; when professor Alice goes to the student record site, the server realizes "it's Alice, she's an adviser" (from her certificate) and provides a customized page with links to the records for her advisees. Furthermore, the PKI frees the IT folks from having to worry about users revealing their master secret (a password) to each new Web site that requires authentication.

Practical Problems. In theory, client-side SSL promises a nice vision. Making it happen in the real world requires overcoming many practical problems. Probably the first on the list is the need to have users with certified key pairs. If, like Dartmouth, a single enterprise is providing enough services to a large enough set of captive users, then setting up an enterprise PKI may be a feasible (albeit nontrivial) approach.

This approach will require overcoming several challenges. For one thing, user key pairs—especially those that a browser may like to wield during SSL—will likely need to be accessible via the OS/browser keystore on the user's platform. Achieving this goal often leads to surprises; for example, the user might have to first manually load the enterprise's CA as a trust root in his or her browser.[5] Another issue is how to make a key pair portable across all the machines a user might use. Currently, the natural solution is to keep the key pair within a USB token, thus also providing some physical protection and two-factor authentication. However, we found that using tokens can negate the platform independence of client-side SSL. All modern browsers speak client-side SSL, but token vendors do not always supply drivers for all modern user platforms! On the back end, getting information services to work with client-side SSL can also lead to various annoyances—such as different vendors having incompatible versions of the same standard interface—that don't qualify as "research problems" but can be just as obstructive to practical progress.

Of course, an enterprise that lacks the critical mass of services and users to justify its own CA faces additional challenges. Will each user even have a certified key pair? If so, can the enterprise build a valid trust path to each one? If, in fact, such trust paths exist, can the Web server and browser figure out ways to discover them? How will the user who has several key pairs know which one to use for this service? (In experiments, we observed that one major browser would offer the user a list— but list only the "Distinguished Name" for each certificate. As a consequence, user Alice would be offered to select from a set of choices, each of which was identified solely by the name "Alice.") If Alice does not have a key pair, why would she bother getting one just for this service?

In theory, these problems can all be solved. In practice, it's probably safe to say that they remain an area of ongoing work.

Proponents of PKI tout the advantage that, unlike passwords, private keys are hard to share. However, in real-world information service settings, this feature can in fact be a bug. As we have noted, for many services requiring password authentication, one can find scenarios whereby users share passwords (a bad thing) because

---

5. This is another instance of the conundrum whereby the CAs the user has no way of trusting being silently trusted by the platform, but the CA that a user automatically trusts requiring extra work.

it's the easiest way to achieve what is arguably a reasonable goal. Administrative assistants to deans may need to log in as their deans. Roommates may need check the email of a student who's away, to see whether a critical job letter has arrived. If client-side SSL or any user authentication/authorization system does not allow for such delegation, it is likely that users will either ignore it or work around it—neither of which is a good outcome. We might hypothesize that, in order to be effective on a large scale in real-world human settings, client-side SSL will need to overcome the limited expressiveness of simple identity certificates. (We've also been doing some research here [MS07, SS07].)

Another set of practical issues in deploying client-side SSL, even in an enterprise setting, is that users may need access to other services that require authentication and authorization but might not easily adapt to the Web or SSL. Such services might include VPNs—although Web-based approaches do exist—network admission, S/MIME email, and so on. To the extent that these other services require different schemes or PKI with different client key pairs, user adoption of client-side SSL may be hindered.

Security Problems. We've been singing the praises of client-side SSL. It is indeed a nice way—using standards, and standards that standard browsers actually support—to get strong authentication on Web browser requests. However, when considering technological solutions to problems, particularly security problems, it's always good to stop and ask: "Does it work?"

When our college, assisted by our lab, started deploying client-side SSL, we asked ourselves this question. Does a Web request packaged within an SSL session established properly using Alice's private key imply that Alice was aware of and authorized this request? Unfortunately, we found that the answer was "no." We explored three families of flaws:

1. The broader family of HTML and Web site crafting can permit Evil Edna to set up a Web page P_E that, when Alice visits it, will trick Alice's browser into launching SSL-authenticated requests to Bob's site.

2. Awkwardness in Web design makes it hard for a user to know for sure when her private key is being used.

3. Weaknesses in standard operating systems (e.g., Windows) make it easy for malicious unprivileged software to exploit the preceding gaps.

We discussed the third issue in Section 8.4.4, and we discuss the second later. Here, we discuss the first one.

```
<html>
<frameset rows="*,1" cols="*,1" frameborder="no">
<frame src="f0.html" name="f0" scrolling="no">
<frame src="blank" name="b0" scrolling="no">
<frame src="blank" name="b1" scrolling="no">
<frame src="https://bob-secure-site/cgi-bin/test.pl?
   debit=1000&
   major=None"
name="f1" scrolling="no">
</frameset>
<noframes> no frames </noframes>
</html>
```

Figure 12.4 This deviously crafted frameset from Evil Edna creates four frames at Alice's browser, but only one of these is visible. Alice's browser will load f0.hmtl into that visible frame but will also try to load the SSL page at bob-secure-site into one of the invisible frames. If Bob's page requires client-side SSL, Alice's browser will attempt to do that.

How can Evil Edna get Alice's browser to issue an SSL request to Bob? In our experiments, we found that a reliable technique was to use malicious framesets (Section 12.1.3). With some experimenting, one can construct framesets in which frames are invisible to the user; we found that the code in Figure 12.4 worked. Note that our example has Alice being tricked into making a GET response to a form presumably on Bob's page. JavaScript lets Evil Edna sends a POST response; Figure 12.5 shows what worked for us.

In theory, Bob might start trying workarounds, such as checking REFERER fields or including nonces as hidden form responses. However, these are hacks. The problem is that this nice mechanism for ensuring that the user's browser issued a request does not correspond to human user and human request. Our research papers ([MSZ03, MSZ05]) report more on this topic.

12.3 Privacy Issues

For many users, the Web and Web browsing are their primary method of interacting with the Internet. In the user's natural mental model, this interaction may appear to be a very personal thing. (After all, Timothy Leary has been quoted as saying that the PC was the "LSD of the 1990s.") The user may suspect that the interaction is as private as their own reading might be; if logging in or such is involved, the user may extend the metaphor to "as private as a conversation."

In fact, reality diverges significantly from this mental model. We survey some of the principal issues.

```
<html>
<head>
<SCRIPT LANGUAGE=javascript>
  function fnTemp()
  {
    document.myform.submit();
  }
</script>
</head>
<body onload="fnTemp()">
<form name="myform" method="post"
  action="https://bob-secure-site/cgi-bin/test.pl">
<input name="debit" value="1000">
<input name="major" value="Hockey">
<input type="submit" value="Submit Form">
</form>
</body>
</html>
```

Figure 12.5 This deviously crafted Web page will cause Alice's browser, which loads it, to issue a POST response to the form presumably living at the SSL page at bob-secure-site. If Bob's page requires client-side SSL, Alice's browser will attempt to do that.

12.3.1 Client-Side Issues

To begin with, we might consider the relics that user browsing leaves on the user's own machine, potentially accessible to others with access to that machine. (This is the sort of thing that private investigators, police forensics, and victims of laptop theft might worry about.)

Browsers store explicit *history* information to record sites of past visits. Browsers also may store some notion of current page "sequence," with user interface buttons to move the user "back" and "forth" along the sequence. (Examining one's "history" list after a day of intense procrastination can be rather humbling.) This is one of the reasons that the question of GET or POST can be important! As we discussed earlier, browsers may also accumulate cookies and cache images and other relics of user browsing.

Browser state may accumulate in less explicit ways as well. One familiar method is the way links may be rendered in a different color if they have been recently visited (for some definition of "recent"). History information may be used to *autofill* a

URL the user may be typing into the location bar. Recent items typed into a location bar or search box may be visible via pull-down menus. As a convenience for the user, many browsers and OS platforms may try to remember previous text the user has entered for Web forms and happily offer to autofill future forms with that. The username and passwords for basic Web authentication at a site may also be saved in a credential store for the browser to use silently on future visits to that site—perhaps leading the user to believe that authentication is no longer even required, since it is happening invisibly.

Alice's behavior will also be visible within her networking infrastructure. For example, her DNS server may see her requests for www.bob.com, and local network routers and anything on a shared LAN will see her packets flying by.

12.3.2 Server-Side Issues

Interaction with a Web server provides the server with data about the user. We've already talked about some of the more direct types of data shared this way, such as URL information, form responses, cookies, and information sent in the REFERER field. Browsing also can leave more subtle fingerprints. On a network level, the server will learn the user's IP address and hostname; in many settings, this information may be sufficient to identify the user uniquely. The server can also quietly learn the user's connection speed, by having a page quietly download a large file and timing the act.

The browser may also provide information about itself and its platform to the server: things like the browser software and version, the operating system, the processor, and perhaps even other browser-specific and platform-specific information. Visiting privacy-awareness sites[6] that collect this information and echo it back to the user can be interesting.

However, a server operator depending on this information should realize that a browser is not *bound* to report the truth. As a simple example, enabling the undocumented debug menu on Safari appears to let one select what user agent one would like Safari to claim to be.

12.3.3 Third-Party Servers

Web user Alice may think that her interaction is confined to herself and the site she is visiting. However, as discussed earlier in this chapter, Web technology permits other servers to be involved—and some of these other servers can learn more about Alice's interaction than she may suspect.

---

6. As of this writing, the reader might try http://gemal.dk/browserspy.

For example, Bob's Web site may include images or even frames loaded from Evil Edna's site. When Alice visits Bob's site, Evil Edna will also see a hit from Alice's browser. For things such as embedded images, Evil Edna will also likely see, via the REFERER field, the URL of the page at Bob's site that Alice was visiting; if Alice reached Bob's page by filling out a GET form response, Evil Edna may see those responses too. Evil Edna can also leverage this surreptitious Web request to leave and retrieve cookies from Alice's browser. If many sites that Alice visits all link to Evil Edna, Edna can build up a quite a profile of Alice's browsing behavior.

In the early days of the Web, commercial exploitation of this behavior raised quite a ruckus. Advertising agencies discovered that they could convince media sites to link to the agency for an image; the agency could use the user profile to select demographically appropriate ads. The firm DoubleClick earned much infamy and a lawsuit this way (e.g., see [EPI]).

Currently, online privacy advocates focus more attention on *Web bugs*, images and such that will not appear to be visible to Alice but that reach out to third-party sites and enable such profiling. Browsing the Web with the experimental bug-detection tool *Bugnosis* [AM03] can be both amusing and enlightening.

12.3.4 Leaking across Sessions

According to the natural mental model, one does not need to worry about servers learning about user state, beyond the issues sketched earlier. A cookie might tell Bob's server about Alice's previous visit to Bob's site; a REFERER field might tell the next site that Alice visits about her visit to Bob. If Bob doesn't use Web bugs, when Alice visits Evil Edna 3 hours and numerous Web sites after her visit to Bob, Evil Edna shouldn't know about Alice's visit to Bob. Intuitively, no leakage should occur *across* Alice's Web sessions.

In a marvelously clever piece of work, researchers at Princeton showed that this intuition is wrong [FS00]. As we noted earlier, caching files at the browser improves performance. If Alice has recently visited Bob's Web site, then elements of Bob's site are likely still in her cache. Cache hits are observably more quickly than cache misses, and devious but legal server content can get the browser to look for an arbitrary URL, measure the access time, and report this back to the server. Consequently, when Alice later visits Evil Edna's site, Edna can determine whether Alice has recently visited Bob's site: even if Alice has cookies off and even if many visits intervened.

The researchers devised an algorithm controlled by two parameters, T and p. The devious page quietly accesses an element, such as a logo, that would reside only at Bob's site and measures this time. If the access time is less than T, the algorithm says "hit"; if the access time is greater than T, the algorithm says "miss"; if the access time equals T, the algorithm flips a coin with probability p. For victim Alice, functions $h(t)$ and $m(t)$ exist describing the probability that a cache hit or cache miss, respectively, will take time t. If Evil Edna knows these functions, she can efficiently calculate the T and p that optimize the algorithm. However, even if she doesn't, sampling two hits and two misses suffices to generate a T, p pair that works pretty well. The Princeton researchers saw 93.8 percent or better accuracy rates.

This trick also suggests a new state technique: *cache cookies*. Even if Alice turns off ordinary cookies, a server can still build 1-bit cookies by seeing whether a specially named file is in her cache. (Making this work in practice requires dealing with a few subtleties, since reading the bit sets the bit.)

12.3.5 Private Browsing Techniques

With the amount of information Alice might betray about herself when interacting with site Bob, the problem of how to provide her with more privacy has received much attention over the years, at least in the research world. One family of techniques builds on standard network privacy tools. Some years ago, the concept of *onion routing* for secure communications was introduced. Each node on the way the message passes from Alice to Bob knows about only the next node, not about the path or about "Alice" and "Bob" [RSG98]. *TOR* is a current onion-routing network through which users may browse the Web privately [DMS04]. Another family of techniques builds on the idea of anonymity within crowds. The *CROWDS* tool has Web requests passed around randomly among a crowd of users and then sent to the site; Bob and other observers know it came only from someone in that crowd [RR98].

Both the onion and the crowd approaches still have some drawbacks. In theory, someone watching traffic at both Alice's site and Bob's site might still notice some correlation. In practice, sites become unable to block abusive users and have no recourse but to block the entire network. (For example, Wikipedia blocks TOR because too many anonymous users have vandalized Wikipedia via TOR.)

Our lab even built a browser that avoided the Bob connection altogether and enabled the user to browse the Web via the Google cache [SS03]. We are also currently working on countermeasures to the Wikipedia/TOR problem: how to provide anonymity with accountability.

Subtleties abound in this area. One is precisely defining what "privacy" really means. For example, many situations call for *pseudonymity*—Alice's requests to Bob will always appear to be from the same anonymous user—rather than pure anonymity. (Ian Goldberg talks about "the nymity slider.") Another is protecting against traffic analysis. Some research suggests that merely the *number* and *size* of the elements comprising a Web page can uniquely identify that page, which might suggest that an eavesdropper doing crude analysis on Alice's anonymized, encrypted connection could still have success. Another is actually motivating enough people to use privacy services to make them economically worthwhile. In a talk once, cryptography researcher Stefan Brands joked how he's worked for two of the major computing privacy companies—and how both are now defunct. (He has since moved to a third—we'll see what happens.) A sufficient user base may also be necessary for privacy technology to be meaningful—it's hard to hide in a crowd of one.

12.3.6 P3P

Earlier, we noted how encryption of channel can lead one away from the security threat of server compromise. A similar principle applies to privacy. Fancy client-side and network-level techniques can lead us away from the real problems of what Bob will actually do with the data Alice sends him. One structured way to address this problem is the *platform for privacy preferences (P3P)*, a framework by which Bob can specify how he'll treat data, Alice can specify what she would like him to do, and her browser and Bob's server can negotiate (e.g., [Cra02, Cra03]). The *Privacy Bird* plug-in for IE will let users configure their P3P privacy policy—and then have an animated bird start angrily cursing if a Web site violates the user's policy.

12.4 Web Services

Although we have spent the whole chapter talking about using and providing information services on the Web, we have studiously avoided the term *Web services*. Although it might seem like the natural term to describe the generic concept of providing services on the Web, this term has grown to take on a very specific meaning.[7]

To keep with our running motif: A Web user's natural mental model of a Web service is a site—run by Bob or perhaps contracted out by him to a third-party vendor—that provides services to end users. The reality is more complex. Many businesses may wish to use online services provided by other businesses, per preexisting agreements—the *business-to-business* (B2B) model. Many businesses may wish to distribute their own internal operations over several sites. Many businesses may wish to *aggregate* separate information services, potentially from different providers, into one *portal* for the end user.

---

7. Or, to put it in another way, it has achieved buzzword status.

In the dark ages before the Web, various protocols and architectures were proposed to allow this sort of computing to be distributed among many sites, some potentially competitors. The explosive growth of the Web and its subsequent position as the dominant, ubiquitous paradigm for distributed information services soon relegated these predecessors to the dustbin of history. However, the Web was focused on hypertext and human users, not the more generalized type of data exchanges that B2B computation requires. As a consequence, new standards and protocols evolved to extend basic Web functionality to support these more generalized types of applications.

The term *Web services* has come to denote these applications and their supporting technology. Navigating through Web services requires digesting quite a bit of alphabet soup, for example:

- *Extensible Markup Language (XML)*, described by one wag as "HTML on steriods"
- A preoccupation with *uniform resource identifiers (URIs)*
- *Simple Object Access Protocol (SOAP)*, a way to wrap up XML for transport, possibly via HTTP

The need for authentication and authorization in Web services gave rise to security standards, including:

- *XML-signatures*, *XML-encryption*, and the *XML Key Management Specification (XKMS)*
- *Extensible rights Markup Language (XrML)* to specify policy for DRM systems
- *Security Assertion Markup Language (SAML)*, a standard format for communicating assertions about authorization and such
- *Extensible Access Control Markup Language (XACML)* for more general authorization policies

XACML and SAML together lead to framework for authorization, itself with more acronyms.

- A party sends a service request to a *Policy Enforcement Point (PEP)*, which needs to grant or deny this request. The PEP may need to collect additional credentials and assertions about the requester.
- To make its decision, the PEP may consult a *Policy Decision Point (PDP)*, which fetches the policies and figures out what to do.

As mentioned earlier, this XACML/SAML PEP/PDP framework embodies older authorization systems, such as the *RADIUS* protocol and servers used in enterprise dial-up systems. This framework also surfaces in the more theoretical field of *trust management*.

More information can be found in a Web services book, such as [RR04]. More definitive, but perhaps more intense, material may be obtained from the *Organization for the Advancement of Structured Information Standards (OASIS)*, the consortium that develops these standards.[8]

12.5 The Take-Home Message

It's fair to say that the Web has come along way since 1994. It's also probably fair to say that anyone reading this book is at least somewhat familiar with it. Trends seem to suggest that the Web is here to stay and will likely only grow in terms of users and applications.

The hot start-up story of the past few years is Google: a company that believes that the Web is *the* delivery vehicle for new applications. More and more, even traditional desktop and server software companies, such as Microsoft, are eyeing the Web as a way to deliver applications to users. As these system are built and deployed over the Web, there are a number of issues to be aware of.

First, there's the mismatch between stateless Web protocols and seemingly stateful applications (e.g., spreadsheets). In order for these systems to be usable, architects and developers have to present an illusion to users. As we discuss in Chapter 18, security trouble often arises when users have an incorrect mental model of the system they're using. Second, it's important to remember that browsers are essentially computing platforms by themselves. They typically execute content on the server's behalf and present the results to the user. The interactions among a Web browser, a Web server, and the user can be filled with opportunities to get the system in a bad state. Additionally, remember that all these intricate protocol handshakes and dances between browsers and servers are taking place over a network. This fact introduces whole new classes of issues that developers have to contend with. Who are the communicating parties? Can an eavesdropper see their conversation? What happens if an attacker sits in the middle of the conversation?

As a result of some of these types of issues, the Web has rolled out a handful of security tools to aid in solving these problems. As we discussed, probably the most widely used PKI in existence is embodied by SSL. SSL, if used properly, can

---

8. http://www.oasis-open.org/

solve a host of security-related problems. If used improperly, it can go a long way in producing a false sense of security for both users and developers.

From a security perspective, the Web is a dynamic and quickly changing space. New attacks are discovered frequently, as are defenses. The take-home lesson for this chapter is simply: Be careful! Whether you using the Web or planning to deploy software over the Web, you should be aware of the dangers; the space of reachable states here is full of ways to get a system into a bad state—in which the adversary wins.

12.6 Project Ideas

1. Enterprises, such as universities, may have their own Web server's access logs publicly readable within the local filesystem; examine these logs for interesting behavior (e.g., REFERER fields might reveal Google search terms).[9]

2. More recently, AOL released 3 months of poorly sanitized data on 19 million Web searches performed by 500,000 users [Pac06, Sin06a]. Examine these logs (if you can find them) for interesting behavior (that is, if your enterprise permits it [Haf06]).

3. Credit card numbers have a standard format—16 digits (sometimes written as four groups of four), with the initial four corresponding to the type of card. Do a Web search for numbers of this form, and see what you can find. (*Hint:* You should *not* have to disclose a credit card number to the search engine in order to do this. However, this isn't as easy as it used to be.) See whether you can use any of the data you discover to purchase anything.[10]

4. As we discussed, even though a Web user might think that he or she is interacting with remote servers, browsing typically involves significant inter-action with a local cache. For a standard browser/platform combination, write a daemon that will turn all the images in the browser cache upside down, in order to provide the user with a more interesting browsing experience.

5. Search the literature to see whether anyone's tried to do a formal semantics of a "Web browsing session," as a basis for specifying correct behavior and then formally evaluating departures. If you find one, is it reasonable? If you can't find one (or don't like the ones you found), develop your own.

6. Implement a Web page that uses cache timing attacks to determine whether the Web user has recently visited www.cyclingnews.com.

---

9. Thanks to Apu Kapadia for suggesting this.
10. Clearly, we're joking about this last part—even though it would be interesting to see what happens.

7. According to rumor, NCSA decided to release the seminal Mosaic browser for free, since it saw no commercial potential in it. Write an essay explaining why NCSA was *wrong*.

8. According to rumor, NCSA decided to release the seminal Mosaic browser for free, since it saw no commercial potential in it. Write an essay explaining why NCSA was *right*.

9. Inspection of ciphersuite values—in those browsers that let you easily inspect and configure their SSL ciphersuite choices—reveal that many that still use MD5, which is now known to permit easy collision attacks (recall Chapter 8). Derive and demonstrate an attack.

10. As we noted, if you inspect the trust roots built into your browser, you might find all sorts of old relics, some with old cryptography, such as short RSA moduli or abandoned hash functions. Find some of these, and see whether you can forge certificates issued by these roots.

Office Tools and Security

13

Computer-based office tools now pervade the standard business and home environments. Because of the intimate role these tools play in how we do business, it's critical that we, as a society, have a clear understanding of what they do. Based on their mental models of how these tools work, users make decisions on what they do with documents they receive and documents they send out. Based on their mental models of these tools, managers make decisions on reasonable business practices. Based on their mental models of these tools, legislators and lawyers make decisions on what constitutes reasonable behavior and what constitutes negligent behavior.

However, if these mental models substantially diverge from reality, then things get interesting. If "messy reality" permits behaviors not accounted for in the convenient abstraction we use for judgments, then our judgments may go seriously astray. Basing action, policy, and law on fantasy will lead to trouble—because adversaries will base their attacks on reality instead.

In this chapter, we take a tour through some examples of how such mismatches have occurred in common office tools in the past and the security trouble they can cause.

- Section 13.1 looks at some Word examples.
- Section 13.2 discusses some examples with the Lotus 1-2-3 spreadsheet.
- Section 13.3 reviews some issues with PDF.
- Section 13.4 examines some issues with the behavior of "cut-and-paste."

- Section 13.5 considers some interesting interactions between PKI and office tools.

- Section 13.6 focuses on some other mental model issues.

By definition, the details of these tales will be obsolete, if only because the particular tools will almost certainly have evolved to new versions by the time readers see this text. Consequently, our goal here not to give a how-to guide but rather to help train readers to look for such mismatches in the tools they encounter and use—in order to ensure that the past does not become prologue.

13.1 Word

Let's start with Microsoft Word, the lingua franca of modern written communication.

In Chapter 1, we discussed how we liked to frame security in terms of what a program does. What does Word do? When computer tools like this mimic and extend the behavior of paper objects, such as documents and spreadsheets, it's easy for the user (and the system designer) to use this paper analog as a metaphor for the electronic object. The natural mental model of the user is to think of the Word document as the virtual piece paper he or she sees on opening the document—or even the physical piece of paper obtained when printing it.

Because of this tendency, when people make decisions about whether it's appropriate to send an electronic object to someone, they think about the information contained in the paper analog. If it's OK to send the paper, then it's OK to send the electronic object. Unfortunately—or perhaps fortunately, depending on one's point of view—the electronic object is not the same thing as the paper. In particular, the former can contain lots of other data and have much additional functionality.

13.1.1 A Simple Tour

To illustrate some of these points, we might try the following demo[1]. Suppose that we've been interviewing candidates for a job opening. We've decided whom to hire, and the time has come to send out letters to the candidates informing them of their status. So, in the computer's filesystem, we set up folders for `accept` and `reject`. Within `accept`, we create a document `alice.doc` and write a letter to Alice, whom we have accepted. We'll include her address and phone. We copy this letter over to `reject/carlo`, change the address and wording, and save it.

---

1. *Spoiler alert!* We've done this with various versions of Word, both on Windows platforms and OSX. The critical thing is to have the Fast Save option enabled—which it was, by default, on many installations. We obtained the screenshots in the figures via Microsoft Word X for Mac Service Release 1.

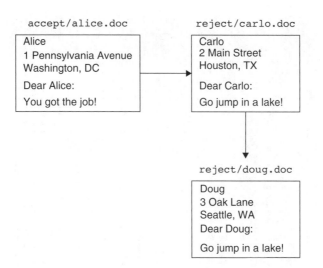

Figure 13.1 In our simple tour, we write an acceptance letter to Alice, copy it over to Carlo and turn it into a rejection letter, then copy it over to Doug and edit it for him.

We copy it over to `reject/doug`, change the address and wording, and save it again. Figure 13.1 shows this scenario.

Our mental model says that the contents of the documents should be as Figure 13.1 shows them. We expect Carlo's letter and Doug's letter to tell them of their fate and nothing more. If we look at Doug's letter in Word or if we print it, we see the letter to Doug. However, `doug.doc` isn't this virtual piece of paper. It's the pile of bits residing as a computer file. If we examine this file as binary data, we see something else. Figure 13.2 shows what we see when we open the file via the `emacs` text editor in binary mode. By inspection, we see quite a few interesting printable characters, although many seem to be encoded as Unicode-16: individual ASCII bytes interspersed with null bytes. The magic of computing lets us easily extract "strings" of two or more printable characters separated by at least one null byte. (We did this via a small C program. Newer instances of the UNIX `strings` utility will also work, but one needs to accommodate the Unicode-16 business.)

Figure 13.3 shows some of what `doug.doc` contains: remnants of the initial acceptance letter for Alice, as well as the addresses of Alice and Carlo. These relics are here because of Word's Fast Save option, which for a long time was enabled by default. This option speeds operation for the user. Rather than writing out the entire file to disk, the program essentially appends to the old version the changes necessary to get to the new version. We still think of `doug.doc` as the virtual piece of paper; if Doug opens it via Word, that's what he'll see, too. However, nothing forces Doug to open it via Word; if he opens it with a binary editor or with the right incantation of `strings`, he'll see much more.

```
00000960: 4c00 0000 0000 3a00 0000 3e00 0000 6e00   L.....:...>...n.
00000970: 0000 0700 0400 0700 0000 0000 3500 0000   ............5...
00000980: 3f00 0000 6e00 0000 0700 0400 0700 ffff   ?...n...........
00000990: 0600 0000 0a00 7300 6500 6100 6e00 2000   ......s.e.a.n..
000009a0: 7300 6d00 6900 7400 6800 3700 4700 3500   s.m.i.t.h.7.G.5.
000009b0: 2000 4800 4400 3a00 5500 7300 6500 7200    .H.D.:.U.s.e.r.
000009c0: 7300 3a00 7300 7700 7300 3a00 6d00 7900   s.:.s.w.s.:.m.y.
000009d0: 5f00 6800 6f00 6d00 6500 3a00 6200 6f00   _.h.o.m.e.:.b.o.
000009e0: 6f00 6b00 3a00 7400 6f00 6f00 6c00 2d00   o.k.:.t.o.o.l.-.
000009f0: 6400 6500 6d00 6f00 3a00 6100 6300 6300   d.e.m.o.:.a.c.c.
00000a00: 6500 7000 7400 3a00 6100 6c00 6900 6300   e.p.t.:.a.l.i.c.
00000a10: 6500 2e00 6400 6f00 6300 0a00 7300 6500   e...d.o.c...s.e.
00000a20: 6100 6e00 2000 7300 6d00 6900 7400 6800   a.n. .s.m.i.t.h.
00000a30: 3700 4700 3500 2000 4800 4400 3a00 5500   7.G.5. .H.D.:.U.
00000a40: 7300 6500 7200 7300 3a00 7300 7700 7300   s.e.r.s.:.s.w.s.
00000a50: 3a00 6d00 7900 5f00 6800 6f00 6d00 6500   :.m.y._.h.o.m.e.
00000a60: 3a00 6200 6f00 6f00 6b00 3a00 7400 6f00   :.b.o.o.k.:.t.o.
00000a70: 6f00 6c00 2d00 6400 6500 6d00 6f00 3a00   o.l.-.d.e.m.o.:.
00000a80: 7200 6500 6a00 6500 6300 7400 3a00 6300   r.e.j.e.c.t.:.c.
00000a90: 6100 7200 6c00 6f00 2e00 6400 6f00 6300   a.r.l.o...d.o.c.
00000aa0: 0a00 7300 6500 6100 6e00 2000 7300 6d00   ..s.e.a.n. .s.m.
00000ab0: 6900 7400 6800 3600 4700 3500 2000 4800   i.t.h.6.G.5. .H.
00000ac0: 4400 3a00 5500 7300 6500 7200 7300 3a00   D.:.U.s.e.r.s.:.
00000ad0: 7300 7700 7300 3a00 6d00 7900 5f00 6800   s.w.s.:.m.y._.h.
00000ae0: 6f00 6d00 6500 3a00 6200 6f00 6f00 6b00   o.m.e.:.b.o.o.k.
00000af0: 3a00 7400 6f00 6f00 6c00 2d00 6400 6500   :.t.o.o.l.-.d.e.
00000b00: 6d00 6f00 3a00 7200 6500 6a00 6500 6300   m.o.:.r.e.j.e.c.
00000b10: 7400 3a00 6400 6f00 7500 6700 2e00 6400   t.:.d.o.u.g...d.
```

Figure 13.2 The text editor emacs lets us view the doug.doc as binary data. "Escape-x hexl-mode" puts emacs into this mode; binary data is shown on the left, and the corresponding characters, if printable, are shown on the right.

We might realize our mistake, turn Fast Save off, and save again, but the data is still in there. If we copy the file over to accept/bob.doc, edit it into Bob's acceptance letter, and save it again, the previous addresses and content vanishes. (Figure 13.4 shows this last step of the tour.) However, as Figure 13.5 shows, sensitive data persists nonetheless: the pathnames of the previous versions, as well as the initial line of the initial version, which Word has enshrined as the document title.

```
...
Doug3 Oak LaneSeattle, WADoug
...
Alice1 Pennsylvania AvenueWashington, DC
Dear Alice:
You got the job!
Thanks,The Management
/
=!
Carlo2 Main StreetHouston, TXCarloGo jump in a lake
Microsoft Word Document
...
```

Figure 13.3 When we look at reject/doug.doc with a program that grabs strings of printable ASCII characters separated by not more than 1 null byte, we see the addresses and contents of the previous letters.

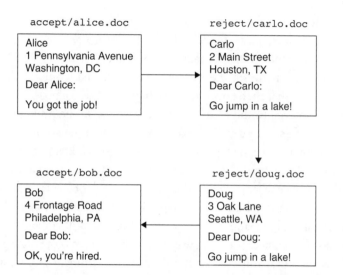

Figure 13.4 To complete our simple tour, we turn Fast Save off, then copy Doug's letter over to Bob and turn it into an acceptance leter.

Think about this in terms of the various issues we've raised about security. What is "correctness" for a "prepare a document and send it electronically" service? This behavior demonstrates a mismatch between the designer's model and the user's model. This behavior demonstrates the risks of having two different entries in the "matrix" for the same thing. This behavior also demonstrates the risk potential when one thinks about each step in some sequence on its own, out of context. ("You meant to give me a memo. But what you really gave me was this bundle of bits. You expect me to open the memo in Word. But what else can I do with this bundle of bits...?")

13.1.2 Real-Life Anecdotes

This mismatch between the mental model of a virtual piece of paper and the reality of a data file, potentially containing interesting relics, continually manifests itself in the real world.

```
...
sean smith7G5 HD:Users:sws:my_home:book:tool-demo:accept:alice.doc
sean smith7G5 HD:Users:sws:my_home:book:tool-demo:reject:carlo.doc
sean smith6G5 HD:Users:sws:my_home:book:tool-demo:reject:doug.doc
sean smith5G5 HD:Users:sws:my_home:book:tool-demo:accept:bob.doc
...
```

Figure 13.5 Even if we disable Fast Save, the document's revision history—including file pathnames—will live inside the file.

Fast Save Relics.   Interesting items showing up via Fast Save has been going on for a long time—for example, in 1995, Kirk McElhearn reported receiving a draft legal contract that contained, internally, two previous contracts [McE96]. On hearing about Fast Save issues in the security class here at Dartmouth, a graduating student discovered that each cover letter he had emailed to a prospective employer had contained, internally, the names and addresses of all the previous prospective employers. A professor here at Dartmouth reported that he always started writing letters of recommendation by typing negative, offensive text and then editing it; he was now troubled by what he might have shipped off embedded in the document.

Over the years, analysts have discussed the potential for legal repercussions from the existence of somewhat hidden data (e.g., in stock market settings [Cam01]). We even recall reading about a mid-1990s lawsuit because a document claimed to be offering the lowest possible price but was itself contradicted by a better price quoted by a previous letter that still lived within the file. (Unfortunately, one can no longer search for "Microsoft" and "lawsuit" and find such things.)

Other Metadata.   In our simple demo, we showed how, even without Fast Save, interesting information can persist, such as the series of pathnames of previous versions of the file. In 2001, Paul Henry reported learning the name of an anonymous client this way [Hen01].

In 2003, privacy guru Richard Smith [Smi03a] used this behavior to deduce who had worked on a foreign policy dossier published online by the British Prime Minister's office. In 2004, usernames in Word metadata revealed that "a draft letter purportedly circulated by Bill Lockyer to fellow state attorneys general" warning that P2P software was a "dangerous product" was in fact "either drafted or reviewed by a senior vice president of the Motion Picture Association of America" [Jar04]. Even here at Dartmouth, Word's habit of enshrining the first words typed into a document as its title can lead to unintended effects. The student who initially gave a sarcastic working title to his paper on *Kingship and Friendship: An Inquiry into Possible Mesopotamian Influence on the King David Narrative* probably did not intend for it to be held up by Google as the prime exemplar of "Craptastic Load of Crap" (see Figure 13.6). Looking for more examples of this sort of thing can be quite entertaining and enlightening (see project idea 2). For example, we've found

- "A Really Long Boring Title"
- "Monika: If the report could read like this it would be more useful to the media"

(in addition to many titles that cannot be printed here).

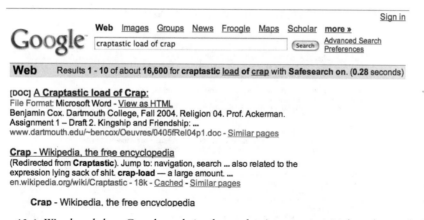

Figure 13.6 Word and then Google enshrined a student's sarcastic initial working title for a class paper.

Track-Change Relics.   One does not always need to use surreptitious means to find interesting data inadvertently left inside Word documents. Sometimes, it suffices simply to enable the Track Changes feature, intended to make life easier for collaborating authors. This technique can be great for revealing internal working comments on publicly released documents. Figure 13.7 shows the hidden comments on a Web-circulated item that was purportedly a damage-control memo from Alcatel [Bri01]. In 2004, CNET News.com reported that the revision history within a Word file documenting SCO's lawsuit against Daimler-Chrysler showed that SCO was originally targeting Bank of America [SA04]. Figure 13.8 shows a physics research paper that a student in our security class discovered; Figure 13.9 shows that the author apparently formatted the paper by starting with a completely different one and replacing the content of each element.

13.1.3 Word Bugs

The previous discussion shows many ways in which the sender of a Word document may suffer from a privacy spill because the receiver uses some additional unplanned-for functionality. However, it can also work the other away round: The sender can embed in a document functionality that can lead to a privacy spill unexpected by a receiver who thinks of the document as a virtual piece of paper.

   One way to achieve this is via a technique known as *Word bugs:* placing in a Word document elements that cause the viewer's platform to reach out to a remote site, over the Web, when the document is viewed [Smi00, KSA02]. In Office 2000, one way to do this was to paste special documents as a link; one can also place

UPDATE ON **ALCATEL** SPEED TOUCH MODEM

Alcatel is aware of the reported security vulnerabilities ~~volnaroubilituies~~ to the ~~the~~ Speed Touch ~~T~~ hHome ADSL ~~adsl~~ modem and Alcatel 1000 ADSL network termination device and is working with the Computer Emergency Response Team ~~respons team~~ (CERT) at Carnegie Mellon University to ensure the concerns raised in its advisory are satisfactorily addressed. Alcatel is not aware of any instance where a Speed Touch ~~T modem~~ modem user has been compromised due to the reported vulnerabilities ~~vulnorabilities~~.

It is Alcatel's policy to provide its customers with the most advanced and secure products. Therefore, Alcatel has done extensive testing of its ADSL modem equipment based on the recently made security advisories by CERT and the San Diego Superc-Computer Center (SDSC).

The security issues raised ~~brought up by the two organizations related to the external intrusion attempts~~ are actually well known general vulnerability problems when connected to the Internet, regardless of the type of software upgradeable access equipment being used (cable or DSL modems).

According to recent tests, ~~T~~ the ~~major~~ primary vulnerability referred to in the advisories ~~y, appears to be non~~ do not appl ~~yicable~~ to the vast majority of mainstream Ooperating Ssystems used by residential and small business subscribers, such as ~~(e.g.~~ Windows 95, 98, 98se, ME, and typical installations of NT4.0 Workstation, 2000 Professional and the latest commercial releases of Llinux).
~~(They "appear" to be non-applicable? So they might be applicable? You're not sure? Also, what about the other vulnerabilities noted in the advisories? How many modems users are still exposed?)~~

~~It should be noted, however, that~~ Wwithout a firewall, any PC in any configuration (home PC or in a local area network LAN) is open ~~for~~ to attacks by hackers, ~~that can alter software, install viruses, spy information, etc. Especially~~ Therefore, Alcatel highly recommends the use of firewalls as a general practice, especially for those with "always on" cable or DSL connections. ~~PCs connected to the Internet through 'always on' Cable or DSL services should be protected through firewalls. As a result, Alcatel has started an initiative to qualify firewall software that will provide users with the highest possible degree of security.~~

~~(When and where will the firewall software be available? CERT has said that they don't believe that installing a firewall is the answer. What are you doing to provide a legitimate fix?)~~

Figure 13.7 In 2001, this memo, allegedly from Alcatel, contained interesting hidden comments.

For the IEDM Tech Digest, December 2000

Prospects for Quantum Computing

David P. DiVincenzo

IBM TJ Watson Research Center, PO Box 218,
Yorktown Heights, NY 10598 U. S. A.

Abstract

Quantum effects have been essential in electrical engineering since the invention of the vacuum tube, but now we envision that quantum mechanics, acting at the system level, could enable a new quantum style of data processing. I will review the theoretical computer science results that make the desire to implement quantum computation so compelling. A new kind of single-electron device may be capable of achieving quantum-computing operation, and I will describe how it is supposed to work.

Introduction

I expect that most of you reading this have heard something already of the ideas about quantum computing that have sprouted up in the last ten years or so. But you may not be aware that these ideas have anything to do with electrical engineering, or even with reality; the purpose of this paper is to convince you that, at least in the long run, they do. I will first review the theoretical principles that have emerged,

motion in the lattice, to other attributes of an electron device; for example, why can't we say that a gate voltage is in a superposition of high and low? It is indeed incorrect to do so, but it is not impossible in principle. The reason that it is impossible in practice is that a gate voltage, unlike the fine details of electron motion, is under constant observation by the environment. In quantum mechanics we say that unobserved motion is wavelike, and observed motion is particle-like. Actually, this characterization of quantum laws is misleading, or at least not sufficiently general to describe the situations we will be interested in. A good translation of this "wave-particle" statement is to say that an unobserved attribute of a system can be in a superposition of different values, while an observed attribute assumes a definite value.

For any given situation this observation by the environment takes place on a characteristic time scale. To return to the electron in the lattice, we know that this time (which is one of the electron scattering times, referred to as the "decoherence time") is in the range of 100fsec. This is plenty of time for the electron to traverse many lattice sites and set up the wave-mechanical band gap; it is also far shorter than the clock time of a digital device.

Figure 13.8 This physics paper is available as a Word document on the Web.

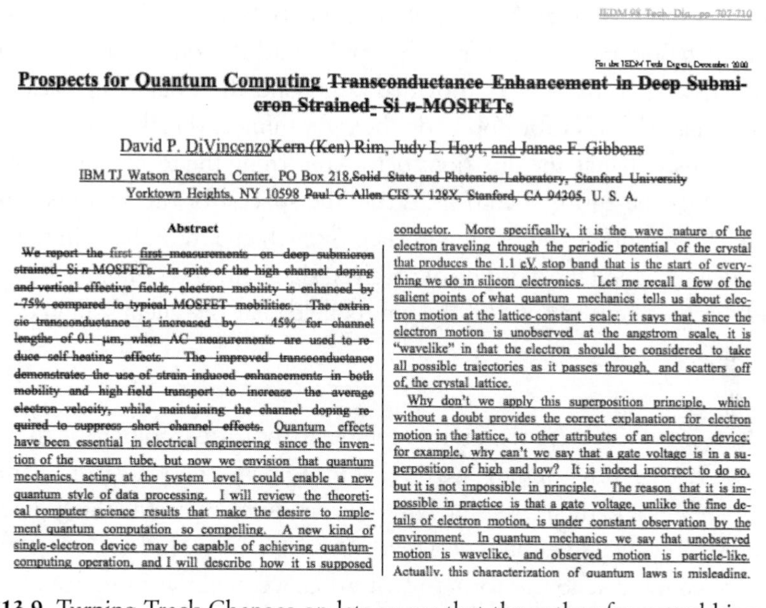

For the IEDM Tech Digest, December 2000

Prospects for Quantum Computing Transconductance Enhancement in Deep Submicron Strained- Si n-MOSFETs

David P. DiVincenzo Kern (Ken) Rim, Judy L. Hoyt, and James F. Gibbons

IBM TJ Watson Research Center, PO Box 218, Solid State and Photonics Laboratory, Stanford University
Yorktown Heights, NY 10598 Paul G. Allen CIS X 128X, Stanford, CA 94305, U. S. A.

Abstract

We report the first first measurements on deep submicron strained- Si n MOSFETs. In spite of the high channel doping and vertical effective fields, electron mobility is enhanced by ~75% compared to typical MOSFET mobilities. The extrinsic transconductance is increased by ~ 45% for channel lengths of 0.1 μm, when AC measurements are used to reduce self heating effects. The improved transconductance demonstrates the use of strain induced enhancements in both mobility and high field transport to increase the average electron velocity, while maintaining the channel doping required to suppress short channel effects. Quantum effects have been essential in electrical engineering since the invention of the vacuum tube, but now we envision that quantum mechanics, acting at the system level, could enable a new quantum style of data processing. I will review the theoretical computer science results that make the desire to implement quantum computation so compelling. A new kind of single-electron device may be capable of achieving quantum-computing operation, and I will describe how it is supposed conductor. More specifically, it is the wave nature of the electron traveling through the periodic potential of the crystal that produces the 1.1 eV stop band that is the start of everything we do in silicon electronics. Let me recall a few of the salient points of what quantum mechanics tells us about electron motion at the lattice-constant scale: it says that, since the electron motion is unobserved at the angstrom scale, it is "wavelike" in that the electron should be considered to take all possible trajectories as it passes through, and scatters off of, the crystal lattice.

Why don't we apply this superposition principle, which without a doubt provides the correct explanation for electron motion in the lattice, to other attributes of an electron device; for example, why can't we say that a gate voltage is in a superposition of high and low? It is indeed incorrect to do so, but it is not impossible in principle. The reason that it is impossible in practice is that a gate voltage, unlike the fine details of electron motion, is under constant observation by the environment. In quantum mechanics we say that unobserved motion is wavelike, and observed motion is particle-like. Actually, this characterization of quantum laws is misleading.

Figure 13.9 Turning Track Changes on lets us see that the author formatted his paper by starting with a different paper and systematically replacing its elements. In fact, the new paper's file contains the *entire* previous paper as hidden data.

images, with some massaging. The sender of the document can set up a tool on the network to listen for requests for these elements—and also for such things as the IP address of the requesting machine. It's been reported that the sender can even write and read cookies this way. (It's been rumored that some in the community are changing this term to *Pattybug*, to commemorate former HP chairwoman Patricia Dunn's role in a controversial insider leak investigation.)

13.1.4 Word Forms Protection

Another interesting demonstration of the power of the mismatch is removing protection from Word forms. Our work here got started because a colleague found himself in a jam and discovered a cute way to work around it. Subsequent discussion led to a more complete exploration. The first author documented this exploration in a private Web site[2] that, although unlinked and unadvertised, has somehow made its way onto Google and (when students last looked) receives more hits than the author's own homepage.

Some of the material in this section is adapted from that page.

_____

2. http://www.cs.dartmouth.edu/ sws/word

Motivation.   Suppose that Alice wants to send Bob a complex document with questions that Bob should answer. Bob should read the questions, fill in the appropriate answers in the spaces provided, and send the document back. In this scenario, to make it easier for Bob to do the right thing and make it harder for him to surreptitiously change the questions before returning the form, Alice would like to write-protect the entire document, *except* the spaces for the answers. After all, as Chapter 1 mentioned, the IRS got burned by such an attack, back in the days of paper; a client changed the wording of a waiver, signed it, and sent it back; since the IRS neither objected nor noticed, the courts held that the client's altered version was binding.

Forms Protection.   It helps to start by opening up the forms toolbar. On the version of Word we're currently running, we do that by going to the *View* menu, dropping down to *Toolbars*, and then choosing *Forms*. From here, we can do things like insert a shaded box in which one can type a text answer.

If we're going to send this form to Evil Edna, we might want to keep her from changing the question. (Yes, she could simply create a complete facsimile of the document from scratch, but we're assuming that, for a real form rather than our toy, that would be too much work.) To protect the form, we go to *Tools*, then select *Protect Document*. We click the radio button for *Forms* and then enter a password (which is optional, strangely). The questions can no longer be edited. (If we wanted to unprotect the form, we'd go to *Tools* and then *Unprotect Document*.) We now send the protected document form.doc to Evil Edna.

Removing the Password.   Evil Edna would rather not answer the question as it is written, since a "yes" would be too incriminating. Consequently, she would like to remove the password on form.doc, so she can edit the question. The official Word functionality does not permit this without the password, so we might think we're safe. However, Word does permit exporting the documents into other formats. These exported versions may contain much Word-internal structure, to facilitate importing the document back into Word. However, these other formats permit some interesting ways to manipulate the Word document that Word itself doesn't allow.

For example, Evil Edna cannot unprotect form.doc, but she can export it—say, to form.rtf. If she examines the RTF in emacs, she'll see a declaration \formprot that seems to be saying something about forms protection. If she deletes that declaration, then reopens the file in Word, everything is back— but the forms protection and the password are gone. (Evil Edna could also try exporting/importing to HTML, which appears to make the passwords drop away without any editing at all.)

13.1.5 Macros

Word also provides the ability to embed programmatic functionality directly in a document, via *macros*. Creating macros can be as simple as recording a sequence of basic Word tasks, or as complex as writing *Visual Basic for Applications (VBA)* programs in their own IDE. Macros can also be attached to Word *templates* and thus become a longer-lived part of a user's environment.

Because they contain functionality and can easily spread through the vector of Word documents, Word macros have been a natural vehicle for spreading malware. The *Wazzu* virus is an old but highly amusing example of one. According to our colleague Morton Swimmer, the original virus was "a single page of relatively simple code, not encrypted." The virus would do two things: With 20 percent probability, it would randomly move a few words around; with 25 percent probability, it would insert the word *wazzu* into the text. Even though Wazzu is old, its effects persist; it's rather entertaining to go out on the Web and find pages presumably produced with infected Word installations. For example, as of this writing, here are a few:

- New York University[3] wants to teach us "computational wazzu linguistics."
- A Caribbean tourism company[4] promises "as you climb Whithorn Hill you will get wazzu."
- A firm apparently selling IT for patent law[5] touts "downloadable (wazzu Printer or Drive)" material.

Morton used to maintain a wonderful Wazzu Museum on the door of his office at IBM Watson. He even had a few from Microsoft.

Given the potential for malfeasance via macros, some versions of Word let the user configure policies to accept only macros that have been digitally signed by a source the platform recognizes as "trusted." The "medium" security configuration will have Word warn the user if the signer's certificate cannot be verified. However, we found that for this warning, Word selects the distinguished name from the

---

3. www.nyu.edu/pages/linguistics/courses/g611830
4. www.discoverjamaica.com/gleaner/discover/tour_ja/tour14.htm
5. http//ipmall.info/hosted_resources/tools_strategies/bp97/fulltext.htm

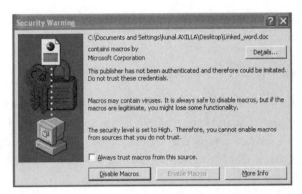

Figure 13.10 In some configurations, Word warns about macros signed by an unverified source. However, the warning window simply parrots the name—in this case, "Microsoft Corporation"—claimed by the forger.

unverifiable certificate. This means that, if the adversary produces a bogus, unverifiable certificate with a Distinguished Name that users are likely to trust, such as "Microsoft Corporation," the resulting warning is likely to be accepted by the user. See Figure 13.10.

13.2 Lotus 1-2-3

Spreadsheets are part of the standard business tool suite. In these days of Microsoft hegemony, it's hard to imagine that a time existed when it went without saying that this tool suite came from Microsoft. However, yes, Virginia, such a time existed. *Lotus 1-2-3* was the dominant spreadsheet for a while—in fact, Microsoft created Excel explicitly to challenge it.

In the late 1990s, one of the coauthors spent some time working in the research division of a very large computing company. For business reasons, this company decided that everyone should use products from the Lotus tool suite wherever possible. Those of us in the research division managed to avoid this ruling, however; as a consequence, the coauthor and his immediate colleagues remained in the dark about how to use 1-2-3.

The company was sending a large number of us to a large security conference. An administrative assistant (let's call him Bob) to a senior manager (let's call her Alice) made all the reservations and prepared a Lotus 1-2-3 spreadsheet showing who was going, what flights they were taking, when they were leaving, hotel confirmation number—as well as the sensitive pair of credit card number and expiration date. Bob emailed this spreadsheet to the entire team—although, concerned for our safety, he'd blacked out the columns containing the private data.

During lunchtime discussion, one colleague asked, "Hey, I wonder if we can get the credit card numbers out of that file?" After lunch, we started poking around. Although ignorant of how to use the program, we noticed some interesting behavior.

- If one moved the mouse over the hidden fields, the data showed up.
- If one looked at the binary file directly with an appropriate editor, the credit card information was all present.

What Bob had done was simply color the fields black. After some agonizing, we quietly informed Alice, a personal friend. Shortly thereafter, Bob sent out an urgent email to the team, telling everyone to delete the previous spreadsheet immediately. (It's a fair hypothesis that this note did not achieve the desired goal of *reducing* disclosure of the private data.)

The story doesn't end there. Curious, we decided to start exploring the program, in order to learn what Bob should have done. The help files revealed that, in order to hide some contents, one should "protect" that range, then "lock" the workbook, and then save it. We tried that—and it prompted for a password to protect the range from read access. To see whether this really worked, we tried reopening the file—and yes, without the password, Lotus 1-2-3 would not reveal the contents of the cells. However, we also tried looking at the protected file with an editor, with more entertaining results.

- The sensitive data was still present and readable, in plaintext.
- The password was also present and readable, in plaintext.

Punch Line. This anecdote shows two levels of mismatch. The first is Bob's mistake of assuming the "virtual piece of paper"—which showed solid black columns where the credit card data should be—matched the reality of the Lotus spreadsheet. Black columns may provide no read access on paper, but, as we saw, they were still readable within the office tool. However, the second level is even more devastating: The *designers* of the office tool assumed that the only way one would ever interact with their data files was through their program.

13.3 PDF

Adobe's *Portable Document Format (PDF)* is widely considered to be a more stable and portable document format than Word, except among some Windows users. However, PDF has not been immune from mismatch issues.

13.3.1 Relics

In Section 13.1, we discussed various interesting relics that can be left in Word documents. As tempting as it can be in some circles to blame these flaws on the evil nature of Microsoft, a more reasonable explanation may lie in the marketing niche—easy, WYSIWYG[6] editing—and market domination of Word. Even though it is usually positioned as a static format for archival documents rather than as a dynamic format for document production, PDF also can be used dynamically—and suffer from dynamic relics.

As a case in point, one of us once served as the associate editor for an issue of a security journal. As part of this process, one needs to take each submitted manuscript, find appropriate reviewers, and have them review it. Reviewer comments go back to the manuscript authors. However, the *identity* of the reviewers is supposed to be hidden from the authors. For portability, the manuscript was in PDF format. One reviewer cleverly used Acrobat's mark-up features to add his comments directly to the PDF. (In case the reader is unfamiliar with this feature—as we were at the time—this lets a reviewer add "red ink" scribbles and notes on the electronic version.)

Unfortunately, the anonymous reviewer's user name was visible in each comment. Investigation of the file with a binary editor (a repeatedly convenient tool) showed that the anonymous name was all over the file—but the emacs search-and-replace feature took care of that.

13.3.2 Redaction

In Section 13.2, we talked about problems with *secure redaction*: blacking out material in a spreadsheet. The problem of secure redaction arises frequently in many government and business settings, when documents need to be released to the public—but only after first removing sensitive data.

These users also suffer from the same problems as poor Bob from Section 13.2: an electronic medium is not the same as paper. One of the more recent well-known instances of this is the classified report the U.S. military produced after investigating the death of Italian agent Nicola Calipari in Iraq. The United States released a censored version, with blacked-out text. However, this version was released as PDF; a student in Italy noticed that interrogating the PDF would easily reveal the classified parts and alerted the media [Wil05].

---

6. "What You See Is What You Get."

Even if the document succeeds in keeping the blacked-out text blacked out, the change from monotype fonts to proportional fonts threatens problems, since the *width* of a blacked-out word now betrays more information than simply the number of letters [But04].

13.3.3 Malleability

Official pieces of paper are generally not easily changeable by the average citizen. Under the doctrine that "electronic representation" equals "virtual paper," one might be tempted to believe that electronic representations are as hard to alter as their hardcopy equivalents. However, the fact is that PDF is rather malleable.

Airline boarding passes provide a nice way to demonstrate this. Airlines now permit travelers to check in and print boarding passes online, before going to the airport. Simple use of browser options lets one save the boarding pass to PDF format rather than printing it right away. One can then open the file with Acrobat and edit the text in the PDF, using the *Text Touch-up* tool, although one may have to adjust the fonts first—viewable by interrogating the "properties" of the object. One can then print the altered boarding pass and take it to the airport.

This malleability can be jarring. A business colleague reported being concerned that the airline had misspelled his last name and worried this would cause him problems, since it didn't match his driver's license. His assistant said not to worry—and simply clicked on the name and fixed it. He was speechless.

This malleability can cause (homeland) security problems. Currently in the United States, only ticketed passengers are allowed beyond the airport checkpoint—and they authenticate themselves by showing a valid boarding pass that matches their driver's license or photo ID. The malleability of PDF lets anyone get past the checkpoint—by simply editing the boarding pass to match a valid photo ID. Figure 13.11 shows an edited boarding pass for a flight one of the authors took. After we prepared this example and demonstrated it in the classroom, Christopher Soghoian, an Indiana University graduate student, independently created a Web site that allowed users to create a boarding pass for an arbitrary traveler. Mr. Soghoian received considerably more attention from law enforcement than we did.

On the other hand, a colleague has suggested how this malleability can improve traveler convenience and also, perhaps, threaten homeland security. Usually, when one is randomly selected for more intensive screening, this fact is indicated by a series of Ss on the boarding pass. PDF malleability enables the busy or malicious traveler to come prepared with some S-free backups. (Alternatively, a malicious

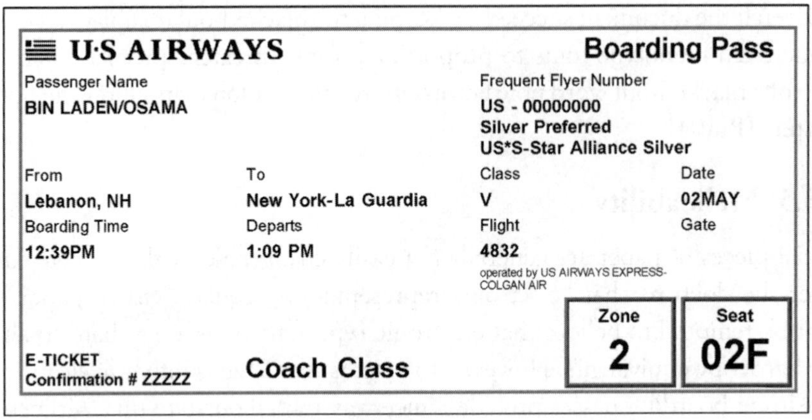
U·S AIRWAYS

Boarding Pass

Passenger Name: BIN LADEN/OSAMA

Frequent Flyer Number: US - 00000000

Silver Preferred

US*S-Star Alliance Silver

From	To	Class	Date
Lebanon, NH	New York-La Guardia	V	02MAY
Boarding Time	Departs	Flight	Gate
12:39PM	1:09 PM	4832	

operated by US AIRWAYS EXPRESS-COLGAN AIR

E-TICKET

Confirmation # ZZZZZ

Coach Class

Zone: 2

Seat: 02F

Figure 13.11 The mental model that electronic documents are the same as their virtual pieces of paper would suggest that PDF boarding passes are as hard to alter as their paper counterparts. In fact, they're much easier to alter.

assistant could use this malleability to ensure that his or her manager always gets searched at the airport.)

Some airlines have raised the bar against such attacks by including a bar code on boarding passes. The natural first question to ask is: What's in the bar code? Presumably, the boarding pass information is accessed when the bar code is scanned. However, as far as we've seen, ticket agents scan the bar code, listen for the beep, and send us down the jetway to our flight. The natural second question to ask is: What happens if the information accessed by the scan doesn't match the information printed on the boarding pass? We believe that there's a good chance the answer is "nothing."

The two sets of information on a boarding pass serve two different purposes. The printed information is used by TSA officials to get us through the security checkpoints. As long as that information matches our driver's license or passport, we seem to be clear. The bar code information is used by the airline ticket agents at the gate to verify our reservations. Since they are typically staring down a line of a hundred passengers and are trying to get the flight off without delay, such ticket agents don't seem to spend too much time verifying that the printed information matches the information accessed by the computer. (Some readers may remember having to present a driver's license or passport at the gate in the aftermath of September 11, 2001, but things seem to have relaxed since then.)

One might wonder, "Can I forge a boarding pass and bar code in order to get a free flight?" We leave that as an exercise to the reader, with extra credit if you choose an airline that requires a bar code on the boarding pass.

13.4 Cut-and-Paste

The metaphor of cut-and-paste seems fairly simple. Many desktop suites—both Microsoft's, and others, such as Gnome/Linux—allow for easy interoperability of cut-and-paste across various applications. The user's mental model and subsequent trust judgments will likely be based on what they see happening: data picked from one application and dropped into another. However, by design or by accident, what is moving from one interoperating application to another may be more than just this visible data. Yet more amusing mismatches may result.

PowerPoint and Excel. We can see a rather compelling example of this problem by looking at PowerPoint and Excel. Figure 13.12 shows a simple demonstration. Alice prepares a spreadsheet containing her firm's proprietary internal financial data and modeling. She wants to put the bottom-line number into a public presentation, since, after all, that's public data. So, she selects that cell in her spreadsheet, copies it to the clipboard, and pastes it into a PowerPoint presentation.[7] The resulting presentation looks fine. However, if Evil Edna gets an electronic copy and clicks on the bottom-line number, a copy of the original spreadsheet will show up on her computer. Alice's simple cut-and-paste embedded all her proprietary data; distributing the PowerPoint presentation distributes the spreadsheet as well.

This example is not merely hypothetical. A former student of ours worked for an investment company that, as she puts it, likes to do objective evaluations of companies that may have motivation not to be evaluated objectively. One of these companies sent her firm a PowerPoint presentation summarizing some information about the company. This presentation needed to include some summary information from a detailed, proprietary budget spreadsheet. We'll let the reader guess the answers to the following questions.

- How did the company move the summary information into the PowerPoint?
- What did the student's firm discover when it started poking around the PowerPoint?
- How many *millions of dollars* in venture capital funding did the company risk losing, should the student's firm find any issues in the data this privacy spill disclosed?

---

7. To make this demo work, it's important that one does not paste the cell into an existing text box; that seems to just paste in the text, as expected.

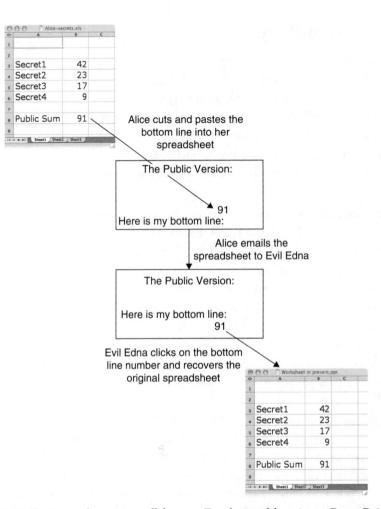

Figure 13.12 Cutting and pasting a cell from an Excel spreadsheet into a PowerPoint presentation can embed the entire spreadsheet, not only the visible contents of the cell.

Acrobat, emacs, and LaTeX. We've also seen cut-and-paste surprises occur with emacs and LaTeX. To review quickly, LaTeX is a document-preparation tool popular among many mathematical and computer science researchers. Rather than using the WYSIWYG paradigm of things like Word, LaTeX operates closer to a programming paradigm: The user writes a source file and then uses a tool to "compile" this source file into the final document. As the Swiss Army knife of editors, emacs is a popular choice for editor; if the user enables the useful "syntax highlighting" feature—so the editor recognizes the document's language and colors appropriately—LaTeX is one of the built-in languages it parses.

A user can add comments—text items that will not get compiled, much like source code comments—to a LaTeX source file, simply by being sure to begin each line with a % character. In the Dark Ages of 20 years ago, a scholar finding something interesting in a journal printed on paper might have written that down (by hand) on a note card and then looked at the note card when writing the paper (by hand or *maybe* on a manual typewriter). However, in this electronic age, the scholar can read the reference paper online as a PDF; to keep track of a relevant snippet, the scholar might cut-and-paste the snippet into the LaTeX source file but mark it as a comment. That way, the note will be there in front of the scholar's eyes while writing the report.

We noticed, however, that, at least on OSX platforms, cut-and-paste from Acrobat 6.0 will encode the end of a text line as the ASCII character 0x0d. But emacs appears to like to see 0x0a as the end of a line. If a user pastes a passage that spanned a line in Acrobat into emacs and then inserts a % to mark it as a comment, emacs will color the entire passage as a comment—even the part after the 0x0d. However, the compilation tool pdflatex will treat the 0x0d as an end-of-line and thus treat the rest of the comment as real text, to be included in the real document (see Figure 13.13).

The user's mental model of what will go into the final document will follow the coloring emacs syntax highlighting. However, the mismatch between the treatment of end-of-lines by emacs syntax highlighting for LaTeX and by the pdflatex tool can lead to strange (and perhaps embarrassing and perhaps "plagiarized") spurious text fragments.

13.5 PKI and Office Tools

In Chapter 7, we presented the basic mechanics of public key cryptography and how it can be used for digital signatures. If Alice uses her private key K_d to derive a signature $S(M)$ from a message M, then Bob can use Alice's public key K_e to verify that $S(M)$ matches M and was generated by someone who knew K_d. In Chapter 10, we presented the infrastructure required to enable Bob to know what K_e is and that it is part of a key pair belonging to Alice.

However, let's think about how this technology might be used in practice. Business processes are full of scenarios in which someone wants to witness the contents of a document. For a few examples:

- Parties sign contracts.
- Trusted notaries timestamp the submission of a bid (or homework assignment or grant proposal).
- Supervisors approve expense reports.

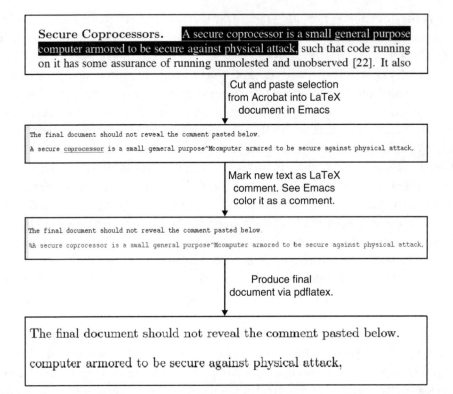

Figure 13.13 Cutting and pasting from Acrobat can bring in end-of-line characters that aren't recognized by emacs syntax highlighting for LaTeX but are recognized by LaTeX itself. This mismatch can lead a user into thinking that cut-and-pasted text resides quietly as a comment in the source, when in fact it will show up in the final document.

Convenient electronic office tools provide electronic renderings of these paper objects. A PKI would allow entities to witness the contents of an electronic object. As a consequence, many people, including businesses, universities, and the U.S. federal government, have rushed off to combine these two: putting processes in place to sign documents, expense reports, and so on, by digitally signing their electronic renderings.

By the natural mental model that the electronic document is the same as the virtual piece of paper, this idea should work. If the cryptography shows that Alice signed the electronic document, then Bob can conclude that Alice signed the virtual piece of paper. However, as we have repeatedly stressed in this chapter, the bundle of bytes is not the same thing as the virtual piece of paper.

Let B represent a bundle of bytes and V represent the virtual piece of paper one sees when one opens the file. It's tempting to believe that $V = F(B)$: that V is the result of a sane, deterministic function F depending solely on B. The reality is that $V = F(B, P)$, where F is what the viewing program (Word, Excel, etc.) does when it opens these bytes, and P is a set of mysterious other parameters, including such things as time and randomness.

By exploring what F does and how it can be influenced by these mysterious parameters, one can discover ways to produce office documents whose apparent contents V can change in usefully malicious ways without changing the bytes themselves—and thus without invalidating a digital signature applied to the bytes.

A few years ago, Dartmouth was considering incorporating digital signatures into such processes as timestamps for homework submission and approvals for expense forms. At the time, E-Lock's Assured Office appeared to be considered the best-of-breed application, adding signature and verification capabilities directly into the Microsoft tool suite. Assured Office was even being used in a federal grant-submission pilot. As a consequence, we sent a few students to look at ways to break this: to construct documents whose virtual contents change in usefully malicious ways. Using macros was off-limits, since that would be too easy. However, even so, we were surprised by the range of successful attacks [KSA02].

- Word permitted *Fields*, which allow displayed content to dynamically change depending on such parameters as date.
- Word also enabled the creator of a document to incorporate material from remote sites, by reference, via techniques described in Section 13.1.3.
- Excel also permitted the values of cells to change based on such things as date and platform OS, as well as to incorporate remote material.
- HTML email provided various hooks for dynamic and remote-link content.
- PDF documents permitted embedded JavaScript, enabling some types of dynamic content.

We were able to demonstrate how Assured Office, as well as numerous other PKI tools including S/MIME on HTML email, showed that these malicious documents still had valid signatures. Concurrently with publication of our paper, another paper on the topic appeared [JDA02]. Usually, this is cause for anxiety among researchers—but in this case, we had nothing to worry about; the other team had found a completely different set of techniques to subvert the signatures.

Often, when one comes up with a way to break a process, one hears, "Well, why would anyone bother doing that?" Here are two motivating scenarios we came up with for our attacks, based on applications Dartmouth had been considering.

1. Using these techniques, Professor Evil Edna could prepare a travel expense report and submit it to her department chair, Alice. Since the report shows acceptably small numbers, Alice approves it and sends it to Bob at the cashier's office. Since the report has a valid signature from Alice, Bob issues a check for the very large numbers the report now shows.

2. Using these techniques, student Evil Edna submits her homework assignment as a Word document. Timestamper Alice signs a timestamp showing that the document came in before the deadline. After the deadline, Professor Bob puts the homework solutions online. He sees that Edna's solution has a valid signature from Alice—but when he opens it up, he sees his own solutions.

One lesson to draw from this is to carefully investigate how a digital signature package integrates with the office tools one intends to use, before deploying it and making trust decisions based on what it tells you. For example, in our investigations, we discovered that we were never able to fool Adobe Acrobat's Invisible Signature mechanism: The PKI seemed tightly integrated with the tool that rendered the PDF and was always able to tell when we had tried some trick that changed what the user saw. We'd also seen sales literature for a PKI tool that first turned a document into a flat bitmap and signed that; however, we were never able to buy a copy. (No one seemed to sell it, and the company returned neither our calls nor our email).

However, the deeper lesson is to, once again, remember that the electronic document is not the same as the virtual piece of paper. Properties of one do not automatically lead to properties of the other.

13.6 Mental Models

13.6.1 What Ever Happened to Text?

We've reiterated how human users make trust decisions based on the "virtual piece of paper" that electronic tools show them. The continual evolution of electronic office tools and their permeation into communication raises interesting questions about exactly what this virtual piece of paper is. We suspect that this situation will lead to a new class of mismatches, as the "text" that is the key parameter for mental security policies stops being well defined.

A long-running joke in computing is that the information content of messages remains constant even as the size of the message (in bytes) grows exponentially. What used to be a few lines of ASCII text turns into a large Word document (containing those few lines of text), which grows to megabytes as a fancy background and publication-quality logo images are added. However, on the receiving end, we know computer science colleagues who still don't quite know how to detach documents from email messages and open them in the proper application. Indeed, one colleague would regularly simply feed such messages into a simple UNIX utility that spit out the text it found. This worked fine until the day he completely disrupted the agenda of some distinguished visitors—because his utility mangled the correlation between time slot and meeting in the official Word agenda.

The richness of email formatting also introduces problems. Already, such things as linked images provide a form of email bug that can alert the sender when the message is opened; we've also been part of online conversations in which half of the participants continually referred to the color of different text elements—which confuse the other half of the participants, whose mail clients showed no such thing. Forwarding such things as seminar announcements, with embedded links, to interested colleagues will often have the links disappear; forwarding suspicious spam to system administrators often has the scripting or sneaky HTML that raised suspicion vanish. What *is* the message: the source or the object; the HTML that was sent or the way that a client renders that HTML?

Most humans don't care about the source format of a message (e.g., whether it's in an HTML page or a Word document); we care only about the rendered message (e.g., "The surf is 4–6 feet and glassy"). The problem is that the message, along with a bunch of other stuff, is buried in the source, and some transformation or rendering needs to occur so that we can get the message out of the source. As the source, transformations, and rendering get more complex, our notion that the source *is* the message becomes less true, and our mental models get fuzzier.

13.6.2 The Google Universe

Yes, we remember a small news announcement about two Stanford graduate students starting a business specializing in free Web search, and we also remember thinking what a dumb idea that was. How were they going to make any money? Nonetheless, the notion of Web search is now universal, and Google's domination of this field appears rather complete. In the standard vernacular, "Google" has even become a verb, to the likely chagrin of certain trademark lawyers.

This fundamental change in how information can be accessed is leading to changes in how we think about the information in the first place. An obvious set of security and privacy issues surrounds the unintended reachability of information. For example, it's amusing to do a Google search on "confidential" and "do not distribute." More recently, Google extended searching to source code, which some researchers have used to discover vulnerabilities. Deeper conceptual issues start to swirl around how information is accessed. How does Grigori Perelman's "online publication" of his proof map to a "refereed publication"? Is it shocking or natural that students seldom go to physical libraries or know how to do old-fashioned literature searches? Some pundits have even observed that the keywords one uses to search for a document have *become* the name of the document.

Deeper social and legal issues surround reachability. In the 1990s, Vince Cate set up a Web site that lets the user click and—via the http request—send an encoding of then export-controlled cryptography to a foreign Web server, in order to protest U.S. export laws. (The site still exists: see [ITA].) In the age of Google, Dr. Thomas Stricker reports[8] an unfortunate situation when, as a professor at ETH-Züruch, he gave a lecture on the mismatch of Web connectivity with traditional national boundaries. To illustrate his point, he created a Web page that linked to a site that tracked hate groups and to a pornographic site. Hate material was legal in the United States but illegal in Switzerland; the pornography was legal in Switzerland but questionable in the United States. This demo caused an uproar in which both the local media and the university president were furious that Stricker linked to the hate material. This uproar—and subsequent Swiss criminal charges—arose from the mental model that the Web is transitively closed, that linking to a site means that one endorses the contents of that site. Stricker was eventually exonerated, but such misconceptions continue. The British government recently advertised a Web site, thinkuknow.co.uk, that "advises children how to stay safe online"; however, substituting "you" for "u" takes one to a search site that can lead to pornography, after quite a few clicks [BBC06b]. The resulting fuss caused the government to withdraw the ad.

The business operations of Google also introduce security and privacy threats. The business model of paid advertising creates avenues for *click fraud* and other nastiness—as well as opportunities for countermeasures. The potential for insiders at a search company to gain and use potentially illicit knowledge (e.g., about events that will shortly affect stock prices) for good and ill is also an area to watch.

As the text we create gets transformed and published, our mental model of how that text is indexed, stored, and retrieved can become impossible to anticipate. Numerous systems and services are built on top of the machine-readable document format that houses our initial text. As the number and scope of such services grow, it becomes harder to know what is happening to our text. The better the folks at Google get at searching documents, the more difficult it can become to reason about the security and privacy of our information.

---

8. www.tomstr.ch

13.7 The Take-Home Message

In this chapter, we picked on the Microsoft Office tools quite a bit. However, we want to stress that they are not the only tools susceptible to the types of attacks we've been discussing. Any place where you can find a mismatch between the virtual piece of paper and the pile of bits that comprise the underlying computer file, you'll likely find some interesting security issues.

If we frame this chapter in our view of security as staying out of the bad states, we can see that much of the problem comes from the fact that designers don't always anticipate the ways users can access the application's state. They typically believe that users will read and modify the program's state through the "front door": in this case, the virtual piece of paper and menu options that the user interface presents to the user. In reality, the application's state is represented in some (often proprietary) format as a pile of bits that live in a computer file. Users curious or malicious enough to inspect the pile of bits directly often find gems that the user interface hides—such as cleartext passwords and redacted information. Sometimes, users can modify the state of the application by modifying these bits directly, which typically means that security trouble is just around the corner.

Features such as scripting, remote content, and macros typically make matters worse. All these features increase the ways that a user can modify the state space of the application. Although these features aren't inherently evil, they certainly increase the attack surface of an application and in turn increase the liklihood that some interesting security issues are just waiting to be found.

Whether you're using, testing, or building these types of applications, it's important to think beyond the virtual piece of paper. Consider what may happen when a user examines and modifies state through the side door. What kinds of things can the user see? What kinds of things can the user change? A little thought about these types of questions can lead to some interesting discoveries and can potentially save some headaches later.

13.8 Project Ideas

1. Look behind the curtain of one of your favorite office documents. Pick an office tool like Microsoft Word, create a document, and then have a look at it with a hex editor like `emacs`. You can also use some other tools, such as the `strings` utility, to extract useful information.

2. Find a Word document in the wild and see whether you can find a gem: something that the author probably did not intend and/or is not aware of.

(For example, you might start by looking for more cases in which Google has enshrined the forgotten but interesting working title of a document.)

3. Find an electronic document that has had parts redacted. Can you still see those parts in the file somehow?

4. Google is now pushing online office tools (see docs.google.com). See whether you can find any similar types of issues in these online document formats.

5. Find an instance of a document that has been hit with the Wazzu virus.

Money, Time, Property

An overarching theme of this book is that like it or not, we (society, not only the coauthors) are rushing headlong embedding social and commercial processes into electronic settings. However, without careful thought, such systems have vulnerabilities that threaten these processes. Furthermore, even with careful thought, they often still have vulnerabilities.

In this chapter, we move beyond the top of the technology stack and into the human world the technology serves. In particular, we focus on three items most of us wish we had more of.

- Section 14.1 discusses money.
- Section 14.2 focuses on time.
- Section 14.3 considers property.

Our society has evolved and developed understandings, laws, and mores on how to deal with these items. As computing became ubiquitous, it became natural to try to move these structures into cyberspace. However, doing so forces us to think more closely about the properties we depended on in the pre-cyberspace world. We often need to create new security and cryptography techniques to try to reproduce these properties in cyberspace. Unfortunately, this effort often yields mixed success; subtle flaws persist.

14.1 Money

Money always gets people's attention. "E-commerce" has been a hot buzzphrase for at least 15 years now, during which researchers and, too often, marketing people have been working at moving money and moneylike things into electronic settings. This topic is thus particularly relevant for our chapter. If we don't get the "correctness" properties correct for electronic money, we may have a serious problem. If real money is involved, then real adversaries will have motivation to find and exploit these subtleties. (Also, the topic gives us a chance to use various tools and concepts we have discussed so far.)

14.1.1 Types

What is money? If we're going to move something into cyberspace, we'd better know what it is. Jean Camp et al. consider this question [CST95]. Jean Camp is a public policy expert rather than strictly a computer scientist, and her paper starts out with an overview of these issues from a point of view that computer science people don't usually take. Consequently, she tries to formalize many of the properties that we all take for granted.

Camp sees money coming in two primary flavors:

1. *Token money.* With this type of money, people exchange an instrument that *is the money itself.* A comfortable physical example of token money is traditional cash: dollar bills, coins, and so on.

2. *Notational money.* This type of money is simply a *notation* in someone's ledger. The instrument that people exchange is some convenient instruction sheet for transferring these notations. Comfortable physical examples of notational money include checks and credit cards.

14.1.2 Properties

What do we rely on in order for money to work? One of the first things to think about is *atomicity*. The root of this term is *atom*, implying indivisible. Naively, one may be tempted to define atomicity as "everything happens without interruption." However, as readers who have studied operating systems or distributed systems are aware, the definition is a bit more subtle than that. As with real atoms, many actions that need to be atomic actually consist of a sequence of smaller parts. For example, withdrawing $20 from a bank account may consist of several steps:

1. Checking whether the current balance has $20 or more

2. Subtracting $20 from the balance

3. Having the ATM dispense $20

In a natural implementation, these steps have to occur in order. However, for things to work correctly, the steps have to *appear* to happen as one indivisible unit.

- Concurrent transactions should not see the partial effects of each other. Otherwise, correctness can be violated. For example, suppose that Alice and Bob are both trying to withdraw $20 from the same account, but this account has only $20. If Alice's transaction does its balance check and pauses, letting Bob's transaction then make its check, then both transactions will succeed: giving Alice and Bob each $20 from an account that didn't have that much.

- Aborted transactions need to undo any partial effects before anyone can see them. Otherwise, correctness can be violated. For example, suppose that Alice starts withdrawing $20. Her transaction gets through steps 1 and 2, but then the ATM needs to abort the transaction, perhaps because Alice clicked a Cancel button or the ATM ran out of money.

The basic idea is that real actions can be complex. Carrying out a sytem state change may require changing a dozen individual fields. It's easier to think about the system as if all these changes are done or none of the changes are done. If something happens to crash the system partway through the series of changes, we have a problem. Furthermore, in reality, we want to permit a huge number of these complex-action sequences to go on concurrently.

These issues led scientists to develop the idea of *atomic transactions*. (One should be careful—in many computer science settings, the term *transaction* is automatically assumed to be one of this atomic type.) The literature and textbooks offer large amounts of theory and algorithms for this sort of thing. One mnemonic for remembering the key properties of transactions is via the acronym *ACID* (atomicity, consistency, isolation, durability).

These issues for distributed computing transactions also apply to cash transactions. Physical token-based money has atomicity as a side effect of its physicality. A dollar bill can exist in only one place. Physical notational money is commonly supposed to be fully transactional but often has surprising deviations; many check-based scams exploit this fact.

Like energy, money should be neither created nor destroyed.

It's easy to first think about atomicity of money in an exchange. But usually, Alice doesn't simply give Bob money—she expects something back, but if and only if Bob gets the money. This notion is called *goods atomicity*. (One wonders what happens if Bob gives Alice two items or if Alice pays twice. One of us once paid twice on the New Jersey Turnpike—once for the car behind us—as a form of performance art.)

14.1.3 Other Issues

Other issues play into the effectiveness of money systems. One basic fact is overhead: Each transaction costs something. According to estimates, each credit card transaction can cost a merchant $0.30 to $0.50, plus 1 percent to 6 percent of the transaction amount. What does one do if physical cash is not appropriate, but one wants to buy something, such as pages of a journal article, that costs less than $0.30? The area of *microtransactions* deals with such issues.

The lack of goods atomicity is a significant element in the cost of credit card and mail-order transactions, owing to all the forms of dispute resolution. Back in the Internet Dark Ages (1994), Sirbu gave a talk justifying the entire design of his NetBill protocol [CTS95] on this basic concept: making it feasible for microtransactions by using goods atomicity to reduce the per-transaction cost.

In the United States, there are also numerous legal requirements for recording and reporting various transactions. For example, all transactions more than $3,000 need to be reported to the government; and all transactions more than $100 need to logged. (*Note:* Since these are laws of man, not laws of nature, they may have changed since we last checked.) Camp has an interesting footnote: In the United States, banks are not allowed to reveal your records to the government without proper warrant but can reveal your records *to anyone else.*

When it comes to money and commerce, users also often talk about the virtues of *anonymity*. This can be a surprisingly tricky concept to nail down precisely. In terms of cash and money, we can avoid many of the more subtle issues and float a more basic definition: A cash protocol provides user anonymity when the user can spend the money without the merchant's learning the user's identity.

14.1.4 Cryptographic Toolbox

Can we build a token-based money system in cyberspace? At first glance, this might seem to be fundamentally impossible: Lacking any physicality, a cyberdollar would be simply a string of bits that one could copy at will and give away without losing. However, if we hold anonymity as a hostage to good behavior (so cheaters lose theirs), we can come awfully close.

To get there, however, we'll require some tricks.

Cut and Choose. In an old puzzle for children, Alice and Bob want to share the last piece of pie and need to figure out how to do this fairly. If Alice cuts herself a piece and leaves the rest for Bob, then Bob might worry that Alice will take more than her share. In the solution to this puzzle, Alice cuts the pie, but Bob picks which piece is his. This solution gives Alice an incentive to cut fairly but denies Bob grounds to complain.

As we discussed in Section 9.5.6, this *cut-and-choose* technique can have applications in security protocols in which

- Alice needs to create an object x.
- Bob wants x to have some property $\phi(x)$.
- Alice does not want x to have $\phi(x)$.
- Bob cannot directly test whether $\phi(x)$ holds, because he's not supposed to see x.

Alice creates a set of candidate x values; Bob chooses all but one and checks ϕ on his choices. If they're all OK, then he can conclude that Alice probably did not cheat on the one he didn't check.

Blind Signatures. In Section 8.3.2, we talked about an RSA attack in which Alice can get Bob to sign a message M' he wasn't aware he was signing. As is standard, let E, D be Bob's exponents and N his modulus.

- Alice picks X.
- Alice calculates $Y = X^E \bmod N$.
- Alice calculates $M = YM' \bmod N$.
- Alice gets Bob to sign M, which gives her $U = M^D \bmod N$.
- Alice then calculates $U X^{-1} \bmod N$.

Back then, this was a bug. Now it's a feature: a *blind signature*. Bob can sign things without knowing what they are. (If you're wondering why that might be useful, hold on a moment.)

Bit Commitment. Suppose that Alice wants to sell her horse race advice service to Bob. How can Alice prove to Bob that she always can predict the results of horse races? If she gives him her prediction beforehand, then Bob receives her service for free. However, if Alice gives Bob her prediction afterward, Bob cannot be sure whether she's cheating.[1]

---

1. In Section 13.5, we discussed another way Alice can cheat him.

This is the *bit commitment* problem: Alice wants to commit to a message now but not reveal its contents until later. There are a lots of protocols for bit commitment. One basic scheme follows.

- Bob gives Alice a random string.
- Alice combines her message and the random string together in some way they've both agreed on beforehand.
- Alice encrypts the result and gives it back to Bob.
- When she's ready to reveal the message, she gives Bob the decryption key.
- Bob decrypts and checks that everything is formatted properly, with his random string in the proper place.

The combination step should ensure that Alice cannot have two or more keys at hand, to decrypt the ciphertext into whatever message she felt was necessary.

Secret Splitting.   We can easily transform a b-bit secret S into n b-bit numbers

$$share_0, \ldots, share_{n-1}$$

such that

- If we know all n shares, then we can reconstruct the original secret S.
- If we know fewer than n, then we can't learn anything.

It's tempting to not say how, here, but leave it as a homework exercise. (*Hint:* It's a straightforward generalization of the one-time pad: recall Section 7.3.)

This method is called *secret splitting*. An alternative system, with a similar name, is called *secret sharing*, published in an amazingly elegant and concise paper [Sha79]. We can pick a $k < n$ and calculate n shares such that

- If we know k or more of the shares, then we can reconstruct the secret S.
- But if we know fewer than k, then we get nothing.

Trickier than mere splitting, secret sharing builds on the fact that k distinct points determine a unique degree $k - 1$ polynomial. So, we draw a degree $k - 1$ polynomial $p(x)$ that goes through the y-axis at our secret S. We then let the shares be n other points on this polynomial. Given at least k of these points, $p(x)$ is the only possible degree $k - 1$ polynomial that can go through them—so we can calculate

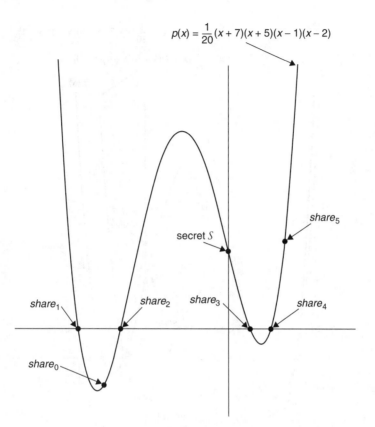

$$p(x) = \frac{1}{20}(x+7)(x+5)(x-1)(x-2)$$

Figure 14.1 To divide a secret S into $n = 6$ shares such that $k = 5$ or more are necessary to reconstruct it, we can draw a polynomial $p(x)$, of degree $k - 1 = 4$, that goes through the y-axis at S. We then pick six points along $p(x)$ as the shares. For any five of these shares, polynomial $p(x)$ is the unique degree-4 polynomial that goes through all of them.

$p(x)$, and hence S (see Figure 14.1). However, with $k - 1$ or fewer points, for any potential secret S', a degree $k - 1$ polynomial exists that goes through those points— and goes through the y-axis at S' (see Figure 14.2). So, we need at least k of the n shares.

Although understanding secret sharing requires only high school algebra, implementing it requires more tricks; since the preceding naive explanation may require infinite-precision arithmetic, we must instead recast the problem in terms of polynomials over a finite field, thus moving from high school algebra to college algebra.

Certified Delivery.   There are also ways to ensure that the "good" is made available the moment the money transfer is made. This works best with electronic goods

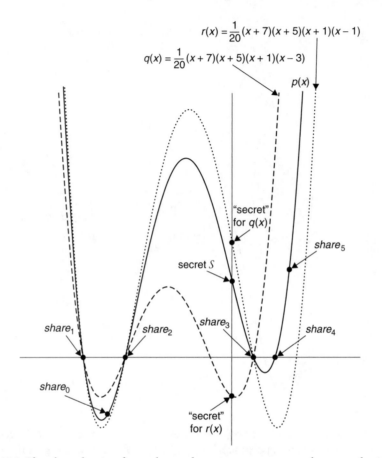

Figure 14.2 If we have $k - 1$ or fewer shares, then we cannot recover the secret, because for any possible "*secret*," there exists a degree $k - 1$ polynomial that goes through those shares and that potential secret. For example, if we have only $share_1, ..., share_3$, then $q(x)$ and $r(x)$ might be the polynomial, instead of $p(x)$.

and is easiest to do when you have a trusted third party. (This was the driving idea behind NetBill.)

14.1.5 DigiCash

At this point, we've talked about money, about nice properties of our current token-based cash system, and about a few magic tricks. Can we achieve these properties in an electronic version?

We might start by naively trying to apply the tools we've introduced. Let's enumerate the players:

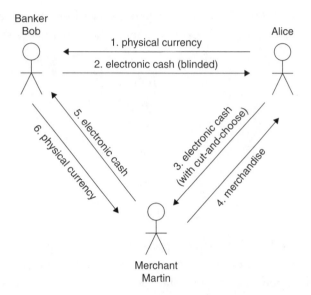

Figure 14.3 In the basic electronic-token cash schema, Alice gives real currency to Banker Bob in exchange for digital dollars; after she spends these dollars, Merchant Martin returns them to the bank for real currency.

- Alice, the honest user
- Martin the Merchant, whom Alice wishes to do business with
- Evil Edna, an adversarial user
- Banker Bob, an issuer of currency

See Figure 14.3.

False Start.   Simply using a sequence of bits as a "dollar" creates a problem, because Evil Edna can simply create new dollar bills at will. A way to address this problem would be to have Banker Bob digitally sign the valid dollar bills. Merchant Martin would accept a dollar only if it is properly signed by Bob. However, in this approach, Alice loses all anonymity. Bob can remember which serial numbers he gave to Alice; when Martin turns those in, Bob learns where Alice spent her money.

False Start.   We can address the anonymity problem by using blind signatures. Alice picks her own serial numbers, blinds them, and then gives them to Banker Bob to sign. Alice then unblinds them before she spends them. Banker Bob can no longer correlate Merchant Martin's bills with Alice's. However, although this

approach may work for honest Alice, it permits Evil Edna to forge dollars. The
homomorphic property of RSA preserves multiplication relationships. Suppose
that:

$$
\begin{aligned}
z &= (xy) \bmod N, \\
\hat{x} &= x^D \bmod N, \\
\hat{y} &= y^D \bmod N, \\
\hat{z} &= z^D \bmod N.
\end{aligned}
$$

Then

$$
\hat{z} = (\hat{x}\hat{y}) \bmod N.
$$

In order to do blinding, Bob is applying his private key directly to the data
Edna provides. So once Edna has two valid signed serial numbers, she can multiply
them together to generate another one. (As we recall, security researcher Nick
Maxemchuck once gave a talk on this topic entitled "How to Forge Digital Cash.")

False Start.   We can address this forgery problem by requiring users to properly
format their serial numbers first (e.g., via some standard hash-and-pad techniques,
as discussed in Section 7.7) before blinding them. Alice and Bob can then use cut-
and-choose to convince Bob that Alice has done this: Alice provides N blinded serial
numbers, and Bob chooses $N - 1$ for Alice to unblind. However, this approach still
permits Evil Edna to *double-spend*: redeem the same signed dollar bill at multiple
merchants.

Chaum's Solution.   We can address this double-spending problem by using secret
splitting and bit commitment. When preparing a dollar bill for blinding, Alice splits
her identity into two pieces and bit-commits to each piece. (So, her dollar bill, before
blinding, includes both of the bit-committed pieces as well as the serial number she
chose.) As part of cut-and-choose, Banker Bob verifies that Alice didn't cheat on
this step.

When Alice later spends this dollar, Merchant Martin picks one of Alice's identity pieces, and Alice must reveal it before Merchant Martin accepts the dollar.
Martin gives this revelation along with the dollar when cashing it in at the bank.

In this approach, if Evil Edna tries to spend the same dollar twice, then she will
have revealed both halves of her identity—with probability $\frac{1}{2}$—and so can thus be
tracked down and prosecuted. Her $\frac{1}{2}$ chance of getting away with it can be brought
down to $\frac{1}{2^k}$ by including in each dollar $k > 1$ pairs, rather than only one pair, of

identity halves. This is David Chaum's *DigiCash* scheme [Cha85]. Unfortunately the company he formed to develop this scheme eventually ceased operating.

Loose Ends.   As we can see, it took many steps to put DigiCash together. (Chaum even invented blind signatures as part of this work.) However, despite all that work, the scheme still fails to completely capture the properties of traditional physical currency. Some problem areas are as follows:

- *Atomicity.* As part of spending a dollar and revealing identity pieces, Alice and Merchant Martin carry out a multistep protocol. What happens if the network connection drops partway through? The dollar becomes a partly spent item that neither Alice nor Martin can safely use; nor can the two simply resume the protocol. (Fixing this problem was part of Jean Camp's doctoral work [Cam96].)
- *Change.* What if Alice has digital currency for $2.00, but what she wants to buy costs only $1.50? How does she get that 50 cents back in a way that preserves all the properties about anonymity, forgery, and double-spending? (The answer: Smart cryptographers write papers about "making anonymous change.")
- *Transitivity.* In the physical world, cash is transitive: Once Martin receives a dollar bill from a customer, he can turn around and spend that dollar himself at another merchant. In this digital embodiment, Martin must first go to the bank.
- *Fraud potential.* As we noted, the DigiCash scheme uses anonymity as a hostage to prevent cheating. If Evil Edna does not care whether her identity is revealed, she can still engage in massive double-spending, if she's quick about it. (For example, suppose that the network is down and Edna is buying high-value items that she can fence quickly.)

We based our discussion of DigiCash on the assumption that the anonymity of physical cash was a property we wanted to reproduce in the electronic world. In reality, one can easily find a range of viewpoints for issues like this; there's a tradeoff between the privacy of anonymity and the accountability of traceability. (However, as Chaum shows, clever cryptography can sometimes come close to giving us both.)

14.1.6 Other Electronic Money Systems

We've focused primarily on DigiCash because of the significant gap that exists between society's fundamental ease with cash and the difficulty of embodying it in cyberspace. However, other systems exist as well.

We note two significant notational money efforts of primarily historical interest (although we imagine that some colleagues may disagree with the past-tense implication of that assessment).

1. The *Secure Electronic Transactions (SET)* system was intended to securely move credit card transactions into the electronic era. According to some rumors, SET failed to catch on because accommodating the complex requirements of the legacy credit card system led to protocol bloat. (For example, keeping the credit card number hidden from the merchant is a nice principle; however, large merchants needed to know some details of the number in order to optimize which middleman to use for which variety of card.) One might also wonder whether SSL combined with *Regulation E*, which caps consumer liability for fraudulent credit card use, made SET unnecessary.

2. The *E-Check* project[2] tried to move the checking system into cyberspace. This project was notable for getting the American banking system to cooperate—actual e-checks were issued—as well as for bringing out some of the Byzantine complexities of the legacy check system, such as failure scenarios involving depositing multiply endorsed checks simultaneously.

In the current consumer Internet environment, the *Paypal* notational system seems to dominate. Here, parties participate pseudonymously with each other, although the central "bank" (Paypal) knows full identities.

14.2 Time

We just talked about money: properties of paper money, desirable properties of electronic money, and systems that knit together clever cryptographic techniques that get most of these properties.

We'll now talk about another property: *time.* Physical documents have physical reality. Society has evolved practices and legal mechanisms to establish that physical documents existed at certain points in time: People send sealed, postmarked envelopes or execute signatures in front of a notary. Often, these processes are supported by properties inherent to the physical mechanisms involved—postage stamps can be hard to reproduce; signatures and legal text can be laid over complicated printed patterns. Legal consequences can also support these mechanisms.

---

2. www.echeck.org

Potentially, even forensics can lend a hand by physically analyzing the age of paper and ink.

In the information age gospel, we keep pushing paper processes into electronic settings. What happens when we do this with timestamping? Stuart Haber and W. S. Stornetta carried out the seminal research work in this space [HS91] and also obtained key patents and started a business[3] in the space—but that's another story. We'll tell one version of this story here.

14.2.1 Digital Timestamping

We might start by thinking about notaries. We'd like to have a trusted party witness that a document (e.g., some bundle of bits) exists "now." Haber and Stornetta call this party the *timestamping service (TSS)*. Given our tools of hashing and cryptography, we might start with the obvious solution.

- The client sends a hash of its document to the TSS.
- The TSS adds the time, signs it, and sends back the signature.

The U.S. Postal Service once considered setting up such a "digital postmarking" service. We pointed out how, using Merkle trees (recall Section 7.6.3), a third party could undercut that business by reselling postmarks. (As we recall, the proposed countermeasure was "We won't allow that," to which we replied, "If you're just timestamping a hash, how can you tell?")

To evaluate timestamping schemes, Haber and Stornetta proposed several metrics. Some are the usual performance issues. How efficient is the scheme? How much record keeping is required? However, exhibiting true security paranoia, they also considered trust issues. What if the TSS wants to cheat? What if the TSS wants to cheat *later*? The obvious solution doesn't fare too well against these trust criteria. At any future point in time, a TSS can forge a timestamp from any time in the past.

To address these flaws, Haber and Stornetta extended the obvious scheme with iterated hashing. They force a "valid timestamp" to depend on all previously issued timestamps—and then take steps to ensure that some of this history is outside the control of all the adversaries, including the TSS. Figure 14.4 sketches such a system.

1. Collect all the hashes during a "tick."
2. Organize them into a Merkle tree.

---

3. http://www.surety.com/

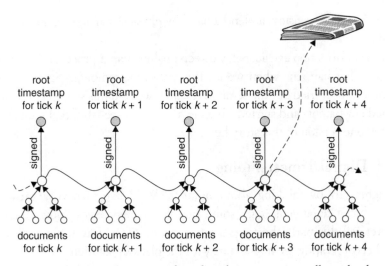

root timestamp for tick k | root timestamp for tick $k+1$ | root timestamp for tick $k+2$ | root timestamp for tick $k+3$ | root timestamp for tick $k+4$

signed | signed | signed | signed | signed

documents for tick k | documents for tick $k+1$ | documents for tick $k+2$ | documents for tick $k+3$ | documents for tick $k+4$

Figure 14.4 The Haber-Stornetta approach to digital timestamping collects the documents in each tick into a Merkle hash tree whose root also depends on the root of the previous tick's tree. A document's timestamp consists of the signed root along with the proof of the document's presence in that tree. At regular intervals, the current root gets published in physical media.

3. Hash in the root of the tree from the *previous* tick and sign the result.

4. Send each client a timestamp consisting of the signed root and the proof that this client's hash contributed to that Merkle tree.

5. Once a week, publish the root as a classified ad in the *New York Times.*

If it wants to forge a timestamp from the past, the TSS needs to go back and change all subsequent timestamps, as well as all the archived copies of the *New York Times.* If the TSS accidentally loses or discloses its private key, the prior timestamps still remain valid.

Haber and Stornetta also considered what might happen when the cryptographic components fail. Naively, we might consider changing the TSS key pair or even upgrading modulus length or algorithms when we predict that the components may no longer continue to be dependable. However, this would leave us with a problem. Suppose that in June, we upgrade the keylength from 1024 bits to 2048 bits because we worry that by December, factoring 1024-bit moduli will be tractable. An adversary who factors the old modulus in December will not be able to forge timestamps issued with the new key pair. However, the adversary could still start issuing signatures with the old key pair, which would complicate life.

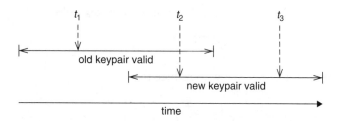

Figure 14.5 Suppose that the TSS timestamps a document at time t_1 using its old key pair and then uses its new key pair to timestamp the existence of that timestamp at time t_2, while both key pairs are valid. A relying party can then verify the validity of the original timestamp at time t_3, even after the original key pair is no longer considered secure.

For example, how can Rita the Relying Party distinguish between the validity of signature S_1 issued by the old key pair in March (when it was still good) and the validity of a signature S_2 issued by the adversary in December?

Figure 14.5 sketches the cute solution Haber and Stornetta proposed. In June, the TSS can use the new key pair to timestamp the existence of S_1. Rita can thus know that S_1 was issued *before* the old key pair became insecure. This approach can extend to digital signatures in general. Indeed, PKI communities are currently discussing how to validate old signatures and old certificates; this approach to timestamp renewal could prove useful there. (This idea is reminiscent of the cryptographic concept of *backward secrecy:* An adversary can't figure out information next week that will let him or her break things from today. A related concept is *forward secrecy*, or *forward security:* an adversary can't figure out information today that will let him or her break things next week.)

Since signatures and Merkle trees both depend on hashing, Haber and Stornetta also proposed using multiple hash functions (e.g., at the time, these might have been MD5 and SHA-1). If one goes, the other will still be valid.

14.2.2 Gluing Hash Functions Together

Interestingly, recent progress (e.g., see [Jou04]) provides some counterintuitive results. Joux considers building such *cascaded* hash functions by concatenating the outputs from two existing hash functions:

$$(F||G)(m) = F(m)||G(m).$$

Suppose that F produces n_F-bit hash values and G produces n_G-bit values. Without loss of generality, let $n_F \leq n_G$. From the Birthday Paradox, we would expect that the best brute-force attack would require searching

$$\sqrt{2^{n_F+n_G}} = 2^{\frac{n_F}{2}} \cdot 2^{\frac{n_G}{2}}$$

values. However, Joux shows how to reduce this to

$$\left(n_G 2^{\frac{n_F}{2}}\right) + \left(2^{\frac{n_G}{2}}\right).$$

To do this, Joux first shows how, if F follows the iterated construction of the Merkle-Damgard model, then building a set of 2^t colliding messages costs only t times as much as building a pair of colliding messages. Let f be the compression function inside F. Suppose that we have a subroutine $C(i)$ that, given i, calculates a collision on f : that is, a pair of blocks b_0 and b_0' such that

$$f(i, b_0) = f(i, b_0').$$

If we call C with the IV of F, we get two messages—b_0 and b_0'—that collide on F. However, if we call C again on $f(\text{IV}, b_0)$, we get another pair of blocks b_1 and b_1'. These two pairs of blocks give four ways to construct messages that all collide under F (see Figure 14.6). The result generalizes. For t calls to C, we end up with a set of 2^t messages that all collide.

Via a brute-force Birthday attack, we can calculate a collision on f by searching $2^{\frac{n_F}{2}}$ values. Via the preceding trick, we can do this $\frac{n_G}{2}$ times and end up with a set of $2^{\frac{n_G}{2}}$ messages that all collide to the same value under F. Thus, this requires searching $n_G 2^{\frac{n_F}{2}}$ values in total—the first term in the better complexity.

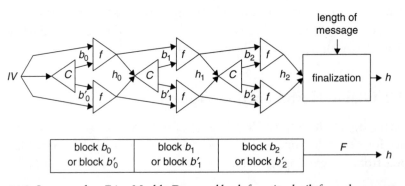

Figure 14.6 Suppose that F is a Merkle-Damgard hash function built from the compression function f, and we have a subroutine C that lets us calculate a collision on f for any given intermediate value. Then $t = 3$ calls to C (above) gives us $2^t = 8$ different messages (below) that all collide to the same value under F.

Because of the Birthday Paradox, we expect that two of these messages will also collide under G. (We discussed the Birthday Paradox in Section 8.3.4.) We need to find which two they are. The tree structure of the way Joux calculated the F-multicollisions lets us find the G birthday collision with $2^{\frac{n_G}{2}}$ calls to G's compression function instead of $\frac{n_G}{2}2^{\frac{n_G}{2}}$ ones.

Punch Line.   Concatenating two hash functions produces a function that, when we consider brute-force attacks, is only slightly stronger than the stronger of the two. Surprise!

14.3 Property

Consider what Alice can do with a book. She can buy one. She can lend or even sell it to Bob; however, she will no longer have a copy. If, like Solomon, she tries to rip the book into two pieces, she'll end up with a mess (unlike Solomon). She can make photocopies of short portions of the book. She might try making a copy of the book with a photocopier, but it's probably not worth her bother: producing something as durable and professional as the original will likely be more expensive than simply buying another copy. It would also be rather difficult for Alice to alter the book in a convincing way or to insert her own chapter into it.

A publisher of traditional media, such as books printed on paper, depends on these behaviors and limits for its business model. If Alice could make an unlimited number of perfect replicas of the book, then she might easily undercut the publisher's legitimate sales. What's worse, she could start selling them wholesale to unscrupulous bookstore operators; pirated and legitimate copies will be indistinguishable downstream. If Alice can easily subdivide the book, she might bet that it's unlikely that two of her friends will need the same page at the same time—and arrange for herself and her friends to all share the same copy. If Alice can easily alter the book, she might insert inflammatory material and then declaim to friends about the garbage that the previously reputable firm decided to publish. (In the pre-Web world, we heard one major publisher refer to this worry as the *binding problem*.)

However, all these properties follow from the physical nature of the medium itself. Things like books and vinyl records have them. Things like CDs start to lose them; things like MP3s and other pure digital content lose them altogether.

The area of *digital rights management (DRM)* examines this general problem of what type of rights users and others should have on digital objects and how to build the objects so that, like books, their substance and construction implicitly provide these properties. As nearly every recent college student knows, the term *DRM* is now a hot button that invokes images of crusading pirates, bumbling industrial technologists, and rapacious lawyers. (Alter the adjectives to obtain the other side of the story.)

Using technologies discussed in this book to design a DRM system—or to defeat one—are good exercises for the reader. In this section, we discuss one family of supporting technology.

14.3.1 Information Hiding and Piracy

Many approaches to the piracy problem reduce to examining a special message connected to the digital object. Developing a workable architecture here requires thinking of ways to handle several challenges. Where does this message come from? Who checks it? What is done with the results of this check? Can an adversary modify or delete the message? How is the message connected to the digital object after all?

Petitcolas, Anderson, and Kuhn provide an exhaustive, if dated, survey of this space [PAK99]. This paper also has one of the longest bibliographies we've seen in a research paper. The authors estimate that in 1995, when they wrote the paper, the cost of forgery was $24 billion—and 100 deaths. The situation has not likely improved.

The general field of *steganography* ("covered writing") goes back millennia. Petitcolas et al. cite many ancient and modern examples. For example, they cite Kahn's story of how, in WWI, a censor changed the message "Father is dead" to "Father is deceased," prompting a query: "Is Father dead or deceased?" [Kah96] However, with respect to copy issues for digital objects, the term usually used is *watermarking*. This term derives from paper makers' centuries-old practice of embedding a background logo in their paper, to establish its quality.

The field of watermarkings gets further divided. *Watermarks* often refer exclusively to embedded messages that identify the owner of the *intellectual property* (e.g., the content of the book). In contrast, *fingerprints* refer to embedded messages that identify the owner of *that particular instance* of the IP.

These concepts then get divided into a more elaborate taxonomy, based on the requirements of the *detector*, the module that looks for the message.

- In *private marking*, the detector requires the unmarked object. In *type I* systems, the detector extracts the mark. In *type II* systems, the detector takes the mark as a parameter and answers yes or no. (And yes, we do not appreciate these types of taxonomies that use nonmnemonic category names!)

- In *semiprivate marking*, the detector does *not* require the unmarked object but still requires the mark.
- In *public marking*, the detector requires only the marked object.

Usually, one thinks of this image marking in the spirit of symmetric cryptography: Installing the marking requires the same privilege as detecting the image. However, *asymmetric marking* is also conceivable. So far, only one direction has been done: Hiding requires the private key. As far as we know, the other direction is still an open problem.

14.3.2 The Prisoner's Problem

Where and how do we hide a message within a larger dataset?

Gus Simmons of Sandia National Laboratory[4] frames one aspect of this challenge as the *Prisoner's Problem* [Sim88]. (No, this is not the same as the *Prisoner's Dilemma*. But well-cultured computer scientists should know what that is, too.) Alice and Bob, in prison, are planning an escape together. They need to rely on the warden to pass messages back and forth. However, any sign of encryption will cause the warden to stop routing the messages! What can they do?

The obvious approach is to use *subliminal channel:* for example, in the randomness in many signature schemes or in the low-order bits of grayscale values in the pixels making up an image. However, Alice and Bob might also find success by moving in the completely opposite direction and using what Scott Craver called a *supraliminal channel:* hiding the message in the "perceptually significant information" that the warden cannot "modify without gross modifications to the transmitted object" [Cra98]. As a basic example, Craver observes that a warden who can change only a small percentage of the bits in a message is unlikely to turn an image of a cow into one of a pig. Although counterintuitive, a supraliminal channel is more likely to survive compression, censorship, editing, and so on.

(Supraliminal channels are an example of a rule of thumb that can be useful to computer security as well as to other avenues of life. If the natural approach seems well fortified, try the opposite approach. It worked for the British in the their raid on Fort Montgomery and Fort Clinton during the American Revolution: Rather than attack the well-fortified river-facing front of the forts, the raiders overran the unguarded rear. And until recently, one could still poke around the

---

4. Which can translate to the "Watermelon National Laboratory" in Spanish.

Figure 14.7 This photograph of Boston contains the README file for the steghide steganographic tool, embedded via steghide (available from steghide.sourceforge.net). The README is 7 KB long, and the image with the embedded README was smaller than the original, owing to compression of the embedded file.

unprotected—but unlabeled—ruins of Fort Montgomery, in the woods, off Route 9W, just north of where the Appalachian Trail crosses the Hudson River.)

14.3.3 Watermarking Examples

Until 2000 or so, *images* seemed to get the most attention (see Figure 14.7). As we mentioned earlier, a naive approach is to embed the message by diddling the least-significant bits in the grayscale or color values in pixels. More advanced schemes do the diddling in some transformed domain; for example, the Petitcolas survey discusses an approach using barely perceptible geometric distortions, and some recent work considers using aspects of images that humans cannot perceive well.

With the dawn of the age of MP3s, iTunes, and Napster, *audio* started appearing in the news. The recording industry established the *Secure Digital Music Initiative (SDMI)* and invited researchers to analyze a set of proposed watermarking schemes. A team of researchers led by Princeton's Ed Felten analyzed these schemes and broke several. Their resulting research report makes for many interesting stories [CWL+01]. On a narrow scope, the paper is notable for reporting how the team used patent searching as a research tool. (It turns out that one of the participating companies had filed patents that shed light on challenge schemes.) The paper also documents how, essentially, the recording industry worried about its own version of the publishing industry's binding problem. On a larger scope, the paper is notable because the Recording Industry Association of America tried legal action to suppress it.

Researchers have also considered how to embed watermarks in *code* (i.e., computer programs). Diddling code so that it still performs correctly but carries a message is an interesting problem that, on the surface, seems to suggest an entertaining duality to the design of polymorphic viruses. (Research topic, anyone?) Watermarks or fingerprints certainly would have been helpful to the RSA Corporation in getting to the bottom of the RC4/Arcfour controversy (recall Section 7.1). A related issue here is *software tamper resistance*. If the adversary changes an important part of the watermark or other protection technology, then the software should stop working. However, the defender must obscure the causality between the adversary's action and the consequence; otherwise, the adversary can simply patch out the response.

14.3.4 Watermarking Applications

So far, we've been discussing issues about how to embed messages in larger digital objects. However, we've not yet fleshed out the larger context of why and how. The technology has two main styles of application.

First, one can use such embedded messages to detect illegitimate use of one's property. In the predigital world, we have encountered road maps in which the map maker embedded features that were minor but fictitious. The hope was not to lead customers astray but to enable detection of unscrupulous map makers copying these maps instead of doing their own surveys. (Unfortunately, one of us tried to bicycle down such a fictitious road.) The CMU Computer Science Department had a tradition of including fictitious names in the departmental directory, which carried a warning that it was not to be used as a source of names for advertising solicitations but was, anyway. In theory, an advertiser sending something to a name that appeared only in this directory was politely advised of its malfeasance.

In the digital world, an intellectual property owner might watermark their works with its identity, so that a Web crawler could easily seek out and identify pirated copies. The owner might even fingerprint each object with the identity of whose copy it is, in order to identify who leaked it.

Alternatively, one can try to use embedded messages to ensure only legitimate use. Various recording industry projects propose schemes whereby the playback device looks for the appropriate watermark before letting the media play. Some proposals even embed less-trivial rights policies (e.g., "The user has the right to make three copies of this, but the copies may not be copied").

In another setting, anonymity schemes have occasionally been compromised owing to *unintended* fingerprinting. As an example, Rao and Rohatgi used dusty old linguistic techniques, previously used to resolve authorship of the *Federalist Papers* and *Primary Colors*, to group Internet postings by author with high probability. Authors who make anonymous postings but have a larger body of postings out there might find their writings linked [RR00]. (Rao and Rohatgi didn't even consider the potential of *syntactic fingerprinting:* looking at patterns of misspellings and punctuation errors.)

14.3.5 Attacks

As we continually note, we like to think about security in terms of keeping the system in a safe state, despite adversarial actions and plain old environmental failure. We've been discussing using steganographic encodings to help ensure various good things—well, good from the defenders' point of view—will happen. How might failures and malice keep these good things from happening?

Historically, the application space tended toward physical-world images, and so security analysis tended to consider basic physical-space actions. How *robust* is the watermark? Will it persist if the image is stretched or distorted, compressed and then decompressed, or photocopied? What does the adversary need to do in order to win: remove all evidence of the watermark or simply render it unreadable or simply determine that it exists? Alternatively, might the adversary benefit from altering the watermark so that it appears to carry a valid but different message from what was installed, or even from inserting a fraudulent watermark into an object that did not have one initially?

This historical bias also tended to consider human-based attacks: Can a *human* perceive or alter the watermark? In the digital world, however, humans can't even perceive the object directly but must instead depend on a computational proxy. Consequently, when considering attacks, we must consider what is *computationally* doable, not only what is humanly doable. In recent practice, the balance seems to be tilting toward the attacker, at least for larger payloads. Naturally arising images, for example, possess many types of natural continuities, that current embedding systems significantly disrupt—a disruption that statistical methods detect.

Defenders also often neglect to consider the case of the adversary's having N watermarked versions of the same item and examining the differences. Petitcolas discusses the *mosaic* attack: breaking the image into a zillion small pieces. Will the watermark persist? What if pieces from different originals are mixed in?

The adversary might also bypass the steganographic process altogether. For example, Alice could simply steal Bob's object and pirate that one instead. Many cynics also cite the *analog hole* problem: For many types of media (e.g., music), the digital object eventually needs to be turned into some type of sensory (analog) output, in order to have value, and one might worry that a pirate can always tap into that.

Ultimately, it's probably an economic argument. To return to this chapter's opening theme, we might ask: Can physical cash be forged? Yes, but one presumes that the Department of the Treasury has deployed technology and processes that make unprosecutable counterfeiting to be so expensive that the amount of profitable counterfeiting stays at an acceptably low level.

14.4 The Take-Home Message

Society's migration of physical processes to electronic ones is probably unavoidable. Furthermore, one could likely enumerate many strong and convincing reasons— economics, accessibility, environment—why this is a Good Thing.

As this chapter has discussed, these physical processes often depend on properties of physical objects. The tools in the security toolbox can help reproduce the necessary properties, but, as this chapter has also discussed, things usually don't work out quite the same way.

14.5 Project Ideas

1. Is DigiCash feasible on a PDA? Why or why not?

2. Reinvent secret splitting. That is, derive a way to easily transform a b-bit secret S into n b-bit numbers $share_0, \ldots, share_{n-1}$, such that if we know all n shares, we can reconstruct the original number, but if we know fewer than n, we can't learn anything.

3. Take a look at the Habner and Stornetta scheme, and then try to implement their timestamping service.

4. Use technologies discussed in this book to design a DRM system—or to defeat one.

5. Consider legal and ethical aspects of DRM hacking.

6. The Digital Millenium Copyright Act (DMCA) makes it illegal to "circumvent" copy protection systems in digital objects. Is the DMCA a good way to protect intellectual property? Why or why not ?

7. Why is the naive approach to embedding a message in an image naive?

Part V

Emerging Tools

Formal Methods
and Security

In the beginning of this book, we framed security as the problem of keeping the system in a safe state despite adversarial actions and plain old failures. Throughout the text, we have presented various tools and techniques that, one hopes, increase the chances that the systems we build and deploy possess this property.

However, it's hard to be sure, and history has given us numerous examples of the system providing a few more services and interfaces, and ways for adversaries and failures to modify system state, than the designers perhaps anticipated. For example, the fingerd[1] architects probably did not intend to offer a service that allowed anyone on the net to inject code and execute it at fingerd's privilege level.

Automated formal methods are becoming an increasingly viable approach to help determine whether the system "works," even for industrial-scale projects. Since this is a security book, we tend to think about "working" in the sense of remaining secure; however, these techniques are also showing promise for other types of reliability, correctness, and robustness.[2]

In theory, the vision sounds straightforward and attractive. We start by picking up a tool, and we write down a description of our system in the language preferred by this tool. Then, we write down the security properties we care about—again, in

---

1. Recall the discussion of fingerd in Section 3.1.
2. In fact, we are showing our bias here, like that famous *New Yorker* cartoon showing a New Yorker's view of the rest of the world. In all honesty, these lesser non-security-specific properties were probably the primary motivation.

terms of the language preferred by this tool. We crank the handle, and—presto—the security assurance pops out the other side. (Of course, when the first author tried this in practice when developing a commercial security product, the reality turned out to be far messier and far more iterative.)

Many tools—both paper based and real code—are emerging to help with this process. In this chapter, we consider this element of the security artisan's toolkit.

- Section 15.1 discusses how to specify what the system does and what the properties we want are.
- Section 15.2 surveys the tools of formal logic, useful for talking about behaviors and goals.
- Section 15.3 focuses on automated tools that let us crank the handle and have security assurance pop out.
- Section 15.4 reviews some case studies.
- Section 15.5 walks through an explicit example.
- Section 15.6 discusses some limits of this technique.

This chapter is a bit thinner than some of the earlier ones, owing to its different scope. Rather than being a core part of the security toolbox, automated formal methods are techniques from outside that have proven surprisingly useful—and perhaps *should* be part of the standard toolbox. We would be remiss in not discussing them.

15.1 Specification

If we're going to achieve this vision of using formal methods to analyze system behavior, we need to formally specify the system itself. The toolbox gives a number of ways to do this. A standard one, which influenced our running characterization of security, is as a *discrete state system* (recall Figure 1.2).

For example, we decompose the system into a set of component elements, such as processes, channels, events, and so on. For each of these elements, we define a set of possible values. We can then define the *state space* of the system as the cross-product of these individual spaces. At any point in time, we could describe the state of the system by a tuple $s \in States$ specifying the state of each component.

In general, not all elements of this cross-product space may actually be valid. For example, for some types of systems, we might want to discuss the hardware state, the running processes, and the I/O channels. However, if the device is being held in hardware reset, its set of currently running processes and output channels must be empty; any other combination is illegal. In such situations, we might want to end up defining a *structural correctness* predicate specifying which subset of *States* should actually be possible.

We might also want to enumerate the sets of actions or events that might change the state of the system. We then define a *transition function* δ on *States* × *Events* that describes how this happens. Exactly what δ maps to—and whether it's strictly a function, mathematically speaking—depend on what we're trying talk about.

- We might want a standard function:

$$\delta \ : \ States \times Events \ \rightarrow \ States.$$

  If the system is in state s, then $\delta(s, e)$ names the unique state that the system goes to if e happens.
- Sometimes, we might want a *partial* function: δ is undefined for some inputs, meaning that the system state doesn't change.
- Sometimes, we might want a *multifunction*: δ can take on many values, meaning that the system might transition in many ways.

We have many choices (see Figure 15.1).

We can then start talking about what the system does. What are its *initial states*? What states are *reachable*? Does it have an *end state*, where execution terminates? Which of these *end states* are "correct"? Does the system have *partial correctness*— all reachable end states are correct—or *total correctness*—and we always reach one of these? (See Figure 15.2.)

Can we put *everything* in this system specification? Of course not. Like it or not, the specification we build is only a *model*. As Chapter 2 discussed, on a

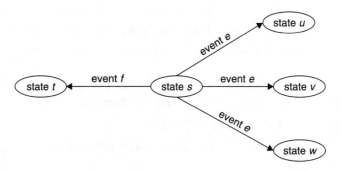

Figure 15.1 If e, f, and g are the events that can happen when the system is in state s, then the state transition function δ shown here would be a partial function, because $\delta(s, g)$ is undefined, and a multifunction, because $\delta(s, e)$ is the set $\{e, v, w\}$.

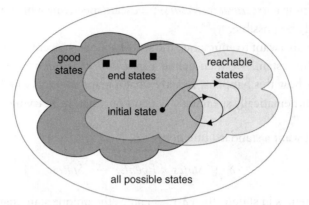

Figure 15.2 This system is *partially correct*. When it terminates, it terminates in a good state—but some executions, such as the one shown by the line, never terminate.

formal-methods project, one of us had a coworker who liked to use the example of trying to decide whether the author should run across a bridge in high winds.

- Maybe we would build a physical model of the bridge, with a physical model of the author on it. We could then subject the toy bridge to the appropriate toy high winds and see what happens.
- If we put the right things in the model, then the behavior of the model might say something reasonable about the behavior of the real thing.
- However, if we missed something important, we might end up sending the real author over the real bridge when we shouldn't, with unfortunate consequences.

With formal modeling, an inevitable fact of life is *abstraction*.

Once we have our system model, we can try to express what's important about the real thing, in terms of the model. So, what is important? How do we specify this? We might begin expressing the desired properties in straightforward human terms.

- "No student can take a sequence of actions that results in that student being able to see another student's GPA, but instructors can."
- "Money is neither created nor destroyed."
- "No student can spend the same dollar more than once."

But this is much trickier than it may appear. Can we state the property in a way that's clear enough to a human reader but precise enough to be expressible in our model?

Sometimes, we might want to do this in terms of *invariants:* predicates that should remain true over the execution. Sometimes, though, we need to recast invariants as "remaining true except when inside a transaction that temporarily must make them false." Consider the invariant that "money is neither created nor destroyed," which, in a banking model, we might express as "the net sum of money should remain constant." On typical hardware, moving money from one bank account to another will require doing the subtraction and the addition in some serial order, which temporarily disrupts the invariant.

In our own experience, we sometimes find that, after we build the model, we cannot easily express the security property we cared about. For example, in the modeling the IBM 4758 (see Chapter 8 in [Smi04c]), we found that what we cared about was not a property of the static state but rather of the sequence of states. "If X happens and then Z happens, then a compensating Y happened in between." Unfortunately, the formal modeling tool we were using did not want to talk about sequences, just states—which required some ugly workarounds.

15.2 Logics

The need to specify predicates about system behavior usually requires tools from mathematical logic. Since computer science curricula frequently omit this topic, we'll briefly discuss it here.

15.2.1 Boolean Logic

Most computer scientists are familiar with basic Boolean logic: formulas built from the operators

- *And* ($\wedge$)
- *Or* ($\vee$)
- *Not* ($\neg$)
- *Implies* ($\Rightarrow$). $A \Rightarrow B$ is true if, whenever A is true, then B is true too; it's equivalent to $(\neg A) \vee B$.

15.2.2 Propositional Logic

Propositional logic adds two more notions:

1. *Axioms*, an initial set of assertions we believe to be true
2. *Inference rules*, which specify how we can derive new "true" assertions from existing ones

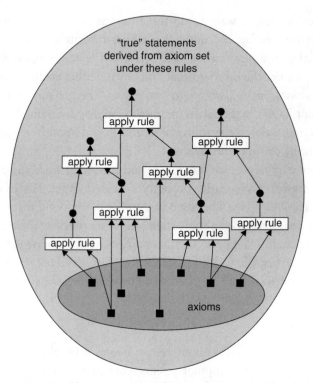

Figure 15.3 In propositional logic, we start with a set of axioms and then keep applying our rules to derive more things we believe are true under these rules.

Inference rules are often written as schema such as:

$$\frac{F_1, F_2}{F_3}$$

This example indicates that if our current set of "assertions believed true" contains one matching the pattern of F_1 and another matching the pattern of F_2, then we can add one matching F_3 to our set. Propositional logic thus lets us reason about what can be derived from axioms using our rule set (see Figure 15.3).

A natural question to ask is whether this set of assertions we conclude are true makes any sense. (If not, then we might need to tune the axioms or inference rules!) Two concepts in particular receive attention:

- *Soundness.* Are all our conclusions actually true?
- *Completeness.* Are we actually able to derive all the true statements we need to?

Of course, for these concepts to be meaningful, we need to have some notion of *ground truth*, in the reality of the system we are modeling.

15.2.3 First-Order Logic

Standard Boolean operators let us reason about things:

$$\text{\textit{Alice is a user}} \quad \wedge \quad \text{\textit{Alice is in group } \texttt{cs58}}$$

First-order logic lets us extend this reasoning about populations of things by giving us two more operators:

1. *For all:* The formula

$$\forall x \in S \; : \; F(x)$$

   is true when assertion $F(x)$ holds for all $x \in S$.

2. *Exists:* The formula

$$\exists x \in S \; : \; F(x)$$

   is true when assertion $F(x)$ holds for at least one $x \in S$.

(See Figure 15.4.)

15.2.4 Temporal Logic

Traditional mathematical proofs start with some assumptions and axioms and conclude with the derived result. As a consequence, traditional approaches to proving

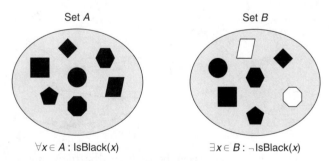

Figure 15.4 In first-order logic, we can reason about populations of things, as well as about the things themselves.

correctness of computer programs start with the *preconditions* assumed true when the program starts and conclude with the *postconditions* true when the program finishes.

However, this tradition implicitly assumes that programs achieve their usefulness by running once and then terminating. This assumption does not hold in many real-world systems, such as a desktop OS or an avionics computer, where "correctness" depends on what the system does while it's running and termination of the system is often an error condition.

Temporal logic gives us tools to talk about the behavior of systems that aren't supposed to terminate [Pnu77]. We have new operators, such as:

- *Always:* The formula

$$\Box F$$

means that assertion F is always true throughout the entire execution.
- *Eventually:* The formula

$$\Diamond F$$

means that assertion F will be true at some future state in the execution.

(See Figure 15.5.)
We can then say things like:

$$\Box (\textit{Alice hits return} \ \Rightarrow \ \Diamond \textit{Alice receives a shell prompt})$$

(Pnueli received the 1996 Turing Award for his role in the development of temporal logic.)

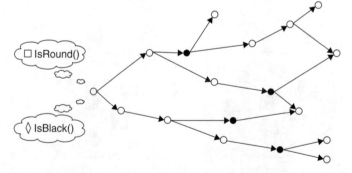

Figure 15.5 In temporal logic, we can reason about what will be true (or not) along sequences of events. In this sketch, it will always be true that we're in a round state, and it will eventually be true that we'll be in a black state.

15.2.5 BAN Logic

When it comes to reasoning about authentication protocols, things get even trickier. We need to reason about how Alice can believe that a message came from Bob, which means that we need to talk about such assertions as: "If Alice believes that only she and Bob know key K, and if she receives a message with a MAC generated from K, then she ought to believe that the message came from Bob."

Authentication logics, such as the seminal *BAN logic* [BAN90], let us reason about such assertions. Until we get to authentication, we've been able to use logic and assertions that implicitly have one type of truth: Assertions are true, in some absolute sense, or they are not. However, when we start talking about multiple, autonomous parties, we need to deal with the fact that none of them can see the *entire* system, and they may have different beliefs and value systems to begin with. To handle these multiple points of view, we need new operators:

- *Believes:* The formula

$$Alice \models X$$

  means that assertion X is one of the things that Alice currently holds to be true. (Consequently, she can use that as an input to her inference rules and derive new things she believes to be true.)

- *Sees:* The formula

$$Alice \lhd X$$

  is true when Alice "sees" or "perceives" message X. Depending on what she believes about the structure and cryptography of X and the channel by which it arrived, she might then add additional "facts" to her belief set.

- *Once said:* The formula

$$Alice \mathrel{\vdash\!\sim} X$$

  is true when, at some point earlier in the execution, Alice "said" X: that is, perhaps she sends that as a message.

    We'll often see this operator used in potentially counterfactual executions. For example:

$$Bob \models (Alice \mathrel{\vdash\!\sim} X).$$

  Maybe Alice really said X, or maybe Bob believes anything he's told and Evil Edna told him that Alice said X.

- *Has jurisdiction over:* The formula

$$Alice \Rightarrow K$$

means that Alice has jurisdiction over K. We can use this operator to start talking about cryptography. For example, if

$$(Bob \models (Alice \Rightarrow K)) \quad \wedge \quad (Bob \vartriangleleft (M \text{ signed by } K))$$

maybe we could conclude that

$$Bob \models (Alice \vdash M).$$

- *Is fresh:* The formula

$$\sharp(X)$$

is true when X is "fresh." Although awkward to define even informally, freshness lets us reason about such things as *nonces:* the random values that parties exchange during cryptographic protocols to help ensure that they're talking to a live entity on the other side and not an adversary replaying old messages. For example, when trying to reason about what server Bob might conclude during an SSL session, we may end up asserting

$$Bob \models \sharp(\texttt{pre\_master\_secret})$$

Figure 15.6 sketches some concepts from BAN logic. Typically, such a logic will also give us some new inference rules about what conclusions Alice might draw from what she sees, based on what she already believes.

15.2.6 Some Security Examples

Less mathematical readers might wonder: What's the point of all these symbols? To shed light here, consider the analogous question of why one has to actually write out a program to get a computer to perform an algorithm: Why isn't a paragraph of prose enough? The answers to these questions have several components:

- *Precision.* English is notoriously ambiguous. (That's why lawyers need to write in legalese instead.) Formal logic lets you specify *exactly* what you mean. Sometimes, we can go even further: Formal logic gives us the tools to be precise about things we otherwise would have skipped altogether. Consider BAN logic. When writing authentication protocols and handshakes, folks

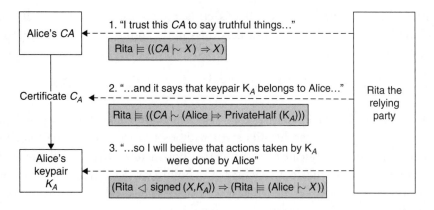

Figure 15.6 BAN logic lets us reason about what parties perceive and conclude during authentication protocols. Here, we revisit the notion of PKI certificate (and Figure 10.1) and try to formally describe what Rita is thinking.

usually write down only the exchange of messages and omit what the parties might conclude from these messages and why. However, whether the protocol "works" depends on this latter material—and if we can't express it, we can't reason about it.

- *Machine readability.* If we want to use our statements about security correctness as inputs to an automated verification process, informal prose will not suffice.

- *Human readability.* Stop laughing. Yes, beyond first-order logic—where there are at least some easy mnemonics (e.g., "Exists" is a backward "E")—the symbols get strange. On the other hand, suppose that you need to consider the implications of a proposed access control rule, something that security artisans need to do. Which makes it easier to see the nuances: a page of dense, ambiguous text or a few lines of clean logic with lots of whitespace?

Let's consider a few more security-specific examples.

File Access. Recall from Section 4.2.3 the UNIX file access rules. When exactly should Alice be allowed to read file F? What if the file has permissions `---rwxrwx` and Alice is both the owner and in its group? With logic, we can say it exactly:

$$((Alice = Owner(F)) \wedge (Perms(F) = \texttt{r********})),$$

$$\vee \ ((Alice \neq Owner(F)) \wedge (Alice \in Group(F)) \wedge (Perms(F) = \texttt{***r*****})),$$

$$\vee \ ((Alice \neq Owner(F)) \wedge (Alice \notin Group(F)) \wedge (Perms(F) = \texttt{*****r**})).$$

Chinese Wall. Recall the Chinese Wall security model from Section 2.2.3. If Alice reads a file now, that changes her access rules in the future. We can use temporal logic to say that action exactly:

$$\square \ \forall X \neq Y \in C \ \left(Reads(Alice, X) \ \Rightarrow \ \neg \lozenge Reads(Alice, Y)\right).$$

PKI. Why should Rita the Relying Party believe that Bob belongs to key pair K_{Bob}? In the standard (X.509) world, Rita starts with a set of trust roots. She somehow gets her hands on a certificate C asserting that Bob matches K_{Bob}. She then tries to find enough other certificates to enable her to build a validated trust path from one of her roots to C. As we sketched in Figure 15.6, we can use BAN logic to talk about what Rita believes about assertions and keys. However, we can use *propositional* logic to talk about how she puts together paths.

- For each trust root CA, the fact that Rita believes the assertions it makes become axioms:

$$Rita \ \models \ (CA \mapsto K_{CA})$$
$$Rita \ \models \ ((CA \mathrel{\vdash\!\!\!\sim} X) \ \Rightarrow \ X).$$

- The certificates Rita encounters become axioms:

$$Rita \ \lhd \ Signed(C, K_C).$$

- The fact that Rita can draw conclusions from digital signatures becomes an inference rule:

$$\frac{Rita \lhd Signed(X, K_A), \quad Rita \models (A \mapsto K_A)}{Rita \models (A \mathrel{\vdash\!\!\!\sim} X)}.$$

- Finally, Rita can then use the inference rule that if Rita believes that a party speaks correctly about certificate assertions, and if she encounters a certificate assertion made by that party, then she believes the assertion:

$$\frac{Rita \models (CA \mathrel{\vdash\!\!\!\sim} X), \quad Rita \models ((CA \mathrel{\vdash\!\!\!\sim} X) \ \Rightarrow \ X)}{Rita \models X}.$$

A "trust path" is simply the repeated application of these inference rules to her axioms that yields the conclusion that $Bob \mapsto K_{Bob}$.

Of course, the reality of X.509 PKI is a bit more complicated. When a CA issues a certificate to another CA, it's usually qualified: "I trust this CA to make assertions of this type" or "I trust this CA to assert bindings about identities in this namespace." Some relying parties also work such predicates into their inference rules. (Revocation is also an issue—but you'll deal with that in project idea 4.)

15.3 Cranking the Handle

Suppose that we have formally specified what our system is and does and we have formally specified the security correctness properties that we care about. How do we go about determining whether these properties always hold for our system? Two general flavors of tools exist:

1. If our state space is finite, then we can decide this question easily—in theory, anyway. We simply run our system model through all the reachable states and check that our properties are true in each one. This is the *model-checking* approach.

2. Even for large or infinite state spaces, we could still logically establish that our properties are always true. For example, it doesn't take a stretch of imagination to see that one might deduce some general relation about what happens to our bank balance after a withdraw operation, instead of evaluating it for each possible balance value. This *theorem-proving* approach tries to logically prove theorems about the model, instead of taking it through every reachable state.

   Rather than trying to exhaustively search the reachable states of the system, we're trying to explore the reachable assertions of a propositional logic system (recall Figure 15.3) to see whether our desired security property is one of them. The inference rules include some basic ones from logic—and probably new ones particular to the kind of system we're modeling.

Doing either by hand is awful. Fortunately, in the past two decades, industrial-strength tools have started emerging to do this verification automatically.

Choosing between the two approaches gives rise to many tradeoffs. Model checkers for real systems deal with *huge* state spaces and consequently need lots of cleverness to make the problem tractable. This cleverness includes abstraction, chunking, and tricks to encode the state space in a memory-efficient manner. In contrast, theorem provers can directly deal with *infinite* spaces. For a trivial example, think of how many cases we'd need to examine to model check the assertion

$$\forall a, b \in \mathbb{Z} \quad (a + b) = (b + a).$$

Model checkers can run by themselves; theorem provers can be painfully inter-active. A positive output of model checker ("no counterexamples") can be less than confidence-inspiring. On the other hand, a positive output from a theorem prover can be hand-checked, in theory. A negative output of a model checker—an explicit counterexample—can be useful for debug/development. But again, on the other hand, a negative output of a theorem prover ("Gosh, darn, we just couldn't prove it") can be less than helpful.

15.4 Case Studies

Clarke and Wing's survey provides many real-world applications of automated formal methods for general properties [CW96]. For instance, Ed Clarke's group found errors in the IEEE futurebus standard. Gerard Holzmann's group found that approximately 55 percent of the original requirements in a large telecom software project were logically inconsistent. (Think about what this might mean in the real world. How much money will you save your company if you can prove that the requirements are logically inconsistent—so *no* system can meet them—before the company spends 2 years trying build such a system?) North Carolina State University used model checking to find flaws in distributed active structural control systems for earthquake protection of buildings. Wing's follow-up paper [Win98] looked at security applications in particular; for example, she discusses how Gavin Lowe used model checking to exhibit a flaw in a protocol that had been around for *18 years*. (We also call attention to citation 21 in her text.)

The use of automated formal methods in security continues to progress. Somesh Jha and colleagues built the *Brutus* model checker and applied it to numerous security protocols, sometimes searching nearly 80 million states [CGP99]. Paul Ammann's group at George Mason has been using model checking to discover paths through which an adversary at machine X can penetrate some other machine Y several hops away in the network [RI00]. Jonathan Herzog, now at the Naval Postgraduate School is using automated formal methods to search for API vulnerabilities in the TCG's TPM (that is, the Trusted Computing Group's Trusted Platform Module system; see Chapter 16). One of us led a team using the *ACL2* theorem prover to verify security properties of the IBM 4758 secure coprocessor [Smi04c, Chapter 8].

15.5 Spinning Your Bank Account

We can demonstrate the use of automated formal methods for security by using the freely available *Spin* model checker [CGP99, Hol04, Spi]. (Spin received the *ACM Systems Award* in 2001.)

```
withdraw(amount) {
   if (balance >= amount) {
      spit out amount;
      balance -= amount;
   }
}
```

Figure 15.7 Sample code a bank computer might execute when a user tries to withdraw money from an ATM.

In Spin, we write a specification of system behavior in *Promela*, a language that looks a lot like C. In practice, we find that it looks so much like C that some students think that they're programming, instead of merely specifying potential behavior.

Consider the sample code in Figure 15.7 for the ATM example from Section 14.1.2. Suppose that Alice and Bob were going to try to withdraw money from the same bank account concurrently. We might wonder whether this code has a race condition: some way that Alice's and Bob's request can interleave in such a way to cause a security problem. To examine this, we can first specify this system in Promela (see Figure 15.8).

The bank account starts out with $100, and Alice and Bob each try to withdraw $100. We conclude our specification with a correctness predicate: the assertion that when both Alice and Bob have finished their actions, the net total of cash they received should not be greater than $100.

We can use Spin in random mode, using the -n option to seed the PRNG. Figure 15.9 shows how this random probing reveals an execution that violates the assertion!

Sharp-eyed readers would have noticed that we failed to provide mutual exclusion for the critical section in the withdraw operation and that this omission permits a TOCTOU bug (recall Section 6.3). Figure 15.10 shows how putting a lock on the section should solve the problem. Using Spin to generate an exhaustive search on this specification confirms that our fix works.

15.6 Limits

Automated formal methods are not yet a silver bullet. For one thing, they still are teetering on the edge of being practical for large systems with real development deadlines. Our colleague who manned the ACL2 engine lamented how it would run for hours, only to say "no, couldn't prove it"; he would then go back to reading Kafka in German.

```
int balance;
int cash;
int done;

proctype withdraw(int atm, amount) {

  if
    :: (balance >= amount) ->
         printf("ATM %d gives $%d\n", atm, amount);
         cash = cash + amount;
         balance = balance - amount;
    :: else ->
         printf("ATM %d says: insufficient funds!\n",atm);
  fi;

  done++;
}


init {

  balance = 100;
  done = 0;

  run withdraw(1,100);
  run withdraw(2,100);

  (done == 2) -> assert (cash <= 100);
}
```

Figure 15.8 Using Promela to specify that the bank running Figure 15.7 should not end up spitting out more cash than an account contains.

More important, we need to remember our original focus: We're doing all this work to try to increase assurance. Does a "proof" from one of these automated formal tools mean that our system is secure? Unfortunately, no—the best it can do is make a statement that some properties hold for an abstract model.

- Jeannette Wing notes that "there will always be a gap between what is in a person's head and the first codification of the system or desired property" [Win98] (which sounds like something Donald Norman would have said—see Chapter 18).

- What about *conformance*? Does our code match the specification? What about the levels of software and hardware translation between the code we're

```
        ATM 2 gives $100
        ATM 1 gives $100
spin: line  30 "bank.spin", Error: assertion violated
spin: text of failed assertion: assert((cash<=100))
#processes: 3
                balance = -100
                cash = 200
                done = 2
 18:    proc  2 (withdraw) line  19 "bank.spin" (state 10)
 18:    proc  1 (withdraw) line  19 "bank.spin" (state 10)
 18:    proc  0 (:init:) line  30 "bank.spin" (state 6)
3 processes created
```

Figure 15.9 Running Spin on the specification from Figure 15.8 reveals a TOCTOU problem in Figure 15.7.

analyzing and the actual execution? Do we have a clear understanding of what our language does when it's compiled? Does our model?

- *Quis custodiet ipso custodes?* (Who watches the watchmen?) How do we know that the verification tool actually works?

- What's actually in the model? Formal methods would not have found the flaws in the protocols from Section 9.5.3 if the model itself did not allow for extra parties, message reflection, and message reuse. Formal methods would not have found the atomicity flaw in DigiCash (Section 14.1.5) if the model did not allow for abnormal termination. Formal methods would not find the SSL timing flaw that Boneh exploited (Section 8.4.1) if the model did not include the dependency of execution time on input parameters.

On the other hand, negative results from a model checker can be very useful because they can tell us the conditions that cause the error.

15.7 The Take-Home Message

Automated formal methods can be one way to provide increased assurance that a system will be secure. Thinking about what properties your system should have (and at what times) and writing them down can often uncover numerous subtleties in the system. Even the attempt to use automated formal methods forces a precision in specifying behavior and security that itself can increase system robustness as well as assist in debugging. For systems in which assurance is critical, this alone can be worth the price of admission.

```
int balance;
int cash;
int done;
bool lock;

#define ACQUIRE(L) atomic { (!L) -> L = true;}
#define RELEASE(L) atomic { assert (L);  L = false; }

proctype withdraw(int atm, amount) {

   ACQUIRE(lock);
   if
     ::  (balance >= amount) ->
           printf("ATM %d gives $%d\n", atm, amount);
           cash = cash + amount;
           balance = balance - amount;
     ::  else ->
           printf("ATM %d says: insufficient funds!\n",atm);
   fi;
   RELEASE(lock);
   done++;
}

init {

   lock = false;
   balance = 100;
   done = 0;

   run withdraw(1,100);
   run withdraw(2,100);

  (done == 2) -> assert (cash <= 100);
}
```

Figure 15.10 Using Promela to specify that the bank running Figure 15.7—but with a lock added around the critical section—should not end up spitting out more cash than an account contains.

However, as we have noted, the tools are still emerging. We do not see them as a default option built in to gcc or Visual Studio—yet. For commercial software, which is often big and ships on a tight schedule, many development shops may not have the time or resources to write the system and then turn around and write the specification. Not to mention that the specification needs to be maintained— changing a single line of code can mean that the specification needs to change as well.

15.8 Project Ideas

1. Consider an online academic information service in a university.

   - Formally specify the correctness condition that "No student can take a sequence of actions that results in that student's being able to see another student's GPA, but instructors can."
   - Would a system that allows students to see both their own GPA and the average GPA within a group of students they specify be correct?
   - Would a system that allows students to teach courses be correct?

2. It's tempting to try to use the $\Rightarrow$ operator to state more cleanly when Alice is allowed to read file F, under UNIX rules:

$$((Alice = Owner(F)) \Rightarrow (Perms(F) = \texttt{r********})),$$
$$\wedge\ ((Alice \in Group(F)) \Rightarrow (Perms(F) = \texttt{***r*****})),$$
$$\wedge\ ((Alice \in Universe) \Rightarrow (Perms(F) = \texttt{*****r**})).$$

   Can you see any problems with this?

3. Pick your favorite authentication protocol (e.g., Kerberos), and model it in BAN logic.

4. Consider the CRL method of distributing certificate revocation in X.509 PKI. Use the tools of formal logic to express when Alice will accept a certificate as valid. Then use the tools to express when she *should* accept a certificate as valid. Is Alice's reasoning system sound and complete?

5. Take some of your own programs, and model them in temporal logic.

6. Go to http://www.spinroot.com and download Spin. Write a few programs—or take some that you've already written—write their specification in Promela, and check them. (*Extra credit:* Read Kafka in German while you wait).

7. Pick your favorite programming language and write a parser that generates a Promela model from a program written in that language. You can use such tools as `lex` and `yacc` or `antlr`.

Hardware-Based Security

We worry about computer security because important social processes keep migrating to distributed computerized settings. When considering security, it's important to take a holistic view—because we care about the security of the social process itself, not only some component. However, in this chapter, we take a reductionist point of view and look at one of the components in particular: the hardware.

Historically, probably the main path toward thinking about hardware security came from considering the protection of computation from adversaries with direct physical access to the computing machinery. We've always liked framing this question in terms of dependency. Alice's interests may depend on certain properties of computation X—perhaps integrity of its action or confidentiality of some key parameters. However, if X occurs on Bob's machine, then whether these properties hold may depend on Bob. For example, if Bob's machine is a standard PC and Bob is root, then he pretty much has free reign over X. He can see and modify data and code at will. As a consequence, preservation of Alice's interests depends on the behavior of Bob, since Bob could subtly subvert the properties that Alice depends on. These circumstances force Alice to trust Bob, whether or not she wants to. If Bob's interests do not coincide with Alice's, this could be a problem.

This main path—reducing Alice's dependency by modifying Bob's computer—leads to several lines of inquiry. The obvious path is using hardware itself to protect data and computation. Another path toward thinking about hardware security comes from considering that computing hardware is the underlying physical environment for computation. As such, the nature of the hardware can directly influence the nature of the computation it hosts. A quick glance at *BugTraq* [Sec06] or the latest Microsoft security announcements suffices to establish that deploying secure systems on conventional hardware has proved rather hard. This observation raises another question: If we changed the hardware, could we make it easier to solve this problem?

In this chapter, we take a long look at this exciting emerging space.

- Section 16.1 discusses how memory devices may leak secrets, owing to physical attack.

- Section 16.2 considers physical attacks and defenses on more general computing devices.

- Section 16.3 reviews some larger tools the security artisan can use when considering the physical security of computing systems.

- Section 16.4 focuses on security approaches that change the hardware architecture more fundamentally.

- Section 16.5 looks at some future trends regarding hardware security.

(The first author's earlier book [Smi04c] provides a longer—but older—discussion of many of these issues. Chapter 3 in particular focuses on attacks.)

16.1 Data Remanence

One of the first challenges in protecting computers against adversaries with direct physical contact is protecting the stored data. Typically, one sees this problem framed as how a device can hide critical secrets from external adversaries, although the true problem is more general than this, as we discuss later. Potential attacks and defenses here depend on the type of beast we're talking about.

We might start by thinking about *data remanence:* what data an adversary might extract from a device after it has intended to erase it.

16.1.1 Magnetic Media

Historically, nonvolatile magnetic media, such as disks or once ubiquitous tapes, have been notorious for retaining data after deletion. On a physical level, the contents of overwritten cells have been reputed to be readable via magnetic-force microscopy; however, a knowledgeable colleague insists that no documented case exists for any modern disk drive. Nonetheless, researchers (e.g., [Gut96]) and government standards bodies (e.g., [NCS91]) have established guidelines for overwriting cells in order to increase assurance that the previously stored data has been destroyed. (The general idea is to write a binary pattern, then its complement, then repeat many times.)

A complicating factor here is the existence of many layers of abstraction between a high-level request to delete data and what actually happens on the device in question. In between, many things could cause trouble.

- For example, a traditional filesystem usually breaks a file into a series of chunks, each sized to occupy a disk sector, and distributes these chunks on the disk according to various heuristics intended to improve performance. Some type of index table, perhaps in a sector of its own, indicates where each chunk is. In such a system, when the higher-level software deletes or even shrinks a file, the filesystem may respond by clearing that entry in that file's index table and marking that sector as "free." However, the deleted data may remain on the disk, in this now-free sector. (Issues such as this led to the *object reuse* worries of the Orange Book world of Chapter 2.)

- *Journaling filesystems*, a more advanced technology, make things even worse. Journaling filesystems treat the disk not as a place to store files so much as a place to store a log of changes to files. As with Word's Fast Save option (see Chapter 13), the history of edits that resulted in a file's current state may be available to the adversary inspecting the disk itself.

- Computing hardware has seen a sort of trickle-down (or perhaps smarting-down) effect, whereby traditionally "dumb" peripherals now feature their own processors and computing ability. Disk controllers are no exception to this trend, leading to yet another level of abstraction between the view the computing system sees and what actually happens with the physical media.

16.1.2 FLASH

In recent years, semiconductor FLASH memory (e.g., in USB thumbdrives) has probably become more ubiquitous than magnetic media for removable storage. FLASH is also standard nonvolatile storage in most embedded devices, such as cell phones and PDAs. The internal structure of a FLASH device is a bit more complex than other semiconductor memories (e.g., see [Nii95]). FLASH is organized into *sectors*, each usually on the order of tens or hundreds of kilobytes. When in "read" mode, the device acts as an ordinary ROM. To write a sector, the system must put the FLASH device into write mode, which requires writing a special sequence of bytes, essentially opcodes, to special addresses in the FLASH device. Typically, the stored bits can be written only one way (e.g., change only from 0 to 1). To erase a sector (e.g., clearing all the bits back to 0), another sequence of magic bytes must be written. Often, FLASH devices include the ability to turn a designated sector into ROM by wiring a pin a certain way at manufacture time.

FLASH gives two additional challenges for system implementers. First, writing and erasing sectors both take nontrivial time; failure, such as power interruption, during such an interval may lead to undetermined sector corruption. Second, each FLASH cell has a relatively small (e.g., 10,000) lifetime of erase-write cycles.

These technical limitations lead to incredible acrobatics when designing a filesystem for FLASH (e.g., [GT05, Nii95]). In order to avoid wearing out the FLASH sectors, designers will use data structures that selectively mark bits to indicate dirty bytes within sectors and rotate usage throughout the sectors on the device. For fault tolerance, designers may try to make writes easy to undo, so that the old version of a file can be recovered if a failure occurs during the nontrivial duration of a write. Even relatively simple concepts, such as a directory or index table, get interesting—if you decide to keep one, then you'll quickly wear out that sector, even if you're clever with the rest of the files.

FLASH architecture has several consequences for security.

- Because of these log-structured and fault-tolerant contortions, old data may still exist in the device even if the higher levels of the system thought it was erased.

- Because an error in a product's ROM can be expensive, at least one vendor includes an undocumented feature to rewrite the ROM sector by writing a magic series of bytes to the chip. (The complexity of the legitimate magic-byte interface makes it hard to otherwise discover such back doors.)

- Because of the large market demand for low-cost thumbdrives and the smarting down of computation into peripherals, much engineering has gone into commercial FLASH drives, leading to a gap between even the API the encapsulated device provides and the internal state.

16.1.3 RAM

Random-access memory (RAM) is the standard medium for memory during active computation. *Dynamic RAM (DRAM)* stores each bit as an electrical charge in a capacitor. Since these charges tend to be short-lived, data remanence is not as much of an issue here. This short lifetime leads to additional functionality: The devices need to continually read and restore the charges, before they decay. (One wonders whether this continual processing of stored data might lead to side-channel exposures.) However, the capacitors do not take much real estate on the chip;

as a consequence, DRAM tends to be favored when large amounts of memory are required.

In contrast, *static RAM (SRAM)* stores each bit via the state in a flip-flop, a small collection of logic gates. This approach takes more real estate but does not require the extra functionality and its extra power. As a consequence, when a device needs memory with the properties of RAM (e.g., none of this sector business) but otherwise nonvolatile, it may end up using battery-backed SRAM, which is sometimes referred to as *BBRAM*.

SRAM, however, is not without remanence issues. Long-term storage of the same bits can cause memory to *imprint* those values and retain them even after power-up. Environmental factors, such as cold temperatures and radiation, can also cause imprinting. (Gutmann [Gut01] and Weingart [Wei00] both provide more discussion of these issues.)

16.1.4 The System

So far, we've discussed properties of the memory medium itself. However, the memory is embedded in the context of a larger system, and this larger context can lead to issues. For example, at many levels in the software stack, software optimization might decide that a write to a data location that will no longer be used is unnecessary and silently eliminate it. This can undo a programmer's efforts to clear sensitive data. Researchers at Stanford recently used a form of virtualization (see Section 16.4.2) to explore this issue of data lifetime in the context of an entire system—and uncovered many surprising cases of data living longer than the designers or programmers intended or believed [CPG+04].

16.1.5 Side Channels

Devices that instantiate computation in the real world must exist as physical machines in the real world. Because of this physical existence, computational actions the device takes can result in real-world physical actions that the designer can easily fail to foresee but that an adversary can exploit. We discussed many examples of this in Section 8.4.

16.2 Attacks and Defenses

16.2.1 Physical Attacks

So far, we've discussed how a computing device may or may not keep secrets from an adversary with physical access. We now discuss some ways an adversary may use physical access to mount an attack. To start with, we might consider the security perimeter: what the designers regarded as the boundary between the internal trusted part of the system and the external part under the potential control of the adversary.

Individual Chips.   Perhaps the first model to consider is the single trusted chip. The designer/deployer wants to trust the internal operation of the chip, but the adversary controls the outside. Over the years, this model has received perhaps the most attention—in the public literature, anyway—owing to the long and widespread use of low-cost *chip cards*—often considered synonymous with *smart cards*—in commercial applications, such as controlling the ability to make telephone calls or to view licensed satellite TV. The ubiquity creates a large community of adversaries; the applications give them motivation; and the cost makes experimentation feasible.

The work of Anderson and Kuhn provides many nice examples of attack techniques on such single-chip devices [AK96, AK97]. Perhaps the most straightforward family of attacks are the many variations of "open up the device and play with it." Various low-cost lab techniques can enable the adversary to open up the chip and start probing: reading bits, changing bits, resetting devices back to special factory modes by re-fusing fuses, and so on. Historically, we've seen a cycle here.

- The vendor community claims that such attacks are either not possible or are far too sophisticated for all but high-end state-sponsored adversaries.
- The adversary community demonstrates otherwise.
- The vendor community thinks a bit, reengineers its defense technology, and the loop repeats.

It's anyone's guess where we will be in this cycle—and whether the loop will keep repeating—when this book is published.

By manipulating the device's environment, the adversary can also use more devious ways to influence the computation of such devices. For an amusing and effective example of attacks, we refer back to Anderson and Kuhn. The device may execute an internal program that brings it to a conditional branch instruction. Let's say that the device compares a register to 0 and jumps to a different address if the two are equal. However, in typical chip card applications, the device obtains its power from an outside source. This means that the adversary can deviously manipulate the power, such as by driving it way out of specification. Generally speaking, the CPU will not function correctly under such conditions. If the adversary applies such a carefully timed spike at the moment the device is executing this comparison instruction, the adversary can cause the CPU to always take one direction of the branch—whether or not it's correct. Finding examples where such an attack lets the adversary subvert the correctness of the system is an exercise for the reader.

In some sense, such environmental attacks are the flip side of side-channel attacks. Rather than exploiting an unexpected communication path coming out of the device, the adversary is exploiting an unexpected communication path going into it. Another example of this family of attack is *differential fault analysis (DFA)*, sometimes also known as the *Bellcore attack*. Usually framed in the context of a chip card performing a cryptographic operation, this type of attack has the adversary somehow causing a transient hardware error: for example, by bombarding the chip with some kind of radiation and causing a gate to fail. This error then causes the chip to do something other than the correct cryptographic operation. In some situations, the adversary can then derive the chip's critical secrets from these incorrect results.

Bellcore attacks were originally suggested as a theoretical exercise (e.g., [BDL97]). However, they soon became a practical concern (e.g, [ABF⁺03]), to the point where countermeasures became a serious concern. How does one design a circuit to carry out a particular cryptographic operation but that also doesn't yield anything useful to the adversary if a transient error occurs? Some researchers have even begun formally studying this model: how to transform a circuit so that an adversary who can probe and perhaps alter the state of a limited subset of wires still cannot subvert the computation [ISW03]. We touch on these attacks again in Section 16.5.

Larger Modules.   Multichip modules provide both more avenues for the attacker and more potential for defense.

Getting inside the chassis is the first step. Here we see another cat-and-mouse game, featuring such defenses as one-way bolt heads and microswitches on service doors, and corresponding counterattacks, such as using a pencil eraser as a drill bit or putting superglue on the microswitch after drilling through the door.

An attacker who can get inside the chassis might start monitoring and manipulating the connections on the circuit boards themselves. The attacker might hook logic analyzers or similar tools to the lines or insert an *interposer* between a memory or processor module and the circuit board, allowing easy monitoring and altering of the signals coming in and out. Other potential attacks misusing debugging hooks include using an *in-circuit emulator (ICE)* to replace a CPU and using a *JTAG* port to suspend execution and probe/alter the internal state of a CPU.[1]

---

1. JTAG stands for Joint Test Action Group, but that's not important. What is important is that the name denotes an industry standard for physical interfaces to ease testing of hardware.

The attacker might also exploit properties of the internal buses, without actually modifying hardware. For one example, the PCI bus includes a *busmastering* feature that allows a peripheral card to communicate directly with system memory, without bothering the CPU. Intended to support *direct memory access (DMA)*, occasionally a desirably form of I/O, busmastering can also support malicious DMA, through which a malicious PCI card reads and/or writes memory and other system resources illicitly.

API Attacks.   When focusing on these subtle ways that an adversary might access secrets by sneakily bypassing the ways a system might have tried to block this access, it's easy to overlook the even more subtle approach of trying to use the front door instead. The APIs that systems offer through which legitimate users can access data are becoming increasingly complex. A consequence of this complexity can be extra, unintended functionality: ways to put calls together that lead to behavior that should have been disallowed. Bond and Anderson made the first big splash here, finding holes in the API for the *Common Cryptographic Architecture (CCA)* application that IBM offered for the IBM 4758 platform [BA01]. More recently, Jonathan Herzog has been exploring the use of automated formal methods to discover such flaws systematically [Her06].

16.2.2 Defense Strategies

As with attacks, we might start discussing defenses by considering the trust perimeter: what part of the system the designer cedes to the adversary.

Chips.   As we observed earlier, attacks and defenses for single-chip modules have been a continual cat-and-mouse game, as vendors and adversaries take turns with innovation. In addition, some new techniques and frameworks are beginning to emerge from academic research laboratories. Researchers have proposed *physical one-way functions:* using a device's physical properties to embody functionality that, one hopes, cannot be accessed or reverse engineered any other way. The intention here is that an adversary who tries to use some type of physical attack to extract the functionality will destroy the physical process that generated the functionality in the first place.

In an early manifestation of this concept, researchers embedded reflective elements within a piece of optical-grade epoxy [PRTG02]. When entering this device, a laser beam reflects off the various obstacles and leaves in a rearranged pattern. Thus, the device computes the function that maps the input consisting of the laser angle to the output consisting of the pattern produced by that input. Since the details of the mapping follow randomly from the manufacturing process, we call this a *random function:* the designer cannot choose what it is, and, one hopes, the adversary cannot predict its output with any accuracy, even after seeing some reasonable number of x, $f(x)$ pairs. (Formalizing and reasoning about what it means for the function to resist reverse engineering by the adversary requires the tools of theoretical computer science—recall Section 7.1 or see the Appendix.)

It's hard to use these bouncing lasers in a computing system. Fortunately, researchers [GCvD02] subsequently explored *silicon physical random functions (SPUF)*, apparently from the earlier acronym *silicon physical unknown functions*. The central idea here is that the length of time it takes a signal to move across an internal connector depends on environmental conditions, such as temperature and, one hopes, on random manufacturing variations. If we instead compare the relative speed of two connectors, then we have a random bit that remains constant even across the environmental variations. Researchers then built up more elaborate architectures, starting with this basic foundation.

Outside the Chip.   Even if we harden a chip or other module against the adversary, the chip must still interact with other elements in the system. The adversary can observe and perhaps manipulate this interaction and may even control the other elements of the system. A number of defense techniques—many theoretical, so far— may apply here. However, it's not clear what the right answer is. Figuring out the right balance of security against performance impact has been an area of ongoing research; many of the current and emerging tools we discuss later in this chapter must wrestle with these design choices.

For example, suppose that the device is a CPU fetching instructions from an external memory. An obvious idea might be to encrypt the instructions and, of course, check their integrity, in order to keep the adversary from learning details of the computation. Although perhaps natural, this idea has several drawbacks. One is figuring out key management: Who has the right to encrypt the instructions in the first place? Another drawback is that the adversary still sees a detailed trace of instruction fetches, with only the opcodes obfuscated. However, there's nothing like the real thing—the most damning indictment of this technique is the way Anderson and Kuhn broke it on a real device that tried it [AK96].

We might go beyond this basic idea and think about using external devices as memory, which makes sense, since that's where the RAM and ROM will likely be. What can the adversary do to us? An obvious attack is spying on the memory contents; encryption can protect against this, although one must take care with using initialization vectors (IVs) or clever key management to prevent the same plaintext from going to the same ciphertext—or the same initial blocks from going to the same initial blocks. (Note, however, that straightforward use of an IV will cause the ciphertext to be one block larger than the plaintext, which might lead to considerable overhead if we're encrypting on the granularity of a memory word.)

Beyond this, two more subtle categories of attacks emerge:

1. *Learning access patterns.* The adversary who can see the buses or the memory devices can see what the trusted chip is touching when. One potential countermeasure here lies in aggregation: If it has sufficient internal storage, the chip can implement virtual memory and *cryptopage* to the external memory, treated as a backing store [Yee94].

   The world of crypto and theory give us a more thorough and expensive technique: *oblivious RAM* (ORAM) [GO96]. In a basic version, the trusted device knows a permutation π of addresses. When it wants to touch location i_1, the device issues the address $\pi(i_1)$ instead. If it only ever touches one address, then this suffices to hide the access pattern from the adversary. If it needs to then touch an i_2, then the device issues $\pi(i_1)$ and then $\pi(i_2)$— unless, of course, $i_2 = i_1$, in which case the device makes up a random i_2' and issues $\pi(i_2')$ instead. The adversary knows that two addresses were touched but doesn't know which two they were or even whether they were distinct. To generalize this technique, the device must generate an *encrypted shuffle* of the external memory; the kth fetch since the last shuffle requires touching k memory addresses. (One might wonder whether we could turn around and use the same technique on the k fetches—in fact, Goldreich and Ostrevsky came up with an approach that asymptotically costs $O(\log^4 n)$ per access.)

2. *Freshness of contents.* Earlier, we mentioned the obvious attack of spying on the stored memory and the obvious countermeasure of encrypting it. However, the adversary might also change memory, even if it's encrypted. An effective countermeasure here is less obvious. Naturally, one might think of using a standard cryptographic integrity-checking technique, such as hashes or MACs, although doing so incurs even more memory overhead. However, if the device is using the external memory for both writing and reading, then we have a problem. If we use a standard MAC on the stored data, then we can replace the MAC with a new value when we rewrite the memory. But then nothing stops the adversary from simply replacing our new value-MAC pair

with an older one! We could stop this attack by storing some per location data, such as the MAC, inside the trusted device, but then that defeats the purpose of using external memory in the first place.

Two techniques from the crypto toolkit can help here. One is the use of *Merkle trees* (recall Section 7.6 and Figure 7.19). Rather than storing a per location hash inside the trusted device, we build a Merkle tree on the hashes of a large set of locations and store only the root inside the device. This approach saves internal memory but at the cost of increased calculation for each integrity/freshness check. Another idea is to use *incremental multiset hashing*, a newer crypto idea, whereby the device calculates a hash of the contents of memory—"multiset"—but can do so in an incremental fashion. (Srini Devadas' group at MIT came up with these ideas—for example, see [CDvD+03, SCG+03].)

The preceding approaches considered how the trusted device might use the rest of the system during its computation. We might also consider the other direction: how the rest of the system might use the trusted device. A general approach that emerged from secure coprocessing research is *program partitioning:* sheltering inside the trusted device some hard to reverse engineer core of the program but running the rest of the program on the external system. Doing this systematically, for general programs, in a way that accommodates the usually limited power and size of the trusted device, while also preserving overall system performance, while also being secure, appears to be an open problem.

However, researchers have made progress by sacrificing some of these goals. For example, theoreticians have long considered the problem of *secure function evaluation (SFE)*, also known as *secure multiparty computation*. Alice and Bob would like to evaluate a function f which they both know, on the input (x_A, x_B), which they each know (respectively), but don't want to share. In 1986, Yao published an algorithm to do this—an inefficient algorithm, to be sure, but one that works [Yao86]. 2004 brought an implementation—still inefficient, but we're making progress [MNPS04].

The economic game of enforcing site licenses on software also used to manifest a version of this program-partitioning problem. Software vendors occasionally provide a *dongle*—a small device trusted by the vendor—along with the program. The program runs on the user's larger machine but periodically interacts with the dongle. In theory, absence of the dongle causes the program to stop running. Many software vendors are moving toward electronic methods and are abandoning the hardware dongle approach. For example, many modern PC games require an original copy of the game CD to be inserted into the machine in order to play the game; a copied CD generally will not work.

Modules.   Building a module larger than a single chip gives the designer more opportunity to consider hardware security, as a system. For example, a larger package lets one more easily use internal power sources, environmental sensing, more robust filtering on the power the device demands from external sources, and so on.

However, colleagues who work in building "tamper-proof hardware" will quickly assert that there is no such thing as "tamper-proof hardware." Instead, they advocate looking at a systems approach interleaving several concepts:

- *Tamper resistance.* It should be hard to penetrate the module.
- *Tamper evidence.* Penetration attempts should leave some visible signal.
- *Tamper detection.* The device itself should notice penetration attempts.
- *Tamper response.* The device itself should be able to take appropriate countermeasures when penetration is detected.

Integrating these concepts into a broader system requires considering many tradeoffs and design issues. Tamper evidence makes sense only if the deployment scenario allows for a trustworthy party to actually observe this evidence. Tamper resistance can work in conjunction with tamper detection—the stronger the force required to break into the module, the more likely it might be to trigger detection mechanisms. Tamper response may require consideration of the data remanance issues discussed earlier. What should happen when the adversary breaks in? Can we erase the sensitive data before the adversary can reach it? These questions can in turn lead to consideration of protocol issues—for example, if only a small amount of SRAM can be zeroized on attack, then system software and key management may need to keep larger sensitive items encrypted in FLASH and to be sure that the sensitive SRAM is regularly inverted. The choice of tamper-response technology can also lead to new tamper-detection requirements, since the tamper-response methods may require that the device environment remain inside some *operating envelope* for the methods to work.

Antitamper, Backward.   Recently, a new aspect of tamper protection has entered the research agenda. U.S. government agencies have been expressing concern about whether the chips and devices they use in sensitive systems have themselves been tampered with somehow—for example, an adversary who infiltrated the design and build process for a memory chip might have included (in hardware) a Trojan horse that attacks its contents when a prespecified signal arrives. We can find ourselves running into contradictions here—to protect against this type of attack, we might need to be able to probe inside the device, which violates the other type of tamper protection. (Some recent research here tries to use the techniques of side-channel analysis—typically used to *attack* systems—in order to discover the presence of hardware-based Trojan horses; the idea is that even a passive Trojan will still influence such things as power consumption. [ABK+07].)

Software.   So far in this section, we've discussed techniques that various types of trusted hardware might use to help defend themselves and the computation in which they're participating against attack by an adversary. However, we might also consider what software alone might do against tamper. The toolkit offers a couple of interesting families of techniques.

- *Software tamper-resistance* (e.g., [Auc96]) techniques try to ensure that a program stops working correctly if the adversary tampers with critical pieces—for example, the adversary might try to run the program without a proper license. Effective use of dongles often requires some notions of software tamper resistance. As noted earlier, if the program simply checks for the dongle's presence and then jumps to the program start, then the adversary might simply bypass this check—so the tamper response needs to be more subtle. Related to this topic are techniques to produce binary code that is difficult to disassemble.
- *Software-based attestation* techniques (e.g., [SLS+05, SPvDK04]) try to assure an external relying party that a piece of software is running on a particular platform in a trustworthy way. The basic idea is that the relying party knows full operational details of the target system and crafts a checksum program that requires using all the resources of the system in order to produce a timely but correct response; a trusted path between the relying party and the target system is usually assumed. These techniques are still early but promising.

16.3 Tools

The previous section discussed foundations: basic issues of hardware attacks and defenses. However, when putting together a secure system, one typically thinks of larger-scale components. Rather than worrying only about how to build a chip that resists an attacker, one might worry about how to use an attack-resistant chip to do something useful within a larger system. In this section, we take a look at some of components in the toolbox.

16.3.1 Secure Coprocessors

If we're thinking about trying to protect computation from an adversary with direct physical access to the computer, the most "natural" approach might be to think about putting armor around the entire computer. However, since effective physical security raises issues about heat dissipation and internal maintenance, we usually can't count on armoring the entire computer system in question, so a more practical compromise is to armor a smaller subsystem and use that in conjunction with a larger *host*. This is the approach taken by *secure coprocessors*. Commercial examples include the IBM 4758 [SW99] and its more recent follow-on, the IBM 4764 [AD04]. (As the reader may conclude from checking out the citations in the bibliography, yes, the authors of this book had something to do with this.)

Generally, this type of device works by hiding secrets inside the armored device and using an interleaving of tamper-protection techniques to ensure that, under attack, the secrets are destroyed before the adversary can get to them. Owing to the relative ease of zeroizing SRAM compared to other forms of storage, secure coprocessors typically end up with a tiered memory architecture: a small amount of battery-backed SRAM contains the nonvolatile but tamper-protected secret; larger DRAM contains runtime data, and FLASH holds nonvolatile but non-secret data.

As a consequence, perhaps the most natural application of a secure coprocessor is to obtain confidentiality of stored data. This can be useful. However, one can also use this "protected secret" architecture to provide other properties. For example:

- *Integrity of public data.* If the secret in question is the private half of a key pair, then the coprocessor can use it to sign statements. A relying party that verifies the signature and believes that the device's physical security works and software is trustworthy, can believe that this statement came from an untampered device. If the statement pertains to the value of a stored data item, then the relying party can trust in the integrity of that value. This property may be useful in such scenarios as metering.

- *Integrity of executing program.* Is the device still running the correct, untampered software? A side effect of the private key approach just discussed is that the relying party can also verify that the software inside the device is still correct—if an adversary has tampered with it, then the private key would have, in theory, been zeroized and thus not available to the modified software.

This property can be useful in many scenarios, such as a trustworthy SSL-protected Web server. With more complex devices that permit updates and reinstallation of software and permit nontrivial software architectures, making this scheme work can become rather tricky. This idea of *outbound authentication*—enabling the untampered entity to authenticate itself as such to the outside world—foreshadowed the subsequent emphasis on *attestation*.

- *Privacy of program execution.* Some scenarios call for the program itself to be public but its execution to be private—that is, not only selected parameters but also operational details, such as which branch is taken after a comparison. For example, consider an auction. The program may need to be public, as all participants need to trust that the program evaluating the bids works correctly. However, exactly what it does when it runs on the secret bids should be secret; otherwise, observers would know details of the bids.

  Outbound authentication, combined with a self-contained computing environment, can provide this property.

- *Secrecy of program code.* Typically, the device may store its software in internal FLASH. However, the device could store much of this software in encrypted form and use its protected secret to decrypt it into DRAM before execution—thus using the protected-secret architecture to provide secrecy of program executables. This property may be useful for protecting proprietary pricing algorithms for insurance or pharmaceuticals.

Using a secure coprocessor in real-world applications may require dealing with some subtle design and architecture issues, owing to the exigencies of commercially feasible physical security. One basic problem is that the device may be too small to accommodate the necessary data; this problem drives some current research, as we discuss later. Another problem arises from the typical lack of human I/O on devices. If an enterprise runs a stand-alone application that has one trusted coprocessor installed but depends on input from an untrustworthy host, then the enterprise may not be benefiting much from the physical security. Nearly anything the adversary might have wanted to do by attacking the coprocessor can be achieved by attacking the host. The true value of the physical security comes into play when other parties and/or other trusted devices come into the picture: for example, remote clients connecting to a coprocessor-hardened server.

Another real-world issue with using a commercial secure-coprocessor platform is believing that it works. In our case, we had it validated against FIPS 140-1; however, going from such a validation to the conclusion that a system using such a device is sufficiently secure is a big step—see Chapter 11.

16.3.2 Cryptographic Accelerators

As discussed earlier in the book, cryptography is a fundamental building block of security in many modern computing scenarios. However, as Chapter 7 made clear, it is based on tasks that are by no means easy for traditional computers. For a basic example, RSA requires modular exponentiation: taking X and Y to X^Y mod N, where X, Y, and N are all very large integers. By current standards, RSA requires integers at least 1024 bits long to be deemed secure; currently, however, standard desktop computers operate on 32-bit words. Implementing 1024-bit modular exponentiation on a 32-bit machine is rather inefficient; this inefficiency can become an obstacle for applications, such as SSL Web servers, that must do this repeatedly.

These issues drive the idea of creating special-purpose hardware to accelerate such otherwise inefficient operations. Hardware for such operations as symmetric encryption and hashing can also be inserted in-line with data transmission (e.g., in a network card or in a disk drive) to make use of encryption in these aspects of system operation more affordable. (For example, building hardware acceleration for digital signature generation and verification into edge routers can greatly improve the performance cost of S-BGP compared to standard BGP—recall Chapter 5.)

Both the nature and the applications of cryptography introduce issues of physical security for cryptographic accelerators. For one thing, cryptographic parameters, such as private keys, may be long-lived, mission-critical data items whose compromise may have serious ramifications. For another thing, application domains, such as banking and the postal service, have a long history of relying on physical security as a component of trying to assure trustworthiness. As a consequence, cryptographic accelerators may tout tamper protection and feature APIs to protect installation and usage of critical secrets. As we noted, such devices tend to be called *hardware security modules (HSMs)* in the literature and in discussions of best practices for such application installations as certification authorities. The same architecture issues we noted earlier apply here as well. Physical security may protect against an adversary directly extracting the keys from the device and may protect against more esoteric attacks, such as subverting the key-generation code the device uses in the first place, in order to make the "randomly" generated keys predictable to a remote adversary. However, physical security on the HSM does not protect against attacks on its host.

For using cryptographic accelerators or HSMs in the real world, we advise consideration of many questions.

- Should you trust that the HSM works? Researchers have shown that one can build a crypto black box that appears to work perfectly but has adversarial back doors, like the one discussed earlier [YY96]. Here, we recommend that you look for FIPS validations—both of the overall module (e.g., via FIPS 140-N) and of the individual cryptographic algorithms used (recall Chapter 11).

- Should you trust that the HSM works too well? From a perhaps a straightforward security perspective, it's better for a device to have false positives—and destroy secrets even though no attack was occurring—than the other way around. From a business perspective, however, this may be a rather bad thing. The necessity to preserve the *operational envelope* in effective tamper protection may create even more opportunities for such false positives (e.g., if the building heat fails at Dartmouth College in the winter, an IBM 4758 would not last more than a day). Using HSMs requires thinking beforehand about continuity of operations.

- What if the manufacturer goes out of business or the device reaches its end of life? In order to make its physical security mean something, an HSM design may make it impossible to export private keys to another type of device. However, what happens should the vendor cease supporting this HSM? (This happened to colleagues of ours.)

- Exactly how can you configure the cryptographic elements? Having hardware support for fast operations does not necessarily mean that you can do the combination of operations you would like to. For example, the IBM 4758 Model 2 featured fast TDES and fast SHA-1, both of which could be configured in-line with the buffers bringing data in or through the device. Doing cryptography this way on large data was much faster than bringing into the device DRAM and then using the relatively slow internal architecture to drive the operation. However, in practical settings, one usually does not want *just* encryption: One wants to check integrity as well. One natural way to do this might be to hash the plaintext and then encrypt it along with its hash. However, doing something like this with the fast IBM hardware requires being able to bring the data through the TDES engine and then sneak a copy of the plaintext into the hash engine on its way out. Unfortunately, our fast hardware did not support this!

- What if new algorithms emerge? For example, the TDES engine in the IBM 4758 Model 2 includes support for standard chaining, such as CBC. Subsequently, Jutla invented a slower chaining method that provided integrity checking for free [Jut01]. We would have liked to use this chaining method, but the hardware did not support it. For another example, one need only consider the recent demise of MD5 hashing and fears of the future demise of SHA-1.

- Should you believe performance benchmarks? The problem here is that cryptographic operations may feature several parameters; in practice, many operations may be joined together (e.g., signatures or hybrid encryption); and HSMs may include internal modules, thus confusing which boundaries we should measure across.

    For example, if one wants to attach a number to an implementation of a symmetric cryptosystem, the natural measure might be bytes per second. IBM did this for the DES engine in the IBM 4758. A customer complained; on examination, we found that the touted speed was what one could get if operations were done with very long data items. Informally, the device had a per byte cost on the data as well as a per operation cost on the overhead of setting up the keys and such. For small data, the per operation cost dominates—and the effective per byte cost could drop an order of magnitude or more.

16.3.3 Extra-CPU Functionality

These armoring approaches run into some fundamental limitations. It seems that the computational power of what can fit inside the armor always lags behind the power of a current desktop system. This delta is probably an inevitable consequence of Moore's Law (see Section 16.5.3) and the economics of chip manufacturing: What gets packaged inside armor lags behind the latest developments.

This situation raises a natural question: Can we use hardware techniques to improve the security of general systems without wrapping the CPUs in armor? In the commercial and research space here, the general trend is to use hardware to increase assurance about the integrity and correctness of the software on the machine.

Boot-Time Checking.   Currently, the dominant approach is to consider boot-time protections. Figure 16.1 sketches an example sequence of what software gets executed when a system boots. The time order of this execution creates a dependency order: If software module S_1 executes before software module S_2, then correct execution of S_2 depends on S_1; if the adversary attacks or modifies S_1, then maybe it will change S_2 before loading it, or maybe it will load something else altogether.

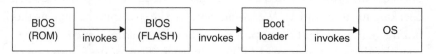

Figure 16.1 At boot time, a well-defined sequence of software modules get executed.

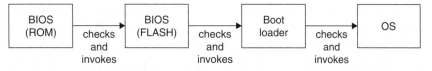

Figure 16.2 In the typical approach to system integrity checking, each element in the boot sequence checks the next before invoking it.

Boot-time approaches exploit the inductive nature of this sequence. By magic, or perhaps by hardware, we check the integrity and correctness of the first element of this chain. Then, before we grow the chain with a new element, a chain element that has been already checked checks this next candidate element. Figure 16.2 sketches an example. (In our 4758 work, we got rather formal about this and included hardware elements in this "chain.")

At the end of the process, we might have some assurance that the system is running correct, unaltered software—that is, if we have some way of knowing whether this verification process succeeded. (One will see the terms *trusted boot* and *secure boot* used for this process—sometimes as synonyms, sometimes to denote slightly different versions of this idea.)

One way to know whether verification succeeded is to add hardware that releases secrets depending on what happens. In the commercial world, the *Trusted Computing Group (TCG)* consortium[2] has developed—and still is developing, for that matter—an architecture to implement this idea in standard commercial machines. The TCG architecture adds a *trusted platform module (TPM)*—a small, inexpensive chip—to the motherboard. At the first level of abstraction, we can think of the TPM as a storehouse that releases secrets, depending on the state of the TPM's *platform configuration registers (PCRs)*. Each PCR can contain an SHA-1 hash value but has some special restrictions regarding how it can be written.

- At boot time, the PCRs are reset to 0s.[3]
- If a PCR currently contains a value v, the host can *extend* a PCR by providing a new value w. However, rather than replacing v with w, the TPM replaces v with the hash of the concatenation of v with w:

$$PCR \quad \longleftarrow \quad H(PCR \parallel w).$$

---

2. The TCG succeeded the *Trusted Computing Platform Alliance (TCPA)*; sometimes, one still sees the acronym of the predecessor consortium used to denote this architecture.
3. The latest specification of the TPM explores some other special conditions under which a PCR can be reset; expect further developments here.

This approach to "writing" PCRs allows the system to use them to securely measure software and other parameters during the boot process (see Figure 16.1). At step $i - 1$, the system could hash the relevant software from module i and store this hash in PCR i. Suppose that module 3 is supposed to hash to h_3 but that, in fact, the adversary has substituted an untrustworthy version that hashes instead to h_3'. If the PCRs permitted ordinary writing, nothing would stop adversarial software later from simply overwriting h_3' with h_3 in PCR 3. However, because the PCRs permit writing only via hash extension, the PCR will contain $H(0 \parallel h_3')$; if the hash function is secure, the adversary will not be able to calculate a v such that

$$H\big(H(0 \parallel h_3') \parallel v\big) = H(0 \parallel h_3).$$

In fact, this hash-extension approach allows the system to measure platform configuration into the PCRs using two dimensions. The system could use each PCR i to record the hash of a critical piece of the boot process. However, the system could also record a sequence of measurements within a single PCR, by successively hash-extending in each element of the sequence. By the properties of cryptographically secure hash functions, the end result of that PCR uniquely reflects that sequence of values, written in that order.

As mentioned, we can think of the TPM as essentially a place to store secrets. When we store a secret here, we can tie it to a specified subset of the PCRs and list a value for each. Subsequently, the TPM will reveal a stored secret only if each PCR in that subset has that specified value. (Note that we qualify this statement with "essentially": The actual implementation of this functionality is a bit more convoluted.) If such a secret is an RSA private key, then it can be stored with a further provision: When the PCRs are correct, the TPM will *use* it on request from the system but will never actually release its plaintext value.

The ability of the PCRs to reflect system configuration and the ability of the TPM to bind things such as RSA private keys to specific configurations enables several usage scenarios.

- Binding a key to a software configuration on that machine enables us to do similar things to what we did with secure coprocessors. The entity consisting of that software on that device can now *authenticate* itself, make verifiable statements about things, and participate in cryptographic protocols.
- If we cook things up so that we have a trusted entity that is much smaller than the entire platform, we can use a TPM-bound private key to make signed *attestations* about the rest of the platform configuration, as expressed by the

PCRs. In the TCG architecture, this entity is part of the TPM itself, but it could also be a separate software module protected by the TPM.

Moving from a rather special-purpose and expensive device (a secure coprocessor) to a generic, ubiquitous platform (standard desktops and laptops) changes the flavor of potential applications, as well. For example, moving Yee's partitioned-computation idea from a coprocessor to an encrypted subsystem or tables (protected by a TPM) can enable a software vendor to lock an application to a particular machine or OS. Attestation can enable an enterprise to shunt unpatched machines to a remedial network, thus promoting better network hygiene—this is called *trusted network connect (TNC)*. Attestation might also enable a powerful corporation to monitor everything on your machine. (Of course, all these scenarios are based on the assumption that the adversary cannot subvert the TPM's security protections!)

Realizing this approach in the real world requires worrying about exactly how to map platform configuration into the PCRs. This part of the design is rather complex and keeps changing, so we won't bother going through it all here. The initial BIOS reports itself to a PCR; as a consequence, the BIOS can break everything and thus is called the *root of trust measurement (RTM)*.[4] Subsequently, things already measured turn around and measure other things; what they are and which PCR they get measured into appear to be determined both by platform-specific specifications and random vendor choices. Platform elements also factor into the hashes; we discovered that doing things as simple as removing a keyboard or replacing a memory card caused the PCRs to change.

As Chapter 4 described, however, the software that comprises a particular application running on a contemporary operating system is by no means a monolithic entity or even a simple stack. How to glue TPM measurements to this complex structure is an area of ongoing research. In our early work here, we introduced a level of indirection—the TPM protects a trusted kernel-based module, which in turn evaluates higher-level entities [MSMW03, MSWM03]. In contrast, our colleagues at IBM Watson extended the hash-extension idea all the way up into Linux application environments [SZJv04].

We stress again that this is an area of active research by many parties. Stay tuned. In particular, as this book goes to press, researchers have developed ways to break the security of current TPM-based PCs simply by using a wire to ground the reset line on the *Low Pin Count (LPC)* bus that connects the TPM to the rest of the system.

---

4. So no, in this case, the acronym RTM does not stand for Read the Manual or Robert Tappan Morris.

This fools the TPM into thinking that the system has rebooted, at which point, the TPM resets all its PCRs, and the host can feed it measurements that simulate booting of the system it would like to impersonate. It looks as though Bernard Kauer [Kau07] got there first, but we were the first to do it on YouTube [Spa].

Runtime Checking.   Using hardware to assist with runtime checks of platform integrity is an area that has also received renewed interest lately. *CoPilot*, an academic project currently being commercialized, is good example of this [PFMA04]. One adds to the standard platform a separate PCI card with busmastering capabilities, so it can take over the PCI bus and probe system memory. At regular intervals, this auxiliary card probes the system memory and looks for signs of malware and corruption.

Realizing this approach in the real world requires intricate knowledge of what the system memory image should look like and requires that what image the card sees is the same reality the host CPU sees. Neither of these tasks is trivial. For example, rootkits typically attack systems not by inserting themselves into something big and relatively static, like executable code, but rather by making subtle modifications to dynamic data structures. The fact that these data structures are *supposed* to change makes it hard for the coprocessor to determine when bad changes have occurred. For another example, malware might restore correct-looking data structures when the coprocessor examines memory or might even maintain a decoy set of structures where the coprocessor expects to find them. Combating this latter set of issues may require using the software-based attestation ideas from earlier to establish a dynamic root of trust within the host CPU.

Strictly speaking, the runtime approach is not necessarily disjoint from the boot-time approach. As the experimental approaches we just discussed illustrate, a boot-time-verified module can easily turn around and verify changes and events during runtime. Even standard uses of a TPM can update PCRs during runtime. As we also mentioned earlier, the TCG is currently examining approaches whereby some PCRs can be reset during special conditions at runtime; such an approach could also extend to doing regular remeasurements during runtime.

Other Approaches.   So far, we've looked at approaches that use hardware either to directly harden the traditional computing platform or to detect tampering afterward. Ongoing research has been looking at more unconventional approaches: transforming the computation somehow so that a conventional, untrusted host does most of the work, but a smaller, trusted unit participates in such a way as to still provide the overall security property. We offer some examples.

- Cryptographic operations can lend themselves to situations in which part of the work can be blinded and then outsourced to a less trusted host. This approach might provide higher throughput and lower latency, while still protecting the private keys within a small hardware TCB.

- Our own *tiny trusted third party* project (e.g., [IS06]) builds on ORAM and Yao's secure multiparty computation to compile a program into a blinded circuit, which a fast untrusted host can execute with the assistance of a small piece of special-purpose hardware. This approach might provide privacy of computational details, even if the computation doesn't fit inside a small hardware TCB.

- In general, one might speculate about the space of functions in which calculating an answer requires significant resources, but verifying it requires very little. Can we build a method to provide integrity in such calculations, with only limited trusted hardware?

At some point, this approach starts to merge into the partitioned computation model with secure coprocessors.

16.3.4 Portable Tokens

It's almost a cliche that computing hardware has been getting small enough and cheap enough that substantial computing power now fits in a pocket. The truth that underlies this cliche also affects hardware-based security. Putting substantial computing and memory, perhaps with physical security, in a package that users can carry around is economically feasible in many situations; the near-ubiquity of USB slots on PCs and laptops—and the emerging ubiquity of Bluetooth and other forms of *near-field communication (NFC)*—make interaction with the standard computing environment rather easy.

Such devices have many security applications. They can be one factor for multifactor authentication. In enterprise-wide PKI installations, users might carry and wield private keys from a portable device rather than trying to bring data around. Perhaps a user's portable device could verify the integrity of a broader and untrusted system (e.g., [SS05]).

Such devices can also enable another type of security application: *honey-tokens*. Black-hat teams have penetrated enterprises by distributing "abandoned" USB memory sticks—with Trojan horses—in the parking lot. Employees of the target enterprise find the memory sticks, bring them inside the enterprise, insert them into computers, and unintentionally invoke the Trojan; the testers thus succeed in running their own code with insider privileges on inside-the-firewall systems. (See [Sta06] for more information and some commentary by such a pen tester.)

16.4 Alternative Architectures

So far, we've considered hardware additions for security that start with a computing environment based on a traditional CPU and then either put armor around it or put armored devices next to it. However, many active areas of current research—and also current industrial development—are exploring changing the traditional CPU instead. Some of this work is explicitly motivated by security; some has other motivations but still has relevance to security.

16.4.1 The Conventional Machine

In Section 4.1.1, we reviewed the basic architecture of a conventional system. As Figure 4.1 showed, memory is an array of indexed locations; let's say that each location is 1 byte wide. The CPU interacts with a memory location by issuing the address of that location on the address bus and indicating the nature of the interaction (e.g, read or write) on a control line. The data in question is then transferred on the data bus; the direction of this transfer depends on whether the operation is a read or a write.

Programs are stored in memory like anything else. The CPU fetches an instruction from memory, internally decodes it, and carries out its operation, which may involve additional reads or writes. The CPU then proceeds to fetch the next instruction.

Current conventional architectures differ from this simple one in three fundamental ways.

1. *Memory management.* In this naive model, the address that the CPU issues is the address that the memory sees. As a consequence, when multitasking, each separate program or process must be aware of the addresses the other ones are using. This clearly creates problems for security and fault tolerance, as well as general ease of programming.

   To avoid these problems and to enable lots of other flexibility, modern systems introduce a level of indirection: A *memory-management unit (MMU)* translates the virtual or logical addresses the CPU issues into physical addresses the memory sees (see Figure 4.2). The MMU can also enforce restrictions, such as read-only, by failing to translate the address, for a write request. The MMU, in conjunction with OS trickery, can enforce more exotic models as well, such as copy on write, whereby memory is shared between two processes until one tries to write to it.

When changing the process or memory domain currently active, the CPU can also instruct the MMU to change *address spaces:* the memory image seen by the CPU.

2. *Privileged instructions.* This is a security book, so our natural inclination is to look at everything—including address translation—from a security perspective. From this perspective, a natural question is: What's the point of using memory management to protect address spaces from rogue programs on the CPU, if the CPU itself is responsible for controlling and configuring the MMU?

This line of thinking led to the introduction of *privilege levels.* (a) The CPU has some notion of its current privilege level. (b) What an instruction or operation does or whether it's even permitted depends on the current privilege level. (c) Transitions between privilege levels—in particular, translations to greater privilege—must be carefully controlled.

In the standard textbook model today, a CPU has two[5] privilege levels: user and kernel—or, sometimes, unprivileged and privileged, respectively. Typically, important protection-relevant tasks, such as changing MMU settings, can be done only in kernel mode. As discussed in Chapter 4, user-level code can transition to kernel mode only via a *system call*, or *trap*, that, via hardware, changes mode but also transfers control to specially designated, and one hopes, trusted code. The standard model uses the terms *user* and *kernel* for privileges because of the general intention that operating system code runs in kernel mode, that code from ordinary users runs in user mode, and that the operating system protects itself (and the users) from the users.

3. *Caching.* In the naive model, a memory location, once translated, "lives" at some place in ROM or RAM; in this simple model, the CPU does one thing at a time and accesses memory as needed. Modern systems have achieved significant performance improvements, however, by throwing these constraints out the window. Memory no longer needs to be bound to exactly one physical device; rather, we can try to *cache* frequently used items in faster devices. Consequently, CPUs may have extensive internal caches of memory—and then play various update games to make sure that various

---

5. Many variations have been explored throughout history; even the standard x86 architecture today has four levels, ring 0 through ring 3. As discussed earlier, in practice, only ring 0 and ring 3 get used—as user and kernel, respectively.

devices, such as other CPUs, see consistent views of memory. Caching enables a CPU to execute sequences of instructions without touching external memory. Caching also motivates the development of fancy heuristics, such as *prefetching*, to attempt to make sure that the right items are in the cache when needed. Processors sometimes separate instruction caches from data caches.

Systems achieve additional performance improvement by doing away with the notion that the CPU execute the instructions one at a time, as written in the program. One way this is done is via *pipelining:* decomposing the execution of an instruction into several stages and making sure that the hardware for each stage is always busy. Another innovation is *superscalar* processing—after decomposing the instruction execution into stages, we add extra modules for some of the stages (e.g., a second arithmetic unit). Since idle hardware is wasted hardware, processors also use aggressive heuristics for *speculative* execution (e.g., guessing the result of a future branch and filling the pipeline based on that assumption) and *out-of-order* execution (e.g., shuffling instructions and registers around at runtime to improve optimization).

(For more information on modern system architectures, consult one of the standard books in the area. Patterson and Hennessy [PH07] is considered the default textbook; Stokes [Sto07] provides a lighter introduction that focuses more directly on the machines you probably use.)

Privilege levels, syscall traps, and memory management all clearly assist in security. (Indeed, consider how susceptible a modern Internet-connected computer would be if it lacked kernel/user separation.) Sometimes, the lack of sufficient control can be frustrating. For example, if the MMU knew when a CPU's memory read was really for an instruction fetch, we could cook up a system in which memory regions had "read but do not execute" permission—thus providing a line of defense against stack-code injection attacks (recall Section 6.1). Indeed, this relatively straightforward idea was touted as the revolutionary *NX* feature by the technical press in recent years.

However, features such as internal caching and pipelining/out-of-order execution make things a bit harder. The relationship between what the internal system is doing and what an external device (such as a PCI card verifying integrity of kernel memory structures) can perceive is much less well defined. For example, suppose that we wanted to ensure that a certain FLASH device could be reprogrammed only when the system was executing a certain trusted module within ROM. Naively, we might add external hardware that sensed the address bus during instruction fetches and enabled FLASH changes only when those fetches were from ROM addresses.

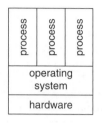

Figure 16.3 In the conventional system model, the OS provides protection between separate processes.

However, if we can't tell which cached instructions are actually being executed at the moment (let alone whether other code is simply "borrowing" parts of ROM as subroutines or even whether a memory read is looking for data or an instruction), then such techniques cannot work.

16.4.2 Virtualization

As Chapter 4 discussed, in the standard software architecture, an operating system provides services to user-level processes and enforces separation between these processes. As Section 16.4.1 discussed, hardware architecture usually reinforces these features. The aspiration here is that we don't want processes interfering with or spying on each other or on the OS, unless it's through a channel explicitly established and monitored by the OS. Figure 16.3 sketches this model.

In many scenarios, this approach to controlled separation may not be sufficient. Rather than providing separation between userland processes, one may prefer separation at the machine level. Rather than an OS protecting processes from each other, an OS and its processes are hoisted from a real machine up to a virtual machine, and another software layer—-usually called a *virtual machine monitor (VMM)*—protects these virtual machines from each other. Figure 16.4 shows one approach—although, as Section 16.5.1 discusses, many approaches exist here.

This idea of creating the illusion of multiple *virtual machines* within one machine is called *virtualization*. Initially explored in the early days of mainframe computing, virtualization has become fashionable again. What's the motivation for virtualization? Since this is a book about security, we tend to think about security first. And indeed, some reasons follow from security.

- For one thing, the API between the OS and userland applications can be extraordinarily rich and complicated. This complexity can make it hard to reason about and trust the properties one would like for this separation.

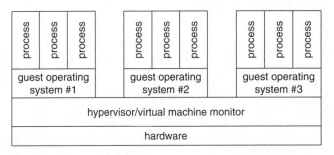

Figure 16.4 In virtualization models, processes are partitioned among virtual machines. Here, we sketch the type I approach, whereby the VMM runs on the hardware and provides separation between separate OS instances. In this case, the VMM is often called a *hypervisor*. Other models exist—see Section 16.5.1.

Complexity of API will also likely lead to complexity of implementation: increasing the size and likely untrustworthiness of the TCB.

- For another example, modern platforms have seen a continual bleeding of applications into the OS. As a consequence, untrustworthy code, such as device drivers and graphics routines, may execute with kernel privileges. (Indeed, some researchers blame this design choice for Windows' endless parade of vulnerabilities.)

Other reasons follow from basic economics.

- The API an OS gives to the application is highly specialized and may thus be unsuitable—for example, one can't easily run a mission-critical Win98 application as a userland process on OSX.
- According to rumor, this practice of giving each well-tested legacy application/OS its own machine leads to CPU utilization percentages in the single digits. Being able to put many on the same machine saves money.

Section 16.5.1 discusses old and new approaches to virtualization and security implications in more detail.

16.4.3 Multicore

Another trend in commercial CPUs is *multicore:* putting multiple processors (*cores*) on a single chip. The vendor motivation for this trend is a bit murky: increased performance is touted, better yield is rumored. However, multicore also raises the potential for security applications: If virtualization can help with a security idea, then wouldn't giving each virtual machine its own processor be much simpler and more likely to work rather than mucking about with special modes?

One commercial multicore processor, CELL, touts security goals; it features an architecture in which userland processes get farmed off to their own cores, for increased protection from both other userland processes and the kernel. (We discuss this further in Section 16.5.3.)

16.4.4 Armored CPUs

Modern CPUs cache instructions and data internally and thus fetch code and data chunks at a time, instead of piecemeal. As we noted earlier, this behavior can make it hard for external security hardware to know exactly what the CPU is doing. However, this difficulty can be a feature as well as a bug, since it also can be hard for an external adversary to observe what's happening.

Consequently, if we assume that the adversary cannot penetrate the CPU itself, we might be able to achieve such things as private computation, by being sure that code lives encrypted externally; integrity of code and data, by doing cryptographic checks as the chunks move across the border; and binding data to code, by keeping data encrypted and decrypting it only internally if the right code came in.

Several research projects have built on this idea. XOM (Stanford) explored this idea to implement execute-only memory via simulators. AEGIS (MIT) made it all the way to real FPGA-based prototypes, which also incorporate the SPUF idea, to provide some grounds for the physical-security assumption.

16.4.5 Tagging

When lamenting the sad state of security in our current cyberinfrastructure, some security old-timers wistfully talk about *tagged* architectures, which had been explored in early research but had been largely abandoned. Rather than having all data items look alike, this approach *tags* each data item with special metadata. Implemented in hardware, this metadata gets stored along with the data in memory, gets transmitted along with it on buses—and controls the ways in which the data can be used. Systems in which permissions are based on capabilities (recall Chapter 4) might implement these capabilities as data items with a special tag indicating so; this keeps malicious processes from simply copying and forging capabilities.

Some of these ideas are finding expression again in modern research. For example, many buffer overflow attacks work because the adversary can enter data, as user input, which the program mistakenly uses as a pointer or address. Researchers at the University of Illinois have built, via an FPGA (field-programmable gate array) prototype, a CPU retrofit with an additional metadata line to indicate that a data item is tainted [CXN+05]. The CPU automatically marks user input as tainted. Attempts to use a tagged data item as an address throw a hardware fault. However, certain comparison instructions—as code does when it sanity checks user input—clear the taint tags. Stanford's *TaintBochs* project uses software-based virtualization to explore further uses of taintedness and tagging in security contexts [CPG+04].

16.5 Coming Trends

So far, we have looked at the basic foundations of physical security and some of the ways it is embodied in tools available for system design. We close the chapter by looking at some new trends.

16.5.1 Virtualization and Security

Much security research—both old and new—is driven by a basic challenge. It can be useful to have separate compartments within a machine, with high assurance that malicious code in one compartment cannot spy on or disrupt the others. However, we often don't want *complete* separation between the compartments—but we want to make sure that only the right types of interaction occur. How do we provide this separation? How do we mediate the interaction? How do we provide assurance that this all works, that this all provides the desired properties, and that it doesn't kill performance?

In some sense, the challenge motivated the notion of separate processes within an operating system. However, most of the field has accepted the unfortunate notion that the standard OS model will not provide an appropriate solution here. This conclusion comes from several beliefs. Standard operating systems provide too rich and complex an interaction space between processes; standard operating systems are written too carelessly; target applications require more than simply the OS-level interface.

As we discussed in Section 16.4.2, these drawbacks have led to renewed thinking about virtualization: other ways to provide these separate virtual compartments and to mediate interaction between them. However, it's not clear what the "right" way to do this is. Right now, in both academia and industry, we see lots of approaches swirling around to enable machines to have highly compartmented pieces. This exploration raises many issues.

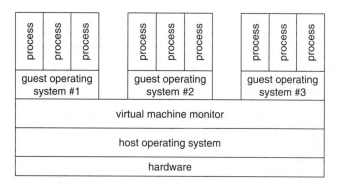

Figure 16.5 In the type II approach to virtualization, the VMM runs above the host operating system.

- What's the right level to split the machine into compartments?

- Should we use hardware-based support?

- Should we use a virtual machine monitor/hypervisor running above the hardware? (This is called a *type I* virtual machine—recall Figure 16.4.)

- Should we use a virtual machine monitor running within or above the host OS? (This is called a *type II* virtual machine—see Figure 16.5.)

- Should we instead virtualize some image above the OS? (Examples here include UML, BSD Jails, and Solaris Zones—see Figure 16.6.) We have seen some researchers call this approach *paenevirtualization*.

- Does the guest software—in particular, the OS—need to be rewritten in order to accommodate the virtualization, or it can be run unmodified? *Paravirtualization* refers to the former approach.

Some projects to watch in this space include *VMWare* [VMW07] and *XEN* [BDF+03, Xen07].

Another set of issues arise pertaining to the mediation between the compartments. How do we define the APIs? How do we have assurance that the APIs, if they work as advertised, work as intended? How do we have assurance that they are implemented correctly? Furthermore, an often neglected issue is how easily human designers and programmers can craft policies that capture the intended behavior. One might remember that these same issues vexed OS design—and one might cynically ask why virtualization research will do any better.

As we discussed earlier, one can take many approaches to providing this illusion. However, if the goal is to provide the illusion of the conventional architecture,

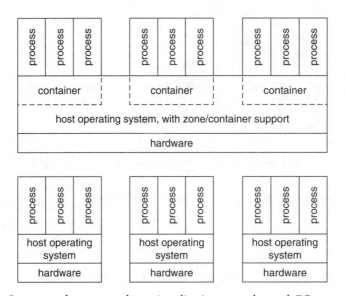

Figure 16.6 In yet another approach to virtualization, an enhanced OS groups processes into sets called *zones* or *containers* (above). One OS installation manages all the containers—however, from the perspective of the userland processes, each container appears to have its own instance of the OS and the machine (below).

doing so with conventional architecture is problematic. The guest system running inside a virtual machine expects to have user and kernel privileges. If guest kernel mode runs inside real user mode, then kernel-mode instructions won't necessarily operate properly. But if guest kernel mode runs inside real kernel mode, then nothing stops the guest from interfering with other virtual machines. (Indeed, the hacker community celebrates its *red pills*.[6] techniques to determine whether a program is running in a virtualized environment, via exploiting such differences. These properties were well known in the security literature, however.) For that matter, even if we could straighten out the privileges for virtual machines, how do we manage them all? Which code should do that, and how does the architecture enforce that? ([U+05] provides a nice overview of these challenges.)

Hardware vendors have been developing a new generation of processor architectures to address these issues. Intel's *Vanderpol technology (VT)*, sometimes defined as *virtualization technology*, removes the privilege and address space obstacles to virtualization. Intel's *LaGrande technology (LT)* adds support for secure management of virtualization; essentially, turning the kernel/user model into a quadrant:

---

6. Named after an instrument in the *Matrix* film series.

kernel/user for VM and kernel/user for hypervisor, which has special privileges. As of this writing, LT details are still limited to innuendo; according to rumor, the reason VT and LT seem to overlap somewhat in functionality is that they were rival, not complementary, projects. (Also, new marketing terms, such as TXT, appear to be supplanting these older project names.) AMD's *Pacifica* and *Presidio* architectures correspond to VT and LT, respectively.

Although not necessarily designed for security, these virtualization-friendly architectures have security applications. Such platforms as an IE/Windows Web-browsing installation, which typically are lost causes for security, can be safely confined in a VM. Watchdog modules that check system integrity no longer have to be constrained to looking at RAM and guessing at the internal state of the CPU; they can run inside the CPU, with their fingers inside the target VM. (*Virtual machine introspection* is a term used for this sort of thinking.) On the other hand, the *SubVirt* project illustrates another type of security application: malware that inserts itself as a malicious hypervisor (wags suggested calling it a "hypervirus") and shifts the victim system into a virtual machine, where it can't easily detect or counteract the malware [KCW+06].

16.5.2   Attestation and Authentication

We began our discussion of hardware-based security by considering how hardware can bind secrets to the correct computational entity. We see the potential for much industrial churn and ongoing research here.

One of the first issues to consider is which *a*-word applies: *attestation* or *authentication* or perhaps even *authorization*. When considering the general scenario of interacting with a remote party, the primary security question is: Who is it? Is it the party I think it is? Resolving this question is generally considered the domain of *authentication*. As discussed in Section 9.7.2, some dissidents instead see authentication as addressing the binding between entity and name and preach that *authorization*, as the binding of entity to property, is the true goal.

When the entity in question is a computational device, both identity and properties depend in part on the basic configuration of the device: what the hardware is and what the software is. However, as some of our own work demonstrated (e.g., [Smi04a]), the question is more subtle. The "correct" device can and perhaps should change software while remaining the same entity; the same hardware with a fresh reinstallation of the same software may in fact be a different entity. Consequently, consideration of the *a*-words in this realm often leads to an initial focus on *attesting* to a manifest of software and hardware configuration.

Some colleagues insist that, if checking software configuration is involved, then it must be attestation. We disagree.

- One cannot have meaningful attestation without authentication. An entity can claim any configuration it wants to; without authentication, the relying party has no reason to believe this claim.

- On the other hand, one can easily have authentication without attestation. When connecting to a hardware-hardened Web server, what the relying party cares about is the fact that it's a hardened Web server. The relying party does not necessarily need to know the full state of libraries and Apache versions—just that they're okay.

Whichever *a*-word one uses, we see two current sets of unresolved problems. The first is the "right" way to implement this structure within a multicompartmented machine. (We use the general term *multicompartmented* because we see this applying to a range of beasts, from SELinux boxes with TPMs to advanced virtualization and multicore.) Should a hardware-based root provide a full manifest for each compartment? Should a hardware-based root provide a manifest for a software-based root that in turn certifies each compartment? (And for that matter, why not other combinations of one or more hardware roots with one or more software roots?)

The second set of unresolved problems pertains to what should get listed in a manifest. What is it that the relying party really wants to know about a remote machine? We often joke that giving a TCG-style set of hashes is akin to the uniformed person at the door providing a DNA sample when asked to prove that he or she is really a bona fide police officer—it's a detailed answer that does not really give the right information. Current researchers are exploring *property-based attestation*, based on third parties' providing bindings, and *semantic remote attestation*, based on programming language semantics. This space will be interesting.

16.5.3 The Future of Moore's Law

In 1965, Gordon Moore observed that the number of tranistors on an integrated circuit doubles every 2 years. Subsequently blurred and transformed (e.g., the timeline is often presented as every 18 months), this curve has now entered popular folklore as *Moore's Law*,[7] usually stated as "every *N* years, the number of transistors on chips will double."

---

7. We have encountered a student who confused Moore's Law with Murphy's Law. The implications are worth considering.

So far, industry has stayed true to Moore's Law. However, insiders (e.g., [Col05]) observe that the causality is a bit more complicated than might meet the eye. Yes, Moore's Law was a good predictor of the trend of technology. But also, the industry came to use Moore's Law as a road map for its business model. For example, the generation N processor might currently be manufactured and the generation $N+1$ almost ready to fab; however, the design for the generation $N+2$ processor, to be fabbed k years later, was already under way and was counting on the fact that chip technology supporting far more transistors would be ready when the processor was ready to be manufactured.

Recently, hardware researchers have begun to express concern about the future of Moore's Law. Among many, the conventional wisdom is that, in order for Moore's Law to continue to hold, the transistors themselves will become less reliable—in terms of increased failure rate during manufacture and also, perhaps, in terms of increased failure rate in the field.

Some conjecture that the increased failure rate at manufacture will lead to a stronger emphasis on *multicore* devices. Committing to one large monolithic processor is risky, since faulty transistors might render the entire chip useless. An architecture that instead consisted of many smaller, somewhat independent modules is safer—the vendor can include a few extra modules in the chip, and sufficiently many should turn out to be good, even with faulty transistors.

However, we might also conjecture that an increased failure rate in the field might lead to a resurgence of work on Bellcore attacks and countermeasures (recall the discussion in Section 16.2.1).

16.5.4 Personal Tokens of the Future

The personal tokens common in the past decade were *smart cards*: credit-card-sized pieces of plastic with small chips on them, typically used in small-value commercial transactions. As we observed in Section 16.3.4, USB devices are common now. What's coming next?

Personal digital assistants (PDAs) are one possible candidate. For designers of security protocols, PDAs offer the advantage of having an I/O channel the user trusts, thus avoiding some of the problems of traditional smart cards. However, one might be cynical as well. As PDAs become more like general-purpose computing environments, the greater their risk of contamination—and the less advantage they offer over a risky general-purpose platform. Some economic observers predict that *cell phones* will displace PDAs. For the security designer, cell phones offer the challenge that it can be harder to experiment and deploy new applications; vendors tend to keep things locked up. (Looking at the students and young professionals who surround us, we might wonder whether iPods might be usable as a personal token.)

16.5.5 RFID

The burgeoning use of *RFID (radio frequency identification)* devices also offers potential for security applications and abuses. Of course, the first step in this discussion is to nail down exactly what RFID devices are. Everyone agrees that these are electronic devices that use some type of close-range radio to communicate. However, the sophistication assigned to these devices varies, from simple replacements for optical barcodes to more complex devices that are armed with environmental sensors, state, and batteries and that participate in interactive protocols with "reader" devices.

Anyone who has tried to wrestle groceries into the right position for a laser to read the barcode printed on them can immediately appreciate the advantages of inexpensive RFID tags that can be read from any orientation, without line-of-sight. Indeed, discussions of application scenarios often begin on such use cases: replacing clumsy optically read tags with easy and efficient RF-read ones, on items such as groceries, library books, warehouse inventory, and passports. No need to manually wrestle the item into the right position—the RF makes the connection automatically!

Of course, the same ease of use that motivates the application of RFID technology is also the source of its security and privacy worries. A machine-readable barcode is typically big enough for a human to see as well—so humans can be aware of its presence. The physical manipulation required for a barcode to be scanned is typically big enough for a human to notice—so humans can make judgments about what's being scanned and when. Humans also understand the notion of "sight" and thus have a good intuition of how to keep an optical tag from being seen.

These artifacts, which made it possible for human end users to control and understand the use of optical identifiers, disappear with RFID. Which objects have tags? Who is reading them and when and from how far away? What are the privacy implications of this quantum leap in automated information gathering?

Of course, the general notion of an inexpensive device communicating over an open medium raises the more standard security questions of physical security of the end device and communications security between them.

Juels's survey [Jue06] and the Garfinkel-Rosenberg anthology [GR05] provide more discussion of this problem space. Recently, NIST even published guidelines for RFID security [KEB+07].

16.6 The Take-Home Message

We often think of our system as the software we've written. However, a complete view of "the system" includes the hardware that executes the instructions we've written. As we've been discussing throughout this chapter, the set of hardware components that we rely on to run our applications can make or break the security of the system. Hardware can aid us in building more secure and resilient systems; it can also make that job much more difficult.

Even if you never design or build a hardware component, understanding the features and limitations of hardware will help you design better systems. Where can we store secrets? Does the hardware protect computation and data? What types of adversaries are they protected from? These types of questions should be part of the standard checklist when it comes to building secure systems; they are certainly part of any good attacker's.

There's something strangely Gödellian in thinking that we can make software more secure by simply writing more, perhaps better, software. If we end up with either incompleteness or inconsistency, there's a good chance that some security trouble is lurking just around the corner. If designed and used correctly, hardware might be able to help. As with anything else, it's no magic bullet. It's a tool that, when applied appropriately, can solve certain issues.

16.7 Project Ideas

1. In Section 16.1.1, we noted that a colleague insists that it's impossible to read data from disks once the cells themselves have been overwritten. Nonetheless, rumors persist (e.g., "just hack the disk controller code to change the head alignment so it reads the edges of the tracks instead!"). Prove our colleague wrong!

2. In Section 16.2.1, we discussed how an attack that forces the CPU to take one direction of the branch—whether or not it's correct—could let the adversary subvert the correctness of the system. Can you find some real code examples of this?

3. Learn a bit about how dongles are used to protect software. Can you think of ways to break them? Can you design a better scheme?

4. Implement modular exponentiation for 1024-bit integers on a 32-bit machine. Time the result of your software-only implementation, and compare it to numbers given by your favorite cryptographic accelerator's hardware implementation.

5. Assume that we had a TPM whose PCRs used MD5 as a hash algorithm instead of SHA1. Knowing that MD5 has some problems (see Chapter 8), think about ways that you can exploit MD5 weaknesses to hack a TPM.

6. Sketch a design for new CPU interfaces that would make it easier to determine what code was being executed in what context. (Extra credit: Prototype your design with OpenSPARC.)

7. One popular use of virtualization is in Linux honeypots that rely on *user-mode linux (UML)*. Design (and code, for extra credit) a red pill to determine whether your program is running on UML. How does "real" virtualization (i.e., under the OS) improve the situation?

17

In Search of the Evil Bit

In Chapter 1, we introduced our favorite way of thinking about systems and security. At any given time, the state of the system is some particular element of the set *States*. We can partition this set into two subsets: *Bad* and *NotBad*. The goal of the adversary is to somehow get the system into a state in the *Bad*. The goal of the system defender is to keep that from happening. However, since we can't always meet our goals, we might settle instead for simply knowing whether the adversary has already achieved his or her goal. (This does not necessarily imply that the adversary has won—we could simply be trying to detect whether the adversary has achieved the first step of a longer-range attack.)

In many defense situations, be useful to decide whether the current state is *Bad* or *NotBad*. We list some real-world examples.

- Are those network packets part of a nefarious attack?
- Is Alice's desktop computer infected with a virus?
- Has a hacker learned Bob's password and is currently doing something illegitimate in his name?
- Is that e-mail message spam?
- Is that credit card transaction fraudulent?
- Is that IRS tax return fraudulent?
- Is that medical claim fraudulent?

It would be rather convenient if we could automatically figure out whether the current state is good or bad. We might broaden a tongue-in-cheek suggestion made in the context of networks [Bel03] and wish for an *evil bit:* a flag that would be set to 1 whenever the system was in a bad state. Then our defense software could simply inspect that flag, and we'd be done.

Of course, no such flag exists. However, a function $F : States \longrightarrow \{1, 0\}$ does exist that labels each state. Since we can't simply check a flag, we'll have to program an implementation of F instead. Unfortunately, even this approach has a few problems.

- The relevant aspect of the system may be in fact the history of states rather than a single static observation. For example, a common pattern of Medicaid fraud is for an individual practitioner to request payment for more hours of service within a day than is humanly possible (sometimes more than 24). We wouldn't see this by looking at each individual billing event; we need to look at longer sequences.

- The relevant pieces of the state may not all be in one place. For example, when we analyzed fraudulent access to an online journal archive, we found an incident of "seriously evil fraudulent action sequence" was split into several disjoint pieces; in each piece, the last hop originated from a different IP address [SS04a]. Looking at each client address's individual access patterns alone would not have revealed this.

- The natural definition of "badness" might not correspond to what the real world needs. For example, one might think that, from the perspective of the issuer, the "bad" criteria for a credit card account would be whether the customer has defaulted on his or her debt. However, the credit card companies we used to work with were more concerned about prediction: given a customer's transaction history, is the individual likely to default soon?

- We may not even have full knowledge of the state of the system. For example, lacking omniscience, we probably cannot always determine with certainty whether a tax return is fraudulent simply by looking at the return. (Indeed, incomplete knowledge, in some form or another, is an overarching theme throughout all these examples.)

(We haven't even gone down the rabbit hole of worrying about whether F is even computable in the first place—recall Section 1.4.1.)

In reality, we may have no idea how to code up F. We do not know how to enumerate all the relevant parameters of the state. If we did, it's not clear that computing

F is even tractable, let alone computable in real time (e.g., rather than reaching an answer 200 years after the person who submitted the tax return has died). It's not clear that a thoughtful human analyst could classify any given system state instance as *Bad* or *NotBad*. It's not clear what the system should do if $F(s) = 1$. So what do we do?

In this chapter, we take a brief look at the field of *artificial intelligence (AI)*. Specifically, we explore what AI tools we can apply to this problem of classifying whether a given state is *Bad* or *NotBad*.

- Section 17.1 looks at some of the basic tools in the AI toolbox.
- Section 17.2 discusses some of the types of problems that these AI tools can solve.
- Section 17.3 walks through one of our lab projects that used some of the AI tools to detect misuse of an online journal collection.
- Section 17.4 examines some of the factors that come into play when trying to build the types of systems we discuss in this chapter.

The field of AI is an interesting one on its own, and volumes have been written about it. In this chapter, we're presenting only enough AI to give readers an appreciation for its intersection with the field of security. As with some other topics in Part V, these tools may lie beyond the boundaries of what security specialists typically pay attention to; however, these tools continue to prove useful for real-world security problems, and the security artisan needs to know that they exist.

Readers seeking more about AI (or more depth on some of the topics in this chapter) should start with the mostly widely used textbook in the field: Russell and Norvig's *Artificial Intelligence: A Modern Approach* [RN02].

17.1 The AI Toolbox

To solve this problem of determining whether a state is bad, we need some way to somewhat efficiently approximate a complex function on a complex data set, even though we may not really know much about the internal structure of either one, and have imperfect information to start with. Within computer science, the field of AI has grappled with just this type of problem. Various related subfields have emerged: *machine learning (ML)*, for building computational systems that "learn"; *computational learning theory (COLT)*, for studying the mathematical complexity theory behind ML; *data mining*, for discovering patterns and correlations in complex data sets; and *statistical inference*. One former colleague liked to sum up the whole collection as *data dredging*, perhaps because of the course-grained, ad hoc connotation of the verb "dredge," or perhaps simply because he liked being cantankerous.

We begin quickly reviewing the overall framework here. We might start by assuming that some deterministic, well-defined function really exists on some state space:

$$F : States \longrightarrow \{0, 1\}$$

We want a real-world computational device that computes F. However, we (or our computational partner) might not be able to see all of *States*. So, let's add an *Obs* function here to describe observation. *Obs(s)* is what we can perceive of $s \in States$. The functions we end up building have to operate not on *States* but on

$$Observables = Obs(States).$$

This might cause our function to stop being *well defined*. That is, there could very well exist $s_1, s_2 \in States$ such that $F(s_1) \neq F(s_2)$ but $Obs(s_1) = Obs(s_2)$. That's too bad.

We thus need to settle for a real-world device that computes some *approximation*:

$$F_A : Observables \longrightarrow \{0, 1\}.$$

This F_A should be "close" to F: that is, $F_A(Obs(s))$ should equal $F(s)$ for *most* s, somehow.

Unfortunately, we have no idea how to program F_A. Instead, we set up a system that, we hope, evolves to a good F_A.

- We set up a "tunable" device that takes its input from *Observables*.
- Each setting K of the knobs causes this device to compute a different function Device (K) on *Observables*.
- We assume that somewhere in *Device*( ), there's a good approximation to F.
- We identify an initial setting of the knobs K_0, which gives some initial function $Device(K_0)$.
- We then use an algorithm, based on positive and negative examples of F and such, to continually refine the knob settings, traversing the space of possible devices until we end up with a K_F such that $Device(K_F) \approx F_A$.

Figure 17.1 sketches this process.

One such mechanism is the *artificial neural network*—"artificial" because it was intended to mimic the natural variety found within brains. A classic textbook

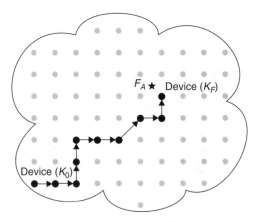

Figure 17.1 In the general ML framework, we want to produce something that calculates the function F_A, but we have no idea how. Instead, we produce a tunable *Device* that can calculate many functions, depending on how we set its knobs. We start it at an initial setting K_0 and then use some automated training process to end up with a setting K_F that, we hope, is a good approximation of F_A.

application example is processing photographs to determine whether a tank is present in the image.

- Here, *States* might be a real-world scenario in which a tank may or may not be hiding. F is true when a tank is present.

- *Observables* might be a set of image bitmaps of these scenarios.

- We want an F_A that takes a bitmap and outputs "1" when there's a tank hidden in the image. As one can see, how to "program" such an F_A is not clear.

- *Device*( ) is a neural network, a simple circuit of threshold gates. Each gate is controllable by a few parameters. The knob settings K correspond to these parameters (see Figure 17.2).

- We might then "train" the network by starting with a "current" knob setting, seeing how the device with that setting works on some sample images—some with tanks, some without—and using a systematic manner to continually tweak the knobs based on what happens.

The meat of the field of computational learning lies in the details. Researchers and deployers need to wrestle with such issues as what *Device*( ) looks like, what *feature set* of the data should be fed to its functions as parameters, how the systematic tweaking works, where the training data comes from, and whether it comes labeled

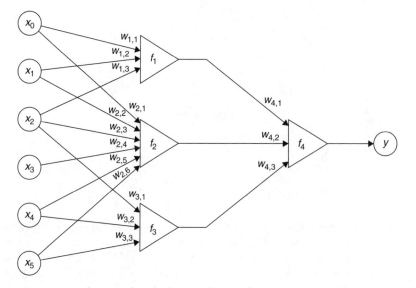

Figure 17.2 A neural network calculates a binary function on its binary inputs (here, $x_0, \ldots, x_5$) via a series of internal gates (here, $f_1, \ldots, f_4$). Typically, each gate is a threshold function on a weighted sum of its inputs. The training process adjusts the weights until the network produces an output y that matches our expected output (e.g., whether a tank is present).

a priori with the right answer—and, for that matter, *why* it is that something in *Device*( ) will be close to F_A.

After the standard textbook example of neural networks for tank detection, one often hears the anecdote that the training produced a network that functioned perfectly on the training data—but it turned out that the tank pictures were taken on a cloudy day. The network had succeeded in learning to distinguish between sunny days and cloudy days, which was not much use in determining whether a tank was present—at least in the general case. (See [Fra98] for some discussion.)

Of course, this discussion began with an implicit assumption—"we don't know how to program this problem"—that is itself questionable. Maybe we *do* know how to program the problem—or at least have some ideas. AI/"data dredging" approaches are certainly free to use such attempts to directly codify expert knowledge, as another element in the arsenal. We can also ask the other question— besides transferring human knowledge into device tuning, can we transfer device tuning into human knowledge? Suppose that we do manage to find some setting of the knobs so that *Device*( ) manages to approximate F_A. Is there a way we can translate this successful approximation into rules or descriptions that humans can understand?

At graduate school, the first author noticed that most students (except for the AI ones) spoke disparagingly about AI. "They have no idea *why* the device works." "It's not really *intelligence.*" "It's all ad hoc." (Of course, one might speculate that the reason for these opinions might stem from student resentment about poor scores on the AI qualifier.) This environment contributed to the author's surprise when he went to Los Alamos and found that everything in the AI toolkit—neural nets, expert systems, fancy mathematical techniques, and more—was being used to help solve security problems. And it was working! If memory serves, a research project using AI techniques to analyze electronic tax returns for fraud actually made a profit—the amount of fraud we found in the client's data set exceeded the funding the client had given us. (Ordinarily, research projects aren't supposed to be profit centers!)

Furthermore, these applications undermined the standard canards.

- "They have no idea *why* the device works." That doesn't matter—it works.

- "It's not really *intelligence.*" That doesn't matter—it's solving a problem that we couldn't otherwise solve.

- "The function isn't really learnable." That doesn't matter—even if we're close enough to identify interesting cases to pass on to a human investigator, we win.

- "They can't effectively test it—how do they know the cases they're missing?" That doesn't matter—if we're finding more bad cases than we were before, we win.

17.2 Application Taxonomy

Simplistic taxonomies are usually wrong. Nonetheless, we might organize the use of these AI tools in security into two categories.

1. The first is *misuse detection*, or, depending on the context, *intrusion detection.* Here, we try to implement a function that recognizes things that are "bad." Naturally, this approach requires some initial characterization or examples of what constitutes "bad things." As a consequence, this approach often prompts the challenge, "But can you handle bad things you've never seen before?"

2. The other approach in our simplistic taxonomy is *anomaly detection*, whereby we try to look for things that are somehow "different" from what we've seen before or from everything else we're seeing. This approach requires some type of metric under which the distinction between "clusters" and "outliers" has significance. This approach also raises the challenge that things that are different are not necessarily bad—and vice-versa.

Table 17.1 Taxonomy of Applications in Security.[a]

	Looking for *Wrong* Things	Looking for *Different* Things
Network	Network-level intrusion detection systems	Detecting trouble via anomalous network flows (e.g., StealthWatch)
Program	Virus scanning	Syscall profiling
User activity	Host-based systems that look for patterns of failed logins, setuid, etc.	Detecting impostors via clickstream anomalies
Application data	Spam filters	Detecting credit card theft via spending anomalies

[a] However tempting it may be to think of its role simply as "intrusion detection," AI techniques can aid security on many levels of the computing infrastructure. This table shows some examples.

These categories provide one axis to consider in the application space. However, we might also consider where in the computer system we decide to apply these tools. (Table 17.1 sketches this resulting taxonomy.)

Historically, perhaps the first application area considered here was *network traffic*. Misuse detection tools scan packet streams to recognize packets that have the signature of known attack patterns—this is often what an *intrusion detection systems* does. Anomaly detection can also be useful here—for example, even in the early 1990s, the *NADIR* system at Los Alamos would monitor for unusual network behavior. Besides picking up attacks, it would also occasionally identify components that were about to fail. Moving to modern times, Dartmouth, as part of its security posture, currently deploys the *StealthWatch* tool[1] to look for unusual network flows. (In our local computing circles, this deployment is known primarily for its false positives—such as blackholing the Computer Science Web server in the first week of classes, owing to the anomalous behavior of many students downloading class programming tools.)

Computer system behavior is another domain to which these tools can be applied. Virus scanning, a standard element of many enterprise security postures, is essentially misuse detection on the platform level: scanning files and executables to see whether any known bad elements are present. Indeed, artifacts of this approach create many of the challenges that face virus scanning. How do we identify and distribute the latest virus signatures? What about *polymorphic* viruses, which change shape and elude signature recognition? In some sense, the source of the term—and the source of the concern—for *zero-day exploits* stem from the pattern-matching nature of this standard defense tactic. We can't recognize something we haven't

1. www.lancope.com/products/

seen. Some recent research tries to generalize from looking for patterns in the literal binary code to looking for patterns in its behavioral semantics [DCJ+07].

Anomaly detection can also be applied to computer system behavior. For example, if we are worried that the adversary might use buffer overflow or other nefarious means to corrupt a userland application, we might wish that the OS had a way of checking whether the "evil flag" was set for any given application. It doesn't, and having the system administrator profile by hand what the "correct behavior" of the application should be (as seen by the OS) is too daunting—there's too much, and it's too hard to get right. However, we could have a component of the OS itself *automatically* generate profiles of an application's behavior and then raise an alarm when the behavior departs from its typical behavior, such as syscalls (e.g., [SAH98]) or more general parameters, such as CPU usage.

Indeed, the difficulty of sitting down and specifying correct behavior for a program is one of the things reputed to make SELinux (see Section 4.5.2) so hard to use. Recall that such "high-assurance" operating systems require a detailed policy saying exactly what each entity can and cannot do. A common practice (e.g., [Fen05]) is to simply run the program on ordinary input, and automatically generate its profile (thus turning its protections into behavioral-level anomaly detection).

Early work in intrusion detection cast a wider net, looking at both system-level and user action, from failed login attempts to file accesses and application invocation. After all, however tempting it might be to consider esoteric implementation flaws, the direct approach of obtaining a user's password and logging in as that person was (and remains) an attractive attack. As a consequence, it becomes useful to be able to see whether a *user's* behavior is evil—because it differs from that *user's* typical behavior or because it fits the pattern for known attacks—and thus merits closer scrutiny. Of course, looking at user behavior can also help identify insider attack, if the legitimate user is in fact the adversary, but there's a price here: Looking at user behavior can also unnerve the legitimate user.

Classic work on intrusion detection includes Dorothy Denning's framework [Den87], as well as the *Intrusion-Detection Expert System (IDES)* [LTG+90]— which in fact incorporated both approaches: looking for not only anomalies but also misuse. Later publications by Becky Bace [Bac00] and Wenke Lee [L+00] can bring the reader into the modern age. In more recent work, Padmanmabhan and Yang [PY, Reh07] examine the potential to use Alice's online Web-browsing behavior (her *clickstream*) to determine whether it's really Alice or an impostor.

We can also use these AI techniques on application-specific data streams. In today's Internet-connected personal computing environments, most users are familiar with spam and use junk mail filtering and other tools to avoid being overly inundated with it. Separating "ham" from spam is a task that might lend itself to careful human effort but not to clear-cut formal rules; as a consequence, many filters explicitly use machine-learning techniques and "training."

Data dredging also proves useful in application settings that many readers might find less conventional. Credit card companies have long monitored the sequence of transactions for any given customer, looking for anomalies in spending patterns that might indicate a stolen card [BH02]. (Of course, this motivates the countermeasure of being able to identify the geographic location corresponding to a stolen credential, in order to avoid obvious triggers [Kre07].) Searching for explicitly "bad" patterns has also been applied to credit card transaction streams in order to identify fraud or customers who are about to default [SFL+97]. We mentioned the IRS; published applications there include looking for fraud within tax returns [Hed96], looking for fraud based on longer streams of taxpayer behavior [Hol05], and looking for taxpayers engaged in illicit tax shelters [DEW06]. Data dredging has also been used to "prevent bad debt events" in telecommunication billing [PEE06]. Data dredging has been used to identify money laundering in broader transaction streams [S+95] and to identify fraudulent securities trading [New05].

17.3 Case Study

To illustrate the use of these AI techniques to help find the evil bit, we discuss a real-world case study: our experience in trying them in our own lab. (See our original reports for more details [Sel03, SS04a].)

17.3.1 The Context

Colleagues of ours operate an online archive of a large number of scholarly journals, mainly in areas other than computer science. The archive works with member institutions, which in turn permit their users to access the archive.

Suppose that user Alice (from university U_A) requests something from the archive. In order to grant this request, the archive server needs to determine whether Alice belongs to a member institution. In fact, the name "Alice" doesn't even matter; authorization doesn't depend on the user's identity. In theory, we could recall Section 9.7.2 and Chapter 10 and derive some fancy way to have Alice cryptographically prove her affiliation. (We leave the design of such a scheme as an exercise for the reader.)

In practice, however, the archive needed to accommodate real-world institutions, each of which already had a different legacy way of authenticating a bona fide user. Few, if any, of these methods would extend beyond the domain of its institution, without further work. Furthermore, the typical archive user is not likely to be a computer aficionado, willing to adopt a fancy new authentication technique.

Consequently, rather than using the cryptographic authentication techniques of Chapter 10, the archive opted to use the network techniques of Chapter 5. To determine whether Alice is authorized, the archive server would examine the IP address of the machine from which she issued the request. The server then does a WHOIS lookup to determine the institution to which this address belongs. If it's a member institution, then the server grants the request.

Although pragmatic, this approach has several drawbacks. On the usability front, even though Alice may be a bona fide member of university U_A's user population, her client's IP address may sometimes lie outside U_A's range. (For example, Alice may be traveling and using her laptop from a conference's wireless network, which has issued her a "foreign" IP address via DHCP, or she may be using network address translation, which gives her an address outside anyone's range.) To address this problem, many member institutions set up *proxy* machines within their own IP space; Alice connects first to one of these machines, which then in turn connects to the archive.

This approach also may have legal drawbacks. In many real-world institutions, not every user who legitimately issues a request from an institution's machine is an official member of that institution's user population. (For example, consider public-access machines in a university library. Just because a library visitor can use such a machine doesn't automatically make that person a student or a staff member.) Chapter 18 considers some of these issues further.

However, what concerns us most are the *security* drawbacks.

- As Chapter 5 discussed, in the current Internet, spoofing the origin IP address is a standard trick in the attacker's arsenal. Attacker Bob could simply forge an address from U_A. (Although it would take a few extra tricks for Bob to also receive the response from the archive.)

- As Chapter 6 discussed, standard operating systems and applications software are rife with security vulnerabilities that can enable remote attackers to run their own code on that machine. Attacker Bob could compromise a machine in U_A and then issue a request.

- Owing either to a concern for usability or to carelessness, some institutions even operated *open proxies*, which required no authentication. If he discovers an open proxy, attacker Bob doesn't need to use any other tricks.

17.3.2 The Problem

What concerned the archive was the fact that human inspection of access logs revealed instances of a suspicious pattern: sequences of requests from the same IP address that appeared to be systematically downloading large chunks of the archive. This was not legitimate use by an Alice at a member U_A but rather piracy by a Bob who had managed to issue requests from a U_A address. The seriousness of this problem led to a challenge: how to stop this piracy. However, the need to accommodate myriad legacy authentication systems led to a constraint: Any solution must not change anything at the client side. Thus, stopping piracy here turned into an "evil bit" problem—when it receives a request X, the server must decide whether X is evil.

However, the nature of this problem differed from the classical ML/AI scenario in a few keys ways.

- First, we need to look at each request in the context of a broader sequence of requests. Any given X, on its own, could very well be legitimate—someone at that IP address could want to see that article in that issue of that journal. We need broader granularity to see a broader pattern of systematic downloading.

- Second, although it's good to detect that illegitimate access to licensed material took place, it would be better to prevent it from happening in the first place. Consequently, once we can train our device to recognize fraudulent sequences of requests, we then want to see whether we can get it to recognize them as evil *early* on, before they've gone too far.

- Finally, we don't have the luxury of a labeled data set. The journal archive provided us with genuine access logs and descriptions of some of the fraudulent behavior they found. But after that, it's up to us.

17.3.3 Techniques

We started by surveying some basic AI techniques to apply to this problem. (The curious reader should consult standard texts, such as Mitchell [Mit97] or Hastie, Tibshirani, and Friedman [HTF01] for more thorough coverage.)

Artificial Neural Networks. We already discussed these (recall Figure 17.2). Training a neural net requires coming up with labeled training data and also picking a *feature set:* How do we encode the data items into the set of values input to the net?

Decision Trees. Suppose again that we have labeled training data and a feature set. We could instead pick one of the features and divide the set according to the choices for that feature and then look at each resulting subset. If all the elements of the subset have the same label, then we're done with that subset. Otherwise, we keep recursing. The resulting structure is called a *decision tree*; once we pick the feature set, the meat of decision tree learning lies in choosing the feature by which to partition the set.

Unlike classic neural networks, the decision tree approach makes it possible for a human to learn why a trained *Device* ended up making the decision it did.

Clustering. In the "clustering" approach, we look at the training data items as points in a multidimensional space and see how they cluster together. More formally, we might start by guessing a set of "archetypes" for each subset of input data we'd like to recognize. For each element in the training set, we put it in a cluster with the closest archetype. It might be that we did a poor job of picking archetypes, however. So, for each cluster, we

- Calculate its *centroid*, the geometric center, according to the axes we used for the space
- Use *that* point as the new archetype
- Start again

The training process is done when iterations no longer result in changes to the clusters. We can then use these clusters to classify data items by seeing which of the clusters they belong to.

Like decision trees, the clustering approach also makes it possible for a human to learn why a trained *Device* ended up making the decision it did—indeed, the final "archetypes" can be considered just that: archetype instances of the various learned categories.

Genetic Algorithms. In the *genetic algorithm* approach, we draw inspiration from genetic evolution to try to evolve the right *Device*( ) setting. This approach requires that our *Device*( ) family let us

- "Mix" two *Device*( ) settings together in order to emulate sexual reproduction
- Randomly mutate *Device*( ) settings in order to emulate mutation
- Evaluate the *fitness* of candidate setting, compared to the F_A that we're trying to approximate, in order to emulate natural selection

We start with a large class of potential settings and then evolve them through generations in which they mix and mutate, but only the fittest survive to the next generation. Whether a human can learn from a trained *Device* here depends on the underlying family we use.

17.3.4 Feature Set

The archive provided us with a large set of logs of individual accesses. As we observed earlier, we needed to look at each access in a broader context. We decided to look at the context of accesses from any given IP address, so we partitioned the set $\mathcal{L}$ of logs into a collection of disjoint subsets $\{\mathcal{L}_i\}$, one for each IP address i that issued a request.

We want our *Device* to make a decision on i; what we can observe is $\mathcal{L}_i$. However, the various $\mathcal{L}_i$ differ in a large number of parameters, and feeding all of these parameters to our magic *Device* will greatly complicate the learning process. Can we instead map them down to a smaller set of more significant fields? We considered what typical normal and fraudulent usage might looked like and identified several features that might help distinguish between the two:

- *Amount of usage.* How many requests did an IP address make during a day? An attacker systematically downloading the database would be making a lot.

- *Download percent.* What was the ratio of download requests versus others? An attacker systematically downloading the database would have a high download percentage.

- *Search percent.* What was the ratio of search requests versus others? An attacker systematically downloading the database would have a low search percentage.

- *Range of download.* An attacker systematically downloading the database would tend to hit heavily on a few journals. To measure this property, we developed a metric based on weighted frequencies of ISSN requests; a low measure here would indicate a skew toward heavy downloading of a few journals.

We can thus map each of our $\mathcal{L}_i$ down to some point p_i in this four-dimensional space $\mathcal{S}$.

Of course, although we picked these features to help distinguish user Alice from attacker Bob, the "wrong" measure on any one does not necessarily indicate an attack. For example, a legitimate proxy machine may register a high usage amount, since it can represent the collective behavior of many individuals.

17.3.5 Experiments

Since we picked features that we hoped would be significant in distinguishing legitimate users from fraudulent ones, we can pick two points in opposite corners of this space as "typical" instances of legitimate and fraudulent users. Let's call these points l_0 and f_0, respectively. Of course, there's no guarantee that these two points are "typical," since getting here was all guesswork. So, instead, we use them as initial centroids for clustering and run through all our $\{p_i\}$ records. This process produced two new cluster centroids: l_1 and f_1. We noticed that only 0.017 percent of the p_i clustered around f_1 but that more than 6.5 percent of the downloads went to these IP addresses. On human inspection, we found that the IP addresses in this cluster included "obvious" cases of fraud, as well as more subtle cases in which obvious fraud was mixed with otherwise legitimate-looking behavior.

So far, so good. However, we don't want to detect an IP address as evil *after* 24 hours of activity. To see how clustering against l_1 and f_1 would work against real-time data, we took each daily log $\mathcal{L}_i$ for each address and broke it into a sequence of incremental partial logs, each adding one more request to the previous. Mapping this sequence into our feature space $\mathcal{S}$ gave us a sequence of points:

$$p_i{}^1, p_i{}^2, p_i{}^3, \ldots p_i{}^{k_i} = p_i.$$

We can then classify each of these points according to our clusters, in order to learn

- For a p_i that landed in the fraudulent cluster, how far in the sequence did we have to go before the $p_i{}^j$ landed in the fraudulent cluster? (That is, for fraudulent addresses, how long did it take us to get around to the right answer?)
- How many of the p_i in the legitimate cluster had an earlier $p_i{}^j$ that landed in the fraudulent ones? (That is, for legitimate addresses, how many appeared to be fraudulent early on?)

For the second question, our analysis showed less than 0.001 percent false positive rate, which was good. For the first question, we still needed to see 65 percent of the downloads, on average, before the device marked the address as fraudulent.

To try to reduce this 65 percent, we used genetic algorithms to try to evolve better cluster centroids. We used our clustering *Device* (with l_1, f_1) to label each p_i and hence each sequence of $p_i{}^j$. We developed a fitness measure that

- Rewarded a centroid pair for quickly recognizing an abnormal $p_i{}^j$ sequence
- Penalized a pair for falsely labeling a legitimate $p_i{}^j$ as fraudulent
- Penalized a pair for falsely labeling a fraudulent $p_i{}^j$ as legitimate

This process yielded an l_2, f_2 centroid pair that reduced the 65 percent down to 40 percent. We could detect the bad guys when they were less than half done.

As a final experiment, we revisited our assumption that our *Device* should operate on IP addresses. What we want to do is recognize bad traffic streams. Although the assumption that attacker Bob may generate his traffic from a single IP address might be a reasonable first guess, this doesn't necessarily have to be true. Indeed, when we examined the logs by hand, we discovered one case in which an attacker from the same IP address had connected to two different open proxies and divided his systematic downloads between the two. To explore this angle, we considered an attacker who might split traffic between two IP addresses, and we then generalized the input space for our *Device*: from "traffic from an IP address" to "traffic from a potential attacker using two IP addresses." To get this latter space, we considered each pair of points p_i, p_j—except that we had to adjust for relative load; otherwise, a fraudulent p_i would make any pair it was part of also appear fraudulent. When we analyzed our logs this way, we found an additional population of potential distributed attacks.

Punch Line.   The reader may be eagerly awaiting a punch line, such as "We then sent these tools back to our external collaborator, who deployed them and saved the world from fraud." Unfortunately, the punch line is rather different. We sent these tools back to the external collaborator, who thanked us but also

- Could not tell us whether any of the potentially fraud cases had been followed up on—let alone what had been discovered

- Could not tell us whether these tools had been incorporated into any antifraud defenses

- Could not tell us anything else about antifraud defenses

Even more unfortunately, these constraints seem endemic to research and development in the use of these data-dredging techniques to hunt for the evil bit in real-world data sets. Those with the real-world problems don't want to disclose to researchers anything that might be useful to an adversary. (Colleagues who work in fraud detection research later told us how lucky we were to actually get real data!)

17.4 Making It Real

As we have seen, securing real-world computing systems leads to scenarios—at lower technical levels and also at higher application levels—where we need to distinguish which items from a large data set are evil. Also, we have seen that we can mine the field of AI for techniques that can and do prove useful in developing automated methods to assist in this classification. However, like so much else in security, doing this effectively requires a fair amount of skill. Which *Device* should we choose? How do we train it? Where do we get the training data? Is the training data genuine or simulated? (Simulated data can exhibit statistical abnormalities that hamper the effectiveness of many techniques.) If the training data is genuine, do we have access to its semantics? (Colleagues who work in AI analysis of credit card data complain that clients won't tell them what the various fields in the data items actually mean.) Will the training data have the same distribution as data encountered in the real world? Will the training data be *labeled* with whether or not each case is evil?

Evaluating whether our technique works also requires a fair amount of skill. First, we have the obvious questions. What fraction of the good cases do we label correctly? What fraction of the bad cases do we label correctly? How do we measure the effectiveness of the *Device* when we use it on live data in the field? (When using it in the field, will we even be able to get ground truth?)

In the beginning of the book, we introduced the notion of "security" in terms of states of the system—but a common problem is that the "system" is often bigger than the technology on which we focus initially. When discussing using AI technology to detect the evil bit, it's important not to lose track of the broader system. For example, timing may be an issue. As we noted in Chapter 1, in many electronic benefits systems, timeliness of correct payments is more important than suppression of fraudulent ones. Besides basic duration, we also need to consider other computational costs—for example, early experimental system-level monitors were reputed to require more computing power than the system itself being monitored.

As the human–computer interaction people remind us, another important aspect of the "system" are the humans. How do we summarize output in a way a human can digest? Can our device express the reasons for its decisions? Of course, another class of humans to consider are the adversaries. How do we keep the detection system secure from the attacker? Does knowing the detection algorithm enable the attacker to avoid it?

Some researchers are going in the other direction: Rather than using AI to solve problems too hard for humans to program, they are designing systems that farm the hard decision tasks out to humans. For an industrial example, Amazon is touting its *Amazon Mechanical Turk* service as "artificial AI": a way for distributed computation to send queries to human decision makers, in real time—for a fee. (The name derives from a chess-playing "robot" that actually concealed a human chess expert.)

17.5 The Take-Home Message

When we hear the term *artificial intelligence,* it's hard to resist the images that Hollywood has produced—from HAL[2] to the antagonists in *The Matrix.* A bit more realistic consideration turns up systems like Deep Blue, IBM's chess-playing machine: although impressive, still a long way off from a self-aware computer. It's almost too easy to write AI off as the field of the future—that always will be.

However, if we pull back the curtain and look at what many of these AI systems are trying to accomplish, we realize that their goals are not so different from ours: classification, recognizing patterns, and finding things that do not fit. The tools in the AI toolbox can help us wade through the enormous state space and complexity of a modern system and help us determine when our system is in a bad one. We've attempted to show that there is an overlap between the AI toolkit and the security toolkit. As usual, there's no magic here, but sometimes the most appropriate tool for a job comes from an unlikely source.

17.6 Project Ideas

1. Pick a simple game like checkers or tic-tac-toe. At each point in a game, a player has a set of possible moves. Write an automated player that uses a decision tree approach to recognize which moves are good. (Hint: Consult Russell and Norvig [RN02] to learn about MINIMAX and alpha-beta pruning.)

2. Using the same game as above, design and implement (and train) a simple artificial neural network to recognize which moves are good.

3. As we discussed in Chapter 6, static-analysis tools look for dangerous fragments of code, such as unsafe functions or improper use of buffers. Write an artificial neural network that looks at C source code and "learns" to determine whether buffers are being used properly.

4. Design a solution to the archive authorization problem we discussed earlier, using cryptography and PKI instead of IP restrictions.

5. See how many computer security issues you could apply parts of the AI toolbox to.

---

2. HAL is the AI system that was featured in Stanley Kubrick's 1968 film *2001: A Space Odyssey.*

Human Issues

Throughout this book, we've been discussing the tools that one needs to build a secure system. Theoretically, at this point, you should be able to construct a system that holds up against a wide array of attacks. For the sake of illustration, let's assume that you've built such a system. You've designed it with security in mind, and you've used threat models to aid in that design. You've locked down all the communication with cryptography, you've tested your code, and maybe you've even formally modeled the entire system. Let's assume that you've used all the tools in the shop, you've used them all correctly, and you've constructed an airtight system that solves your problem. One question remains: can anyone really use the system? So far, we've been talking about technology, engineering, and mathematics. But there's more to the picture than that.

Some argue that there seems to be an inverse correlation between the security of a system and the usability of that system, and striking a balance between the two is more art than engineering. One thing's for sure: a secure system that no one can use solves no one's problem. Complicating matters further is the fact that each system and situation is unique. In practice, we've been asked by a customer to build whizz-bang security features into products, only to be asked by the same customer for a way to circumvent these features, owing to their complexity. We've also been in situations in which we could give security complexity to certain types of users (e.g., administrators) but had to minimize the security impact on other types of users (e.g., end entities).

Others argue that the issue is more complex than simply a tradeoff between usability and security. They argue that there are three forces at work: usability, security, and a reasonable price. It's possible to get any two properties in the set but not all three. For example, you can build cheap usable systems, and you can build cheap secure systems, but a secure usable system will be prohibitively expensive.

Unfortunately, there are no rules to follow that are guaranteed to produce a usable and secure system. Ultimately, building such a system takes judgment, which is refined only with practice. In this last chapter of the book, we hope to provide some basic guidelines that can serve as a starting point for such judgment.

- Section 18.1 looks at the core of the problem: humans. We examine the importance of the system model that gets built inside a human's mind and the consequences of a system deviating from that picture.

- Section 18.2 explores the work of Donald Norman and covers a number of his main ideas. Norman's principles provide a solid foundation on which to start reasoning about usability issues. We also present some more recent principles for designing user interfaces for security systems.

- Section 18.3 discusses some other nontechnological forces at work in human space that affect that crafting of secure systems.

- Section 18.4 focuses on the fundamental concept that secure systems are designed to facilitate: trust.

As with some other chapters in Part V, this one is thinner than those earlier in the book. As before, this difference stems from the fact that this material is, by definition, "emerging." It's important for the security artisan to be aware of these human issues, but we can't give you polished conclusions, because the field doesn't have them yet![1]

18.1 The Last Mile

Most, if not all, computer systems are built to solve a human problem or enhance a human process. As you might imagine, such systems eventually interact with real human users—perhaps to collect input or to guide processing. The communications industry uses the term "the last mile" to refer to the final stage in connecting the customer to the communication provider. In modern computing systems, the

---

1. But perhaps you can help with that.

last mile includes the interactions between the systems and the humans they were designed to serve.

As it flows in and out of the machines, devices, and miles of network cable that comprise a modern computing system, data eventually crosses a human/computer boundary. Such boundaries are often abstractions, metaphors, and interfaces that are familiar and, one hopes, understandable to a human. A poorly designed interface can not only be frustrating for humans to use but also allow, or even encourage, users to put the system in a state that it should not be in. (By now, we hope that it's an automatic response for you to assume that such scenarios mean that security trouble is right around the corner.)

Of course, the preceding discussion focused on only one class of humans: the end users. We also need to think about all the other humans involved, such as the system administrators, the developers, and the folks on both the development side and the procurement side trying to match system behavior to human process requirements. Furthermore, good technology doesn't magically permeate the world; we need to also think about the human processes that cause technology to succeed and fail in the marketplace.

In their textbook, Charlie Kaufman, Radia Perlman, and Mike Speciner give an accurate account [KPS02, p. 237] of the difficulty involved when considering the human aspects of secure system design:

> Humans are incapable of securely storing high-quality cryptographic keys, and they have unacceptable slow speed and accuracy when performing cryptographic operations. (They are also large, expensive to maintain, difficult to manage, and they pollute the environment. It is astonishing that these devices continue to be manufactured and deployed. But they are sufficiently pervasive that we must design our protocols around their limitations.)

Although the passage is intended to be humorous—at least we find it so—it underscores an important point. Good systems and good protocols must be designed with humans in mind. Time and time again, we see secure systems that are carefully and correctly designed and implemented but are so difficult to use that they become effectively useless. Ignoring usability issues can make a system counterproductive— the security features can become so cumbersome that users will use them incorrectly, circumvent them, or simply stop using the system altogether.

In 2000, Alma Whitten and Doug Tygar's seminal paper, "Why Johnny Can't Encrypt," established that the fancy cryptography in a popular secure email package was much less effective than intended because users found it too hard to use correctly [WT99]. Although it took a while, this paper opened up a branch of research in looking at what Johnny can and cannot do. We offer a few examples.

- Back in the dark ages, our own lab did a user study showing that a sample user population understood our phishing-resistant browser trusted-path techniques but found them slightly irritating [YS02].
- Dhamija and colleagues showed how a sample user population exhibits misunderstandings that phishing exploits [DTH06].
- Schecter and colleagues showed that a sample user population cannot understand the current state of the art in browser security indicators [SDOF07].
- Jackson and colleagues showed that a sample user population cannot effectively use IE7's new features to warn of phishing—and that reading the IE7 help file makes things worse [JSTB07].
- Garfinkel and Miller did a "Johnny 2" study showing that a sample user population does a better job understanding their key continuity PKI email scheme than Whitten's users understood PGP [GM05].

Anyone familiar with a modern version of the Windows OS has likely felt the pain that follows from trying to do day-to-day tasks as a nonadministrator. Although standard good practice is to use a lower-privilege account, users often take the easy way out and run the system with elevated privileges. (Orange Book graybeards would recognize this as the "system high" phenomenon.) Taking an informal poll among a classroom of students will typically confirm this practice—that is, if enough Windows users are in the room.

In Chapter 4, we discussed how SELinux formally instantiated a reference monitor that could provide MLS (multi-level security) and other security properties. In Chapter 6, we discussed how formal analysis established that it called the reference monitor in the correct places. Consequently, one might assume that SELinux ensures that system behavior faithfully follows the Linux Security Module policy—so the security artisan can use it as a basis for building secure systems.

However, this conclusion overlooks a critical step: We first have to write the policy for SELinux. In practice, we have found the process of translating security goals into SELinux policy to be tenuous, at best. We've run across more than one instance in which people trying to use SELinux found it so difficult to configure and use that they simply gave up and uninstalled the system. One time, the system had to be reinstalled because the user's policy had accidentally locked out the ability for anyone to administer the machine. Writing a policy that "worked" ended up like the bad old days of programming: random cutting-and-pasting until the policy seems to permit the correct behaviors. Of course, this process says nothing about whether the policy prohibits the incorrect ones—so much for assurance! As a consequence, we've begun investigation into *policy engineering* to solve these problems in the design, development, and maintenance of policy, much as software engineering was intended to solve them for the design, development, and maintenance of software. (See [BFMS07] for more information.)

In 1999, Anne Adams and Angela Sasse pointed out that, although many secure-system designers have not stressed the importance of human issues, the hacker community has given human issues the recognition they deserve [AS99]. In Chapter 12, we saw examples of how poor mental models can lead to spoofing attacks on such systems as Web browsers. But some of the most successful attacks to date do not involve exploiting a software vulnerability of any kind. Rather, an attacker can often exploit a human process or faulty mental model of a system to gain access. Many attackers assert that such *social engineering attacks* are still a ripe source of real-world attack vectors. Sometimes, the days that it can take to plan and execute a simple attack on a system can be avoided with a simple trick phone call or a trip to an organization's dumpster. Readers interested in learning more about social engineering should refer to Kevin Mitnick's *The Art of Deception*; it is an excellent source of information on the topic [MS02].

In our own experience, we've found social engineering to be an endless source of amusement. [Smi04b] summarizes some password-theft social engineering experiments we tried at Dartmouth.

- Two students offered plastic dinosaurs or squirt guns in exchange for a subject's Dartmouth userid and password. They got an 80 percent success rate. (Students who also gave a friend's userid/password got a plastic dinosaur *and* a squirt gun.)

- A student sent out a fake email survey with a link to an official-looking site that asked for userid and password; he got an 83 percent success rate.

- A student walked around asking people to participate in a survey and offering them his laptop, connected to an official-looking site protected by SSL with a self-signed cert. He got a 93 percent success rate—including faculty!

When a student wishes to buy even an $80 piece of software and charge it to a research grant, the Dartmouth Computing Store typically demands to see student ID and verifies the charge with the professor in charge of the grant. A female grad student in our lab still chortles about being able to walk out with a $2,000 computer, without showing *any* identification (Dartmouth or otherwise) and without having any professor authorization checked. (Interestingly, the BBC reports on a psychology study showing that the sight of attractive women disrupts a male's ability to think rationally [BBC06b].)

From our own experiences in dealing with enterprise customers, we've found that they think that usability and human issues are extremely important. In an enterprise IT environment, "software that's hard to use" translates into "software that's expensive to use." Often, a system's usability annoyances can become an expensive problem when the system is in the hands of tens- or hundreds-of-thousands of users, which is a common size for many modern enterprises. The real dollar cost of owning such a system is incurred by the administrators who spend time configuring and maintaining the software, by the end users who have to undergo training and lose productive time wrestling with the system's complexity, and by the help desk infrastructure that has to be in place to respond to confused users.

As a community, we are just beginning to realize the important role that humans play when building secure systems. Users have known that humans are important for years; all the whizz-bang cryptography and security features are useless if users can't actually use them. Furthermore, if the security of the system prevents users from getting real work done, they'll often try to find a way around it. The hacker community too has recognized the importance of humans for years; it has continuously paid attention to the weakest link in almost any system: the humans. Finally, customers have known how important usability is for years; a system that is difficult to use is an expensive system to buy. Only in recent times has the secure systems community begun to acknowlege the link between usability and security.

18.2 Design Principles

In 2003, one of us was invited to attend the ACM/CHI Workshop Human-Computer Interaction and Security Systems. The workshop aimed to introduce the human/ computer interaction community and the security community. A somewhat detailed account of the workshop can be found in the resulting article, "Humans in the Loop" [Smi03c].

For us, one of the resonating outcomes of the workshop was the introduction to the work of Donald Norman—in particular, his classic 1988 book *The Design of Everyday Things* [Nor02]. Norman doesn't directly focus on human/computer interaction; rather, he considers the broader topic of human/device interaction. Norman's book is chock-full of design anecdotes involving such things as car radios, doors, and water faucets. Nevertheless, a number of his design principles and patterns are highly relevant to the areas of human/computer interaction and security.

We now review a number of Norman's principles.

18.2.1 It's Not Your Fault

Humans tend to blame themselves when they can't use a device correctly. This fact seems particularly true of nontechnologists who attempt to use technology. How many folks do you know who claim that they can't program their VCR because "it's too complicated"? The implication here is that the user feels that the task is too complicated to figure out. This sentiment is even more prevalent in areas where the technology is more complex and/or abstract, such as modern computing systems. For example, anecdotes abound of computer help desks dealing with users stuck because a prompt said "hit the Enter key to continue" but the computer did not have an Enter key, just a Return key.

Although we are quick to blame ourselves when we can't use something correctly, Norman points out that we can usually trace such a lack of usability back to a fundamental design problem that neither users nor designers seemed to notice.

Consequently, when building systems, we find it best to adopt the philosophy that the customer is always right. It's acceptable to force users to think and behave a certain way when using a system; in fact in many cases, the designer's insight (and thus the system's approach) to a problem may be its selling point. But when that approach is difficult to use or understand and users complain (or, worse, stop using the system), then it's the designer's responsibility to fix it. This is especially true of commercial software; software that's easier than its competitors to use has a competitive advantage.

18.2.2 Conceptual Models

As part of how we humans interact with the world, we like to make theories about the mechanisms underlying how something works—even if there is no underlying mechanism. We then use this theory, right or wrong, to guide how we interact with things (see Figure 18.1).

A great example involves how to use a thermostat to control the temperature in a room. If we're cold and we'd like to get the room to temperature X very quickly, which is the best strategy?

- Should we turn the control to the maximum temperature?
- Should we turn the control to X?

Figure 18.1 Humans use conceptual models of how a system works in order to guide their interaction with it.

To help us decide on the right course of action, we refer to our mental model of how the device works. Whether our decision works depends on whether the model matches reality. In the preceding case, real-world experience can easily give us two conflicting models:

1. If we think that the control setting correlates to the intensity of the heat produced, then we should turn the control the maximum temperature.

2. If we think that the control setting correlates to the room temperature at which the furnace shuts off, then turning the control to X suffices.

(By the way, the former is the correct model for automobile heating but not for home furnaces.)

Numerous security problems have their root in the discrepancy between the picture of the system in a user's mind and reality.

- For one example, a colleague deployed PKI to the employee population at his large enterprise. The private keys lived on USB tokens. To unlock the token, a user entered a passphrase via the interface on his or her PC. To protect against brute-force guessing, the token would lock itself out—requiring certificate revocation—if more than a few incorrect passphrases were entered.

Unfortunately, should a user enter the wrong passphrase, the PC interface asked something like "Passphrase rejected—try again?"

— In the mental model of most users, this query was asking whether they wanted to try typing the passphrase again, so they clicked "yes."

— However, in the reality of the system, the PC-based interface was asking *whether the PC should try the same incorrect passphrase again.* Clicking "yes" once or twice quickly killed the token.

This mismatch led to the cost and hassle of reissuing far more tokens than expected and of revoking far more certificates than planned. (We briefly discussed this in Chapter 10.)

- For another example, in an old version of Microsoft Outlook, a user who was preparing to send encrypted email would be given a "Cancel" option.

— In the mental model of most users, selecting "Cancel" would cancel the sending of the email.

— In the reality of the system, selecting "Cancel" would cause the program to cancel the encryption—but send the email anyway [Stu98].

- For yet more examples, we only need to look at how a user decides whether "deleting" a file actually renders its contents unavailable or whether it's safe to type a password into a Web page allegedly from that user's bank.

(We leave further examples to the reader.)

Any system with real users is bound to have an enormous state space. As we've discussed throughout this book, large and complex state spaces don't fit into developers' heads, much less the heads of end users. As a result, users are often left to draw their own conclusions about how the system reacts to specific stimuli; this map of causes to effects comprises the user's mental model of the system.

We would even go further than Norman and cite the fact that real systems consist of many layers (e.g., design, high-level application code, machine code, OS, OS machine code, hardware). All these layers must work together for the system to be secure. However, most users *and most developers* likely have mental models sufficiently rich (that is, to enable sound judgments) for only a few. One might trace such amusements as side-channel analysis on cryptography or Appel's use of a lightbulb to subvert Java typesafety[2] to this inability to see all the layers.

---

2. See [GA03]. First, fill memory with a data structure deviously constructed so that flipping one bit makes an integer and an integer pointer live at the same address; then, use the heat from a light bulb to induce this bit flip. For classroom demos, we have better luck with a hairdryer.

Naturally, a user's mental picture of the system is limited. For starters, it typically contains only the portions of the state space that are presented to the user via the user interface, command line, and so on. Additionally, most end users of the system will have no idea what the internal state space of any system looks like. In fact, it's likely that an overwhelming majority of the system's users have never seen or written software at the level at which developers do.

Ideally, the user's limited view of the system should be a proper subset of the system's "good" states: No matter what the user does, the system should never wind up in an unsafe state. In reality, this is rarely the case; many systems fall into bad states because of incongruent mental models. Often, the system designers and implementers have a mental model that does not account for all the possible inputs that users can supply to the system. Many of these inputs can transition the system into a bad state. Additionally, nonmalicious end users often mistakenly assume that bad states are unreachable from the interface they are presented and thus perform dangerous actions without an understanding of the consequences.

Sometimes, the actual metaphor that a system presents to users encourages them to render faulty models. In Chapter 13, we discussed how word processors, such as Microsoft's Word, attempt to get users to think of their electronic document as a piece of paper. That metaphor isn't accurate. Microsoft Word documents contain a Turing-complete scripting engine that will execute arbitrary scripts. Additionally, the documents can contain links to the Web and retrieve data from external sites to include in the document on each viewing. Word documents are no more flat pieces of paper than are Web pages, and this mismatch between the metaphor and the real system can lead users to make bad assumptions about their documents— assumptions that can result in security trouble.

As a system builder, it will be your job to present good mental models. The central tradeoff in this area is between transparency and expressiveness. Some argue that the security of the system should be *transparent*[3]—the user shouldn't have to think about it at all. In effect, a tranparent system in this regard means that, regardless of what actions the user takes, the system cannot wind up in a bad state. Users are not burdened with making security-relevant decisions; in return, the application attempts to guarantee to stay in a good state. Others argue that the system should be *expressive* and let the user know when the system is dealing with security-related information or is at a point where a transition into an unsafe state is possible. Proponents of expressiveness claim that security-related decisions are

---

3. Yes, we realize that "transparent" has at least two distinct meanings when it comes to computer systems. Sorry about that.

best made in context and that the best source of context is the human using the system.

So, who is right? In our experience, we've found that they both are. There are situations in which users shouldn't have to deal with security. For example, systems that communicate potentially sensitive information over the network shouldn't ask the user whether to encrypt the traffic and what key lengths and algorithms to use. That part of the system's security should be invisible. However, the same system may need to be expressive when it comes to authenticating a machine or user across the network. The system itself may have no clue as to whether to trust a remote server, but the system's user may know immediately.

Unfortunately, there are no hard-and-fast rules on when to make a portion of the system invisible or expressive. This decision is often made on a case-by-case basis. However, in practice, we often use at least one heuristic to help us decide: If the portion of the system is dealing with trust, it should be expressive; otherwise, try to make it invisible. We discuss trust in more detail in Section 18.4, but we can say here that humans are much better than machines at making trust decisions. Security decisions that don't directly involve trust (e.g., how to secure data at rest or in transit) typically don't benefit from user intervention, although we're sure that you'll come across counterexamples out in the real world.

18.2.3 Mapping

In order to use a device for its intended purpose, a human must eventually manipulate its set of controls. Controls can be quite simple (such as the controls used to open a door), or much more complex (such as in an airplane cockpit). Regardless of the level of complexity, the device has some mapping between a control-change event (e.g., a button press) and a transition in the state of the system (e.g., the missles are launched).

How do users understand these mappings? If it's not in the device in the world, it has to be in the head. In developing mental models, humans essentially try to deduce what these mappings are. Often, humans will manipulate the controls, observe the result, and remember the cause-and-effect relationship. Sometimes, these mappings are very straightforward (e.g., pressing the red button always launches the missiles). Other times, the mapping can be more complex (e.g., pushing the flight stick forward might move the plane in different directions, depending on the orientation of the plane). Regardless of the complexity, a user must be able to grasp the mapping in order to use the device effectively.

As a case in point, consider how tricky it is to figure out how to adjust the balance (left-right) and fading (front-back) on an unfamiliar car radio. To start with, although only one of these transitions has a left-right orientation, the controls for *both* do. One of us used to own a car whose radio had both controls overloaded on one knob, making matters even worse. Norman likes to cite sinks in a dormitory room at the University of Sheffield that required an instruction sheet to use. One of us once encountered a hotel room shower at Johns Hopkins that also required instructions; we tried for 5 minutes to start the shower, in vain, until noticing that instructions were on the counter.

As we've discussed at great lengths, our definition of security involves keeping the system out of bad states. We hope that, by now, you appreciate the fact that the state space in a modern system is enormous. Such state spaces don't fit into the developers' heads, much less the users'. Users typically have a very limited mental model of the system, based on the control mappings that the users have observed. Even subtle inconsistencies in the control mappings can break a user's model and lead the person to use things incorrectly. If the system's designers haven't anticipated the user's behavior, the system can get into a bad state, which as you know, can have security ramifications.

18.2.4 Constraints, Affordances, and Feedback

System designers have three tools at their disposal to guide users into creating appropriate mental models of the system and thus using the system correctly, or at least in such a way that doesn't send it into states that they aren't anticipating. Norman calls these tools *constraints*, *affordances*, and *feedback*.

Constraints limit what the controls can do. Ideally, they should be used as a way to disallow input or control events that send the system into a bad state. For example, a Web form that asks users to enter their phone numbers can constrain the input to allowing only the right number of digits and blocking all alphabetical characters. One can also imagine cases in which certain controls (e.g., a Next button on a wizard) are inaccessible until certain conditions have been met (e.g., the user has accepted the End User License Agreement). Although constraints aren't perfect, they certainly play a big part in keeping the system in a good state. (And we certainly get frustrated at Web sites that expect a credit card number to be entered a certain special way but give no clues to that.)

Norman uses the term *affordances* to describe actions that are perceivable by the user. As a system designer, one can use this concept to build controls that, by their construction and appearance, naturally suggest their proper use. A classic example of this can be found on doors. Well-designed doors that need a push to open present

Figure 18.2 This entrance to a sandwich shop near Dartmouth is a wonderful example of a "Norman door." The design of the handle implies "pull," but in fact, the user must *push* on it to open the door.

the user a simple push pad. Push doors that present a handle for users to grasp are confusing—do you grab and pull or grab and push? Although this ambiguity is often resolved with a simple user experiment or a sign with clear instructions ("push" or "pull"), this is unnecessary complexity. A well-designed door handle suggests its own proper use. Norman is somewhat embarrassed that doors whose design misleads the user are now called "Norman doors" (see Figure 18.2).

As part of the way humans interact with the world, we evaluate actions and plan strategy based on our perception of what our actions did. The observable result of our actions is usually called *feedback*. For a system designer, this feedback can help guide users into constructing accurate mappings beween control-change events and system state changes. As we've been discussing throughout this section, an accurate understanding of this mapping is the basis for a good mental model of the system. Thus, it's important that significant control-change events and other important state changes generate some change that the user can perceive.

18.2.5 Yee's Principles

A more recent set of principles for designing the user interface of security systems came from Ka-Ping Yee in 2002, while he was a graduate student at Berkeley [Yee02]. Unlike Norman, Yee focused on the specific problem of UI design for security systems. As such, Yee's principles cover a number of the concepts we've been discussing throughout this chapter and are worth mentioning.

"The path of least resistance" aims to take into account the fact that humans often search for the easiest way to accomplish a given task. Although this is true in the real world, it also applies to software. Thus, if the easiest way to accomplish the task (i.e., "the path of least resistance") is secure, then users will naturally take the most secure path through the system.

"Active authorization" states that the system interface should allow users to grant authority to others in a way that's obvious to both the granter and the grantee. Furthermore, if a user is explicitly granting authority to another party, the system should give *only* that authority to the receiving party—no more and no less.

"Revocability" means that the system should give users a way to take such granted authority away from other users. For example, Alice should be allowed to limit other users' access to her resources.

"Visibility" refers to the requirement that the system's UI should allow any user to get an accurate view of the authority that other users have to that user's resources. *"Self-awareness"* is the complement to visibility. At any time, the UI should allow a user to see his or her authority with respect to other users' resources.

The *"trusted path"* principle states that a user must have a secure channel from the UI to any entity, such as a process, that can modify authority for the user. A secure channel in this context is one that cannot be spoofed or tampered with.

"Expressiveness" requires that the method of setting security policy in the system should allow the user to set the policy to reflect the user's mental model. The security policy language should allow users to do what they want to do.

The principle of *"relevant boundaries"* states that the UI should make it clear to the user where the distinctions between objects are. For example, if Alice is trying to restrict access to an object she owns (e.g., a file or a directory), then the UI should allow her to restrict access to that object. If the boundary is too big, then the action Alice performs will be too coarse-grained. For example, if the UI allows Alice to operate only on directories, then she will end up changing the permissions on all the files in her directory, which may not be the intended effect. If it's too small, Alice may have to perform multiple actions to get the desired effect. For instance, if the UI allows Alice to modify permissions only on files and she wants to lock down a directory, she will have to manually change the permissions on each file in the directory.

"Identifiability" is a principle that refers to the notion that, in order for users to clearly express their intentions, objects and actions in the system need to be uniquely identifiable. Furthermore, objects that are the same should appear the same to the user, and objects that are different should appear different.

Finally, the principle of *"foresight"* specifies that the UI should clearly communicate to the user the security consequences of his or her decisions. The idea here is that users decide to take actions based on what they think will happen as a result (i.e., based on their mapping between controls and the system state). If the system fails to give users the appropriate feedback, then they are likely to miscalculate the result of their action and thus cause security trouble.

18.3 Other Human-Space Issues

So far, we've been focusing exclusively on technology and on individual human psychology. However, other aspects of human society also play into secure system design.

Economics.   One area beginning to receive attention is *economics*. One angle to look at is how economic forces promote or discourage secure products in the computer system and software marketplace. As anyone who has worked in development can testify, the software industry has a strong pressure to be first to market and patch later; taking longer to build a secure system can lead to market death. On the procurement end, it can be hard to justify spending more for "security" when it's perceived to provide negative functionality—if that.

Another angle looks at the consumer end and cost. What is the *return on investment (ROI)* on security? If an enterprise's CFO asks its CIO whether they should be spending less or more on security, how can they answer? (Figure 18.3 sketches

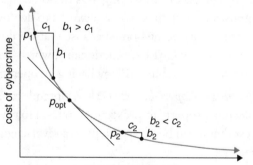

Figure 18.3 To make a rational decision on investing in cybersecurity, enterprise management needs to be able to evaluate its return on investment. In this sketch, adapted from Dr. Scott Dynes' reading of Gordon and Loeb [GL02], the gray curve shows the tradeoff between the cost of cybercrime and the cost of cybersecurity. At point p_1, investing in security makes sense, because the benefit outweighs the cost. At point p_2, it does not. Point p_{opt} is the optimal point for the enterprise: Spending any more isn't worth it, but neither is spending any less. (Unfortunately, in the real world, finding what this gray curve looks like and where one lies on it remain significant challenges.)

this problem.) Other researchers take a societywide view, examining how those who benefit from information security practices are not necessarily those who shoulder their cost. If Bob is careless with configuration and patching on his Internet-connected machine and it gets borrowed by spammers, the entire Internet suffers; however, Bob may turn a deaf ear to the clamoring for him to clean up his machine, since it's not affecting him. Researchers compare this phenomenon to the older, noncyber metaphor of the *tragedy of the commons.*

Dan Geer and colleagues compare the current security marketplace to the medical marketplace in the late 1800s—there is a real problem and potential for real solutions but not much to guide the consumer to make effective choices. Geer has repeatedly called for a quantitative theory of information risk management that is as solid as we have for other types of risk management. This is an area of active research. See [And01, GL02] for some good surveys here.

Action at a Distance.   Another human-space activity worth noting for its potential effect on securing systems is the arena of law and treaty. In Chapter 11, we surveyed such things as HIPAA and HSPD12 that drove computer security standards and testing. More activity looms; we provide a few examples.

- The *Communications Assistance for Law Enforcement Act (CALEA)* intends to make it easier for U.S. law enforcement to wiretap electronic communications, when permitted by law. As of this writing, it is rumored that university lawyers are forcing campuses with open wireless networks to deploy campuswide authentication for network admission—because that would be cheaper than building in the appropriate CALEA functionality, which would be required if the university remained a "public ISP" by having an open network.

- The *Digital Millennium Copyright Act (DMCA)* intends to make it easier for owners of intellectual property to prosecute pirates. However, some readings of the act suggest that it can be used to suppress reverse engineering and vulnerability analysis.

- Europe has enacted several privacy laws intended to enforce privacy of citizen data. One effect was the immediate complication of life for international corporations that do business both in the United States and in Europe, since the laws can lead to some ambiguous situations.

- The *Basel II* accord in the finance industry intends to ensure that financial firms retain reserve funds sufficient to cover emergencies, including infosec emergencies. Firms need to justify why the amount they reserve is sufficient—money reserved is not money invested, so reducing the reserve leads to increased profit. Consequently, as a side effect of this accord, investment banks suddenly find themselves with an ability to calculate a meaningful ROI on security technology.

Again, this is another area where action at a distance can change the security game.

18.4   Trust

So far in this chapter, we've been discussing what system designers can do to make their systems usable. We've discussed the importance of humans and have outlined a number of concepts and principles that designers can use to guide them in their task. We now step back and think about the underlying entity that any secure system must facilitate: trust.

Of course, having worked with a sociologist, we're hesitant to give a formal definition of "trust." What do we mean when we say "Alice trusts Bob"? That Bob's interests somehow encapsulate Alice's? That Alice voluntarily *chooses* to accept the risk that Bob might do her harm? That Alice has no choice but to trust Bob, because she has no other way of constraining his behavior? (This latter definition was the original type of trust embodied in the term *trusted computing base.*) See [CNM02] for some representative discussion here. Bravely, we'll sidestep that issue and move ahead.

18.4.1   Why Trust Is Important

Secure systems must facilitate different types of trust to solve different types of problems. First and foremost, a secure system must itself be "trustable" to its users. That is, the system must be trustworthy to the users—and the users must have the ability to know that. If users are going to use the system to accomplish tasks that require sensitive information, such as personal or classified material, then they need some assurance that the system will handle that information appropriately while the information is at rest and in transit.

Multiuser systems have another dimension of trust problems to contend with in order to establish their trustworthiness. In these types of systems, the actions of one user can affect the integrity of the entire system. For example, a user who accidentally destroys system information can effectively deny service to everyone. A malicious user who releases a virus or installs spyware or some other form of malware on the system can deny service, compromise other users' information, or even take complete control of the system. Furthermore, such a malicious user may compound problems by disabling reporting mechanisms, such as logging, thus allowing the problems to go unnoticed for a long period of time.

In multiuser systems, cooperation among the users is necessary to ensure the system's integrity. Such cooperation is often difficult when users are *vulnerable* (the outcome of their actions can depend on the actions of others) and *uncertain* (users don't know what other users will do and cannot immediately determine who is trustworthy and who is not). Ultimately, trust is necessary for cooperation and coexistence in conditions of uncertainty and vulnerability. If users are being asked to share the system with others, they need some assurance that the system will protect them.

In addition to being trustable, a secure system must also allow users to make sound trust judgments about the other entities they must deal with. Such entities might include other users, processes, or the results of computations—all of which can be either local or remote. No matter how much a user trusts the system to safeguard his or her infomation, behave as expected, and provide protection from other users, a user who has no basis for trusting the other agents that operate on his or her infomation can't use the system to securely solve any real problems.

In short, much of the work that goes into secure systems is about trust. But trust is a human phenomenon—machines do not trust; they merely obey. System builders must realize that trust is a human issue and that using principles and techniques such as those described in this chapter can help them build trustable systems that enable users to make reasonable trust judgments.

18.4.2 Facilitating Trust

Many of the tools we've been discussing throughout the book can be viewed as mechanisms to facilitate trust. The topics in Part II—OS, network, and implementation security—are aimed at making systems themselves trustworthy—from the OS to the installed applications to the communication channels between multiple systems. The topics discussed in Part III—cryptography, authentication, and PKI—can aid in making systems trustworthy but are also useful in enabling users to make valid trust judgments about other actors and agents that operate on the user's behalf. In Part IV, we've been covering emerging tools—formal methods, hardware, and AI—that can allow system builders to formally reason about the trust of the system, enlist the help of system hardware to facilitate trust, and have the system itself attempt to detect when it is in an untrustworthy state.

As we've been discussing in this chapter, good interface design goes a long way toward making the system trustable. Ulitmately, users want to believe that the system will help and encourage them to do the correct thing and warn them when they are about to do the wrong thing. As we discussed in Section 18.2.4, constraints, affordances, and feedback can help users build accurate mental models, which are essential in establishing system–user trust.

In order for users in a multiuser environment to trust the system, they need some assurance that their information is safe from others. Many of Yee's principles address this issue. They note that giving users a clear and accurate picture of who can access their infomation, an expressive mechanism to state their intentions, and appropriate controls to grant and revoke access are necessary steps in establishing such trust as well. Many of the tools to implement these principles—such as authentication and authorization—were discussed in Part II.

Finally, if users are going to use the system for any real problem, they need to be able to make reasonable trust judgments about the entities that they interact with. Users need to have some basis on which to trust the computational entities that run on the user's behalf (and their results). In the course of performing computations, the system may pass data to other users and/or machines, meaning that such entities must be trustable as well. In Chapters 7 and 10, we discussed how cryptography and various cryptographic protocols can help build the foundation for these types of trust judgments to occur. In this chapter, we've highlighted the importance of building usable interfaces for such features.

18.5 The Take-Home Message

Humans play a vital part to the security of the system. The attacker community has acknowledged this fact for some time; the systems community is beginning to follow suit. Ultimately, a user's actions are going to influence how the system transitions through the state space. An otherwise well-built system can end up in bad states quite often if the interface makes it easy to get the system in such a state or makes it difficult for users to steer away from such states.

It's important to build mental models and mappings that encourage the user to use the system the way you intended it to be used. When mental models and reality diverge, the system is headed for trouble. There is no "correct" way to build a usable interface; each system will pose a different set of challenges. However, as we've discussed throughout this chapter, a number of techniques and principles can help.

18.6 Project Ideas

1. Pick a modern mail client, and see whether you can actually get encryption and signing to work. Can you think of ways in which the UI can be improved?

2. Try encrypting a subset of the files you use on a daily basis. How could you improve the UI?

3. Talk to your local computer help desk about the problems users report. See whether you can mine that data to produce evidence supporting or refuting Norman's principles.

4. Pick a random sample of vulnerabilities from BugTraq [Sec06] (or from your favorite source, if you don't like BugTraq) and see what percentage of them can be linked to poor interface design.

The Take-Home Lesson

Crafting a secure system is hard. Many factors contribute to this problem.

- The artisan must look at the entire system, including many levels of hardware and software technology, user interface design, manufacturing, sales, maintenance—as well as laws, standards, social practices, psychology (and probably a few other things we're missing).
- The components and application of this system continue to undergo revolutionary changes. Would you walk over a bridge built 30 years ago? (Of course!) But would you trust a cryptosystem designed 30 years ago? Would you hook up a PC, whose last patch was only 10 months ago, to the Internet?
- The science and engineering behind bridge building are well understood. In contrast, "security" is still an unfinished field. What does it mean for a system to be secure? How do we measure that? How do we achieve that?

System security is a space filled with complexity and tradeoffs but few methods to tell you whether you've succeeded. Unfortunately, the state of the art and technology haven't given us—the system-building community—any clearly defined, accepted, and effective methodology. We have to rely on our judgment, creativity, and experience and, of course, our tools. It is for this reason that we claim that building secure systems is still a *craft,* as opposed to an art or an engineering discipline.

We hope that this book has helped sharpen your judgment, creativity, and curiosity in this domain. We purposely provided a detailed bibliography so that you could learn more about what those before us have done. Although reading does not completely substitute for direct experience, we intend for it to help you avoid reinventing the wheel and to stay clear of the common pitfalls. Finally, we hope that you have discovered a number of tools to help you in your own endeavors. We encourage you to keep looking for such tools—even from seemingly different worlds, such as the realms of automated formal method, AI, and human/device interaction.

Finally, we hope that this book has given you a little bit of the skepticism necessary to be successful in this field. It's hard to build a secure system if you can't think like your adversary. The bibliography is chock-full of instances in which people took things apart, challenged some principle, or put things together the wrong way. Many times, such exercises led to interesting results. We encourage you to think differently about the systems you use and build. We are continuously asking ourselves, "I wonder what would happen if . . . ."

The future of our society depends on system security. We need skilled security artisans to make that happen. It's up to you.

Exiled Theory

Among some of our engineering colleagues, "theory" has a bad reputation, seeming to have connotations of "impractical" and "divorced from reality." This reputation is unfortunate, particularly in computer science. Computation itself is an abstract, mathematical concept. The rigor of mathematics lets us talk precisely about it. In this sense, "theoretical" computer science can lead us toward, rather than away from, the heart of what's really going on here.

The tools of theoretical computer science help illuminate many aspects of the security craft. In this appendix, we provide deeper discussion of some of the topics in this space, broached briefly earlier in the book.

- Section A.1 offers some background on relations, orders, and lattices.
- Section A.2 offers some background on functions.
- Section A.3 introduces computability theory.
- Section A.4 compares the frameworks of computability theory, complexity theory, and information theory.
- Section A.5 provides more detail on quantum mechanics and quantum computing.

A.1 Relations, Orders, and Lattices

The primary security models in this Orange Book world depend on the mathematical concepts of orders and lattices. We quickly review these definitions here.

A *relation* R on a set S is a subset of $S \times S$, except that we write it in infix notation. That is, we write aRb when a is related to b within this relation.

An *order* on a set is a relation R that satisfies these properties:

- *Transitive.* If aRb and bRc, then aRc.
- *Reflexive.* For any a, we have aRa.
- *Antisymmetric.* If aRb and bRa, then $a == b$.

A nice intuitive example of an order is $\leq$ on the integers.

We say that an order is *total* when, for any distinct x, y, we have either xRy or yRx. (Again, think of $\leq$ on the integers.) In contrast, a *partial order* does not require that all distinct pairs be orderable. Some pairs can be incomparable.

- "I love each of my daughters more than I love the raccoon that lives behind the garage."
- "But I can't tell you whether I love my older daughter more than I love my younger daughter."

(If one wants to be pedantic about it, a total order is merely a special case of a partial order.)

In a partial order, an element c is the *least upper bound* of elements a and b if c satisfies these properties:

- aRc.
- bRc.
- If aRd and bRd, then cRd.

Intuitively, the first two conditions mean that c is indeed an upper bound of a and b; the third condition means that it is "smaller" than any other upper bound of a and b. We can similarly define a *greatest lower bound*.

A *lattice* is a partially ordered set such that any two elements have a least upper bound and a greatest lower bound. Infinite lattices can be a bit strange to think about. However, suppose instead that we have a finite one, built from taking the transitive closure of a simple relation, and we draw it as a directed graph:

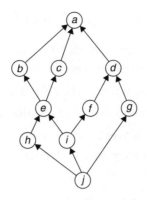

Figure A.1 This directed graph is an example of a simple lattice, where $n_1 \leq n_2$ if and only if a directed path exists from n_1 to n_2. We see that node e is the greatest lower bound of nodes b and c. Nodes $e, h, i,$ and j are all lower bounds of these two nodes, but $h \leq e, i \leq e,$ and $j \leq e$.

- A node for each element of the set
- An edge for each pair under the simple relation
- Paths for the transitive relation

The resulting structure will actually look a bit like what we call a lattice in ordinary English. Each pair of nodes needs to have a unique least upper bound, which forces us to have a regular lattice-work structure. The graph itself will have distinctive *top* and *bottom* elements. Figure A.1 sketches these concepts.

A.2 Functions

A mathematical *function* f from a set D to a set R is a map that takes each element $x \in D$ to some element $f(x) \in R$. A *partial function* can leave some $f(x)$ undefined. The set D here is called the *domain* of f; the set R is its *range*. Sometimes, this is all expressed mathematically as

$$f \, : \, D \longrightarrow R.$$

Sometimes, the value $f(x) \in R$ is said to be the *image* of x under f; the value x is said to be the *preimage* of the value $f(x)$.

There are no requirements that D and R be distinct; folks often talk about just one set (e.g., "a function on the integers") when $D = R$.

We sometimes distinguish some special properties of functions.

- A function f is *one to one* (or *injective*) if for any $x \neq y \in D$, we have $f(x) \neq f(y)$. Each x goes to its very own image.
- A function f is *onto* (or *surjective*) when f hits every element in its range R.
- A function f that is both injective and surjective is a *bijection*.
- The word *homomorphic* derives from the phrase *same form*. A function is *homomorphic* when it preserves some interesting form of its domain set, such as some special relations.

We might blunder and somehow manage to introduce an f such that it's not clear which element of R some x maps to. In this case, our function f is not *well defined*.

A.3 Computability Theory

Given a function $f : D \longrightarrow R$, our first reaction, as computer people, might be to think about how we would compute it: how we would write a program that takes $x \in D$ as an input and spits out $f(x)$.

The field of the *theory of computation* developed precise mathematical characterizations of what things "programs" can do. This characterization leads to a surprising, counterintuitive result: There exist well-defined functions that *cannot be computed*.

We quickly present this result.

A.3.1 Things Can Be Uncountable

We start with *countability*.

Recall the set of natural numbers:

$$\mathbb{N} = \{1, 2, \dots\}.$$

The set $\mathbb{N}$ is clearly infinite; other sets are infinite as well. Mathematically, we say that a set S is *countable* when we can put S in one-to-one correspondence with $\mathbb{N}$. One might ask: Are there any infinite sets that *are not* countable? The answer is yes. For example, consider the real numbers between 0 and 1:

$$R = \{r \in \mathbb{R} \ : \ 0 < r < 1\}.$$

Since each element of R is between 0 and 1, we can write each in decimal as 0, followed by a decimal point, followed by some number of digits, perhaps a

$r_1 = 0.$	2	4	7	4	9	0	$\cdots$
$r_2 = 0.$	9	3	1	1	6	8	$\cdots$
$r_3 = 0.$	6	5	0	6	2	3	$\cdots$
$r_4 = 0.$	2	2	8	3	9	0	$\cdots$
$r_5 = 0.$	5	1	4	0	7	8	$\cdots$
$r_6 = 0.$	3	4	7	6	5	9	$\cdots$

Figure A.2 If the real numbers between 0 and 1 were countable. we could enumerate them as $r_1, r_2 \ldots$.

nonterminating sequence of them. We'll also define a *Twist*() function that twists a digit to be something very different:

$$Twist(d) = \begin{cases} 7 & \text{if } d{\neq}7 \\ 5 & \text{otherwise.} \end{cases}$$

We can show that R is not countable, using something called *Cantor's diagonalization technique*. If R were countable, we could enumerate it as $r_1, r_2, \ldots$ and hit the entire set. We could use this enumeration and the decimal representation to build a table: Row n would contain r_n, and column k would contain the kth decimal digit. (See Figure A.2.)

From this table, we can construct another element of R (call it s) by going along the diagonal but twisting things at each step—we let the nth digit of s be *Twist(d)*, where d is the nth digit of r_n. (See Figure A.3.) This new number s is clearly in R. But it also cannot be in this table—for if $s = r_m$ for some m, what would the mth digit of s be? Cool, eh?

A.3.2 Things Can Be Uncomputable

We can use the same principle to show that there are uncomputable functions. Let P be the set of possible programs and I be the set of possible inputs to these programs. When we get serious about formalizing P and I, we end up with sets that are countable. So, we can use these facts to build a table: Row n talks about

s = 0.							
$r_1 = 0.$	7 / 2̸	4	7	4	9	0	...
$r_2 = 0.$	9	7 / 8̸	1	1	6	8	...
$r_3 = 0.$	6	5	7 / 0̸	6	2	3	...
$r_4 = 0.$	2	2	8	7 / 8̸	9	0	...
$r_5 = 0.$	5	1	4	0	7 / 1̸	8	...
$r_6 = 0.$	3	4	7	6	5	7 / 0̸	...
⋮	⋮	⋮	⋮	⋮	⋮	⋮	⋱

Figure A.3 By moving along the diagonal and twisting the digit there so it's different, we produce a real number s that cannot be in this enumeration.

program p_n; column k talks about what happens when we run programs on input i_k. In entry n, k, we write *Halt* or *Not Halt*, depending on whether $P_n(i_k)$ halts or runs forever. (See Figure A.4.)

We can define a new *Twist*() function:

$$Twist(d) = \begin{cases} Halt & \text{if } d = Not\ Halt \\ Not\ Halt & \text{if } d = Halt. \end{cases}$$

From this table, we can construct a function f by going along the diagonal but twisting things at each step:

$$f(i_n) = Twist(p_n(i_n)).$$

(See Figure A.5.)

Semantically, this function f returns *Halt* on i_n exactly when P_n does *not* halt on input i_n. Consequently, *no program can compute f!* All possible programs appear in this table. So, if f were computable, it must be computed by p_m for some m. However, how can $p_m(i_m)$ behave the same as $f(i_m)$? If $p_m(i_m)$ halts, then $f(i_m)$ must say *Not Halt*, so $p_m \neq f$; if $p_m(i_m)$ does not halt, then $f(i_m)$ must halt, so $p_m \neq f$. Cool, eh?

The uncomputable problem of deciding, yes or no, whether a given program halts on a given input is called the *Halting Problem*. One can use this idea as a

	i_1	i_2	i_3	i_4	i_5	i_6	
p_1	Halt	Halt	Halt	Not Halt	Not Halt	Not Halt	⋯
p_2	Not Halt	Not Halt	Not Halt	Halt	Halt	Not Halt	⋯
p_3	Halt	Halt	Not Halt	Not Halt	Halt	Halt	⋯
p_4	Not Halt	Halt	Halt	Halt	Not Halt	Not Halt	⋯
p_5	Not Halt	Halt	Not Halt	Halt	Not Halt	Halt	⋯
p_6	Halt	Not Halt	Halt	Not Halt	Not Halt	Not Halt	⋯
⋮	⋮	⋮	⋮	⋮	⋮	⋮	⋱

Figure A.4 Because the Turing machines are countable, we can enumerate them (down the rows here). Because their possible inputs are countable, we can enumerate them as well (across the columns here). Each machine on each input either halts or doesn't; in this table, we show what happens.

$f() =$	i_1	i_2	i_3	i_4	i_5	i_6	
p_1	**Not Halt** ~~Halt~~	Halt	Halt	Not Halt	Not Halt	Not Halt	⋯
p_2	Not Halt	**Halt** ~~Not Halt~~	Not Halt	Halt	Halt	Not Halt	⋯
p_3	Halt	Halt	**Halt** ~~Not Halt~~	Not Halt	Halt	Halt	⋯
p_4	Not Halt	Halt	Halt	**Not Halt** ~~Halt~~	Not Halt	Not Halt	⋯
p_5	Not Halt	Halt	Not Halt	Halt	**Halt** ~~Not Halt~~	Halt	⋯
p_6	Halt	Not Halt	Halt	Not Halt	Not Halt	**Halt** ~~Not Halt~~	⋯
⋮	⋮	⋮	⋮	⋮	⋮	⋮	⋱

Figure A.5 By moving along the diagonal and twisting the entry there so it's different, we produce a function f that cannot be computed by a Turing machine in this enumeration.

springboard into a world of fascinating theoretical and practical work and uncomputable functions. (Sipser's *Introduction to the Theory of Computation* covers these problems in detail [Sip97].) As a young postdoc, one of us was once asked to write a program (for the U.S. Postal Service) that essentially solved the Halting Problem. Citing Alan Turing's classic 1930s paper [Tur37] in our final report [Smi05] was cause for much mirth (at least among the authors of the report).

A.4 Frameworks

Section A.3 showed how functions exist that cannot be computed. This existence can be useful when we want to talk rigorously about hard tasks: For example, we can show that in order to do this task, we have to solve the Halting Problem. This is an example of a *computation-theoretic* argument framework.

Theory also gives us other frameworks to reason about things. Among computable functions, we can start rigorously reasoning about the time and space resources (and types of computational devices) it takes to compute them. This theory gives us a way to talk about the *complexity* of computable problems. Informally, we say a problem has complexity $O(f(n))$ if the resources it requires to solve an instance of size n grows by not more than $f(n)$, asymptotically. A problem has *complexity* $\Omega(f(n))$ if the required resource grows by at least $f(n)$ asymptomatically. (Note however, that complexity theory usually assumes that the problem's parameters are written down in binary.)

The resulting framework gives another way to talk about hard tasks. For example, we can show that doing this task requires doing a function that, although computable, takes more resources than is feasible. This is an example of a *complexity-theoretic* argument framework.

Many aspects of cryptography are even weaker than complexity-theoretic. For one example, no clear complexity-theoretic bound underlies the security of SHA-1. For another example, everyone suspects that factoring is hard, but no one really knows; furthermore, breaking RSA might be even easier. We also thus sometimes see a tacit "cryptographic" framework—where one simply hopes that certain key functions are intractable. (We then argue that breaking our scheme requires breaking one of these hopefully intractable functions.)

Chapter 7 discussed yet another framework: the use of *information theory* to characterize the raw information present in message. If the information isn't there, then the adversary can't get it. However, if the information *is* there, that doesn't mean that the adversary *can* get it. When it comes to considering computation in the real world, information theory has a glaring deficiency—it neglects to take into account the feasibility (or even the possibility) of actually extracting the information from the message.

Conundrum.   As a thought exercise about these frameworks, suppose that Alice wants to send a 20-character ASCII message M to Bob. She can choose many encodings:

- M_1. She encodes each bit of M as an instance of the *satisfiability* problem, over a number of variables polynomial in $|M|$. (Satisfiable means that the bit is 1.)
- M_2. She encodes each bit of M as an instance of the *Halting Problem*. (Halts means that the bit is 1.)
- M_3. She encrypts the message with TDES.
- M_4. She sends the message in plaintext but deletes the least-significant bit of each byte.

(The satisfiability problem comes from complexity theory: One is given a Boolean formula consisting of ANDs and ORs of variables and their negations and needs to answer: Is there a truth assignment to the variables that satisfies this formula?)

How much information about M is present in each of Alice's formats? Information theory tells us that M_1, M_2, and M_3 contain *all* the information. However, decoding M_1 is intractable, and decoding M_2 is, in general, not even computable. If Alice wants to minimize information exposed to an eavesdropper, she should choose M_4—even though that gives away half the message right away; any sensible implementer would choose M_3.

(Whenever we asked a local theoretician about this problem, he told us we were giving him a headache.)

A.5 Quantum Physics and Quantum Computation

Chapter 8 talked about how, if we use the properties of quantum mechanics to build new kinds of computers, we can factor efficiently—and thus break RSA. This section gives some more detail.

A.5.1 Evolution of Physics

To tell this story, let's broaden our scope from cryptography to the *universe.* How does the universe *work?*

Throughout history, humans seem to want to have a mathematical model that seems "natural" and "intuitive," and also actually explains the way the universe works. Searching for such a model raises deeper philosophical issues. Does the universe work this way because the model is natural? Or does the model seem natural (to us) because that's the way the universe works?

Newtonian mechanics was a model that proved rather satisfying. It explained how balls bounced. It gave us calculus. Unfortunately, the Newtonian model did not quite explain all observable phenomenon. This shortfall gave rise, in the early part of the twentieth century, to *relativity:* a clean model that explains such things as how the measured speed of light remains constant. Relativity isn't quite as "obvious" as the Newtonian model, but if one accepts a few things on faith, then it's still somewhat intuitive.

However, when scientists started examining the physics of very small stuff, things got strange. Explaining this strangeness led to a new model: *quantum mechanics*. The quantum model is elaborate, bizarre, and unintuitive—there is no "obvious" reason why the universe should work that way. The model appears sufficiently artificial and complex that a graduate student who proposed this as a theory to his or her adviser would probably be gently encouraged to go think a bit more.

However strange, the quantum model is the simplest model that we've come up with that actually explains the observed phenomenon. We now delve into this strange world.

A.5.2 Quantum Mechanics

We start with a simplified sketch. Consider an object O that might be in any state in some set S_O. For example, O might be a photon, with S_O being various polarizations; O might be a 1-bit register, with $S_O = \{0, 1\}$. For simplicity, we'll assume that S_O is finite. Intuitively, we think of the object O as actually being in exactly one state $s \in S_O$. For example, the photon has a vertical polarization right now, or the bit equals 1.

The Natural Intuitive Model.   We might describe the state of the object O with a *vector*, with an entry v_s for each $s \in S_O$. The entry is 1 for the state s that O actually is in and 0 for all other entries.

Perhaps we're not certain which state the object is in. In this case, we might assign each $s \in S_O$ a number $P(s)$ describing the probability that object O is in state s. For each s, $P(s)$ is a real number in the range $0 \leq P(s) \leq 1$; over all $s \in S_O$, the $P(s)$ sum to 1. We can extend our vector description to handle this uncertainty, simply by setting each entry $v_s = P(S)$. The object O is in exactly one of these states, but we don't know which one.

Suppose instead that we have two of these objects: O_1 and O_2. If these two objects interact, we simply need to figure out what state each was in beforehand and then what state each goes to after the interaction. If we have uncertainty about what states they are in, we simply need to work through the probabilities. That is, we work through each choice of $s_1 \in S_O$ and $s_2 \in S_O$.

For example, suppose that t_1 and t_2 are the new states of O_1 and O_2, respectively, when O_1 is in s_1 and O_2 is in s_2. If v_1 and v_2 be the vectors of O_1 and O_2, respectively, then the probability that O_1 is in s_1 and O_2 is also in s_2 is $v_1[s_1] \cdot v_2[s_2]$. So, we add $v_1[s_1] \cdot v_2[s_2]$ to the probability that O_1 goes to t_1 and also to the probability that O_2 to t_2. And so on.

The Unnatural Quantum Model.   The quantum model is like this intuitive model but branches out in a few surprising directions.

As before, if object O can be in one state from a set S_O of states, we can describe its state with a vector v consisting of an entry for each element of S_O. However, now, we express uncertainty by using *complex* numbers[1]. Each such entry is called an *amplitude*; the squared moduli[2] of the amplitudes sum to 1.

Quantum mechanics adopts the convention of writing states using "$| \rangle$" notation: for example, $|0\rangle$ and $|1\rangle$ for a 1-bit register. We then describe the state of the object as $w|0\rangle + v|1\rangle$, where $w, v \in \mathbb{C}$ are the amplitudes. Naively, we might suspect that these amplitudes are like probabilities; if the object has more than one nonzero amplitude, then it is still in one state, but which state that is is somehow reflected by the amplitude. However, it is stranger than that—more than one nonzero amplitude means that we cannot know what state the object is in, because it literally *is in more than one state*. This arrangement is called a *superposition of states*.

An object's ability to be in multiple states simultaneously leads to some surprising things. For one thing, we might wonder about why we never actually see an object in more than one state at one time. Something called the *collapse of the wave function* is responsible for this. If we make an observation of an object that is in a superposition of states, the object collapses into one state. Which state we see is determined probabilistically by the amplitudes—if object is in $w|0\rangle + v|1\rangle$, the object goes to $|0\rangle$ with probability $|w|^2$ and $|1\rangle$ with probability $|v|^2$. What's

---

1. Recall that the complex numbers $\mathbb{C}$ are numbers of the form $w = a + bi$, where $a, b \in \mathbb{R}$ and $i = \sqrt{-1}$.
2. For a complex $w = a + bi$, the *squared moduli* $|w|^2 = a^2 + b^2$.

even stranger here is that the object *stays* in the state we see. Observing the object changes the state of the object—its state *becomes* the state we observe.

Being in more than one state at a time also affects what happens when two objects interact. In the simpler uncertainty model, we merely had to think about the probability that objects O_1 and O_2 were in some particular states and then figure out what happens in that combination. However, with superposition of states, each state in O_1's superposition interacts with each state in O_2's superposition, all at the same time. Every state in the superposition contributes in an interaction. Furthermore, because these amplitudes are complex, we can end up with *constructive interference* and *destructive interference* between states. In fact, these phenomena caused the optical conundrums that helped motivate quantum theory in the first place.

A.5.3 The Root-Not Gate

To understand the computational implications of this model, let's consider a new kind of logic gate: *ROOT-NOT*. (Deutsch gives a nice discussion of this concept [Deu89].) We're familiar with the comfortable world of Boolean gates. Can we build a Boolean gate G such that G composed with G is *NOT*? Can we build a Boolean gate G that flips coins?

Our initial answer is: of course not! If $G \circ G = NOT$, then we must have:

$$G(G(1)) = 0,$$
$$G(G(0)) = 1.$$

We can then work through the possibilities. If $G(1) = 1$, then $G(G(1)) = 1$, which breaks the rule. So, $G(1) = 0$. Similarly, we can establish that $G(0) = 1$. But then $G(G(1)) = G(0) = 1$, which also breaks the rule. So, we're stuck.

However, suppose that we build gates that use complex amplitudes and superpositions of states and operate on *qubits*. (The field defines a *qubit* to be a superposition of $|0\rangle$ and $|1\rangle$.) Then we might build a G that acts on the $|0\rangle$ and $|1\rangle$ components of its input as follows:

$$G(|0\rangle) = \frac{i}{\sqrt{2}}|0\rangle + \frac{1}{\sqrt{2}}|1\rangle$$
$$G(|1\rangle) = \frac{1}{\sqrt{2}}|0\rangle + \frac{i}{\sqrt{2}}|1\rangle.$$

What happens when we run G on $|0\rangle$ and then run G again on the result?

$$G(G(|0\rangle)) = G\left(\frac{i}{\sqrt{2}}|0\rangle + \frac{1}{\sqrt{2}}|1\rangle\right)$$

$$= \frac{i}{\sqrt{2}}G(|0\rangle) + \frac{1}{\sqrt{2}}G(|1\rangle)$$

$$= \frac{i}{\sqrt{2}}\left(\frac{i}{\sqrt{2}}|0\rangle + \frac{1}{\sqrt{2}}|1\rangle\right) + \frac{1}{\sqrt{2}}\left(\frac{1}{\sqrt{2}}|0\rangle + \frac{i}{\sqrt{2}}|1\rangle\right)$$

$$= -\frac{1}{2}|0\rangle + \frac{i}{2}|1\rangle + \frac{1}{2}|0\rangle + \frac{i}{2}|1\rangle$$

$$= i|1\rangle.$$

When the wave function collapses, we see 1! Similarly, $G(G(|1\rangle))$ yields $|0\rangle$. G composed with itself is *NOT*—hence G is *ROOT-NOT*.

What happens if we feed $|0\rangle$ to G and observe the result? If we look at the amplitudes, we see that we will observe $|0\rangle$ with probability $\frac{1}{2}$ and $|1\rangle$ with probability $\frac{1}{2}$. So, one stage of G flips a coin, but running two stages of G inverts the original input. Yes, this is counterintuitive. But yes, this is how the universe works.

This *ROOT-NOT* gate gives a flavor of the power of quantum computing. Compare things like *ROOT-NOT* to standard Boolean gates—we can do things in a few steps that are much more complicated in the traditional model.

Bibliography

This bibliography lists the papers, books, and Web publications cited in the book. This list is comprehensive, in that we have tried to paint a complete picture of system security, and these are its supporting citations. However, this list is certainly not *exhaustive*. We have cited works that were historically relevant or gave more detail on a topic or were good examples of the idea being discussed. However, by no means could we cite *all* important works in the literature—that bibliography alone would take another book.

[AA04]   D. Atkins and R. Autstein. RFC 3833: Threat Analysis of the Domain Name System (DNS), August 2004. www.ietf.org/rfc/rfc3833.txt.

[AAL⁺05a]   R. Arends, R. Autstein, M. Larson, D. Massey, and S. Rose. RFC 4033: DNS Security Introduction and Requirements, March 2005. www.ietf.org/rfc/rfc4033.txt.

[AAL⁺05b]   R. Arends, R. Autstein, M. Larson, D. Massey, and S. Rose. RFC 4034: Resource Records for the DNS Security Extensions, March 2005. www.ietf.org/rfc/rfc4034.txt.

[AAL⁺05c]   R. Arends, R. Autstein, M. Larson, D. Massey, and S. Rose. RFC 4035: Protocol Modifications for the DNS Security Extensions, March 2005. www.ietf.org/rfc/rfc4035.txt.

[ABF⁺03]   C. Aumüller, P. Bier, W. Fischer, P. Hofreiter, and J.-P. Seifert. Fault Attacks on RSA with CRT: Concrete Results and Practical Countermeasures. In *Cryptographic Hardware and Embedded Systems—CHES 2002*, pp. 260–275. Springer-Verlag LNCS 2523, 2003.

[ABK⁺07]   D. Agrawal, S. Baktir, D. Karakoyunlu, P. Rohatgi, and B. Sunar. Trojan Detection Using IC Fingerprinting. In *Proceedings of the 2007 IEEE Symposium on Security and Privacy*, pp. 296–310. IEEE Computer Society Press, May 2007.

[AD04]   T. W. Arnold and L. P. Van Doorn. The IBM PCIXCC: A New Cryptographic Coprocessor for the IBM eServer. *IBM Journal of Research and Development* 48(3/4): 2004.

[AES06]   AESec Corporation, June 2006. http://www.aesec.com.

[AK96]   R. Anderson and M. Kuhn. Tamper Resistance—A Cautionary Note. In *Proceedings of the 2nd USENIX Workshop on Electronic Commerce*, pp. 1–11, 1996.

[AK97]   R. Anderson and M. Kuhn. Low Cost Attacks on Tamper Resistant Devices. In *Proceedings of the 1997 Security Protocols Workshop*, pp. 125–136. Springer-Verlag LNCS 1361, 1997.

[Ale96]   Aleph One. Smashing the Stack for Fun and Profit. *Phrack* (49): 1996.

[AM03]   A. Alsaid and D. Martin. Detecting Web Bugs with Bugnosis: Privacy Advocacy through Education. In *Privacy Enhancing Technologies—PET 2002*. Springer-Verlag LNCS 2482, 2003.

[And01]   R. Anderson. Why Information Security Is Hard—An Economic Perspective. In *Proceedings of the 17th Annual Computer Security Applications Conference (ACSAC)*, 2001.

[AS99]   A. Adams and M. A. Sasse. Users Are Not the Enemy: Why Users Compromise Security Mechanisms and How to Take Remedial Measures. *Communications of the ACM* 42:41–46, 1999.

[AS04]   Y. Ali and S. W. Smith. Flexible and Scalable Public Key Security for SSH. In *Public Key Infrastructure: EuroPKI 2004*, pp. 43–56. Springer-Verlag, LNCS 3093, June 2004.

[Auc96]   D. Aucsmith. Tamper Resistant Software: An Implementation. In *Proceedings of the First International Workshop on Information Hiding*, pp. 317–333. Springer-Verlag LNCS 1174, 1996.

[BA01]   M. Bond and R. Anderson. API-Level Attacks on Embedded Systems. *IEEE Computer* 34:64–75, 2001.

[Bac00]   R. G. Bace. *Intrusion Detection*. Macmillan, 2000.

[BAN90]   D. Burrows, M. Abadi, and R. Needham. *A Logic of Authentication*. Digital Equipment Corporation, February 1990. DEC SRC Research Report 39.

[BB03]   D. Boneh and D. Brumley. Remote Timing Attacks Are Practical. In *Proceedings of the 12th USENIX Security Symposium*, August 2003.

[BBC06a]   BBC. "Porn-link" Safety Advert Banned, August 2006. http://news.bbc.co.uk/1/hi/uk_news/5277012.stm.

[BBC06b]   BBC. Sex Cues Ruin Men's Decisiveness, April 2006. http://news.bbc.co.uk/2/hi/health/4921690.stm.

[BDF+03]   P. Barham, B. Dragovic, K. Fraser, S. Hand, T. Harris, A. Ho, R. Neugebauer, I. Pratt, and A. Warfield. Xen and the Art of Virtualization. In *SOSP '03: Proceedings of the Nineteenth ACM Symposium on Operating Systems Principles*, pp. 164–177, 2003.

[BDL97]   D. Boneh, R. A. DeMillo, and R. J. Lipton. On the Importance of Checking Cryptographic Protocols for Faults. In *Advances in Cryptology, Proceedings of EUROCRYPT '97*, pp. 37–51. Springer-Verlag LNCS 1233, 1997. A revised version appeared in the *Journal of Cryptology* in 2001.

[BDSG04]   D. Balfanz, G. Durfee, D. Smetters, and R. Grinter, In Search of Usable Security: Five Lessons from the Field. *IEEE Security and Privacy* 2(5): 19–24, 2004.

[Bel89]   S. Bellovin. Security Problems in the TCP/IP Protocol Suite. *Computer Communications Review* 2(19):32–48, 1989.

[Bel03]   S. Bellovin. RFC 3514: The Security Flag in the IPv4 Header, April 2003. www.ietf.org/rfc/rfc3514.txt.

[Ber05]   D. Bernstein. Cache-Timing Attacks on AES, April 2005. `cr.yp.to/antiforgery/cachetiming-20050414.pdf`.

[BFIK99a]   M. Blaze, J. Feigenbaum, J. Ioannidis, and A. Keromytis. IETF RFC 2704: The KeyNote Trust-Management System, version 2, September 1999.

[BFIK99b]   M. Blaze, J. Feigenbaum, J. Ioannidis, and A. Keromytis. The Role of Trust Management in Distributed Systems. *Secure Internet Programming* 1603:185–210, 1999. Lecture Notes in Computer Science.

[BFL96]   M. Blaze, J. Feigenbaum, and J. Lacy. Decentralized Trust Management. In *Proceedings of the 1996 IEEE Symposium on Security and Privacy*, pp. 164–173. IEEE Computer Society Press, May 1996.

[BFMS07]   S. Bratus, A. Ferguson, D. McIlroy, and S. W. Smith. Pastures: Towards Usable Security Policy Engineering. In *Proceedings of the Second International Conference on Availability, Reliability and Security (ARES 2007)*, pp. 1052–1059. IEEE Computer Society, April 2007.

[BFS98]   M. Blaze, J. Feigenbaum, and M. Strauss. Compliance-Checking in the PolicyMaker Trust Management System. In *Proceedings of Second International Conference on Financial Cryptography (FC '98)* 1465: 254–274, 1998.

[BGW01]   N. Borisov, I. Goldberg, and D. Wagner. Intercepting Mobile Communications: The Insecurity of 802.11. In *Proceedings of the 7th Annual International Conference on Mobile Computing and Networking*, pp. 180–189. ACM Press, 2001.

[BH02]   R. Bolton and D. Hand. Statistical Fraud Detection: A Review. *Statistical Science* 17(3):235–255, 2002.

[Bib77]   K. Biba. *Integrity Considerations for Secure Computer Systems*. The MITRE Corporation, April 1977. Technical Report ESD-TR-76-372.

[BIH+93]   R. Bird, I. Gopal, A. Herzberg, P. Janson, S. Kutten, R. Molva, and M. Yung. Systematic Design of a Family of Attack-Resistant Authentication Protocols. *IEEE Journal on Selected Areas in Communications* 11(5):679–693, 1993.

[Bih99]   E. Biham. Cryptanalysis of Triple Modes of Operation. *Journal of Cryptology: The Journal of the International Association for Cryptologic Research* 12(3):161–184, 1999.

[Bir89]   A. Birrell. *An Introduction to Programming with Threads*. DEC Systems Research Center, January 1989. Technical Report 35.

[BL76]   D. Bell and L. LaPadula. *Secure Computer Systems: Unified Exposition and Multics Interpretation*. The MITRE Corporation, March 1976. Technical Report ESD-TR-75-306, MTR 2997 Rev. 1.

[ble02]   blexim. Basic Integer Overflows. *Phrack*, 0x0b(0x3c), 2002.

[BMG01]   B. Blakley, E. McDermott, and D. Geer. Information Security Is Information Risk Management. In *Proceedings of New Security Paradigm Workshop*. ACM, 2001.

[Bor64]   J. L. Borges. The Library of Babel, in *Labyrinths: Selected Stories & Other Writings*, translated by James E. Irby. New York: New Directions, 1964.

[BR94]   M. Bellare and P. Rogaway. Optimal Asymmetric Encryption—How to Encrypt with RSA. In *Advances in Cryptology—Eurocrypt '94*, pp. 92–111. Springer-Verlag, 1994.

[Bri01]   M. Bristow. Alcatel Admits More Than They Meant To. *The Risks Digest*, 21(35), 2001.

[BS03]   S. Brostoff and A. Sasse. Ten Strikes and You're Out: Increasing the Number of Login Attempts Can Improve Password Usability. In *ACM Workshop on Human-Computer Interaction and Security Systems*, April 2003.

[BSD05]   S. Bhatkar, R. Sekar, and D. DuVarney. Efficient Techniques for Comprehensive Protection from Memory Error Exploits. In *14th USENIX Security Symposium*, August 2005.

[Bus04]   George W. Bush. Homeland Security Presidential Directive/HSPD12, August 2004. www.whitehouse.gov/news/releases/2004/08/20040827-8.html.

[But04]   Declan Butler. Censored Words Unmasked, May 2004. www.nature.com/news/2004/040510/full/040510-8.html.

[BV98]   D. Boneh and R. Venkatesan. Breaking RSA May Not Be Equivalent to Factoring. In *Eurocrypt '98*, pp. 59–71. Springer-Verlag LNCS 1233, 1998.

[Cam96]   L. J. Camp. Privacy & Reliability in Internet Commerce. Ph. D. thesis, Carnegie Mellon University, August 1996.

[Cam01]   Peter Campbell. France Telecom Inadvertent Disclosure Blamed on "Computer Error." *The Risks Digest* 21(65), 2001.

[CDFT98]   J. Callas, L. Donnerhacke, H. Finney, and R. Thayer. RFC 2440: OpenPGP Message Format, November 1998. www.ietf.org/rfc/rfc2440.txt.

[CDvD+03]   D. Clarke, S. Devadas, M. van Dijk, B. Gassend, and G. Suh. Incremental Multiset Hash Functions and Their Application to Memory Integrity Checking. In *Advances in Cryptology—ASIACRYPT*, pp. 188–207. Springer-Verlag LNCS 2894, 2003.

[CEE+01]   D. Clark, J. Elien, C. Ellison, M. Fredette, A. Morcos, and R. Rivest. Certificate Chain Discovery in SPKI/SDSI. *Journal of Computer Security* 9(4):285–322, 2001.

[CER]   CERT's OCTAVE Approach Homepage. www.cert.org/octave.

[CGP99]   E. Clarke, O. Grumberg, and D. Peled. *Model Checking*. MIT Press, 1999.

[Cha85]   D. Chaum. Security without Identification: Transaction Systems to Make Big Brother Obsolete. *Communications of the ACM* 28(10):1030–1044, 1985.

[CHJ99]   D. Coppersmith, S. Halevi, and C. Jutla. ISO 9796-1 and the New Forgery Strategy, 1999. grouper.ieee.org/groups/1363/contrib.html. Research contribution to P1386.

[Cig]   Cigital Labs. ITS4: Software Security Tool. www.cigital.com/its4.

[CJM00]   E. M. Clarke, S. Jha, and W. Marrero. Verifying Security Protocols with Brutus. ACM Transactions on Software Engineering and Methodology 9 (4): 443–487, 2000.

[CNM02]   L. J. Camp, H. Nissenbaum, and C. McGrath. Trust: A Collision of Paradigms. In *Proceedings of the 5th International Conference on Financial Cryptography*, pp. 91–105. Springer-Verlag LNCS 2339, 2002.

[CNS99]   J. Coron, D. Naccache, and J. Stern. On the Security of RSA Padding. *Lecture Notes in Computer Science* 1666:1–18, 1999.

[COB03]   D. Chadwick, A. Otenko, and E. Ball. Role-Based Access Control with X.509 Attribute Certificates. *IEEE Internet Computing*, 2003.

[Coh63]   J. Cohen. On the Nature of Mathematical Proofs. In *A Stress Analysis of a Strapless Evening Gown: Essays for a Scientific Age*. Prentice-Hall, 1963.

[Col05]   R. P. Colwell. *The Pentium Chronicles: The People, Passion, and Politics Behind Intel's Landmark Chips*. Wiley-IEEE Computer Society Press, 2005.

[Com06]   G. Combs. Wireshark, 2006. www.wireshark.org/.

[Cor]   Core Security Technologies. Core Impact, 2006. www.coresecurity.com.

[COS04]   COSO: The Committee of Sponsoring Organizations of the Treadway Commission. Enterprise Risk Management—Integrated Framework, 2004. www.coso.org/publications.htm.

[Cov]   Coverity Inc. Prevent. www.coverity.com/products/prevent.html.

[CPG+04]   J. Chow, B. Pfaff, T. Garfinkel, K. Christopher, and M. Rosenblum. Understanding Data Lifetime via Whole System Simulation. In *Proceedings of the 13th USENIX Security Symposium*, 2004.

[cpp]   CppUnit. cppunit.sourceforge.net.

[CPW+98]   C. Cowan, C. Pu, J. Walpole, P. Bakke, S. Beattie, A. Grier, P. Wagle, Q. Zhang, and H. Hinton. StackGuard: Automatic Adaptive Detection and Prevention of Buffer-Overflow Attacks. In *Proceedings of the 7th Annual Usenix Security Symposium*, pp. 63–78, January 1998.

[Cra98]   S. Craver. On Public-Key Steganography in the Presence of an Active Warden. In *Proceedings of the Second International Conference on Information Hiding*, Springer-Verlag LNCS 1525, 1998.

[Cra02]   L. Cranor. *Web Privacy with P3P*. O'Reilly, 2002.

[Cra03]   L. Cranor. Designing a Privacy Preference Specification Interface: A Case Study. In *ACM/CHI2003 Workshop on Human-Computer Interaction and Security Systems*, 2003.

[CRK+07]   P.-C. Cheng, P. Rohatgi, C. Keser, P. A. Karger, G. M. Wagner, and A. Schuett Reninger. Fuzzy Multi-Level Security: An Experiment on Quantified Risk-Adaptive Access Control. In *Proceedings of the IEEE Symposium on Security and Privacy*, May 2007.

[CST95]   L. J. Camp, M. Sirbu, and J. D. Tygar. Token and Notational Money in Electronic Commerce. In *1st USENIX Workshop on Electronic Commerce*, 1995.

[CT91]   T. Cover and J. Thomas. *Elements of Information Theory*. Wiley, 1991.

[CTS95]   B. Cox, J. D. Tygar, and M. Sirbu. Netbill Security and Transaction Protocol. In *1st USENIX Workshop on Electronic Commerce*, pp. 77–88, 1995.

[CW87]   D. Clark and D. Wilson. A Comparison of Commercial and Military Computer Security Policies. In *Proceedings of the IEEE Symposium on Security and Privacy*, pp. 184–194, 1987.

[CW96]   E. Clarke and J. Wing. Formal Methods: State of the Art and Future Directions. *ACM Computing Surveys* 28:626–643, 1996.

[CWHWW03]   N. Cam-Winget, R. Housley, D. Wagner, and J. Walker. Security Flaws in 802.11 Data Link Protocols. *Communications of the ACM* 46(5), 2003.

[CWL+01]   S. Craver, M. Wu, B. Lie, A. Stubblefield, B. Swartzlander, D. Wallach, D. Dean, and E. Felten. Reading between the Lines: Lessons from the SDMI Challenge. In *Proceedings of the 10th USENIX Security Symposium*, August 2001.

[CXN+05]   S. Chen, J. Xu, N. Nakka, Z. Kalbarczyk, and R. K. Iyer. Defeating Memory Corruption Attacks via Pointera Taintedness Detection. In *Proceedings of the International Conference on Dependable Systems and Networks*, pp. 378–387, 2005.

[DCJ+07]   M. Dalla Preda, M. Christodorescu, S. Jha, and S. Debray. A Semantics-Based Approach to Malware Detection. In *Proceedings of the 34th Annual Symposium on Principles of Programming Languages (POPL 2007)*, 2007.

[Den76]   D. Denning. A Lattice Model of Secure Information Flow. *Communications of the ACM* 19(5):236–243, 1976.

[Den87]   D. Denning. An Intrusion-Detection Model. *IEEE Transactions on Software Engineering*, SE-13(2):222–232, 1987.

[Der96]   M. Dery. Escape Velocity: Cyberculture at the End of the Century. Grove Press, 1996.

[Deu89]   D. Deutsch. Quantum Computational Networks. In *Proceedings of the Royal Society of London* A425: 73–90, 1989.

[DEW06]   D. DeBarr and Z. Eyler-Walker. Closing the Gap: Automated Screening of Tax Returns to Identify Egregious Tax Shelters. *SIGKDD Explorations* 8(1):11–16, 2006.

[DH76]   W. Diffie and M. Hellman. New Directions in Cryptography. *IEEE Transactions on Information Theory*, IT-22(6):644–654, 1976.

[DLS97]   B. Dole, S. Lodin, and E. Spafford. Misplaced Trust: Kerberos 4 Session Keys. In *Proceedings of 4th Symposium on Network and Distributed System Security*, pp. 60–71. IEEE Press, 1997.

[DMS04]   R. Dingledine, N. Mathewson, and P. Syverson. Tor: The Second-Generation Onion Router. In *Proceedings of the 13th USENIX Security Symposium*, August 2004.

[DMS06]   M. Dowd, J. McDonald, and J. Schuh. *The Art of Software Security Assessment*. Addison-Wesley, 2006.

[DNS]   DNSSEC.NET. DNS Threats and DNS Weaknesses. www.dnssec.net/dns-threats.php.

[DNSW01]   M. Donner, D. Nochin, D. Shasha, and W. Walasek. Algorithms and Experience in Increasing the Intelligibility and Hygiene of Access Control in Large Organizations. In *Proceedings of the IFIP TC11/ WG11.3 Fourteenth Annual Working Conference on Database Security*. Kluwer, 2001.

[Dob96a]   H. Dobbertin. The Status of MD5 after a Recent Attack. *CryptoBytes* 2(2), 1996. The technical newsletter of RSA Laboratories.

[Dob96b]   H. Dobbertin. Cryptanalysis of MD5 Compress, May 1996. www.cs.ucsd.edu/users/bsy/dobbertin.ps. Announcement on Internet.

[DoD85]   Department of Defense Trusted Computer System Evaluation Criteria, December 1985. DoD 5200.28-STD. This is better known as the Orange Book, owing to the color of the hardcopy cover.

[DPS07]   N. D'Cunha, M. Pala, and S. W. Smith. *Programming Languages Security: A Survey for Practitioners*. Department of Computer Science, Dartmouth College, forthcoming.

[DR06]   T. Dierks and E. Rescorla. RFC 4346: The Transport Layer Security (TLS) Protocol, Version 1.1, April 2006. `www.ietf.org/rfc/rfc4346.txt`.

[DTH06]   R. Dhamija, J. D. Tygar, and M. Hearst. Why Phishing Works. In *Proceedings of the Conference on Human Factors in Computing Systems (CHI2006)*, 2006.

[Dwo05]   M. Dworkin. *Recommendation for Block Cipher Modes of Operation: The CMAC Mode for Authentication*. NIST Special Publication 800-38B, May 2005.

[Dwo07]   M. Dworkin. *Recommendation for Block Cipher Modes of Operation: Galois/Counter Mode (GCM) and GMAC*. NIST Special Publication 800-38D (Draft), June 2007.

[EAH+01]   Y. Elley, A. Anderson, S. Hanna, S. Mullan, R. Perlman, and S. Proctor. Building Certification Paths: Forward vs. Reverse. In *Network and Distributed System Symposium Conference Proceedings*, 2001.

[eey]   eEye Digital Security. `www.eeye.com`.

[EFF98]   EFF: The Electronic Frontier Foundation. *Cracking DES: Secrets of Encryption Research, Wiretap Politics, and Chip Design*. O'Reilly, 1998.

[EFL+99]   C. Ellison, B. Frantz, B. Lampson, R. Rivest, B. Thomas, and T. Ylnen. RFC 2693: SPKI Certificate Theory, September 1999. `www.ietf.org/rfc/rfc2693.txt`.

[Eld06]   Eldos. SecureBlackbox—Completely Managed SSL Components for .NET Framework, 2006. `www.eldos.com/sbb/net-ssl.php`.

[Ell96]   C. Ellison. Establishing Identity without Certification Authorities. In *Proceedings of the Sixth Annual USENIX Security Symposium*, pp. 67–76, July 1996.

[Ell99]   C. Ellison. RFC 2692: SPKI Requirements, September 1999. `www.ietf.org/rfc/rfc2692.txt`.

[Ell02]   C. Ellison. Improvements on Conventional PKI Wisdom. In *Proceedings of the 1st Annual PKI Research Workshop*, April 2002.

[EPI]   EPIC Opposes DoubleClick Class Action Settlement. `www.epic.org/privacy/internet/cookies/`.

[ER89]   M. Eichin and J. Rochlis. With Microscope and Tweezers: An Analysis of the Internet Virus of November 1998. In *Proceedings 1989 IEEE Symposium on Security and Privacy*, pp. 326–343, 1989.

[F+99]   J. Franks et al. RFC 2617: HTTP Authentication: Basic and Digest Access Authentication, June 1999. `www.ietf.org/rfc/rfc2617.txt`.

[Fen05]   Kevin Fenzi. Tuning Your SELinux Policy with Audit2allow. *SysAdmin* 14(8), 2005.

[Fey84]   R. Feynman. *Surely You're Joking, Mr. Feynman! (Adventures of a Curious Character)*. Norton, 1984.

[Fil06]   Filter Worldwide. Bluecasting: The Proximity Marketing System, 2006. `www.bluecasting.com`.

[Fis88]   D. Fiske. Another ATM Story. *The Risks Digest* 6(66), 1988.

[FK92]   D.F. Ferraiolo and D. R. Kuhn. Role Based Access Control. In *15th National Computer Security Conference*, 1992.

[FMS01]   S. Fluhrer, I. Mantin, and A. Shamir. Weaknesses in the Key Scheduling Algorithm of RC4. *Selected Areas in Cryptography*, 2001.

[Fra98]   Neil Fraser. Neural Network Follies, September 1998. http://neil.fraser.name/writing/tank/.

[Fre06]   The FreeS/WAN Project. Linux FreeS/WAN, 2006. www.freeswan.org.

[FS00]   E. Felten and M. Schneider. Timing Attacks on Web Privacy. In *ACM Conference on Computer and Communications Security*, pp. 25–32, 2000.

[FSSF01]   K. Fu, E. Sit, K. Smith, and N. Feamster. Dos and Don'ts of Client Authentication on the Web. In *Proceedings of the 10th USENIX Security Symposium*, August 2001.

[Fyo06a]   Fyodor. NMap Network Scanner, 2006. www.insecure.org/nmap/.

[Fyo06b]   Fyodor. Remote OS Detection via TCP/IP Fingerprinting, 2006. www.insecure.org/nmap/osdetect.

[GA03]   S. Govindavajhala and A. Appel. Using Memory Errors to Attack a Virtual Machine. IEEE Symposium on Security and Privacy May, 2003.

[Gar05]   S. Garfinkel. Design Principles and Patterns for Computer Systems That Are Simultaneously Secure and Usable. Ph. D. thesis, Massachussets Institute of Technology, 2005.

[GCvD02]   B. Gassend, D. Clarke, M. van Dijk, and S. Devadas. Silicon Physical Random Functions. In *Proceedings of the 9th ACM Conference on Computer and Communications Security*, pp. 148–160, 2002.

[GHT05]   C. Gebotys, S. Ho, and C. Tiu. EM Analysis of Rijndael and ECC on a Wireless Java-Based PDA. In *Workshop on Cryptographic Hardware and Embedded Systems*, 2005.

[GKS+04]   N. Goffee, S. H. Kim, S. W. Smith, W. Taylor, M. Zhao, and J. Marchesini. Greenpass: Decentralized, PKI-Based Authorization for Wireless LANs. In *3rd Annual PKI Research and Development Workshop Proceedings*. NIST/NIH/Internet2, April 2004. www.cs.dartmouth.edu/~sws/papers/greenpass-pki04-final.pdf.

[GL02]   L. A. Gordon and M. P. Loeb. The Economics of Information Security Investment. *ACM Transactions on Information and System Security* 5(4):438–457, 2002.

[GM82]   S. Goldwasser and S. Micali. Probabilistic Encryption & How to Play Mental Poker Keeping Secret All Partial Information. In *Proceedings of the Fourteenth Annual ACM Symposium on Theory of Computing*, 1982.

[GM00]   M. Girault and J.-F. Misarsky. Cryptanalysis of Countermeasures Proposed for Repairing ISO 9796-1. In *Proceedings of Eurocrypt 2000*, pp. 81–90. Springer-Verlag LNCS 1807, 2000.

[GM05]   S. Garfinkel and R. Miller. Johnny 2: A User Test of Key Continuity Management with S/MIME and Outlook Express. In *Symposium on Usable Privacy and Security*, 2005. SOUPS 2005.

[GO96]   O. Goldreich and R. Ostrovsky. Software Protection and Simulation on Oblivious RAMs. *Journal of the ACM* 43(3):431–473, 1996.

[GR05]   S. Garfinkel and B. Rosenberg (eds). *RFID : Applications, Security, and Privacy.* Addison-Wesley, 2005.

[Gri00]   F. Grieu. A Chosen Message's Attack on the ISO/IEC 9796-1 Signature Scheme. In *Proceedings of Eurocrypt 2000*, pp. 70–80. Springer-Verlag LNCS 1807, 2000.

[Gri06]   J. Grieves. Personal conversation. Jay Grieves co-created Symantec's Policy Manager product, 2006.

[GT05]   E. Gal and S. Toledo. Algorithms and Data Structures for FLASH Memories. *ACM Computing Survey* 37(2):138–163, 2005.

[Gut96]   P. Gutmann. Secure Deletion of Data from Magnetic and Solid-State Memory. In *Proceedings of the 6th USENIX Security Symposium*, pp. 77–89, 1996.

[Gut97]   P. Gutmann. How to Recover Private Keys for Microsoft Internet Explorer, Internet Information Server, Outlook Express, and Many Others—or—Where Do Your Encryption Keys Want to Go Today? 1997. `www.cs.auckland.ac.nz/~pgut001/pubs/breakms.txt`.

[Gut01]   P. Gutmann. Data Remanence in Semiconductor Devices. In *Proceedings of the 10th USENIX Security Symposium*, pp. 39–54, 2001.

[Gut02]   P. Gutmann. PKI: It's Not Dead, Just Resting. *IEEE Computer* 35(8):41–49, 2002.

[Gut04]   P. Gutmann. Why the Internet Isn't Secure Yet, Dammit. In *AusCERT Asia Pacific Information Technology Security Conference; Computer Security: Are We There Yet?* 2004.

[GW96]   I. Goldberg and D. Wagner. Randomness and the Netscape Browser. *Dr. Dobb's Journal*, pp. 66–70, 1996.

[Haf06]   K. Hafner. Researchers Yearn to Use AOL Logs, but They Hesitate. *The New York Times*, 2006.

[Has88]   J. Hastad. Solving Simultaneous Modular Equations of Low Degree. *SIAM Journal on Computing* 17:336–341, 1988.

[Hay03]   T. Hayes. A Vulnerability in SSL/TLS Implementations of Ciphersuites that Use Block Ciphers, 2003. `www.mozilla.org/projects/security/pki/nss/news/vaudenay-cbc.html`.

[HB05]   G. Hoglund and J. Butler. *Rootkits, Subverting the Windows Kernel.* Addison Wesley, 2005.

[Hed96]   S. R. Hedberg. AI & Taxes. *IEEE Intelligent Systems and Their Applications* 11(2), 1996.

[Hen01]   P. Henry. The Old Ones Are the Best Ones: Hidden Info in MS Word Documents. February 2001.

[Her06]   J. Herzog. Applying Protocol Analysis to Security Device Interfaces. *IEEE Security and Privacy*, 4(4):84–87, 2006.

[HHE+04]   S. Harris, A. Harper, C. Eagle, J. Ness, and M. Lester. *Gray Hat Hacking: The Ethical Hacker's Handbook.* McGraw-Hill, 2004.

[Hig07]   K. J. Higgins. CSRF Bug Runs Rampant, June 2007. `www.darkreading.com/document.asp?doc_id=127731&WT.svl=news1_1`.

[HL03]   M. Howard and D. LeBlanc. *Writing Secure Code.* Microsoft, 2003.

[HM96]   N. Haller and C. Metz. RFC 1938: A One-Time Password System, May 1996. `www.apps.ietf.org/rfc/rfc1938.html`.

[HM04]   G. Hoglund and G. McGraw. *Exploiting Software: How to Break Code.* Addison-Wesley, 2004.

[Hog06]   G. Hoglund. 2006. www.rootkit.com.

[Hol04]   G. Holzmann. *The Spin Model Checker.* Addison-Wesley, 2004.

[Hol05]   W. J. Holstein. An Algorithm as a Pickax. *The New York Times,* 2005.

[Hou06]   R. Housley. Personal commmunication, April 2006.

[HPS04]   Y. Hu, A. Perrig, and M. Sirbu. SPV: Secure Path Vector Routing for Securing BGP. In *Proceedings of SIGCOMM 2004,* pp. 179–192, August 2004.

[HRU76]   M. A. Harrison, W. L. Ruzzo, and J. D. Ullman. Protection in Operating Systems. *Communications of the ACM* 19(8):461–470, 1976.

[HS91]   S. Haber and W. S. Stornetta. How to Time-Stamp a Digital Document. *Journal of Cryptology* 2:99–111, 1991.

[HTF01]   T. Hastie, R. Tibshirani, and J. Friedman. *The Elements of Statistical Learning.* Springer-Verlag, 2001.

[IEE04]   IEEE Std 1003.1, 2004 Edition, 2004. www.unix.org/version3/ieee_std.html.

[Inf07]   Information Systems Audit and Control Association. Control Objectives for Information and Related Technology, 2007. www.isaca.org/cobit.htm.

[Int04]   Internet Explorer URL Spoofing Vulnerability, February 2004. Secunia Advisory SA10395.

[IS06]   A. Iliev and S. W. Smith. Faerieplay on Tiny Trusted Third Parties. In *Second Workshop on Advances in Trusted Computing (WATC '06),* November 2006.

[ISC]   ISC. BIND Vulnerabilities. www.isc.org/index.pl?/sw/bind/bind-security.php.

[ISO97]   ISO 9796: Information Technology—Digital Signature Scheme Giving Message Recovery—Mechanisms Using Redundancy, 1997. www.iso.org.

[ISO05]   ISO 17799: Information Technology—Security Techniques: Code of Practice for Information Security Management, 2005. www.iso.org/iso/en/prods-services/popstds/informationsecurity.html.

[ISS]   Internet Security Systems. www.iss.net.

[ISW03]   Y. Ishai, A. Sahai, and D. Wagner. Private Circuits: Securing Hardware against Probing Attacks. In *Advances in Cryptology, Proceedings of CRYPTO '03.* Springer-Verlag LNCS, 2003.

[ITA]   ITAR Civil Disobedience: International Arms Trafficker Training Page. http://online.offshore.com.ai/arms-trafficker/.

[Jar04]   Xeni Jardin. P2P in the Legal Crosshairs, March 2004. www.wired.com/news/digiwood/0,62665-1.html.

[JDA02]   A. Jøsang, D. Povey, and A. Ho. What You See Is Not Always What You Sign. In *Proceedings of AUUG2002,* September 2002.

[JK03]   J. Jonsson and B. Kaliski. RFC 3447: Public Key Cryptography Standards (PKCS) #1, 2003. www.ietf.org/rfc/rfc3447.txt.

[Jou04]   A. Joux. Multicollisions in Iterated Hash Functions. Application to Cascaded Constructions. In *Advances in Cryptology, Prcoeedings of CRYPTO '04,* pp. 306–316. Springer-Verlag LNCS 3152, 2004.

[JSTB07]   C. Jackson, D. Simon, D. Tan, and A. Barth. An Evaluation of Extended Validation and Picture-in-Picture Phishing Attacks. In *Proceedings of Usable Security*, 2007.

[Jue06]   A. Juels. RFID Security and Privacy: A Research Survey. *IEEE Journal on Selected Areas in Communications* 24(2), 2006.

[jun]   JUnit. `junit.sourceforge.net`.

[Jut01]   C. Jutla. Encryption Modes with Almost Free Message Integrity. Lecture Notes in Computer Science, 2045, 2001.

[Kah96]   D. Kahn. *The Codebreakers: The Comprehensive History of Secret Communication from Ancient Times to the Internet*, Scribner, (rev. ed.). 1996.

[Kas07]   K. Kaspersky. *Hacker Disassembling Uncovered, 2nd ed.* A-List Publishing, 2007.

[Kau07]   B. Kauer. *OSLO: Improving the Security of Trusted Computing*. Technische Universitat Dresden, Department of Computer Science, Technical Report 2007.

[KCW+06]   S. King, P. Chen, Y. Wang, C. Verbowski, H. Wang, and J. Lorch. SubVirt: Implementing Malware with Virtual Machines. In *Proceedings of the IEEE Symposium on Security and Privacy*, May 2006.

[KEB+07]   T. Karygiannis, B. Eydt, G. Barber, L. Bunn, and T. Phillips. *Guidelines for Secure Radio Frequency Identification (RFID) Systems*. NIST Special Publication 800-98, April 2007.

[Ken03]   S. Kent. Securing the Border Gateway Protocol: A Status Update. In *Seventh IFIP TC-6 TC-11 Conference on Communications and Multimedia Security*, October 2003.

[Ken06]   S. Kent. An Infrastructure Supporting Secure Internet Routing. In *Public Key Infrastructure, Third European PKI Workshop: Theory and Practice*, pp. 116–129. Springer-Verlag LNCS 4043, 2006.

[KJJ]   P. Kocher, J. Jae, and B. Jun. Differential Power Analysis. `www.cryptography.com/resources/whitepapers/DPA.html`.

[KLA+04]   J. Koziol, D. Litchfield, D. Aitel, C. Anley, S. Eren, N. Mehta, and R. Hassell. *The Shellcoder's Handbook: Discovering and Exploiting Security Holes*. J. Wiley, 2004.

[Kli05]   V. Klima. Finding MD5 Collisions on a Notebook PC Using Multimessage Modifications. In *Proceedings of the 3rd International Conference Security and Protection of Information*, May 2005.

[Kli06]   V. Klima. *Tunnels in Hash Functions: MD5 Collisions within a Minute* (extended abstract). IACR ePrint archive, Technical Report 2006/105, March 2006.

[KLS00]   S. Kent, C. Lynn, and K. Seo. Secure Border Gateway Protocol. *IEEE Journal of Selected Areas in Communications* 18(4):582–592, 2000.

[KM00]   R. Kohlas and U. Maurer. Confidence Valuation in a Public-Key Infrastructure Based on Uncertain Evidence. In *Proceedings of the Third International Workshop on Practice and Theory in Public Key Cryptosystems*, pp. 93–112. Springer-Verlag, 2000.

[KM00b]   R. Kohlas and U. Maurer. Reasoning About Public-Key Certification: On Bindings Between Entities and Public Keys. Journal on Selected Areas in Communications, pp. 551–560, 2000

[Ko96]   P. Kocher. Timing Attacks on Implementations of Diffie-Hellman, RSA, DSS, and Other Systems. In Advances in Cryptology—Crypto 96. Springer-Verlag, LNCS 1109, 1996.

[Kor78]   L. Kornfelder. Toward a Practical Public-Key Cryptosystem, 1978. B.S. thesis, Department of Electrical Engineering, MIT.

[Kot06]   M. Kotadia. Mac OS X Hacked in under 30 Minutes, March 6 2006. `www.zdnet.com.au/news/security/soa/Mac_OS_X_hacked_in_less_than_30_minutes/0,2000061744,39241748,00.htm`.

[KPS02]   C. Kaufman, R. Perlman, and M. Speciner. In Chapter 15 *Network Security—Private Communication in a Public World*, 2nd ed. Prentice Hall, 2002.

[KR07]   J. F. Kurose and K. W. Ross. Computer Networking: A Top-Down Approach, Fourth Edition. Addison-Wesley, 2007.

[Kre07]   B. Krebs. Tracking the Password Thieves. *The Washington Post*, 2007.

[KRV04]   C. Kruegel, W. Robertson, and G. Vigna. Detecting Kernel-Level Rootkits through Binary Analysis. In *Proceedings of the 20th Annual Computer Security Applications Conference (ACSAC)*, December 2004.

[KSA02]   K. Kain, S. W. Smith, and R. Asokan. Digital Signatures and Electronic Documents: A Cautionary Tale. In *Advanced Communications and Multimedia Security*, pp. 293–307. Kluwer, 2002.

[KSRW04]   T. Kohno, A. Stubblefield, A. Rubin, and D. Wallach. Analysis of an Electronic Voting System. In *IEEE Symposium on Security and Privacy*, May 2004.

[KZB+91]   P. Karger, M. Zurko, D. Bonin, A. Mason, and C. Kahn. A Retrospective on the VAX VMM Security Kernel. *IEEE Transactions on Software Engineering* 17:1147–1165, 1991.

[L+00]   W. Lee et al. Adaptive Intrusion Detection: A Data Mining Approach. *Artificial Intelligence Review* 14(6):533–567, 2000.

[Lam74]   B. W. Lampson. Protection. *ACM Operating Systems Review* 8(1):18–24, 1974. Reprinted from the *Proceedings of the 5th Princeton Conference on Information Sciences and Systems*, 1971.

[Lam83]   B. Lampson. Hints for Computer System Design. In *9th ACM Symposium on Operating Systems Principles*, 1983.

[Lan81]   C. Landwehr. Formal Models for Computer Security. *ACM Computing Surveys* 13(3), 1981.

[LBM+93]   C. Landwehr, A. Bull, J. McDermott, and W. Choi. A Taxonomy of Computer Program Security Flaws, with Examples. Naval Research Laboratory, November, 1993.

[Lev03]   S. Levy. *Crypto: How the Code Rebels Beat the Government Saving Privacy in the Digital Age*. Diane Publishing, 2003.

[LGF03]   N. Li, B. Grosof, and J. Feigenbaum. Delegation Logic: A Logic-Based Approach to Distributed Authorization. *ACM Transactions on Information and System Security (TISSEC)* 6(1):128–171, 2003.

[Lip81]   R. Lipton. How to Cheat at Mental Poker. In *Proceedings, AMS Short Course on Cryptography*, 1981.

[Lip04]   S. Lipner. The Trustworthy Computing Security Development Lifecycle. In *Proceedings of the 20th Annual Computer Security Applications Conference (ACSAC)*, December 2004.

[LS01]   P. Loscocco and S. Smalley. Integrating Flexible Support for Security
              Policies into the Linux Operating System. In *Proceedings of the FREE-
              NIX Track: 2001 USENIX Annual Technical Conference (FREENIX 01)*,
              2001.

[LTG⁺90]   T. Lunt, A. Tamaru, F. Gilham, R. Jagannathan, P. Neumann, and C. Jalali.
              IDES: A Progress Report. In *Proceedings of the Sixth Annual Computer
              Security Applications Conference*, Dec. 1990.

[LWM03]   N. Li, W. Winsborough, and J. Mitchell. Beyond Proof-of-Compliance:
              Safety and Availability Analysis in Trust Management. In *Proceedings of
              the 2003 IEEE Symposium on Security and Privacy*, pp. 123–139. IEEE
              Computer Society Press, May 2003.

[LWW05]   A. Lenstra, X. Wang, and B. Weger. Colliding X.509 Certificates, 2005.
              Cryptology ePrint Archive, Report 2005/067. eprint.iacr.org.

[Mau96]   U. Maurer. Modeling a Public-Key Infrastructure. In *European Symposium
              on Research in Computer Security (ESORICS)*. Springer-Verlag, LNCS,
              1996.

[McC03]   J. McCabe. *Network Analysis, Architecture and Design*. Morgan Kaufmann,
              2003.

[McE96]   Kirk McElhearn. Hidden File Info that You Do Not Know About. *The
              Risks Digest* 18(41), 1996.

[McG06]   G. McGraw. *Software Security: Building Security In*. Addison-Wesley, 2006.

[McL85]   John McLean. A Comment on the "Basic Security Theorem" of Bell and
              LaPadula. *Information Processing Letters* 20(2):67–70, 1985.

[Met06]   The Metasploit Project. The Metasploit Framework, 2006. www.
              metasploit.com.

[MFS90]   B. Miller, L. Fredriksen, and B. So. An Empirical Study of the Reliability of
              UNIX Utilities. *Communications of the ACM* 33(12), 1990.

[Mic]   MSDN Platform SDK, 2006. msdn.microsoft.com/library/
              default.asp?url=/library/en-us/sdkintro/sdkintro/
              devdoc_platform_software_development_kit_start_pa-
              ge.asp.

[Mic03]   S. Micali. NOVOMODO: Scalable Certificate Validation and Simplified
              PKI Management. In *1st Annual PKI Research Workshop—Proceedings*.
              NIST Special Publication 800-62, 2003.

[Mic04]   Settings May Not Be Applied with URL with Short Filename, June 2004.
              Microsoft Knowledge Base KB179148. support.microsoft.com/
              kb/q179148/.

[Mic06]   Microsoft. FXCop Code Scanner, 2006. www.gotdotnet.com/team/
              fxcop.

[Mit97]   T. Mitchell. *Machine Learning*. McGraw-Hill, 1997.

[MIT06]   MITRE Corporation. Common Vulnerabilities and Exposures, 2006. cve.
              mitre.org.

[MNPS04]   D. Malkhi, N. Nisan, B. Pinkas, and Y. Sella. Fairplay: A Secure Two-
              Party Computation System. In *Proceedings of the 13th USENIX Security
              Symposium*, August 2004.

[MS02]   K. Mitnick and W. Simon. *The Art of Deception: Controlling the Human
              Element of Security*. Wiley, 2002.

[MS05a]   J. Marchesini and S. W. Smith. Modeling Public Key Infrastructure in the
             Real World. In *Public Key Infrastructure: EuroPKI 2005*. Springer-Verlag
             LNCS, June 2005.

[MS05b]   J. Marchesini and S. W. Smith. SHEMP: Secure Hardware Enhanced
             MyProxy. In *Proceedings of Third Annual Conference on Privacy, Security
             and Trust*, October 2005.

[MS07]   C. Masone and S. W. Smith. Towards Usefully Secure Email. *IEEE Technol-
             ogy and Society (Special Issue on Security and Usability)* 26(1):25–34, 2007.

[MSK05]   S. McClure, J. Scambray, and G. Kurtz. *Hacking Exposed*. McGraw-Hill,
             2005.

[MSMW03]   R. MacDonald, S. W. Smith, J. Marchesini, and O. Wild. *Bear: An Open-
             Source Virtual Coprocessor based on TCPA*. Technical Report TR2003-471,
             Department of Computer Science, Dartmouth College, 2003.

[MSWM03]   J. Marchesini, S. W. Smith, O. Wild, and R. MacDonald. *Experimenting
             with TCPA/TCG Hardware, Or: How I Learned to Stop Worrying and Love
             the Bear*. Technical Report TR2003-476, Department of Computer Science,
             Dartmouth College, 2003.

[MSZ03]   J. Marchesini, S. W. Smith, and M. Zhao. Keyjacking: Risks of the Current
             Client-Side Infrastructure. In *2nd Annual PKI Resarch Workshop*. NIST,
             April 2003.

[MSZ05]   J. Marchesini, S. W. Smith, and M. Zhao. Keyjacking: The Surprising
             Insecurity of Client-side SSL. *Computers and Security* 4(2):109–123, 2005.

[Mur06]   S. Murphy. RFC 4272: BGP Security Vulnerabilities Analysis, January 2006.
             `www.ietf.org/rfc/rfc4272.txt`.

[MvOV96]   A. Menezes, P. van Oorschot, and S. Vanstone. *Handbook of Applied
             Cryptography*. CRC Press, 1996.

[Nat94]   *National Training Standard for Information Systems Security (INFOSEC)
             Professionals*. NSTISSI No. 4011. June 1994.

[nco]   NCover: Code Coverage for .NET. `ncover.org`.

[NCS87]   NCSC. Trusted Network Interpretation of the Trusted Computing System
             Evaluation Criteria, July 1987. NCSC-TG-005 Version 1.

[NCS91]   NCSC. A Guide to Understanding Data Remanence in Automated Infor-
             mation Systems, September 1991. NCSC-TG-025 Version 2. This is also
             known as the Forest Green Book.

[NCS95]   NCSC. Final Evaluation Report: Gemini Computers, Inc., Gemini Trusted
             Network Processor Version 1.01, June 1995.

[Nel81]   B. Nelson. Remote Procedure Call. Ph. D. thesis, Department of Computer
             Science, Carnegie-Mellon University, 1981.

[Neu95]   P. Neumann. *Computer-Related Risks*. Addison-Wesley, 1995.

[New05]   Newswise. Securities Fraud Targeted by New Computing Tool, October
             2005. `www.newswise.com/articles/view/515259/`.

[Nii95]   Hideto Niijima. Design of a Solid-State File Using FLASH EEPROM. *IBM
             Journal of Research and Development* 39(5):531–545, 1995.

[NIS01]   NIST. Federal Information Processing Standard 140-2: Security Re-
             quirements for Cryptographic Modules, May 2001. `http://csrc.
             nist.gov/cryptval/140-2.htm`.

[NIS02]   NIST. Federal Information Processing Standard 198: The Keyed-Hash Message Authentication Code (HMAC), March 2002. http://csrc.nist.gov/publications/fips/fips198/fips-198a.pdf.

[NIS07a]   NIST. Federal Information Processing Standards, 2007. http://csrc.nist.gov/publications/fips.

[NIS07b]   NIST. Role Based Access Control, 2007. http://csrc.nist.gov/rbac.

[Nor02]   D. Norman. *The Design of Everyday Things*. Basic Books, 2002.

[NSAa]   The NSA Security-Enhanced Linux Site. www.nsa.gov/selinux/.

[NSAb]   The NSA Verona Site. www.nsa.gov/verona.

[Ope97]   The Open Group. DCE 1.1: Remote Procedure Call, 1997. www.opengroup.org/onlinepubs/9629399.

[Ope06]   OpenBSD Web site, 2006. www.openbsd.org.

[Opp04]   P. Oppenheimer. *Top-Down Network Design*. Cisco Press, 2004.

[OV06]   A. Ornaghi and M. Valleri. Ettercap NG, 2006. ettercap.sourceforge.net.

[Pac06]   John Paczkowski. No, no, no, you weren't supposed to tear down THAT wall. Good Morning Silicon Valley, 2006. http://blogs.siliconvalley.com/gmsv/2006/08/aol_just_cant_d.html.

[PAK99]   F. Petitcolas, R. Anderson, and M. Kuhn. Information Hiding—A Survey. *Proceedings of the IEEE* 87:1062–1078, 1999.

[Pas06]   Passfaces. Passfaces home page, 2006. www.realuser.com.

[PaX06]   The PaX Team. Homepage of the PAX Team. pax.grsecurity.net/.

[PEE06]   C. A. R. Pinheiro, A. G. Evsukoff, and N. F. F. Ebecken. Revenue Recovering with Insolvency Prevention on a Brazilian Telecom Operator. *SIGKDD Explorations* 8(1):65–70, 2006.

[PFMA04]   N. Petroni, T. Fraser, J. Molina, and W. A. Arbaugh. Copilot—A Coprocessor-Based Kernel Runtime Integrity Monitor. In *Proceedings of the 13th USENIX Security Symposium*, pp. 179–194, 2004.

[PH07]   D. Patterson and J. Hennessy. *Computer Organization and Design, 3rd ed. rev.* Morgan Kaufmann, 2007.

[Pie00]   M. Pietrek. Under the Hood. *Microsoft Systems Journal*, 2000.

[Pnu77]   A. Pnueli. The Temporal Logic of Programs. In *Proceedings of the 18th IEEE Symposium Foundations of Computer Science (FOCS 1977)*, pp. 46–57, 1977.

[Pro06]   N. Provos. Systrace, 2006. www.systrace.org.

[PRTG02]   R. Pappu, B. Recht, J. Taylor, and N. Gershenfeld. Physical One-Way Functions. *Science* 297:2026–2030, 2002.

[PT04]   D. Price and A. Tucker. Solaris Zones: Operating System Support for Consolidating Commercial Workloads. In *Proceedings of the 18th Large Installation Systems Administration Conference (USENIX LISA 04)*, 2004.

[PY]   B. Padmanabhan and Y. Yang. Clickprints on the Web: Are There Signatures in Web Browsing Data? Working paper. http://ssrn.com/abstract=931057.

[QD91]   J. Quisquater and Y. Desmedt. Chinese Lotto as an Exhaustive Code-Breaking Machine. *Computer* 24(11):14–22, 1991.

[RA00]   R. Ritchey and P. Ammann, Using Model Checking to Analyze Network Vulnerabilities. In Proceedings 2000 IEEE Computer Society Symposium on Security and Privacy pages 156–165, May, 2000.

[Ray99]   E. Raymond. *The Cathedral and the Bazaar: Musings on Linux and Open Source by an Accidental Revolutionary.* O'Reilly, 1999.

[RCBC06]   N. Ratha, J. Connell, R. Bolle, and S. Chikkerur. Cancelable Biometrics: A Case Study in Fingerprints. In *Proceedings of the 18th International Conference on Pattern Recognition—Volume 04*, pp. 370–374, 2006.

[Reh07]   J. Rehmeyer. Tiny Behavioral Differences Can Reveal Your Identity Online. *Science News* 171(2), 2007.

[Res00]   E. Rescorla. *SSL and TLS: Designing and Building Secure Systems.* Addison-Wesley, 2000.

[Ric99]   J. Richter. *Programming Applications for Microsoft Windows*, 4th ed. Microsoft, 1999.

[Ric02]   G. Richarte. Four Different Tricks to Bypass StackShield and StackGuard Protection, 2002. `www.coresecurity.com/files/files/11/StackguardPaper.pdf`.

[RL96]   R. Rivest and B. Lampson. SDSI—A Simple Distributed Security Infrastructure. `http://theory.lcs.mit.edu/~rivest/sdsi10.html`, April 1996.

[RN02]   S. Russell and P. Norvig. *Artificial Intelligence: A Modern Approach*, 2nd ed. Prentice Hall, December 2002.

[Ros06]   D. Rosato. Five Dirty Secrets of Airfares. *Money Magazine*, 2006. Published online.

[RR98]   M. K. Reiter and A. D. Rubin. Crowds: Anonymity for Web Transactions. *ACM Transactions on Information and System Security* 1(1):66–92, 1998.

[RR00]   J. R. Rao and P. Rohatgi. Can Pseudonymity Really Guarantee Privacy? In *Proceedings of the 9th USENIX Security Symposium*, 2000.

[RR04]   J. Rosenberg and D. Remy. *Securing Web Services with WS-Security.* SAMS, 2004.

[RSA]   RSA Laboratories. Public Key Cryptography Standards. 2007 `www.rsa.com/rsalabs/node.asp?id=2124`.

[RSA78]   R. Rivest, A. Shamir, and L. Adleman. A Method for Obtaining Digital Signatures and Public-Key Cryptosystems. *Communications of the ACM* 21(2):120–126, 1978.

[RSG98]   M. G. Reed, P. F. Syverson, and D. M. Goldschlag. Anonymous Connections and Onion Routing. *IEEE Journal on Selected Areas in Communications* 16(4):482–494, 1998.

[Rus05]   M. Russinovich. Sony, Rootkits and Digital Rights Management Gone Too Far, October 2005. `www.sysinternals.com/blog/2005/10/sony-rootkits-and-digital-rights.html`.

[Rus07]   M. Russinovich. DebugView for Windows, January 2007. `www.microsoft.com/technet/sysinternals/utilities/debugview.mspx`.

[S⁺95]   T. Senator et al. The Financial Crimes Enforcement Network AI System. *AI Magazine* 16(4), 1995.

[SA04]   Stephen Shankland and Scott Ard. Hidden Text Shows SCO Prepped
            Lawsuit against BOFA, March 2004. `http://news.com.com/2100-`
            `7344-5170073.html?tag=nl.`

[Sab00]   T. Sabin. Pwdump2, 2000. `www.bindview.com/Services/razor/`
            `Utilities/Windows/pwdump2_readme.cfm.`

[SAH98]   A. Somayaji S. A. Hofmeyr, S. Forrest. Intrusion Detection Using Sequences
            of System Calls. *Journal of Computer Security* 6(3):151–180, 1998.

[SCFY96]   R. S. Sandhu, E. J. Coyne, H. L. Feinstein, and C. E. Youman. Role-Based
            Access Control Models. *IEEE Computer* 29(2):38–47, 1996.

[SCG+03]   G. Suh, D. Clarke, B. Gassend, M. Dijk, and S. Devadas. Efficient Memory
            Integrity Verification and Encryption for Secure Processors. In *International
            Symposium on Microarchitecture (MICRO-36)*, 2003.

[Sch96]   B. Schneier. *Applied Cryptography*, 2nd ed. Wiley, 1996.

[Sch00]   B. Schneier. *Secrets & Lies: Digital Security in a Networked World*. Wiley,
            2000.

[Sch01]   R. Schell. Information Security: Science, Pseudoscience, and Flying Pigs. In
            ACSA/ACM Annual Computer Security Applications Conference, December
            2001.

[Sch05]   B. Schneier. Schneier on Security. A weblog covering security and se-
            curity technology, February 18, 2005. `www.schneier.com/blog/`
            `archives/2005/02/cryptanalysis_o.html.`

[SDOF07]   S. Schechter, R. Dhamija, A. Ozment, and I. Fischer. The Emperor's New
            Security Indicators: An Evaluation of Website Authentication and the
            Effect of Role Playing on Usability Studies. In *Proceeding of the IEEE
            Symposium on Security and Privacy*, 2007.

[Seca]   Secure Software Inc. RATS: Rough Auditing Tool for Security. `www.`
            `securesoftware.com/resources/download_rats.html.`

[Secb]   Security Innovation. Holodeck. `www.securityinnovation.com/`
            `holodeck/index.shtml.`

[Sec06]   Security Focus. The BugTraq Mailing List, 2006. `www.securityfocus.`
            `com.`

[Sel03]   P. Selgiman. An Implementation of Machine Learning Algorithms to Detect
            Abnormal Data Access from Online Journal Archives, 2003. B.A. thesis,
            Department of Computer Science, Dartmouth College.

[SFL+97]   S. J. Stolfo, D. Fan, W. Lee, A. Prodromidis, and P. Chan. Credit Card Fraud
            Detection Using Meta-Learning: Issues and Initial Results. In *Proceedings of
            the AAAI-97 Workshop on AI Methods in Fraud and Risk Management*, 1997.

[Sha79]   A. Shamir. How to Share a Secret. *Communications of the ACM* 22(11):612–
            613, 1979.

[Sim88]   G. Simmons. The Prisoners' Problem and the Subliminal Channel. In
            Proceedings of CRYPTO '88, pp. 51–67, 1988.

[Sin06a]   Ryan Singel. FAQ: AOL's Search Gaffe and You, August 2006. `www.`
            `wired.com/news/politics/privacy/0%2C71579-0.html.`

[Sin06b]   A. Singh. *Max OS X Internals: A Systems Approach*. Addison-Wesley, 2006.

[Sip97]   M. Sipser. *Introduction to the Theory of Computation*. PWS Publishing, 1997.

[SL05]   E. Skoudis and T. Liston. *Counter Hack Reloaded : A Step-by-Step Guide to
            Computer Attacks and Effective Defenses*. Prentice Hall, 2005.

[SLS+05]   A. Seshadri, M. Luk, E. Shi, A. Perrig, L. van Doorn, and P. Khosla. Pioneer: Verifying Code Integrity and Enforcing Untampered Code Execution on Legacy Systems. In *Proceedings of the 20th ACM Symposium on Operating Systems Principles*, pp. 1–16, 2005.

[SM03]   A. Sabelfeld and A. Myers. Language-Based Information-Flow Security. *IEEE Journal on Selected Areas in Communications* 21(1), 2003.

[Smi00]   R. Smith. Distributing Word Documents with a "Locating Beacon," August 2000.   www.securiteam.com/securitynews/5CP13002AA.html.

[Smi03a]   R. Smith. Microsoft Word Bytes Tony Blair in the Butt, June 2003. www.computerbytesman.com/privacy/blair.htm.

[Smi03b]   S. W. Smith. A Funny Thing Happened on the Way to the Marketplace. *IEEE Security and Privacy* 1(6):74–78, 2003.

[Smi03c]   S. W. Smith. Humans in the Loop: Human-Computer Interaction and Security. *IEEE Security and Privacy*, 1(3):75–79, 2003.

[Smi04a]   S. W. Smith. Outbound Authentication for Programmable Secure Coprocessors. *International Journal on Information Security*, 2004.

[Smi04b]   S. W. Smith. Probing End-User IT Security Practices—via Homework. *The Educause Quarterly* 27(4):68–71, 2004.

[Smi04c]   S. W. Smith. *Trusted Computing Platforms: Design and Applications.* Springer, 2004.

[Smi05]   S. W. Smith. Turing Is from Mars, Shannon Is from Venus: Computer Science and Computer Engineering. *IEEE Security and Privacy* 3(2):66–69, 2005.

[SMS04]   S. W. Smith, C. Masone, and S. Sinclair. Expressing Trust in Distributed Systems: The Mismatch Between Tools and Reality. In *Forty-Second Annual Allerton Conference on Communication, Control, and Computing*, September 2004.

[Sol06]   Solar Designer. Linux Kernel Patch from the Openwall Project, 2006. www.openwall.com.

[Sou06]   Sourcefire. Snort, 2006. www.snort.org.

[Spa]   E. Sparks. TPM Reset Attack. www.cs.dartmouth.edu/~pkilab/sparks/.

[Spa89]   E. Spafford. The Internet Worm: Crisis and Aftermath. *Communications of the ACM* 32:678–687, 1989.

[Spi]   On-the-fly, LTL Model Checking with SPIN. www.spinroot.com.

[SPP+04]   H. Shacham, M. Page, B. Pfaff, E.-J. Goh, N. Modadugu, and D. Boneh. On the Effectiveness of Address-Space Randomization. In *CCS '04: Proceedings of the 11th ACM Conference on Computer and Communications Security*, pp. 298–307, 2004.

[SPvDK04]   A. Seshadri, A. Perrig, L. van Doorn, and P. Khosla. SWAtt: Software-Based Attestation for Embedded Devices. In *Proceedings of the IEEE Symposium on Security and Privacy*, May 2004.

[SRS+04]   L. Subramanian, V. Roth, I. Stoica, S. Shenker, and R. Katz. Listen and Whisper: Security Mechanisms for BGP. In *Proceedings of First Symposium on Networked Systems Design and Implementation (NSDI 2004)*, March 2004.

[SS75]   J. Saltzer and M. Schroeder. The Protection of Information in Computer Systems. *Proceedings of the IEEE* 63(9):1278–1308, 1975.

[SS03]   A. Shubina and S. W. Smith. Using Caching for Browsing Anonymity. *ACM SIGecom Exchanges* 4.2:11–20, 2003.

[SS04a]   P. Seligman and S. W. Smith. Detecting Unauthorized Use in Online Journal Archives: A Case Study. In *Proceedings of the IADIS International Conference WWW/Internet 2004* 1: 209–217, October 2004.

[SS04b]   F. Swiderski and W. Snyder. *Threat Modeling.* Microsoft Press, 2004.

[SS05]   S. Sinclair and S. W. Smith. PorKI: Making User PKI Safe on Machines of Heterogeneous Trustworthiness. 21st Annual Computer Security Applications Conference, IEEE Computer Society. December, 2005.

[SS07]   N. Santos and S. W. Smith. Limited Delegation for Client-Side SSL. In *6th Annual PKI Research and Development Workshop.* NIST, 2007.

[Sta06]   S. Stasiukonis. Social Engineering, the USB Way, June 2006. www.darkreading.com/document.asp?doc_id=95556&WT.svl=column1_1.

[STH85]   R. R. Schell, T. F. Tao, and M. Heckman. Designing the GEMSOS Security Kernel for Security and Performance. In *Proceedings of the 8th National Computer Security Conference*, pp. 108–119, 1985.

[Sto07]   J. Stokes. *Inside the Machine.* No Starch Press, 2007.

[STT88]   W. R. Shockley, T. F. Tao, and M.F. Thompson. An Overview of the GEMSOS Class A1 Technology and Application Experience. In *Proceedings of the 11th National Computer Security Conference*, pp. 238–245, 1988.

[Stu98]   M. Stutz. Security Bugaboo in MS Outlook?, May 1998. www.wired.com/science/discoveries/news/1998/05/12249.

[Suna]   Sun Microsystems. General FAQs for Solaris 10. ie.sun.com/practice/software/solaris/faqs_general.jsp.

[Sunb]   Sun Microsystems. OpenSolaris. www.opensolaris.org/os/.

[Sun88]   Sun Microsystems. RFC 1057: Remote Procedure Call Protocol Specification: Version 2, 1988. www.ietf.org/rfc/rfc1057.txt.

[Sun04]   Sun Microsystems. Package javax.net.ssl, 2004. java.sun.com/j2se/1.5.0/docs/api/javax/net/ssl/package-summary.html.

[SW99]   S. W. Smith and S. Weingart. Building a High-Performance, Programmable Secure Coprocessor. *Computer Networks* 31:831–860, 1999.

[SWT01]   D. Song, D. Wagner, and X. Tian. Timing Analysis of Keystrokes and Timing Attacks on SSH. In *10th USENIX Security Symposium*, August 2001.

[SZJv04]   R. Sailer, X. Zhang, T. Jaeher, and L. van Doorn. Design and Implementation of a TCG-Based Integrity Measurement Architecture. In *Proceedings of the 13th USENIX Security Symposium*, pp. 223–238, 2004.

[Tan02]   A. Tanenbaum. *Computer Networks.* Prentice Hall, 2002.

[TC04]   A. Tucker and D. Comay. Solaris Zones: Operating System Support for Server Consolidation. In *USENIX 3rd Virtual Machine Research and Technology Symposium*, 2004.

[Ten06]   Tenable. Nessus Vulnerablity Scanner, 2006. www.nessus.org.

[Tho84]   K. Thompson. Reflections on Trusting Trust. *Communications of the ACM* 27:761–763, 1984.

[TPCF]   M. Two, C. Poole, J. Cansdale, and G. Feldman. NUnit. www.nunit.org.

[Tri]   M. V. Tripunitara. The Page of Spaf's Analogies. http://homes.cerias.purdue.edu/~tripunit/spaf-analogies.html.

[Tri06]   Tripwire. Tripwire, 2006. www.tripwire.com.

[Tur37]   A. Turing. On Computable Numbers, with an Application to the Entschei-
            dungsproblem. *Proceedings of the London Mathematical Society, ser. 2*, 42,
            1937.

[TvO04a]   J. Thorpe and P. van Oorschot. Graphical Dictionaries and the Memorable
            Space of Graphical Passwords. In *Proceedings of the 13th Annual USENIX
            Security Symposium*, 2004.

[TvO04b]   J. Thorpe and P. van Oorschot. Towards Secure Design Choices for
            Implementing Graphical Passwords. In *Proceedings of the 20th Annual
            Security Applications Conference*, December 2004.

[U+05]   R. Uhlig et al. Intel Virtualization Technology. *IEEE Computer*, 38(5):48–56,
            2005.

[U.S.96]   U.S. Congress. Health Insurance Portability and Accountability Act, 1996.
            www.hhs.gov/ocr/hipaa/.

[U.S.99]   U.S. Congress. Gramm-Leach-Bliley Act, 1999. www.ftc.gov/
            privacy/glbact/glbsub1.htm.

[U.S.02]   U.S. Congress. Sarbanes-Oxley Act, 2002. www.legalarchiver.org/
            soa.htm.

[VM97]   J. Voas and G. McGraw. *Software Fault Injection: Innoculating Programs
            Against Errors*. Wiley, 1997.

[VM01]   J. Viega and G. McGraw. *Building Secure Software: How to Avoid Security
            Problems the Right Way*. Addison-Wesley, 2001.

[VMC02]   J. Viega, M. Messier, and P. Chandra. *Network Security with OpenSSL:
            Cryptography for Secure Communications*. O'Reilly, 2002.

[VMW07]   VMware: Virtualization, Virtual Machine and Virtual Server Consolidation,
            2007. www.vmware.com/.

[Wag]   D. Wagner. BOON: Buffer Overrun detectiON. www.cs.berkeley.
            edu/~daw/boon/.

[WBV+05]   Y. Wang, D. Beck, B. Vo, R. Roussev, and C. Verbowski. Detecting Stealth
            Software with Strider GhostBuster. In *Proceedings of the IEEE International
            Conference on Dependable Systems and Networks (DSN)*, June 2005.

[WCS+02]   C. Wright, C. Cowan, S. Smalley, J. Morris, and G. Kroah-Hartman. Linux
            Security Modules: General Security Support for the Linux Kernel. In
            Proceedings of the 11th USENIX Security Symposium, pp. 17–31, 2002.

[Wee01]   S. Weeks. Understanding Trust Management Systems. In *Proceedings of
            2001 IEEE Symposium on Security and Privacy*, pp. 94–105. IEEE Computer
            Society Press, May 2001.

[Wei00]   S. Weingart. Physical Security Devices for Computer Subsystems: A
            Survey of Attacks and Defenses. In *Cryptographic Hardware and Embedded
            Systems—CHES 2000*, pp. 302–317. Springer-Verlag LNCS 1965, 2000.

[WFLY04]   X. Wang, D. Feng, X. Lai, and H. Yu. *Collisions for Hash Functions MD4,
            MD5, HAVAL-128 and RIPEMD, 2004*. Cryptology ePrint Archive, Report
            2004/199. eprint.iacr.org.

[WI06]   S. Weiler and J. Ihren. RFC 4470: Minimally Covering NSEC Records
            and DNSSEC On-line Signing, April 2006. www.ietf.org/rfc/
            rfc4470.txt.

[Wie96]   M. Wiener. Efficient DES Key Search. Reprinted in *Practical Cryptography for Data Internetworks*, IEEE Press, 1996 Originally presented at the rump session of Crypto '93.

[Wil05]   David Willey. Italy Media Reveals Iraq Details, May 2005. `http://news.bbc.co.uk/2/hi/europe/4504589.stm`.

[Win98]   J. Wing. A Symbiotic Relationship between Formal Methods and Security. In *Proceedings from Workshops on Computer Security, Fault Tolerance, and Software Assurance*, 1998.

[Win06]   N. Wingfield. "Worms" Turn on Apple Macs, Bigger Target as Sales Boom, Wall Street Journal, February 27 2006, Page B1.

[WKvO05]   T. Wan, E. Kranakis, and P. van Oorschot. Pretty Secure BGP (psBGP). In *The 12th Annual Network and Distributed System Security Symposium (NDSS'05)*, February 2005.

[Woj98]   R. Wojtczuk. Defeating Solar Designer's Non-executable Stack Patch, January 1998. `www.insecure.org/sploits/non-executable.stack.problems.html`.

[WT99]   A. Whitten and J. D. Tygar. Why Johnny Can't Encrypt: A Usability Evaluation of PGP 5.0. In *USENIX Security*, 1999.

[WYY05a]   Y. Yin, X. Wang, and H. Yu. Finding Collisions in the Full SHA-1, August 2005. `202.194.5.130/admin/infosec/download.php?id=2`. Presented at the rump session of CRYPTO 2005.

[WYY05b]   X. Wang, H. Yu, and Y. Yin. Efficient Collision Search Attacks on SHA-0, August 2005. `202.194.5.130/admin/infosec/download.php?id=1`. Presented at the rump session of CRYPTO 2005.

[Xen07]   The Xen Virtual Machine Monitor, 2007. `www.cl.cam.ac.uk/research/srg/netos/xen/`.

[xsh06]   xshadow. The Vanquish Rootkit, 2006. `www.rootkit.com/project.php?id=9`.

[Yao86]   A. C. Yao. How to Generate and Exchange Secrets. In *27th Annual Symposium on Foundations of Computer Science*, pp. 162–167, 1986.

[Yee94]   B. S. Yee. Using Secure Coprocessors. Ph. D. thesis, Carnegie Mellon University, May 1994.

[Yee02]   K.-P. Yee. User Interaction Design for Secure Systems. In *Proceedings of the 4th International Conference on Information and Communication. Security (ICICS 02)*. Inst. for Infocomm Research/Chinese Academy of Sciences, 2002.

[Yee04]   K.-P. Yee. Aligning Security and Usability. *IEEE Security and Privacy* 2(5): 48–55, 2004.

[YH06]   E. Young and T. Hudson. OpenSSL, 2006. `www.openssl.org`.

[YS02]   E. Ye and S. W. Smith. Trusted Paths for Browsers. In *Proceedings of the 11th USENIX Security Symposium*, August 2002.

[YY04]   A. Young and M. Yung, Malicious Cryptography: Exposing Cryptovirology. Wiley, 2004.

[YY96]   A. Young and M. Yung. The Dark Side of Black-Box Cryptography, or: Should We Trust Capstone? In *Advances in Cryptology—Crypto 96*, pp. 89–103. Springer-Verlag LNCS 1109, 1996.

[ZEJ02]   X. Zhang, A. Edwards, and T. Jaeger. Using CQUAL for Static Analysis
               of Authorization Hook Placement. In Proceedings of the 11th USENIX
               Security Symposium, pp. 33–48, 2002.

[Zim95]   P. Zimmerman. *The Official PGP User's Guide*. MIT Press, 1995.

[ZSN05a]   M. Zhao, S. Smith, and D. Nicol. Aggregated Path Authentication for
               Efficient BGP Security. In *Proceedings of the 12th ACM Conference on
               Computer and Communications Security (CCS 2005)*, November 2005.

[ZSN05b]   M. Zhao, S. W. Smith, and D. Nicol. Evaluating the Performance Impact
               of PKI on BGP Security. In *4th Annual PKI Research and Development
               Workshop*. NIST/NIH/Internet2, April 2005.

Index

3DES. *See* TDES (Triple DES).

A

AA (attribute authority), 266
Abstraction, 51–52, 394
Access control. *See also* Permissions; Privileges.
  ACEs (access control entries), 71
  ACLs (access control lists), 71
  attribute-based, 245
  DAC (discretionary access control),
    29, 34, 71–72
  filesystem, 70–72
  hygiene, 223
  MAC (mandatory access control),
    29, 34, 72, 92
  methods. *See* Authenticating; Authentication;
    Authorization.
  RBAC (role-based access control),
    32–33, 245
  Web security, 316–317
  WLANs (wireless LANs),
    116–118
  XACML (Extensible Access Control Markup
    Language), 335
Access control matrix. *See also* State.
  computability theory, 16
  definition, 7
  domains, 8
  examples, 7, 8–9
  objects, 7
  policy engineering flaws, 8–9
  principals, 8
  reducing complexity, 8
  safe states, 16–18
  safety problem, 17–18
  security policies, 8
  software engineering flaws, 8–9
  subjects, 7
Access patterns, learning, 420
Access points, WLANs, 113
ACEs (access control entries), 71
ACLs (access control lists), 71
Acquiring and Implementation domain, 287
Acrobat, 356–357. *See also* PDF (Portable
  Document Format).

Action at a distance, 482–483
Active authorization, 480
Active Web page content, 309–310
ActiveX controls, 309
Ad hoc networking, 113
Adams, Anne, 471
Address Resolution Protocol (ARP), 92
Address space, 125–126, 435
Address space randomization (ASR), 131–132
Addresses (memory), 62–63, 65
admin users, 69–70
Adversaries, 18–19
AEGIS, 439
AES (Advanced Encryption Standard)
  block ciphers, 166
  cache timing attacks, 205–206
  key length, 171–172
Affordances, 478–479
AI (artificial intelligence)
  Amazon Mechanical Turk service, 465
  case study
    archetypes, 461
    artificial neural networks, 460
    clustering, 461
    context, 458–459
    decision trees, 460–461
    experiments, 462–464
    feature set, 462
    genetic algorithms, 461
    problem statement, 459–460
    results, 464
    techniques, 460–461
  polymorphic viruses, 456
  in real-world systems, 464–465
  tools
    anomaly detection, 455–456
    COLT (computational learning
      theory), 451
    computer system behavior, 456
    data dredging, 452, 457–458
    data mining, 451
    IDES (Intrusion-Detection Expert System), 457
    intrusion detection, 456–457
    misuse detection, 455–456
    ML (machine learning), 451

AI (artificial intelligence) (*continued*)
  network traffic, 456
  neural networks, 454–455
  processing photographs, 453
  statistical inference, 451
  StealthWatch, 456
  tank detection, 454–455
  zero-day exploits, 456
Airline boarding passes, 353–354
AJAX (asynchronous JavaScript and XML), 314
Aleph One, 127
Algorithms, cryptographic, 159
Always operator, 398
Amazon Mechanical Turk service, 465
Amazon.com, cookies, 315
Ammann, Paul, 404
Amplitude, 499
Analog hole problem, 387
And operator, 395
Anderson, Ted, 192
Anecdotes. *See* Case studies; Examples.
Anomaly detection, 455–456
Anonymity, electronic money, 373–374
Anonymous SSL, 320
ANSI (American National Standards Institute), 280
Antitamper, backward, 422–423
API attacks, 418
API hooking, 81
APIs (application program interfaces), 73–74
Application layer, 94–96
Applied Cryptography, 157–158
Archetypes, 461
Architecture, computer, 62–63. *See also* Hardware security, alternative architectures.
Argument validation
  input assumptions
    escape sequences, 137–138
    format string bugs, 133–134
    fuzz testing, 133
    integer overflow, 134–137
  internal validation, 138–139
  reverse engineering, 133
  SQL injection, 137–138
Arguments, stack frame, 126
Armored CPUs, 439
ARP (Address Resolution Protocol), 92
ARP cache poisoning, 107
The Art of Deception, 79, 471
The Art of Software Security Assessment, 295
Articles. *See* Books and publications.
Artificial intelligence (AI). *See* AI (artificial intelligence).
Artificial neural networks, 460
ASR (address space randomization), 131–132
Assurance requirements, 33–34
Asymmetric cryptography, 175
Asymmetric marking, 383
Asynchronous JavaScript and XML (AJAX), 314
Atallah, Mike, 225

ATMs
  examples, 10–11, 14
  jackpotting, 14
  PIN discrepancies, 14
Atomicity, 366–368, 375
Attack surface, 295
Attacks. *See also* specific attacks.
  brute force, 192–194
  bucket brigade, 225–226
  chess grandmaster, 225–226, 234
  cryptography. *See also* Public-key cryptosystems, breaking; Symmetric-key cryptosystems, breaking.
    blinding, 205
    cache timing, 205–206
    chosen-ciphertext, 161
    chosen-plaintext, 160–161
    ciphertext-only, 160–161
    EMF (electromagnetic field), 206–207
    factoring versus breaking, 208–209
    hardware side-channel, 206–207
    keyjacking, 207–208
    known-plaintext, 160–161
    meet-in-the-middle, 169–170
    square-and-multiply, 183–184, 203–205
    strategies, 160–161
    timing attacks on RSA, 203–205
  dictionary, 218
  hardware. *See* Hardware security, attacks.
  man-in-the-middle, 225–226
  mosaic, 386
  network
    ARP cache poisoning, 107
    automation, 108–109
    banner grabbing, 105–106
    exploits, 108–109
    IP spoofing, 108
    MAC flooding, 107
    MAC spoofing, 108
    man-in-the-middle, 107
    objectives, 105
    packet routing, determining, 106
    penetration tests, 109
    ping sweeping, 106
    promiscuous mode, 106–107
    scanning, 105–106
    sniffing, 106–107
    spoofing, 107–108
    TTL (time-to-live) field, 106
    vulnerabilities, 108–109
  oracle, 235
  OS
    botnets, 78
    bots, 78
    DDoS (distributed DoS), 78
    DoS (denial of service), 78
    dumpster diving, 79
    exploits, 79–80
    keyloggers, 80–82
    privilege escalation, 78